Contemporary Authors®

ISSN 0010-7468

Contemporary Authors®

**A Bio-Bibliographical Guide to
Current Writers in Fiction, General Nonfiction,
Poetry, Journalism, Drama, Motion Pictures,
Television, and Other Fields**

volume 244

THOMSON

★

GALE

Detroit • New York • San Francisco • San Diego • New Haven, Conn. • Waterville, Maine • London • Munich

Contemporary Authors, Vol. 244

Project Editor
Julie Mellors

Editorial
Michelle Kazensky, Joshua Kondek, Lisa Kumar, Tracey Matthews, Mary Ruby

Permissions
Margaret Chamberlain-Gaston, Edna Hedblad, Shalice Shah-Caldwell

Imaging and Multimedia
Lezlie Light

Composition and Electronic Capture
Carolyn Roney

Manufacturing
Drew Kalasky

LIBRARY OF CONGRESS CATALOG CARD NUMBER 62-52046

ISBN 0-7876-7873-2
ISSN 0010-7468

This title is also available as an e-book.
ISBN 1-4144-1004-2
Contact your Thomson Gale sales representative for ordering information.

Printed in the United States of America
10 9 8 7 6 5 4 3 2 1

Contents

Indexing note: All *Contemporary Authors* entries are indexed in the *Contemporary Authors* cumulative index, which is published separately and distributed twice a year.

As always, the most recent Contemporary Authors cumulative index continues to be the user's guide to the location of an individual author's listing.

Preface

Contemporary Authors (*CA*) provides information on approximately 120,000 writers in a wide range of media, including:

- Current writers of fiction, nonfiction, poetry, and drama whose works have been issued by commercial publishers, risk publishers, or university presses (authors whose books have been published only by known vanity or author-subsidized firms are ordinarily not included)

- Prominent print and broadcast journalists, editors, photojournalists, syndicated cartoonists, graphic novelists, screenwriters, television scriptwriters, and other media people

- Notable international authors

- Literary greats of the early twentieth century whose works are popular in today's high school and college curriculums and continue to elicit critical attention

A *CA* listing entails no charge or obligation. Authors are included on the basis of the above criteria and their interest to *CA* users. Sources of potential listees include trade periodicals, publishers' catalogs, librarians, and other users of the series.

How to Get the Most out of *CA*: Use the Index

The key to locating an author's most recent entry is the *CA* cumulative index, which is published separately and distributed twice a year. It provides access to *all* entries in *CA* and *Contemporary Authors New Revision Series* (*CANR*). Always consult the latest index to find an author's most recent entry.

For the convenience of users, the *CA* cumulative index also includes references to all entries in these Thomson Gale literary series: *Authors and Artists for Young Adults, Authors in the News, Bestsellers, Black Literature Criticism, Black Literature Criticism Supplement, Black Writers, Children's Literature Review, Concise Dictionary of American Literary Biography, Concise Dictionary of British Literary Biography, Contemporary Authors Autobiography Series, Contemporary Authors Bibliographical Series, Contemporary Dramatists, Contemporary Literary Criticism, Contemporary Novelists, Contemporary Poets, Contemporary Popular Writers, Contemporary Southern Writers, Contemporary Women Poets, Dictionary of Literary Biography, Dictionary of Literary Biography Documentary Series, Dictionary of Literary Biography Yearbook, DISCovering Authors, DISCovering Authors: British, DISCovering Authors: Canadian, DISCovering Authors: Modules* (including modules for Dramatists, Most-Studied Authors, Multicultural Authors, Novelists, Poets, and Popular/Genre Authors), *DISCovering Authors 3.0, Drama Criticism, Drama for Students, Feminist Writers, Hispanic Literature Criticism, Hispanic Writers, Junior DISCovering Authors, Major Authors and Illustrators for Children and Young Adults, Major 20th-Century Writers, Native North American Literature, Novels for Students, Poetry Criticism, Poetry for Students, Short Stories for Students, Short Story Criticism, Something about the Author, Something about the Author Autobiography Series, St. James Guide to Children's Writers, St. James Guide to Crime & Mystery Writers, St. James Guide to Fantasy Writers, St. James Guide to Horror, Ghost & Gothic Writers, St. James Guide to Science Fiction Writers, St. James Guide to Young Adult Writers, Twentieth-Century Literary Criticism, 20th Century Romance and Historical Writers, World Literature Criticism,* and *Yesterday's Authors of Books for Children.*

A Sample Index Entry:

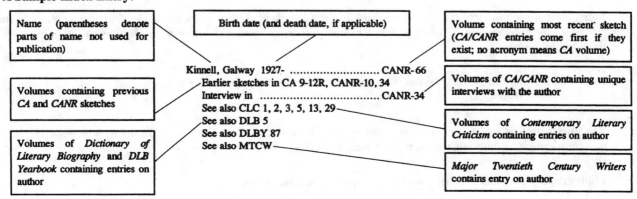

How Are Entries Compiled?

The editors make every effort to secure new information directly from the authors; listees' responses to our questionnaires and query letters provide most of the information featured in *CA*. For deceased writers, or those who fail to reply to requests for data, we consult other reliable biographical sources, such as those indexed in Thomson Gale's *Biography and Genealogy Master Index,* and bibliographical sources, including *National Union Catalog, LC MARC,* and *British National Bibliography.* Further details come from published interviews, feature stories, and book reviews, as well as information supplied by the authors' publishers and agents.

An asterisk (*) at the end of a sketch indicates that the listing has been compiled from secondary sources believed to be reliable but has not been personally verified for this edition by the author sketched.

What Kinds of Information Does An Entry Provide?

Sketches in *CA* contain the following biographical and bibliographical information:

- **Entry heading:** the most complete form of author's name, plus any pseudonyms or name variations used for writing

- **Personal information:** author's date and place of birth, family data, ethnicity, educational background, political and religious affiliations, and hobbies and leisure interests

- **Addresses:** author's home, office, or agent's addresses, plus e-mail and fax numbers, as available

- **Career summary:** name of employer, position, and dates held for each career post; resume of other vocational achievements; military service

- **Membership information:** professional, civic, and other association memberships and any official posts held

- **Awards and honors:** military and civic citations, major prizes and nominations, fellowships, grants, and honorary degrees

- **Writings:** a comprehensive, chronological list of titles, publishers, dates of original publication and revised editions, and production information for plays, television scripts, and screenplays

- **Adaptations:** a list of films, plays, and other media which have been adapted from the author's work

- **Work in progress:** current or planned projects, with dates of completion and/or publication, and expected publisher, when known

- **Sidelights:** a biographical portrait of the author's development; information about the critical reception of the author's works; revealing comments, often by the author, on personal interests, aspirations, motivations, and thoughts on writing

- **Interview:** a one-on-one discussion with authors conducted especially for *CA*, offering insight into authors' thoughts about their craft

- **Autobiographical essay:** an original essay written by noted authors for *CA*, a forum in which writers may present themselves, on their own terms, to their audience

- **Photographs:** portraits and personal photographs of notable authors

- **Biographical and critical sources:** a list of books and periodicals in which additional information on an author's life and/or writings appears

- **Obituary Notices** in *CA* provide date and place of birth as well as death information about authors whose full-length sketches appeared in the series before their deaths. The entries also summarize the authors' careers and writings and list other sources of biographical and death information.

Related Titles in the *CA* Series

Contemporary Authors Autobiography Series complements *CA* original and revised volumes with specially commissioned autobiographical essays by important current authors, illustrated with personal photographs they provide. Common topics include their motivations for writing, the people and experiences that shaped their careers, the rewards they derive from their work, and their impressions of the current literary scene.

Contemporary Authors Bibliographical Series surveys writings by and about important American authors since World War II. Each volume concentrates on a specific genre and features approximately ten writers; entries list works written by and about the author and contain a bibliographical essay discussing the merits and deficiencies of major critical and scholarly studies in detail.

Available in Electronic Formats

GaleNet. *CA* is available on a subscription basis through GaleNet, an online information resource that features an easy-to-use end-user interface, powerful search capabilities, and ease of access through the World-Wide Web. For more information, call 1-800-877-GALE.

Licensing. *CA* is available for licensing. The complete database is provided in a fielded format and is deliverable on such media as disk, CD-ROM, or tape. For more information, contact Thomson Gale's Business Development Group at 1-800-877-GALE, or visit us on our website at www.galegroup.com/bizdev.

Suggestions Are Welcome

The editors welcome comments and suggestions from users on any aspect of the *CA* series. If readers would like to recommend authors for inclusion in future volumes of the series, they are cordially invited to write the Editors at *Contemporary Authors*, Thomson Gale, 27500 Drake Rd., Farmington Hills, MI 48331-3535; or call at 1-248-699-4253; or fax at 1-248-699-8054.

Contemporary Authors Product Advisory Board

The editors of *Contemporary Authors* are dedicated to maintaining a high standard of excellence by publishing comprehensive, accurate, and highly readable entries on a wide array of writers. In addition to the quality of the content, the editors take pride in the graphic design of the series, which is intended to be orderly yet inviting, allowing readers to utilize the pages of *CA* easily and with efficiency. Despite the longevity of the *CA* print series, and the success of its format, we are mindful that the vitality of a literary reference product is dependent on its ability to serve its users over time. As literature, and attitudes about literature, constantly evolve, so do the reference needs of students, teachers, scholars, journalists, researchers, and book club members. To be certain that we continue to keep pace with the expectations of our customers, the editors of *CA* listen carefully to their comments regarding the value, utility, and quality of the series. Librarians, who have firsthand knowledge of the needs of library users, are a valuable resource for us. The *Contemporary Authors* Product Advisory Board, made up of school, public, and academic librarians, is a forum to promote focused feedback about *CA* on a regular basis. The six-member advisory board includes the following individuals, whom the editors wish to thank for sharing their expertise:

- **Anne M. Christensen,** Librarian II, Phoenix Public Library, Phoenix, Arizona.

- **Barbara C. Chumard,** Reference/Adult Services Librarian, Middletown Thrall Library, Middletown, New York.

- **Eva M. Davis,** Youth Department Manager, Ann Arbor District Library, Ann Arbor, Michigan.

- **Adam Janowski, Jr.,** Library Media Specialist, Naples High School Library Media Center, Naples, Florida.

- **Robert Reginald,** Head of Technical Services and Collection Development, California State University, San Bernadino, California.

- **Stephen Weiner,** Director, Maynard Public Library, Maynard, Massachusetts.

International Advisory Board

Well-represented among the 120,000 author entries published in *Contemporary Authors* are sketches on notable writers from many non-English-speaking countries. The primary criteria for inclusion of such authors has traditionally been the publication of at least one title in English, either as an original work or as a translation. However, the editors of *Contemporary Authors* came to observe that many important international writers were being overlooked due to a strict adherence to our inclusion criteria. In addition, writers who were publishing in languages other than English were not being covered in the traditional sources we used for identifying new listees. Intent on increasing our coverage of international authors, including those who write only in their native language and have not been translated into English, the editors enlisted the aid of a board of advisors, each of whom is an expert on the literature of a particular country or region. Among the countries we focused attention on are Mexico, Puerto Rico, Germany, Luxembourg, Belgium, the Netherlands, Norway, Sweden, Denmark, Finland, Taiwan, Singapore, Spain, Italy, South Africa, Israel, and Japan, as well as England, Scotland, Wales, Ireland, Australia, and New Zealand. The sixteen-member advisory board includes the following individuals, whom the editors wish to thank for sharing their expertise:

- **Lowell A. Bangerter,** Professor of German, University of Wyoming, Laramie, Wyoming.

- **Nancy E. Berg,** Associate Professor of Hebrew and Comparative Literature, Washington University, St. Louis, Missouri.

- **Frances Devlin-Glass,** Associate Professor, School of Literary and Communication Studies, Deakin University, Burwood, Victoria, Australia.

- **David William Foster,** Regent's Professor of Spanish, Interdisciplinary Humanities, and Women's Studies, Arizona State University, Tempe, Arizona.

- **Hosea Hirata,** Director of the Japanese Program, Associate Professor of Japanese, Tufts University, Medford, Massachusetts.

- **Jack Kolbert,** Professor Emeritus of French Literature, Susquehanna University, Selinsgrove, Pennsylvania.

- **Mark Libin,** Professor, University of Manitoba, Winnipeg, Manitoba, Canada.

- **C. S. Lim,** Professor, University of Malaya, Kuala Lumpur, Malaysia.

- **Eloy E. Merino,** Assistant Professor of Spanish, Northern Illinois University, DeKalb, Illinois.

- **Linda M. Rodríguez Guglielmoni,** Associate Professor, University of Puerto Rico—Mayagüez, Puerto Rico.

- **Sven Hakon Rossel,** Professor and Chair of Scandinavian Studies, University of Vienna, Vienna, Austria.

- **Steven R. Serafin,** Director, Writing Center, Hunter College of the City University of New York, New York City.

- **David Smyth,** Lecturer in Thai, School of Oriental and African Studies, University of London, England.

- **Ismail S. Talib,** Senior Lecturer, Department of English Language and Literature, National University of Singapore, Singapore.

- **Dionisio Viscarri,** Assistant Professor, Ohio State University, Columbus, Ohio.

- **Mark Williams,** Associate Professor, English Department, University of Canterbury, Christchurch, New Zealand.

CA Numbering System and Volume Update Chart

Occasionally questions arise about the *CA* numbering system and which volumes, if any, can be discarded. Despite numbers like "29-32R," "97-100" and "243," the entire *CA* print series consists of only 295 physical volumes with the publication of *CA* Volume 244. The following charts note changes in the numbering system and cover design, and indicate which volumes are essential for the most complete, up-to-date coverage.

CA First Revision	• 1-4R through 41-44R (11 books) *Cover:* Brown with black and gold trim. There will be no further First Revision volumes because revised entries are now being handled exclusively through the more efficient *New Revision Series* mentioned below.
CA Original Volumes	• 45-48 through 97-100 (14 books) *Cover:* Brown with black and gold trim. 101 through 244 (144 books) *Cover:* Blue and black with orange bands. The same as previous *CA* original volumes but with a new, simplified numbering system and new cover design.
CA Permanent Series	• *CAP*-1 and *CAP*-2 (2 books) *Cover:* Brown with red and gold trim. There will be no further Permanent Series volumes because revised entries are now being handled exclusively through the more efficient *New Revision Series* mentioned below.
CA New Revision Series	• CANR-1 through CANR-149 (149 books) *Cover:* Blue and black with green bands. Includes only sketches requiring significant changes; **sketches are taken from any previously published CA, CAP, or CANR volume.**

If You Have:	You May Discard:
CA First Revision Volumes 1-4R through 41-44R and *CA Permanent Series* Volumes 1 and 2	*CA* Original Volumes 1, 2, 3, 4 Volumes 5-6 through 41-44
CA Original Volumes 45-48 through 97-100 and 101 through 244	**NONE:** These volumes will not be superseded by corresponding revised volumes. Individual entries from these and all other volumes appearing in the left column of this chart may be revised and included in the various volumes of the *New Revision Series*.
CA New Revision Series Volumes *CANR*-1 through *CANR*-149	**NONE:** The *New Revision Series* does not replace any single volume of *CA*. Instead, volumes of *CANR* include entries from many previous *CA* series volumes. All *New Revision Series* volumes must be retained for full coverage.

A Sampling of Authors and Media People
Featured in This Volume

Victoria Gotti

Gotti is a novelist, entrepreneur, actor, and editor. The daughter of convicted murderer and mafia boss John Gotti, Victoria grew up inside one of history's most notorious organized crime families. Gotti has been a columnist for major American newspapers, an editor, a fashion designer and entrepreneur with her own clothing line, and a regular guest on a variety of television programs. Gotti also suffers from a cardiac condition called mitral valve prolapse, and because of this she published the book *Women and Mitral Valve Prolapse: A Comprehensive Guide to Living and Coping with M.V.P. and Its Symptoms.*

Amy Grant

Singer and songwriter Grant was one of the first genuine stars of the world of Christian contemporary music, and she was also one of the first Christian musicians to successfully cross over to mainstream music. Her debut album, *Amy Grant,* was released when she was only sixteen years old. Her album *Age to Age,* released in 1982, was the first Christian contemporary album to go platinum. Grant has also won multiple Grammy Awards for best female gospel performance.

Ferreira Gullar

Gullar is a one-time political exile and a successful Brazilian poet and playwright. The author first gained widespread acclaim in South America with his volume of experimental poetry titled *A luta corporal: poemas.* Gullar has reached celebrity status in Brazil and South America, and his most famous work, *Poema sujo,* was translated into English as *Dirty Poem.* In 2002 his work earned him the prestigious Prince Claus Award.

Tom Hanks

Hanks is considered one of the most popular and most successful actors in Hollywood. He won back-to-back Oscar awards for best actor in 1993 and 1994 for his roles in the major motion pictures *Philadelphia* and *Forrest Gump.* His success continued with his similarly highly-praised roles in *Apollo 13* and *Saving Private Ryan.* Aside from acting, Hanks is the author of the screenplay for the film *That Thing You Do!,* which he also directed. In 2002 Hanks was awarded the Life Achievement Award by the American Film Institute.

Libby Hathorn

Hathorn is an Australian writer who publishes poetry, picture books, drama, novels, short stories, and nonfiction for children, young adults, and adults. Best known in the United States for her critically acclaimed novel *Thunderwith,* Hathorn has created works ranging from serious stories of troubled youth to lighthearted, fast-paced comedies. In several books Hathorn has combined her interest in young people with her concerns about the environment, poverty, and homelessness. She has won numerous awards for her work, including the Prime Minister's Centenary Medal in 2003. An autobiographical essay by Hathorn is included in this volume of *CA.*

Jane Johnson

Johnson began her career as an editor of fantasy and science fiction. She wrote her first novel under the joint pseudonym Gabriel King in 1997. When author J.R.R. Tolkien's "Lord of the Rings" series was being filmed as a movie trilogy, Johnson, writing as Jude Fisher, created a number of "Visual Companions" to accompany the movies. In 2002 Johnson began writing her own series and produced the "Fool's Gold Trilogy."

Kazuo Koike

Koike is a prolific Japanese graphic novelist who found success with his "Lone Wolf and Cub" comic books, which were first serialized in Japan beginning in 1970, and by the late 1980s had sold some eight million copies. Later published in the United States as a series of twenty-eight book-length collections between 2000 and 2002, "Lone Wolf and Cub" has also been adapted for television. In addition to comic books, Koike has written screenplays, poetry, and fiction; hosted television programs; and mentored young Japanese artists and writers.

Zell Miller

A former U.S. senator and governor of Georgia, Miller is a controversial but stalwart figure in American politics. He entered politics in 1959, starting as the mayor of Young Harris, Georgia, and was then elected to the state senate in 1960. Characterized as a conservative democrat, Miller held a number of key posts throughout his forty-five-year career in public office. Miller sparked controversy when he diverged from the Democratic Party to support George W. Bush over John Kerry in the 2004 U.S. presidential election. Miller has also been the author of several successful books, including *A National Party No More: The Conscience of a Conservative Democrat.*

Acknowledgments

Grateful acknowledgment is made to those publishers, photographers, and artists whose work appear with these authors's essays. Following is a list of the copyright holders who have granted us permission to reproduce material in this volume of *CA*. Every effort has been made to trace copyright, but if omissions have been made, please let us know.

Photographs/Art

Hathorn, Libby: All photographs reproduced by permission of Libby Hathorn.

A

* Indicates that a listing has been compiled from secondary sources believed to be reliable, but has not been personally verified for this edition by the author sketched.

ABOULELA, Leila 1964-

PERSONAL: Born 1964, in Cairo, Egypt; married; children: two sons. *Education:* University of Khartoum, B.A., 1985; London School of Economics, two M.A.s. *Religion:* Muslim.

ADDRESSES: Home—Dubai, United Arab Emirates, and Aberdeen, Scotland. *Agent*—c/o Author Mail, Grove/Atlantic, Inc., 841 Broadway, 4th Fl., New York, NY 10003.

CAREER: Writer.

AWARDS, HONORS: Caine Prize for African Writing, 2000, for short story "The Museum."

WRITINGS:

The Translator (novel), Polygon (Edinburgh, Scotland), 1999.
Coloured Lights (short stories; includes "The Museum"), Polygon (Edinburgh, Scotland), 2001.
Minaret (novel), Grove Press (New York, NY), 2005.

Also author of the radio play *The Sea Warrior* for the British Broadcasting Corporation (BBC); author of an adaptation of *The Translator* for the BBC; contributor to *Opening Spaces: An Anthology of Contemporary African Women's Writing,* edited by Yvonne Vera, Heinemann, 2000.

SIDELIGHTS: Fiction writer Leila Aboulela was born in Cairo, Egypt, the daughter of an Egyptian mother and a Sudanese father. The family soon moved to Khartoum, Sudan, where Aboulela spent her childhood. Until the age of seven, she attended a Catholic school, despite being Muslim, then switched for several years to the Khartoum American School before returning to a Catholic school at the age of eleven. English was an important part of her education at both institutions, and proved useful when she later moved to England to further her studies after graduating from the University of Khartoum in 1985. It was only then, outside the confines of her upbringing, that Aboulela felt free to embrace her religion, which she believes to be a more-vital part of her personality and her writing that her nationality.

In an interview with Anita Sethi for the *Observer,* Aboulela explained: "I grew up in a very westernised environment and went to a private, American school. But my personality was shy and quiet and I wanted to wear the hijab but didn't have the courage, as I knew my friends would talk me out of it." Aboulela remarked of her life in London: "I didn't know anybody. It was 1989 and the word 'Muslim' wasn't even really used in Britain at the time; you were either black or Asian. So then I felt very free to wear the hijab." That freedom, however, helped to highlight the differences in culture that Aboulela witnessed. In her writing, she concentrates on that sense of separation between Muslims and Christians, as well as the feeling of displacement inherent in moving between very different nations, as she has done frequently for both her education and for work.

Aboulela won critical acclaim and the inaugural Caine Prize for African Writing with her short story "The

Museum." The story, which has some autobiographical elements, follows a young Muslim woman named Shadia in her move from Sudan to Aberdeen, Scotland, where she meets a young man and struggles with the radical cultural differences that pummel her from every direction. Aboulela's first novel, *The Translator,* was also well received by critics. *Coloured Lights,* her collection of short stories, gathers eleven stories, including "The Museum," and continues to address the state of flux experienced by characters whose lives are caught between eastern and western cultures. Natalie Brierley, in a review for *New Statesman,* commented that Aboulela's "stories move so briskly that we receive only fleeting glimpses of people's lives, but they are intimate all the same." Writing for *New Internationalist,* Peter Whittaker stated that "overall, this is an excellent collection which signals the emergence of a strong new fictional talent."

Minaret, Aboulela's second novel, tells the story of Najwa, a wealthy Sudanese girl who finds herself exiled from her country and working as a maid in London. Starr E. Smith, in a review for *Library Journal,* singled out the book for its "clear and precise writing, sympathetic characters, and positive portrayals of Muslim religious practices." A reviewer for *Publishers Weekly* remarked of Aboulela that, "aside from some stilted dialogue, she draws Najwa's odyssey of exile, loss and found faith beautifully," while a contributor for *Kirkus Reviews* concluded that *Minaret* is "a low-key, affecting account of one bruised young woman's search for wisdom and solace."

BIOGRAPHICAL AND CRITICAL SOURCES:

PERIODICALS

African Business, April, 2002, review of *Coloured Lights,* p. 49.
Kirkus Reviews, July 1, 2005, review of *Minaret,* p. 697.
Library Journal, July 1, 2005, Starr E. Smith, review of *Minaret,* p. 63.
Middle East, November, 2001, Fred Rhodes, review of *Coloured Lights,* p. 45.
New Internationalist, December, 2001, Peter Whittaker, review of *Coloured Lights,* p. 32; August, 2005, Louise Gray, Peter Whittaker, Malcolm Lewis, and Talia Whyte, review of *Minaret,* p. 30.

New Statesman, September 11, 2000, Jason Cowley, "Glittering Prize," about the inaugural Caine Prize for African Writing and "The Museum," p. 57; July 30, 2001, Natalie Brierley, review of *Coloured Lights,* p. 41.
Publishers Weekly, July 11, 2005, review of *Minaret,* p. 56.
World and I, August, 2002, Charles R. Larson, "Halal Novelist: Western and Islamic Civilizations Dialogue in Sudanese Writer Leila Aboulela's Fiction," p. 250.

ONLINE

Observer Online, http://books.guardian.co.uk/ (October 25, 2005), Anita Sethi, "Keep the Faith," interview with Leila Aboulela.*

* * *

ABRAMS, Floyd 1936-

PERSONAL: Born July 9, 1936, in New York, NY; son of Isidore and Rae (Eberlin); married Efrat Surasky, December 25, 1963; children: Daniel, Ronnie. *Education:* Cornell University, B.A., 1956; Yale University, LL.B., 1960.

ADDRESSES: Home—New York, NY. *Office*—Cahill Gordon and Reindel LLP, 80 Pine St., 17th Fl., New York, NY, 10005-1790. *E-mail*—fabrams@cahill.com.

CAREER: Princeton University, Princeton, NJ, research assistant in department of politics, 1960-61; U.S. District Court, Wilmington, DE, clerk to Paul Leahy, 1961-63; admitted to the Bar of New York State, 1961; Cahill, Gordon & Reindel (law firm), New York, NY, associate, 1963-70, partner, 1970—. Yale University, New Haven, CT, visiting lecturer, 1974-80 and 1986-89; Columbia University, New York, NY, visiting lecturer, 1981-85, William J. Brennan, Jr., visiting professor in Graduate School of Journalism, 1993. Member of First Amendment advisory council, The Media Institute, 2004.

MEMBER: American Bar Association (chair of rights of expression committee, individual rights section, 1976-79, Ross essay prize, chair of freedom of speech and press committee, litigation section, 1977-79, forum committee, 1979-80, amicus curiae committee, 1980-82), Bar Association of the City of New York (member of state legal committee, 1965-67, chair of communications committee, 1992-94).

AWARDS, HONORS: Anvil of Freedom award, Estlow International Center for Journalism and New Media, 2003-04; Hubert H. Humphrey First Amendment Freedoms Prize, Anti-Defamation League, 2003.

WRITINGS:

Shield Law Protection for the Press (sound recording; broadcast on National Public Radio, 1978), Center for the Study of Democratic Institutions (Santa Barbara, CA), 1982.
(With Richard Willard) *National Security and the First Amendment* (debate transcript), American Bar Association (Chicago, IL), 1984.
(With Diane Orentlicher) *Kampuchea, after the Worst: A Report on Current Violations of Human Rights,* Lawyers Committee for Human Rights (New York, NY), 1985.
Speaking Freely: Trials of the First Amendment, Viking (New York, NY), 2005.

Member of board of editors, *New York Law Journal,* 1983—, and *Legal Times,* 1989.

SIDELIGHTS: Floyd Abrams earned his law degree from Yale University in 1960, then went on to serve as a law clerk for Paul Leahy in the U.S. District Court of Wilmington, Delaware. In 1963, he joined the law practice of Cahill, Gordon & Reindel in New York City and was named a partner in the firm in 1970. Abrams specializes in First Amendment rights and has served as chair and as a member of several committees within the American Bar Association. Among his many achievements, he acted as co-counsel for the *New York Times* in the 1971 "Pentagon Papers" case, which involved the publication of top-secret documents detailing U.S. involvement in the Vietnam War. In addition, he successfully defended the National Broadcasting Company, Inc. (NBC) in a libel action brought against it by performer Wayne Newton, and participated in a variety of other cases dealing with magazines, book publishers, and film and television companies, some of which have gone to the U.S.

Supreme Court. In 2003, Abrams was awarded the Anti-Defamation League's Hubert H. Humphrey First Amendment Freedoms Prize. Abraham H. Foxman, in a report posted on *ADL.org,* remarked that "Abrams is a tireless defender of the First Amendment. . . . His record shows a deep-seated commitment to the ideals of freedom that the Framers envisioned and intimate knowledge of the importance the rights detailed in the First Amendment have to the survival of a healthy democracy." Abrams himself, quoted by a contributor to *Broadcasting,* stated: "I do care a lot about the First Amendment and about the rights of journalists to report and the essentiality of keeping the government out of the picture." He continued: "The uniqueness of this country is brought about in large part by the uniqueness of having a written, legally enforced protection against governmental entry into the . . . control of what journalists say, what they think, what they do."

Abrams has written several volumes about the First Amendment and how it fits in with the other concerns of the country, such as national security and human rights. In *Speaking Freely: Trials of the First Amendment,* published in 2005, Abrams provides a thorough discussion of the previous fifty years of First Amendment litigation, focusing in particular on nine cases that were important both to his own career and to the way free speech is interpreted and practiced in the United States. The cases reviewed include the Pentagon Papers, which marked Abrams's first appearance in front of the U.S. Supreme Court; *McConnell vs. the Federal Election Commission,* a trial concerning political campaign regulation; and the Brooklyn Museum case, which involved the city's threat to withdraw funding for the museum due to an exhibit they found in poor taste. Alec Foege, in a review for the *Recorder,* remarked that "the main flaw of *Speaking Freely* is that the outcome of each of Abrams' battles rarely matches the drama of the fight." Abrams closes the book by comparing American law to that of England, Europe, and the world as a whole. A contributor for *Kirkus Reviews* remarked that "Abrams's . . . approach is pitched at a higher level than much that passes for today's commentary on current events." He concluded that the book is comprised of "complex yet lucidly conveyed points of constitutional interpretation." In a review for *Publishers Weekly,* a contributor wrote that the author "conveys the nuance of constitutional law, the grappling for incremental advances in precedent, the interplay between the needs of his clients and the larger cause of free speech." Robert Corn-Revere, in a review for *Legal Times,* remarked of Abrams's effort: "Written for an intelligent lay audience and not necessarily for free speech specialists or other lawyers, the book provides a very readable account of some of Abrams' most famous First Amendment cases." He added that "it is a book of ideas, outlining the importance of free expression to the democratic scheme and illustrating the challenges involved in preserving it."

BIOGRAPHICAL AND CRITICAL SOURCES:

PERIODICALS

America's Intelligence Wire, July 6, 2005, "News Conference on CIA Leak Investigation."

Bond Buyer, March 30, 2005, Lynn Hume, "Can Raters Be Regulated?: Lawyer, Cases Cite First Amendment Protection," p. 1.

Broadcasting, October 24, 1983, "The First Amendment and Its Favorite Son," p. 95.

Chicago Tribune, July 17, 2005, Stevenson Swanson, "Celebrated First Amendment Attorney Continues Fight for Free Press."

Electronic Media, March 15, 1999, Jon Lafayette, "Libel Expert Feels a Chill: 'Tailwind' Lawyer Sees Media Antagonism on the Rise," interview with Floyd Abrams, p. 27.

Kirkus Reviews, February 1, 2005, review of *Speaking Freely: Trials of the First Amendment,* p. 157.

Legal Times, May 2, 2005, Robert Corn-Revere, "Championing the First Amendment," review of *Speaking Freely.*

National Law Journal, July 25, 2005, Pierce O'Donnell, review of *Speaking Freely.*

Publishers Weekly, February 14, 2005, review of *Speaking Freely,* p. 65.

Recorder, June 17, 2005, Alec Foege, "Speech, Speakers, and the Lawyer Who Backs Them," review of *Speaking Freely.*

ONLINE

Anti-Defamation League Web site, http://www.adl.org/ (November 7, 2003), "Renowned Attorney, Floyd Abrams, Honored with ADL Hubert H. Humphrey First Amendment Freedoms Prize."

Columbia University School of Journalism Web site, http://www.jrn.columbia.edu/ (October 25, 2005), "Floyd Abrams."*

*   *   *

ACEVEDO, Chantel

PERSONAL: Born in Hialeah, FL; married Orlando Acevedo (a chemist). *Education:* University of Miami, A.B., M.F.A., both 1997.

ADDRESSES: Home—Hamden, CT. *Office*—St. Margaret's-McTernan School, Chase Collegiate School, 565 Chase Parkway, Waterbury, CT 06708. *Agent*—Judith Weber, Sobel-Weber Associates, Inc., 146 E. 19th St., New York, NY 10003. *E-mail*—cacevedo@smmct.org.

CAREER: Writer and educator. St. Margaret's-McTernan School, Chase Collegiate School, Waterbury, CT, English teacher and dean of students.

AWARDS, HONORS: Fred Shaw Fiction Prize, 1998, and Pushcart Prize nomination, both for "Blue Exile"; Fulbright Memorial Fund grant, 2001; Fulbright Hays grant, 2004.

WRITINGS:

Love and Ghost Letters (novel), St. Martin's (New York, NY), 2005.

Also author of short stories and poems, including "Blue Exile," "The Tourist's Gift," "The Storyteller and the Little Revolution," "The Longest Walk," and "A Love That Hurts."

SIDELIGHTS: Chantel Acevedo is the daughter of two Cuban-American immigrants and Acevedo grew up in Miami, Florida, in the midst of a large extended family of Cuban exiles. Cuban culture and nostalgia pervaded her childhood and her grandmother told her stories of family members left behind. This consciousness, based on a Cuba that she can imagine but has never seen in person, pervades Acevedo's fiction, which she has been publishing since the late 1990s. Her novel *Love and Ghost Letters* tells the story of Josefina, a young woman from a wealthy family in pre-Castro Cuba. Captivated by a romantic but poor man, she marries him and leaves her comfortable home for a poverty-stricken village. Although she comes to believe that her father is dead, he has actually immigrated to Miami; now he begins sending her letters and money that are delivered by her village butcher. Josefina believes the letters are from heaven and falls in love with the man who delivers them.

Acevedo's debut novel was fairly well received by critics, and a *Kirkus Reviews* contributor called *Love and Ghost Letters* a "multigenerational story of life and love in Cuba." However, some reviewers complained that the story lacked a real sense of the details of Cuban life and deemed it unfocused. Marjorie Kehe, reviewing the book for the *Christian Science Monitor,* wrote that "Acevedo is a fine storyteller and although her tale ultimately bogs down, it unfolds with a leisurely pleasure that feels like magical realism."

BIOGRAPHICAL AND CRITICAL SOURCES:

PERIODICALS

Christian Science Monitor, August 29, 2005, Marjorie Kehe, "Longed for, but Never Quite Attained," review of *Love and Ghost Letters.*
Kirkus Reviews, June 15, 2005, review of *Love and Ghost Letters,* p. 649.

ONLINE

Chantel Acevedo Home Page, http://www.chantelacevedo.com (October 5, 2005).
Chantel Acevedo Web log, http://yucababy.easyjournal.com/ (October 5, 2005).
St. Margaret's-McTernan School: Chase Collegiate Parent's Association Web site, http://smmt-parents.org/ (October 5, 2005), author profile.*

*　　　*　　　*

ADAMS, Diane 1960-

PERSONAL: Born 1960; married. *Education:* University of Redlands, B.A.; studied at Art Center College of Design.

ADDRESSES: Home—Redlands, CA. *Agent*—c/o Author Mail, Peachtree Publishers, 1700 Chattahoochee Ave., Atlanta, GA 30318.

CAREER: Art and writing teacher.

WRITINGS:

Zoom! (picture book), illustrated by Kevin Luthardt, Peachtree Publishers (Atlanta, GA), 2005.

SIDELIGHTS: Diane Adams, an art and writing instructor; with the publication of *Zoom!,* she also became a children's book author. Geared toward preschoolers and students in the younger grades, this picture book tells the story of one young boy's triumph over his own fears. Encouraged by his eager father, the little boy reluctantly agrees to go on the Dino Coaster at the local amusement part. After the two reach the top and begin the first huge drop of the roller-coaster ride, explained *School Library Journal* contributor Grace Oliff, "the roles are reversed, with the child obviously thrilled and Dad clearly not." Throughout the ride, the illustrations by Kevin Luthardt show the boy beaming and waving his arms enthusiastically, the fear gone from his face. At the same time his father has the look of someone caught in a trap and wishing to be anywhere else. The story itself "unspools in singsongy couplets with plenty of heavy-duty action words," noted a *Publishers Weekly* reviewer, capturing the "lurching," "jerking," and "rumbling" of the roller coaster car as it speeds around the track. In the end of course, it is the little boy who decides to go around for a second time, while his father sits on the nearest bench.

BIOGRAPHICAL AND CRITICAL SOURCES:

PERIODICALS

Publishers Weekly, April 11, 2005, review of *Zoom!,* p. 53.
School Library Journal, May, 2005, Grace Oliff, review of *Zoom!,* p. 76.*

*　　　*　　　*

ADAMS, Simon 1955-

PERSONAL: Born 1955, in Bristol, England. *Education:* Studied at London University and Bristol University. *Hobbies and other interests:* Walking, cycling.

ADDRESSES: *Home*—London, England. *Agent*—c/o Author Mail, Heinemann Library, 100 N. LaSalle, Ste. 1200, Chicago, IL 60602.

CAREER: Editor and freelance writer. Children's book editor until 1990; writer, 1990—.

WRITINGS:

NONFICTION

(With Ann Kramer) *Revolution and Technology: Rapid Change and the Growth of the Modern World,* Warwick Press (New York, NY), 1990.

(With Ann Kramer) *Exploration and Empire: Empire Builders, European Expansion, and the Development of Science,* Warwick Press (New York, NY), 1990.

(With Ann Kramer and John Briquebec) *Illustrated Atlas of World History,* Random House (New York, NY), 1992.

The DK Visual Timeline of the 20th Century, DK Publishing (New York, NY), 1995.

(With others) *The DK Geography of the World,* DK Publishing (New York, NY), 1996.

Titanic (juvenile), DK Publishing (New York, NY), 1999, revised edition, 2004.

World War II (juvenile), DK Publishing (New York, NY), 2000, revised edition, 2004.

Kids' London, DK Publishing (New York, NY), 2000.

World War I (juvenile), photographs by Andy Crawford, DK Publishing (New York, NY), 2001, revised edition, 2004.

The Best Book of Volcanoes (juvenile), edited by Karen Dolan, Kingfisher (New York, NY), 2001.

The Best Book of Weather (juvenile), illustrated by Mike Saunders and Roger Stewart, Kingfisher (New York, NY), 2001.

The Presidents of the United States (juvenile), Two-Can (Minnetonka, MN), 2001, revised edition published as *The Presidents of the United States: Completely Revised and Updated to Include the 2004 Election,* 2005.

Codebreakers: From Hieroglyphics to Hackers (juvenile), DK Publishing (New York, NY), 2002.

Leicester and the Court: Essays on Elizabethan Politics, Manchester University Press (New York, NY), 2002.

(With Mary Atkinson and Sarah Phillips) *Children's World Atlas,* DK Publishing (New York, NY), 2003.

Mahatma Gandhi: The Father of Modern India (juvenile), Raintree Steck-Vaughn (Austin, TX), 2003.

Castles and Forts (juvenile), Kingfisher (New York, NY), 2003.

Winston Churchill: From Army Officer to World Leader (juvenile), Raintree Steck-Vaughn (Austin, TX), 2003.

(With David Murdoch) *Texas* (juvenile), DK Publishing (New York, NY), 2003.

The Cold War (juvenile), Sea-to-Sea Publications (North Mankato, MN), 2004.

The Role of the United Nations (juvenile), Sea-to-Sea Publications (North Mankato, MN), 2004.

Life in Ancient Rome (juvenile), Kingfisher (New York, NY), 2004.

The Russian Republics (juvenile), Sweet Apple Media (North Mankato, MN), 2005.

Northern Ireland (juvenile), Sweet Apple Media (North Mankato, MN), 2005.

Alexander: The Boy Soldier Who Conquered the World (juvenile), National Geographic Society (Washington, DC), 2005.

The Balkans (juvenile), Sweet Apple Media (North Mankato, MN), 2005.

Elisabeth I: The Outcast Who Became England's Queen (juvenile), National Geographic Society (Washington, DC), 2005.

Propaganda in War and Peace: Manipulating the Truth, Heinemann Library (Chicago, IL), 2005.

Contributor to over sixty books on historical topics, including *The Thirty Years' War,* edited by Geoffrey Parker, Routledge & Kegan Paul (Boston, MA), 1984.

SIDELIGHTS: Simon Adams is an English writer who specializes in works of history for juvenile readers. His *World War II* is a "highly visual introduction" to that conflict, according to *Booklist* contributor Carolyn Phelan. In the book, each major event of the war—such as the Battle of Britain or the development and use of the atomic bomb—is covered in a single paragraph accompanied by a picture. Adams gives the same treatment to the other major military conflict of the twentieth century with *World War I.* Again Adams blends a good deal of illustrated material with minimal text to examine major aspects of the war, from its causes to its conclusion. Hazel Rochman in *Booklist* found that the approach "provides a quick, informative overview." With *Castles and Forts* Adams explores another aspect of warfare, looking at forts and hilltop castles around the world, from the Great Wall of China to medieval castles. *School Library Journal* contributor Susan Shaver commended this title for being "colorful and accessible."

Adams has also explored the world of politics and world leaders with other titles. Leaders of the United States is the subject of *The Presidents of the United States,* in which each president is profiled in two pages with accompanying quotations from the person being profiled. For *School Library Journal* contributor William McLoughlin, "a fascinating part of each entry is the quotation that has come to define the man and his vision of the office." International world leaders are the focus of two biographies from Adams: *Mahatma Gandhi: The Father of Modern India* and *Winston Churchill: From Army Officer to World Leader.* With the former title, Adams provides, according to *School Library* contributor Kristen Oravec, an "insightful" as well as a "well researched" look at one of the most famous of world leaders. Adams particularly details how Gandhi's religious beliefs influenced his political life. The author also shows how Gandhi was able to stand up against the British Empire to forge a new nation and, in so doing, influence other future leaders, such as Martin Luther King, Jr. With his biography of British Prime Minister Winston Churchill, Adams follows the course of Churchill's life from his early years in the military in India and South Africa to his rise to a seat in Parliament and leadership of his country through the difficult years of World War II. *School Library Journal* reviewer Vicki Reutter called Adams's title "rock-solid."

BIOGRAPHICAL AND CRITICAL SOURCES:

PERIODICALS

Booklist, November 1, 1996, review of *The DK Geography of the World,* p. 534; November 15, 1999, Ellen Mandel, review of *Titanic,* p. 615; November 1, 2001, Carolyn Phelan, review of *World War II,* p. 526; December 15, 2001, Hazel Rochman, review of *World War I,* p. 718.
Childhood Education, summer, 2002, Stephanie J. Frickert, review of *The Best Book of Weather,* p. 240.

Kliatt, July, 2002, Janet Julian, review of *Codebreakers: From Hieroglyphics to Hackers,* p. 48.
Publishers Weekly, April 9, 2001, review of *The Presidents of the United States,* p. 76.
School Library Journal, July, 2001, William McLoughlin, review of *The Presidents of the United States,* p. 116; April, 2002, Patricia Manning, review of *The Best Book of Weather,* p. 128; April, 2003, Kristen Oravec, review of *Mahatma Gandhi: The Father of Modern India,* p. 171; July, 2003, Vicki Reutter, review of *Winston Churchill: From Army Officer to World Leader,* p. 135; December, 2003, Paul J. Bisnette, review of *Children's World Atlas,* p. 94, Susan Shave, review of *Castles and Forts,* p. 163; April, 2004, review of *Mahatma Gandhi: The Father of Modern India,* p. S54.

ONLINE

Education Oasis, http://www.educationoasis.com/ (September 9, 2005), "Simon Adams."*

*   *   *

AJAK, Benjamin 1982-

PERSONAL: Born 1982, in Sudan; son of farmers; immigrated to United States, 2001.

ADDRESSES: Home—San Diego, CA. *Agent*—c/o Author Mail, PublicAffairs, 250 W. 57th St., Ste. 1321, New York, NY 10107.

CAREER: Writer, truck driver, and actor. Has acted in television programs and films, including *Master and Commander, Judging Amy,* 2002, and *Threat Matrix,* 2003.

WRITINGS:

(With Judy Bernstein, Alephonsion Deng, and Benson Deng) *They Poured Fire on Us from the Sky: The True Story of Three Lost Boys from Sudan,* PublicAffairs (New York, NY), 2005.

SIDELIGHTS: For sidelights, see Deng, Benson.

BIOGRAPHICAL AND CRITICAL SOURCES:

BOOKS

Ajak, Benjamin, and Judy Bernstein, Alephonsion Deng, and Benson Deng, *They Poured Fire on Us from the Sky: The True Story of Three Lost Boys from Sudan,* PublicAffairs (New York, NY), 2005.

PERIODICALS

Del Mar Times (Del Mar, CA), May 27, 2005, Erin Spry, "From Death March to New Life on Coast."
Good Times Weekly, July 14, 2005, Christa Martin, review of *They Poured Fire on Us from the Sky.*
Kirkus Reviews, March 1, 2005, review of *They Poured Fire on Us from the Sky,* p. 272.
Library Journal, April 1, 2005, Maria C. Bagshaw, review of *They Poured Fire on Us from the Sky,* p. 107.
Los Angeles Times Magazine, January 5, 2003, David Weddle, "What the Lost Boys of Sudan Found in America."
Publishers Weekly, April 11, 2005, review of *They Poured Fire on Us from the Sky,* p. 40.
San Diego Union-Tribune, June 12, 2005, Wendy L. Smith, review of *They Poured Fire on Us from the Sky.*

ONLINE

BookLoons, http://www.bookloons.com/ (September 29, 2005), Mary Ann Smyth, review of *They Poured Fire on Us from the Sky.*
BookPage, http://www.bookpage.com/ (September 29, 2005), Anne Bartlett, review of *They Poured Fire on Us from the Sky.*
Insight News, http://www.insightnews.com/ (September 29, 2005), Terry Schlichenmeyer, review of *They Poured Fire on Us from the Sky.*
PublicAffairs Books Web site, http://www.publicaffairs books.com/ (September 29, 2005).
They Poured Fire on Us from the Sky Web site, http://www.theypouredfire.com/ (September 29, 2005).*

AKHTAR, Salman 1946-

PERSONAL: Born July 31, 1946.

ADDRESSES: Office—Department of Psychiatry and Human Behavior, Jefferson Medical College, Thomas Jefferson University, 833 Chestnut E., Ste. 210, Philadelphia, PA 19107. *E-mail*—Salman.Akhtar@jefferson.edu.

CAREER: Jefferson Medical College, Philadelphia, PA, professor of psychiatry; Inter-Act Theater Company, Philadelphia, scholar-in-residence.

AWARDS, HONORS: Best paper of the year award, *Journal of the American Psychoanalytic Association.*

WRITINGS:

PSYCHOLOGY

New Psychiatric Syndromes: DSM-III and Beyond, J. Aronson (New York, NY), 1983.
(Editor, with Selma Kramer) *The Trauma of Transgression: Psychotherapy of Incest Victims,* J. Aronson (Northvale, NJ), 1991.
(Editor, with Henri Parens) *Beyond the Symbiotic Orbit: Advances in Separation-Individuation Theory: Essays in Honor of Selma Kramer, M.D.,* Analytic Press (Hillsdale, NJ), 1991.
Broken Structures: Severe Personality Disorders and Their Treatment, J. Aronson (Northvale, NJ), 1992, revised edition, 2002.
(Editor, with Selma Kramer) *When the Body Speaks: Psychological Meanings in Kinetic Clues,* J. Aronson (Northvale, NJ), 1992.
(Editor, with Selma Kramer) *Mahler and Kohut: Perspectives on Development, Psychopathology, and Technique,* J. Aronson (Northvale, NJ), 1994.
(Editor, with Selma Kramer and Henri Parens) *The Birth of Hatred: Developmental, Clinical, and Technical Aspects of Intense Aggression,* J. Aronson (Northvale, NJ), 1995.
Quest for Answers: A Primer of Understanding and Treating Severe Personality Disorders, J. Aronson (Northvale, NJ), 1995.

(Editor, with Selma Kramer and Henri Parens) *The Internal Mother: Conceptual and Technical Aspects of Object Constancy,* J. Aronson (Northvale, NJ), 1996.

(Editor, with Selma Kramer) *Intimacy and Infidelity: Separation-Individuation Perspectives,* J. Aronson (Northvale, NJ), 1996.

(With others) *Lacan avec la psychanalyse américaine,* edited by Judith Feher-Gurewich and Michel Tort, Denoël (Paris, France), 1996.

(Editor, with Selma Kramer) *The Seasons of Life: Separation-Individuation Perspectives,* J. Aronson (Northvale, NJ), 1997.

(Editor, with Vamik Volkan) *The Seed of Madness: Constitution, Environment, and Fantasy in the Organization of the Psychotic Core,* International Universities Press (Madison, CT), 1997.

(Editor, with Selma Kramer) *The Colors of Childhood: Separation-Individuation across Cultural, Racial, and Ethnic Differences,* J. Aronson (Northvale, NJ), 1998.

(Editor, with Selma Kramer) *Brothers and Sisters: Developmental, Dynamic, and Technical Aspects of the Sibling Relationship,* J. Aronson (Northvale, NJ), 1999.

Inner Torment: Living between Conflict and Fragmentation, J. Aronson (Northvale, NJ), 1999.

Immigration and Identity: Turmoil, Treatment, and Transformation, J. Aronson (Northvale, NJ), 1999.

Thicker than Blood: Bonds of Fantasy and Reality in Adoption, J. Aronson (Northvale, NJ), 2000.

(Editor, with Henri Parens) *Does God Help?: Developmental and Clinical Aspects of Religious Belief,* J. Aronson (Northvale, NJ), 2001.

Three Faces of Mourning: Melancholia, Manic Defense, and Moving On, J. Aronson (Northvale, NJ), 2001.

(Editor, with Vamik Volkan) *Cultural Zoo: Animals in the Human Mind and Its Sublimations,* International Universities Press (Madison, CT), 2003.

(Editor, with Vamik Volkan) *Mental Zoo: Animals in the Human Mind and Its Psychology,* International Universities Press (Madison, CT), 2003.

New Clinical Realms: Pushing the Envelope of Theory and Technique, J. Aronson (Northvale, NJ), 2003.

(Editor, with Henri Parens) *Real and Imaginary Fathers: Development, Transference, and Healing,* J. Aronson (Lanham, MD), 2004.

(Editor) *Freud along the Ganges: Psychoanalytic Reflections on the People and Culture of India,* Other Press (New York, NY), 2005.

Objects of Our Desire: Exploring Our Intimate Connections with the Things around Us, Harmony Books (New York, NY), 2005.

(Editor, with Harold Blum) *The Language of Emotions: Development, Psychopathology, and Technique,* J. Aronson (Northvale, NJ), 2005.

POEMS

The Hidden Knot, Adams Press (Chicago, IL), 1985.
Turned to Light, Adams Press (Chicago, IL), 1998.
Nadi ke pas: Intikhab-i kalam, Star Pablikishanz (Delhi, India), 2004.

Also author of *Kubahku,* 1976, and of two other books of poetry.

ADAPTATIONS: The play *Parinday* (title means "Birds"), based on *Immigration and Identity: Turmoil, Treatment, and Transformation,* aired on British Broadcasting Corporation.

SIDELIGHTS: Psychiatrist Salman Akhtar is the author of many books, both works about psychoanalysis—generally in English—and poetry, often in his native Urdu. His best-known work may be *Objects of Our Desire: Exploring Our Intimate Connections with the Things around Us,* published in 2005. In this volume Akhtar "takes readers on a quirky tour of the ordinary objects that populate our lives," Marianne Le explained in *Library Journal.* Akhtar examines the way that almost all physical objects in the world figure in people's attempts to make sense of their lives and construct their personalities. In one chapter, he discusses the importance of children's favorite blankets or stuffed animals, which, he claims, help young children "create the experiential realm between the inner world and external reality." In another chapter, he examines the urge that all people have, to a greater or lesser extent, to amass "stuff," an urge he views as rooted in childhood experiences. Akhtar also turns his attention to specific objects with which people have spiritual relationships, such as Jerusalem's Wailing Wall, the Hindu diety Ganesha, and the Muslim Dome of the Rock, and discusses the transition of human bodies from "persons" to "objects" at death. "Among the highlights are some intriguing thing-related factoids," noted a *Kirkus Reviews* contributor, citing the fact that "the inventor of the Frisbee instructed his family that after death his remains should be incorporated into limited edition Frisbees."

Akhtar examines the psychology of immigrants in *Immigration and Identity: Turmoil, Treatment, and Transformation*. This book examines the experiences of voluntary immigrants from many perspectives, including historical, external, and internal, but the author is quick to point out that every immigrant's experience is different. After explaining the psychological conflicts an immigrant is likely to face, Akhtar then gives some advice to psychoanalysts who find themselves working with such patients. "Akhtar beautifully captures the kaleidoscopic nature of an immigrant's identity in this rich and enlightening book," Azmaira Maker wrote in *International Migration Review*.

BIOGRAPHICAL AND CRITICAL SOURCES:

BOOKS

Akhtar, Salman, *Objects of Our Desire: Exploring Our Intimate Connections with the Things around Us*, Harmony Books (New York, NY), 2005.

PERIODICALS

International Migration Review, summer, 2001, Azmaira Maker, review of *Immigration and Identity: Turmoil, Treatment, and Transformation*, p. 606.
Kirkus Reviews, June 15, 2005, review of *Objects of Our Desire: Exploring Our Intimate Connections with the Things around Us*, p. 669.
Library Bookwatch, July, 2005, review of *Cultural Zoo: Animals in the Human Mind and Its Sublimations*.
Library Journal, July 1, 2005, Marianne Le, review of *Objects of Our Desire*, p. 103.
Publishers Weekly, June 6, 2005, review of *Objects of Our Desire*, p. 52.*

*   *   *

ALEGRÍA, Fernando 1918-2005

OBITUARY NOTICE— See index for *CA* sketch: Born September 26, 1918, in Santiago, Chile; died of kidney failure, October 29, 2005, in Walnut Creek, CA. Educator and author. Alegría was an award-winning Chilean author of novels, poetry, and criticism, who spent much of his life living and teaching in the United States. Fostering a love of literature from his boyhood, his first writings were published in *La Nación* in Santiago while he was attending the Academia de Humanidades. After graduating from the University of Chile, he moved to the United States for his graduate education. Alegría completed his master's degree at Bowling Green State University in 1941, followed by a Ph.D. from the University of California at Berkeley in 1947. By this time he was already a published author and had won the Latin American Prize of Literature in 1943 for the children's book *Lautaro: Joven libertador de Arauco* (1943; 5th edition, 1965). After he completed his doctorate, Alegría remained at Berkeley as an instructor and later professor of Spanish and Portuguese until 1967, when he joined the faculty at Stanford University. During this time, he solidified his reputation as a writer with *Caballo de copas* (1957; 2nd edition, 1961), a novel that expresses his love of horses and which was translated in 1964 as *My Horse Gonzales*. Although he taught in America, Alegría spent a great deal of his time in Chile, where he was a friend of President Salvador Allende. Allende, in fact, appointed Alegría to be the cultural attaché at the Chilean Embassy in Washington, DC, in 1970. In Chile, the author was also known for his "Viva Chile M!," a poem about a devastating earthquake that was set to music and became very popular. Alegría served as cultural attaché until 1973, when Allende was assassinated in a military coup. The author later wrote about the coup in *El paso de los gansos* (1980); he also fictionalized Allende's life in *Allende: mi vecino, el presidente*, translated as *Allende: A Novel* (1993). Having been a friend to the former president, Alegría was forced into exile and would not return to his homeland until political restrictions were lifted in 1987, the same year he retired from teaching as a professor emeritus. As an educator, Alegría was best known for being a pioneer in the study of Latin-American literature. He helped students and teachers become more familiar with the writings of South and Central American writers, editing such collections as *Novelistas contemporaneos hispanoamericanos* (1964), *Chilean Writers in Exile: Eight Short Novels* (1982), and *Paradise Lost or Gained? The Literature of Hispanic Exile* (1992). Among his other writings are *Ten Pastoral Psalms* (1968), *Amerika (manifiestos de Vietnam)* (1970), *The Chilean Spring* (1980), and *The Funhouse* (1986).

OBITUARIES AND OTHER SOURCES:

PERIODICALS

Los Angeles Times, November 23, 2005, p. B8.
San Francisco Chronicle, November 20, 2005, p. B5.

ALEXANDER, Max 1957-

PERSONAL: Born February 17, 1957, in Grand Rapids, MI; son of James and Marianne (Helko) Sterling; married Sarah Rachel Baldwin (June 14, 1986); children: Harper, Whit. *Education:* Columbia University, B.A., 1987. *Politics:* Democrat.

ADDRESSES: Agent—c/o Author Mail, Carroll & Graf, 245 W. 17th St., 11th Fl., New York, NY 10011-5300.

CAREER: Writer, editor, and farmer. *Variety* and *Daily Variety,* executive editor, Los Angeles, CA, 1990-97; *People,* senior editor, New York, NY, 1997-99; farmer, 1999—.

WRITINGS:

(With Clark Frasier and Mark Gaier) *The Arrows Cookbook: Cooking and Gardening from Maine's Most Beautiful Farmhouse Restaurant,* foreword by Jeremiah Tower, photography by John Kernick, Scribner (New York, NY), 2003.

Man Bites Log: The Unlikely Adventures of a City Guy in the Woods, Carroll & Graf (New York, NY), 2004.

Editor of *Ernest Shackleton,* by George Plimpton. Also contributor to *Reader's Digest, This Old House, Martha Stewart Living, Bon Appetit, Country Home,* and *New York Times Book Review.*

SIDELIGHTS: Max Alexander went from being an editor in New York City and Los Angeles, California, to being a freelance writer and farmer in Maine. He and his wife and two sons decided, like many before them, that the hectic and chaotic world of big-city living was not for them. Instead, their lives now consist of farming, gardening, making wine, writing, and dealing with the new experiences and struggles that result from living off of the land. Alexander shares his and his family's experiences in the essay collection *Man Bites Log: The Unlikely Adventures of a City Guy in the Woods.*

The book was well received by critics who found the stories, by turns, endearing and amusing. Indeed, Loree Davis, writing in *Library Journal,* noted that "Alexander takes us on a familiar journey—but he does it well." A *Publishers Weekly* critic echoed the sentiment, stating that "City slicker-in-the-woods has been done before, as Alexander readily admits, but it's done here with honesty, charm, and a good dose of self-deprecation." The city-to-country lifestyle continued to hold an appeal for Alexander and his family; as of 2005, they were still living in Maine. The family set up the *Faraway Farm, Maine* Web site to discuss pertinent issues with others who share their lifestyle.

Alexander has also coauthored *The Arrows Cookbook: Cooking and Gardening from Maine's Most Beautiful Farmhouse Restaurant.* Alexander collaborated on the book in 2003 with Clark Frasier and Mark Gaier, both of whom had also moved to Maine to farm. They then opened a very popular restaurant that utilized their produce. Alexander provided the blurbs and sidelines that appear throughout the cookbook.

BIOGRAPHICAL AND CRITICAL SOURCES:

BOOKS

Alexander, Max, *Man Bites Log: The Unlikely Adventures of a City Guy in the Woods,* Carroll & Graf (New York, NY), 2004.

PERIODICALS

Kirkus Reviews, September 1, 2004, review of *Man Bites Log,* p. 843.

Library Journal, October 15, 2004, Loree Davis, review of *Man Bites Log,* p. 69.

Publishers Weekly, April 21, 2003, review of *The Arrows Cookbook: Cooking and Gardening from Maine's Most Beautiful Farmhouse Restaurant,* p. 55; October 11, 2004, review of *Man Bites Log,* p. 66.

ONLINE

Faraway Farm, Maine Web site, http://www.faraway maine.com/ (October 19, 2005).

*   *   *

ALLRED, Michael D.
(Michael Dalton Allred)

PERSONAL: Born in OR; married June 22, 1981; wife's name Laura (an artist); children: three. *Hobbies and other interests:* Film, rock-and-roll music.

ADDRESSES: Office—c/o Dark Horse Comics, 10956 SE Main St., Milwaukie, OR 97222.

CAREER: Comic-book artist and writer. Worked as a television journalist in Europe. Member of rock band Gear. Writer, director, and producer of film *Astroesque,* 1998; producer, with Shane Hawks, of film *Eyes to Heaven,* 1999.

WRITINGS:

COMICS

The Complete Madman Comics, Volume 2, Dark Horse Comics (Milwaukie, OR), 1996.

The Superman/Madman Hullabaloo! (originally published as issues 1-3 of *Superman/Madman Hullabaloo!* comic-book series), Dark Horse Comics/DC Comics, (Milwaukie, OR), 1998.

Red Rocket 7 (originally published as issues 1-7 of *Red Rocket 7* comic-book series), Dark Horse Comics (Milwaukie, OR), 1998.

Madman Boogaloo! (originally published as *Nexus Meets Madman* and *Madman/The Jam* comic-book series), Dark Horse Comics/DC Comics, (Milwaukie, OR), 1999.

(Illustrator) Shane Hawks, *Feeders,* Dark Horse Comics (Milwaukie, OR), 1999.

The Complete Madman Comics, Volume 3, Dark Horse Comics (Milwaukie, OR), 2000.

(Illustrator, with others) *Green Lantern/Superman: Legend of the Green Flame,* DC Comics (New York, NY), 2000.

The Complete Madman Comics, Volume 4, Dark Horse Comics (Milwaukie, OR), 2001.

Author of other comics series, including *Graphique Musique* (later titled *Graphik Muzik* and *Tales of Ordinary Madness.* Author of screenplay *Astroesque.*

ADAPTATIONS: Graphik Muzik was adapted by Robert Cooper, Richard L. Albert, and Nicholas Johnson as the film *G-Men from Hell,* directed by Christopher Coppola, Sawmill Entertainment, 2001.

SIDELIGHTS: Michael D. Allred has written and illustrated a variety of comic-book series, creating such characters as amnesiac superhero Frank Einstein of *Madman* and space alien Red Rocket 7 of the series of the same name and also drawing characters originated by others, such as Superman. Allred has described himself as a "frustrated filmmaker," and his work displays the influence of science-fiction movies and film noir, as well as showcasing his love of rock-and-roll music. Allred had been a broadcast journalist and was trying to develop a career in movie-making when he began working on comics. "It's storytelling in a very visual medium much like film," he told *Washington Times* reporter Joseph Szadkowski, adding: "I realized that if I honed my artistic skills, I could draw my own movies."

One of Allred's early projects, *Graphique Musique* (later *Graphik Muzik*), was "kind of an umbrella title that allowed me to do anything I wanted," he remarked in an interview with Shawna Ervin for the Dark Horse Comics Web site. One of the characters he developed in this series is Einstein, who is driven to discover the truth about himself and his past, as he can remember nothing. Einstein was one of Allred's favorite creations, and he proved popular with readers too. Wanting to go further with the character, Allred made Einstein the costumed protagonist of *Madman.* "Rather than creating a character from scratch, I liked this Frank Einstein character so much that I saw his backstory was really the genesis of this new character," he told Ervin. Writing about Einstein gives Allred the opportunity of "rediscovering the world through his eyes," the author continued, adding that "Frank Einstein used to be the crazy, unpredictable character, and as the series progresses and more crazy characters are introduced, he's becoming the sane, stable one."

One of the characters who has appeared in *Madman,* Mott from the planet Hoople, is an homage to the rock group Mott the Hoople, reflecting Allred's interest in rock and roll music. Another title, *Red Rocket 7,* explores the music world further. In this series, a space alien known as Red Rocket lands in the northwestern United States and is cloned six times, with each clone, numbered two through seven, gaining an intensified version of one of the original Red Rocket's talents. Red Rocket 7 has a gift for music, and he "integrates himself and takes part in Rock 'n' Roll history," Allred told Tom Fassbender in an interview for the Dark Horse Comics Web site. "He's there at the beginning and finds himself at all these key events as this musical art form changes and grows and progresses." The character encounters Elvis Presley, Little Richard, and the Beatles, among others. Szadkowski called *Red Rocket 7* "a very inspired work" and "an intriguing tale." Allred's band, the Gear, released a concept CD, *Son of Red Rocket 7,* in conjunction with a collection of the comics.

Son of Red Rocket 7 is "not a soundtrack per se," Allred told Fassbender; he explained, "When I would listen to music I would often read comics—when I think of certain comic books I think of the music that I was listening to at the time. I wanted to have that kind of experience for this." Allred allowed that the project is "unconventional," but told Fassbender: "I feel very strongly about expanding comics. Comics is the untapped art medium. Music has been done so many ways, as have films and novels. . . . comic books are so untapped when you compare them to other art forms. There's so much to be done."

BIOGRAPHICAL AND CRITICAL SOURCES:

PERIODICALS

Washington Times, July 8, 1995, Joseph Szadkowski, "Michael Allred's 'Madness' Helped Hone His Artistic Talents," p. B4; November 22, 1997, Joseph Szadkowski, "Rocket Is Blast of Sci-fi, Rock," p. B4.

ONLINE

Dark Horse Comics Web site, http://www.darkhorse. com/ (February 1, 1999), Shawna Ervin, interview with Michael D. Allred; (December 30, 2003) Tom Fassbender, interview with Allred.
Michael D. Allred Home Page, http://www.aaapop. com (November 26, 2003).*

*   *   *

ALLRED, Michael Dalton
    See ALLRED, Michael D.

*   *   *

AMIS, Vivian 1961-

PERSONAL: Born January 23, 1961, in Wiesbaden, Germany; naturalized U.S. citizen; daughter of Peter and Brigitta (Pfeiffer) Liebschwager; married Angel Alfredo, 1986 (marriage ended, 1996); married Rafael Quinones (a granite installer); children: Caroline Bruhn, Brian, Charlene, Rebecca. *Education:* Attended a trade school for beauticians.

ADDRESSES: *Home*—10102 Singing Oaks Ct., Tampa, FL 33615. *Office*—P.O. Box 261274, Tampa, FL 33685-1274. *E-mail*—vivamis123@verizon.net.

CAREER: Writer. Spiritual healer and teacher of spiritual consciousness. Worked as a sales associate at Dillards, a bank analyst, and an office manager of lifeguards, all in Tampa, FL. Healing Arts Alliances, member.

WRITINGS:

The Essentials of Life, I-nspire Direct (Clearwater, FL), 2004.

Contributor to periodicals.

WORK IN PROGRESS: *Reflections,* on the spiritual understanding of relationships; research on spiritual color therapy and spiritual numerology.

SIDELIGHTS: Vivian Amis told *CA:* "My primary motivation for writing is to make a difference in people's everyday lives. God is my main motivation. Jesus's life teachings influence my work. I feel a strong need to interpret the Bible and the teachings of Jesus into a usable, understandable language. In meditation I receive messages that I pass on in my teachings: books, classes, and consultations.

"I experienced a healing at the age of eleven. A spiritual experience at the age of twenty-seven put me on my path to seek the truth of our being."

*   *   *

ANDERSEN, Deborah Lines 1948-

PERSONAL: Born July 10, 1948, in Suffern, NY. *Education:* Mount Holyoke College, A.B. (with distinction), 1970; Wesleyan University, M.A.T., 1972; Simmons College, M.S.L.S., 1977; State University of New York at Albany, Ph.D., 1996.

ADDRESSES: Home—New Fadum Farm, 1167 Delaware Turnpike, Delmar, NY 12054-5517. *Office*—School of Information Science and Policy, State University of New York at Albany, Albany, NY 12222. *E-mail*—dla@albany.edu.

CAREER: Writer. Junior high school English teacher in Glastonbury, CT, 1971; high school English teacher and dramatics coach in Suffield, CT, 1971-73, and Winchester, MA, 1973-77; New York State Library, Albany, reference librarian, 1977-82; State University of New York at Albany, adjunct professor, 1992-93, 1996-97, visiting assistant professor and academic coordinator of Korean Partnership Program, 1997-98, assistant professor of information science and policy, 1998—. University of Glasgow, visiting professor at Humanities Advanced Technology and Information Institute, 2003. Workshop and conference presenter; consultant to New York State Forum for Information Resources Management and to regional and city libraries. New Fadum Farm (sheep and wool enterprise), owner and operator, 1982—; Altamont Fair, mentor and demonstrator of fiber production techniques, 1987—, director of sheep barn fiber activities, 1999—; Hancock Shaker Museum, fiber arts interpreter, 1997.

MEMBER: International System Dynamics Society (vice president for publications, 2004—), American Library Association, American Association for History and Computing (member of executive committee and policy council, 1999-2006), American Historical Association, Beta Phi Mu.

AWARDS, HONORS: Award for best article, American Association for History and Computing, 1999, for "Academic Historians, Electronic Information Access Technologies, and the World Wide Web: Longitudinal Study of Factors Affecting Use and Barriers to That Use."

WRITINGS:

(Editor) *Digital Scholarship in the Tenure, Promotion, and Review Process*, M.E. Sharpe (Armonk, NY), 2004.

Contributor to books, including *History.edu: Essays on Teaching with Technology*, edited by Trinkle and Merriman, M.E. Sharpe (Armonk, NY), 2000. Contributor of articles and editorials to periodicals, including *System Dynamics Review*, *Public Library Quarterly*, *Pantaneto Forum*, and *Journal of Education for Library and Information Science*. Associate editor, *Journal of the Association for History and Computing*, 1998—.

SIDELIGHTS: Deborah Lines Andersen told *CA:* "Computers are changing the way we do everything in our lives. In the academic world we find that more and more faculty members are using computing, not just to type their manuscripts, but also to give new forms and functions to the way that they do research, teaching, and publication. The World Wide Web allows academics to pursue new venues for dissemination of their work—creating virtual communities of scholars around the world.

"Tenure, promotion, and review are critical to academics who wish to continue at universities and colleges. Digital scholarship has made their work richer and more accessible, but it has also made evaluating this work more difficult. Academics were once reviewed based upon books or articles produced on paper. Now, although they may choose paper formats, they may also select the World Wide Web, CD-ROM, DVD, computer simulations, or a wealth of other media—textual, auditory, and/or visual—in which to display and disseminate their scholarship.

"My research and teaching focus to a large degree on evaluation for policy formation and redesign. *Digital Scholarship in the Tenure, Promotion, and Review Process* specifically addresses the issues, methods, and policies involved both in creating nontraditional scholarship and in evaluating that scholarship for academic advancement."

*   *   *

APPLEGATE, Shannon

PERSONAL: Daughter of Rex Applegate (deceased); children: six.

ADDRESSES: Agent—c/o Author Mail, Thunder's Mouth Press, 245 W. 17th St., 11th Fl., New York, NY 10011-5300.

CAREER: Writer, lecturer, teacher, and historian. Applegate Pioneer Cemetery, sexton, Yoncalla, OR, 1997—. Chair of Oregon Commission on Historic Cemeteries. Also worked as a museum director, arts programs coordinator, historical properties manager, and chef.

AWARDS, HONORS: National literary award, Coordinated Council of Literary Magazines, 1977; selection among Oregon's Best 100 Literary Works, 1800-2000, for *Skookum: An Oregon Pioneer Family's History and Lore.*

WRITINGS:

Skookum: An Oregon Pioneer Family's History and Lore, Beech Tree Books (New York, NY), 1988.
(Editor, with Terence O'Donnell) *Talking on Paper: An Anthology of Oregon Letters and Diaries,* Oregon State University Press (Corvallis, OR), 1994.
Living among Headstones: Life in a Country Cemetery (memoir), Thunder's Mouth Press (New York, NY) 2005.

Contributor of essays to book and periodicals. Work included in anthology *The Stories That Shape Us,* Norton, 1995.

WORK IN PROGRESS: Minus Tides, a novel.

SIDELIGHTS: Shannon Applegate was working as a writer, historian, and writing teacher when she inherited the position of sexton at the Applegate Pioneer Cemetery in Yoncalla, Oregon. The cemetery had been passed down through her family for generations, but her father had tried to get the city to take over after he retired so that Applegate would not have to inherit the responsibility and upkeep of the small cemetery. The city refused, and Applegate became sexton in 1997. Already a writer, Applegate saw much material for a book in the little cemetery. She learned about its upkeep and about the Yoncalla inhabitants who had ancestors buried there, and *Living Among Headstones: Life in a Country Cemetery* was the result.

The book ponders Applegate's family's past as well as the past and history of other Yoncalla families and residents. In addition, the book considers the symbolic meaning behind many funereal traditions, and reports on the modern issues that the cemetery faces on a daily basis. A *Kirkus Reviews* contributor noted that "what the author says about being a small-town sexton is fresh and interesting." Furthermore, *Eugene Weekly* contributor Molly Templeton called the author's writing "pragmatic and straightforward," noting that Applegate is "also deeply in touch with the emotions that she sets gently on the page, even through the stranger, sadder parts of her life as a cemetery sexton."

BIOGRAPHICAL AND CRITICAL SOURCES:

BOOKS

Applegate, Shannon, *Living among Headstones: Life in a Country Cemetery,* Thunder's Mouth Press (New York, NY), 2005.

PERIODICALS

Eugene Weekly, June 2, 2005, Molly Templeton, "An Unusual Responsibility: Living with Death in a Small Oregon Town."
Kirkus Reviews, April 1, 2005, review of *Living among Headstones,* p. 393.
Oregonian, May 29, 2005, Joanna Rose, review of *Living among Headstones.*
Seattle Times, June 17, 2005, David Takami, review of *Living among Headstones.*

ONLINE

Oregon State University Press Web site, http://oregon state.edu/ (October 19, 2005), author profile.

*   *   *

ARDELIUS, Lars 1926-

PERSONAL: Born 1926, in Sweden; married.

ADDRESSES: Agent—c/o Author Mail, Norstedts Tryckerigatan, Box 4, Stockholm 2052, Sweden.

CAREER: Has worked as a salesman, psychologist, and teacher.

AWARDS, HONORS: Nordiska Radets Litteraturpris nomination, for *Barnsben.*

WRITINGS:

Svävningar, Norstedt (Stockholm, Sweden), 1963.
Plagiat, Norstedt (Stockholm, Sweden), 1968.
(With others) *Refuserat* (Swedish drama), Bonnier (Stockholm, Sweden), 1969.
Gösta Berglunds Saga, Norstedt (Stockholm, Sweden), 1970.
Kronprinsarna, Norstedt (Stockholm, Sweden), 1972.
Smorgasbordet, Norstedt (Stockholm, Sweden), 1974.
Och kungen var kung, Norstedt (Stockholm, Sweden), 1976.
(With Gunnar Rydström) *Författarnas litteraturhistoria* (biography), three volumes, Författarförlaget (Stockholm, Sweden), 1977– 78
Tid och otid (sequel to *Och kungen var kung*), Norstedt (Stockholm, Sweden), 1978.
Svävningar och Rök, PAN/Norstedt (Stockholm, Sweden), 1979.
Spritt språngande och Plagiat, PAN/Norstedt (Stockholm, Sweden), 1979.
(With others) *Författarnas litteraturhistoria: de utländska författarna* (literary history and criticism) three volumes, Författarförlaget (Stockholm, Sweden), 1980– 82
Provryttare, Norstedt (Stockholm, Sweden), 1981.
Nya drömboken, Norstedt (Stockholm, Sweden), 1982.
Ogjort (biography), Författarförlaget (Stockholm, Sweden), 1983.
Större än störst, Norstedt (Stockholm, Sweden), 1985.
Barnsben (autobiography), Norstedt (Stockholm, Sweden), 1986.
Skjuta i höjden (autobiography), Legenda (Stockholm, Sweden), 1988.
Livtag (autobiography; title mean "A Grapple with Life"), Legenda (Stockholm, Sweden), 1991.
Kurage! (historical novel), Norstedt (Stockholm, Sweden), 1993.
Resandes ensak (stories), Norstedt (Stockholm, Sweden), 1995.
Bitvargen (autobiography), Norstedt (Stockholm, Sweden), 1997.
Lilla sockerstunden: berättelser, Norstedt (Stockholm, Sweden), 1998.

Världens ställe, Norstedts (Stockholm, Sweden), 2000.
Ett hål i naturen: om konst, Atlantis (Stockholm, Sweden), 2002.
Ingen ålder, Norstedt (Stockholm, Sweden), 2003.
En lyckad begraving, Norstedts (Stockholm, Sweden), 2005.

Author of television plays, including *Badarna,* 1968; *Rätt man,* 1968; and *Vådaren,* 1969. Work represented in anthologies, including *Förord,* Rabén & Sjögren (Stockholm, Sweden), 1969.

SIDELIGHTS: Lars Ardelius is a Swedish author of fiction who has also written several autobiographies, including *Barnsben,* which was nominated for a literature prize. In *Livtag,* he writes of his family, various jobs, and the writing community of which he has been a part. Ardelius notes his preferences in the areas of both literature and fine art and comments on his life as a child, his politics, and his struggle with alcoholism. Ardelius is also open about his fragile relationship with is father, who ended his life and left a note that blamed his son, in part, for his suicide.

Bitvargen is an account of Ardelius's life from age forty-five to sixty. He writes touchingly of his sister's death from alcoholism at the age of thirty-five. Charlotte Schiander Gray reviewed the book in *World Literature Today,* noting that "Ardelius's accounts of his writing, his periods of writer's block, and his searches for inspiration are illustrative and at times humorous" and that his "extensive portrayals of people and events are part of a continual quest for meaning and identity."

BIOGRAPHICAL AND CRITICAL SOURCES:

BOOKS

Ardelius, Lars, *Barnsben,* Norstedt (Stockholm Sweden), 1986.
Ardelius, Lars, *Skjuta i höjden,* Legenda (Stockholm, Sweden), 1988.
Ardelius, Lars, *Livtag,* Legenda (Stockholm, Sweden), 1991.
Ardelius, Lars, *Bitvargen,* Norstedt (Stockholm, Sweden), 1997.

PERIODICALS

World Literature Today, autumn, 1992, Joran Mjoberg, review of *Livtag,* p. 1992; summer, 1994, Charlotte Schiander Gray, review of *Kurage!,* p. 590; summer, 1996, Charlotte Schiander Gray, review of *Resandes ensak,* p. 716; spring, 1998, Charlotte Schiander Gray, review of *Bitvargen,* p. 396.*

* * *

ARSENAULT, Mark 1967-

PERSONAL: Born 1967, in MA. *Education:* Assumption College (Worcester, MA), B.A., 1989.

ADDRESSES: Office—Providence Journal, 75 Fountain St., Providence, RI 02902. *E-mail*—Mark0079@cox.net; marsenau@projo.com.

CAREER: Writer and journalist. *Gardner News,* MA, reporter, 1989-92; *Marlboro Enterprise,* Marlboro, MA, reporter and night city editor, 1992-94; *Sun,* Lowell, MA, reporter, 1994-98; *Providence Journal,* Providence, RI, general assignment reporter, 1998—. Also worked as a newspaper delivery boy, newspaper truck diver, Sunday paper section inserter, and paste-up artist.

AWARDS, HONORS: Pulitzer Prize finalist, 2003, for *Providence Journal* coverage of February, 2003, Station nightclub fire.

WRITINGS:

Spiked (novel), Poisoned Pen Press (Scottsdale, AZ), 2003.
Speak Ill of the Living (novel), Poisoned Pen Press 2005.

SIDELIGHTS: Mark Arsenault began his career as a paper boy before working as a reporter for a number of newspapers. It is no wonder, then, that when Arsenault wrote his first mystery novel, *Spiked,* the protagonist was a journalist. The book met with much critical success and has been followed up by the equally successful *Speak Ill of the Living.*

The story in *Spiked* revolves around Eddie Bourque, a journalist in Lowell, Massachusetts. Eddie is covering the next city council election when his partner is killed. He then turns his attention instead to investigating the death of his friend and in the process puts himself into danger. According to *Booklist* contributor Frank Sennett, Arsenault "has a fine ear for the rhythms of a low-rent paper," while a *Publishers Weekly* critic stated: "A fine writer, Arsenault keeps the tension building right up to the surprise ending."

Arsenault's second mystery novel, *Speak Ill of the Living,* is the story, according to a *Midwest Book Review* critic, of a "car-jacking, a banker's murder, and a subsequent kidnapping with a puzzling corpse." The protagonist is once again journalist Eddie Bourque, who is following the story in the hope that it will advance his career. This time, the mystery takes Eddie to prison where his brother Henry, whom he barely knows, says he knows what has happened and that he is innocent of the crime he was imprisoned for. Writing in the *Midwest Book Review,* Harriet Klausner called the novel "a cleverly constructed mystery" in which "Arsenault uses misinformation to create a fantastic journalistic thriller."

BIOGRAPHICAL AND CRITICAL SOURCES:

PERIODICALS

Booklist, July, 2005, Frank Sennett, review of *Spiked,* p. 1868; January 1, 2005, Frank Sennett, review of *Speak Ill of the Living,* p. 824.
Kirkus Reviews, December 1, 2004, review of *Speak Ill of the Living,* p. 1118.
Library Journal, July, 2005, Rex Klett, review of *Spiked,* p. 129.
Midwest Book Review, February, 2005, Harriet Klausner, Review of *Speak Ill of the Living;* April, 2005, review of *Speak Ill of the Living.*
Publishers Weekly, June 16, 2003, review of *Spiked,* p. 54.

ONLINE

All Readers, http://www.allreaders.com/ (October 19, 2005), Harriet Klausner, review of *Speak Ill of the Living.*

BookLoons, http://www.bookloons.com/ (October 19, 2005), Mary Ann Smyth, review of *Speak Ill of the Living.*

Mark Arsenault Home Page, http://www.mark arsenault.net (October 19, 2005).*

* * *

AUDOUX, Marguerite 1863-1937

PERSONAL: Born July 7, 1863, in Sancoins, France; died February 1, 1937, in France.

CAREER: Worked as a dressmaker and a shepherdess.

AWARDS, HONORS: Prix Femina, 1910, for *Marie-Claire.*

WRITINGS:

Marie-Claire (novel), E. Fasquelle (Paris, France), 1910, translation by John Nathan Raphael, Hodder & Stoughton (New York, NY), 1911.
Valserine, and Other Stories, Hodder & Stoughton (New York, NY), 1912, reprinted, Books for Libraries Press (Freeport, NY), 1970.
L'atelier de Marie-Claire (novel), E. Fasquelle (Paris, France), 1920, translation by F.S. Flint published as *Marie Claire's Workshop,* Thomas Seltzer (New York, NY), 1920.
De la ville au moulin (novel), E. Fasquelle (Paris, France), 1926.
Douce lumière (novel), Grassett (Paris, France), 1937.

SIDELIGHTS: French author Marguerite Audoux was honored in the year of her death, 1937, with the launch of a magazine named after her novel *Marie-Claire.* The life of the protagonist of the story in many ways resembles that of Audoux herself. At the age of three, her mother died of tuberculosis, and her father left her and her sister in the care of an aunt. They were then placed in an orphanage, and Audoux was apprenticed to a tailor. Her interest in literature blossomed when she found a book of stories in the attic of the house on a rural farm where she later worked as a shepherdess. Later, Audoux moved to Paris, where she took on a variety of jobs before opening her own dressmaking shop. She was one of the "group of Carnetin," writers who met regularly in the village of Seine-et-Marne in 1908. Critics found it difficult to believe that the author of *Marie-Claire* could be the woman who had come from a peasant background and who supported herself with her sewing until she died.

Nina Hellerstein, presenting a study of Audoux's life and work in the *French Review,* wrote that the author's four novels and other writings are "virtually forgotten. This neglect is all the more surprising in that *Marie-Claire* is an exceptionally interesting and powerful work." Hellerstein noted that "the novel, like all autobiographical fiction, is far from a simple reproduction of 'real' experience. Its most notable qualities are the result of conscious construction and a complex narrative technique that transforms the raw material of memory into a compelling tale of loss and of self-discovery."

BIOGRAPHICAL AND CRITICAL SOURCES:

BOOKS

Philip, Anne Glenday, editor, *Marie-Claire à Villevieille,* Clarendon Press (Oxford, England), 1953.

PERIODICALS

French Review, December, 1995, Nina Hellerstein, "Narrative Innovation and the Construction of Self in Marguerite Audoux's *Marie-Claire,*" pp. 246-254.*

* * *

AZZARELLO, Brian

PERSONAL: Male.

ADDRESSES: Agent—c/o Author Mail, Marvel Enterprises, Inc., 10 E. 40th St., New York, NY 10016.

CAREER: Writer and comic-book creator.

AWARDS, HONORS: Eisner Award, for *100 Bullets: Hang Up on the Hang Low.*

WRITINGS:

"100 BULLETS SERIES;" COLLECTIONS

First Shot, Last Call, illustrated by Eduardo Risso and Dave Johnson, Vertigo (New York, NY), 2000.

Split Second Chance, illustrated by Eduardo Risso and Dave Johnson, Vertigo (New York, NY), 2001.

Hang Up on the Hang Low, illustrated by Eduardo Risso, Vertigo (New York, NY), 2001.

A Foregone Tomorrow, illustrated by Eduardo Risso, Vertigo (New York, NY), 2002.

The Counterfifth Detective, Vertigo (New York, NY), 2003.

Six Feet under the Gun, Vertigo (New York, NY), 2003.

OTHER

Hellblazer: Hard Time, illustrated by Richard Corben and Tim Bradstreet, Vertigo (New York, NY), 2000.

Startling Stories: Banner, illustrated by Richard Corben, Marvel (New York, NY), 2001.

(With others) *The Incredible Hulk,* Marvel (New York, NY), 2002.

Johnny Double, DC Comics (New York, NY), 2002.

Hellblazer: Good Intentions, illustrated by Marcelo Frusin, Vertigo (New York, NY), 2002.

Cage, illustrated by Richard Corben, Marvel (New York, NY), 2002.

Cage: Volume 1, illustrated by Richard Corben, Marvel (New York, NY), 2003.

Hellblazer: Freezes Over, illustrated by Marcelo Frusin, Guy Davis, and Steve Dillon, Vertigo (New York, NY), 2003.

Batman/Deathblow: After the Fire, DC Comics (New York, NY), 2003.

Sgt. Rock: Between Hell and a Hard Place, illustrated by Joe Kubert, Vertigo (New York, NY), 2003.

Writer for comic-book series, including *Batman, Spider-Man,* and *Hellblazer;* creator and sole writer of *100 Bullets* comic-book series.

SIDELIGHTS: Comic-book writer Brian Azzarello has worked on a number of comic-book series, including *Hellblazer,* which *Comic World News* online reviewer Scott Woods wrote "has always been a great idea." English protagonist John Constantine's magical adventures have included the political, the raunchy, the comic, and the frightening, and have always provided a "massively entertaining read," said Woods. "It has primarily been a real world-flavored comic with real people issues weaved throughout the macabre characters, situations and multi-dimensional rifts."

Woods noted that the series' central character and antihero with a heart was, for a time, "simply meandering. . . . You'd think with a character with as much backstory as Constantine . . . he'd have more to do than tease hookers and hitchhike across America." Woods praised the contributions of Azzarello and artist Richard Corben, who were responsible for a number of issues, including the story arcs *Hard Time* (numbers 146-150), *Freezes Over* (numbers 158-161), and *Good Intentions* (numbers 151-156).

In *Hellblazer: Hard Time,* Constantine has been sentenced to a maximum-security prison for the murder of his friend, Lucky Fermin, and there he comes up against gangs, brutal guards, and the man who rules it all. In *Hellblazer: Good Intentions,* the now released Constantine travels to West Virginia to see Lucky's family and finds himself caught up in a series of bizarre events that threaten their little town. Constantine continues his back roads journey in *Hellblazer: Freezes Over.*

The character Deathblow, featured in *Batman/Deathblow: After the Fire,* was a minor DC Comics character and friend of Batman who died while investigating a pyromaniac villain named Firebug, who was suspected in the death of an intelligence officer and friend of Batman. The story goes back and forth in time, recounting the undercover operations of both Batman and such organizations as the Central Intelligence Agency. *Booklist* reviewer Ray Olson wrote that, although Batman is "brutal and nihilistic," he "remains heroic." Mary Harvey reviewed *Batman/Deathblow* for *Rambles* online, saying that it "gets credit . . . for tackling the well-worn theme of covert agency corruption, where cat-and-mouse style chess games pit one agency against another. . . . Trying to find its voice through the character/narrator of Batman, a hero whose missions could not be further removed from that of an assassin's, is a twist that's unique enough to get the reader's attention."

Silver Bullet Comic Books contributor Ray Tate also reviewed *Batman/Deathblow,* saying that "ultimately, it's Batman's honesty that saves him from ending up fallen on the chessboard the government has created." Tate wrote that "the story itself is a mirror to our own world," and noted that, because Batman is the hero, Azzarello had to find a way to have him remain so. "He finds a means without diminishing the themes of betrayal or the labyrinthine means in which the bad-men who run the world achieve their goals."

Marvel revived a superhero in their graphic novel *Sgt. Rock: Between Hell and a Hard Place,* written by Azzarello and drawn by veteran Rock penciller Joe Kubert. The World War II setting finds three captive Germans killed while in the custody of East Company. *Entertainment Weekly* contributor Tom Sinclair noted that since the new version is published by DC Comics' Vertigo imprint, Azzarello could have "upped the carnage quotient," but instead tells the story nearly as it was originally told forty years earlier. "Understand, that's not necessarily a bad thing," wrote Sinclair; "it's refreshing to find a creator who doesn't feel compelled to reinvent the wheel for the sake of it."

Azzarello's popular *100 Bullets* contains stories of revenge in which an agent named Graves gives a gun and one hundred untraceable bullets to people who have been wronged, thereby providing them with a way to kill their abusers without being caught. In the first volume, *First Shot, Last Call,* Latina gangbanger Dizzy Cordova is given the opportunity to avenge the murders of her husband and child, who were killed in a drive-by shooting, while a bartender is likewise able to seek atonement for his ruined life. *Mad Review* online contributor The Dean, noted that in subsequent issues, readers learn that Dizzy "was recruited for a cadre of elite operatives waging a secret war at the highest levels of economics and power. Bit by bit, we discover the selection process utilized by Graves and the manipulative Mr. Shepherd is not so random after all." *Entertainment Weekly* contributor Ken Tucker called the *100 Bullets* series "a rarity: a nonsuperhero book that imputes equal-opportunity heroism and villainy to its female characters."

In the second story arc, published in book form as *Split Second Chance,* details of the manipulative Graves's past begin to surface. The third collection, *Hang Up on the Hang Low,* earned Azzarello an Eisner award. Here Graves initiates a young man named Loop Hughes into his web of conspiracy, and Loop, who finds his long-lost mob-boss father, is drawn into mob enforcement.

Azzarello's *100 Bullets* series has continued to reveal more and more of the nature of Graves's beneficiaries and opponents. In the fifth collection, titled *The Counterfifth Detective,* the man who receives the gun and bullets is private investigator Milo Garret, whose face, ever since an automobile accident, must be swathed in bandages. Gordon Flagg commented in *Booklist* that Eduardo Risso's art "perfectly suits Azzarello's sparse, hardboiled scripts; this is one of the most effective writer-artist teams in comics."

BIOGRAPHICAL AND CRITICAL SOURCES:

PERIODICALS

Booklist, May 1, 2003, Gordon Flagg, review of *100 Bullets: The Counterfifth Detective,* p. 1531; May 15, 2003, Ray Olson, review of *Batman/ Deathblow: After the Fire,* p. 1626.
Entertainment Weekly, January 26, 2001, Ken Tucker, review of *100 Bullets,* p. 96; November 21, 2002, Tom Sinclair, review of *Sgt. Rock: Between Hell and a Hard Place,* p. L2T42.
Publishers Weekly, May 7, 2001, review of *100 Bullets: Split Second Chance,* p. 226.

ONLINE

Comic World News, http://www.comicworldnews.com/ (December 7, 2003), Scott Woods, review of *Hellblazer.*
Mad Review, http://madreview.com/ (May 17, 2000), The Dean, review of *100 Bullets.*
Rambles, http://www.rambles.net/ (May 10, 2003), Mary Harvey, review of *Batman/Deathblow.*
Silver Bullet Comic Books Online, http://www.silver bulletcomicbooks.com/ (December 7, 2003), Ray Tate, review of *Batman/Deathblow.**

B

BA Jin 1904-2005
(Li Fei-kan, Li Yaotang, Pa Chin)

OBITUARY NOTICE— See index for *CA* sketch: Born November 25, 1904 (one source says November 24), in Chengtu, Szechwan, China; died of cancer, October 17, 2005, in Shanghai, China. Author. Widely recognized as one of the greatest writers of twentieth-century China, Ba was a prolific author of novels, short stories, and nonfiction who was often praised for his critical social examinations of pre-communist China. Born Li Yaotang to an aristocratic family in which he enjoyed a number of privileges, including a good education, Ba nevertheless bristled under what he considered an unjust feudal system and the influence of the West. He became interested in leftist writings and began producing them himself under his adopted pen name, Ba Jin. He began to travel as well, including to Paris, where in 1927 he wrote *Destruction,* his first novel. Returning to China, he then produced a trilogy of novels, beginning with *Chia* (1931), which was later translated as *The Family* (1958) and became his most famous book. With the founding of the People's Republic in 1949, Ba spent much of his writing efforts on his work as a foreign correspondent covering Korea, Japan, and Vietnam. He also was a committee member of the China Association of Literary Workers and the Cultural and Educational Commission, as well as vice chair of the All-China Federation of Literary and Art Circles and chair of the China People's Union of Chinese Writers. Despite his loyalty to the government, even Ba was not immune to the Cultural Revolution of the 1960s and 1970s, when Chinese intellectuals and others were rounded up and sent to labor camps. While enduring forced labor at one such camp, Ba lost his wife when she became sick and was denied medical treatment. Nevertheless, even after leaving the camp he never overtly criticized his government. In the 1980s, however, he told interviewers that he planned to write a novel about the Cultural Revolution, although it was never published. Ba continued to write into the early 1990s; he was named chair of the Chinese Writers Association in 1981 and by the mid-1980s began to call for more freedom of speech for writers. Awarded the Special Fukuoka Asian Commemorative Prize in 1990, Ba never won the Nobel Prize many felt he deserved, although he was twice nominated. His works continue to remain a prominent part of Chinese literary history.

OBITUARIES AND OTHER SOURCES:

PERIODICALS

Los Angeles Times, October 18, 2005, p. B9.
New York Times, October 18, 2005, p. C19.
Washington Post, October 18, 2005, p. B6.

*　　*　　*

BAAB, Lynne M.

PERSONAL: Married. *Education:* Attended Fuller Theological Seminary (Pasadena, CA); University of Washington, Ph.D. candidate, completion expected in 2007.

ADDRESSES: Home—Seattle, WA. *Agent*—c/o Author Mail, InterVarsity Press, P.O. Box 1400, Downers Grove, IL 60515.

CAREER: Association for Psychological Type, consultant, 1993-97; Bethany Presbyterian Church, Seattle, WA, associate pastor, 1997-2004.

WRITINGS:

Personality Type in Congregations: How to Work with Others More Effectively, Alban Institute (Bethesda, MD), 1998.

Embracing Midlife: Congregations as Support Systems, Alban Institute (Bethesda, MD), 1999.

A Renewed Spirituality: Finding Fresh Paths at Midlife, InterVarsity Press (Downers Grove, IL), 2002.

Beating Burnout in Congregations, Alban Institute (Bethesda, MD), 2003.

Sabbath Keeping: Finding Freedom in the Rhythms of Rest, InterVarsity Press (Downers Grove, IL), 2005.

SIDELIGHTS: Presbyterian minister Lynne M. Baab has written several titles that deal with ministerial issues, including *A Renewed Spirituality: Finding Fresh Paths at Midlife* and *Sabbath Keeping: Finding Freedom in the Rhythms of Rest.* In the former, Baab looks at a common sentiment: the desire of middle-aged people to renew commitments to religious faith and give something back to the world. Although in *Publishers Weekly* a commentator noted that Baab's insights are not original and are sometimes "unsophisticated, she honestly and simply confronts the spirituality of midlife." Similarly, based on the personal experiences of Baab and her husband, *Sabbath Keeping* deals with another issue religious faithful face: how to keep Sunday a holy day in a society that is always on the go. According to Graham Christian in *Library Journal,* this is a "brief but heartfelt book on the advantages of Sabbath observance." As Baab explains in the text, "The frantic pace, the exhaustion that accompanies it and the resulting emptiness call us back to a rhythm that includes stopping and resting." Calling the work "winsome, passionate and persuasive," a *Publishers Weekly* contributor predicted that it "will convince many Christians of the continuing relevance of the Fourth Commandment."

Baab told *CA:* "Writing books is incredibly enriching for me. I always learn an incredible amount from the reading and interviews I do for each book and from the writing process itself. My faith in God is deepened, I am more committed to living a life of wholeness and love, and with each book I continue to grow in gratitude and awe for the creative process. I've seen through writing books that creativity requires both a spark of inspiration and a surprising amount of diligent and painstaking work. But the work is always worth the pain. The growth and life that has come to me from writing books is a great privilege."

BIOGRAPHICAL AND CRITICAL SOURCES:

BOOKS

Baab, Lynne M., *Sabbath Keeping: Finding Freedom in the Rhythms of Rest,* InterVarsity Press (Downers Grove, IL), 2005.

PERIODICALS

Library Journal, March 1, 2005, Graham Christian, review of *Sabbath Keeping: Finding Freedom in the Rhythms of Rest,* p. 92.

Publishers Weekly, April 29, 2002, review of *A Renewed Spirituality: Finding Fresh Paths at Midlife,* p. 63; December 20, 2004, review of *Sabbath Keeping,* p. 54.

ONLINE

InterVarsity Press Web site, http://ivpress.gospelcom. net/ (August 18, 2005).

*   *   *

BACON, Edmund N. 1910-2005
(Edmund Norwood Bacon)

OBITUARY NOTICE— See index for *CA* sketch: Born May 2, 1910, in Philadelphia, PA; died October 14, 2005, in Philadelphia, PA. City planner, architect, and author. Bacon, the father of actor Kevin Bacon, was an accomplished and influential city planner who profoundly changed the character of his hometown of Philadelphia. Studying architecture at Cornell University, he graduated in 1932 and then traveled to China and Europe, an experience from which he would take home many ideas concerning architecture and planning concepts. Further study at the Cranbrook Academy of Art in Michigan was followed by a job with the Institute of Research and Planning in Flint, Michigan. Returning to Philadelphia in 1940, he joined the U.S. Navy when the United States entered World War II. With the war over, Bacon was hired by the Philadelphia City Planning Commission. Resolved to improve the city aesthetically and make it a more livable place, he spearheaded many projects that changed the city dramatically. At times, he would come into conflict with building preservationists or other groups, but Bacon remained steadfast in his vision. One of his positions was that no building in Philadelphia should be taller than the top of the statue of William Penn atop the City Hall. It was an idea that was respected until the mid-1980s, and Bacon protested vigorously when structures such as One Liberty Place began to exceed the limit, which he felt was disrespectful to the state's founding father. Bacon was also responsible for the demolition of unsightly areas of the city, such as the old railroad yard, and he headed the construction of the residential area of Society Hill. After retiring in 1970, Bacon remained active by teaching at the University of Pennsylvania and the University of Illinois as an adjunct professor, by producing a series of films called *Understanding Cities,* and by serving as vice president of design at the real-estate-development firm Mondev International Ltd. Despite being officially retired, he remained a prominent figure in his hometown. In 2002 he protested a ban on skateboarding in a city park, and subsequently criticized city plans to redesign the Independence Mall plaza and the Benjamin Franklin Parkway. The writer of an important text that was widely used in colleges, *Design of Cities* (1967; revised edition, 1974), Bacon was also the author of *Archetype, Architecture: A Lecture Sponsored by the Erwin S. Wolfson Fellowship Fund* (1990). In recognition of his many contributions, he was presented with such honors as the American Institute of Planners Distinguished Service Award, the Philadelphia Award, and the American Institute of Architects Medal.

OBITUARIES AND OTHER SOURCES:

PERIODICALS

Chicago Tribune, October 17, 2005, section 4, p. 9.
Los Angeles Times, October 15, 2005, p. B15.
New York Times, October 18, 2005, p. C19.
Washington Post, October 16, 2005, p. C8.

*   *   *

BACON, Edmund Norwood
See BACON, Edmund N.

*   *   *

BAHARLOO, Morteza 1961-

PERSONAL: Born 1961, in Darab, Fars, Iran; immigrated to United States, 1978; married; children: Sahar Claire, Yasmine Grace. *Education:* Attended Oregon State University School of Pharmacy. *Hobbies and other interests:* Writing, painting, poetry.

ADDRESSES: Office—Healix, Ltd., 14140 Southwest Freeway, 4th Fl., Sugar Land, TX 77478. *Agent*—Amy Rennert Agency, 98 Main St., No. 302, Tiburon, CA 94920. *E-mail*—author@mortbaharloo.com; Mbaharloo@healix.cc.

CAREER: Writer and entrepreneur. Healix, Ltd. (a health care company), Houston, TX, chairman and cofounder, 1989—.

WRITINGS:

The Quince Seed Potion (novel), Bridge Works (Bridgehampton, NY), 2004.

Author of three novellas and a travelogue in Farsi.

SIDELIGHTS: Although Morteza Baharloo has written novellas in his native language, Farsi, *The Quince Seed Potion* was his first novel published in English. In it Baharloo provides readers with the "engrossing, elegantly told story of a sweetly pathetic, supremely loyal family retainer," to quote *Booklist* reviewer Whitney Scott. This servant, Sarveali, who was sold to the Kahn family when only six years old, has lived an impotent life, both literally and figuratively, as the slave of a handsome young man and against the backdrop of a radically changing Iran. An *Advocate* critic likened *The Quince Seed Potion* to Pearl S. Buck's *The Good Earth* for just this portrayal of an ancient nation on the road to change. Yet, told in the first person, this tale is more than the tale of a man who kills his adulterous wife in a drunken rage, is imprisoned, and becomes addicted to opium. According to Lawrence E. Butler, writing in *Lambda Book Report,* "the portrayal is sympathetic, giving some sense of dignity and purpose to [Sarveali's] obsession. Even his slide into opium addiction is treated gently, both by the author and by the characters around him." Butler continued, "The language throughout is strong, blunt and gorgeous, always witty and often obscene. It perfectly fits the casual cynicism and polished brutality of the world that surrounds Sarveali. Descriptions are spare, but the details richly suggestive of both the rural feudal world and the westernized cities of Twentieth Century Iran." Scott also suggested that Baharloo's readers might gain a "humanizing perspective on a history too many Americans know only through authoritarian stereotypes."

BIOGRAPHICAL AND CRITICAL SOURCES:

PERIODICALS

Advocate, March 1, 2005, "From the 'Axis of Evil' to the Literary Realms of Spanglish," review of *The Quince Seed Potion,* p. S34.
Booklist, October 15, 2004, Whitney Scott, review of *The Quince Seed Potion,* p. 388.
Kirkus Reviews, September 15, 2004, review of *The Quince Seed Potion,* p. 879.
Lambda Book Report, January-March, 2005, Lawrence Butler, "Devoted Servant," review of *The Quince Seed Potion,* p. 44.

ONLINE

Morteza Baharloo Home Page, http://www.morteza baharloo.com (August 18, 2005).*

*　　*　　*

BALESTRINI, Nanni 1935-

PERSONAL: Born July 2, 1935, in Milan, Italy. *Education:* Attended Università Cattolica, Milan, Italy.

ADDRESSES: Agent—c/o Author Mail, Baldini & Castoldi, vi Crocefisso 21/A, 21121, Milan, Italy.

CAREER: Poet, journalist, and novelist. *Quindici* (journal), founder, 1967-69; Potere operaio (worker's rights political action group), founder, c. 1968; Marsilio (publishers), Milan, Italy, member of staff, c. 1972; *Arena* (magazine), cofounder, c. 1977; Gallimard (publisher), Paris, France, member of staff, beginning late 1970s; *Change International* (journal), founder, 1983; *Compagni* (magazine), founder. Organizer of poetry festivals, including Veneziea Poesia II: Festival della Parola, 1997. *Exhibitions:* Creator of computer-generated art exhibited in galleries in Italy, including Galleria Emilio Mezzoli, Modena, 2002.

AWARDS, HONORS: Nominated chevalier, Order of Arts and Letters, 1996.

WRITINGS:

Il sasso appeso, Scheiwiller (Milan, Italy), 1961.
Come si agisce (poetry; title means "How to Act"), Feltrinelli (Milan, Italy), 1963.
Altri procedimenti 1964-1965, Scheiwiller (Milan, Italy), 1965.
Tristano (novel), Feltrinelli (Milan, Italy), 1966.
Ma noi facciamone un'altra: poesie 1964-1968, Feltrinelli (Milan, Italy), 1968.
Prendiamoci tutto. Conferenza per un romanzo. Letteratura e lotta di classe (pamphlet), Feltrinelli (Milan, Italy), 1972.
Vogliamo tutto (novel; also see below), Feltrinelli (Milan, Italy), 1973, preface by Franco Berardi, Derive Approdi (Rome, Italy), 2004.
(With Dario Argento) *Le cinque giornate* (screenplay; title means "The Five Days"), Bompiani (Milan, Italy), 1974.
Ballates distese (poems), Geiger (Turin, Italy), 1975.
(With Dario Argento) *Profondo Thrilling* (screenplay), Sonzongno (Milan, Italy), 1975.
La violenza illustrata (novel; title means "Violence Illustrated"), Einaudi (Turin, Italy), 1976.
Poesie pratiche 1954-1969, Einaudi (Turin, Italy), 1976.
Ballate della signorina Richmond: primo libro (poetry), Cooperativa Scrittori (Rome, Italy), 1977.
Blackout (poetry), Feltrinelli (Milan, Italy), 1980.

Ipocalisse: 49 sonetti, Provenza 1980-1983 (poetry), Scheiwiller (Milan, Italy), 1986.

Gli invisibili (novel; also see below), Bompiani (Milan, Italy), 1987, translated by Liz Heron as *The Unseen,* Verso (London, England), 1989.

Il ritorno della signorina Richmond: terzo libro, 1984-1986 (poetry), Becco Giallo (Treviso, Italy), 1987.

La signorina Richmond se ne va: secondo libro (poetry), Corpo 10 (Milan, Italy), 1988.

Osservazioni sul volo degli uccelli. Poesie 1954-1956, Scheiwiller (Milan, Italy), 1988.

(With Primo Moroni) *L'orda d'oro 1968-1977; la grande ondata riboluzionaria e creativa, politica ed esistenziale,* SugarCo (Milan, Italy), 1988.

L'editore (novel; also see below), Bompiani (Milan, Italy), 1989.

Il pubblico del labirinto: quarto libro della signorina Richmond, 1985-1989, Scheiwiller (Milan, Italy), 1992.

I furiosi, Bompiani (Milan, Italy), 1994.

Estremi rimedi, Piero Manni (Lecce), 1995.

Una mattina ci siam svegliati, Baldini & Castoldi (Milan, Italy), 1995.

(Translator) *I novissimi: Poetry for the Sixties,* Sun & Moon Press (Los Angeles, CA), 1995.

Le avventure complete della signorina Richmond, Testo & Immagine (Turin, Italy), 1999.

La grande Rivolta (contains *Vogliamo tutto, Gli invisibili* and *L'editore*), Bompiani (Milan, Italy), 1999.

L'ombelico del mondo (television script), RAI, 2000.

Elettra: operapoesia (recording), Luca Sossella (Rome, Italy), 2001.

(Editor, with Alfredo Giuliani) *Grupo 63: l'antologia,* Teston & Immagine (Turin, Italy), 2002.

Parma 22: una resistenza antifascista, edited by Margherita Becchetti, Giovanni Ronchini, and Andrea Zini, Derive Approdi (Rome, Italy), 2002.

Sfinimondo, preface by Pietro Cataldi, Bibliopolis (Naples, Italy), 2003.

Sandokan: storia di camorra, Einaudi (Turin, Italy), 2004.

Contributor to *Mutazioni: balletto in 6 quadri,* Suvini Zerboni (Milan, Italy), 1964; *Lucio Fontana. Foto, photos: Ugo Mulas,* A. Mauri (Milan, Italy), c. 1968; *Vivere a Milano: 15 documenti fotografici per la presentazione di 15 manifesti,* by Aldo Vito Bonasia, C.S.-A.P.P. (Milan, Italy), 1976; *Sulla neoavanguardia,* Bastogi (Foggia, Italy), 1983; *Ut pictura poesis: "com la pintura, aizi és la poesia,"* Fundacio Cazio de Pensions (Barcelona, Spain), 1988; and *Sottotiro: 48 stron-*

cature, by Enzo Golino, Manni (Lecce), 2002. Also contributor to anthologies, including *Critica e teoria* edited by Renato Barilli and Angelo Guglielmi, 1976; *I poeti per Montale,* Bozzi (Genoa, Italy), c. 1978; *Teatro italiano* (dramas), Sampietro (Bologna, Italy), 1983; and *The Quality of Light: Modern Italian Short Stories,* Serpent's Tail (New York, NY), 1993. Also contributor of poems/lyrics to sound recording *The Condor,* Soul Note (Milan, Italy), 1986. Member of editorial board, *Il Verri,* c. 1958.

SIDELIGHTS: Part of the Italian "novissimi" movements of the second half of the twentieth century, poet and novelist Nanni Balestrini was the youngest member of "Gruppo 63," the avant-garde group whose members were born in Milan under Luciano Aneschi's auspices. In work representative of the post-World War II Neo-avant-garde movement that swept through Italian literature in the 1960s, Balestrini "strives to revive language" and "seeks to affirm language as the object of artistic expression," wrote a contributor to the *Dictionary of Literary Biography.* In the company of such writers as Umberto Eco and Eduardo Sanguineti, Balestrini immersed himself in this expression. He served on the editorial board of *Il Verri,* a journal founded by Aneschi, organized meetings and conferences of writers, and was considered articulate in expressing his own ideological position.

Inspired to write experimental works, Balestrini published *Come si agisce,* a collection of poems. Following his compulsion to break established "rules," he then wrote *Tristano,* a novel based on the Germanic myth that does not have a traditional plot or characters. According to the *Dictionary of Literary Biography* contributor, it was within the text of *Tristano* that Balestrini began to employ a "collage effect" called *laisses,* in which "various stylistic devices converge in the creation of a deranged structure." Ronald Bottrall, writing in the *Times Literary Supplement,* called Balestrini "the most persistently experimental of all contemporary Italian poets." Concerning *Ideologia e linguaggio,* Balestrini once stated, "The structures of [poetry], already tottering, proliferate in an unforeseen manner in unexpected directions." Bottrall, in reviewing Balestrini's *Ma noi facciamone un'altra: poesie 1964-1968,* called the writer a "powerful and impressive poet." According to Michael Caesar and Peter Hainsworth in *Writers & Society in Contemporary Italy,* Balestrini's collected work "constitute[s] a complete rejection of conventional language."

During the 1960s and 1970s, Balestrini actively participated in the political left in Italy, and his writing became highly politicized. To help promote his political, as well as literary, ideology, he founded the journal *Quindici,* which suspended publication after three years of operation. He also founded *Compagni,* a magazine tied to the workers' political movement. His concern for the working classes is also seen in the novel *Vogliamo tutto,* which is about the Fiat auto plant strikes of 1969. A reviewer for the *Times Literary Supplement* called *Vogliamo tutto* an "energetic, talented book every line of which tingles with heat and feeling." By the mid-1970s his political activism had become so problematic for the state that a warrant was issued for his arrest and the writer was forced to flee to Paris.

During the 1980s, Balestrini continued to write and be involved in political and cultural events. Living in Paris and working for the publishing firm of Gallimard, he founded the journal *Change International* and helped organize an international poetry festival at Cogolin. Returning to the use of collage and *laisses,* he wrote *Gli invisibili,* later translated as *The Unseen.* Gabrielle Barfoot, reviewing the book in *World Literature Today,* noted that because the novel "is written entirely without punctuation," it "is at first rather disconcerting, but the reader soon falls into the rhythm of the words." Gilbert Reid, writing in the *Times Literary Supplement,* commented that in *The Unseen* Balestrini "succeeds in conveying the heedlessness, the brutality and the stupidity" of the "Autonomy" movement of Italy during the 1970s. In the same review, Reid called Balestrini's style of narrative in the 1989 novel *L'editore* "breathless and unpunctuated." *Times Educational Supplement* reviewer Frances Spalding noted that Balestrini's "short unpunctuated paragraphs tell the story" in *The Unseen* and that "the segmented text operates like a series of vivid slides."

In more recent years, which included a stay in Berlin, Germany, during the late 1980s, Balestrini has continued to pursue his avant-garde philosophy with regard to the art of words. During the 1990s he began to create computer-generated artwork, such as faxing collages of newspaper headlines, and was increasingly active in poetry workshops and public readings. He also expanded into scriptwriting with *L'ombelico del mondo,* a television special produced on the French network RAI in 2000. His 2002 joint editorship, with Alfredo Giuliani, of *Grupo 63: l'antologia,* collects the work of Balestrini and many of his literary colleagues from the 1960s.

BIOGRAPHICAL AND CRITICAL SOURCES:

BOOKS

Caesar, Michael, and Peter Hainsworth, editors, *Writers and Society in Contemporary Italy,* St. Martin's Press (New York, NY), 1984, pp. 36-61.
Dictionary of Literary Biography, Thomson Gale (Detroit, MI), Volume 128: *Twentieth-Century Italian Poets,* 1993, Volume 196: *Italian Novelists since World War II, 1965-1995,* 1999.
Esposito, Roberto, *Le ideologie della neoavanguardia,* Liguori Editore (Naples, Italy), 1976.
L'invenzione della realtà: conversazioni su la letterature e altro, A. Guida (Naples, Italy), 1994.

PERIODICALS

Arts, September, 1991, Robert Mahoney, "Take Over," p. 85.
Booklist, Emilie L. Perillo, review of *Vogliamo tutto,* p. 511.
Lingua e Stile, 1977, Niva Lorenzini, "L'itinerario realistico del materiale verbale nella poesia di Balestrini," pp. 481-511.
Times Educational Supplement, February 2, 1990, Frances Spalding, review of *The Unseen,* p. 27.
Times Literary Supplement, September 25, 1969, Ronald Bottrall, "Escaping from the Morass," p. 1100; September 29, 1972, "Life in Turin," p. 1139; October 5, 1990, Gilbert Reid, "A Brutal Time Recalled," p. 1074.
World Literature Today, spring, 1988, Gabrielle Barfoot, review of *Gli invisibili,* p. 261.

ONLINE

Nanni Balestrini Home Page, http://nannibalestrini. arsed.it (May 4, 2001).*

*   *   *

BALMAIN, Julianne
(Nadia Gordon)

PERSONAL: Female.

ADDRESSES: Home—San Francisco, CA. *Agent*—c/o Author Mail, Publicity Department, Chronicle Books, 85 2nd St., 6th Fl., San Francisco, CA 94105. *E-mail*—julianne@juliannebalmain.com.

CAREER: Writer.

WRITINGS:

"CRAFTY GIRL" SERIES

(With Jennifer Traig) *Beauty: Things to Make and Do* (juvenile), Chronicle Books (San Francisco, CA), 2001.

(With Jennifer Traig) *Cool Stuff: Things to Make and Do* (juvenile), Chronicle Books (San Francisco, CA), 2001.

UNDER PSEUDONYM NADIA GORDON; "SUNNY MCCOSKEY NAPA VALLEY MYSTERY" SERIES

Sharpshooter, Chronicle Books (San Francisco, CA), 2002.

Death by the Glass, Chronicle Books (San Francisco, CA), 2003.

Murder Alfresco, Chronicle Books (San Francisco, CA), 2005.

OTHER

The Queen's Amulet (juvenile), illustrated by Matilda Harrison, Chronicle Books (San Francisco, CA), 1999.

Office Kama Sutra: Being a Guide to Delectation & Delight in the Workplace (humor), illustrated by Thorina Rose, Chronicle Books (San Francisco, CA), 2001.

Abroad: A Travel Organizer and Journal, illustrated by Bas De Graf, Chronicle Books (San Francisco, CA), 2001.

The Kama Sutra Deck: 50 Ways to Love Your Lover, Chronicle Books (San Francisco, CA), 2004.

Kama Sutra Journal, Chronicle Books (San Francisco, CA), 2005.

WORK IN PROGRESS: Book four in the "Sunny McCoskey Napa Valley" series.

SIDELIGHTS: Under her own name and a pseudonym, Julianne Balmain has written a variety of books, including mysteries, juvenile titles, and adult humor, all for San Francisco-based publisher Chronicle Books.

Balmain is perhaps best known for publishing, as Nadia Gordon, the "Sunny McCoskey Napa Valley Mystery" series, about California café owner and chef, Sunny McCoskey. The plot of series debut *Sharpshooter* revolves around the murder of a famous vineyard owner and Sunny's efforts to prove her friend innocent of the crime. Robyn Glazer, writing on the *Romantic Times* Web site, found the locale and plot attractive, and called it an "attention-grabbing read, as Gordon combines a smart mystery with interesting details about wine." On the other hand, a *Kirkus Reviews* contributor expressed some reservations, describing the novel as "long on Napa Valley culture, short on logical deduction," yet a "pleasant debut." More laudatory were *Booklist* reviewer Barbara Bibel, who dubbed *Sharpshooter* "a promising debut with a strong plot and colorful characters," and Rex Klett, reviewing it for *Library Journal,* who wrote: "The attractive locales, sturdy plot, and interesting characters make this initial entry in a new series a good choice for regional and larger public libraries."

In *Death by the Glass,* which Klett called "a likable second" in *Library Journal,* Balmain recounts Sunny's involvement in the case of a murdered restaurant owner because her new lover has been accused of the crime. "Sunny's adventures offer readers an amusing romp in the culinary underworld," wrote Bibel in *Booklist,* while a *Kirkus Reviews* writer decided that "Sunny's neurotic habit of sticking her toque where it doesn't belong is the only sour note among the otherwise delectable details."

BIOGRAPHICAL AND CRITICAL SOURCES:

PERIODICALS

Booklist, June 1, 2002, Barbara Bibel, review of *Sharpshooter,* p. 1691; August, 2003, Barbara Bibel, review of *Death by the Glass,* p. 1960.

Kirkus Reviews, May 15, 2002, review of *Sharpshooter,* p. 707; July 15, 2003, review of *Death by the Glass,* p. 939; April 1, 2005, review of *Murder Alfresco,* p. 387.

Library Journal, July, 2002, Rex Klett, review of *Sharpshooter,* p. 125; August, 2003, Rex Klett, review of *Death by the Glass,* p. 140.

Publishers Weekly, August 2, 1999, *The Queen's Amulet,* p. 86; October 1, 2001, "Getting down to

Business," review of *Office Kama Sutra: Being a Guide to Delectation & Delight in the Workplace,* p. 53.

Teen, July, 2001, review of *Cool Stuff: Things to Make and Do,* p. 105.

ONLINE

Nadia Gordon Home Page, http://www.nadiagordon. com (August 18, 2005).

Reviewing the Evidence, http://reviewingtheevidence. com/ (October 8, 2005), Barbara Buhrer, review of *Death by the Glass.*

Romantic Times Online, http://www.romantictimes. com/ (August 18, 2005), Robyn Glazer, review of *Sharpshooter*; Kim Colley, review of *Death by the Glass.*

*   *   *

BANK, Barbara J. 1939-

PERSONAL: Born December 13, 1939, in Chicago, IL; daughter of Julius C. and Anna (Damm) Bank; married Bruce Jesse Biddle (a professor), June 19, 1976. *Education:* Illinois State University, B.S., 1961; University of Iowa, M.A., 1968, Ph.D., 1974. *Politics:* Progressive.

ADDRESSES: Home—924 Yale, Columbia, MO 65203. *E-mail*—bankb@missouri.edu.

CAREER: Writer. University of Missouri—Columbia, began as instructor, became professor of sociology and women's studies, now professor emeritus.

WRITINGS:

(Editor, with Peter M. Hall) *Gender, Equity, and Schooling: Policy and Practice,* Garland Publishing (New York, NY), 1997.

(With Harriet M. Yelom) *Contradictions in Women's Education: Traditionalism, Careerism, and Community at a Single-Sex College,* Teachers College Press (New York, NY), 2003.

BÁNK, Zsuzsa 1965-

PERSONAL: Born 1965, in Frankfurt am Main, Germany. *Education:* Attended universities in Mainz, Germany, and Washington, DC.

ADDRESSES: Home—Frankfurt am Main, Germany. *Agent*—c/o Author Mail, Harcourt, 6277 Sea Harbor Dr., Orlando, FL 32887.

CAREER: Writer, bookseller, and freelance editor.

AWARDS, HONORS: Aspekte Literaturpreis and Literaturförderpreis der Jürgen-Ponto-Stiftung, both 2002, and Deutscher Bücherpreis, 2003, all for *The Swimmer*; Bettina von Arnim Preis, 2003, for story "Unter Hunden"; Adalbert von Chamisso Preis, 2004.

WRITINGS:

Der Schwimmer (novel), S. Fischer (Frankfurt am Main, Germany), 2002, translation by Margot Bettauer Dembo published as *The Swimmer,* Harcourt (Orlando, FL), 2004.

The Swimmer has been translated into Hungarian.

WORK IN PROGRESS: Another novel.

SIDELIGHTS: In her debut novel, *The Swimmer,* Zsuzsa Bánk portrays a dysfunctional Hungarian family against the turbulent backdrop of the 1950s. After the mother, Katalin, deserts the family and heads to the West, the alcoholic father, Kalman, and children Kata and Isti leave their family farm. While they move in and out of the homes of various relatives, Kata tries to make a coherent life for herself and her younger brother Isti, but the only activity that brings together this suffering family is swimming.

The novel caught the attention of reviewers. Told from the perspective of the daughter, this story "can, and does, tug the heartstrings," wrote *Booklist* reviewer Whitney Scott, the critic praising Bánk for her "skillful characterizations and detailed descriptions of the countryside." Among the work's admirers number *Library Journal* reviewer Edward Cone, who, dubbed

The Swimmer a "remarkable" tale, and a *Publishers Weekly* critic who noted that "the novel's delicate treatment of Kata's stoicism and powerlessness makes the denouement of this resonant narrative especially heartbreaking." In *Kirkus Reviews* a contributor likened the novel to the fictional works of Jerzy Kosinski and the memoir of Agota Kristof, writing that its "spareness provides *The Swimmer* with its impact."

BIOGRAPHICAL AND CRITICAL SOURCES:

PERIODICALS

Booklist, December 1, 2004, Whitney Scott, review of *The Swimmer,* p. 634.
Kirkus Reviews, December 15, 2004, review of *The Swimmer,* p. 1152.
Library Journal, October 15, 2004, Edward Cone, review of *The Swimmer,* p. 52.*

*　　*　　*

BARASH, Nanelle R.

PERSONAL: Daughter of David P. Barash (a psychology professor) and Judith Eve Lipton (a psychiatrist). *Education:* Attended Swarthmore College, 2003—.

ADDRESSES: Agent—c/o Author Mail, Delacorte Press, 1745 Broadway, New York, NY 10019.

CAREER: Writer.

WRITINGS:

(With David P. Barash) *Madame Bovary's Ovaries: A Darwinian Look at Literature,* Delacorte (New York, NY), 2005.

SIDELIGHTS: Nanelle R. Barash published *Madame Bovary's Ovaries: A Darwinian Look at Literature* while studying biology and literature at Swarthmore College. She wrote the book with her father, David P. Barash, a psychology professor at the University of Washington in Seattle. The project stemmed from a paper Nanelle wrote on Virgil's *Aeneid* for Overlake School, in which she used her father's suggestion of applying Darwinian analysis. David later wrote about the subject in the *Chronicle of Higher Education* and received praise for her article in the *New York Times.*

Madame Bovary's Ovaries presents many well-known literary texts as illustrations that support Charles Darwin's theory of natural selection. For example, Othello's jealousy is akin to that of male elk and elephant seals. In Jane Austen's *Pride and Prejudice,* the young women naturally seek the most impressive males, just as female bluethroats show a preference for males with the brightest throat feathers. Other analysis treats the works of such authors as William Faulkner, D.H. Lawrence, Frank Norris, Amy Tan, Jonathan Franzen, and August Wilson.

As a work aimed at a general readership, a *Publishers Weekly* critic found *Madame Bovary's Ovaries* to be "a surprisingly lighthearted romp through both literature and the animal kingdom." A *Science News* reviewer found it to be a "well-researched and humorous narrative." According to a *Kirkus Reviews* writer, the study offers "an amusing, learned and literate look at the naked apes who populate the pages of our most celebrated fiction."

Other reviewers suggested that *Madame Bovary's Ovaries* skirts interesting issues. John Derbyshire remarked in the *National Review* that controversial aspects of sociobiology are avoided and concluded: "Half a loaf is better than no bread, and it is a very good thing that popular books setting human nature in its biological, evolutionary context are being published." Writing for *Library Journal,* Rebecca Bollen Manalac advised that "it can serve as a lay reader's introduction to evolutionary biology" rather than literary criticism. In a review for the *Seattle Times,* Bill Dietrich commented that, "like all one-stop solutions, the book seems to explain some lives better than others. . . . The book is silent on homosexuality, celibacy, human sacrifice or mothers who kill their own children." Still, he recommended the book to "any English teacher or book club hoping to provoke spirited discussion."

BIOGRAPHICAL AND CRITICAL SOURCES:

PERIODICALS

Kirkus Reviews, April 1, 2005, review of *Madame Bovary's Ovaries: A Darwinian Look at Literature,* p. 394.

Library Journal, May 15, 2005, Rebecca Bollen Manalac, review of *Madame Bovary's Ovaries,* p. 117.

National Review, June 20, 2005, John Derbyshire, review of *Madame Bovary's Ovaries,* p. 52.

Publishers Weekly, March 28, 2005, review of *Madame Bovary's Ovaries,* p. 67.

Science News, July 16, 2005, review of *Madame Bovary's Ovaries,* p. 47.

Seattle Times, May 2, 2005, Bill Dietrich, review of *Madame Bovary's Ovaries.*

Star Tribune (Minneapolis, MN), July 31, 2005, Peter Moore and Karin Winegar, review of *Madame Bovary's Ovaries.**

*   *   *

BARBERO, Alessandro 1959-

PERSONAL: Born 1959, in Turin, Italy. *Education:* Degree in medieval history, 1981; Scuola Normale Superiore di Pisa, 1987, Ph.D.

ADDRESSES: Agent—c/o Author Mail, University of California Press, 2120 Berkeley Way, Berkeley, CA 94704-1012. *E-mail*—alessandro.barbero@lett.unipmn.it.

CAREER: Università del Piemonte Orientale, Vercelli, Italy, professor of medieval history.

AWARDS, HONORS: Strega prize, 1996, for *Bella vita e guerre altrui di Mr. Pyle, gentiluomo.*

WRITINGS:

NOVELS

Bella vita e guerre altrui di Mr. Pyle, gentiluomo, Mondadori (Milan, Italy), 1995.

Romanzo russo: Fiutando i futuri supplizi, Mondadori (Milan, Italy), 1998.

L'ultimo rosa di Lautrec, Mondadori (Milan, Italy), 2001.

Poeta al comando, Mondadori (Milan, Italy), 2003.

HISTORY

Un santo in famiglia: vocazione religiosa e resistenze sociali nell'agiografia latina medievale, Rosenberg & Sellier (Turin, Italy), 1991.

(With Chiara Frugoni) *Dizionario del medioevo,* Laterza (Rome, Italy), 1994.

Un'oligarchia urbana: politica ed economia a Torino fra tre e quattrocento, Viella (Rome, Italy), 1995.

(With Chiara Frugoni) *Medieoevo: storia di voci, racconto di immagini,* Laterza (Rome, Italy), 1999.

Carlo Magno: un padre dell'Europa, Laterza (Rome, Italy), 2000, translation by Allan Cameron published as *Charlemagne: Father of a Continent,* University of California Press (Berkeley, CA), 2004.

Valle d'Aosta medievale, Liguori (Naples, Italy), 2000.

La cavalleria medievale, Jouvence (Rome, Italy), 2002.

Il ducato di Savoia: amministrazione e corte di uno stato franco-italiano: 1416-1536, Laterza (Rome, Italy), 2002.

La guerra in Europa dal rinascimento a Napoleone, Carocci (Rome, Italy), 2003.

La battaglia: storia di Waterloo, Laterza (Rome, Italy), 2003, translation by John Cullen published as *The Battle: A New History of Waterloo,* Walker (New York, NY), 2005.

SIDELIGHTS: Alessandro Barbero is the author of two different types of works: novels and scholarly pieces about medieval and early modern European history. The two styles complement each other in Barbero's work; his novels are often historical fiction and, as *Spectator* contributor Eric Christiansen speculated in a review of one of Barbero's nonfiction titles, his ability to "hold the attention with arresting details" in those works comes from his background as a novelist. All of Barbero's books were originally written in his native Italian, but a few have been translated into English.

Barbero's first work to be translated into English was *Carlo Magno: un padre dell'Europa,* published in English as *Charlemagne: Father of a Continent.* "The author of this rich, scholarly but accessible study provides an intimate portrait of the man—right down to his shirt and underpants—and a sensitive analysis of his government and times," commented a *Publishers Weekly* contributor. In his biography Barbero debunks some myths about Charlemagne, for example claiming that the "pincers movement" of troops in battle that Charlemagne pioneered was not the result of some great strategic insight, but rather a practical necessity caused by the difficulty of maneuvering vast numbers of slow-moving men and beasts at once. Barbero also examines some of the costs of Charlemagne's rule on the peasants in his territories—peasants who were expected to provide enough surplus food and oxen to keep Charlemagne's army moving and fighting, and who could expect harsh physical punishment if they failed to do so. With explanations such as these, noted a reviewer for the *Economist,* "Barbero chips away at the emperor's legacy until little more than a mediocrity remains." "All this is well discussed by Professor Barbero," Christiansen wrote, adding that the author "has a lightness of touch indispensable in approaching a subject which has constipated generations of continental scholars."

In *The Battle: A New History of Waterloo,* Barbero examines the final days of the career of French Emperor Napoleon Bonaparte. Barbero's history of the Battle of Waterloo, in which Napoleon was defeated by British, Prussian, and other forces, "is a resounding piece of reportage drawing heavily on the memories of those who fought it—and who remembered the grimmest of details," noted a *Kirkus Reviews* contributor. These personal memories, filled with decapitations via cannonballs and swords and other grisly forms of death, are not for the faint of heart. As Barbero walks readers through the action of the battle, "he folds in background information and includes incisive and accessible description and analysis of arms, equipment, and tactics," David Lee Poremba commented in *Library Journal.* In addition to the battle itself, Barbero also discusses its strategic implications. The Battle of Waterloo, Barbero argues, helped to propel Great Britain to its nineteenth-century prominence in world affairs. In addition, he shows how Napoleon's final campaigns came very close to bankrupting France. "The narrative is unusually accessible," wrote a *Publishers Weekly* critic, "and as experienced readers march on, they will find some novel insights and analyses."

BIOGRAPHICAL AND CRITICAL SOURCES:

PERIODICALS

Economist (U.S.), September 18, 2004, review of *Charlemagne: Father of a Continent,* p. 88.

Kirkus Reviews, May 15, 2005, review of *The Battle: A New History of Waterloo,* p. 569.
Library Journal, July 1, 2005, David Lee Poremba, review of *The Battle,* p. 96.
Publishers Weekly, June 7, 2004, review of *Charlemagne,* p. 39; May 16, 2005, review of *The Battle,* p. 53.
Spectator, October 9, 2004, Eric Christiansen, "Big Daddy of Europe?," p. 49.
World Literature Today, autumn, 1999, review of *Romanzo russo: Fiutando i futuri supplizi,* p. 711.

ONLINE

RIA International Web site, http://www.italica.rai.it/ (October 18, 2005), "Biografia di Alessandro Barbero."

*   *   *

BARBIERI, Heather Doran 1963-

PERSONAL: Born 1963; married; children: three. *Education:* Attended University of Washington.

ADDRESSES: Home—Seattle, WA. *Agent*—c/o Author Mail, Soho Press, 853 Broadway, New York, NY 10003. *E-mail*—heather@heatherbarbieri.com.

CAREER: Writer. Has held editorial jobs at newspapers and magazines.

AWARDS, HONORS: Waller Literature Award, 1984; James W. Hall Fiction Prize, 1985; Seattle Artists literary fellow, 1994-95; Ian St. James International Short Fiction Award, 1995; So to Speak Short-Short Fiction Award, 2001; Society of Children's Book Writers and Illustrators work-in-progress grant, 2003; Washington State Arts Commission Artist Trust literary fellow, 2004.

WRITINGS:

Snow in July (novel), Soho Press (New York, NY), 2004.

Contributor of short fiction to anthologies, including *The Pursuit of Happiness,* Leftbank Books, 1995; *Writing for Our Lives,* Running Deer Press, 1996; *Pleasure Vessels,* Angela Royal Publishing, 1997; *Explorations 2000,* University of Alaska Southeast, 2001; and *So to Speak,* George Mason University, 2001.

SIDELIGHTS: Heather Doran Barbieri's first novel, *Snow in July,* is the story of two sisters from Butte, Montana: Meghan is a drug addict with two children, and Erin is a recent high-school graduate who works at a vintage clothing store and lives with their mother. At one time, Meghan was the ambitious star of the family. After the death of their alcoholic father, her confidence crumbled and now her younger sister tries to hold things together. When Erin, the narrator, responds to a call from Meghan's preschool-aged daughter Teeny, the children and then Meghan move back to the family home. Meghan finds a job and begins to address her addictions, but when former associates threaten the family tension between the two sisters grows accordingly.

Reviewers were most impressed with the author's handling of family ties and descriptive passages. Writing for *Library Journal,* Elaine Bender stated that in *Snow in July* Barbieri "effectively captures the setting and atmosphere." A *Kirkus Reviews* critic remarked: "Barbieri handles the complex sibling relationship with finesse," and *Seattle Weekly* critic Colleen Smith advised that *Snow in July* can deliver "intricate, commanding descriptions of landscape or memory."

Barbieri told *CA:* "I am the descendent of Irish-American Butte miners who instilled me with the joy of storytelling and importance of family. An avid reader, my favorite books include anything by Edna O'Brien and William Trevor, as well as Pat Barker's 'Regeneration' series, Mary Karr's and Ruth Reichl's memoirs, *The Star of the Sea, Cry the Beloved Country, To the Lighthouse, The Sheltering Sky, The English Patient, The Assault, 100 Years of Solitude, Mrs. Caliban, Jonathan Strange & Mr. Norrell, Possession, Heart of Darkness, The White Bone,* and *The Sweet Hereafter,* among others. Beloved childhood books include *A Wrinkle in Time, Jessamy, The Witch of Blackbird Pond, Watership Down,* and the works of Joan Aiken."

BIOGRAPHICAL AND CRITICAL SOURCES:

PERIODICALS

Booklist, September 15, 2004, Rebecca Maksel, review of *Snow in July,* p. 205.

Kirkus Reviews, September 15, 2004, review of *Snow in July,* p. 880.

Library Journal, November 1, 2004, Elaine Bender, review of *Snow in July,* p. 72.

Seattle Weekly, February 16, 2005, Colleen Smith, review of *Snow in July.*

*　　*　　*

BARON, Devorah
　　See BARON, Dvora

*　　*　　*

BARON, Dvora 1887-1956
　　(Devorah Baron)

PERSONAL: Born 1887, in Ouzda, Russia; died 1956, in Israel; married Yosef Aharonovitch (a journalist); children: Tsipora (daughter). *Religion:* Jewish.

CAREER: Writer. *Young Worker,* literary editor.

AWARDS, HONORS: Bialik prize; Brenner prize.

WRITINGS:

Sipurim (title means "Stories"), Davar (Tel Aviv, Israel), 1926.

(Translator) Gustave Flaubert, *Madam Bovari,* [Tel Aviv, Israel], 1932.

Ketanot (stories; title means "Small Things"), Omanut (Tel Aviv, Israel), 1933.

Mah She-Hayah (stories; title means "What Has Been"), Davar (Tel Aviv, Israel), 1939.

Le-'et 'Atah (stories; title means "For the Time Being"), 'Am 'Oved (Tel Aviv, Israel), 1942.

Stories (in English), World Zionist Organization (Jerusalem, Israel), 1942.

Mi-Sham (stories; title means "From over There"), 'Am 'Oved (Tel Aviv, Israel), 1945.

Ha-Lavan (stories; title means "The Brickmaker"), 'Am 'Oved (Tel Aviv, Israel), 1946.

Shavirim (stories; title means "Sunbeams"), 'Am 'Oved (Tel Aviv, Israel), 1948.

Parashiyot: Sipurim Mekubatsim (stories; title means "Chapters"), Mosad Bi'alik (Jerusalem, Israel), 1950.

Hulyot: Sipurim (title means "Links: Stories"), 'Am 'Oved (Tel Aviv, Israel), 1952.

Me-Emesh: Sipurim (title means "From Yesterday: Stories"), 'Am 'Oved (Tel Aviv, Israel), 1954.

Agav-Urha: Asupah Me-'Izvonah (stories; title means "By the Way"), Sifriyat Po'alim (Merhavyah, Israel), 1960.

The Thorny Path, edited by Itzhak Hanoch, translation by Joseph Schacter (stories; includes "A Day in Rami's Life," "What Has Been," and "Wickedness,"), Institute for the Translation of Hebrew Literature (Jerusalem, Israel), 1969.

Yalkut Sipurim (title means "Collected Stories"), Hotsa 'at Yahedov (Tel Aviv, Israel), 1969.

Ha-Golim (novel; title means "Exile"), 'Am 'Oved (Tel Aviv, Israel), 1970.

Sheloshah Sipurim (title means "Three Stories"), Ha-Mahlakah Le-Hinukh Ule-Tarbut La-Golah (Jerusalem, Israel), 1974.

Ha-Mahatsit Ha-Rishonah: Devorah Baron-Hayehay vi-Yetsiratah, 648-683 (title means "The First Half: Early Stories"), Mosad Bi'alik (Jerusalem, Israel), 1988.

Keritut: Ve-Sipurim Aherim (title means "Divorcing and Other Stories"), 'Am 'Oved (Tel Aviv, Israel), 1997.

Parashiyot: Sipurim Mekubatsim, introductory essay by Asher Barash, Mosad Bi'alik (Jerusalem, Israel), 2000.

"The First Day" and Other Stories, edited by Chana Kronfeld and Naomi Seidman, translation by Naomi Seidman, University of California Press (Berkeley, CA), 2001.

Fradel/Shifra (two stories), Babel (Tel Aviv, Israel), 2001.

Work represented in numerous anthologies, including *Stories from Women Writers of Israel,* Star Publications (New Delhi, India), 1995. Translator of works by Jack London, Anton Chekhov, and others into Hebrew.

Individual stories have been published in Arabic, Chinese, Dutch, English, German, Hindi, Portuguese, Romanian, Spanish, and Yiddish.

SIDELIGHTS: Considered the first modern Hebrew woman writer, Dvora Baron was noted for a fluid writing style that gives her characters subtle emotional depths, thus leading readers to care about them even though her stories are sometimes considered simplistic in nature. According to Sarah Coleman, writing for the Web site *Feminista!,* Baron's approximately eighty short stories can be divided into two groups. The first are "unrestrained and passionate, dealing with wild emotions." Coleman classifies the second, later group of stories as "more measured and polished, less wild." In fact, Baron would come to refer to her earlier writings as her "rags."

Baron's stories focus primarily on life in an eastern European shtetl, a small town inhabited predominantly by a Jewish population, much like the town in Russia where she spent her early years. Her topics include divorce ("Fradl"), incest ("Grandma Heny"), domestic violence ("A Quarreling Couple"), and the fate of the disenfranchised. More often than not, her writings focus on women in a traditional, male-dominated society defined by numerous restrictions on the female sex. Her stories are realistic in nature and reflect the influence of Baron's profound knowledge of biblical and rabbinical literature.

Baron's own life is as interesting and disturbing as that of any of her fictional characters. Born near Minsk, Russia, and the daughter of a rabbi, she received a good education in days when most women received little formal schooling. As a result, she developed an early interest in writing and literature, and by the time she was a teenager, her stories were being published in a local newspaper. Baron moved to Minsk when she was fifteen and supported herself by tutoring and writing as she continued her education with the intent of becoming a teacher. Baron immigrated to Palestine in 1910 during the first Russian Revolution, during which her hometown was destroyed.

After moving to Palestine, Baron met Yosef Aharonovitch, editor of the *Young Worker,* and began to edit the influential Zionist newspaper's literary section. She and Aharonovitch married and soon had a daughter. Members of the literary intelligentsia, the Jewish couple was forced into exile in 1915 and went to live in Alexandria, Egypt. They eventually returned to Tel Aviv, and Baron continued to write, but her life was to take a drastic turn in the 1930s. It was then, after the deaths of her beloved brother and her husband, that she became a recluse, confining herself to her bedroom for the remainder of her life. A rigid vegetarian obsessed with hygiene, Baron would not allow her daughter, Tsipora, to go to school. Tsipora ended up taking care of her mother until Baron died in 1956.

Baron was criticized in her own time for writing too much about the shtetl life of her past even though she was part of a modern ideological Zionist movement. Nevertheless, her stories are often remarkably modern in their point of view. For example, she writes from the perspectives of a one-day-old girl in "The First Day" and of a female Jewish dog in "Liska." As Coleman stated in *Feminista!*, Baron's stories are also important because they "offer a unique perspective into a world that has mostly been chronicled by men, seen through the rose-tinted spectacles of nostalgia."

BIOGRAPHICAL AND CRITICAL SOURCES:

BOOKS

Lieblich, Amia, *Conversations with Dvora: An Experimental Biography of the First Modern Hebrew Woman Writer,* edited by Chana Kronfeld and Naomi Seidman, translation by Seidman, University of California Press (Berkeley, CA), 1997.

ONLINE

Feminista!, http://www.feminista.com/ (August 31, 2005), Sarah Coleman, "One Feminist Icon, Char-Broiled: A Rediscovered Writer Engenders Thoughts on Feminism and Art."*

*   *   *

BAT-MIRIAM, Yocheved 1901-1980(?)

PERSONAL: Born 1901, in Keplits, White Russia (now Belarus); died 1980 (some sources say 1979), in Israel; children: one son. *Education:* Attended University of Odessa and University of Moscow. *Religion:* Jewish.

CAREER: Poet.

AWARDS, HONORS: Israel prize, 1972.

WRITINGS:

POETRY

Me-Rahok (title means "From Afar"), Keren Zangvil be-London (Tel Aviv, Israel), 1931, reprinted, Ha-Kibuts ha-me'uhad (Tel Aviv, Israel), 1985.

Rey'ayon (title means "Interview"), Davar (Tel Aviv, Israel), 1940, reprinted, 1983.

Demuyot me-Ofek (title means "Images from the Horizon"), Mahbarot le-Sifrut (Tel Aviv, Israel), 1941.

Erets Yisra'el (title means "Land of Israel"), Mahberto Lesifrut (Tel Aviv, Israel), 1942.

Shirim la-Geto (title means "Ghetto Verse"), Sifriyat Po'Alim (Merhavyah, Israel), 1943.

Shirim (title means "Verse"), Sifriyat Po'alim (Merhavyah, Israel), 1963.

SIDELIGHTS: Born in White Russia (now Belarus), Jewish poet Yocheved Bat-Miriam found it difficult to get her verse published after a Soviet communist regime took power in her homeland. The year was 1922 and Bat-Miriam was in her early twenties. However, her poems soon began to appear in Hebrew journals in other countries. In 1929, she moved to Palestine, and her first volume of Hebrew poetry, *Me-Rahok,* was published in 1931.

Written when she was a young woman, Bat-Miriam's initial poems are deeply personal and romantic. Much of her poetry focuses on the Jewish home and the lot of Jewish women, and she also wrote about the Bible, focusing primarily on the Bible's female figures. She was a traditionalist in her poetry, looking back longingly on Jewish heritage and the Russian Jews' long-lost way of life. A reflection of this traditionalism is that Bat-Miriam, a small and fragile woman, almost always wore traditional black garments and was known to address people in the third person, an antiquated manner of addressing people respectfully.

In *Erets Yisra'el,* Bat-Miriam focuses her muse on creating nationalistic poems of Israel, then her adopted homeland. She also wrote about Jewish ghetto life. Throughout her poetry, Jewish women figure as heroines; her poetic narrator has many burdens but always strives to make life easier for others. Bat-Miriam quit writing poetry after her son died during Israel's War of Independence in 1948.*

BEBEL, August 1840-1913
(Ferdinand August Bebel)

PERSONAL: Born February, 1840, in Cologne, Germany; died August, 1913, in Passugg, Switzerland. *Politics:* Socialist.

CAREER: Politician. Worked as a master turner in Leipzig, Germany, beginning c. 1860; cofounder of Saxon People's Party, 1866; elected to Constituent Reichstag of North German Confederation, beginning 1867; cofounder and chief spokesperson for Social Democratic Party, Eisenach, beginning 1969; elected to German Reichstag, beginning 1871.

MEMBER: Federation of German Workers' Societies (national chairman, beginning 1867).

WRITINGS:

Der deutsche Bauerkrieg mit Berücksichtigung der hauptsälichsten sozialen Bewegungen des Mittelalters, W. Bracke Jr. (Braunschweig, Germany), 1876.

Die Frau und der Sozialismus, Volksbuchhandlung (Zürich-Hottingen, Switzerland), 1879, 66th edition, Deitz (Berlin, Germany), 1990, translated as *Woman in the Past, Present, and Future,* Modern Press (London, England), 1885, J.W. Lovell (New York, NY), 1886, published as *Woman under Socialism,* New York Labor News Press (New York, NY), 1904, 50th Jubilee edition published as *Woman and Socialism,* Socialist Literature Co. (New York, NY), 1910, published as *Woman: Past, Present, and Future,* Boni & Liveright (New York, NY), 1918, selections published as *Frau und der Sozialismus: Selections,* Progress Publishers (Moscow, USSR), 1971.

Charles Fourier, sein Leben und seine Theorien, J.H.W. Dietz (Stuttgart, Germany), 1888, 3rd edition, 1907.

Zur Lage der Arbeiter in den Bäckereien, J.H.W. Dietz (Stuttgart, Germany), 1890.

Die Sozialdemokratie und das allgemeine Stimmrecht. Mit besonderer Berücksichtigung des Frauenstimmrechts und Proportional-Wahlsystems, T. Glocke (Berlin, Germany), 1895.

Aus meinem Leben (autobiography), three volumes, J.H.W. Dietz (Stuttgart, Germany), 1910–14, translated as *Bebel's Reminiscences,* Socialist Literature Co. (New York, NY), 1911, abridged edition published as *My Life,* two volumes, T.F. Unwin (London, England), 1912.

Speeches of August Bebel, [Berlin, Germany], 1926, International Publishers (New York, NY), 1928.

August Bebels Briefwechsel mit Friedrich Engles (correspondence), edited by Werner Blumenberg, Mouton (The Hague, Netherlands), 1965.

Coeditor, *Vorwärts.*

SIDELIGHTS: A key figure in the German Socialist movement, August Bebel rose from a childhood of poverty to become one of the most influential thinkers of his day. A cofounder, with Wilhelm Liebknecht, of the German Social Democratic Party, Bebel's oratorical gifts made him a political figurehead amid the rising tide of Marxism that swept the unified German states after the Austro-Prussian war of 1866.

Born in Cologne in 1840, Bebel was the son of a Prussian petty officer who died when August was a young boy. After obtaining a rudimentary education at a school for impoverished boys in Wetzlar, he apprenticed as a turner, a vocation that ultimately led him to settle in Leipzig in 1860. Living in the hub of German political activity, Bebel quickly became involved in politics, joining the radical Gewerblicher Bildungsverein (Industrial Educational Association, or IEA) and becoming immersed in the study of European political, social, and economic history. He also studied the works of Ferdinand Lassalle and, with the encouragement of fellow IEA member Liebknecht, those of Karl Marx and Friederich Engels. Marx in particular would be a major influence on Bebel's growing socialist beliefs.

A commanding speaker, Bebel attained prominence as a leader in labor circles, and later, in the realm of politics. From his election to the North German Constituent Reichstag in 1867 as a representative of his own Saxon People's Party, he would go on to represent Dresden and, later, Hamburg, in the German Reichstag. A founder, with Liebknecht, of the German Social Democratic Party and instrumental in aligning it with other social-reform factions, Bebel, by the time of his death in 1913, had become a cornerstone of the growing social democratic movement.

Bebel believed that the social change he viewed as necessary could best be achieved through the reform of existing social and political structures, rather than by the revolutionary tactics that would later be advocated by Vladimir Lenin. *Woman and Socialism,* published as *Die Frau und der Sozialismus* in 1879, was an outgrowth of such beliefs, an attempt to mobilize an existing women's movement under the banner of socialism.

Basing his work on the central tenet of Marxism—that political and social structures are determined by the economic conditions of *all* people—Bebel maintained that the antagonisms between women of different social classes were diminished due to more pressing common interests; that both laboring women and the well-heeled wives of the bourgeois class, despite their differences, might unite to fight for social, economic, and political equality. The aims of the bourgeois suffrage movement, which focused on higher education, professional careers, and the right to hold public office in its bid for equality between the sexes, would do nothing to ameliorate the underlying cause of women's historic inequality. This was, in Bebel's view, the social institutionalization through marriage and other societal norms, of the financial, physical, sexual, and mental slavery of women.

For Bebel, of course, the cause of female equality was secondary to the class struggle; indeed, *Women and Socialism* can be viewed as a political propaganda aimed at a female audience. The "duty of the proletarian woman," he wrote, "to join the men of her class in the struggle for a thoroughgoing transformation of society, to bring about an order that by its social institutions will enable both sexes to enjoy complete economic and intellectual independence"—in other words, to work with men toward the abolishment of capitalism—overshadows the work.

Gaining additional popularity after the formation of the Second International in Paris in 1889, Bebel's tract has been widely read throughout Western Europe and the United States. It has undergone numerous translations and has been reprinted dozens of times. Although the inclusion of now-outdated statistical data has rendered portions of the work obsolete, abridged versions of *Women and Socialism* are still read and studied.

BIOGRAPHICAL AND CRITICAL SOURCES:

BOOKS

Feminist Writers, St. James Press (Detroit, MI), 1996.

Heckart, Beverly, *From Basserman to Bebel: The Grand Bloc's Quest for Reform in the Kaiserreich, 1900-1914,* Yale University Press (New Haven, CT), 1975.

Maehl, William Harvey, *August Bebel, Shadow Emperor of the German Workers,* American Philosophical Society (Philadelphia, PA), 1980.

Marx-Aveling, Eleanor, and Edward Aveling, *Thoughts on Women and Society,* edited by Joachim Müller and Edith Schotte, International Publishers (New York, NY), 1986.

Women in the German Democratic Republic: On the 100th Anniversary of the Publication of August Bebel's Book "Women and Socialism," Verlag Zeit im Bild (Dresden, Germany), 1978.

PERIODICALS

Labor History, February, 1998, Ralph Walz, review of *Aus meinem Leben,* p. 84.*

*　　*　　*

BEBEL, Ferdinand August
　　See BEBEL, August

*　　*　　*

BECKLUND, Laurie

PERSONAL: Female. *Education:* Immaculate Heart College, B.A.; Columbia University, M.A.

ADDRESSES: Home—Los Angeles, CA. *Agent*—Penguin Group, c/o Gotham Books Publicity, 375 Hudson St., New York, NY 10014. *E-mail*—becklund@ pacbell.net.

CAREER: Journalist and author. Former reporter for *Los Angeles Times;* worked for *CBS News* as a journalist and Web site developer. Consultant for journalism software and for University of Southern California online journalism program.

AWARDS, HONORS: Pulitzer Prize, 1992, for team coverage of Los Angeles riots for *Los Angeles Times;* Society of Professional Journalists award, 1993, for best writing nationwide.

WRITINGS:

NONFICTION

(With Chris Oyler and Beth Polson) *Go toward the Light,* Harper & Row (New York, NY), 1988.

(With J.B. Strasser) *Swoosh: The Unauthorized Story of Nike, and the Men Who Played There,* Harcourt (San Diego, CA), 1991.

(With Zainab Salbi) *Between Two Worlds: Escape from Tyranny: Growing up in the Shadow of Saddam,* Gotham (New York, NY), 2005.

SIDELIGHTS: Laurie Becklund is an award-winning journalist who has cowritten several nonfiction books on topics as diverse as the Nike athletic shoe company and Saddam Hussein. In *Swoosh: The Unauthorized Story of Nike, and the Men Who Played There,* Becklund teamed up with her sister, J.B. Strasser, a former advertising executive for the shoe company, to tell the story of Nike's rise to prominence in the 1970s and 1980s. Strasser's husband was an executive for the company during its early days, when Americans took up running and fitness and turned Nike and its "swoosh" logo into a populist status symbol.

Becklund and Strasser chart Nike's humble beginnings in the late 1960s, when Phil Knight, a former track star, decided to meld his interest in sports with his degree in accounting. In relating the young company's freewheeling ways, when those at the top refused to bog themselves down with job titles, Becklund and Strasser, according to a writer in *Publishers Weekly,* "chart a business-sports phenomenon in captivating detail." Reviewers also noted the authors' apparent admiration for Knight's nontraditional business methods and their waning enthusiasm as Nike grows into a billion-dollar powerhouse.

Becklund also helped write Zainab Salbi's memoir, *Between Two Worlds: Escape from Tyranny: Growing up in the Shadow of Saddam.* Salbi's father was one of Saddam Hussein's advisors, and she grew up simultaneously admiring and fearing the Iraqi leader. Under Hussein's dictatorship, Salbi and others learned to forget friends and acquaintances who had been killed by Hussein in order to maintain what little peace of mind they still possessed. When Salbi is a teenager, Hussein becomes interested in her, prompting her parents to ship her off to the United States and into an arranged marriage.

A critic for *Kirkus Reviews* called Becklund's prose in *Between Two Worlds* "flat" but concluded that "Salbi's story has value for those hoping to understand the strangeness and ubiquity of Saddam's regime." Conversely, a writer for *Publishers Weekly* called the book an "engrossing memoir" and "an enlightening revelation of how, by barely perceptible stages, decent people make accommodations in a horrific regime."

BIOGRAPHICAL AND CRITICAL SOURCES:

PERIODICALS

Kirkus Reviews, August 1, 2005, review of *Between Two Worlds: Escape from Tyranny: Growing up in the Shadow of Saddam,* p. 836.

Library Journal, August 1, 2005, Sadiq Alkoriji, review of *Between Two Worlds,* p. 97.

Publishers Weekly, November 22, 1991, review of *Swoosh: The Unauthorized Story of Nike, and the Men Who Played There,* p. 45; July 18, 2005, review of *Between Two Worlds,* p. 196.

Time, January 20, 1992, Richard Stengel, review of *Swoosh,* p. 53.

Washington Free Press, January-February, 1998, Doug Nufer, "Two Tales of One Nike."*

*   *   *

BENNETT, Jonathan 1970-

PERSONAL: Born 1970, in Australia; immigrated to Canada.

ADDRESSES: *Home*—Peterborough, Ontario, Canada. *Agent*—c/o Dean Cooke, The Cooke Agency, 278 Bloor St. E., Ste. 305, Toronto, Ontario M4W 3M4, Canada. *E-mail*—jc_bennett@hotmail.com.

CAREER: Writer and educator. Writing instructor at Ryerson University, Toronto, Ontario, Canada; Trent University, Peterborough, Ontario; and George Brown College, Toronto.

WRITINGS:

After Battersea Park (novel), Raincoast Books (Vancouver, British Columbia, Canada), 2001.

Verandah People (short stories), Publishers Group West (Berkeley, CA), 2003.

Here Is My Street, This Tree I Planted (poems), ECW Press, 2004

Contributor to periodicals, including *Globe & Mail, Quill & Quire,* and *Descant.*

WORK IN PROGRESS: A novel.

SIDELIGHTS: Jonathan Bennett, an Australian transplanted to Canada, writes in many genres. His first published book, *After Battersea Park,* is a novel about identical twin brothers who were separated at age four. The two were raised thousands of miles apart, Curt in Australia and William in Canada, yet their lives have eerie similarities. Both have artistic careers, the former as a jazz musician and the latter as a visual artist, and both have difficulties in their personal relationships stemming from a fear of abandonment. Circumstances eventually propel the two to a reunion in Hawaii, but this does not result in the kind of resolution a reader might expect. "In lesser-skilled hands, this scenario would conclude with a kind of hackneyed happiness, a predictably pat ending where both men use each other to 'figure out' themselves," Mark Sampson explained in the *Danforth Review.* Instead, readers are "given something much richer, much truer." "In remarkably concise fashion," Joanne Wilkinson noted in *Booklist,* "Bennett's story encompasses two decades and three continents while limning themes of family and cultural identity."

Bennett's next book, *Verandah People,* is a short-story collection featuring twelve tales set in Australia, in Sydney and the surrounding area. All of the stories feature tragedies, many from the point of view of those who are left behind to try to cope after others are killed. In "Landmarks," a man cannot stop having nightmares about a girl who drowned after her hair tangled in a pool filter; in "Out Walking," a soon-to-be-married woman's life is shattered when a body falls to the street outside the window of a store where she is shopping. A *Kirkus Reviews* contributor commended "Bennett's sometimes unpolished but ravishing language" and "his ability to animate lives within a landscape that dwarfs the human" in this title.

From *Verandah People,* Bennett turned to poetry with the publication of *Here Is My Street, This Tree I Planted.* He began working on the poems, Bennett explained to *Poetics.ca* interviewer Stephen Brockwell, after some people criticized *After Battersea Park* for swinging "from plotted, garden-variety prose, to whole scenes written in a far denser way: prose poems, almost. . . . I was so bloody worried about my voice and if it sounded Australian or Canadian, that I never thought to consider that I might have multiple urges, that is, not just to write novels and stories, but poems, too."

BIOGRAPHICAL AND CRITICAL SOURCES:

PERIODICALS

Booklist, September 15, 2001, Joanne Wilkinson, review of *After Battersea Park,* p. 190.

Kirkus Reviews, August 15, 2004, review of *Verandah People,* p. 757.

ONLINE

Danforth Review Onlin, http://www.danforthreview. com/ (October 18, 2005), Mark Sampson, review of *After Battersea Park.*

Jonathan Bennett Home Page, http://www. jonathanbennett.com (October 18, 2005).

Poetics.ca, http://www.poetics.ca/ (October 28, 2005), Stephen Brockwell, "A Time and a Place: An Interview with Jonathan Bennett."*

            *   *   *

BEYER, Marcel 1965-

PERSONAL: Born November 23, 1965, in Tailfingen, Germany. *Education:* Studied German and English literature in Siegen, Germany.

ADDRESSES: Home—Dresden, Germany. *Agent*—c/o Author Mail, Harcourt, 15 E. 26th St., New York, NY 10010.

CAREER: Writer, editor, and translator.

WRITINGS:

Das Menschenfleisch (novel), Suhrkamp (Frankfurt am Main, Germany), 1991.

Friederike Mayröcker: eine Bibliographie, 1946-1990,
    P. Lang (New York, NY), 1992.

(Editor, with Karl Riha) Rudolf Blümner, *Ango Laïna
    und andere Texte,* Edition Text + Kritik (Munich,
    Germany), 1993.

(Editor, with Karl Riha) Johannes Baader, *Ich segne
    die Hölle!: Gedichte 1915-1933,* Universität-
    Gesamthochschule Siegen (Siegen, Germany),
    1995.

Flughunde (novel), Suhrkamp (Frankfurt am Main,
    Germany), 1995, translation by John Brownjohn
    published as *The Karnau Tapes,* Harcourt Brace
    (New York, NY), 1997.

Falsches Futter (poems), Suhrkamp (Frankfurt am
    Main, Germany), 1997.

Spione (novel), DuMont (Cologne, Germany), 2000,
    translation by Breon Mitchell published as *Spies,*
    Harcourt (New York, NY), 2005.

(Editor, with Klaus Reichert and Klaus Kastberger)
    Friederike Mayröcker, *Gesammelte Prosa,* Su-
    hrkamp (Frankfurt am Main, Germany), 2001.

Erdkunde (poems), DuMont (Cologne, Germany),
    2002.

Nonfiction (essays), DuMont (Cologne, Germany),
    2003.

Vergesst mich (fiction), DuMont (Cologne, Germany),
    2006.

SIDELIGHTS: German author Marcel Beyer has
garnered critical acclaim for both his novels and
poems. Writing for the *Germany-Poetry International
Web site,* Alexander Gumz called Beyer "one of the
most talked about—and actually read—young authors
in Germany today" and "one of the most important
poets of his generation."

Set mostly during the last five years of World War II,
Beyer's 1995 novel, *Flughunde* (published in English
as *The Karnau Tapes*), alternates between fact and fiction and different points of view. One of the book's
narrators is Hermann Karnau, an engineer obsessed
with recording and analyzing the full range of human
sounds—from the playful chatter of children to the
painful cries of dying soldiers. *Flughunde* is also told
from the point of view of eight-year-old Helga Goebbels, the daughter of Nazi propaganda chief Joseph
Goebbels. Hermann and Helga find themselves
together in Adolf Hitler's bunker in the days before
Hitler's suicide. During this time, Hermann makes the
last recording of Hitler's voice and witnesses the grim
fate of Helga and her siblings at the hands of their
mother. "What distinguishes this text from all others is
the attempt to reconstruct the Third Reich from the
perspective of the history of voice and ear and their
technological reproducibility, amplification, and
transmission by phonograph, tape recorder, micro-
phone, and loudspeaker," noted Ulrich Schonherr of
the English translation in the *Germanic Review.* Schonherr described Hermann as "an eerie figure because he
turns out to be an extremely sensitive observer and
critic of totalitarian culture, despite numerous cor-
respondences between his voice project and the evolution of fascist power politics." Schonherr also felt that
young Helga "undoubtedly embodies the strongest narrative counterweight to the barbarism of the male-
dominated National Socialist culture, despite her age.
. . . Helga's narrative voice evolves as the strongest
moral authority in the text."

Reviews of *Flughunde* were mostly positive. As *World
Literature Today* contributor Robert Schwarz commented, "Large parts of *Flughunde* are superbly done
and show a master hand of creative writing. It is a
relentless book, maintaining a fine balance between
external events and interior voice." A reviewer for
Publishers Weekly noted of the English translation that
"the plot meanders during the book's early stages,"
but concluded that, overall, "the narrative finds its true
tone."

Beyer's next novel, *Spione* (published in English as
Spies), features an unnamed narrator and his cousins
who search for information about their grandfather's
mysterious past. The story switches viewpoints and
moves backward and forward in time as the four
"spies" try to uncover their family's hidden secrets. A
critic for *Publishers Weekly* called the English translation a "love story wrapped in a drama wrapped in a
mystery," and a contributor to *Kirkus Reviews* remarked that *Spies* is "a bit labored and opaque, but
atmospheric, increasingly engrossing and ultimately
very rewarding."

Among Beyer's other writings are the novel *Das Menschenfleisch* and a volume of poetry titled *Erdkunde.*
In addition, Beyer has also edited and translated the
works of many renowned authors.

BIOGRAPHICAL AND CRITICAL SOURCES:

PERIODICALS

Germanic Review, fall, 1998, Ulrich Schonherr, "To-
    pophony of Fascism: On Marcel Beyer's *The Kar-
    nau Tapes,*" p. 328.

Journal of European Studies, June, 1994, Richard Sheppard, review of Rudolf Blümner, *Ango Laïna und andere Texte,* p. 197.

Kirkus Reviews, May 15, 2005, review of *Spies,* p. 555.

Library Journal, November 15, 1997, Robert E. Brown, review of *The Karnau Tapes,* p. 75.

Publishers Weekly, September 22, 1997, review of *The Karnau Tapes,* p. 67; June 6, 2005, review of *Spies,* p. 37.

World Literature Today, fall, 1996, Robert Schwarz, review of *Flughunde,* p. 945.

ONLINE

Germany-Poetry International Web site, http://www.germany.poetryinternational.org/ (July 1, 2005), Alexander Gumz, biography of Marcel Beyer.

*   *   *

BINGAMAN, Kirk A. 1960-

PERSONAL: Born January 22, 1960, in Chambersburg, PA; son of C.F. (an educator and minister) and Joyce (a teacher's aide; maiden name, Wagaman) Bingaman; children: Anne. *Ethnicity:* "Caucasian." *Education:* Messiah College, B.A., 1987; Princeton Theological Seminary, M.Div., 1990; Graduate Theological Union, Ph.D., 2000. *Religion:* Presbyterian.

ADDRESSES: Office—San Francisco Theological Seminary, 105 Seminary Rd., San Anselmo, CA 94960. *E-mail*—kbingaman@sfts.edu.

CAREER: Writer, counselor, and educator. San Francisco Theological Seminary, San Anselmo, CA, pastoral counselor and adjunct professor of pastoral care and counseling, 2001—.

MEMBER: American Academy of Religion, American Association of Pastoral Counselors.

WRITINGS:

Freud and Faith: Living in the Tension, State University of New York Press (Albany, NY), 2003.

SIDELIGHTS: Kirk A. Bingaman told *CA:* "My motivation for writing has been doctoral research and subsequent research in the academic field of theological education. What has influenced my work has been the lived experience of my students. In other words, the writing process for me begins with the practicalities of the experiential realm and from there moves into the realm of theoretical and theological reflection. My book, *Freud and Faith: Living in the Tension,* was inspired, first and foremost, by the lively discussions within the context of the seminary classroom."

*   *   *

BLAKE, Victoria

PERSONAL: Born in Oxford, England. *Education:* Attended Oxford University.

ADDRESSES: Home—West London, England. *Agent*—c/o Author Mail, Orion Publishing Group, Orion House, 5 Upper Saint Martin's La., London WC2H 9EA, England.

CAREER: Writer. Duckworth Publishers, London, England, solicitor. Also worked as a bookseller.

WRITINGS:

"SAM FALCONER" NOVELS

Bloodless Shadow, Orion Publishing Group (London, England), 2003, Berkley Books (New York, NY), 2005.

Cutting Blades, Orion Publishing Group (London, England), 2005.

SIDELIGHTS: In an interview with Ayo Onatade for *Shots* online, author Victoria Blake revealed that prior to publishing her first crime novel, *Bloodless Shadow,* she had unsuccessfully tried to publish two other books. Deciding to give writing one final try, Blake ventured into the crime genre. She commented that while she had read "tons of crime" throughout her life, she had been "frightened by the plotting aspects" of writing a crime novel. Nevertheless, Blake finished—and published—*Bloodless Shadow,* her first book in a series about private investigator Samantha Falconer.

In *Bloodless Shadow,* Blake introduces Samantha "Sam" Falconer, a four-time world judo champion turned private investigator. After agreeing to investigate the disappearance of a prominent psychiatrist's missing wife, Sam must return to Oxford, England, a city she associates with painful memories she had hoped to leave behind.

Blake's debut novel was met with mixed reviews. A contributor to *Publishers Weekly* stated that *Bloodless Shadow* is "engaging" and remarked upon "the smoothly interwoven plot lines and the authentic settings." A critic for *Kirkus Reviews* felt that the "by-the-numbers plotting" does little to grab readers' attention. On the other hand, *Shots* contributor Onatade noted that "Sam's private life is quite fascinating. . . . It will be interesting to see how this series develops and how Ms. Falconer handles herself in the future."

In Blake's second 'Sam Falconer' novel, *Cutting Blades,* the detective is once again investigating a missing person, this time a talented rower from Oxford University. *Cutting Blades,* like *Bloodless Shadow,* reveals more secrets from Sam's past as she attempts to solve a string of intertwined mysteries. A reviewer for the *CrimeSquad* Web site observed that while the plot in *Cutting Blades* is interesting, "it is the marvelous canvas of different characters that always hold your attention." The reviewer concluded that it is the "fascinating" characters that "urge you to turn the pages."

BIOGRAPHICAL AND CRITICAL SOURCES:

PERIODICALS

Kirkus Reviews, June 15, 2005, review of *Bloodless Shadow,* p. 664.
Library Journal, July 1, 2005, Rex E. Klett, review of *Bloodless Shadow,* p. 56.
Publishers Weekly, June 6, 2005, review of *Bloodless Shadow,* p. 43.

ONLINE

CrimeSquad, http://www.crimesquad.com/ (October 10, 2005), review of *Cutting Blades.*

Orion Publishing Group Web site, http://www.orionbooks.co.uk/ (October 10, 2005).
Shots Online, http://www.shotsmag.co.uk/ (October 10, 2005), Ayo Onatade, review of *Bloodless Shadow* and interview with Victoria Blake.*

*   *   *

BLOCK, Barbara
(Isis Crawford)

PERSONAL: Born in New York, NY; children: three sons. *Education:* New York University, B.A.; Columbia University, M.A.; attended Hunter College and School of Visual Arts. *Hobbies and other interests:* Travel, animals.

ADDRESSES: Home—Syracuse, NY. *Agent*—Evan Marshall, Evan Marshall Agency, Six Tristam Place, Pine Brook, NJ 07058-9445.

CAREER: Writer. Also operated a catering business, Syracuse, NY, specializing in desserts.

WRITINGS:

"ROBIN LIGHT MYSTERY" SERIES

Chutes and Adders, Kensington Books (New York, NY), 1994.
Twister, Kensington Books (New York, NY), 1995.
In Plain Sight, Kensington Books (New York, NY), 1996.
The Scent of Murder, Kensington Books (New York, NY), 1997.
Vanishing Act, Kensington Books (New York, NY), 1998.
Endangered Species, Kensington Books (New York, NY), 1999.
Blowing Smoke, Kensington Books (New York, NY), 2001.
Rubbed Out, Kensington Books (New York, NY), 2002.
Salt City Blues, Severn House Publishers (London, England), 2004.

AS ISIS CRAWFORD

A *Catered Murder* (mystery), Kensington Books (New
   York, NY), 2003.
A *Catered Wedding* (mystery), Kensington Books
   (New York, NY), 2004.

Also contributor of articles and reviews to periodicals.

SIDELIGHTS: Barbara Block is an author living in
Syracuse, New York, who uses her town's locale as
the setting for a series of mystery novels featuring
Robin Light, a "hard-drinking sloppily dressed, heavy-
smoking amateur sleuth and exotic pet-store owner,"
according to a reviewer for *Publishers Weekly.* A des-
sert caterer, Block has also used this experience to pen,
under the pseudonym Isis Crawford, a series dealing
with catering sisters who become involved in murder
investigations.

Block's "Robin Light" mysteries began with the 1994
title *Chutes and Adders,* dubbed a "sharp-edged and
wry mystery" by a reviewer for *Publishers Weekly.* Her
debut novel starts out at a hectic pace, when Robin's
pet shop assistant, John, is killed by a poisonous snake
that was lurking in a package addressed to him. When
the police search for the missing snake in the store,
they find instead a packet of 50,000 dollars and a handwritten list of animals that leads them to believe that
Robin is dealing in endangered species. But Robin
recognizes the writing; it belongs to her recently
deceased husband Murphy, who died of a cocaine
overdose. The pet store was Murphy's, and Robin,
once a freelance journalist, has taken over running it
since his death. Now the police think Robin, Murphy,
and John were involved in smuggling animals and that
she may have killed John. Thus, Robin is thrust into
the role of unwilling sleuth trying to clear her own
name in what Stuart Miller described in *Booklist* as a
"terrific first novel." Miller went on to commend the
"appealing central character and a truly enthralling plot
with a wham-bang ending." For the *Publishers Weekly*
contributor, "Robin is an engaging, if stubborn and
reckless, amateur sleuth."

Robin is drawn into a second murder investigation in
Twister when a friend of hers named Lynn is found
kneeling over a dead man's body; the deceased also
was carrying one of Robin's cards from her days as a

journalist. Lynn's father hires Robin to get to the bottom of matters in this "intricate story with another hair-
raising ending," as Miller noted in *Booklist.* Similar
praise came from a *Publishers Weekly* contributor who
concluded: "Block skillfully carries readers through
the turbulence to a satisfying conclusion."

Robin's fame as an amateur sleuth brings her clients
in her third outing, *In Plain Sight,* but when a woman
who has consulted her to find some damaging information on her husband later turns up dead, Robin has a
bigger case on her hands. Block has developed the
technique of involving an animal in the finale of each
of her books, and *In Plain Sight* finds bats taking
center stage. Miller, again writing in *Booklist,* felt this
installment is "not to be missed." Block's 1997 addition to the series, *The Scent of Murder,* stirs up the past
and involves dealings with Robin's dead husband,
Murphy. Miller noted in *Booklist* that "Block's gripping denouements are especially good," while a *Publishers Weekly* contributor found the novel a "complex,
satisfying story of family greed and corruption."

A missing-person case forms the heart of Robin's next
case, *Vanishing Act,* as the pet-shop owner is on the
track of a missing college student. More back-story is
also provided, with subplots including the strained
relations between Robin and her black, ex-cop
boyfriend, George. A reviewer for *Publishers Weekly*
complained that, "although tightly written, stereotypes
abound" in this fifth in the series. Miller, reviewing
the same title in *Booklist,* however, had a higher assessment of the book, deeming it "a fine addition to
this excellent series." In *Blowing Smoke,* the children
of an aging and wealthy woman seek Robin's help,
claiming she is being fooled and swindled by her
much-younger husband and by a man who claims he
can talk to dead animals. Things heat up when the pet
psychic is found dead. Miller praised the "corking-
good plot [that] will keep you turning the pages until
the very end" in a *Booklist* review, while Rex E. Klett,
writing in *Library Journal,* found the same book "a
pleasing page-turner." Block's eighth "Robin Light"
book, *Rubbed Out,* involves complicated plot twists
including a missing girl, a missing 200,000 dollars,
and the Russian mob. A contributor for *Kirkus Reviews*
was critical of this installment in the series, noting that
"the suspense never keeps pace with the florid plot
complications." Klett, however, reviewing the title in
Library Journal, thought it "an exciting challenge for
a tough heroine," and a critic for *Publishers Weekly*

called it "an exciting read with an attractive and strangely plausible heroine."

Robin Light returns in the 2005 installment, *Salt City Blues,* investigating the murder of a local low-life, Freddy, during one cold and dark Christmas season. The police put his slaying down to a gang killing, but Robin takes a look at Freddy's fancy and expensive belongings, and is not so sure. A critic for *Kirkus Reviews* felt this novel presents "a depressing tale, but one with enough twists and turns to make sharing Robin's blues worthwhile." Barbara Bibel, writing in *Booklist,* had praise for Block's amateur sleuth, calling Robin "a welcome addition to the ranks of female detectives."

Block's two novels under the pseudonym Isis Crawford feature sisters Libby and Bernie, who run a catering business in a fictional upstate New York town. Also part of the cast is their wheel-chair-bound father, Sean, who is retired from the police. As with the animals in her books featuring Robin Light, Block peppers these catering mysteries with recipes and food chat. In *A Catered Murder,* the sisters are hired to cater a dinner for a local celebrity, a best-selling author of vampire books, but when the author dies at the dinner table, the sisters find themselves dragged into the role of amateur detectives in an attempt to clear the good name of their catering firm. A reviewer for *Publishers Weekly* commended the "naturally flowing narrative, lively and likable characters, and plenty of clever word play" in this series opener. In the second installment of the series, *A Catered Wedding,* the sisters investigate the murder of a young woman, shot through the heart by an arrow, shortly before her wedding. Bridget Bolton, writing for *Reviewing the Evidence,* thought this novel is "fluently written, and is a quick and enjoyable read."

Block told *CA:* "I love stories, always have, always will. I love words. I was one of those kids that used to read the dictionary for fun. My favorite class has always been creative writing. When I was younger I used to read three books a week. Fiction was my refuge. It was my substitute for the brothers and sisters I didn't have. I lived at the library. Then life intruded and I grew up. I got a job, got married, had children and pets, and I abandoned my first love. Eventually though it called me back and I found myself scribbling random observations on the margins of my shopping lists. The scribblings grew into a book and even though

that one wasn't published, nor the one after that, the third one was.

"The most surprising thing I've learned as a writer is that everything you need to know to finish your book is contained in the first three chapters."

BIOGRAPHICAL AND CRITICAL SOURCES:

PERIODICALS

Booklist, August, 1994, Stuart Miller, review of *Chutes and Adders,* p. 2025; July, 1995, Stuart Miller, review of *Twister,* p. 1862; July, 1996, Stuart Miller, review of *In Plain Sight,* p. 1806; June 1, 1997, Stuart Miller, review of *The Scent of Murder,* p. 1665; July, 1998, Stuart Miller, review of *Vanishing Act,* p. 1862; May 1, 2001, Stuart Miller, review of *Blowing Smoke,* p. 1622; March 15, 2005, Barbara Bibel, review of *Salt City Blues,* p. 1269.
Kirkus Reviews, September 15, 2002, review of *Rubbed Out,* p. 1352; March 15, 2005, review of *Salt City Blues,* p. 318.
Library Journal, August, 1997, Rex E. Klett, review of *The Scent of Murder,* p. 139; September 1, 1998, Rex E. Klett, review of *Vanishing Act,* p. 220; June 1, 2001, Rex E. Klett, review of *Blowing Smoke,* p. 224; November 1, 2002, Rex E. Klett, review of *Rubbed Out,* p. 132; November 1, 2004, Rex E. Klett, review of *A Catered Murder,* p. 58; May 1, 2005, Rex E. Klett, review of *Salt City Blues,* p. 65.
Publishers Weekly, July 4, 1994, review of *Chutes and Adders,* p. 55; May 15, 1995, review of *Twister,* p. 58; July 8, 1996, review of *In Plain Sight,* p. 78; June 9, 1997, review of *The Scent of Murder,* p. 41; June 22, 1998, review of *Vanishing Act,* p. 88; June 4, 2001, review of *Blowing Smoke,* p. 61; November 4, 2002, review of *Rubbed Out,* p. 66; November 24, 2003, review of *A Catered Murder,* p. 45; November 8, 2004, review of *A Catered Wedding,* p. 39.

ONLINE

AllReaders.com, http://www.allreaders.com/ (August 13, 2005), Harriet Klausner, review of *Blowing Smoke, Rubbed Out, A Catered Murder,* and *A Catered Wedding.*

New Times Online (Syracuse, NY), http://www. newtimes.com/ (March 9, 2005), Bethany Root, "Killer Catering."

Reviewing the Evidence, http://www.reviewingthe evidence.com/ (August 13, 2005), Bridget Bolton, review of *A Catered Wedding.*

*   *   *

BLOCK, Leo 1920-

PERSONAL: Born June 15, 1920, in Russia; naturalized U.S. citizen; married; wife's name Shirley Mae. *Ethnicity:* "Russian." *Education:* University of Southern California, B.Eng. (cum laude), M.S.; also attended Naval War College. *Politics:* "Conservative." *Religion:* Eastern Orthodox. *Hobbies and other interests:* Sailing his thirty-foot sloop, history.

ADDRESSES: Home and office—409 Calle Delicada, San Clemente, CA 92672. *Agent*—New England Publishing Associates, P.O. Box 5, Chester, CT 06412. *E-mail*—leoblock1@aol.com.

CAREER: Writer, engineer, and historian. Rheem Manufacturing, design and development engineer for forced-air and gravity furnaces in South Gate, CA, and Chicago, IL, 1948-50; Holly Co., Pasadena, CA, design engineer of wall heaters, floor furnaces, forced-air furnaces, and air conditioning equipment, 1952-58; Day and Night—Payne, La Puente, CA, project engineer for advanced engineering of gas-fired, forced-air furnaces, water heaters, and air conditioning units, 1958-60; Transicold Corp., Montebello, CA, chief engineer of refrigeration for long-haul trailers, 1960-65; Raypak, Inc., Westlake Village, CA, vice president of operations and of engineering for gas-fired boilers, water heaters, and swimming pool and spa heaters, 1976-83; consultant to gas appliance manufacturers and expert witness in technical litigations regarding carbon monoxide poisoning, 1983—. Waste King Universal Corp., engineering manager for gas cooking appliances, 1959-60, 1965-66; holder of more than twenty U.S. patents and several foreign patents. Coneyo Valley Chamber of Commerce, member of board of directors. *Military service:* U.S. Navy; became chief petty officer. U.S. Naval Reserve; became captain. U.S. Coast Guard, licensed captain for 100-ton vessels, both power and sail.

MEMBER: American Society of Gas Engineers.

AWARDS, HONORS: International Appliance Technical Conference Award, 1990, as coauthor of technical paper "Thermophotovoltaics: A New Cogeneration Technology for Gas Appliances."

WRITINGS:

Diesel Engines: A Boat Owner's Guide to Operation and Maintenance, Cornell Maritime Press (Centreville, MD), 1991.
To Harness the Wind: A Short History of the Development of Sails, Naval Institute Press (Annapolis, MD), 2003.

Contributor to professional journals and boating magazines, including *Sea, Indoor Air Review, Custom Builder, Yachting, Gas Industries, Appliance Engineer,* and *Air Conditioning, Heating, and Refrigeration News.*

WORK IN PROGRESS: Pacific Destroyer: The Enlisted Man's Life aboard a U.S. Navy Fleet Destroyer in World War II.

SIDELIGHTS: Leo Block told *CA:* "In 1990 books about diesel engines described how to overhaul and rebuild diesel engines, but a boat owner needed a book, written in non-technical language, that described how to operate and maintain a diesel engine to minimize the need for costly repairs. My first book, *Diesel Engines: A Boat Owner's Guide to Operation and Maintenance,* was published in 1991 to fill this need. The next printing will include descriptions of electronic diesel engines that feature a computer-controlled fuel injection system.

"After formal retirement, I became an avid sailor, and history was always my avocation. This resulted in my second book, *To Harness the Wind: A Short History of the Development of Sails.* This book explains, in layman's language, how today's sails originated and describes the development of the two classic sailing rigs: the 'square rig' and the 'fore-and-aft rig.'"

*   *   *

BOGART, Leo 1921-2005

OBITUARY NOTICE— See index for *CA* sketch: Born September 23, 1921, in Lvov, Poland; died of babesiosis, October 15, 2005, in New York, NY. Sociologist, businessperson, marketing executive, and author. A longtime vice president of market planning and research for the Newspaper Advertising Bureau, Bogart was a prominent voice against sex and violence in television and the pandering of companies to the youth market at the expense of quality programming. Brought to the United States with his family when he was only two years old, he was a bright student with a gift for languages. Eventually fluent in seven languages, when he joined the U.S. Army Signal Intelligence Corps during World War II he was naturally selected to help intercept German communications. A 1941 graduate of Brooklyn College, after the war Bogart completed his master's and doctoral degrees in sociology at the University of Chicago in 1948 and 1950 respectively. While still studying for his Ph.D., he worked as an opinion and communications research specialist for the Standard Oil Company. He quickly rose to the top of his profession as a marketing specialist, becoming vice president of market planning for McCann-Erickson, Inc., in 1952 and director of market research for Revlon in 1958. It was while with the Newspaper Advertising Bureau from 1960 to 1989 that Bogart focused on how mass media affect popular culture. He became increasingly disturbed by the way money was changing the content of programming for the worse, writing about this in his *Commercial Culture: The Media System and the Public Interest* (1995) and *Over the Edge: How the Pursuit of Youth by Marketers and the Media Has Changed American Culture* (2005). After retiring in 1989, Bogart was an adjunct professor of marketing at New York University from 1990 to 1992 and wrote a business column for *Presstime* magazine. He was the author of over half a dozen books on such subjects as public opinion, the media, and politics. Among his other titles are *Strategy in Advertising* (1968; revised edition, 1984), *Premises for Propaganda: The Cold War Operating Assumptions of the U.S. Information Agency* (1976), *Finding Out: Personal Adventures in Social Research: Discovering What People Think, Say, and Do* (2003), and the memoir *How I Earned the Ruptured Duck: From Brooklyn to Berchtesgaden in World War II* (2004).

OBITUARIES AND OTHER SOURCES:

BOOKS

Bogart, Leo, *How I Earned the Ruptured Duck: From Brooklyn to Berchtesgaden in World War II,* Texas A&M University Press (College Station, TX), 2004.

PERIODICALS

Grand Rapids Press, October 20, 2005, p. B7.
New York Times, October 19, 2005, p. A20.

*   *   *

BOGUE, E. Grady 1935-
(Ernest Grady Bogue)

PERSONAL: Born December 9, 1935, in Memphis, TN; son of Emery Grady (a farmer) and Ardell (a postal worker) Bogue; married Linda Young; children: Karin, Michele, Barrett, Sara, Michael. *Ethnicity:* "Caucasian." *Education:* Memphis State University, B.S. (cum laude), 1957, M.A., 1965, D.Ed., 1968. *Hobbies and other interests:* Playing French horn (including performances with symphony orchestras in Georgia and Tennessee).

ADDRESSES: Office—College of Education, University of Tennessee, Knoxville, TN 37996. *E-mail*—bogue@utk.edu.

CAREER: Writer, administrator, and educator. Department of the Navy, civilian instructor and division chair at Naval Air Technical Training Center, Memphis, TN, 1961-64; 1967-71; Memphis State University, Memphis, director of university records, 1964-69, director of institutional research, 1969-71, assistant vice president for academic affairs, 1971-74, adjunct faculty, 1973-74; American Council on Education, fellow in academic administration, 1974-75; Tennessee Higher Education Commission, Nashville, associate director for academic affairs, 1975-80; Louisiana State University, Shreveport, chancellor, 1980-90, chancellor emeritus, 1990—, professor of education, 1980. University of Tennessee, visiting professor, 1991-92, professor of educational administration and policy studies, 1991—. Vanderbilt University, adjunct faculty at George Peabody College for Teachers, 1975; Tennessee State University, adjunct faculty, 1975-76; University of Georgia, visiting professor, 1991; speaker at other institutions; consultant in management development and program evaluation. Member of Northwest Louisiana Biomedical Research Foundation; past affiliate of numerous civic organizations and institutions, including Shreveport Symphony, Shreveport Chamber of Commerce, Shreveport Opera, and Shreveport-Bossier Vocational Technical Institute. *Military service:* U.S. Air Force, maintenance officer for ground electronics installations, 1958-61.

MEMBER: American Association for Higher Education, Association for Institutional Research, American Management Association, American Association of State Colleges and Universities, American Council on Education (member of Commission on Leadership Development), Southern Association of Colleges and Schools, Phi Kappa Phi, Phi Delta Kappa, Kappa Delta Pi, Omicron Delta Kappa, Tarshar Society.

AWARDS, HONORS: Distinguished service award, American Association of Collegiate Registrars and Admissions Officers, 1980; named distinguished alumnus, Memphis State University, 1986; distinguished service award, American Association of State Colleges and Universities, 1990.

WRITINGS:

(With Robert L. Saunders) *The Educational Manager: Artist and Practitioner,* Charles E. Jones Publishing (Worthington, OH), 1976.

The Enemies of Leadership, Phi Delta Kappa (Bloomington, IN), 1985.

A Journey of the Heart: Celebrations of the Call to Teaching, Phi Delta Kappa (Bloomington, IN), 1990.

(With Robert L. Saunders) *The Evidence for Quality,* Jossey-Bass Publishers (San Francisco, CA), 1992.

Leadership by Design: Strengthening Integrity in Higher Education, Jossey-Bass Publishers (San Francisco, CA), 1994.

(With Jeffery Aper) *Exploring the Heritage of American Higher Education: The Evolution of Philosophy and Policy,* Oryx Press (Phoenix, AZ), 2000.

(With George Keller, Cameron Fincher, and John Thelin) *100 Classic Books on Higher Education,* Phi Delta Kappa (Bloomington, IN), 2001.

(With Kimberely Bingham Hall) *Quality and Accountability in Higher Education: Improving Policy, Enhancing Performance,* Greenwood Press (Westport, CT), 2003.

Contributor to books, including *Administering Human Resources,* edited by Francis M. Trusty, McCutchan Publishing (Berkeley, CA), 1971; *Challenges of Re-*

trenchment, edited by James R. Mingle, Jossey-Bass Publishers (San Francisco, CA), 1981; *The Politics and Programatics of Institutional Research,* edited by James W. Firnberg and William F. Lasher, Jossey-Bass Publishers, 1983; *Community in Higher Education,* edited by William McDonald, Jossey-Bass Publishers, 2001; and *Performance Funding Policy in the United States,* edited by Joseph Burke, State University of New York Press (Albany, NY), 2003. Contributor of more than fifty articles and reviews to academic journals, including *Trusteeship, Vital Speeches, Planning for Higher Education, Innovative Higher Education, State Education Leader, Harvard Business Review, International Journal of Institutional Management in Higher Education, National Forum, Educational Forum,* and *Leader to Leader.*

BIOGRAPHICAL AND CRITICAL SOURCES:

PERIODICALS

Journal of Higher Education, January-February, 2005, Trudy W. Banta, review of *Quality and Accountability in Higher Education: Improving Policy, Enhancing Performance,* p. 112.

*   *   *

BOGUE, Ernest Grady
    See BOGUE, E. Grady

*   *   *

BONDS, John Bledsoe 1939-

PERSONAL: Born December 16, 1939, in Meridian, MS; son of Fay (a mail clerk) and Virginia Carolyn (a college teacher; maiden name, Bledsoe) Bonds; married Elizabeth Hutson Rollins (an executive), June 9, 1962; children: John Bledsoe, Jr., Margaret Lynn Bonds Podlich. *Ethnicity:* "Mixed." *Education:* Rice University, B.A.; George Washington University, M.S.; Brown University, M.A.; University of South Carolina, Ph.D. *Hobbies and other interests:* Yachting.

ADDRESSES: Home—253 Hobcaw Dr., Mount Pleasant, SC 29464. *Office*—Department of History, 427A Capers, The Citadel, 171 Moultrie St., Charleston, SC 29409. *E-mail*—john.bonds@bigfoot.com.

CAREER: Writer, officer, educator, and musician. U.S. Navy, career line officer, 1962-88, retiring as captain; U.S. Sailing, Newport, RI, executive director, 1988-94; The Citadel, Charleston, SC, visiting assistant professor of history, 1997—. Also works as professional jazz musician.

MEMBER: Yacht and sailing clubs.

AWARDS, HONORS: Military awards include Meritorious Service Medal, Bronze Star, and Joint Services Commendation Medal.

WRITINGS:

Bipartisan Strategy: Selling the Marshall Plan, Praeger Publishers (Westport, CT), 2002.

Author of articles and book reviews.

WORK IN PROGRESS: Research on strategic limitations, 1946-48.

BIOGRAPHICAL AND CRITICAL SOURCES:

PERIODICALS

Naval War College Review, winter, 2004, Robert S. Wood, review of *Bipartisan Strategy: Selling the Marshall Plan,* p. 154.
Political Science Quarterly, winter, 2003, Robert A. Divine, review of *Bipartisan Strategy,* p. 686.

*   *   *

BONSANTI, Alessandro 1904-1984

PERSONAL: Born November 15, 1904, in Florence, Italy; died February 18, 1984. *Education:* Attended University of Florence.

CAREER: Solaria (journal), co-director, 1932-34; Conservatory of Music, Bologna, Italy, teacher of the history of theater; *Letteratura* (literary journal), founder, 1937; Gabinetto Scientifico-Letterario Vies-

sieux, Florence, Italy, director, 1941-80; *Il mondo* (periodical), founder, 1945; Archivio Contemporaneo, curator, 1979-83; elected mayor of Florence, 1984. *Military service:* Italian army, 1925-26.

WRITINGS:

La serva amorosa (novel; title means "The Amorous Maid"), Solaria (Florence, Italy), 1929.
I capricci dell'Adriana (stories; title means "Adriana's Whines"), Solaria (Florence, Italy), 1934.
Racconto militare (novel; title means "A Military Story"), Parenti (Florence, Italy), 1937.
Dialoghi e altre prose (title means "Dialogues and Other Stories"), Parenti (Florence, Italy), 1940.
Introduzione al gran viaggio (title means "Introduction to the Long Trip"), Tuminelli (Rome, Italy), 1944.
La vipera e il toro (title means "The Viper and the Bull"), Sansoni (Florence, Italy), 1955.
Sopra alcuni personaggi eventuali (title means "On Some Potential Characters"), Carpena (Sarzana, Italy), 1956.
I cavalli di bronzo (title means "The Bronze Horses"), Sansoni (Florence, Italy), 1956.
Racconti lontani, Mondadori (Milan, Italy), 1962.
La buca di San Colombano (novel; title means "San Columbano's Pit"), three volumes, Mondadori (Milan, Italy), 1964.
La nuova stazione di Firenze (novel; title means "The New Railroad Station in Florence"), Mondadori (Milan, Italy), 1965.
Teatro domestico (title means "Domestic Plays"), Mondadori (Milan, Italy), 1968.
Portolani d'agosto, 1971-1974, Mondadori (Milan, Italy), 1978.

SIDELIGHTS: Italian novelist and playwright Alessandro Bonsanti enjoyed a fifty-year publishing career that produced works ranging from short stories to the 2,000-page, three-volume novel *La buca di San Colombano.* His career peaked in the 1950s and 1960s, when he emerged as the best-known representative of the *prosa dell'arte,* or artistic prose, "a literary movement inspired by the neobaroque mode of artistic expression, prevalent especially in the seventeenth century, which is marked by extravagant and elaborate forms," as Andrea Guiati described it in the *Dictionary of Literary Biography.* Guiati explained that "Bonsanti was a conservative writer. Indifferent to experimentation, he was not interested in the literary trends of his time, which stressed formal innovation and immersion in social and political problems."

Born in the city of Florence on November 15, 1904, Bonsanti spent much of his youth in the Italian countryside. That rural atmosphere would later provide the backdrop for much of his fiction. Before he began to write, Bonsanti studied engineering at the University of Florence and, after serving in the army for a year from 1925 to 1926, he moved to Milan and took a job as a bank teller. Two years later he published "Briganti in Maremma," a short story about a nineteenth-century Tuscan farmer who seduces the mistress of an outlaw whom he is harboring. Within a year, he had moved back to Florence and published his first novel, *La serva amorosa.*

La serva amorosa also concerns a love affair. In this story Nino, a young nobleman with a long history of romantic conquests, seduces Guilia, a grocer's daughter. Guilia appreciates the higher standard of living which her involvement with Nino grants her, but she does not find happiness. Although the book has a clear moral undertone, "Bonsanti remains largely unconcerned with morality and religion per se, choosing optimism in life as the defining element of his narrative," Guiati said.

Many of Bonsanti's works feature Giovanni Borghini, a semi-autobiographical character who appears for the first time in *Racconto militare* as a bank teller who wants to be a writer. In many of the books about Borghini, the reader learns little about the character's current circumstances, since most of the stories are Borghini's reminisces about his past. In one novel, *La nuova stazione di Firenze,* begun in 1954 but not published until 1965, Borghini spends most of the book telling an architect with whom he shares a train compartment about his youth. Borghini speaks of Italy's fascist regime and of writing for the journal *Solaria,* a journal Bonsanti actually edited in the early 1930s. Borghini also appears in *I cavalli di bronzo,* this time as a professor who wants to be a writer. This story, set in Borghini's present, tells of a young couple's dispute with family members over whether they should marry in America or in their home village. The dispute is ended when the couple dies in a plane crash.

Bonsanti's most famous work may be *La buca di San Colombano.* The massive novel begins in the present, with all its characters at the end of life, and then traces events backwards to a time when they were all young with a world of possibilities in front of them. "No Italian novelist of the twentieth century has treated the process of aging in such lyrical detail as Bonsanti," Guiati wrote of the book in the *Dictionary of Literary Biography.*

In the late 1960s Bonsanti turned his attention to writing plays, publishing several of them in a small volume titled *Teatro domestico.* The work contains *Don Giovanni,* which had originally appeared in his previous work *Letteratura,* as well as two new plays, *Ottaviano* and *Maria Stuarda.* As with *La buca di San Colombano,* these plays have memory at their center. *Ottaviano* features the Emperor Octavian preparing to dictate his autobiography, even though he already knows that no matter what he says, he will be condemned by future historians. The other two plays "are marked by long monologues dwelling on the beauty of youth and the sorrows of old age," stated Guiati.

Throughout his career, Bonsanti usually worked at something else in addition to his writing. From 1932 to 1934, he co-directed *Solaria* with fellow writer Alberto Carocci, and in 1937 he founded the literary journal *Letteratura.* Around the same time, Bonsanti also took a job teaching the history of theater at the Conservatory of Music in Bologna. In the early 1940s, he again moved to Florence, where he became director of the Gabinetto Scientifico-Letterario Viessieux, a position he held from 1941 until 1980. Toward the end of his life he turned his attention to politics. Bonsanti was elected mayor of Florence shortly before he died in February of 1984.

BIOGRAPHICAL AND CRITICAL SOURCES:

BOOKS

Dictionary of Literary Biography, Volume 177: *Italian Novelists since World War II,* Thomson Gale (Detroit, MI), 1997.*

*   *   *

BOOTH, Wayne C. 1921-2005
(Wayne Clayson Booth)

OBITUARY NOTICE— See index for *CA* sketch: Born February 22, 1921, in American Fork, UT; died of complications from dementia, October 10, 2005, in

Chicago, IL. Critic, educator, and author. A University of Chicago English professor, Booth was best known as a literary critic who often wrote on the interaction between author and reader. Raised in a Mormon family, Booth's first aspiration was to be a missionary in Chicago. However, he began to grow critical of religious teachings and turned instead to literature. He earned a B.A. at Brigham Young University in 1944, then served in the U.S. Army as an infantry clerk in Paris during the final two years of World War II. He returned home in 1946 to attend the University of Chicago, where he completed his M.A. in 1947 and his Ph.D. in 1950. His first job as a teacher was at Haverford College, where he was an assistant professor for three years. He then joined the Earlham College faculty as an English professor and department chair. In 1962, Booth returned to Chicago, where he embarked on a long career that would last until his 1992 retirement as George M. Pullman Professor of English emeritus; even then, he continued to teach courses as late as the summer of 2005. Booth's publishing career began auspiciously with the classic *The Rhetoric of Fiction* (1961). He would write many more books on literary criticism, including *Critical Understanding: The Powers and Limits of Pluralism* (1979), *The Company We Keep: An Ethics of Fiction* (1988), and *The Rhetoric of Rhetoric: The Quest for Effective Communication* (2004). As a critic, Booth believed that it was possible to have more than one valid interpretation of a work of fiction—this became known as critical pluralism—and he also became known for coining such phrases as "the unreliable narrator" and "the implied author." He was ultimately a significant contributor to the art of literary criticism for asserting that criticism and fiction are purely subjective arts and cannot be honed down into pure objective terms. This was directly in contrast to the then-dominant school known as New Criticism. In addition, Booth contributed to his discipline significantly as the founder of the important journal *Critical Inquiry*. At the time of his death, he had just completed the memoir *My Many Selves: The Quest for a Plausible Harmony* (2006).

OBITUARIES AND OTHER SOURCES:

BOOKS

Booth, Wayne C., *For the Love of It: Amateuring and Its Rivals,* University of Chicago Press (Chicago, IL), 1999.

Booth, Wayne C., *My Many Selves: The Quest for a Plausible Harmony,* Utah State University (Logan, UT), 2006.

PERIODICALS

Chicago Tribune, October 13, 2005, section 1, p. 13.
Los Angeles Times, October 14, 2005, p. B8.
New York Times, October 11, 2005, p. A25.
Times (London, England), October 14, 2005, p. 80.

*   *   *

BOOTH, Wayne Clayson
    See BOOTH, Wayne C.

*   *   *

BORN, James O.

PERSONAL: Married; wife's name Donna; children: John, Emily.

ADDRESSES: Home—Palm Beach County, FL. *Agent*—c/o Putnam Publicity, Penguin Group, 375 Hudson St., New York, NY 10014.

CAREER: Law enforcement agent and novel writer. U.S. Marshals Service, Miami/West Palm Beach, FL, deputy marshal, 1986-87; Drug Enforcement Agency, West Palm Beach, FL, investigator, c. 1987-91; Florida Department of Law Enforcement, special agent, c. 1991—.

WRITINGS:

Walking Money, Putnam (New York, NY), 2004.
Shock Wave, Putnam (New York, NY), 2005.
Escape Clause, Putnam (New York, NY), 2006.

SIDELIGHTS: A special agent with the Florida Department of Law Enforcement, James O. Born first became interested in writing crime fiction during long hours spent on wearisome surveillance missions. Born's early attempts at writing—nearly fifteen years before his first book was published—were influenced by the works of military fiction writers Tom Clancy and W.E.B. Griffin, as well as by a side job providing technical advice to crime writer Elmore Leonard. In a 2005 interview with *Mystery Ink Online* contributor David J. Montgomery, Born shared how his career with the Drug Enforcement Agency (DEA) inspired his books: "When I was an agent with the DEA I would set up on these incredibly boring surveillances, following smugglers all over south Florida, waiting for the little lead or piece of information that would break the case. During that time I'd imagine what would happen if. . . . Rarely was anything as exciting as what I imagined nor were my actions as courageous as I had imagined. I thought, 'Man, I could put this in a book for every cop that dreamed of doing something more.'"

Accuracy is as important to Born as is establishing a realistic character. "It took fifteen years of rejection before I sold a novel but I've always tried to stay true to the underlying principles of the physics of police work," Born wrote in a 2005 article for *Web Mystery Magazine*. "I like seeing accurate detail, not something a writer learned on *Law and Order* or *CSI*. A good story is much more important than perfect detail, but the little things can add up to turn off a realism junkie."

Born's first published novel, *Walking Money*, follows Florida law enforcement agent Bill Tasker as he struggles against an attempted framing by an F.B.I. officer. *Library Journal* contributor Craig Shufelt called the book "an amusing comic crime novel" and "an enjoyable and entertaining read." A reviewer for *Publishers Weekly* remarked: "Putting 17 years of service with various law enforcement agencies to excellent use, Born delivers a riveting, serpentine tale. . . . This is a terrific debut." Connie Fletcher wrote in a review for *Booklist* that Born's "background lends authority not only to the plot but also to the dialogue, the edgy cop humor, and the glitzy-grotesque South Florida setting," producing "a sleek and slick caper."

Walking Money was quickly followed by *Shock Wave*, a second Tasker novel that follows the agent as he tracks a deranged bomber. "Top thrillwork, with a Jerry Bruckheimer ending [and] much welcome humor" wrote a *Kirkus Reviews* contributor. A contributor to *Publishers Weekly* commented: "An eccentric cast and a credible plot lift Born's second Florida-set crime novel."

BIOGRAPHICAL AND CRITICAL SOURCES:

PERIODICALS

Booklist, May 1, 2004, Connie Fletcher, review of *Walking Money,* p. 1502.
Kirkus Reviews, March 1, 2005, review of *Shock Wave,* p. 243.
Library Journal, July, 2004, Craig Shufelt, review of *Walking Money,* p. 66.
Publishers Weekly, May 31, 2004, review of *Walking Money,* p. 49; March 21, 2005, review of *Shock Wave,* p. 37.

ONLINE

James O. Born Home Page, http://www.jamesoborn. com (September 22, 2005).
Mystery Ink Online, http://www.mysteryinkonline. com/ (May 17, 2005), David J. Montgomery, author interview.
Web Mystery Magazine, http://lifeloom.com/web mysterymagazine/ (September 22, 2005), James O. Born, "Writer Cops."

*   *   *

BOST, Pierre 1901-1976

PERSONAL: Born September 5, 1901, in Lasalle France; died December 10, 1976, in Paris, France. *Education:* Educated at Lycée and Sorbonne.

CAREER: Staff member with *Gazette de France, Nouvelle Revue Française,* and Grasset Editions, 1924-27; Secretary of the Senate, 1927-33; *Marianne,* editor, 1933-35; editor of *Marie-Claire.*

WRITINGS:

BOOKS

Hercule et mademoiselle (stories), Nouvelle Revue Française (Paris, France), 1924.
Prétextat, Nouvelle Revue Française (Paris, France), 1925.

Homocide par imprudence, [Paris, France], 1925.

Les Vieillards, [Paris, France], 1925.

Crise de croissance, [Paris, France], 1926.

Faillite, Nouvelle Revue Française (Paris, France), 1928.

Anaïs, [Paris, France], 1930.

Le cirque et le music-hall, [Paris, France], 1931.

Le scandale, Nouvelle Revue Française (Paris, France), 1931, translated and published at *The Offence*, [London, England], 1932.

Porte-Malheur, Gallimard (Paris, France), 1932.

Un an dans un tiroir, Gallimard (Paris, France), 1945.

Monsieur l'admiral va bientôt mourir, Gallimard (Paris, France), 1945.

La Haute-Fourche, [London, England], 1946.

(With others) *La puissance et la gloire* (based on the novel by Graham Greene), [Paris, France], 1953, published as *The Power and the Glory*, [London, England], 1959.

(With C.A. Puget) *Un nommé Judas*, [Paris, France], 1954.

Traité de navigation côtière, Pierre Bost (Montrouge, France), 1984.

(Editor) *Code du plaisancier en rivière: ouvrage de code à l'intention des candidats au permis rivière*, Pierre Bost (Quimper, France), 1991.

Anna Boine, Greco & Greco (Milan, Italy), 1993.

SCREENPLAYS

L'héritier des Mondésir, 1940.

Croisières sidérales, 1942.

L'homme qui joue avec le feu, 1942.

Dernier atout, 1942.

Une étoile au soleil, 1943.

La chèvre d'or, 1943.

Madame et le mort, 1943.

La libération de Paris, 1944.

Patrie, 1945.

Les jeux sont faits, 1947.

Le château de verre, 1950.

Les sept péchés capitaux, 1952.

La voce del silenzio, 1952.

La conciencia acusa, 1953.

Destinées, 1954.

Une fille nommée Madeleine, 1954.

El amor de Don Juan, 1956.

Gervaise, 1956.

Oeiil pour oeil, 1957.

Le vent se Lève, 1958.

Ein gewisser Judas (televison), 1958.

Pantalaskas, 1959.

The Power and the Glory (produced for stage and television, 1959; revivied, 2001), Samuel French (New York, NY), 1959.

Che gioia vivere, 1960.

Umorismo negro, 1965.

François Malgorn, séminariste ou celui qui n'était pas appelé (television), 1972.

Le château perdu (television), 1973.

Molière pour rire et pour pleurer (television miniseries), 1973.

Lucien Leuwen (television miniseries), 1973.

Le juge et l'assassin, 1974.

Un dimanche à la campagne (based on a novel by Bost), 1984.

Der grüne Berg, 1990.

SCREENPLAY ADAPTATIONS; WITH JEAN AURENCHE

Douce, 1943.

La symphonie pastorale, 1946.

La septième Porte, 1946.

Le diable au corps (title means "Devil in the Flesh"), 1947.

Au-delà des grilles, 1949.

Occupe-toi d'Amélie, 1949.

Dieu a besoin des hommes, 1950.

L'auberge rouge, 1951.

Les jeux interdits, 1951.

Le blé en herbe, 1953.

Les orgueilleux, 1953.

Le rouge et le noir (title means "The Red and the Black"), 1954.

Chiens perdus sans collier, 1955.

Gervaise, 1955.

La traversée de Paris, 1956.

En cas de malheur, 1958.

Le joueur, 1958.

La jument verte, 1959.

Le chemin des écoliers (television), 1959.

Les régates de San Francisco, 1960.

Tu ne tueras point, 1961.

Le crime ne paie pas, 1962.

Le rendezvous, 1962.

Le meurtrier, 1963.

Le magot de Josefa, 1964.

Les amitiés particulières, 1964.

Paris brûle-t-il? (title means "Is Paris Burning?"), 1966.

Le Franciscain de Bourges, 1967.

L'horloger de Saint-Paul (also known as *The Clock-maker*; based on the novel by Georges Simenon), 1974.

ADAPTATIONS: *Monsieur l'admiral va bientôt mourir* was adapted for film by Bertrand Tavernier as *A Sunday in the Country,* 1984.

SIDELIGHTS: Pierre Bost was a French writer who contributed to a great many important films, particularly during the 1940s and 1950s. For many of these screenplays, including *Douce, La symphonie pastorale, Le diable au corps, Le rouge et le noir,* and *Gervaise,* he collaborated with Jean Aurenche. According to R.F. Cousins, writing in the *International Dictionary of Films and Filmmakers,* "the two writers formed a unique partnership translating for the screen an impressive array of literary classics."

Director Bertrand Tavernier honored Bost after the writer's death with a film version of Bost's novel *Monsieur l'admiral va bientôt mourir,* which the director titled *A Sunday in the Country.* In the 1970s, Tavernier had hired Bost and Aurenche to write the screenplay for an adaptation of Georges Simenon's novel *The Clockmaker,* as well as for several other films.

Bost and Denis Cannan wrote a stage version of Graham Greene's *The Power and the Glory* in 1956. The play was revived in New York for the first time in 2003. The story is set in 1930s Mexico and is the story of the last Catholic priest to survive after the socialist government had banned the Church. In a review of the revival, *Back Stage* critic Victor Gluck noted that "the ordeals of this little-known episode of religious persecution mounted in power, with some later scenes riveting in their tension." Bost's impressive output, which includes many books, places him among the most prolific of French writers.

BIOGRAPHICAL AND CRITICAL SOURCES:

BOOKS

International Dictionary of Films and Filmmakers, Volume 4: *Writers and Production Artists,* 3rd edition, St. James Press (Detroit, MI), 1993.

PERIODICALS

Back Stage, March 7, 2003, Victor Gluck, review of *The Power and the Glory,* p. 64.

Los Angeles Times, January 27, 1985, Sheila Benson, "Deceptive Surface of a Tavernier 'Sunday'," Calendar section, p. 20.*

*   *   *

BOUTS, Dirk
See GRESHOFF, Jan

*   *   *

BOWEN, Euros 1904-1988

PERSONAL: Born September 12, 1904, in Treorci, Rhondda Valley, Wales; died 1988. *Education:* University of Wales, B.A., B.D.; University of Oxford, M.A.; also attended St. David's College, Lampteter. *Religion:* Anglican.

CAREER: Poet and cleric. Wrexham, Denbighshire, curate; Llangywair and Llanuwchllyn, near Bala, Merionethshire, rector, until 1973. Member, Church of Wales Standing Liturgical Advisory Commission, 1967-74.

MEMBER: Academi Gymreig (secretary).

AWARDS, HONORS: Crown at National Eisteddfod of Wales, 1948, for poem "O'r Dwyrain," and 1950, for poem "Difodiant."

WRITINGS:

POEMS

Achlysuron, Gwasg Gomer (Llandysul, Wales), 1970.

Cylch o gerddi, Gwasg y Brython (Liverpool, England), 1970.

Elfennau, Gwasg Gomer (Llandysul, Wales), 1972.

Poems, Gwasg Gomer (Llandysul, Wales), 1974.

Cynullion, Gwasg Gomer (Llandysul, Wales), 1976.

O'r Corn aur, Gwasg Gee (Denbigh, Wales), 1977.

Trin cerddi, Llyfrau'r Faner (Y Bala, Wales), 1979.

Beirdd simbolaidd Ffrainc, Gwasg Prifysgol Cymru (Cardiff, Wales), 1980.

Amrywion, Gwasg Gomer (Llandysul, Wales), 1980.

Dan Groes y Dean, Gwasg Gee (Denbigh, Wales), 1980.

(With Enid Luff) *Lux in tenebris* (includes musical score), Primavera (London, England), 1980.

Masg Minos, Gwasg Gee (Denbigh, Wales), 1981.

Gwynt yn y canghennau, Gwasg Gee (Denbigh, Wales), 1982.

O bridd i bridd, Gwasg Gee (Denbigh, Wales), 1983.

Detholion, Yr Academi Cymreig (Cardiff, Wales), 1984.

Buarth bywyd, Gwasg Gwynedd (Caernarfon, Wales), 1986.

Goleuni'r eithin, Gwasg Gee (Denbigh, Wales), 1986.

Yr alarch, Gwasg Gregynog (Y Drenewydd, Wales), 1987.

Oes y Medwsa, Cyhoeddiadau Barddas (Caernarfon, Wales), 1987.

Lleidr tân, Gwasg Gwynedd (Caernarfon, Wales), 1989.

Dathlu bywyd, Cyhoeddiadau Barddas (Aberystwyth, Wales), 1990.

Euros Bowen: Priest-Poet (anthology), edited by Cynthia Davies and Saunders Davies, Church in Wales Publications (Penarth, Wales), 1993.

TRANSLATIONS

Virgil, *Bugeilgerddi Fyrsil,* Gwasg Prifysgol Cymru (Cardiff, Wales), 1975.

Athanasius, Saint, Patriarch of Alexandria, *De incarnatione—Ymgnawdoliad y Gair,* Argrafffty'r M.C. (Caernarfon, Wales), 1976.

Sophocles, *Oidipos yn Colonos,* Gwasg Prifysgol Cymru (Cardiff, Wales), 1979.

Sophocles, *Electra,* Gwasg Prifysgol Cymru (Cardiff, Wales), 1984.

Sophocles, *Philoctetes,* Gwasg Prifysgol Cymru (Cardiff, Wales), 1991.

SIDELIGHTS: After earning degrees from the University of Wales and the University of Oxford, Euros Bowen became an Anglican priest. He followed a tradition of combining learning with religious duties, translating a variety of texts into Welsh from the original Greek, Latin, and French languages. Begin-ning in the winter of 1947, he wrote volumes of his own poetry, verse steeped in imagery of nature, life, and rebirth and strongly influenced by his readings and translations of European literature. Regarding the use of imagery, he preferred to avoid the more decorative style, relying instead on images that evoked deeper expressions. He experimented frequently in his work, going so far as to invent some new poetic forms. Bowen was awarded the crown at the National Eisteddfod in 1948 for his poem "O'r Dwyrain" and again in 1950 for "Difodiant."

Bowen made frequent use of *cynghanedd,* a Welsh poetic technique employing assonance and internal rhyming patters. Tim Saunders, in an article for *World Literature Today,* remarked that Bowen "used *cynghanedd* both in the traditional ways and in bold experiments which often aroused controversy. He gave the prose poem fresh colors with it and applied it to vers libre in order to create a new sense of form." In a review of *O'r Corn aur* for *World Literature Today,* Bedwyr Lewis Jones commented of Bowen's work that "poems such as these are celebrations of creative renewal; they stir the reader's response."

BIOGRAPHICAL AND CRITICAL SOURCES:

BOOKS

Stephens, Meic, editor, *Oxford Companion to the Literature of Wales,* Oxford University Press (New York, NY), 1986.

PERIODICALS

World Literature Today, winter, 1979, Bedwyr Lewis Jones, review of *O'r Corn aur,* p. 169; summer, 1993, Tim Saunders, review of *Euros Bowen: Priest-Poet,* p. 651.

Y-Traethodydd Aberystwyth, Volume 123, 1968, pp. 98-107; Volume 128, 1973, pp. 177-185.

ONLINE

Archive Network Wales, http://www.archivesnetwork wales.info/ (September 23, 2005).

Western Illinois University Web site, http://www.wiu. edu/ (September 23, 2005).*

BOYNTON, Robert S.

PERSONAL: Male. *Education:* Haverford College, B.A.; Yale University, M.A., 1988.

ADDRESSES: Office—Department of Journalism, New York University, Arthur Carter Hall, 10 Washington Place, New York, NY 10003. *E-mail*—Robert.Boynton@nyu.edu.

CAREER: Journalist and professor. New York University, New York, NY, director of magazine journalism program and assistant professor of journalism.

WRITINGS:

The New New Journalism: Conversations with America's Best Nonfiction Writers on Their Craft, Vintage Books (New York, NY), 2005.

Contributing editor and writer for publications, including *New Yorker, Harper's, Atlantic Monthly, New York Times Magazine, New York Times Book Review, Lingua Franca, New Republic, Nation, Los Angeles Times Book Review, Village Voice, New York Observer, Newsday, Salon, Columbia Journalism Review, Washington Post, Time Digital, Philadelphia Inquirer, Chicago Tribune, Manhattan, Inc.,* and *Rolling Stone.*

SIDELIGHTS: Director of New York University's magazine journalism program, Robert S. Boynton has been a prolific writer for and contributing editor to many of the world's most notable magazines. As a professor, Boynton takes a personal interest in the research techniques and creative processes of what he calls the "new new journalists," a contemporary group of reporters who rely on innovative journalistic methods. *The New New Journalism: Conversations with America's Best Nonfiction Writers on Their Craft* is a compilation of Boynton's interviews with nineteen prominent features writers, who answer questions ranging from how they conduct interviews, organize and/or take notes, and commence writing projects to how they feel about various ethical issues facing modern journalists.

Vanessa Bush, a contributor to *Booklist,* described *The New New Journalism* as "a fascinating book that makes the reader want to go out and get every book the writers have written as well as those mentioned as sources of inspiration." A *Publishers Weekly* reviewer remarked that "this batch of discussions is a gold mine of technique, approach and philosophy for journalists, writers and close readers alike." Writing for the *Weekly Standard,* Diane Scharper commented: "Part history of the movement, part close-up of its practitioners, this book . . . makes new (or new new) journalism more alluring than ever." *Kliatt* reviewer Daniel Levinson called the book a "marvelously thoughtful and intelligent collection of interviews."

BIOGRAPHICAL AND CRITICAL SOURCES:

PERIODICALS

Booklist, February 15, 2005, Vanessa Bush, review of *The New New Journalism: Conversations with America's Best Nonfiction Writers on Their Craft,* p. 1038.
Kliatt, July, 2005, Daniel Levinson, review of *The New New Journalism,* p. 34.
Publishers Weekly, February 7, 2005, review of *The New New Journalism,* p. 53.
Weekly Standard, May 23, 2005, Diane Scharper, review of *The New New Journalism,* p. 39.

ONLINE

New New Journalism Web site, http://www.newnewjournalism.com/ (November 10, 2005).
Robert S. Boynton Home Page, http://www.robertboynton.com (September 22, 2005).

* * *

BRABNER, Joyce

PERSONAL: Married Harvey Pekar (a comic-book writer); children: Danielle (foster daughter).

ADDRESSES: Home and office—Cleveland, OH. *Agent*—c/o Author Mail, Dark Horse Comics, 10956 SE Main St., Milwaukie, OR 97222.

CAREER: "Comic-book journalist," writer, and peace activist.

WRITINGS:

(Editor) *Real War Stories* (graphic journalism), Central Committee for Conscientious Objectors (Philadelphia, PA), 1987.

(Editor and contributor) *Brought to Light* (graphic journalism; includes "Flashpoint: The La Penca Bombing") drawings by Tom Yeates and Bill Sienkiewicz), Eclipse Books (Forestville, CA), 1989.

(With husband, Harvey Pekar) *Our Cancer Year,* illustrated by Frank Stack, Four Walls Eight Windows (New York, NY), 1994.

Author of comic-book journalism series *Real War Stories;* author of "Joyce's Blog," on *Harvey Pekar's Home Page.*

SIDELIGHTS: Joyce Brabner and her husband, the comic book writer and retired Veterans Administration hospital file clerk Harvey Pekar, became famous with the 2003 release of the film *American Splendor,* based on Pekar's autobiographical comic book series by the same name. The series—which won an American Book Award in 1987—detail Pekar's humdrum life in Cleveland, Ohio, his comic meeting of and hasty marriage to third wife Brabner, and their life with their foster daughter, budding cartoonist Danielle. The universal appeal of *American Splendor* is owed to Pekar's candid and insightful portrayal of the everyday, middle-class, working life in America. Actress Hope Davis, who plays Brabner in the film, is quoted in the production notes on the *American Splendor Movie Web site* as saying, "Joyce is probably the most colorful character I've ever played. She's extremely intellectual, a very opinionated and forthright person."

Brabner collaborated with Pekar on a 1994 graphic novel, *Our Cancer Year,* the story of Pekar's diagnosis of and treatment for lymphoma, just as the couple was buying a house for the first time, and as Joyce was involved with collecting the stories of international war survivors during the escalation of the Gulf War, in the winter of 1991. The novel chronicles their struggle with these and smaller everyday events as they deal with the physical and emotional rigors of Pekar's chemotherapy and its excruciating side effects. Chris Faatz, in a review of the book for the *Nation,* wrote: "This book is an in-your-face picture of that time, full

of fear and pain and desperation, and love and heroism as well." Joseph Witek, writing in the *Review of Contemporary Fiction,* commented: "The same honesty that *American Splendor* routinely brings to the mundane happenings of daily life permeates *Our Cancer Year.*" Witek also wrote that the authors and illustrator "have demonstrated that comics created with intelligence and unflinching candor can be deeply moving literature." Ray Olson, in *Booklist,* found that "few prose-only cancer survivors' accounts are as good," while a *Publishers Weekly* contributor noted that the book "is distinguished by Brabner's great tenderness and determination in the middle of Pekar's medical nightmare." Stuart Sherman, in a review for the *Chicago Tribune,* wrote: "The book beautifully conveys a sense of battles raging and worlds collapsing everywhere, on every scale: in one man's mind and body, in Cleveland homes, streets, and hospital beds, on the war-shredded map of the Middle East."

In the late 1980s, Brabner began collecting and publishing, in comic-book format, stories of soldiers and citizens from around the world who had survived war and were willing to tell the real stories of devastation and suffering—so different from U.S. military propaganda designed to interest American youth in joining the armed forces. The result was the ongoing series *Real War Stories,* for which she once faced federal court charges after a conflict with the Defense Department. Leslie J. Gastwirt, in *Library Journal,* observed that the stories counteract "the *Rambo*-like fantasies misleading today's youth." Sherman, in his *Chicago Tribune* review of *Our Cancer Year,* pointed out that Brabner, in *Real War Stories,* writes "to make her readers both wary and committed. In her stories there are innocents and villains, huge conspiracies to expose, a world to change."

Under the sponsorship of the Christic Institute, Brabner also wrote "Flashpoint: The La Penca Bombing," published together with a story by the English comic book writer Alan Moore in the 1989 graphic journalism work *Brought to Light.* Both stories deal with the controversial Iran-contra scandal, narcotics smuggling, and U.S. arming of right-wing groups in the Third World. "Flashpoint' reveals the discovery by journalists Martha Honey and Tony Avrigan of an attempt to assassinate Nicaraguan contra leader Eden Pastora in a 1984 bombing at La Penca, while Moore's "Shadowplay" follows a bloody, long-term covert CIA operation in Nicaragua. Ray Olson, of *Booklist,* called the stories "lucid précis of events" that were obscured by mainstream journalism. Richard Gehr, in a review for the *Village Voice,* commented that "Flashpoint" "offers a crammed portrait of an international crew of mercenaries, thieves, adventurers, and misdirected patriots." A *Publishers Weekly* contributor called Brabner's story "a straightforward and competently illustrated journalistic account" of the assassination attempt. Roger Sabin, in a review for *New Statesman & Society,* however, perceived it as "not a serious piece of investigative journalism . . . but a colourful and entertaining rendering by writers and artists" who use their techniques as a film director uses cameras and lighting. But, said Sabin, "This is not to belittle its achievement in any way."

BIOGRAPHICAL AND CRITICAL SOURCES:

PERIODICALS

Booklist, March 1, 1989, Ray Olson, review of *Brought to Light,* p. 1072; September 15, 1994, Ray Olson, review of *Our Cancer Year,* p. 89.

Financial Times of Canada, December 4, 1994, Liam Lacey, "Harvey and Joyce's Comic Confidences," p. C1.

Library Journal, October 15, 1987, Leslie J. Gastwirt, "A Conscientious Comic Book" (review of *Real War Stories*), p. 52.

Nation, December 26, 1994, Chris Faatz, review of *Our Cancer Year,* p. 810.

New Statesman & Society, February 17, 1989, Roger Sabin, "Serious Comic" (review of *Brought to Light*) p. 37.

Publishers Weekly, February 17, 1989, review of *Brought to Light,* p. 73; August 8, 1994, review of *Our Cancer Year,* p. 420.

Review of Contemporary Fiction, summer, 1996, Joseph Witek, review of *Our Cancer Year,* p. 196.

Tribune Books (Chicago, IL), November 20, 1994, Stuart Sherman, review of *Our Cancer Year,* p. 7.

Village Voice, April 4, 1989, Richard Gehr, "Tales from the Dark Side" (review of *Brought to Light*) pp. 48-49.

ONLINE

American Splendor Movie Web site, http://www. americansplendormovie.com/ (November 1, 2003), "About the Production."

Beek's Books, http://www.rzero.com/ (August 6, 2003), review of *Our Cancer Year.*

Harvey Pekar's Home Page, http://www.harveypekar. com/ (October 20, 2003), "Joyce's Blog."

OTHER

American Splendor (film), HBO, 2003.*

*   *   *

BRANDS, Joh. G.
    See GRESHOFF, Jan

*   *   *

BRAZAITIS, Thomas Joseph
    See BRAZAITIS, Tom

*   *   *

BRAZAITIS, Tom 1940-2005
    (Thomas Joseph Brazaitis)

PERSONAL: Born August 8, 1940, in Cleveland, OH; died of cancer March 30, 2005, in Washington, DC; married Sheila Loftus (divorced); married Eleanor Clift (a journalist), c. 1990; children: (first marriage) Mark, Sarah; stepchildren (second marriage): Edward, Woody, Robert. *Education:* John Carroll University, B.S.S., teacher's certificate.

CAREER: Journalist. Worked for weekly newspapers, Cleveland, OH, c. 1960s; *Plain Dealer,* Cleveland, 1971-2005, began as a beat reporter, became Washington correspondent, 1974, bureau chief, 1970-98, senior editor and op-ed writer, 1998-2005. Founding co-president, Regional Reporters's Association, Washington. *Military service:* U.S. Army, 1962-64; attained rank of first lieutenant.

AWARDS, HONORS: Woodrow Wilson visiting fellow.

WRITINGS:

(With wife, Eleanor Clift) *War without Bloodshed: The Art of Politics,* Scribner (New York, NY), 1996.

(With Eleanor Clift) *Madam President: Shattering the Last Glass Ceiling,* Scribner (New York, NY), 2000, revised edition published as *Madam President: Women Blazing the Leadership Trail,* Routledge (New York, NY), 2003.

SIDELIGHTS: For Sidelights, see Clift, Eleanor.

BIOGRAPHICAL AND CRITICAL SOURCES:

PERIODICALS

Booklist, June 1, 1996, Mary Carroll and Gilbert Taylor, review of *War without Bloodshed: The Art of Politics,* p. 1640.
Library Journal, July, 2000, Robert F. Nardini, review of *Madam President: Shattering the Last Glass Ceiling,* p. 119.
New York Times Book Review, July 30, 2000, Joyce Purnick, review of *Madam President,* p. 26.
Political Science Quarterly, spring, 2004, Kathleen Knight, review of *Madam President,* p. 218.
Presidential Studies Quarterly, spring, 1997, Nelson W. Polsby, review of *War without Bloodshed,* p. 399.
Publishers Weekly, April 29, 1996, review of *War without Bloodshed,* p. 57; June 19, 2000, review of *Madam President,* p. 69.
Washington Monthly, July, 2000, Myra MacPherson, review of *Madam President,* p. 46.

ONLINE

Eagles Talent Connection Web site, http://eaglestalent. com/ (September 12, 2005), author profile.

OBITUARIES

PERIODICALS

Washington Post, March 31, 2005, p. B7.*

*   *   *

BRIDGES, Karl F. 1964-

PERSONAL: Born March 14, 1964, in Vincennes, IN; son of William (a poet) and Karen (a freelance writer) Bridges; married; wife's name Rita (a librarian). *Education:* Franklin College, B.A., 1986; Miami University, Oxford, OH, A.M., 1988; University of Illinois, M.L.S., 1991. *Politics:* "Conservative." *Religion:* Church of England (Anglican).

ADDRESSES: Home—24 Baycrest, Apt. 404, South Burlington, VT 04503. *Office*—100 Bailey Howe Library, University of Vermont, Burlington, VT 05403. *E-mail*—karl.bridges@uvm.edu.

CAREER: Writer and librarian. Eastern Illinois University, Charleston, librarian, 1991-98; University of Vermont, Burlington, librarian, 1998—. Consultant in Web-site development.

MEMBER: American Library Association, Association of College and Research Libraries, Vermont Library Association.

WRITINGS:

(Editor) *Expectations of Librarians in the Twenty-first Century,* Greenwood Press (Westport, CT), 2003.

Contributor to periodicals, including *Illinois Libraries, American Libraries, Wilson Library Bulletin, Computers in Libraries,* and *Library Instruction Roundtable News.*

WORK IN PROGRESS: 100 Novels You Should Read, for Libraries Unlimited, completion expected in 2006; research on Herodotus and his influence on nineteenth-century education.

SIDELIGHTS: Karl F. Bridges told *CA:* "Influences on my work include William Bridges (both of them), Stephen Bridges (for the art), Sally Hanley, Agathon, those unnamed people who were sensible enough to fire me (or refuse to hire me) for jobs for which I was unsuitable and which would have made me (and them) unhappy, and, most of all, my wife Rita, whose taste and culture greatly exceed my own. Cultural influences include the classics, England, the Clash, television, and Max Beerbohm.

"I don't know if I have a particular motivation for writing other than, sometimes, I see problems that are interesting enough to be worth commenting on. I'm fortunate enough to be in a profession (and a society) that encourages me to express an opinion—even though not everyone agrees with me.

"How do I get things written? I'm fortunate to be married to a beautiful woman who doesn't think it strange to find her husband sitting in the living room studying Attic Greek or Ge'ez rather than folding socks. So, I have rather more time than the average person. So, in sum, thanks to her I have more than I deserve.

"I don't know if I have any advice for other people who want to write, other than to say—simply do it. Writing is like lying: one has to practice it regularly in order to be any good at it. I suppose, being a librarian, I should say something about libraries. So: Go there. Read a book. Be nice to the librarian."

BIOGRAPHICAL AND CRITICAL SOURCES:

PERIODICALS

Booklist, December 1, 2003, Sarah Watstein, review of *Expectations of Librarians in the Twenty-first Century,* p. 698.
Library Resources and Technical Services, April, 2004, Betty Landesman, review of *Expectations of Librarians in the Twenty-first Century,* p. 159.

*   *   *

BROEG, Bob 1918-2005
(Robert M. Broeg)

OBITUARY NOTICE— See index for *CA* sketch: Born March 18, 1918, in St. Louis, MO; died of pneumonia, October 28, 2005, in Creve Coeur, MO. Journalist and author. Broeg was a Baseball Hall of Fame sports writer and longtime editor for the *St. Louis Post-Dispatch.* His love of sports started when he was a young boy, when he began writing on the subject at the age of nine. Graduating from the University of Missouri in 1941, he was a reporter for the Associated Press in Jefferson City, Missouri for a year, followed by a year in Boston. With the onset of World War II, Broeg served in the U.S. Marine Corps Reserve for the duration. In 1945, he joined the *St. Louis Post-Dispatch* as a sports writer, and was promoted to sports editor in 1958. Originally covering the former St. Louis Browns team, he became a staunch fan of the Cardinals, in addition to his notable love for his alma mater's football team. Impressive for his extensive

knowledge of baseball and football, Broeg was a mainstay for his newspaper through 1984. Afterward, he continued to work with the *St. Louis Post-Dispatch* as a contributing editor and occasional columnist. Among his memorable contributions to sports journalism, many will always remember Broeg for giving ballplayer Stan Musial the nickname Stan the Man; Musial was also the subject of his biography *Stan Musial: "The Man's" Own Story* (1964). Broeg was inducted into the writer's wing of the Baseball Hall of Fame in 1979; in addition, he was the recipient of a Knute Rockne Club Sportswriter of the Year award, a University of Missouri journalism medal, and the J.G. Taylor Spink Award for meritorious contributions to baseball writing. He was also the author of numerous books, including *Bob Broeg's Redbirds: A Century of Cardinals' Baseball* (1981), *My Baseball Scrapbook* (1983), and *The 100 Greatest Moments in St. Louis Sports* (2000).

OBITUARIES AND OTHER SOURCES:

BOOKS

Broeg, Bob, *Bob Broeg: Memories of a Hall of Fame Sportswriter,* Sagamore (Champaign, IL), 1995.

PERIODICALS

Los Angeles Times, November 1, 2005, p. B9.
St. Louis Post-Dispatch, October 29, 2005, p. 5.
Washington Post, October 30, 2005, p. C10.

*   *   *

BROEG, Robert M.
See BROEG, Bob

*   *   *

BRONNEN, Arnolt 1895-1959
(A.H. Schelle-Noetzel)

PERSONAL: Born August 19, 1895, in Vienna, Austria; died October 12, 1959, in East Berlin, German Democratic Republic (now Berlin, Germany); son of Ferdinand (a professor) and Martha (an author; maiden name, Schelle) Bronnen; children: Barbara. *Education:* Studied law and philosophy in Vienna, Austria.

CAREER: Dramatist. Worked as a department store sales clerk and in a bank, c. 1920-22; freelance writer; dramaturge for Universum Film AG (movie studio), 1928-33, and for Dramatische Funkstunde (radio broadcasting company), 1933-35; program director for a television studio, until 1939; *Neue Zeit* (newspaper), Linz, Austria, editor, 1945-50; Neues Theater, Vienna, Austria, director, beginning 1951; *Berliner Zeitung* (newspaper), East Berlin, German Democratic Republic, theater critic and publicist, 1955-59. *Military service:* Austrian Army; served during World War I; served in the Dolomites; wounded in action, 1916; prisoner of war in Sicily; enlisted in army in Austria, 1944-45; jailed for treason briefly in 1944.

WRITINGS:

PLAYS

Vatermord (one-act; first produced in Frankfurt am Main, Germany, April 22, 1922), Fischer (Berlin, Germany), 1920.

Anarchie in Sillian (first produced in Berlin, Germany, at Deutsches Theater, April 6, 1924), Rowohlt (Berlin, Germany), 1924.

Katalaunische Schlacht (first produced in Frankfurt am Main, Germany, at Schauspielhaus, November 28, 1924), Rowohlt (Berlin, Germany), 1924.

Die Geburt der Jugend (first produced in Berlin, Germany, at Lessing-Theater, December 13, 1925), Rowohlt (Berlin, Germany), 1922.

Die Exzesse: Lustspiel (first produced in Berlin, Germany, at Lessing-Theater, June 7, 1925), Rowohlt (Berlin, Germany), 1923.

Rheinische Rebellen (first produced in Berlin, Germany, at Staatliches Schauspielhaus, May 16, 1925), Rowohlt (Berlin, Germany), 1925.

Ostpolzug (first produced in Berlin, Germany, at Staatliches Schauspielhaus, January 29, 1926), Rowohlt (Berlin, Germany), 1925.

(Adapter) Heinrich von Kleist, *Michael Kohlhaas* (first produced in Frankfurt an der Oder, Germany, at the Stadttheater, October 4, 1929; adapted and broadcast for radio, 1929), radio and stage versions published together as *Michael Kohlhaas: Für Funk und Bühne bearbeitet,* Rowohlt (Berlin, Germany), 1929, revised edition published as *Michael Kohlhaas: Schauspiel nach der Novelle Heinrich von Kleists,* Pallas (Salzburg, Austria), 1948.

Reparationen: Lustspiel (first produced in Mannheim, Germany, at the Nationaltheater, January 30, 1930), Rowohlt (Berlin, Germany), 1926.

Sonnenberg (radio play), Hobbing (Berlin, Germany), 1934.

"N," first produced in Linz, Austria, at the Landestheater, April 24, 1948.

Gloriana (first produced in Stuttgart, Germany, at the Württembergisches Staatstheater, November 8, 1951) 1977.

Die jüngste Nacht, first produced in Linz, Austria, at Volkshochschule-Studio, May 6, 1952.

Stücke (collected plays), edited by Hans Mayer, Athenäum (Kronberg, Germany), 1977.

Die Kette Kolin (first produced in Karlsruhe, Germany, at Badisches Staatstheater, March 8, 1981), 1958.

OTHER

Die Septembernovelle, Rowohlt (Berlin, Germany), 1923.

Napoleon's Fall, Rowohlt (Berlin, Germany), 1924.

Film und Leben, Barbara La Marr (novel), Rowohlt (Berlin, Germany), 1928.

(With Max Brod, Axel Eggebrecht, and others) *Die Frau von Morgen, wie wir sie wünschen,* edited by Friedrich M. Huebner, Seeman (Leipzig, Germany), 1929.

O.S. (novel), Rowohlt (Berlin, Germany), 1929.

Roßbach, Rowohlt (Berlin, Germany), 1930.

Erinnerung an eine Liebe, Rowohlt (Berlin, Germany), 1933.

(As A.H. Schelle-Noetzel) *Kampf im Äther; oder, Die Unsichtbaren* (novel), Rowohlt (Berlin, Germany), 1935.

Arnolt Bronnen gibt zu Protokoll: Beiträge zur Geschichte des modernen Schriftstellers, Rowohlt (Berlin, Germany), 1935.

Deutschland, kein Wintermärchen: eine Entdeckungsfahrt durch die Deutsche Demokratische Republik, Verlag der Nation (Berlin, Germany), 1956.

(Editor and translator) Aesop, *Sieben Berichte aus Hellas: Der antike Aisopos-Roman neu übersetzt und nach dokumentarischen Quellen ergänzt,* Rowohlt (Hamburg, Germany), 1956.

Viergespann, Aufbau (Berlin, Germany), 1958.

Tage mit Bertolt Brecht: Geschichte einer unvollendeted Freundschaft, Desch (Munich, Germany), 1960.

Begegnungen mit Schauspielern: 20 Portraits aus dem Nachlaß, edited by Harald Kleinschmidt, Henschel (Berlin, Germany), 1967.

Sabotage der Jugend: Kleine Arbeiten, 1922-1934, edited by Friedbert Aspetsberger, Institut für Germanistik, Universität Innsbruck (Innsbruck, Austria), 1989.

Werke (collected works), five volumes, edited by Friedbert Aspetsberger, 1989.

Contributor to periodicals, including *Der Abend.*

SIDELIGHTS: Best known as a playwright, Arnolt Bronnen entered the spotlight as a controversial writer who created scenes of eroticism and violence for the stage during the heady days of Germany's Weimar Republic. A friend of famous dramatist Bertolt Brecht, Bronnen also wrote experimental plays for the theater that mixed realism with expressionism. While his early plays, such as *Vatermord,* were influenced by the playwright's predilection for combining eroticism and violence, his later dramas primarily involve political themes that reflect the author's extreme evolution from right-wing National Socialist to left-wing Communist.

After serving in the Austrian army during World War I, Bronnen moved to Berlin to begin his career in the theater. He worked as a sales clerk and for a bank for the next two years while completing his early plays. The first of these, *Vatermord,* was first performed in 1922 in Frankfurt am Main, Germany. The story of a family dominated by the father, the play outraged audiences when they viewed the sexual relationship between a mother and her son, who later kills his own father. When the play was performed in Berlin, it incited a riot that required police intervention. Another early play, *Die Geburt der Jugend,* is a highly idealized example of antiauthoritarianism. Originally written when Bronnen was nineteen, the play is about a group of students who rebel against their schoolteachers. In the final scene, they flee into the woods, where they celebrate a union with nature, becoming "a collective body growing toward divinity," as Ward B. Lewis described it in the *Dictionary of Literary Biography.*

Although Bronnen continued to write sexually charged plays laced with violence, such as *Anarchie in Sillian* and *Die Exzesse: Lustspiel,* he was also becoming a political writer by the mid-1920s. *Katalaunische Schlacht* mixes these two sides of the playwright in a story about immoral soldiers who desert their posts and rob their dead comrades of their possessions. After the war, Hiddie, the wife of one of the deserters who has died, is pursued by three of the other men who intend to rape her. In the end, cornered by the men on an ocean steamer, she kills herself. The play's unflattering portrayal of German soldiers at a time when nationalism was heating up in that country doomed it to disaster. Bronnen, therefore, switched gears to produce *Rheinische Rebellen,* a much more patriotic work that clearly favored Germany's designs to regain the Rheinland region then occupied by France.

After the production of his epic play *Ostpolzug* in 1926, a work that depicts Alexander the Great in a modern light as he conquers Mt. Everest and the world, Bronnen released two novels that clearly illustrated his right-wing politics at the time. *O.S.* concerns the disputed territory of Upper Silesia that Germany wished to wrest from Poland, and *Roßbach* "glorified Adolf Hitler's attempted putsch in Munich," related Lewis. Bronnen wished to be officially declared an Aryan, disguising the fact that his father was Jewish and making contact with Joseph Goebbels, the head of Nazi propaganda. However, the attempt failed; not only this, but the fact that Bronnen was a Jew, led to his being fired from his job at a radio network. By 1940, his works were banned by the Nazis, and three years later Bronnen fled back to Austria. Though he re-enlisted in the army there, he was jailed for treason in 1944.

After the war, Bronnen lived in Austria and found work as editor of the newspaper *Neue Zeit.* His plays now took a distinctly anti-right turn as his politics began to shift toward communism. In 1948, for example, the play *"N"* was performed. "Ostensibly a historical drama about Napoleon, 'N' is actually a veiled attack on Hitler," noted Lewis. Bronnen's transition to the left was complete by 1951, when he became director of the Viennese Neues Theater, which performed plays emphasizing communist themes. In 1955, he moved to East Berlin at the invitation of East Germany's cultural minister. Here he worked as theater critic and publicist for the *Berliner Zeitung* and continued to produce such left-wing plays as *Die Kette Kolin.* Unfortunately, the reputation he still had from his earlier plays, which were considered bourgeois by the East Germans, prevented Bronnen from rediscovering success in his final years.

BIOGRAPHICAL AND CRITICAL SOURCES:

BOOKS

Dictionary of Literary Biography, Volume 124: *Twentieth-Century German Dramatists, 1919-1992,* Thomson Gale (Detroit, MI), 1992.

PERIODICALS

Modern Language Review, October, 1991, Alfred D. White, "Modernism in German Literature: A Review Article," pp. 924-928.
Theatre Survey, November, 1998, Lynn Dierks, "Arnolt Bronnen's *Vatermord* and the German Youth of 1922," pp. 25-38.*

*   *   *

BRUMWELL, Stephen 1960-

PERSONAL: Born 1960, in Portsmouth, England; married; one daughter. *Education:* University of Leeds, B.A. (with first class honors), 1993, M.A. (with distinction), 1994, Ph.D., 1998.

ADDRESSES: Agent—c/o Author Mail, Da Capo Press, Eleven Cambridge Center, Cambridge, MA 02142.

CAREER: Cornish Times, Cornwall, England, reporter, 1979-82; *Evening Herald,* Plymouth, England, senior reporter, 1982-90; University of Leeds, Leeds, England, tutor in modern history, 1994-98, lecturer in modern history, 1998-99; freelance scholar and writer, 2000—

AWARDS, HONORS: W.M. Keck Foundation and Fletcher Jones Foundation fellow to Huntington Library, 1999.

WRITINGS:

Cassell's Companion to Eighteenth-Century Britain, Sterling Publishing (New York, NY), 2001.

Redcoats: The British Soldier and War in the Americas, 1755-1763, Cambridge University Press (New York, NY), 2002.
White Devil: An Epic Story of Revenge from the Savage War That Inspired "The Last of the Mohicans," Weidenfeld & Nicolson (London, England), 2004, published as *White Devil: A True Story of War, Savagery, and Vengeance in Colonial America,* Da Capo Press (Cambridge, MA), 2005.
Wolfe: Soldier of Empire, Humbledon & London Books (London, England), 2005.

Author of introduction, *Through So Many Dangers: The Adventures & Memoirs of Robert Kirk, Late of the Royal Highland Regiment,* Purple Mountain Press; contributor to *British Military Greats,* Cassell.

SIDELIGHTS: An historian particularly noted for his studies of the British army in eighteenth-century America, Stephen Brumwell is the author of *Redcoats: The British Soldier and War in the Americas, 1755-1763* and *White Devil: A True Story of War, Savagery, and Vengeance in Colonial America.*

In *Redcoats* Brumwell provides a comprehensive examination of the men who fought for England during the French-and-Indian War. Drawing on numerous memoirs, letters, courts-martial records, and other archival materials, he recreates the individuals who enlisted for financial or patriotic reasons, or to escape the drudgery of rural life. In doing so, he finds a number of soldiers who displayed remarkable intelligence and initiative, and in turn, an army that adapted to the unique terrain and unconventional fighting style of colonial North America. This is in sharp contrast to the image of the British army as being hopelessly hidebound, relying on the American frontiersmen to win the kind of war European troops were incapable of waging. This is the view of the French-and-Indian War that comes from General Braddock's resounding defeat by unconventional forces in the forest in 1755. But as Brumwell reveals, this is not the end of the story, but, rather, the beginning. In the wake of this defeat, Brumwell shows, the British were forced to rethink their tactics and create a different kind of army. In fact, Brumwell reveals that George Washington's own Continental Army would use many of these innovations to defeat that same British army in the Revolutionary War. As a result, according to *Military*

Book Review contributor Michael Russert, "Brumwell has successfully created a fascinating and insightful book that should be of interest to all interested in Eighteenth Century warfare." For *Albion* contributor Jeremy Black, "this is an excellent example of military history, that will at once be of value to scholars working on eighteenth-century Britain and also to those interested in the struggle for empire."

In *White Devil* Brumwell turns to a specific incident in the French-and-Indian War, and to one of those unconventional warriors celebrated in the more-traditional histories of the period. In 1759, Robert Rogers was ordered to take his group of rangers and punish the Abenaki, a Native-American tribe that supported the French and had massacred English settlers at Fort William Henry. Rogers' response was a brutal slaughter of the Abenaki village, an incident that became the source of James Fennimore Cooper's novel *The Last of the Mohicans.* In addition to narratives written or retold by survivors on both sides, Brumwell draws on 250 years of archival materials on Native American and European relations "to explore the truth behind this controversial episode from America's aggressive past," in the words of *Library Journal* contributor Dale Farris. The result, for Len Barcousky writing in the *Pittsburgh Post-Gazette,* is a "fast-moving tale of courage, cruelty, hardship and savagery."

BIOGRAPHICAL AND CRITICAL SOURCES:

PERIODICALS

Albion, spring, 2003, Jeremy Black, review of *Cassell's Companion to Eighteenth-Century Britain,* p. 262.

Booklist, September 15, 2002, Jeremy Black, review of *Redcoats: The British Soldier and War in the Americas, 1755-1763,* p. 134.

Contemporary Review, October, 2004, review of *White Devil: An Epic Story of Revenge from the Savage War that Inspired "The Last of the Mohicans,"* p. 254.

Library Journal, February 15, 2002, T.J. Schaeper, review of *Redcoats,* p. 158; March 1, 2005, Dale Farris, review of *White Devil: A True Story of War, Savagery, and Vengeance in Colonial America,* p. 97.

Pittsburgh Post-Gazette, July 3, 2005, Len Barcousky, review of *White Devil.*

Spectator (London, England), September 28, 2002, Hugh Cecil, "An Army Emerges with Honour," p. 66.

ONLINE

Military Book Review Online, http://www.themilitary bookreview.com/ (September 12, 2005), Michael Russert, review of *Redcoats.*

Stephen Brumwell Home Page, http://www.vleggaar. nl/brumwell (September 12, 2005).*

*   *   *

BUCKLEY, David 1965-

PERSONAL: Born 1965. *Education:* Liverpool University, Ph.D.

ADDRESSES: Agent—c/o Author Mail, Chicago Review Press, 814 N. Franklin St., Chicago, IL 60610.

CAREER: Freelance biographer.

WRITINGS:

David Bowie: The Complete Guide to His Music, Omnibus Press (Chester, NY), 1996, 2nd edition, 2004.

The Stranglers: No Mercy, Hodder & Stoughton (London, England), 1997.

Strange Fascination: David Bowie, the Definitive Story, Virgin (London, England), 1999.

R.E.M. Fiction: An Alternative Biography, Virgin (London, England), 2002.

The Thrill of It All: The Story of Bryan Ferry and Roxy Music, Chicago Review Press (Chicago, IL), 2005.

SIDELIGHTS: A biographer of rock musicians, David Buckley has produced well-researched studies of David Bowie, Bryan Ferry, and the Stranglers. After publishing a short guide to Bowie's music and an official biography of the Stranglers, Buckley was able to publish a biography of his rock music idol, David Bowie. *Strange Fascination: David Bowie, the Definitive Story* is a heavily documented study that explores the cultural themes and the biographical details that have been such a powerful influence in Bowie's music.

Buckley next produced *R.E.M. Fiction: An Alternative Biography* after his publisher rejected his idea of doing a study of Roxy Music. He persevered, however, and eventually published *The Thrill of It All: The Story of Bryan Ferry and Roxy Music.* Buckley had interviewed Ferry while researching his biography of David Bowie, but he found a reluctance on the part of band members to participate in the new venture. Nevertheless, he undertook the extensive research and wideranging interviews that have marked his biographies. He describes Ferry's compelling rise from coalminer's son to rock star, as well as the artistic influences and personal battles the musician encountered along the way, particularly his difficult relationship with keyboardist Brian Eno, who left Roxy Music a few years after its formation. Reviewing the book for *Artforum International,* Greeta Daval felt that, "as a history, the book is perfectly competent—but readers seeking an account as original and thought-provoking as the band itself should look elsewhere." Other reviewers were more impressed, *Library Journal* contributor Matthew Moyer concluding: "this is the best Ferry/Roxy read yet."

BIOGRAPHICAL AND CRITICAL SOURCES:

PERIODICALS

Artforum International, summer, 2005, Geeta Daval, review of *The Thrill of It All: The Story of Bryan Ferry and Roxy Music,* p. S55.

Library Journal, June 1, 2005, Matthew Moyer, review of *The Thrill of It All,* p. 129.

School Library Journal, September, 2001, Barbara Hoffert, review of *Strange Fascination: David Bowie, the Definitive Story,* p. S74.

ONLINE

Roxy Music Web site, http://www.vivaroxymusic.com/ (December 20, 2004), "The Thrill of It All—David Buckley Interview."*

BUJO, Bénézet 1940-

PERSONAL: Born April 4, 1940, in Drodro, Congo; son of Michel Ngodya and Léonie Dyedha. *Education:* Completed habilitation and doctorate in theology. *Religion:* Roman Catholic.

ADDRESSES: Home—Bunia, Democratic Republic of Congo. *Office*—University of Freiburg, Av. de l'Europe 20, Freiburg, CH-1700 Switzerland. *E-mail*—benezet.bujo@unifr.ch.

CAREER: Writer and educator. University of Freiburg, Freiburg, Switzerland, professor of theology.

WRITINGS:

Morale africaine et foi chrétienne, Faculté de Théologie Catholique (Kinshasa, Congo), 1976.

Les exigences du message évangelique. De l'orthodoxie à l'orthopraxie, Editions Saint Paul Afrique (Kinshasa, Congo), 1980.

Les dix commandements: pourquoi faire?, Editions Saint Paul Afrique (Kinshasa, Congo), 1980, translation published as *Do We Still Need the Ten Commandments?,* Editions Saint Paul Afrique (Nairobi, Kenya), 1990.

Die Begründung des Sittlichen: zur Frage des Eudämonismus bei Thomas von Aquin, F. Schöningh (Paderborn, Germany), 1984.

Afrikanische Theologie in ihrem gesellschaftlichen Kontext, Patmos (Düsseldorf, Germany), 1986, translation by John O'Donohue published as *African Theology in Its Social Context,* Orbis Books (Maryknoll, NY), 1992.

African Christian Morality at the Age of Inculturation, Saint Paul Publications-Africa (Nairobi, Kenya), 1990.

Die ethische Dimension der Gemeinschaft. Das afrikanische Modell im Nord-Sud-Dialog, University of Freiburg (Freiburg, Germany), 1993, translation published as *The Ethical Dimension of Community: The African Model and the Dialogue between North and South,* Pauline Publications Africa (Nairobi, Kenya), 1998.

Christmas: God Becomes Man in Black Africa, Paulines Publications Africa (Nairobi, Kenya), 1995.

Utamadunisho na kanisa la mazingira: nija ya kujitegemea katika yote, Paulines Publications Africa (Nairobi, Kenya), 1999.

Wider den Universalanspruch westlicher Moral: Grundlagen afrikanischer Ethik, Herder (Freiburg, Switzerland), 2000, translation by Brian McNeil published as *Foundations of an African Ethic: Beyond the Universal Claims of Western Morality,* Crossroad Publishing (New York, NY), 2001.

Le notre Père. Son impact sur la vie quotidienne. Méditation d'un théologien africain, Editions Paulines (Kinshasa, Congo), 2001, translation published as *The Impact of the Our Father on Everyday Life: Meditations of an African Theologian,* Paulines Publications Africa (Nairobi, Kenya), 2002.

(Editor, with Juvénal Ilunga Muya) *Théologie africaine au XXIe siècle. Quelques figures,* Editions Universitaires (Freiburg, Switzerland), 2002, translation by Silvano Borruso published as *African Theology in the Twenty-first Century: The Contribution of the Pioneers,* Paulines Publications Africa (Nairobi, Kenya), 2003.

Buzo's writings have also been published in Swahili and Italian.

WORK IN PROGRESS: Théologie africaine au XXIe siècle, Volumes 2-3, for Editions Universitaires; *Christliche Ehe und Ethik. Ein nicht westliches konzept.*

SIDELIGHTS: Bénézet Bujo told *CA:* "As a Christian theologian, writing is an essential part of my apostolate. In my work I have been influenced by various theologians: Thomas Aquinas; German theologians Karl Rahner, Johann Baptist Metz, Walter Kasper, and Alfous Auer; Belgian and French theologians Edward Schillebeeckx and M.-D. Chenu; African theologians N. Mulago and E. Mueng; and German philosophers J. Habermas and K.O. Apel."

"I began with the study of Thomas Aquinas in order to learn his method and his spirit of dealing with the problems of his time. This was the subject of my doctoral thesis and the topic of my habilitation. After having studied Thomas and the Western authors (philosophers and theologians), I began to study their cultural backgrounds and the relativity of their methods and teachings. This gave me the input to develop my own view on theological questions in the context of my African culture.

"What inspires me to write as I do is that all the systems I studied could not answer the burning questions in black Africa. I thought black Africa needs its own way of thinking."

*   *   *

BURKE, Alafair
(Alafair S. Burke)

PERSONAL: Born in Fort Lauderdale, FL; daughter of James Lee (a crime writer) and Pearl (an artist) Burke. *Education:* Reed College, B.A., 1991; Stanford Law School, J.D. (with distinction), 1994.

ADDRESSES: Home—New York, NY. *Office*—Hofstra University School of Law, 121 Hofstra University, Hempstead, NY 11549; fax: 516-463-4962. *E-mail*—lawasb@hofstra.edu.

CAREER: U.S. Court of Appeals for the Ninth Circuit, law clerk to Judge Betty B. Fletcher, 1994-95; deputy district attorney, Portland, OR, 1995-99; Phillips, Lytle (law firm), Buffalo, NY, associate, 1999-2001; Hofstra University School of Law, Hempstead, NY, associate professor of criminal law, 2001—. Oregon Uniform Criminal Jury Instructions Committee, member, 1996-98, secretary, 1998-99; Northeast People of Color Conference planning committee, member, 2003—. Commentator on legal issues for radio and television programs, including *Court TV.*

MEMBER: Women's Bar Association of the State of New York, Order of the Coif, Phi Beta Kappa.

AWARDS, HONORS: Stessin Prize for Outstanding Scholarship, Hofstra University, 2003, 2004.

WRITINGS:

"SAMANTHA KINCAID" MYSTERIES

Judgment Calls, Henry Holt (New York, NY), 2003.
Missing Justice, Henry Holt (New York, NY), 2004.
Close Case, Henry Holt (New York, NY), 2005.

OTHER

Contributor of articles to legal reviews.

SIDELIGHTS: Alafair Burke is the author of a series of mystery novels centered on Samantha Kincaid, an assistant district attorney in Portland, Oregon. Burke knows whereof she writes; she spent five years at that very job in the late 1990s. However, despite Kincaid and Burke sharing a job and a law school, Burke claims that the character's personality is not based on herself. "She's much more brazen and confrontational than I am," Burke told *Book Place* online interviewer Lucy Watson. "She's also funnier, taller, thinner, and much more neurotic, and she could beat me in a race without breaking a sweat."

In the first "Samantha Kincaid" mystery, *Judgment Calls,* Kincaid is presented with a case that the police would like her to prosecute, but not with enough evidence to do so. The crime's victim is a thirteen-year-old, heroin-addicted prostitute who has been raped, seriously beaten, and left for dead, and Kincaid hopes to be able to dig up enough evidence to charge the perpetrators with attempted murder. However, as she investigates, she finds out that this assault is only a small part of a much larger web of crimes. *Judgment Calls* is "narrated in a crisp first person and injected with good-natured humor," commented a *Publishers Weekly* contributor, and is also "tightly plotted and detail laden." "Burke . . . writes with both a clarity and a self-assuredness that belies her first-novelist status," Craig Shufelt wrote in *Library Journal,* and *Booklist* reviewer Mary Frances Wilkens noted that she also "blends courtroom drama and criminal investigation with surprising aplomb."

In the next installment, *Missing Justice,* Kincaid investigates the murder of Clarissa Easterbrook, an administrative-law judge who generally oversaw routine civil cases. The evidence all seems to point to a disgruntled janitor whom Easterbrook had evicted, but Kincaid begins to worry that the man is being framed. The book reads like "a deftly extended episode of *Law & Order,*" commented a *Kirkus Reviews* critic, while a *Publishers Weekly* contributor noted that Burke "does a good job of integrating the political and personal lives of her characters, with the detectives of the Major Crimes Unit being particularly well drawn."

Kincaid's personal life is a major part of the plot in Burke's third mystery, *Close Case.* Her investigation in this novel centers on the murder of Percy Crenshaw,

a journalist. Kincaid's romantic relationship with a detective on the force has been progressing nicely, until his partner uses some questionable tactics when interrogating a suspect in Crenshaw's murder. Kincaid is stuck in the middle, forced to choose between doing her job ethically and trusting her boyfriend's and his partner's judgment in their interrogations. *Close Case* is a "superb legal thriller," Stacy Alesi concluded in *Library Journal,* "Burke hits her stride in this third outing," praised a *Kirkus Reviews* contributor, who also noted the "plausible moral dilemmas for Samantha . . . and surprises that are still popping up on the final pages."

Burke's father, James Lee Burke, also writes mysteries, although of a very different style than his daughter's. As the younger Burke often points out in interviews, she was the family's original mystery writer, borrowing her father's typewriter to compose mysteries such as "Murder at the Roller Disco" as a child, at a time when her father was still writing in other genres. "What I really think I inherited from my family more than any particular writing style . . . is a narrative tradition," Burke commented in an interview on her Home Page. "The Burkes are people who tell stories, and I grew up watching my father work a full-time job and then come home and write every single day to get his stories on paper."

BIOGRAPHICAL AND CRITICAL SOURCES:

PERIODICALS

Booklist, May 1, 2003, Mary Frances Wilkens, review of *Judgment Calls,* p. 1536.
Kirkus Reviews, June 1, 2003, review of *Judgment Calls,* p. 766; April 15, 2004, review of *Missing Justice,* p. 363; May 15, 2005, review of *Close Case,* p. 564.
Library Bookwatch, May, 2005, review of *Judgment Calls.*
Library Journal, May 15, 2003, Craig Shufelt, review of *Judgment Calls,* p. 122; May 15, 2004, Craig Shufelt, review of *Missing Justice,* p. 119; June 15, 2005, Stacy Alesi, review of *Close Case,* p. 64.
Publishers Weekly, September 30, 2002, John F. Baker, "Carrying on the Burke Franchise," p. 14; May 26, 2003, review of *Judgment Calls,* p. 43;

May 31, 2004, review of *Missing Justice*, p. 55;
May 30, 2005, review of *Close Case*, p. 42;
August 22, 2005, review of *Close Case*, p. 49.

South Florida Sun-Sentinel, August 6, 2003, Oline H.
Cogdill, review of *Judgment Calls*.

ONLINE

Alafair Burke Home Page, http://www.alafairburke.
com (October 18, 2005).

BookLoons, http://www.bookloons.com/ (October 28,
2005), Hilary Williamson, interview with Burke.

BookPage, http://www.bookpage.com/ (October 18,
2005), Jay MacDonald, "Like Father, like
Daughter: For the Burkes, Crime Fiction Is All in
the Family."

Book Place, http://www.thebookplace.com/ (October
18, 2005), Lucy Watson, interview with Burke.

Bookreporter, http://www.bookreporter.com/ (October
18, 2005), Kate Ayers, review of *Judgment Calls*.

Brothers Judd Web site, http://www.brothersjudd.com/
(June 30, 2004), Mary-Ellen Walker, review of
Missing Justice.

Hofstra University School of Law Web site, http://
www.hofstra.edu/ (October 18, 2005), "Alafair S.
Burke."

January Online, http://www.januarymagazine.com/
(November 9, 2005), Sarah Weinman, review of
Judgment Calls.

Novel View, http://www.anovelview.com/ (October 28,
2005), interview with Burke.

Shots: The Crime & Mystery Magazine, http://www.
shotsmag.co.uk/ (October 18, 2005), Ali Karim,
interview with Alafair Burke.*

*   *   *

BURKE, Alafair S.
See BURKE, Alafair

*   *   *

BURKE, Monte

PERSONAL: Male.

ADDRESSES: Office—Forbes, 60 5th Ave., New York,
NY 10011. *Agent*—Simon Green, Pom Inc., 611
Broadway, No. 907B, New York, NY 10012. *E-mail*—
Monte@monteburke.com.

CAREER: Forbes, New York, NY, staff writer.

WRITINGS:

(Coeditor) *Leaper: The Wonderful World of Atlantic
Salmon Fishing*, Lyons Press (Guilford, CT),
2001.

*Sowbelly: The Obsessive Quest for the World Record
Largemouth Bass*, Dutton (New York, NY), 2005.

Frequent contributor to *Field & Stream* and other out-
doorsman journals.

SIDELIGHTS: An avid angler, Monte Burke applies
his journalistic skills to his hobby in *Sowbelly: The
Obsessive Quest for the World Record Largemouth
Bass*. Since George Washington Parry allegedly caught
a 22-pound, 4-ounce bass in 1932 that was immediately eaten, serious anglers have been trying to
surpass his feat. While also engaged in this attempt,
Burke encounters an assortment of interesting characters who devote large amounts of time and energy to
their quest. "Unsponsored and comparatively unknown,
this eccentric yet elite bunch delightfully gets its due
from Monte Burke," according to Deborah Weisberg
in the *Pittsburgh Post-Gazette*. These characters
include Mike Long, who fishes in disguise in order to
throw off the competition; Porter Hall, whose obsession helped end his marriage; and Bob Crupi, who also
risked divorce when he chose to fish rather than be
present at the birth of his daughter. He also describes
the opportunists and outright frauds who plague the
true anglers. In addition, "Burke sprinkles ruminations
on the science and details of bass fishing, nicely sewing together a well-paced tale," noted a *Publishers
Weekly* reviewer. Among other subjects, he covers attempts to breed a super bass and the surprising
popularity of a sport that claims over eleven million
devotees and may be on the verge of achieving
mainstream success on the order of NASCAR races.
The result, for *Booklist* reviewer Alan Moores, is an
"engaging, informed account of the sport."

BIOGRAPHICAL AND CRITICAL SOURCES:

PERIODICALS

Booklist, February 11, 2005, Alan Moores, review of
*Sowbelly: The Obsessive Quest for the World
Record Largemouth Bass*, p. 928.

Business Record (Des Moines, IA), May 9, 2005, review of *Sowbelly,* p. 25.

Library Journal, March 1, 2005, Jim Casada, review of *Sowbelly,* p. 94.

Pittsburgh Post-Gazette, July 24, 2005, Deborah Weisberg, review of *Sowbelly.*

Publishers Weekly, February 7, 2005, review of *Sowbelly,* p. 56.

ONLINE

Alabama Booksmith, http://www.alabamabooksmith. com/ (September 12, 2005), review of *Sowbelly.*

Monte Burke Home Page, http://www.monteburke.com (September 12, 2005).

Southern Living Online, http://www.southernliving. com/ (September 12, 2005), review of *Sowbelly.*

*   *   *

BURNS, Charles 1955-

PERSONAL: Born 1955, in Washington, DC; married Susan Moore (a painter); children: two daughters. *Education:* Evergreen State College, B.F.A., 1977; University of California, Davis, M.F.A., 1979.

ADDRESSES: Home—Philadelphia, PA. *Agent*—c/o Author Mail, Fantagraphics Books, 7563 Lake City Way NE, Seattle, WA 98115.

CAREER: Graphic artist, cartoonist, illustrator, and writer; Mark Morris Dance Company, concept and set designer for *The Hard Nut* (contemporary ballet), 1991. Worked in art gallery; created a campus magazine; experimented with photographic novels. *Exhibitions: Charles Burns,* Pennsylvania Academy of the Arts, Morris Gallery, 1999.

AWARDS, HONORS: Pew Fellowship in the Arts, 1993; multiple Harvey and Eisner award nominations for *Black Hole* series, 1994-2003; included on *Comics Journal* list of Top 100 English-Language Comics of the Century, for *Black Hole* series.

WRITINGS:

Big Baby in Curse of the Molemen, Raw Books & Graphics, 1986, published as *Curse of the Molemen,* Kitchen Sink Press (Princeton, WI), 1991.

Hard-Boiled Defective Stories, edited and designed by Art Spiegelman and François Mouly, Pantheon/ Raw Books (New York, NY), 1988.

Skin Deep: Tales of Doomed Romance (originally published in *Big Baby* comic-books series, 1988– 91), edited by Art Spiegelman and R. Sikoryak, Penguin (New York, NY), 1992.

Blood Club, Kitchen Sink Press (Princeton, WI), 1992.

Charles Burns's Modern Horror Sketchbook, Kitchen Sink Press (Northampton, MA), 1993.

(With Gary Panter) *Facetasm: A Creepy Mix & Match Book of Gross Face Mutations!,* Gates of Heck (New York, NY), 1998.

El Borbah (originally published in comic-book format), Fantagraphics Books (Seattle, WA), 1999.

Big Baby (originally published in comic-book format), Fantagraphics Books (Seattle, WA), 2000.

Contributor to *Raw* magazine, *Rolling Stone, Village Voice, Heavy Metal, National Lampoon, Death Rattle, Face, New Yorker, Time,* and *New York Times Magazine;* contributor to publications in Italy, including *Vanity,* in France, including *Métal Hurlant,* and in Spain, including *El Vibora.* Creator or contributor of self-syndicated comic strips to newspapers and to comics anthologies, including *Freak Show: The Residents,* Dark Horse Comics, 1992, and *All-American Hippie Comix,* Kitchen Sink Press (Princeton, WI), reprint edition, 1995. Illustrator for album covers for musicians, including Iggy Pop. Author-illustrator of *Black Hole* comic-books series, Kitchen Sink Press, 1994-98, Fantagraphics Books, 1998-2003.

ADAPTATIONS: Live-action version of comic-book character "Dog Boy" serialized for MTV's *Liquid Television.*

SIDELIGHTS: American cartoonist and graphic novelist Charles Burns is a leading figure of the modern countercultural "comix" movement. He is best known for his stark black-and-white drawings and his surreal characters and stories. Burns's style of illustration has been compared to that of the cartoonist Chester Gould, who created the "Dick Tracy" comic strips of the mid-twentieth century. Burns was an early contributor to editor Art Spiegelman's avant-garde magazine *Raw* and has contributed illustrations and cartoons to numerous magazines and anthologies. As the author of a news release from the Pennsylvania Academy of the Arts posted on the *Absolutearts* Web site wrote, "Dark, funny, and disturbing, [Burns's] gothic imagery and texts are emblematic of our millenial age."

Some of Burns's most famous cartoon characters are the 400-pound Mexican wrestler-private detective El Borbah; the odd and imaginative suburban boy Tony, called Big Baby, who tries to come to terms with the world of adults; and Dog Boy, an otherwise-normal teenage boy whose heart was transplanted from a dog and contributes to his strange canine behavior.

The collection *Hard-Boiled Defective Stories* follows El Borbah through five adventures, in which he rescues missing persons, investigates a suicide, and exposes a scheme at a sperm bank. Ray Olson, in *Booklist,* commented that for lovers of "Dick Tracy" and 1940s *Batman* serials, "El Borbah looks awfully good." C. Carr, writing for the *Village Voice Literary Supplement,* concluded in a review of Burns's book: "as always, he's drawn an ugly world so cleanly and coldly you'd think he was using a knife." Mark Pawson, in a review for *Variant* online, described Burns's black-and-white lines as "ultra-clean" and "scalpel-sharp."

Big Baby in Curse of the Molemen shows Tony's vivid imagination. He dreams up a horror story as workers dig up the neighbors' backyard to build a swimming pool. In a *Village Voice Literary Supplement* review, Carr wrote that Burns's "drawings in sharp blacks and whites—no grays—vibrate with more drama than usual. And help us to develop an overactive imagination like Tony's."

The collection *Skin Deep: Tales of Doomed Romance* features three stories—"Dog Days," a Dog Boy adventure; "Burn Again," a tale of the junkie evangelist Bliss Blister and his strange encounters; and "A Marriage Made in Hell," in which a returning veteran's reconstructive surgery makes a mockery of his marriage. A *Publishers Weekly* contributor called these stories "thoroughly amusing recreations of trashy pop entertainment," while Margot Mifflin, in *Entertainment Weekly,* observed that *Skin Deep* shows Burns "alternately at his bleakest and most uncharacteristically wholesome." Olson, in *Booklist,* called Burns "probably the best of the noir satirists" and said that readers who can laugh at their passions "may be quite tickled by Burns' japes."

Burns collaborated with illustrator Gary Panter in the 1993 book *Facetasm: A Creepy Mix & Match Book of Gross Face Mutations!,* a horror version of children's mix-and-match books, in which readers can combine portions of faces on three horizontal panels to make up to 7,000 different weird faces. Pawson called the combinations "creepy" and "gross." Marc Spiegler, in a review of the book for *Wired,* commented that the faces "seem drawn from fever dreams" and show "the intermediary stage as a human turns ghoulish."

Burns writes often about teen angst, especially in his acclaimed 2003 comix series *Black Hole,* which is set in the 1970s and deals with the Teen Plague, an outbreak of fictitious sexually transmitted disease that affects only teens and causes bizarre transformations in victims' bodies. In an online interview with Alan David Doane for *Comic Book Galaxy,* Burns said that many of the stories from *Black Hole* are based on autobiographical information, including "a lot of my socialization, growing up," although it is disguised. A contributor to *Whole Earth* called Burns's work in this series a combination of "stunning graphic style . . . and a truly warped mind."

Burns was also a concept and set designer for the contemporary ballet *The Hard Nut,* first performed in 1991 and based on Tchaikovsky's *The Nutcracker.* Dale Harris, in a review of the production for the *Wall Street Journal,* said its "dark, absurdist view of childhood, its terrors and fierce loyalties," seem spawned by Burns's influence. Harris also praised the "brilliant black and white sets," inspired by Burns, as well as the cast's colorful costumes. Martha Duffy, in *Time,* called the ballet a "radical reworking of *The Nutcracker*" that is "rude, boisterous, and more than a little, well, nutty."

Burns's work has been very popular both in Europe and in the United States. In the interview with Doane, he acknowledged the influence and inspiration of Gould and of cartoonist Harvey Kurtzman and others. He explained that his style and characters have developed over a long period and that he prefers black-and-white images over color. Burns called his work "low-fidelity comics."

BIOGRAPHICAL AND CRITICAL SOURCES:

BOOKS

Clute, John, and Peter Nicholls, editors, *Encyclopedia of Science Fiction,* St. Martin's Press (New York, NY), 1993.

PERIODICALS

Booklist, August, 1988, Ray Olson, review of *Hard-Boiled Defective Stories,* p. 1878; November 15, 1992, Ray Olson, review of *Skin Deep: Tales of Doomed Romance,* p. 570.
Books, June, 1990, "Comics for Grown-Ups," p. 4.
Entertainment Weekly, December 4, 1992, Margot Mifflin, review of *Skin Deep,* p. 60.
Publishers Weekly, October 19, 1992, review of *Skin Deep,* p. 74; October 11, 1993, review of *Skin Deep,* p. 56.
Time, December 28, 1992, Martha Duffy, review of *The Hard Nut,* p. 67.
Village Voice Literary Supplement, February, 1986, C. Carr, review of *Big Baby in Curse of the Molemen,* p. 3; May, 1988, C. Carr, review of *Hard-Boiled Defective Stories,* p. 3.
Wall Street Journal, January 4, 1993, Dale Harris, "A Cracked 'Nutcracker'," p. A7.
Whole Earth, spring, 1998, review of *Black Hole,* p. 28.

ONLINE

Absolutearts, http://www.absolutearts.com/ (October 8, 1999), "Indepth Arts News: *Charles Burns.*"
Artbabe, http://www.artbabe.com/ (August 6, 2003), "Charles Burns."
Comic Book Galaxy, http://www.comicbookgalaxy.com/ (December 28, 1999), Alan David Doane, "Interview: Charles Burns."
Fantagraphics Books Web site, http://www.fantagraphics.com/ (August 6, 2003), "The Charles Burns Library" and "Charles Burns Biography."
Lambiek, http://www.lambiek.net/ (August 4, 2003), "Charles Burns."
Little Lit, http://www.little-lit.com/ (August 6, 2003), "Charles Burns Spookyland."
Variant, http://www.variant.randomstate.org/ (August 6, 2003), Mark Pawson, "Zine & Comics Review."
Wired, http://www.wired.com (August 6, 2003), Marc Spiegler, "The Many Faces of Disgust" (review of *Facetasm: A Creepy Mix & Match Book of Gross Face Mutations!*).*

*   *   *

BUSSE, Richard C. 1948-

PERSONAL: Born September 18, 1948, in Philadelphia, PA. *Education:* San Diego State University, B.S., 1971; University of California, L.L.D., 1974.

ADDRESSES: Office—Busse & Hunt, 521 American Bank Building, 621 Southwest Morrison, Portland, OR 97205-3818.

CAREER: Lawyer. Multnomah County, OR, chief deputy county counsel, 1975-81; attorney in private practice, 1981—; Busse & Hunt, Portland, OR, senior partner. Frequent speaker and writer on issues of employment law.

MEMBER: International Society of Barristers.

WRITINGS:

Employees' Rights: Your Practical Handbook to Workplace Law, Sphinx Publishers (Naperville, IL), 2004.
Fired, Laid Off, or Forced Out: A Complete Guide to Severance, Benefits, and Your Rights When You're Starting Over, Sphinx Publishers (Naperville, IL), 2005.
Your Rights at Work: All You Need to Know about Workplace Law, and How to Use It to Protect Your Job, Sphinx Publishers (Naperville, IL), 2005.

Frequent contributor to employment law journals.

SIDELIGHTS: Richard C. Busse is an employment lawyer who has established a very successful and highly regarded practice representing plaintiffs in disputes with employers. Drawing on that experience, he has published a number of books apprising employees of their rights and their options in dealing with difficult work situations. *Employees' Rights: Your Practical Handbook to Workplace Law* provides practical advice on challenging discrimination, protecting personal privacy, and the proper limits of disciplinary action. *Booklist* contributor Mary Frances Wilkins found that "the information here is quite useful, both thorough and easy to understand." Much of Busse's practice is designed to protect employees and prevent unfair termination, but he also counsels those who face being let go or who actually have been laid off. *Fired, Laid Off, or Forced Out: A Complete Guide to Severance, Benefits, and Your Rights When You're Starting Over* is designed for them. After discussing ways to defuse a hostile situation or enlist the help of human-relations personnel to prevent termination, Busse turns to those who have exhausted these options or are otherwise unable to keep their jobs. As *Library Journal* reviewer Joan Pedzich explained, "Busse covers what to do when termination is imminent and provides measured, practical guidance on documentation, behavior, and performance." This includes advice on negotiating a severance package, handling oneself in an exit interview, and deciding if a legitimate wrongful-termination lawsuit is appropriate.

BIOGRAPHICAL AND CRITICAL SOURCES:

PERIODICALS

Booklist, February 1, 2004, Mary Frances Wilkens, review of *Employees' Rights: Your Practical Handbook to Workplace Law,* p. 939.

Library Journal, March 1, 2005, Joan Pedzich, review of *Fired, Laid Off, or Forced Out: A Complete Guide to Severance, Benefits, and Your Rights When You're Starting Over,* p. 99.*

* * *

BUTLER, Amy
See GREENFIELD, Amy Butler

* * *

BUYS, Paul
See GRESHOFF, Jan

C

CADWALLADR, Carole

PERSONAL: Female.

ADDRESSES: Agent—c/o Author Mail, Dutton Books, 375 Hudson St., New York, NY 10014.

CAREER: Novelist and journalist. Has worked as a tour guide for American schoolchildren in Europe, a holiday representative in Turkey, and a guidebook writer in Prague, Lebanon, and the former Soviet Union; Daily Telegraph, London, England, travel writer.

WRITINGS:

The Family Tree (novel), Dutton (New York, NY), 2005.

Contributor to travel magazines.

SIDELIGHTS: Long known as a travel writer in Great Britain, Carole Cadwalladr turned her attention to fiction with her debut novel The Family Tree. While her own life and career have taken her to foreign lands, Cadwalladr's novel looks inward, to the strange ways that memory works. As she put it in an autobiographical profile for Powells.com, "The question of memory and how you mould the facts of your past to fit the facts of your present is a game that all the characters play." The main character, Rebecca Monroe, and her sister, Tiffany, remember the same incidents from childhood very differently, and these differing memories serve to shape their characters. At the same time, their grandmother is struggling with Alzheimer's and a loss of identity compounded by her habit of telling stories to herself that have become substitutes for actual memories. Throughout the story, the characters try to fit their memories into a seamless narrative that leads logically to the present, a process that Rebecca's biologist husband calls "retrofitting." Rebecca herself is writing a doctoral thesis on popular culture, and she sees the same phenomenon in celebrity biographies, which seem to embrace the idea that success was inevitable, given the talent and perseverance of their subjects, despite the many examples to the contrary.

The novel itself evolved in a somewhat haphazard way, as Cadwalladr explained in an interview with the BookBrowse Web site: "I wish I could say that I had some grand design for the novel, but I'd be lying. And the structure, the multiple plot lines, was something that evolved along the way." The story begins with Rebecca's attempts to discover the truth about her grandparents' relationship through interviews with relatives, and develops along three lines, set in the 1940s, the 1970s, and the present. As reviewer Susanne Bardelson noted in the School Library Journal, "The author makes sense of the tangled ties among the generations and navigates them with humor and compassion." Along the way, she confronts racism, mental illness, and the realities of marriage, as well as the larger questions of nature versus nurture in the ways we develop and the curious interplay between our experiences and our attitudes.

Much of The Family Tree involves Rebecca's relationship with her manic-depressive mother, Doreen, a relationship that overshadows her own marriage to a scientist "whose questions about whether we're doomed to repeat our parents' mistakes are the book's subtle framework," according to *People* contributor Judith Newman. Similarly, *Entertainment Weekly* reviewer Jennifer Reese noted that "Cadwalladr raises a host of questions about the interaction of the generations (to what extent do the misadventures of our ancestors affect our own lives? Or is it all genetic?) but to her credit never forces answers." In addition, a *Publishers Weekly* reviewer felt that the author's "mastery of time and place, wry humor and sporadic bouts of self-doubt will endear her to readers."

BIOGRAPHICAL AND CRITICAL SOURCES:

PERIODICALS

Booklist, December 1, 2004, Misha Stone, review of *The Family Tree,* p. 634.
Boston Globe, February 3, 2005, Karen Campbell, "A Lot Is Buried under This 'Family Tree.'"
Entertainment Weekly, December 24, 2004, Jennifer Reese, review of *The Family Tree,* p. 72.
Guardian (London, England), March 6, 2005, Flora Hood, review of *The Family Tree.*
Kirkus Reviews, September 15, 2004, review of *The Family Tree,* p. 881.
Library Journal, October 1, 2004, Barbara Love, review of *The Family Tree,* p. 66.
New York Times, January 23, 2005, Patricia T. O'Conner, "Genealogy Is Destiny."
People, February 14, 2005, Judith Newman, review of *The Family Tree,* p. 59.
Publishers Weekly, November 8, 2004, review of *The Family Tree,* p. 33.
San Francisco Chronicle, January 9, 2005, Summer Block, "Fruit of Love Doesn't Fall Far from The Tree," p. E2.
School Library Journal, June, 2005, Susanne Bardelson, review of *The Family Tree,* p. 188.
Telegraph (London, England), June 3, 2005, Julia Flynn, review of *The Family Tree.*

ONLINE

BookBrowse, http://www.bookbrowse.com/ (September 15, 2005), interview with Carole Cadwalladr.

BookPage, http://www.bookpage.com/ (September 15, 2005), Emily Zibart, review of *The Family Tree.*
Carole Cadwalladr Home Page, http://www.cadwalladr.com (September 15, 2005).
New York Daily News Online, http://www.nydailynews.com/ (September 15, 2005), Sherryl Connelly, review of *The Family Tree.*
Powells.com, http://www.powells.com/ (September 15, 2005), autobiographical sketch.*

*   *   *

CALDWELL, Sally 1945-

PERSONAL: Born July 13, 1945, in Dallas, TX; daughter of Walter Jack (a musician) and Ola Elizabeth (a nurse; maiden name, Burris) Caldwell. *Ethnicity:* "White." *Education:* Southern Methodist University, B.A., 1966, M.A., 1968; University of North Texas, Ph.D., 1974.

ADDRESSES: Home—P.O. Box 2495, Wimberley, TX 78676. *Office*—Department of Sociology, Texas State University, San Marcos, TX 78666. *E-mail*—sc14@txstate.edu.

CAREER: Writer and educator. Texas State University, San Marcos, member of sociology faculty.

WRITINGS:

Statistics Unplugged, Wadsworth/Thomson Learning (Belmont, CA), 2004.

*   *   *

CAMMARATA, Joan F. 1950-

PERSONAL: Born December 22, 1950, in NY; daughter of John (a civil engineer) and Angelina (an executive secretary; maiden name, Guarnera) Cammarata; married Richard M. Montemarano (a regional manager), August 9, 1975. *Education:* Fordham University, B.A., 1972; Columbia University, M.A., 1974, M.Phil., 1977, Ph.D., 1982. *Hobbies and other interests:* Piano, gardening, cooking, needlework.

ADDRESSES: Home—New Rochelle, NY. *Office*—Manhattan College, Riverdale, NY 10471. *E-mail*—joan.cammarata@manhattan.edu.

CAREER: Writer and educator. Manhattan College, Riverdale, NY, adjunct assistant professor, 1982-84, assistant professor, 1984-90, associate professor, 1990-96, professor of Spanish literature and language, 1996—. Fordham University, adjunct instructor, 1980-81; Iona College, New Rochelle, NY, adjunct assistant professor, 1982-84; New York University, New York, NY, scholar-in-residence, 1991-92, 1997-98. *Modern Language Studies,* member of editorial board.

MEMBER: Asociación Internacional de Hispanistas, Modern Language Association of America, American Association of Teachers of Spanish and Portuguese, American Council on the Teaching of Foreign Languages, Association of Literary Scholars and Critics, Cervantes Society of America, Hispanic Institute, Renaissance Society of America, Northeast Modern Language Association (president, 1998-99), South Atlantic Modern Language Association, New York State Association of Foreign Language Teachers.

AWARDS, HONORS: Grants from National Endowment for the Humanities, Andrew W. Mellon Foundation, and Program for Cultural Cooperation between Spanish Ministry of Education and U.S. Universities.

WRITINGS:

Mythological Themes in the Works of Garcilaso de la Vega, Editorial Porrúa (Madrid, Spain), 1983.
(Editor) *Women in the Discourse of Early Modern Spain,* University Press of Florida (Gainesville, FL), 2003.

WORK IN PROGRESS: Letters from Teresa: The Cultural Politics of Feminine Epistolography in Sixteenth-Century Spain, a study of the letters of St. Teresa of Ávila; research on the appropriation and authenticity of feminine discourse in early modern Spain.

*   *   *

CAPOUYA, Emile 1925-2005

OBITUARY NOTICE— See index for *CA* sketch: Born 1925 in New York, NY; died October 13, 2005, in East Meredith, NY. Editor, publisher, and author. Capouya was a literary editor, as well as an educator and cofounder of New Amsterdam Books. Born in Manhattan and growing up in the Bronx, his first taste of working on literary magazines was at DeWitt Clinton High School, where he counted James Baldwin among his peers. With high school over, he joined the merchant marine during World War II. After the war, he found work as a stevedore in New York City, where he also attended Columbia University; he would later also attend Oxford University. Eventually, Capouya gained employment as an editor for New Directions, the publishing house where he helped publish the writings of such authors as Tennessee Williams, Ezra Pound, and James Joyce. In 1969, he joined the *Nation* staff as a literary editor; later, he also began contributing reviews and articles to such periodicals as the *Saturday Review* and the *New York Times.* In 1971, Capouya added teaching to his resume, becoming a faculty member for both the Bernard M. Baruch College of the City University of New York and at the Juilliard School. Other posts included working for the *New American Review* as an editor and at Hippocrene Books as editorial director. Leaving the *Nation* in 1981, Capouya went on to found New Amsterdam Books with his wife, Keitha, with whom he would edit the Petr Alekseevich book *The Essential Kropotkin* (1975). Capouya was also the author of *In the Sparrow Hills: Stories* (1993), which won the Sue Kaufman Prize from the American Academy and Institute of Arts and Letters, and the novella *The Rising of the Moon* (2003).

OBITUARIES AND OTHER SOURCES:

PERIODICALS

Los Angeles Times, November 9, 2005, p. B11.
New York Times, November 7, 2005, p. A23.
Washington Post, November 10, 2005, p. B6.

*   *   *

CARMON, Haggai 1944-

PERSONAL: Born November 5, 1944, in Tel Aviv, Israel; immigrated to U.S., 1985; son of Yehiel and Ida Carmon; married Rakeffet Avissara, March 7, 1978; children: Ittai, Dria, Irin, Yahel. *Education:* Tel Aviv University, B.A., 1969, LL.B., 1981; St. John's University, M.A., 1987.

ADDRESSES: Office—Carmon & Carmon, 767 3rd Ave., 24th Fl., New York, NY 10017. *E-mail*—haggai@carmonlaw.com.

CAREER: Carmon & Co., New York, NY, and Israel, partner, 1983—; Carmon & Carmon, New York, NY, partner. Advisor to Israeli Prime Minister Shimon Peres, 1981-84; U.S. Department of Justice, Washington, DC, representative in Israeli litigation, 1985—; adviser to federal agencies on asset recovery and intelligence gathering outside United States; legal counsel to U.S. Embassy in Tel Aviv. *Military service:* Israeli Air Force, served three years.

MEMBER: Israel-American Chamber of Commerce and Industry (vice president; member of board of directors, 1979-85), American Bar Association, Association of Trial Lawyers of America, New York State Bar Association.

AWARDS, HONORS: Honorary chief delegate to United States, Israeli Labor Party, 1985-87.

WRITINGS:

Zehut Meshuleshet, Yedi'ot Aharonot (Tel Aviv, Israel), 2003, published as *Triple Identity* (novel), Steerforth Press (Hanover, NH), 2005.

Contributor to professional journals.

SIDELIGHTS: As an attorney who works closely with both the U.S. government and the government of Israel on complex legal disputes, Haggai Carmon is no stranger to international intrigue. Nor to danger; he was brutally stabbed and almost killed outside a European bank while on a secret mission, and that incident became the inspiration for his first novel, *Triple Identity.* Like Carmon, protagonist Dan Gordon undertakes assignments to retrieve stolen assets for federal government agencies. On one such assignment, he is sent to track down Raymond DeLouise, suspected of stealing ninety million dollars, DeLouise also turns out to be Dov Peled and Bruno Popescu, each with a different nationality. When DeLouise is found dead, Gordon is forced to unravel his "triple identity," a search that soon puts him on the trail of a possible Iranian plot to acquire nuclear weapons. The result is an espionage story with the added twist that the protagonist may be mistaken about Iran's intentions. For a *Kirkus Reviews* contributor, the storytelling is marred by "Dan's compulsion to tiresome exposition, often by interjecting bromides from his Mossad trainers into potentially suspenseful scenes." A *Publishers Weekly* reviewer also found "occasionally stiff or silly writing," but commended the author's "ear for high-level intelligence deception."

BIOGRAPHICAL AND CRITICAL SOURCES:

PERIODICALS

Kirkus Reviews, May 1, 2005, review of *Triple Identity,* p. 491.
Publishers Weekly, May 30, 2005, review of *Triple Identity,* p. 36.

ONLINE

Jewish.com, http://jewish.com/ (July 19, 2005), Alana B. Elias Kornfeld, "Attorney Puts Experience to Work in Writing Thriller about Israeli Agent."
Triple Identity Web site, http://www.tripleidentity.com/ (September 12, 2005).*

*   *   *

CARROLL, Sean B. 1961(?)-

PERSONAL: Born c. 1961. *Education:* Tufts University School of Medicine, Ph.D., 1983; postdoctoral research at University of Colorado, Boulder.

ADDRESSES: Office—Laboratory of Genetics, University of Wisconsin, Madison, 425-G Henry Mall, Madison, WI 53706.

CAREER: University of Wisconsin—Madison, professor of molecular biology, genetics, and medical genetics; Howard Hughes Medical Institute, Chevy Chase, MD, investigator.

WRITINGS:

(With Jennifer K. Grenier and Scott D. Weatherbee) *From DNA to Diversity: Molecular Genetics and the Evolution of Animal Design,* Blackwell Science (Malden, MA), 2001, 2nd edition, 2005.

Endless Forms Most Beautiful: The New Science of Evo Devo and the Making of the Animal Kingdom, Norton (New York, NY), 2005.

Contributor to scientific journals.

SIDELIGHTS: Sean B. Carroll is a leader in the use of DNA evidence to deepen the understanding of evolution, which has traditionally relied on fossil and other morphological evidence. This new science of evolutionary developmental biology, dubbed "Evo Devo," is "concerned with the making and evolution of form," as Carroll explained to Andrew Albanese in an interview for the *Library Journal.* "There is an intimate connection between development, the process of making a complex creature beginning with a simple egg, and evolution. All changes in form are due to changes in development."

In *Endless Forms Most Beautiful: The New Science of Evo Devo and the Making of the Animal Kingdom,* "Carroll combines clear writing with the deep knowledge gained from a lifetime of genetics research,"as a *Publishers Weekly* reviewer put it, to give the general reader a basic understanding of this science and its goals. Among the revelations are the discovery of "Hox genes" that determine the shape of an animal from head to toe and apparently occur in every vertebrate. Carroll describes the complicated method of switches that allow certain genes to develop everything from legs and arms to wings and flippers. "Admittedly, taking in all the details of these discoveries in the early chapters can be heavy going," noted a *Kirkus Reviews* contributor, "but if the reader persists, there are delights to come." These include explanations of the eyespots on butterfly wings, the unique stripe patterns of zebras, and why some people grow red hair. Carroll continues to push the frontiers of Evo Devo, exploring such large questions as the constant recurrence of certain forms in widely varied species and the truly mysterious origins of new behaviors within the animal kingdom, such as the beginning of bird songs and the creation of long-term parental care of the young.

BIOGRAPHICAL AND CRITICAL SOURCES:

PERIODICALS

Capital Times (Madison, WI), April 21, 2005, P.J. Slinger, "UW Prof Tells How Genes Work."

Kirkus Reviews, February 1, 2005, review of *Endless Forms Most Beautiful: The New Science of Evo Devo and the Making of the Animal Kingdom,* p. 159.
Library Journal, March 1, 2005, Walter L. Cressler, review of *Endless Forms Most Beautiful,* p. 105, and Andrew Albanese, "Q&A: Sean B. Carroll," p. 107.
Publishers Weekly, February 28, 2005, review of *Endless Forms Most Beautiful,* p. 55.
Science, June 22, 2001, Gregory A. Wray, review of *From DNA to Diversity: Molecular Genetics and the Evolution of Animal Design,* p. 2256.
Science News, July 9, 2005, review of *Endless Forms Most Beautiful,* p. 31.
Scientist, May 19, 2003, "Sean B. Carroll" (interview), p. 11.

ONLINE

Howard Hughes Medical Institute Web site, http://www.hhmi.org/ (September 12, 2005), profile of Sean B. Carroll.
University of Wisconsin—Madison, Department of Genetics Web site, http://www.genetics.wisc.edu/ (September 12, 2005), profile of Sean B. Carroll.*

*   *   *

CASEY, Karen

PERSONAL: Married; husband's name Joe. *Education:* University of Minnesota—Twin Cities, Ph.D.

ADDRESSES: *Home*—Minneapolis, MN; and Naples, FL. *Agent*—c/o Author Mail, Conari Press, P.O. Box 612, York Beach, ME 03910-0612. *E-mail*—karen@womens-spirituality.com.

CAREER: Taught at University of Minnesota—Twin Cities, Minneapolis, MN; author of self-help books.

WRITINGS:

Each Day a New Beginning, Hazelden Press (Center City, MN), 1982.

(With Martha Vanceburg) *The Promise of a New Day,* Hazelden Press (Center City, MN), 1983, published as *The Promise of a New Day: A Book of Daily Meditations,* HarperSanFrancisco (San Francisco, CA), 1996.

The Love Book, illustrations by David Spohn, Hazelden Press (Center City, MN), 1985.

(Compiler) *If Only I Could Quit: Becoming a Nonsmoker,* Harper/Hazelden (New York, NY), 1987, published as *If Only I Could Quit: Recovering from Nicotine Addiction,* Hazelden (New York, NY), 1996.

A Woman's Spirit, HarperSanFrancisco (San Francisco, CA), 1994.

Daily Meditations for Practicing the Course, Hazelden Press (Center City, MN), 1995.

A Life of My Own: Meditations on Hope and Acceptance, Hazelden Press (Center City, MN), 1995.

In God's Care: Daily Meditations on Spirituality in Recovery, Hazelden Press (Center City, MN), 1996.

Keepers of the Wisdom: Reflections from Lives Lived Well, Hazelden Press (Center City, MN), 1996.

Girls Only!: Daily Thoughts for Young Girls, Holy Cow! Press (Duluth, MN), 1999.

Girl to Girl: Finding Our Voices, Hazelden Information and Educational Services (Center City, MN), 2000.

The Miracle of Sponsorship: Recovery Stories of Hope and Renewal, Hazelden Information and Educational Services (Center City, MN), 2000.

Each Day a New Beginning: A Meditation Book and Journal for Daily Reflection, Hazelden Press (Center City, MN), 2001.

Timeless Wisdom: A Collection of Karen Casey's Best Meditations, Hazelden Information and Educational Services (Center City, MN), 2001.

Fearless Relationships: Simple Rules for Lifelong Contentment, Hazelden Press (Center City, MN), 2003.

The Little Red Book for Women, Hazelden Press (Center City, MN), 2004.

Change Your Mind and Your Life Will Follow: Twelve Simple Principles, Conari Press (York Beach, ME), 2005.

SIDELIGHTS: The author of numerous bestselling self-help books, Karen Casey has written inspirational guides drawing on the twelve steps of recovery programs and the principles of the Course on Miracles.

A number of her books are addressed primarily to female audiences, including her first book, *Each Day a New Beginning,* which is directed at women in recovery. In *Girls Only!: Daily Thoughts for Young Girls* "Casey called upon memories of her own painful childhood as an aid in constructing a year's worth of meditations for girls," in the words of *School Library Journal* contributor Cindy Darling Codell. Casey deals with issues large and small, from coping with a bad-hair day to surviving dysfunctional families and searching for God. She also provides numerous quotations from women who overcame hardship to find their way in the world. Similarly, *Girl to Girl: Finding Our Voices* provides inspirational quotes in a daily-meditation format, but also adds short tales about girls who overcame hardship to achieve their goals.

Other books by Casey are aimed at a wider audience. Titles such as *The Promise of a New Day, Keepers of the Wisdom: Reflections from Lives Lived Well,* and *Fearless Relationships: Simple Rules for Lifelong Contentment* provide advice and meditation exercises for anyone seeking a deeper spirituality or a more meaningful existence. *Change Your Mind and Your Life Will Follow: Twelve Simple Principles* expounds on one of the primary principles of Alcoholics Anonymous: "Let Go and Let God." "Casey firmly believes that the work of someone's life belongs only to that person and to God, and that we should thus each tend only our own garden," explained a *Publishers Weekly* reviewer. For Casey, spirituality is individual and personal, and thus nonjudgmental. Rather than look outward to condemn others and find rules and regulations for life, one should calm one's own ego, learn from personal experiences, and "make friends" with your own emotions, even anger and fear, in order to find your own path. *Library Journal* contributor Deborah Bigelow commends the book as being "easy to digest" and appealing to "someone needing a psychological boost."

As in *Change Your Mind and Your Life Will Follow,* much of Casey's writing draws on her own faith and her experiences in drawing on a higher power to overcome addictions. The principles of Alcoholics Anonymous animate many of her meditations, but there is no attempt to impose a particular program or a particular interpretation of God on her readers. Instead, Casey seeks to inspire both those in recovery and the general reader with a hopeful outlook that embraces the possibility of achieving inward peace and a positive self-image. *Each Day a New Beginning* has sold over three million copies, and millions of readers continue to draw inspiration from her subsequent books and her frequent public appearances.

BIOGRAPHICAL AND CRITICAL SOURCES:

PERIODICALS

Library Journal, May 15, 2005, Deborah Bigelow, review of *Change Your Mind and Your Life Will Follow: Twelve Simple Principles,* p. 134.

Publishers Weekly, March 21, 2005, review of *Change Your Mind and Your Life Will Follow,* p. 46.

School Library Journal, March, 2000, Cindy Darling Codell, review of *Girls Only!: Daily Thoughts for Young Girls,* p. 249.

ONLINE

Women's Spirituality Web site, http://www.womens-spirituality.com/ (September 15, 2005), profile of Karen Casey.

*   *   *

CHADWICK, Paul 1957-

PERSONAL: Born September 3, 1957, in Seattle, WA; son of Stephen F., Jr. (an attorney) and Diane (Halsey) Chadwick; married Elizabeth Moon (a painter), September 14, 1985; child: Stephen. *Education:* Art Center College of Design, B.F.A., 1979.

ADDRESSES: Home—Seattle, WA. *Office*—c/o Dark Horse Comics, 10956 SE Main St., Milwaukie, OR 97222.

CAREER: Author of graphic novels, 1985—; creator of *Concrete,* 1986—. Storyboard artist at Walt Disney Studios, Paramount, Metro-Goldwyn-Mayer, and others, 1979-85; freelance artist at Marvel Comics, DC Comics, and others; painted covers at DAW Books, Del Ray, Tor, and *Magazine of Fantasy and Science Fiction,* 1980-89.

AWARDS, HONORS: Harvey Award for Best Cartoonist, 1988, 1989, and for Best New Series, 1988, all for *Concrete;* Eisner Award for Best New Series, 1988, for Best Writer/Artist, 1989, for Best Continuing series, 1988, 1989, and for Best Black-and-White series, 1988, 1989, all for *Concrete;* Harvey Award for Best Single Issue, 1991, for *Concrete Celebrates Earth Day;* Harvey Award for Best Finite Series, 1992, for *Concrete: Fragile Creature;* Inkpot Award for Outstanding Achievement in Comic Arts, 1994.

WRITINGS:

COMIC BOOKS AND GRAPHIC NOVELS

(Self-illustrated) *Concrete: Complete Short Stories 1986-1989,* Dark Horse Comics (Milwaukie, OR), 1990.

(Self-illustrated) *The Complete Concrete* (contains *Concrete* issues 1-10), Dark Horse Comics (Milwaukie, OR), 1994.

(Self-illustrated) *Concrete: Fragile Creature* (contains *Fragile Creature* issues 1-4), Dark Horse Comics (Milwaukie, OR), 1994.

(Self-illustrated) *Concrete: Killer Smile* (contains *Killer Smile* issues 1-4), Dark Horse Comics (Milwaukie, OR), 1995.

(Self-illustrated) *Concrete: Short Stories 1990-1995,* Dark Horse Comics (Milwaukie, OR), 1996.

(Self-illustrated) *Concrete: Think like a Mountain* (contains *Think Like a Mountain* issues 1-7), Dark Horse Comics (Milwaukie, OR), 1997.

(Self-illustrated) *Strange Armor: The Origin of Concrete* (contains *Strange Armor* issues 1-5), Dark Horse Comics (Milwaukie, OR), 1998.

(Self-illustrated) *The World Below* (four issues), Dark Horse Comics (Milwaukie, OR), 1999.

(Self-illustrated) *The World Below II* (four issues), Dark Horse Comics (Milwaukie, OR), 2000.

Contributor to comic-book series and graphic novels, including *Dark Horse Maverick 2000,* Dark Horse Comics, 2000, *Grendel: Black, White, and Red,* Dark Horse Comics, 2000, *9-11: Artists Respond,* Volume 1, Dark Horse Comics, 2002, and to several issues of *Star Wars.*

SIDELIGHTS: Paul Chadwick has won a devoted fan following with his stories about Concrete, an environmentally conscious hero in a body of stone. Chadwick has won several awards for the comic-book series, which features "superb storytelling and artwork," according to *Washington Times* contributor Joseph Szadkowski, the critic further calling it "a sequential art legend." Chadwick is the creator of another comic-book series, *The World Below,* about an underground community of aliens interacting with explorers from the surface world, and he has also contributed to other comics and anthologies.

The eponymous protagonist of *Concrete* starts out as an ordinary human named Ron Lithgow, a speech-writer for a U.S. senator. Then beings from another planet kidnap him and place his brain inside a giant stone body. "Concrete bears little resemblance to a human, except in his eyes, which Mr. Chadwick fills with great emotion and movement," Szadkowski observed. Because of his situation, Concrete faces many challenges; "A lot of the stories are about coping with that condition in a world of ordinary people," Chadwick told Roger A. Ash, in an interview for the Westfield Comics Web site. Among other things, as Chadwick told Michael Gilman in an interview for the Dark Horse Comics Web site, "he's got an existential dilemma: how to make something of his life . . . how to make it worthwhile." Something Concrete frequently finds worthwhile is battling despoilers of the natural environment.

In the *Think like a Mountain* story arc, for instance, Concrete becomes involved with activists from the radical environmental group Earth First! The members of Earth First! are known for sometimes destroying property and otherwise breaking the law in the name of preserving nature. When they try to enlist Concrete's aid in keeping loggers out of an old-growth forest in the Pacific Northwest, he is wary at first, but they are persuasive, and his support for them grows. "I'm sympathetic to Earth First!, at the same time being uncomfortable with what they do," Chadwick told Ash. "Putting Concrete in this position is a way of sorting out my own feelings about it." Concrete's environmentalism is not the only aspect of the character that reflects his creator. The series is "autobiographical, at least emotionally," Chadwick told Szadkowski, adding that as a shy teenager, he pictured himself "encased in stone."

While Chadwick has frequently said he considers *Concrete* his life's work, he also has felt the need to branch out. The comic-book series *The World Below* is one of the things that has grown out of that need. The concept of the series is that a wealthy entrepreneur has bank-rolled an underground exploratory mission; he had made a lot of money from patenting the technology of an unusual aircraft found in a sinkhole, and now he wants the explorers to find out what else is down there. "What they don't know," Chadwick told Shawna Ervin-Gore in a interview for the Dark Horse Comics Web site, "is that this was a colony for sunlight-shunning aliens who, over the centuries, imported creatures and robots from across the galaxy. Something awful happened; order collapsed; chaos reigns in *The World Below.* The poor saps haven't a clue what they're getting into!"

"Chadwick, known for his contemplative 'Concrete,' is showing his adventurous side in 'The World Below,'" commented reviewer Bill Radford in the Colorado Springs *Gazette* when the first issue came out. However, *The World Below* did not prove as popular with readers as *Concrete.* After ending the series, Chadwick began doing *Concrete* stories for anthologies, and also considered the possibility of a *Concrete* feature film, with Chadwick doing the screenplay. Film is a medium familiar to him; he worked as an art director and storyboard artist on motion pictures such as *The Big Easy, Pee-wee's Big Adventure,* and *The Philadelphia Experiment.* "I've got to keep my eye on my long-term commitment to *Concrete,*" he told Radford. "Because the small but dedicated following that I've got is a treasure."

BIOGRAPHICAL AND CRITICAL SOURCES:

PERIODICALS

Gazette (Colorado Springs, CO), March 25, 1999, "New Comic Explores 'The World Below'"; April 7, 2000, Bill Radford, "Comic Strip Creator Turns Attention Back to *Concrete.*"
Washington Times, February 17, 1996, Joseph Szadkowski, "Environmental Lessons," p. E4; March 23, 1996, Szadkowski, "Paving Concrete Career," p. B4.

ONLINE

Dark Horse Comics Web site, http://www.darkhorse. com/ (December 1, 1995), Michael Gilman, interview with Paul Chadwick; (December 30, 2003) Shawna Ervin-Gore, interview with Paul Chadwick.

Westfield Comics Web site, http://westfieldcompany. com/ (December 15, 1995), Roger A. Ash, interview with Paul Chadwick.*

*   *   *

CHAN, Cassandra
(Cassandra M. Chan)

PERSONAL: Female.

ADDRESSES: Home—Port St. Lucie, FL. *Agent*— Jennifer Jackson, Donald Maas Literary Agency, 160 W. 95th St., Ste. 1B. New York, NY 10025. *E-mail*— chan@worldnet.att.net.

CAREER: Mystery writer.

WRITINGS:

The Young Widow (mystery), St. Martin's Minotaur (New York, NY), 2005.

Work appears in anthologies, including *Murder Most Cozy,* Signet (New York, NY). Contributor of short stories to mystery publications, including *Alfred Hitchcock's Mystery Magazine.*

WORK IN PROGRESS: A second Bethancourt/Gibbons novel.

SIDELIGHTS: Mystery writer Cassandra Chan perfected her protagonists, independently wealthy English detective Phillip Bethancourt and Scotland Yard Detective Inspector Jack Gibbons, over the course of seventeen years of short stories published in mystery magazines. In the style of cozy British mysteries, her debut novel *The Young Widow* presents her sleuthing duo to a wider audience. Here Gibbons is assigned the poisoning case of wealthy Geoffrey Berowne, and Bethancourt, his friend from university days, helps him out. Suspicion initially falls on the victim's young widow, Annette, whose earlier husbands, also older than she, met similar ends. Gibbons becomes romantically involved with Annette and Bethancourt attempts to keep the investigation on course in this "sprightly

debut," as a *Publishers Weekly* contributor described the book. A critic for *Kirkus Reviews* noted: "Chan's debut keeps you guessing until the end." Higher praise came from *Library Journal* contributor Rex E. Klett, who called the novel a "fascinating police procedural in the finest tradition," and from *Best Reviews* contributor, Harriet Klausner, who also found it "a fine English police procedural."

BIOGRAPHICAL AND CRITICAL SOURCES:

PERIODICALS

Kirkus Reviews, March 1, 2005, review of *The Young Widow,* p. 261.
Library Journal, June 1, 2005, Rex E. Klett, review of *The Young Widow,* p. 104.
Publishers Weekly, June 20, 2005, review of *The Young Widow,* p. 60.

ONLINE

Best Reviews, http://www.bestreviews.com/ (September 11, 2005), Harriet Klausner, review of *The Young Widow.*
Cassandra Chan Home Page, http://home.att.net/~c. chan (September 11, 2005).*

*   *   *

CHAN, Cassandra M.
See CHAN, Cassandra

*   *   *

CHAYKIN, Howard 1950-
(Howard Victor Chaykin)

PERSONAL: Born October 7, 1950, in Newark, NJ; son of Leon and Rosalind (Pave) Chaykin.

ADDRESSES: Agent—c/o Author Mail, DC Comics, 1700 Broadway, New York, NY 10019.

CAREER: Writer, illustrator, and graphic artist.

WRITINGS:

The Scorpion, Atlas Comics (New York, NY), 1975.

(Illustrator) Samuel R. Delany, *Empire: A Visual Novel,* Berkley Publishing (New York, NY), 1978.

Cody Starbuck, Star*Reach (Berkeley, CA), 1978.

(With Michael Moorcock) *The Swords of Heaven, the Flowers of Hell,* HM Communications (New York, NY), 1979.

(With Alfred Bestor) *The Stars My Destination,* Byron Preiss Publications, 1979.

Chaos, First Comics (Evanston, IL), 1983.

(Writer and illustrator) *Howard Chaykin's American Flagg!: Hard Times,* First Comics (Chicago, IL), 1985.

American Flagg!: Special, First Comics (Chicago, IL), 1986.

Time2 and Time2: The Satisfaction of Black Mariah, First Comics (Chicago, IL), 1986.

(With Denny O'Neill) *Ironwolf,* DC Comics (New York, NY), 1986.

The Shadow: Blood and Judgement, DC Comics (New York, NY), 1987.

Black Hawk, DC Comics (New York, NY), 1987.

(Writer and illustrator) *American Flagg: Southern Comfort,* Graphitti Designs (Anaheim, CA), 1987.

Black Kiss, Vortex Comics (Toronto, Ontario, Canada), 1988–89.

(Writer and illustrator) *Howard Chaykin's American Flagg: State of the Union,* Graphitti Designs (Anaheim, CA), 1989.

(Illustrator) Archie Goodwin, *Marvel Comics Presents Wolverine, Nick Fury: The Scorpio Connection,* Marvel Comics (New York, NY), 1990.

Blood and Justice, DC Comics (New York, NY), 1991.

(Illustrator) Byron Preiss, *Alfred Bester's The Stars My Destination: The Graphic Story Adaptation,* Epic Comics (New York, NY), 1992.

(With John Francis Moore) *Ironwolf: Fires of the Revolution,* DC Comics (New York, NY), 1993.

(With John Francis Moore and Mark Chiarello) *Batman and Houdini: The Devil's Workshop,* DC Comics (New York, NY), 1993.

(Writer and illustrator) *Batman: Dark Allegiances,* DC Comics (New York, NY), 1996.

(Illustrator) Roy L. Thomas, *Classic Star Wars: A New Hope,* Dark Horse Comics (Milwaukie, OR), 1996.

Batman: Thrillkiller, illustrated by Dan Brereton, DC Comics (New York, NY), 1998.

(With Gil Kane, Kevin Nowland, and Matt Hollingsworth) *Superman: Distant Fires,* DC Comics (New York, NY), 1998.

(With David Tischman) *Son of Superman,* illustrated by J.H. Williams and Mick Gray, III, DC Comics (New York, NY), 1999.

American Century: Scars and Stripes, illustrated by Marc Laming and John Stokes, DC Comics (New York, NY), 2001.

(With David Tischman) *American Century: Hollywood Babylon,* illustrated by Marc Laming and John Stokes, DC Comics (New York, NY), 2002.

(With David Tischman) *American Century: White Lightning,* illustrated by Marc Laming and John Stokes, DC Comics (New York, NY), 2003.

(With David Tischman and Niko Henrichon) *Barnum: In Secret Service to the U.S.A.,* DC Comics (New York, NY), 2003.

Mighty Love, DC Comics (New York, NY), 2004.

Creator of comic-book series, including *Time2, American Flagg!,* and *American Century;* writer and/or illustrator of ongoing series, including *War of the Worlds, Sword of Sorcery, Cody Starbuck, Iron Wolf, Star Wars, The Scorpion, Heavy Metal, Spider-Man, Batman, The Shadow Black Hawk, Black Kiss, Power and Glory,* and *Angel and the Ape.* Writer for television series, including *The Flash, The Viper, Earth: Final Conflict,* and *Mutant X.*

ADAPTATIONS: *Heavy Metal* was adapted as an animated film, Columbia TriStar, 1981.

SIDELIGHTS: Howard Chaykin's long career as a writer and graphic artist began in the early 1970s with his illustrations for *War of the Worlds* for Marvel Comics and *Sword of Sorcery* for DC Comics. Over the years, he has freelanced for numerous comic-book publishers and has worked on some of the most popular series, as well as creating several of his own.

In the early 1980s, Chaykin took a two-year hiatus and came back with *American Flagg!,* the series for which he is perhaps most well known. John Painz, who interviewed Chaykin for *Comics2Film* online, said that the two years "seemed to stew for Chaykin, who created one of the greatest comic heroes in . . . a long time." Painz wrote that *American Flagg!* "was obviously a springboard for Chaykin, to experiment, push the boarders, and create fine work. This formula has worked well for many other artists . . . but it seems that Chaykin pioneered the idea of change in comics, creating strange and new panel concepts, creating a multitude of different uses for type as not only type but as an important design element."

The story is set during the World War II era and features Reuben Flagg, a patriot on the order of the old Western lawman, but one who revels in the junk of American culture, including porn films and comic books. The story also features a plethora of long-legged females sporting garter belts and sexy hosiery as they go about flying jets and toting automatic weapons.

In an *Atlantic Monthly* article titled "Comic Books for Grownups," Lloyd Rose commented on "the brutal, porny, stylish worlds" of *American Flagg!* and *The Shadow.* Rose wrote that Chaykin "seems to have taken his inspiration from between-the-wars American illustrators like James Montgomery Flagg and J.C. Leydendecker. This nostalgic style gives the books their visual charm, but they're fair from quaint. The style is matched to a hectic, razzle-dazzle sense of movement—the images rush and tumble past you, the sound effects screech across the page." Rose noted that Chaykin's fictional future tends to be an exaggeration of contemporary society, with its more violent cities, more vicious politics, and ever-widening gap between rich and poor. Painz called Chaykin's writing "smart, funny, sexy, downright dirty in some points, and violent. Reading the *American Flagg!* series now . . . it's obvious where a lot of writers got their inspiration. *American Flagg!* is a beautiful science fiction epic."

In an article for *Extrapolation,* Tim Blackmore commented that "Chaykin's graphic language (and panache) grew more sophisticated as he worked on [*American*] *Flagg!* Early in the run he had used 'playing card' heads . . . to frame his page. . . . The later [*American*] *Flagg!* tetralogies . . . hinted at something even more striking. Panels which had been organized according to complex grid systems now started to move, dropping a half unit on the page, overlapping each other in an organic way. As Chaykin began to push even harder, he discovered ways of pulling the reader into the page by using his overlapping panels to zoom in on various characters. As the motion on the page became more fluid, readers became accustomed to lightning cross-cutting." Blackmore noted Chaykin's development of a page consisting of

four panels held together by a small square in the center and said that such pages "work on a minimum of four levels. They introduce the subject, context, plot, and subplot, and often include symbolic action proleptic of the story. As these page designs matured and the artist became comfortable with such panel manipulation, striking mixtures of video and audio began to emerge. It almost became possible for the reader to 'hear' the page."

In a *New Statesman & Society* article, Roz Kaveney commented on Chaykin's contributions to the *Black Hawk* comic-book series featuring a chubby fighter pilot who travels with an equally plump female Soviet agent in a digital, post-economic-crash world. Kaveney called Chaykin a "mad-dog talent," but added that he has "a real vigour and a commitment to nonlinear narrative and innovative use of the comic's grid that compels respect."

Son of Superman, which Chaykin wrote with David Tischman, is a projection of what Jon Kent, the son of superhero Clark Kent and Lois Lane, would be like. They have also created a futuristic version of the Justice League, now a joint venture between government and big business, and the even-more-evil Lex Luther. Wonder Woman and Aquaman are ambassadors, and Batman is identified with Wayne Industries. Luther owns the largest company in the world.

In the authors' story arc, Superman has been missing for seventeen years, and Lois is writing and living in Hollywood with Jon, who becomes enmeshed in the plans of Lana Lang and husband Pete Wilson to take down the U.S. government, as he learns more of the whereabouts of his father. Michael Vance reviewed the book for *Comic Box* online and gave "very high marks" to Chaykin and Tischman and said that Superman's son "is as believable as a teenage kid looking to score a date, and as a fledgling superhero seeking to fill his father's boots."

The book was reviewed for *Mad Review* online by The Dean, who wrote that Chaykin "plots this all masterfully, without much of his trademark social sarcasm and the formula fits here. With an assist from David Tischman, they craft a story that is not dark, grim, or gritty. Rather, *Son of Superman* is uplifting and hopeful, for once a bright future rather than a apocalyptic one."

Chaykin writes but does not draw *American Century,* called "adult-but-mainstream comics fare, boasting rough language, brutal violence, and blatant sex," by *Booklist* critic Gordon Flagg. World War II veteran Harry Block is recalled to serve in Korea, but his patriotism has ebbed. After faking his death and stealing some money, he heads to Guatemala to live the life of an expatriate. Jeff Jensen wrote in *Entertainment Weekly* that the story is "steeped in his [Chaykin's] rich blend of ribald dialogue, epic narrative, and political intrigue."

A *Publishers Weekly* contributor reviewed *Barnum!: In Secret Service to the U.S.A.,* saying that it "will delight enthusiasts of the circus, comics, or American history." Circus founder P.T. Barnum saves the life of President Grover Cleveland and then becomes an undercover intelligence agent, traveling with the circus and its performers across the country as they gather information on the evil Nikola Tesla. The reviewer noted that although circus people are often portrayed as undesirables, in this story, they are able to "use their skills of deception and illusion." Included are characters representing actual performers in the early sideshows of the Barnum circus.

Chaykin has also written for television series, including *Mutant X,* which is about people who have gained extraordinary powers because, without their knowledge, they were used as test subjects in a government experiment conducted by the Genetic Security Agency. Mutant X is the name of a small group of these people that is headed by the former chief of Genomax, played by Adam Kane, who did not know his work was being used for this dastardly purpose. Adam has become a multimillionaire as a result of his early investment in the internet and he is now using his fortune to build and operate a mountain fortress called Sanctuary.

Other characters include Shalimar Fox (Victoria Pratt), a beautiful young woman with superhuman strength and speed; computer whiz Jesse Kilmartin (Forbes March), who finds a family in the group and who can alter the density of his body; Brennan Mulwray (Victor Webster), whose body has unusual electrical abilities; and Lexa Pierce (Karen Cliche), who has a past in intelligence work.

Resa Nelson, in *SciFi.com* interviewed Chaykin, asking him how *Mutant* is different from other television series with a comic-book premise. Chaykin replied that "first and foremost, I believe, in contemporary adventure, the characters that Arnold Schwarzenegger plays, the characters that Bruce Willis plays, are superheroes. They are transcendentally superhuman. In my world, *Mutant* is in the grand tradition of all great ensemble shows in televison from *Mission: Impossible* to *The A Team,* with the added lagniappe of an enhanced genetic ability."

Nelson asked Chaykin how creating comics differs from creating for television. He said that comics "is material for audiences with a catalog of preconceived notions. The language is encoded with certain ideas and expectations. When you confound and contradict those expectations, you either succeed beyond your own wildest expectations or you fail so miserably that your audience is confused. Television, because it's a mass-market medium, is a much flatter audience. The audience doesn't bring the same sort of expectations to the material as a comic-book audience would."

BIOGRAPHICAL AND CRITICAL SOURCES:

BOOKS

Clute, John, and Peer Nicholls, editors, *Encyclopedia of Science Fiction,* St. Martin's Press (New York, NY), 1993, p. 209.

PERIODICALS

Atlantic Monthly, August, 1986, Lloyd Rose, "Comic Books for Grown-Ups," p. 77.
Booklist, October 15, 2001, Gordon Flagg, review of *American Century: Scars and Stripes,* p. 367.
Entertainment Weekly, March 30, 2001, Jeff Jensen, review of *American Century,* p. 64.
Extrapolation, summer, 1990, Tim Blackmore, "The Bester/Chaykin Connection: An Examination of Substance Assisted by Style," pp. 101-124.
New Statesman & Society, December 18, 1987, Roz Kaveney, review of *Black Hawk,* p. 42.
Publishers Weekly, November 3, 2003, review of *Barnum: In Secret Service to the U.S.A.,* p. 56.

ONLINE

Comic Box, http://www.thecomicbox.com/ (December 17, 2003), Michael Vance, review of *Son of Superman.*

Comics2Film, http://www.comics2film.com/ (December 17, 2003), John Painz, interview with Chaykin.

Mad Review, http://madreview.com/ (December 17, 2003), The Dean, review of *Son of Superman.*

SciFi.com, http://www.scifi.com/ (December 17, 2003), Resa Nelson, interview with Chaykin.*

* * *

CHAYKIN, Howard Victor
See CHAYKIN, Howard

* * *

CHEEK, Gene 1951-

PERSONAL: Born March 2, 1951, in Winston-Salem, NC; son of Jesse and Sallie Cheek; married (divorced); children: three daughters.

ADDRESSES: Home and office—Lakey Gap Acres, Black Mountain, NC 28711. *E-mail*—Gene3251@ buncombe.main.nc.us.

CAREER: Worked as a house painter. *Military service:* Served in U.S. Navy.

WRITINGS:

The Color of Love: A Mother's Choice in the Jim Crow South (memoir), Lyons Press (Guilford, CT), 2005.

SIDELIGHTS: Gene Cheek was born in North Carolina, and his *The Color of Love: A Mother's Choice in the Jim Crow South* is a telling documentation of not only his own childhood but also of the atmosphere of the segregated South. As an adult, Cheek served in the U.S. Navy and worked in California and Washington; it was after his return to North Carolina that he began to write his memoir.

Cheek was the son of Jesse, a brutal alcoholic, and Sallie, his hard-working and loving mother. Although she tried to keep the family intact, Sallie separated from her husband and then fell in love with Cornelius Tucker, a kind, black coworker, and became pregnant by him. Sallie was still married to Jesse, who had since completely abandoned his family, and he brought charges against her because of her interracial relationship. Sallie's lawyer failed to appear in court, and the testimony overwhelmingly accused her of being a bad mother. Her punishment was to be the loss of one of her children. Cheek, at twelve, volunteered to be placed in the custody of the state rather than have his mother give up the new baby, his half-brother, so he spent his high school years in a home for boys.

Cheek wrote his memoir as vengeance for the mistreatment of his mother, the cruelty of his father and family, and the years he spent in the foster-care system. In doing so, he eventually came to understand and forgive the actions of the past. *Library Journal* reviewer Janet Ingraham Dwyer called *The Color of Love* "an honest look at the lasting pain caused by injustice," while a *Publishers Weekly* contributor deemed it "a mesmerizing yarn."

BIOGRAPHICAL AND CRITICAL SOURCES:

BOOKS

Cheek, Gene, *The Color of Love: A Mother's Choice in the Jim Crow South,* Lyons Press (Guilford, CT), 2005.

PERIODICALS

Kirkus Reviews, February 1, 2005, review of *The Color of Love,* p. 160.
Library Journal, February 15, 2005, Janet Ingraham Dwyer, review of *The Color of Love,* p. 138.
Publishers Weekly, March 21, 2005, review of *The Color of Love,* p. 45.

ONLINE

Curled up with a Good Book, http://www.curledup. com/ (October 4, 2005), review of *The Color of Love.*
Gene Cheek Home Page, http://www.genecheek.com (October 4, 2005).

Smoky Mountain News Online, http://www.smoky mountainnews.com/ (May 18, 2005), Jeff Minick, review of *The Color of Love.**

*   *   *

CHEYETTE, Fredric L. 1932-

PERSONAL: Born January 13, 1932, in New York, NY; son of Irving Cheyette (a professor); married Susan Ross Huston (deceased); children: Oren, Dina, Tamara. *Education:* Princeton University, B.A., 1953; Harvard University, Ph.D., 1959.

ADDRESSES: Office—Department of History, Amherst College, Amherst, MA 01002. *E-mail*—flcheyette@ amherst.edu.

CAREER: Writer and educator. Amherst College, Amherst, MA, professor of history, 1963—.

AWARDS, HONORS: David Pinkney Award, Society for French Historical Studies, 2001, Kayden National Book Award, University of Colorado, 2001, and Ralph Waldo Emerson Prize, Phi Beta Kappa, 2002, all for *Ermengard of Narbonne and the World of the Troubadours.*

WRITINGS:

(Editor) *Lordship and Community in Medieval Europe: Selected Readings,* Holt, Rinehart & Winston (New York, NY), 1968.
(Editor and translator, with Susan R. Huston) Colette Beaune, *The Birth of an Ideology: Myth and Symbol of Nation in Late-Medieval France,* University of California Press (Berkeley, CA), 1991.
Ermengard of Narbonne and the World of the Troubadours, Cornell University Press (Ithaca, NY), 2001.

*   *   *

CHILDS, Laura
[A pseudonym]
(Gerry Schmitt)

PERSONAL: Married; husband a college professor.

ADDRESSES: Agent—C/o Author Mail, Penguin Group, c/o Berkley Prime Crime Publicity, 375 Hudson St., New York, NY 10014. *E-mail*—laura@laura-childs.com.

CAREER: Novelist. Copywriter and producer at national advertising agencies; Mission Critical Marketing (marketing and advertising firm), Minneapolis, MN, former owner, chief executive officer, and creative director.

WRITINGS:

"TEA SHOP MYSTERIES" SERIES

Death by Darjeeling, Berkley Prime Crime (New York, NY), 2001.
Gunpowder Green, Berkley Prime Crime (New York, NY), 2002.
The English Breakfast Murder, Berkley Prime Crime (New York, NY), 2003.
Shades of Earl Grey, Berkley Prime Crime (New York, NY), 2003.
The Jasmine Moon Murder, Berkley Prime Crime (New York, NY), 2004.
Chamomile Mourning, Berkley Prime Crime (New York, NY), 2005.
Blood Orange Brewing, Berkley Prime Crime (New York, NY), 2006.

"SCRAPBOOKING MYSTERIES" SERIES

Keepsake Crimes, Berkley Prime Crime (New York, NY), 2003.
Photo Finished, Berkley Prime Crime (New York, NY), 2004.
Bound for Murder, Berkley Prime Crime (New York, NY), 2004.

SIDELIGHTS: Laura Childs is the pseudonym of Gerry Schmitt, a mystery novelist and former marketing director whose "Tea Shop Mysteries" and "Scrapbooking Mysteries" books have as their protagonists women entrepreneurs who also solve crimes. The "Tea Shop Mysteries" series centers on Theodosia Browning, who, like their author, once worked in advertising, and who is now proprietor of the Indigo Tea Shop in a historic section of Charleston, South Carolina. The

"Scrapbooking Mysteries" are set in another richly historic, atmospheric area, the French Quarter of New Orleans, and focus on Carmela Bertrand, who sells scrapbooks and related craft supplies at a store called Memory Mine. The former series includes recipes, the latter tips on making scrapbooks, and several reviewers have described both as falling into the "cozy" category of mysteries, without extensive descriptions of violence. Child once told an interviewer for *In the Library Reviews* online that the idea for her first series came from her editor, who "wanted 'a mystery featuring a snoopy woman who owns a tea shop!'" According to the pseudonymous novelist, "The rest of the concept sprang from my imagination." The author explained that, that while working in advertising, she met many women who wanted to do what Theodosia has done—leave the corporate world and operate a small business. The scrapbook series, the author continued, "was completely my idea. . . . I figured that old photos and new clippings—the stuff that goes into scrapbooks—would yield a bounty of clues!" The popularity of her mystery novels enabled the author to sell her advertising firm and write full-time.

Death by Darjeeling introduces Theodosia; her valued employees, Drayton and Haley, who help her prepare teas and bakery goods; and her dog, Earl Grey, a dalmatian-labrador mix. The story finds Theo providing refreshments during a tour of landmark Charleston homes; one of the participants, a local real estate developer, dies after drinking poisoned tea. Theo, wishing to keep her business above suspicion, decides to seek out the poisoner, and in the process learns of the conflicts between developers and historic preservationists.

This debut and others in the series have won praise for their portrayals of engaging people and places. *Death by Darjeeling* "offers readers a good setting and a promising cast of characters," commented Jennifer Monahan Winberry in a review for *Mystery Reader* online, the critic adding that it is "a good beginning" to the series. The follow-up, *Gunpowder Green*, takes its title from a special tea Theo and Drayton have created for a party connected with a yacht race; the party turns deadly, however, when the finishing-line gun explodes and kills the man firing it. Theo alone thinks this was no accident, so she begins to investigate. "The story line engages the audience from the start," remarked Harriet Klausner, writing for *AllReaders.com*. Winberry, again contributing to *Mystery Reader,* called the

novel "a delightful cozy that will warm readers the way a good cup of tea does," while *Romantic Times* reviewer Toby Bromberg deemed it "a charming mystery of manners."

The sixth book in the series, *Chamomile Mourning,* revolves around murder at another gala event; the victim, an auction-house owner, is shot and falls from a balcony into a cake Theo's shop has catered for the party. His widow believes his girlfriend is the murderer, as do the police, but Theo has other ideas. A *Publishers Weekly* commentator thought this novel the best so far in the series and termed its author "a master of Southern local color." In a similar vein, a *Kirkus Reviews* critic described the book as an "homage to the Low Country and all things tea-related," while Klausner, reviewing for *MBR Bookwatch,* noted that Charleston itself is one of the story's primary characters, providing "the ambience that makes this series so special." As for human protagonist Theo, she "is one of the most realistic and likeable characters" in mystery fiction, Klausner observed.

Keepsake Crimes inaugurates the scrapbook series as its heroine, Carmela, sets up in business after her husband leaves her. After a man dies during the Mardi Gras parade, her estranged husband, Shamus, is suspected of murder; he was seen fighting with the deceased. Shamus seeks Carmela's aid, and she finds a customer's scrapbook helpful in her search for the true perpetrator. As with the other series, some reviewers found Child's protagonist and locale particularly appealing. In *AllReaders.com,* Klausner dubbed Carmela "plucky and likable" and noted that the novel powerfully evokes the atmosphere of New Orleans and Mardi Gras. It is also "well-written" and truly mysterious, with a wide selection of suspects, Klausner related.

The next in the series, *Photo Finished,* concerns the murder of the disreputable owner of the antiques shop located next door to Carmela's shop, Memory Mine, while the third, *Bound for Murder,* finds Carmela investigating the killing of a friend's fiancée, Reviewing the former book, Klausner wrote on *AllReaders.com* that it is fast-paced and full of action, while also offering "a heroine that is impossible to not like" and a "realistic" view of New Orleans. *Romantic Times* commentator Shari Melnick added that the novel "exudes Southern charm and humor," and is "sure to please fans of light-hearted mysteries." Discussing the latter, *Romantic Times* contributor Cindy Harrison called it "truly suspenseful" and described its characters and setting as "beguiling."

BIOGRAPHICAL AND CRITICAL SOURCES:

PERIODICALS

Kirkus Reviews, April 1, 2005, review of *Chamomile Mourning,* p. 386.
Library Journal, September 1, 2004, Rex E. Klett, review of *The Jasmine Moon Murder,* p. 121; May 1, 2005, Rex E. Klett, review of *Chamomile Mourning,* p. 66.
Publishers Weekly, April 18, 2005, review of *Chamomile Mourning,* p. 47.
Romantic Times, March, 2002, Toby Bromberg, review of *Gunpowder Green*; January, 2004, Shari Melnick, review of *Photo Finished*; November, 2004, Cindy Harrison, review of *Bound for Murder.*

ONLINE

AllReaders.com, http://www.allreaders.com/ (September 28, 2005), David Loftus, review of *Death by Darjeeling*; Abby White, review of *The English Breakfast Murder*; Harriet Klausner, reviews of *Gunpowder Green, Shades of Earl Grey, The English Breakfast Murder, The Jasmine Moon Murder, Chamomile Mourning, Keepsake Crimes, Photo Finished,* and *Bound for Murder.*
In the Library Reviews, http://www.inthelibraryreview. com/ (October 13, 2005), interview with "Laura Childs."
Laura Childs Home Page, http://www.laurachilds.com (September 28, 2005).
MBR Bookwatch Online, http://www.midwestbook review.com/ (October 13, 2005), Harriet Klausner, review of *Chamomile Mourning.*
Mystery Reader, http://www.themysteryreader.com/ (June 3, 2001), Jennifer Monahan Winberry, review of *Death by Darjeeling*; (May 23, 2002) Jennifer Monahan Winberry, review of *Gunpowder Green.**

* * *

CITINO, David 1947-2005

OBITUARY NOTICE— See index for *CA* sketch: Born March 13, 1947, in Cleveland, OH; died of complications from multiple sclerosis, October 17, 2005, in Columbus, OH. Educator and author. Citino was an

English professor at Ohio State University, where he was also named the university's poet laureate. Completing his undergraduate work at Ohio University in 1969, he then earned an M.A. and Ph.D. at Ohio State University in 1972 and 1974 respectively. Upon completion of his studies, he remained at Ohio State as an assistant professor at the Marion campus. Upon becoming a full professor in 1985, he moved to the Columbus campus, where he was still a faculty member at the time of his death. An active poet and editor, Citino was on the editorial board at Ohio State University Press, for which he also served as poetry editor. Over the span of his career, he earned numerous awards for his writing and teaching, including the Prize Poems Award in 1977 from Iowa State University Press and *Poet and Critic,* a National Book Critics Circle notable book citation for his *Broken Symmetry* (1997), the Ohio State University Alumni Distinguished Teaching Award, and the Nancy Dasher Award from the College English Association of Ohio. In 2002 he was named poet laureate of the university. Among Citino's other publications are *Last Rites and Other Poems* (1980), *The House of Memory* (1990), and *The Invention of Secrecy* (2001). More recently, he completed the essay collection *Paperwork* (2003), coedited the fifth edition of *The Bible as Literature* (2006), and was contributing editor for *The Eye of the Poet: Six Views of the Art and Craft of Poetry* (2002).

OBITUARIES AND OTHER SOURCES:

PERIODICALS

Chronicle of Higher Education, October 28, 2005, p. A62.
Grand Rapids Press, October 23, 2005, p. B6.

ONLINE

Ohio State University Web site, http://www.osu.edu/ (October 17, 2005).

* * *

CLAGETT, Marshall 1916-2005

OBITUARY NOTICE— See index for *CA* sketch: Born January 23, 1916, in Washington, DC; died October 21, 2005, in Princeton, NJ. Historian, educator, and author. Clagett was a scholar of the history of science, specializing in research on ancient civilizations and how their discoveries extended their influence all the way through medieval Europe. He completed both his B.A. and M.A. at George Washington University in 1937, continuing on to Columbia University, where he earned his Ph.D. in 1941. When the United States entered World War II, Clagett enlisted in the Navy and saw action in the Pacific theater. He attained the rank of lieutenant commander before being decommissioned. Returning to Columbia to teach for a year, he then moved on to the University of Wisconsin at Madison. Here he rose to full professor of history in 1954 and directed the Institute for Research in the Humanities from 1959 to 1964. That year, he joined the Institute for Advanced Study in Princeton as a professor, remaining there until his 1986 retirement as professor emeritus. As a scholar and author, Clagett was known for his ambitious, multi-volume works on the history of ancient-to-medieval science. Among these works are the four-volume *Archimedes in the Middle Ages* (1964-80) and the three-volume *Ancient Egyptian Science: A Source Book* (1989-99).

OBITUARIES AND OTHER SOURCES:

PERIODICALS

Los Angeles Times, October 30, 2005, p. B13.
New York Times, October 26, 2005, p. C24.

* * *

CLEAVE, Chris 1973-

PERSONAL: Born May 14, 1973, in London, England; married; children: Louis. *Education:* Balliol College, Oxford, B.A.

ADDRESSES: Home—London, England. *Agent*—Jennifer Joel, International Creative Management, 40 W. 57th St., New York, NY 10019.

CAREER: Journalist and author. *Telegraph,* London, England, sub-editor; *lastminute.com,* journalist.

WRITINGS:

Incendiary (novel), Knopf (New York, NY), 2005.

Contributor of articles to London *Telegraph* and other newspapers and magazines.

ADAPTATIONS: Incendiary was optioned for film by Archer Street/Film Four.

WORK IN PROGRESS: A novel set in London.

SIDELIGHTS: Chris Cleave's first novel had one of the more ironic debuts in the history of publishing. *Incendiary,* a tale of a terrorist bombing in London that claimed a thousand lives, was released on July 7, 2005, the very day a series of terrorist bombings in the London Underground took the lives of over fifty people. In Cleave's tale, suicide bombers strike a soccer match between popular London teams Arsenal and Chelsea. The nameless narrator of this novel is watching the events on television, in the process of making love to a journalist neighbor while her policeman husband and son are at the soccer match and lose their lives. The tragedy inspires the widow to write a long letter to Osama bin Laden detailing the mundane and sorrowful events of her life in the aftermath of the killings. She relates her tale in a mixture of London slang, for she is largely uneducated and living on a housing estate. Sent into an emotional tailspin, she attempts suicide, then recovers to volunteer with police efforts to stop further bombings. Meanwhile, London descends into a police state with Muslims persecuted. The narrator begins an affair with her husband's former boss on the anti-terrorist squad, but as she begins to learn inside information from this new lover, she is manipulated by others to reveal what appears to be a government cover-up regarding the stadium bombing. Then a second bomb attack strikes the city.

Cleave's novel, inspired by the terrorist bombings in Madrid in 2004 and by events in the United States in 2001, met with a wide range of critical assessment. Jennifer Reese, writing in *Entertainment Weekly,* felt that the novel, with its blending of heartfelt prose, dark humor, and thriller components "timely but chaotic." Simon Baker, writing in the *New Statesman,* had similar concerns, dubbing the characterization "weak" and further noting that the author's "adherence to the epistolary format comes to seem forced." Baker concluded that Cleave's "too-slender grip on character and structure makes *Incendiary* a novel whose quality falls short of its ambition." Questions of taste arose from *New York Times* reviewer Michiko Kakutani, who found *Incendiary* an "egregious book." Kakutani did, however, praise Cleave's "keen enough eye for social detail," further commenting that he "endows his heroine with his powers of observation." For John Dugdale, reviewing the novel for the London *Times,* Cleave's work is actually "two different novels jammed together," and "fusing them proves impossible."

Other reviewers had a more positive assessment of *Incendiary.* Writing in the *San Francisco Chronicle,* Tamara Straus initially felt that the book "reads a bit too much like a Hollywood screenplay," but went on to note that "Cleave has achieved something rare: a black comedy about the war on terrorism and terrorism itself." Similarly Brigitte Weeks, writing in the *Washington Post Book World,* found that the "power of this novel lies in its extraordinary momentum." Richard Eder, reviewing the same work in the *Los Angeles Times,* thought Cleave's widow—"a younger version of Mother Courage"—is "the saving narrator of this book." These sentiments were echoed by an *Economist* reviewer, who observed that Cleave has created "a distinctive narrative voice and a captivating heroine." Eder went on to note that the novel is "told in graphic detail somewhere between surreal nightmare and savage social irony." Further praise came from a *Kirkus Reviews* critic who termed the book "provocative," and "an oddly elegant debut." Likewise, a reviewer for *Publishers Weekly* called *Incendiary* an "impressive, multilayered debut." Higher praise was added by *Newsweek* contributor Malcolm Jones, who deemed it a "stunning debut" and possibly the "strangest epistolary novel every written." Jones also termed the novel a "haunting work of art."

BIOGRAPHICAL AND CRITICAL SOURCES:

PERIODICALS

Bookseller, December 10, 2004, "Incendiary Debut," p. 6; April 1, 2005, Benedicte Page, "Writing a Letter to bin Laden," p. 24; June 17, 2005, review of *Incendiary,* p. 13.

Economist (U.S.), July 16, 2004, "Dear Osama," review of *Incendiary,* p. 79.

Entertainment Weekly, August 5, 2005, Jennifer Reese, review of *Incendiary,* p. 69.

Kirkus Reviews, June 15, 2005, review of *Incendiary,* p. 652.

Library Journal, July 1, 2005, Sarah Conrad Weisman, review of *Incendiary,* p. 65.

Los Angeles Times, August 29, 2005, Richard Eder, "London Is Warned, Too Late," review of *Incendiary.*

M2 Best Books, July 11, 2005, "Novel about London Terrorist Attack Released on Day of Bombings."

New Statesman, July 18, 2005, Simon Baker, "Them and Us," review of *Incendiary,* p. 56.

Newsweek, August 1, 2005, Malcolm Jones, "Dear Osama Bin Laden," review of *Incendiary,* p. 54.

New York Times, July 29, 2005, Michiko Kakutani, "Bombing Victim's Wife Writes to bin Laden, with Proposition," review of *Incendiary.*

People, August 22, 2005, Lisa Ingrassia, review of *Incendiary,* p. 52.

Publishers Weekly, July 11, 2005, review of *Incendiary,* p. 61.

San Francisco Chronicle, August 14, 2005, Tamara Straus, "One Woman's Letter to Osama bin Laden," review of *Incendiary.*

Times (London, England), July 10, 2005, John Dugdale, "Thrillers: From Arsenal to the Holy Land," review of *Incendiary.*

Washington Post Book World, July 31, 2005, Brigitte Weeks, "Letter to Osama," review of *Incendiary,* p. 3.

ONLINE

Age Online, http://www.theage.com.au/ (July 16, 2005), Jeff Glorfield, review of *Incendiary.*

Bookbrowse.com, http://www.bookbrowse.com/ (October 3, 2005), "Chris Cleave."

Chris Cleave Home Page, http://www.chriscleave.com (October 3, 2005).

Guardian Online, http://books.guardian.com.uk/ (July 16, 2005), Alfred Hickling, "Reality Bites," review of *Incendiary.**

*   *   *

CLIFT, Eleanor

PERSONAL: Married Tom Brazaitis, c. 1990 (died March 30, 2005); children: (former marriage) Edward, Woody, Robert; (with Brazaitis) Mark, Sarah (stepchildren).

ADDRESSES: Agent—c/o Eagles Talent Connection, Inc., 57 West South Orange Ave., South Orange, NJ 07079.

CAREER: Newsweek, contributing editor; *McLaughlin Group,* Public Broadcasting System (PBS), panelist; Fox News Network, political analyst. Iowa State University, Mary Louise Smith Chair in Women and Politics. Appeared in films, including *Independence Day* and *Murder at 1600,* and in televison series, including *Murphy Brown.*

WRITINGS:

(With husband, Tom Brazaitis) *War without Bloodshed: The Art of Politics,* Scribner (New York, NY), 1996.

(With husband, Tom Brazaitis) *Madam President: Shattering the Last Glass Ceiling,* Scribner (New York, NY), 2000, revised edition published as *Madam President: Women Blazing the Leadership Trail,* Routledge (New York, NY), 2003.

Author of the column "Capitol Letter," posted weekly at http://www.newsweek.com and http://www.msnbc.-com.

SIDELIGHTS: Eleanor Clift was married to journalist Tom Brazaitis, now deceased. Together they wrote two books, the first being *War without Bloodshed: The Art of Politics.* The book contains profiles of eight of the most powerful people in Washington, including House Speaker Newt Gingrich, Senator Daniel Patrick Moynihan, lobbyists Michael Bromberg and Paul Equale, pollsters Stanley Greenberg and Frank Luntz, Congresswoman Maxine Waters, and Senator Bob Dole's chief of staff Sheila Burke. *Booklist* reviewers Mary Carroll and Gilbert Taylor called the volume "less cynical than realistic about the exercise of (and limits on) power within government."

Brazaitis and Clift also wrote *Madam President: Shattering the Last Glass Ceiling,* which was revised and retitled *Madam President: Women Blazing the Leadership Trail.* In considering when the United States will elect its first female president, the authors profile women in politics who have learned how to campaign, raise money, and successfully win positions of power.

They include Democrats Geraldine Ferraro, Shirley Chisholm, and Bella Abzug, as well as women who have formed organizations to support female politicians, like Emily's List founder Ellen Malcolm, Barbara Lee of the White House Project, and Karen Strickler of Fifty Plus One.

The authors also look at films that portray women in political positions, including a 1960s story in which Polly Bergen resigns the presidency upon discovering that she is pregnant, much as real-life governor Jane Swift of Massachusetts did because her family needed her. They also study the role of vice president as played by Glenn Close in the film *Air Force One.* Kathleen Knight reviewed the revised edition in *Political Science Quarterly,* noting that the authors "do much more to make the leap from imagination to reality by providing a detailed survey of the field of possible contenders." They profile more experienced female politicians and the newer crop of possible candidates that have emerged as senators, representatives, and governors, including Hillary Clinton.

Brazaitis and Clift conclude that although most people tell pollsters they would vote for a woman president, they are not inclined to actually do so. In order for a woman to be successful, they say, she would have to be conventional, middle-of-the-road, and noncontroversial. As Joyce Purnick commented in the *New York Times Book Review,* "the central question remains whether enough women will be elected to higher office to create a critical mass. Because only then will the country accept that women politicians can be just as good, bad and in-between as most men politicians."

BIOGRAPHICAL AND CRITICAL SOURCES:

PERIODICALS

Booklist, June 1, 1996, Mary Carroll and Gilbert Taylor, review of *War without Bloodshed: The Art of Politics,* p. 1640.

Library Journal, July, 2000, Robert F. Nardini, review of *Madam President: Shattering the Last Glass Ceiling,* p. 119.

New York Times Book Review, July 30, 2000, Joyce Purnick, review of *Madam President,* p. 26.

Political Science Quarterly, spring, 2004, Kathleen Knight, review of *Madam President,* p. 218.

Presidential Studies Quarterly, spring, 1997, Nelson W. Polsby, review of *War without Bloodshed,* p. 399.

Publishers Weekly, April 29, 1996, review of *War without Bloodshed,* p. 57; June 19, 2000, review of *Madam President,* p. 69.

Washington Monthly, July, 2000, Myra MacPherson, review of *Madam President,* p. 46.

ONLINE

Eagles Talent Connection, Inc., http://eaglestalent. com/ (September 12, 2005), author profile.

OBITUARIES

PERIODICALS

Washington Post, March 31, 2005, p. B7.*

*   *   *

CLINE, Catherine Ann 1927-2005

OBITUARY NOTICE— See index for *CA* sketch: Born July 27, 1927, in West Springfield, MA; died of a heart attack, October 12, 2005, in Washington, DC. Historian, educator, and author. Cline was a professor emeritus at the Catholic University of America and an authority on British history. She graduated from Smith College in 1948, then earned her master's degree at Columbia University in 1950 and her doctorate at Bryn Mawr College in 1957. Having previously taught at Smith College and St. Mary's College in the early 1950s, Cline joined the staff of the Notre Dame College of Staten Island in 1954, and became a full professor of history in 1961. She then joined the Catholic University of America faculty as an associate professor in 1968. Promoted to full professor in 1973, she chaired the history department from 1973 to 1976 and again from 1979 to 1982, before retiring in 1996. Cline contributed articles to professional journals and was the author of the books *Recruits to Labour: The British Labour Party, 1914-31* (1963) and *E.D. Morel, 1873-1924: The Strategies of Protest* (1980).

OBITUARIES AND OTHER SOURCES:

PERIODICALS

Washington Post, October 17, 2005, p. B4.

COLE, Joshua 1961-
(Joshua H. Cole)

PERSONAL: Born December 12, 1961. *Education:* Brown University, B.A. (with honors), 1983; University of California, Berkeley, M.A., 1986, Ph.D., 1991.

ADDRESSES: Office—Department of History, University of Michigan, Ann Arbor, MI 48109. *E-mail*—joshcole@umich.edu.

CAREER: Writer, historian, and educator. Institute for Advanced Study, Princeton, NJ, research assistant at School of Social Sciences, 1989-90; Cambridge University, Cambridge, England, postdoctoral research fellow of Pembroke College in Berlin, Germany, 1991-92; Centre de Recherches d'Histoire des Mouvements Sociaux et du Syndicalisme, Paris, France, postdoctoral research fellow in Paris and Berlin, 1992-93; University of Georgia, Athens, assistant professor, 1993-2000, associate professor of history, 2000-04, fellow of Humanities Center, 1994; University of Michigan, Ann Arbor, associate professor of history, 2004—.

AWARDS, HONORS: Mellon fellowship in the Humanities, Mellon Foundation, 1984; Council for European Studies grant, 1986; travel grant, Social Science Research Council, 1987; Bourse Chateaubriand, 1987; grant for Germany, German Academic Exchange Service/Goethe Institute, 1991; postdoctoral fellow at Centre National des Oeuvres Universitaires et Scolaires, 1992; grant from National Endowment for the Humanities, 1994; international travel award, University of Georgia, 2003.

WRITINGS:

The Power of Large Numbers: Population, Politics, and Gender in Nineteenth-Century France, Cornell University Press (Ithaca, NY), 2000.

Contributor to books, including *Capital Cities at War: Paris, London, Berlin, 1914-19,* edited by Jay Winter and Jean-Louis Robert, Cambridge University Press (Cambridge, England), 1997; and *Identity, Memory, and Nostalgia: Algeria 1800-2000,* edited by Patricia Lorcin, Syracuse University Press (Syracuse, NY).

Contributor to academic journals, including *Journal of European Studies, French Historical Studies, History of the Human Sciences, Journal of Family History,* and *Frency Politics, Culture, and Society.*

WORK IN PROGRESS: Editing *Perspectives from the Past: Primary Sources in Western Civilization,* Volume 2, with James M. Brophy, Steven Epstein, and others, for W.W. Norton.

BIOGRAPHICAL AND CRITICAL SOURCES:

PERIODICALS

History: Review of New Books, summer, 2000, Dora Dumont, review of *The Power of Large Numbers: Population, Politics, and Gender in Nineteenth-Century France,* p. 165.
Journal of Modern History, June, 2003, Silvana Patriarca, review of *The Power of Large Numbers,* p. 424.
Population and Development Review, September, 2000, Etienne van de Walle, review of *The Power of Large Numbers,* p. 601.

* * *

COLE, Joshua H.
    See COLE, Joshua

* * *

CONNORS, Rose 1956(?)-

PERSONAL: Born c. 1956. *Education:* Mount St. Mary's College, B.A., 1978; Duke University School of Law, J.D., 1984.

ADDRESSES: *Home*—Chatham, MA. *Agent*—Nancy Yost, Lowenstein Yost Associates, 121 W. 27th St., Ste. 601, New York, NY 10010.

CAREER: Author and lawyer. Trial attorney in MA, 1984—.

MEMBER: Massachusetts Association of Criminal Defense Lawyers.

AWARDS, HONORS: Mary Higgins Clark Award, c. 2002, for *Absolute Certainty.*

WRITINGS:

"MARTHA NICKERSON" NOVEL SERIES

Absolute Certainty, Scribner (New York, NY), 2002.
Temporary Sanity, Scribner (New York, NY), 2003.
Maximum Security, Scribner (New York, NY), 2004.
False Testimony, Scribner (New York, NY), 2005.

WORK IN PROGRESS: Another novel in the "Martha Nickerson" series.

SIDELIGHTS: Attorney and author Rose Connors made a successful fiction debut with her 2002 novel *Absolute Certainty,* a courtroom drama that won the Mary Higgins Clark Award. Since then she has added several other tales to this series featuring the plucky defense lawyer Martha "Marty" Nickerson. Set on Cape Cod, these novels also deal with Marty's partner in law and in life, Harry Madigan. Together, the pair excels at both amateur detective work and courtroom pyrotechnics. Reviewing the author's 2005 addition to the series, *False Testimony,* a critic for *Kirkus Reviews* observed: "Connors continues to be one of the most entertaining writers on the courthouse circuit."

In *Absolute Certainty* Connors introduces her attorney protagonist, at the time an assistant district attorney. Marty Nickerson has just won the conviction of a man for murdering a college student, but her celebration is short-lived when the following day the body of another student is found. While the local authorities want to play down the similarities in the crimes, Marty is not convinced, and begins to investigate, aided by Harry Madigan, the public defender of the convicted man. In doing so, she also risks her career. *Booklist* reviewer Sue O'Brien found *Absolute Certainty* both an "engrossing courtroom drama" and a "satisfying, often poignant debut novel." A contributor for *Kirkus Reviews* was less impressed, dubbing the mystery aspect of the book "folderol," but at the same time praising "Connors's strong sense of pace and skeptical reflections about the morality of the legal system." Higher praise came from a *Publishers Weekly* contributor who felt that Connors's "first novel offers sleek, straightforward entertainment."

Connors's second novel in the series, *Temporary Sanity,* finds Marty no longer with the district attorney's office. She has now become a defense attorney, partnering with Harry Madigan, In this installment, Marty is dealing with two separate murder cases. In the first she is presented with the seemingly impossible task of defending Buck Hammond, who is caught on television in the act of shooting the man who raped and killed Hammond's young son. The second case involves the murder of an abusive boyfriend and parole officer. In both of these, Marty uses as a partial defense the fact that both victims deserved what they got. Her temporary-insanity plea for Hammond seems to be going over well with the judge in that case, but when the judge is assaulted and replaced by another, things go decidedly bad for Marty until she finds a common thread linking these acts of violence. This second installment earned positive critical assessments. A contributor for *Kirkus Reviews* felt that the novel "moves [Connors] up to the big time." The same critic concluded, "For fans of legal intrigue . . . it doesn't get any better than this." O'Brien, writing in *Booklist,* praised Connors's narration for its "touches of humor," as well as its "explanations of the laws involved." Leslie Madden, reviewing the same work in *Library Journal,* noted that it "features strong, likable characters and clean writing." Similarly, a reviewer for *Publishers Weekly* concluded that "this excellent sophomore effort should help [Connors] build name recognition."

The third novel in the "Martha Nickerson" series, *Maximum Security,* deals with another murder, that of wealthy Herbert Rawlings. Police think the man's widow, Louisa, did it, and Harry convinces Marty to take the case. He cannot defend Louisa himself, as he had a relationship with her long ago in law school. That affair fell apart when Louisa realized Harry was headed for the low-paying realms of public defender; her continuing greed now presents a clear motive in the killing. Marty reluctantly takes on the case and enlists the firm's newest member, Kevin Kydd, to help gather evidence. Kydd, however, ends up in Louisa's bed, and suddenly the firm is compromised, as well. Marty needs to find a likelier candidate for the killing, such as the dead man's daughter or her boyfriend. This third outing earned a cooler critical reception than Connors's other efforts. A critic for *Kirkus Reviews* called it a "fast-moving, deeply ordinary case," that is obviously a "breather" for the author. O'Brien also had mixed sentiments in her *Booklist* review, noting that while it is an "enjoyable legal thriller," the "whodunit aspects" do not add up to much.

False Testimony, fourth in the series, offers two more cases for Marty and Harry to tackle. One involves a missing female staff worker for a Massachusetts senator with presidential aspirations, and the second deals with the murder of a local Catholic priest by a young ex-convict. The man's defense is that the priest made sexual advances to him. While Harry takes on the defense of the ex-con, Marty finds herself in deep water when the body of the missing staffer washes up near the senator's home and allegations and gossip of sexual misconduct run rampant. A contributor for *Publishers Weekly* called this installment "another excellent, fast-moving courtroom drama headed by a plucky, energetic heroine."

BIOGRAPHICAL AND CRITICAL SOURCES:

PERIODICALS

Booklist, July, 2002, Sue O'Brien, review of *Absolute Certainty,* p. 1824; May 15, 2003, Sue O'Brien, review of *Temporary Sanity,* p. 1648; August, 2004, Sue O'Brien, review of *Maximum Security,* p. 1904.
Kirkus Reviews, July 15, 2002, review of *Absolute Certainty,* p. 973; June 1, 2003, review of *Temporary Sanity,* p. 768; June 15, 2004, review of *Maximum Security,* p. 549; May 15, 2005, review of *False Testimony,* p. 556.
Library Journal, May 15, 2003, Leslie Madden, review of *Temporary Sanity,* p. 122.
Publishers Weekly, July 22, 2002, review of *Absolute Certainty,* p. 162; June 16, 2003, review of *Temporary Sanity,* p. 50; June 6, 2005, review of *False Testimony,* p. 38.

ONLINE

AllReaders.com, http://www.allreaders.com/ (September 13, 2004), Harriet Klausner, review of *Absolute Certainty, Maximum Security,* and *Temporary Sanity.*

BookBrowser, http://www.bookbrowser.com/ (June 14, 2002), Harriet Klausner, review of *Absolute Certainty.*

Book Loons, http://www.bookloons.com/ (October 5, 2005), G. Hall, review of *Absolute Certainty;* Mary Ann Smith, review of *Temporary Sanity.*

Mystery Reader, http://www.themysteryreader.com/ (October 5, 2005), review of *Maximum Security.*

Romance Junkies, http://www.romancejunkies.com/ (October 5, 2005), Tammy Kelley, review of *Maximum Security.*

Romantic Times Book Club Web site, http://www.romantictimes.com/ (September 13, 2004), Toby Bromberg, review of *Absolute Certainty.*

Shots Online, http://www.shotsmag.co.uk/ (October 31, 2005), John Escott, review of *Temporary Sanity.**

*   *   *

COOPER, Chester L. 1917-2005
(Chester Lawrence Cooper)

OBITUARY NOTICE— See index for *CA* sketch: Born January 13, 1917, in Boston, MA; died of congestive heart failure, October 30, 2005, in Washington, DC. Diplomat, government official, and author. From the 1940s through the 1960s, Cooper was involved with various U.S. government departments as an official working on sensitive international issues. Just before World War II, he earned his B.A. in 1939 and an M.A. in business administration in 1941 from New York University. He then enlisted in the U.S. Army, where he was assigned to work in China with the Office of Strategic Services (OSS). After the war, when the OSS evolved into the Central Intelligence Agency (CIA), Cooper continued his work there and was stationed in Washington, DC. From 1953 to 1955, he was staff assistant for the National Security Council and, from 1955 to 1958, liaison officer for the U.S. Embassy in London. During this time, Cooper was involved with the delicate relations between the United States and Great Britain when the latter country invaded Egypt. Returning to Washington in 1958 to work for the Office of National Estimates, he found himself again involved with international diplomacy when Secretary of State Dean Acheson sent Cooper to England with evidence that the Soviets were building missiles in Cuba. A senior staff member of the National Security Council from 1962 to 1966, and with the U.S. Depart-

ment of State from 1966 to 1970, Cooper worked on the challenge of negotiating with North Vietnam during the Vietnam War, including attending delicate negotiations in Hanoi. He left government service in 1970 to become director of the international division of the Institute for Defense Analysis for two years. During the rest of the early 1970s, he was a fellow at the Woodrow Wilson International Center for Scholars. From 1975 to 1983, Cooper was deputy director of the Institute for Energy Analysis in Tennessee. He then spent two years in Laxenburg, Austria, as deputy director and then acting director for the International Institute for Applied Systems Analysis. His work on environmental and energy issues continued as coordinator of international programs for Resources for the Future in Washington, DC, from 1985 to 1992, and as deputy director of Battelle Pacific Northwest Laboratories at the University of Maryland from 1992 to 2001. Cooper also had a number of interesting avocations during his lifetime. These ranged from his youthful musical endeavors in the 1930s, when he played with Chet Cooper and His Melodians, a group for which Leonard Bernstein also sometimes played. In later life, he was fascinated with creating miniature circuses that included hundreds of tiny clay figures and scale models of tents and other circus paraphernalia. Over the years, he created three complete, detailed circus scenes, which are now displayed at the Cleveland Clinic, the National Institutes of Health, and at Children's Hospital. Cooper was also the author or editor of several books, including *The Lost Crusade: America in Vietnam* (1970), *The Lion's Last Roar: Suez, 1956* (1978), *Science for Public Policy* (1987), and the memoir *In the Shadows of History: Fifty Years behind the Scenes of Cold War Diplomacy* (2005).

OBITUARIES AND OTHER SOURCES:

BOOKS

Cooper, Chester L., *In the Shadows of History: Fifty Years behind the Scenes of Cold War Diplomacy,* Prometheus Books, 2005.

PERIODICALS

New York Times, November 7, 2005, p. A23.
Washington Post, November 3, 2005, p. B8.

COOPER, Chester Lawrence
    See COOPER, Chester L.

*   *   *

CORRICK, Martin

PERSONAL: Male. *Education:* University of East Anglia, M.A.

ADDRESSES: Office—Department of English, School of Humanities, University of Southampton, University Rd., Highfield, Southampton SO17 1BJ, England. *E-mail*—navigationlog@bigfoot.com; m.corrick@ btopenworld.com.

CAREER: Aircraft engineer and pilot. University of Southampton, Southampton, England, visiting fellow and lecturer in creative writing and literature.

WRITINGS:

The Navigation Log (novel), Random House (New York, NY), 2003.
After Berlin (novel; sequel to *The Navigation Log*), Gardners Books, 2005.

SIDELIGHTS: Martin Corrick's first novel, *The Navigation Log,* is set in England in the early twentieth century. It is the story of identical twins Tom and William Anderson, born in London on the eve of the 1918 armistice. Their mother, Constance, is a reclusive artist who reacts to the unexpected pregnancy and birth by immediately having another child, Stella, to whom she devotes herself. Felix, their father and a postal worker and lay minister, gives the responsibility of raising the boys to his housekeeper, Millie, who is also his lover. The story continues forward for two decades, during which William becomes a scholar and teacher and Tom a pilot during World War II. A *Kirkus Reviews* writer felt that the separate stories of the two brothers "dovetail toward a satisfying close, in a momentarily peaceful churchyard echoing with complex images of death and rebirth."

Other characters in the novel include widow Marigold Jennings and spinster Miss Betty, neighbors who interject atmosphere and background. Both brothers seek love, but one finds it elusive. A *Publishers Weekly* contributor wrote that, "if Corrick's purpose was to construct a kaleidoscopic picture of a wartime generation through the seemingly aimless trajectory of particular lives, he has succeeded well." *Booklist* reviewer Meredith Parets called *The Navigation Log* "an understated and moving debut."

BIOGRAPHICAL AND CRITICAL SOURCES:

PERIODICALS

Booklist, April 1, 2003, Meredith Parets, review of *The Navigation Log,* p. 1375.
Kirkus Reviews, February 1, 2003, review of *The Navigation Log,* p. 158.
Library Journal, December, 2002, Barbara Love, review of *The Navigation Log,* p. 176.
Publishers Weekly, March 24, 2003, review of *The Navigation Log,* p. 56.

ONLINE

Martin Corrick Home Page, http://www.martincorrick. co.uk (October 31, 2005).
University of Southampton Web site, http://www. english.soton.ac.uk/ (October 5, 2005), profile of and comments by Corrick.*

*   *   *

COWAN, M. Deborah Larsen
    See LARSEN, Deborah

*   *   *

COWELL, Andrew 1963-

PERSONAL: Born November 22, 1963, in Atlanta, GA; son of W. James (a minister) and Norma B. (a schoolteacher) Cowell; married Punhan Aki (an editor), June 14, 1992; children: Anthony Kawena. *Ethnicity:* "White." *Education:* Harvard University, B.A., 1986; University of California, Berkeley, M.A., 1990, Ph.D., 1993.

ADDRESSES: Home—4485 Hamilton Ct., Boulder, CO 80305. *Office*—Department of French and Italian, Campus Box 238, University of Colorado, Boulder, CO 80309-0238; fax: 303-492-8338. *E-mail*—james. cowell@colorado.edu.

CAREER: Writer and educator. University of Colorado, Boulder, assistant professor, 1995-2002, associate professor of French and Italian and linguistics, 2002—, director of Center for the Study of Indigenous Languages of the West, 2002—, chair of department of French and Italian, 2004—.

WRITINGS:

At Play in the Tavern: Signs, Coins, and Bodies in the Middle Ages, University of Michigan Press (Ann Arbor, MI), 1999.

Telling Stories: Arapaho Narrative Traditions (transcription; with videotape), Wyoming Council for the Humanities (Laramie, WY), 2001.

(Editor and translator, with Alonzo Moss, Sr.) Paul Moss, *Hinono'einoo3itoono: Arapaho Historical Traditions,* University of Manitoba Press (Winnipeg, Manitoba, Canada), 2005.

Contributor to books, including *The Question of the Gift,* edited by Mark Osteen, Routledge (New York, NY), 2002. Contributor to scholarly journals, including *Examplaria, Romanic Review, Cultural Studies, Poetics Today, International Journal of American Linguistics, Oral Tradition, American Indian Quarterly, Algonquian and Iroquoian Linguistics, Anthropological Linguistics, Names,* and *Studies on Voltaire and the Eighteenth Century.*

WORK IN PROGRESS: The Medieval Warrior Aristocracy: Gifts, Violence, Performance, and the Sacred; The Arapaho Language, for University Press of Colorado; and *Performing Identity and Negotiating Change: Arapaho Language and Performance.*

BIOGRAPHICAL AND CRITICAL SOURCES:

PERIODICALS

Medium Aevum, spring, 2001, Alan Hindley, review of *At Play in the Tavern: Signs, Coins, and Bodies in the Middle Ages,* p. 152.

**CRAIG, Gordon A. 1913-2005
(Gordon Alexander Craig)**

OBITUARY NOTICE— See index for *CA* sketch: Born November 26, 1913, in Glasgow, Scotland; died of heart failure, October 30, 2005, in Portola Valley, CA. Historian, educator, and author. Craig, a professor emeritus at Stanford University, was widely considered a leading authority on the modern history of Germany. Although born in Scotland, he spent much of his life in the United States, having immigrated there via Canada in 1925. Here he attended Princeton University, where he received his B.A. in 1936, M.A. in 1939, and Ph.D. in 1941. He also attended Balliol College, Oxford, as a Rhodes scholar in 1938. Craig first became fascinated with Germany while he was in college. He had traveled there before the beginning of the war and was both amazed by the rich history and disgusted by the Nazi's wholesale attack on its own culture. During the war, Craig enlisted in the U.S. Marines, becoming an officer and also serving as a political analyst for the Office of Strategic Services. After the war, he returned to Princeton, where he taught history until 1961. That year, he moved to the West Coast to join the Stanford faculty as a professor of history. Here he was named J.E. Wallace Sterling Professor of Humanities in 1969 and chaired the history department from 1972 to 1975 and from 1978 to 1979, when he retired as professor emeritus. Colleagues of Craig often credited his academic work with boosting Stanford's reputation as a nationally respected institution. A former president of the American Historical Association, Craig was a prolific author best known for his *Germany, 1866-1945* (1978) and for the American Book Award-nominated *The Germans* (1982). Among his other publications are *The Politics of the Prussian Army, 1640-1945* (1955), *The Triumph of Liberalism: Zurich in the Golden Age, 1830-1869* (1988), and *Theodor Fontane: Literature and History in the Bismarck Reich* (1999).

OBITUARIES AND OTHER SOURCES:

PERIODICALS

Independent (London, England), December 23, 2005, p. 45.
Los Angeles Times, November 7, 2005, p. B11.
New York Times, November 9, 2005, p. C17.

Times (London, England), November 16, 2005, p. 65.
Washington Post, November 9, 2005, p. B6.

*   *   *

CRAIG, Gordon Alexander
   See CRAIG, Gordon A.

*   *   *

CRAWFORD, Isis
   See BLOCK, Barbara

*   *   *

CRISWELL, Millie

PERSONAL: Married; husband's name Larry; children: one daughter, one son.

ADDRESSES: Home—Virginia. *Agent*—c/o Author Mail, Harlequin, 225 Duncan Mill Rd., Don Mills, Ontario M3B 3K9, Canada.

CAREER: Novelist.

AWARDS, HONORS: Career Achievement Award, *Romantic Times*; National Readers Choice Award, Oklahoma Romance Writers; Maggie Award, Georgia Romance Writers; Dorothy Parker Award of Excellence; Reviewer's Choice Award.

WRITINGS:

ROMANCE NOVELS

Brazen Virginia Bride, Zebra Books (New York, NY), 1990.
California Temptress, Zebra Books (New York, NY), 1991.
Desire's Endless Kiss, Zebra Books (New York, NY), 1991.
Temptation's Fire, Kensington (New York, NY), 1992.

Phantom Lover, HarperPaperbacks (New York, NY), 1993.
Promise of Eden, Pinnacle Books (New York, NY), 1993.
Diamond in the Rough, HarperCollins (New York, NY), 1994.
Mail-Order Outlaw, HarperCollins (New York, NY), 1994.
Wild Heather (first volume in "Flowers of the West" trilogy), Warner Books (New York, NY), 1995.
Sweet Laurel (second volume in "Flowers of the West" trilogy), Warner Books (New York, NY), 1996.
Prim Rose (third volume in "Flowers of the West" trilogy), Warner Books (New York, NY), 1996.
Desperate, Warner Books (New York, NY), 1997.
Dangerous, Warner Books (New York, NY), 1998.
Defiant, Warner Books (New York, NY), 1998.
True Love, Warner Books (New York, NY), 1999.
The Trouble with Mary, Ivy Books (New York, NY), 2001.
The Pregnant Ms. Potter, Harlequin (New York, NY), 2001.
What to Do about Annie?, Ivy Books (New York, NY), 2001.
(With Liz Ireland and Mary McBride) *A Western Family Christmas* (omnibus), Harlequin (New York, NY), 2001.
The Trials of Angela, Ivy Books (New York, NY), 2002.
Staying Single, Harlequin (New York, NY), 2003.
Mad about Mia, Ivy Books (New York, NY), 2004.
Suddenly Single, Harlequin (New York, NY), 2004.
Body Language, Harlequin (Don Mills, Ontario, Canada), 2004.
No Strings Attached, Harlequin (Don Mills, Ontario, Canada), 2005.

Also author of *The Wedding Planner,* 2000, and *The Marrying Man,* 2000.

SIDELIGHTS: Millie Criswell is the author of numerous romance novels, both historical romances and contemporary romantic comedies. In the historical trilogy "Flowers of the West," Criswell tells the stories of three sisters from Kansas who are in search of husbands. The second book of the series, *Sweet Laurel,* opens as Laurel Martin sets out to become an opera singer in Denver, Colorado. However, her singing talents are not up to the opera company's standards, and she is forced to accept work singing in the Aurora

Borealis saloon. This establishment is owned by Chance Rafferty, a gambler and a charming rogue, and although Laurel is initially shocked at the coarseness of her new surroundings, she soon finds herself intrigued by Chance and his world. Martin sister Rose Elizabeth, whose story is told in *Prim Rose,* the third volume in the trilogy, has no desire to leave the family farm, even after it is sold to British purchaser Alexander Warrick, duke of Moreland. In fact, she refuses to leave and taunts the duke by referring to him as "'your dukeness,' 'your ineptness,' 'your majesticness,' etc.," explained a *Publishers Weekly* reviewer.

Desperate, Dangerous, and *Defiant* form another historical trilogy, this one focusing on the Bodine brothers. *Desperate* centers on Rafe Bodine, a former Texas Ranger whose pregnant wife was raped and murdered. While Rafe is out looking for the perpetrators so that he can take his revenge, he meets up with Emmaline St. Joseph, a Bostonian society lady who has become stranded while on her way to California to found an orphanage. "This is a tightly plotted book and a good read," wrote a *Publishers Weekly* contributor. In *Dangerous,* both Ethan Bodine, a Texas Ranger, and horticulturalist Wilhemina Granville are trying to track down Rafe, who is now wanted for the shooting of one of the men he was seeking in *Desperate.* There is a five-hundred-dollar bounty on Rafe's head, and Wilhemina hopes to earn the money and save her aunt's house from the man who holds its mortgage. Criswell "gets the job done in a dependably entertaining fashion," in *Dangerous,* related a *Publishers Weekly* critic. Travis, the youngest Bodine brother and a lawyer, tries to save Rafe from the executioner in *Defiant.* He has one major distraction in his quest: ex-fiancée Hannah Louise Barkley, also a lawyer, who is hired to work on the case as well. *Defiant* "is great fun, filled with action, witty dialogue and entirely endearing secondary characters," commented a *Publishers Weekly* contributor.

In 2000 Criswell branched out into contemporary romantic comedy with the publication of *The Trouble with Mary.* This book and its sequels, including *What to Do about Annie?* and *Mad about Mia,* are about the family and friends of the Russos, an Italian-American family living in Maryland. Mary Russo, thirty-three years old and the protagonist of the first book, longs for her first sexual relationship and for freedom from her smothering mother. When Mary's boss commits suicide, she resolves to take a step toward independence by opening her own Italian restaurant. She succeeds in founding the restaurant, but its future seems less secure after newspaper food critic Dan Gallagher writes a scathing review of it. When Mary goes to the newspaper to make a complaint, sparks fly between her and Dan. *The Trouble with Mary* is "a hilarious contemporary romance chock-full of delightful characters and wonderful-sounding recipes," Patty Engelmann noted in *Booklist.*

What to Do about Annie? centers on Annie Goldman, a Jewish woman who is Mary's best friend. When Annie was a teenager she was engaged to Mary's brother Joe, but he broke off the engagement and became a priest. Now, fifteen years later, Joe leaves the clergy and asks Annie if they can try again. "Criswell's dialogue is sharp and humorous," wrote a *Publishers Weekly* critic, "and her colorful characters liven up the narrative." Kristin Ramsdell, writing in *Library Journal,* also praised the book, calling it "fast-paced, hilarious, and thoroughly delightful." In *The Trials of Angela,* described by *Booklist* reviewer Engelmann as "a terrifically enjoyable performance spiked with great lawyer jokes," the romantic couple is Joe Franco (Mary Russo's cousin) and Angela DeNero, two lawyers and old friends who find themselves serving as counsel for opposite sides in a bitter custody battle. Angela's younger sister Mia gets her day in *Mad about Mia,* which Engelmann in *Booklist* called "a funny and heartwarming story."

BIOGRAPHICAL AND CRITICAL SOURCES:

PERIODICALS

Booklist, January 1, 2001, Patty Engelmann, review of *The Trouble with Mary,* p. 927; July, 2001, Patty Engelmann, review of *What to Do about Annie?,* p. 1990; September 15, 2001, review of *The Trouble with Mary,* p. 211; April 1, 2002, Patty Engelmann, review of *The Trials of Angela,* p. 1311; December 15, 2003, Patty Engelmann, review of *Mad about Mia,* p. 733.

Library Journal, August, 2001, Kristin Ramsdell, review of *What to Do about Annie?,* p. 88; November 15, 2001, Kristin Ramsdell, review of *A Western Family Christmas,* p. 55; January, 2002, review of *What to Do about Annie?,* p. 51.

Publishers Weekly, February 19, 1996, review of *Sweet Laurel,* p. 211; October 28, 1996, review of *Prim Rose,* p. 77; May 26, 1997, review of

Desperate, p. 83; January 26, 1998, review of *Dangerous,* p. 89; July 20, 1998, review of *Defiant,* p. 216; November 20, 2000, review of *The Trouble with Mary,* p. 52; May 28, 2001, review of *What to Do about Annie?,* p. 57; March 25, 2002, review of *The Trials of Angela,* p. 48.

ONLINE

Fantastic Fiction, http://www.fantasticfiction.co.uk/ (October 22, 2005), "Millie Criswell."
Millie Criswell Home Page, http://www.milliecriswell. com (October 7, 2005).*

*   *   *

CROUCH, Blake 1978-

PERSONAL: Born 1978, in Statesville, NC. *Education:* University of North Carolina, Chapel Hill, B.A., 2000.

ADDRESSES: Home—CO. *Agent*—Linda Allen Literary Agency, 1949 Green St., Ste. 5, San Francisco, CA 94123. *E-mail*—blakecrouch1@yahoo.com.

CAREER: Writer.

WRITINGS:

FICTION

Desert Places: A Novel of Terror, St. Martin's Minotaur (New York, NY), 2004.
Locked Doors, Thomas Dunne Books (New York, NY), 2005.

SIDELIGHTS: Blake Crouch published his first novel, *Desert Places: A Novel of Terror,* in 2004. Crouch's book features a successful suspense and thriller writer who is unwillingly thrust into the horrors he creates. Andrew Thomas, successful horror novelist, receives an anonymous letter one day at his North Carolina home, and his life is changed forever. The unnamed writer tells him that the body of a young woman has been buried in Thomas's backyard, along with evidence that will incriminate him in the murder. The letter writer goes on to tell him that he must call the telephone number enclosed in the letter to avoid having the local police come searching for the body. At first, Thomas thinks this is some twisted joke, but while searching his yard he finds the body of a local woman who has been missing. After calling his anonymous tormentor, Thomas is maneuvered to a hotel where he is drugged and kidnapped by a serial killer who must be stopped.

A *Publishers Weekly* critic felt that "Crouch shows real talent here," and praised the author's "smart, tight prose" and "narrative energy." Praise also came from *Agony Column Book Reviews and Commentary* online writer Rick Kleffel, who felt Crouch "brings art and innovation to aspects of the novel where it's usually in short supply." Kleffel went on to note that Crouch manages "to keep up a positively blistering pace without ever seeming forced." Likewise, an online reviewer for *Curled Up with a Good Book* commented that Crouch's debut thriller is "effective in its darkness, depravity and the sense of terror it inspires."

Crouch followed up *Desert Places* with the sequel, *Locked Doors,* which finds horror novelist Thomas holed up in Alaska, now on the run as a supposed serial killer. Reading about new murders carried out by the real killer, Thomas is lured out of hiding and gives chase. A subplot involves another horror writer who discovers Thomas's whereabouts and has plans of his own. This time around, a critic for *Kirkus Reviews* found the book "blunt but expertly paced and viscerally effective, with many surprises and genuine chills." A *Publishers Weekly* contributor allowed that in *Locked Doors* "the action is nonstop, the violence visceral." Writing for *BookReporter* online, Joe Hartlaub found that "Crouch is quite simply a marvel." The critic went on to explain that the author "changes perspective, points of view, and tense at whim, challenging you to hang on and ride with him. And it's easy to do."

BIOGRAPHICAL AND CRITICAL SOURCES:

PERIODICALS

Booklist, December 1, 2003, Michael T. Gannon, review of *Desert Places: A Novel of Terror,* p. 650.

Capital Times (Madison, WI), May 20, 2004, Rob Thomas, review of *Desert Places.*

Charlotte Observer, July 29, 2005, "Crouch Splatters N.C. with Blood."

Durango Herald, May 4, 2004, Nathaniel Miller, "Finger on Pulse of Depravity."

Kirkus Reviews, November 1, 2003, review of *Desert Places,* p. 1284; May 1, 2005, review of *Locked Doors,* p. 491.

Publishers Weekly, December 8, 2003, review of *Desert Places,* p. 48; June 6, 2005, review of *Locked Doors,* p. 40.

Record and Landmark, (Statesville, NC), August 4, 2005, Chyna Broadnax, "Native Son Finds Success Writing Thrillers."

ONLINE

Agony Column Book Reviews and Commentary, http://trashotron.com/agony/ (April 16, 2004), Rick Kleffel, review of *Desert Places.*

Allreaders.com, http://www.allreaders.com/ (September 12, 2005), Harriet Klausner, review of *Desert Places.*

Blake Crouch Home Page, http://www.blakecrouch.com (September 12, 2005).

BookReporter, http://www.bookreporter.com/ (September 12, 2005), Barbara Lipkien Gershenbaum, review of *Desert Places;* Joe Hartlaub, review of *Locked Doors.*

Curled Up with a Good Book, http://www.curledup.com/ (September 12, 2005), review of *Desert Places.*

MysteryOne, http://www.mysteryone.com/ (September 12, 2005), "Interview with Blake Crouch."

*   *   *

CUNNINGHAM, Sophie

PERSONAL: Female. *Education:* Graduated from Monash University.

ADDRESSES: Agent—c/o Author Mail, Text Publishing, Swann House, 22 William St., Melbourne, Victoria 3000, Australia. *E-mail*—mail@sophiecunningham.com.

CAREER: Editor, author, and journalist. McPhee Gribble/Penguin, on staff, 1992-94; Allen & Unwin, London, England, on staff, 1995-2003; freelance writer and journalist, 2003—.

WRITINGS:

Geography (novel), Text Publishing (Melbourne, Victoria, Australia), 2004.

Contributor of articles and reviews to periodicals, including *Australian Book Review.*

WORK IN PROGRESS: Two novels, *Dharma Is a Girl's Best Friend;* and *Serendip.*

SIDELIGHTS: Australian writer Sophie Cunningham published her first novel, *Geography,* in 2004. Her debut title deals, as Aviva Tuffield noted in the Melbourne *Age,* with "an obsessional love affair between the narrator Catherine and a much older Australian expat[riot], Michael—a long-distance relationship founded almost solely on passionate sex and notable for Michael's atrocious behaviour." Highly autobiographical in nature, the book took four years to write. Tuffield noted, however, that reading the novel "is not akin to rifling through someone's diary; it's an accomplished work of fiction and while partly based on first-hand experiences, those elements have been distilled into lean pacy prose and pitch-perfect dialogue."

Catherine's story is narrated to Ruby, a woman she meets in Sri Lanka on the way to a meditation retreat. The two women end up traveling together through southern India, and Catherine relates her torrid, seven-year, long-distance romance with the two-decades older Michael, whom she met in Los Angeles at the height of the Rodney King riots. Their affair lasted through the 1990s, the two meeting perhaps only once or twice a year. Finally, Catherine ended the affair, aware of Michael's infidelities. Ruby, Catherine's new traveling partner is a lesbian, and by the end of the book the two women have formed a bond apart from men. For a *Kirkus Reviews* critic, this first novel is a "bodice-ripper debut with a lesbian twist, too self-conscious to be erotic." However, Erica Keiko Iseri, reviewing the novel in *Antipodes,* felt that it is much more than a romance novel, or simply a novel of obsession. For Iseri, "there is nothing tedious or unremarkable" about the notion of compassion demonstrated in the novel, both by Catherine's family and friends.

Cunningham told *CA:* "*Geography* is often described as highly autobiographical, but it is not. I strove to create a kind of intimacy between the reader and the narrator, Catherine, by using the First Person. I wanted my heroine's voice to be like that of a friend who was telling the reader her secrets. I was uncertain about this approach as I knew that some would read 'I' as me rather than considering Catherine a constructed, fictional voice. But after re-reading one of my favourite novels, *Jane Eyre* by Charlotte Brontë, which is also written in the first person, I decided it was the best way to give the reader some insight into my heroine's behaviour."

BIOGRAPHICAL AND CRITICAL SOURCES:

PERIODICALS

Age (Melbourne, Victoria, Australia), May 2, 2004, Aviva Tuffield, "Stripped Bare."
Antipodes, Erica Keiko Iseri, review of *Geography,* p. 181.
Arena, December, 2004, Ben Cook, review of *Geography,* p. 39.
Kirkus Reviews, May 1, 2005, review of *Geography,* p. 492.

ONLINE

Sophie Cunningham Home Page, http://www.sophie cunningham.com (September 12, 2005).

*   *   *

CURRAN, Colleen 1974-

PERSONAL: Born 1974.

ADDRESSES: Home—Richmond, VA. *Agent*—Eric Simonoff, Janklow & Nesbit Associates, Inc., 445 Park Ave., New York, NY 10022. *E-mail*—colleen@ colleencurran.com.

CAREER: Author, editor, and educator. *Richmond.com,* associate editor; James River Writers, executive director. Creative writing instructor.

WRITINGS:

FICTION

Whores on the Hill (novel), Vintage Contemporaries (New York, NY), 2005.

Contributor of stories to *Jane, Richmond,* and *Meridian,* and to the anthology *Dictionary of Failed Relationships: 26 Stories of Love Gone Wrong,* Three Rivers Press, 2003.

WORK IN PROGRESS: A collection of short stories.

SIDELIGHTS: Colleen Curran's 2005 debut novel, *Whores on the Hill,* details the experiences of a trio of girls in an all-girl's high school in Milwaukee, Wisconsin, where Curran herself grew up. Describing this first work in *Richmond.com,* Katherine Houstoun called it an "emotionally-charged novel [that] depicts female teenagedom in vivid coloration, ranging from the vibrant firecracker hues of high school parties, youthful freedom and first loves to the darker shades of suicide, depression and betrayal." Jennon Bell, writing in *On Milwaukee* online, termed the book a "no-holds-barred account of what it is like to be 15 and ready to take over the world, plaid skirt and all."

Curran attended a Catholic high school, and her trio of fifteen-year-old fictional friends do so as well. Thisbe is a transfer student to Sacred Heart Holy Angels, and quickly becomes friends with two other girls, Juli and Astrid. Together they sport punk attire and experience firsts such as first love, first kisses, and even first orgasms. There is an edgier side to their lives as well, when love turns violent and emotions curdle into psychological distress.

Curran wrote her book, as she has noted on her home page, to give a voice to teenagers who are entering sexuality and the world at large. Her title comes from what she discovered was an almost universal negative manner of describing students at all-girls high schools. While Bell found the novel "lightning fast and sexually charged," a critic for *Kirkus Reviews* had further praise, dubbing *Whores on the Hill* an "arresting first novel," and one that is "quick-moving" as well as "cleanly written." Overall, this same critic deemed *Whores on the Hill* "a promising start."

BIOGRAPHICAL AND CRITICAL SOURCES:

PERIODICALS

Kirkus Reviews, March 1, 2005, review of *Whores on the Hill,* p. 245.
Publishers Weekly, January 24, 2005, Natalie Danford, "This Is Your . . . Novel?," p. 114.

ONLINE

Beatrice, http://www.beatrice.com/ (June 21-26, 2005), "Author2Author: Colleen Curran and Martha O'Connor."
Colleen Curran Home Page, http://www.colleen curran.com (October 5, 2005).
On Milwaukee.com, http://www.onmilwaukee.com/ (May 16, 2005), Jennon Bell, "Curran's Novel Traces Milwaukee's Heavenly Heathens," review of *Whores on the Hill.*
Richmond.com, http://www.richmond.com/ (May 10, 2005), Katherine Houstoun, "Girls Gone Wild."*

*　　　*　　　*

CZERNER, Thomas B. 1938-

PERSONAL: Born September 27, 1938, in Prague, Czechoslovakia; son of Max and Irma (Froelich) Czerner; married Cynthia Silvert Wax, November 21, 1967; children: Suzanne, Elizabeth. *Education:* University of Illinois, Urbana, B.A., 1959; University of Illinois, Chicago, M.D., 1962.

ADDRESSES: *Office*—3838 California St., San Francisco, CA, 94118-1522.

CAREER: Doctor and educator. Opthalmologist in private practice, San Francisco, CA. University of California School of Medicine, San Francisco, clinical professor of ophthalmology, 1971—; senior faculty consultant to Ophthalmology Residency Training Program, California Pacific Medical Center. *Military service:* U.S. Navy, 1962-64; attained rank of lieutenant commander.

WRITINGS:

What Makes You Tick?: The Brain in Plain English, Wiley (New York, NY), 2001, published as *What Makes the Brain Tick?,* Wiley (Chichester, England) 2001.

SIDELIGHTS: Czech-born Thomas B. Czerner is a practicing physician and a professor of ophthalmology at San Francisco's University of California School of Medicine. His interest in the eye's connection to brain activity "shines through," according to a *Science News* reviewer, in his 2001 book, *What Makes You Tick?: The Brain in Plain English.* In his book Czerner serves up "reader-friendly reports of advances in neuro-science," according to the same reviewer. Reviewing the British edition in *Chemistry and Industry,* neuro-scientist Amy Johnston called Czerner's concise approach a "whistle-stop tour of the human brain and mind." Johnston deemed Czerner's book "a good introduction for the reader who would like to taste the field and perhaps delve further in the future," while a *Science for Success* critic appraised *What Makes You Tick?* as "a fascinating look at how our brain functions."

BIOGRAPHICAL AND CRITICAL SOURCES:

PERIODICALS

Chemistry and Industry, December 17, 2001, Amy Johnston, review of *What Makes the Brain Tick?,* p. 805.
Science News, March 9, 2002, review of *What Makes You Tick?: The Brain in Plain English,* p. 159.

ONLINE

Science for Success, http://www.scienceforsuccess. com/ (September 13, 2005), review of *What Makes You Tick?*

D

D'AMMASSA, Don 1946-
(Donald Eugene D'Ammassa)

PERSONAL: Born April 24, 1946; married Sheila D'Ammassa, 1968; children: one son. *Education:* Michigan State University, B.A.

ADDRESSES: Agent—c/o Author Mail, Five Star, 295 Kennedy Memorial Dr., Waterville, ME 04901. *E-mail*—dammassa@ix.netcom.com.

CAREER: Writer, businessperson, and administrator. Taunton Silversmiths, production control manager and vice president, 1971-92; Computer Network Administrator, Air Products and Chemicals, computer network administrator, 1993-c. 2004. *Military service:* U.S. Army, 1968-71; served in Vietnam war.

WRITINGS:

FICTION

Blood Beast, Pinnacle (New York, NY), 1988.
Twisted Images (short stories), Necronomicon Press (West Warwick, RI), 1995.
Servants of Chaos, Leisure Books (New York, NY), 2002.
Haven, Five Star (Waterville, ME), 2004.
Murder in Silverplate, Five Star (Waterville, ME), 2004.
Scarab, Five Star (Waterville, ME), 2004.

Short fiction has appeared in anthologies, including *Hotter Blood: More Tales of Erotic Horror,* 1991; *Deathport,* 1993; *The Ultimate Zombie,* 1993; *Borderlands 4,* 1994; *Return to the Twilight Zone,* 1994; *Shock Rock II,* 1994; *100 Vicious Little Vampire Stories,* 1995; *100 Wicked Little Witch Stories,* 1995; *Adventures in the Twilight Zone,* 1995; *Blood Muse,* 1995; *Peter Straub's Ghosts,* 1995; *The Ultimate Alien,* 1995; *Singers of Strange Songs: A Celebration of Brian Lumley,* 1997; *Terminal Frights,* 1997; *In the Shadow of the Gargoyle,* 1998; and *Whitley Strieber's Aliens,* 1998. Contributor of short fiction to periodicals.

NONFICTION

Encyclopedia of Science Fiction, Facts on File (New York, NY), 2004.
Encyclopedia of Fantasy and Horror Fiction, Facts on File (New York, NY), 2006.

Book reviewer for *Science-Fiction Chronicle* and other publications; contributor to many reference books.

WORK IN PROGRESS: A sequel to *Scarab.*; *The Sinking Land,* a novel, for Lost Continent Library.

SIDELIGHTS: A reader of science fiction and horror since he was fourteen years old, Don D'Ammassa began his career primarily as a science-fiction and horror short-story writer before producing several novels. Commenting on the author's short fiction, a contributor to the *St. James Guide to Horror, Ghost, and Gothic Writers* noted that the author's "best . . .

work deals with mental disorders" and that "D'Ammassa avoids the more visceral brands of horror." Commenting on his writing process, the author said in an online interview for *Book of Dark Wisdom:* "I usually get a single image or scene in my mind. The story then expands in both directions over the course of time and eventually I sit down and write it. I find it very difficult to write a story unless I can watch the movie version of it in my mind first."

D'Ammassa originally wrote his novel *Scarab* nearly a decade before it was published. Although it was accepted for publication at that time, it was eventually set aside by the publishers. The author rewrote it and submitted it to another house, which released the novel in 2004. *Scarab* tells the story of a serial killer living on the planet Tashista who is known as the Scarab. The killer's victims are the Nashamata, who come from the poor section of the city of Soshambe. Because of Soshambe's rigid class demarcations, not much is done to stop the killer until a city official is found slain in the district. Unable to solve the case, the local police call in an amateur detective named Sandor Dyle. The Scarab has claimed twenty-seven victims, and Dyle is known for the ability to trace a criminal's patterns to capture the perpetrator. Writing for *AllSciFi.com,* Harriet Klausner noted: "This science fiction police procedural is action packed, exciting and will appeal to readers of both genres." In a review in *Booklist,* David Pitt wrote that "there are many excellent things about this novel," citing D'Ammassa's "highly detailed, internally consistent world" and dubbing the book an "entertaining take on a traditional mystery format."

In *Haven* D'Ammassa presents another science-fiction murder mystery coupled with a political conspiracy on the planet Meadow. Avery, who creates virtual, sensory movies, starts hallucinating from stress because of a strange viral infection. He goes to Meadow to relax but discovers a body that disappears when he reports it to the police. Convinced that he was not hallucinating, he enlists the help of Dona Tharmody, a technician who has worked for several years on the planet. Because she is well connected to Meadow's leaders, Dona seeks the help of some political elites, only to involve herself and Avery in a complicated political conspiracy that may make them targets for death as they investigate the murder. D. Douglas Fratz, a contributor to *SciFi.com,* noted: "All of the characters and plot elements play integral roles in the story. . . .

Haven is an extremely well crafted mystery/suspense/ adventure novel." Fratz also noted, however, that the novel "is almost totally devoid of the kind of thematic power and sense of wonder evoked by superior science fiction." Jackie Cassada, writing in the *Library Journal,* called the effort a "taut mystery-suspense adventure."

Murder in Silverplate follows the investigation of a series of slayings at a plant that manufactures silver-plated giftware. The first death is made to look like an accident, but then several more employees are killed, including the company's chief executive officer. Vicki Antonelli, who is a quality-control manager at the plant, starts to investigate the deaths. Also on the case is Vicki's estranged father, Detective Walter Henderson, who begins to suspect that there may be more than one murderer involved and that the deaths may involve a complicated conspiracy. "Detective Henderson remains baffled, but pretty, perky Vicki puts on her Nancy Drew hat and saves the day," noted a *Kirkus Reviews* contributor. Another reviewer writing in *Publishers Weekly,* commented that "D'Ammassa . . . paints a credible portrait of a work force either demoralized or Machiavellian enough to treat murder as a labor-saving device for climbing the corporate ladder."

BIOGRAPHICAL AND CRITICAL SOURCES:

BOOKS

St. James Guide to Horror, Ghost, and Gothic Writers, St. James Press (Detroit, MI), 1998

PERIODICALS

Booklist, April 15, 2004, David Pitt, review of *Scarab,* p. 1431.
Kirkus Reviews, September 15, 2004, review of *Murder in Silverplate,* p. 892
Library Journal, December 1, 2004, Jackie Cassada, review of *Haven,* p. 105.
Publishers Weekly, March 22, 2004, review of *Scarab,* p. 68; November 1, 2004, review of *Murder in Silverplate,* p. 47.

ONLINE

AllReaders.com, http://www.allreaders.com/ (September 25, 2005), Harriet Klausner, review of *Murder in Silverplate.*

AllSciFi.com, http://www.allscifi.com/ (September 25, 2005), Harriet Klausner, reviews of *Haven* and *Servants of Chaos.*

Book of Dark Wisdom, http://www.darkwisdom.com/ (September 25, 2005), interview with author.

Council for the Literature of the Fantastic Web site, http://www.uri.edu/artsci/english/clf/ (September 25, 2005), information about author.

SciFi.com, http://www.scifi.com/ (September 25, 2005), D. Douglas Fratz, review of *Haven.*

*   *   *

DAESCHNER, J.R. 1970(?)-

PERSONAL: Born c. 1970, in CO; married. *Education:* University graduate; graduate studies in Latin America.

ADDRESSES: Home—London, England. *Agent*—Lizzy Kremer, David Higham Associates, 5–8 Lower John St., Golden Square, London W1F 9HA, England.

CAREER: Freelance journalist and author.

AWARDS, HONORS: Fulbright scholarship.

WRITINGS:

True Brits: A Tour of Twenty-first-Century Britain in All Its Shin-Kicking, Bog-Snorkeling, and Cheese-Rolling Glory, Arrow/Random Group (London, England), 2004, published as *True Brits: A Tour of Twenty-first-Century Britain in All Its Bog-Snorkeling, Gurning, and Cheese-Rolling Glory,* Overlook Press (New York, NY), 2005.

Contributor of articles to newspapers, including *New York Times, International Herald Tribune,* and London *Times.*

SIDELIGHTS: An American freelance journalist living in England, J.R. Daeschner dissects odd cultural traditions and fetishes of his adopted country in *True Brits: A Tour of Twenty-first-Century Britain in All Its Bog-Snorkeling, Gurning, and Cheese-Rolling Glory.* A resident in England for a decade, Daeschner was inspired to design his unorthodox tour after hearing of a shin-kicking contest in the village of Chipping

Campden in the Cotswolds. From there it was not a large leap to participate in a bog-and-mud-snorkeling contest in the Welsh village of Llanwrtyd Wells, or a cheese-rolling contest in Gloucestershire involving villagers leaping off a cliff, or to the hugely politically incorrect Padstow Darkie Day celebration, in which villagers blacken their faces and play minstrel songs.

Critics on both sides of the Atlantic responded warmly to Daeschner's book. Writing in London's *Observer,* Stephanie Merritt found *True Brits* an "immensely funny guide to British customs." Similarly, Richard Dickey, writing in *Library Journal,* called the work "an insightful travel narrative" and "a fun collection." For a *Kirkus Reviews* critic, the book is an "atmospheric, modestly entertaining travelogue," while for a *Publishers Weekly* reviewer *True Brits* is "a lighthearted romp."

BIOGRAPHICAL AND CRITICAL SOURCES:

PERIODICALS

Cornish Guardian, April 15, 2004, "'Local Yokels' in New Book," review of *True Brits: A Tour of Twenty-first-Century Britain in All Its Shin-Kicking, Bog-Snorkeling, and Cheese-Rolling Glory.*

Kirkus Reviews, February 1, 2005, review of *True Brits: A Tour of Twenty-first-Century Britain in All Its Bog-Snorkeling, Gurning, and Cheese-Rolling Glory,* p. 161.

Library Journal, March 1, 2005, Richard Dickey, review of *True Brits,* p. 102.

Observer (London, England), April 11, 2004, Stephanie Merritt, "Bill Bryson Meets Tony Hawks," review of *True Brits.*

Publishers Weekly, January 31, 2005, review of *True Brits,* p. 57.

Time, June 4, 2004, Michael Brunton, "Oddball Olympics Bog Snorkeling, Anyone?," review of *True Brits.*

Western Mail (Cardiff, Wales), March 31, 2004, Claire Hill, "Bog Event Makes Book."

ONLINE

BookPage, http://www.bookpage.com/ (September 24, 2005), Lacey Galbraith, "Travelogues Take Readers a World Away," review of *True Brits.*

True Brits Web site, http://www.truebrits.tv/ (September 24, 2005).*

DALTON, Coco
  (Coco Pekelis Dalton, Coco Pekelis)

PERSONAL: Daughter of Carla Pekelis (a writer); married David Dalton (a writer); children: Toby.

ADDRESSES: Agent—c/o Author Mail, St. Martin's Press, 175 5th Ave., New York, NY 10010.

CAREER: Writer.

WRITINGS:

(As Coco Pekelis) *Everything I Know I Learned on Acid,* Acid Test Productions (Petaluma, CA), 1996.
(With Peggy Lipton and husband, David Dalton) *Breathing Out,* St. Martin's Press (New York, NY), 2005.

SIDELIGHTS: Coco Dalton is the author of *Everything I Know I Learned on Acid* (which was published under her maiden name, Coco Pekelis), and is coauthor, with husband David Dalton and actor Peggy Lipton, of Lipton's autobiography *Breathing Out.* Lipton first gained fame as one of the trio of hip detectives on the 1960s television series *The Mod Squad.* Her autobiography reveals her love affairs with the likes of Paul McCartney of Beatles fame and Elvis Presley, both rock-and-roll legends. She also recounts her eventual marriage to musician and music producer Quincy Jones that led her to retire from acting and concentrate on her family until the marriage broke up a decade or so later. Lipton and her coauthors also discuss the actor's difficult youth, her battle with depression, and her eventual spiritual awakening under the tutelage of a guru. Writing in the *Detroit Free Press,* John Smyntek commented that "you don't often see 'literary style' and 'celebrity bio' in the same sentence, but Lipton's coauthors . . . have done a great job of bite-sizing and not super-sizing her life." Smyntek went on to note that the Daltons "mostly keep the revelations chatty," and he gave Lipton "credit for linking up with the right storytellers." A contributor to the *Books in Review* Web site called the book an "easy and very interesting read," while a *Kirkus Reviews* contributor wrote: "People who love star autobiographies will no doubt find this satisfying."

BIOGRAPHICAL AND CRITICAL SOURCES:

PERIODICALS

Detroit Free Press, June 26, 2005, John Smyntek, "Cowriters Keep Lipton's Life Light," review of *Breathing Out.*
Entertainment Weekly, May 13, 2005, Margeaux Watson, review of *Breathing Out,* p. 94.
Kirkus Reviews, March 15, 2005, review of *Breathing Out,* p. 338.
Publishers Weekly, April 11, 2005, review of *Breathing Out,* p. 41.

ONLINE

Books in Review, http://www.geocities.com/pett projects/bookreviews.html (September 14, 2005), review of *Breathing Out.*
Ear Candy, http://www.earcandymag.com/ (September 14, 2005), review of *Breathing Out.**

*   *   *

DALTON, Coco Pekelis
  See DALTON, Coco

*   *   *

D'AMMASSA, Donald Eugene
  See D'AMMASSA, Don

*   *   *

DANCER, Rex
  See KILIAN, Michael D.

*   *   *

DAVIES, Idris 1905-1953

PERSONAL: Born 1905, in Rhymney, Caerphilly, Wales; died of cancer, 1953. *Education:* Attended Loughborough College and University of Nottingham.

CAREER: Poet. Worked variously as a miner and a primary school teacher.

WRITINGS:

Tonypandy, and Other Poems, Faber & Faber (London, England), 1945.

Selected Poems, Faber & Faber (London, England), 1953.

Collected Poems of Idris Davies, edited by Islwyn Jenkins, Gomerian Press (Llandysul, Wales), 1972.

Caneuon y weriniaeth (title means "Songs of the Welsh Republic"), Welsh Socialist Party (Pontypridd, Wales), 1989.

(With others) *Five Settings of Poems* (includes musical score), Mansel Thomas Trust (Mangor, Wales), 1990.

Fe'm ganed i yn Rhymni (poems; title means "I Was Born in Rhymney"), Gomer (Llandysul, Wales), 1990.

Poems of Idris Davies: The Central Achievement, introduction and notes by Anthony Conran, University of Wales Press (Cardiff, Wales), 1990.

Places (poems for children), National Language Unit of Wales (Treforest, Wales), 1991.

The Angry Summer: A Poem of 1926, introduction and notes by Anthony Conran, University of Wales Press (Cardiff, Wales), 1993.

The Complete Poems of Idris Davies, edited and introduced by Dafydd Johnston, University of Wales Press (Cardiff, Wales), 1994.

SIDELIGHTS: Welsh working-class poet Idris Davies was born in 1905 in Rhymney, Wales, the son of a coal miner. Davies learned Welsh at home and English in the local elementary school. At the age of fourteen, he ended his schooling and went to work at the mine where his father served as the chief winder. It was there that a coworker introduced him to the work of nineteenth-century poet Percy Bysshe Shelley. Davies devoured the poetry, soon realizing that the literary form was especially appropriate for relating political ideas and causes, particularly socialism and human dignity. In 1926 Davies lost a finger in a work accident. Shortly after his recovery, a prolonged miners' strike, followed by the closure of the mine where he had worked, forced him to look for another means of employment. He returned to school, completing his education first through correspondence courses and

then at Loughborough College and the University of Nottingham. In 1932 he began teaching at a primary school in London's East End. His love of poetry led him to frequent the nearby Griff's Bookshop, where he became acquainted with a group of Welsh writers who would influence his own work.

Davies began publishing his poems in newspapers and small journals, but got his first significant exposure with the advent of *Wales,* a magazine run by the literary journalist, editor, and poet Keidrych Rhys. Subsequently, Davies published several volumes of poetry with themes involving the conditions of southern Wales during the Depression, the outbreak of World War II, and human suffering. His early experiences as a coal miner and growing up in a community populated by other miners had a strong influence on his writing, and despite the narrowness of his background, he managed to write broadly, in a way that many readers could identify with. As Derek Stanford remarked in *Books and Bookmen,* "It was no doubt natural that Idris Davies . . . should have been considered . . . as a *poet of statement.*" Stanford further noted, "Today, as we read these poems, we stress less the moral content in them and accent instead the lyrical and aesthetic aspect. They are still 'poetic documents,' but the fact that their bearing on the world of action is now considerably smaller enables us to appreciate the more their imaginative and descriptive qualities."

Rather than limiting himself to a specific style of poetry, Davies experimented with varying rhythms and rhyming schemes. He excelled at writing in the ballad form, a skill that led to many of his poems being adopted as songs by folk and rock singers through the decades. "The Bells of Rhymney," a ballad based on a mining accident, was set to music by Pete Seger. Many artists went on to perform the song, including the Byrds, Jimmy Page, Judy Collins, Cher, and Bob Dylan.

BIOGRAPHICAL AND CRITICAL SOURCES:

BOOKS

Stephens, Meic, editor, *Oxford Companion to the Literature of Wales,* Oxford University Press (New York, NY), 1986.

PERIODICALS

Anglo-Welsh Review, Volume 87, 1987, John Pikoulis, "Idris Davies: Poetry and Propaganda," pp. 91-104.

Books and Bookmen, October, 1972, Derek Stanford, review of *Collected Poems of Idris Davies,* p. R12.

New Welsh Review, winter, 1998-99, "Idris Davies's Middle Years," pp. 22-25.

Times Literary Supplement, September 8, 1995, Valentine Cunningham, "Whistling in the Grime," review of *The Complete Poems of Idris Davies,* p. 27.

ONLINE

New Hope International Review Online, http://www. nhi.clara.net/ (September 25, 2005), "Idris Davies: A Carol for the Coalfield."

University of Wales Press Web site, http://www.uwp. co.uk/ (September 25, 2005).*

*   *   *

DAWES, Christopher
(Push)

PERSONAL: Male.

ADDRESSES: Home—London, England. *Agent*—c/o Author Mail, Omnibus Press, 257 Park Ave. S., 20th Fl., New York, NY 10010.

CAREER: Music journalist and author, beginning mid-1980s. *Melody Maker,* editor of dance section; edited magazines *Musik* and *Mondo.*

WRITINGS:

(As Push; with Mireille Silcott) *The Book of E: All about Ecstasy,* Omnibus Press (New York, NY), 2000.

Rat Scabies and the Holy Grail, Sceptre (London, England), 2005.

Has written for *Sounds* and *Melody Maker.*

SIDELIGHTS: British-based music journalist Christopher Dawes, who also uses the pen name Push, has written about all kinds of pop music. His career began in the mid-1980s, and includes creating a dance section for *Melody Maker,* editing the clubbing magazine *Muzik,* and editing the men's magazine *Mondo.* His first book was *The Book of E: All about Ecstasy,* written with Mireille Silcott. He has also written an account of his travels with punk rocker Rat Scabies, who was once drummer for the Damned. *Rat Scabies and the Holy Grail* reveals the inspiration for a quest that takes the two men into rural France.

Dawes and Scabies meet as neighbors in the village of Brentford, England. The drummer, who is known for setting his drums on fire while continuing to play them, proves to be an interesting and unpredictable friend. He convinces Dawes to join him in his search for the Holy Grail, which begins with investigating reports that a French priest made a mysterious discovery in the late nineteenth century. Their bizarre adventure requires historical research, the purchase of metal detectors, and possibly joining the Masonic Order.

Reviews of *Rat Scabies and the Holy Grail* described it as a quirky but entertaining book. A *Kirkus Reviews* writer called it "a dizzy and highly enjoyable caper," while June Sawyers commented in *Booklist* that "Dawes has a droll humor and a winning style." *Entertainment Weekly* writer Tom Sinclair recommended the narrative as a "post-punk Travels with My Aunt."

BIOGRAPHICAL AND CRITICAL SOURCES:

PERIODICALS

Booklist, June 1, 2005, June Sawyers, review of *Rat Scabies and the Holy Grail,* p. 1742.

Bookseller, February 4, 2005, review of *Rat Scabies and the Holy Grail,* p. 37.

Entertainment Weekly, July 15, 2005, Tom Sinclair, review of *Rat Scabies and the Holy Grail,* p. 78.

Kirkus Reviews, May 1, 2005, review of *Rat Scabies and the Holy Grail,* p. 522.*

*   *   *

DEITCH, Kim 1944-

PERSONAL: Born May 21, 1944; son of Gene Deitch (a cartoonist and animator).

ADDRESSES: *Home*—New York, NY. *Agent*—c/o Author Mail, Pantheon Books, 1540 Broadway, New York, NY 10036.

CAREER: Cartoonist and writer. Editor of *Gothic Blimp Works,* 1969. *Exhibitions:* Exhibitor of original drawings at galleries, including La Luz de Jesus Gallery, Los Angeles, CA, 1994; and Bess Cutler Gallery, New York, NY, 1995. Group exhibits include *Kartoon Fever,* Four Color Images, 1994; and *Comix by the Bit,* Cartoon Art Museum, San Francisco, CA, 1995.

WRITINGS:

Hollywoodland, Fantagraphics Books (Westlake Village, CA), 1987.
Beyond the Pale! Krazed Komics and Stories, Fantagraphics Books (Seattle, WA), 1989.
A Shroud for Waldo, Fantagraphics Books (Seattle, WA), 1992.
All Waldo Comics (collection), Fantagraphics Books (Seattle, WA), 1992.
(Illustrator) Lewis Carroll, *Alice's Adventures Under Ground,* Cottage Classics (San Francisco, CA), 2000.
(With brother, Simon Deitch) *Boulevard of Broken Dreams,* Pantheon Books (New York, NY), 2002.

Author-illustrator of comic books, including *Corn Fed Comics, Shadowland,* and *No Business like Show Business;* of comic-book series *The Search for Smilin' Ed;* and of children's comic-book series *Nickelodeon.* Contributor of comics, articles, and interviews to periodicals, including *East Village Other, Raw, Bijou Funnies, Arcade, Comics Journal, Pictopia, Weirdo, Tales of Sex and Death, Details, Zero Zero,* and *Little Lit.* Contributor of comics to anthologies, including *Thrilling Murder Comics,* San Francisco Comic Book Co. (San Francisco, CA), 1971; *Lean Years,* Cartoonists Co-op Press (San Francisco, CA), 1974; and *The Narrative Corpse,* Raw Books (Richmond, VA), 1995.

SIDELIGHTS: Veteran comic-book author and illustrator Kim Deitch has been heavily influenced by the animation industry, in which his father, Gene Deitch, worked. Kim has been drawing comics since 1967 and is considered one of the most influential creators of "underground" comics. He is known for such characters as the Sixties flower child "Sunshine Girl," the sex-crazed dual personality "Uncle Ed," and the blue cartoon cat "Waldo," a main character in his 2002 graphic novel *Boulevard of Broken Dreams.* Often collaborating with his brother, Simon, Deitch has widely published his comics in periodicals and anthologies, as well as in graphic novels. He is noted for his complex characters and narratives and his bold, intricate drawings.

Beyond the Pale! Krazed Komics and Stories is a collection featuring autobiographical comic-book stories, including "Keep 'em Flying," in which Deitch is hypnotized and winds up on another planet with Waldo the cat, and "Two Jews from Yonkers," in which the cartoonist becomes involved with drugs and the pope. A contributor to *Publishers Weekly* described the book as having "Sunday-morning-funnies charm as interpreted by a hippie/Bowery bum."

A Shroud for Waldo brings back the biblical Judas Iscariot as a cat demon, which turns out to be Waldo. In a hospital detoxification ward, Waldo finds an orderly who is actually an immortal spirit from Jesus' day. The orderly discovers a shroud with none other than Waldo's image on it. A *Publishers Weekly* contributor was disappointed with the book, calling the illustrations "amazing" but overdone and the story "directionless and lackluster."

For *All Waldo Comics,* Deitch compiles *Waldo* strips from several sources, beginning with late-1960s newspapers, thus bringing many of his earlier works back into print. Gordon Flagg, of *Booklist,* found this countercultural collection to have "a certain period charm thanks to . . . drugs, sex, and a conspiratorial CIA."

A collaboration between Deitch and his brother Simon Deitch, the graphic novel *Boulevard of Broken Dreams* contains three chapters: "The Boulevard of Broken Dreams," "The Mishkin File," and "Waldo World." It features Waldo as both a demonic talking cat and a doll and is an allegory of the rise and fall of animation in America. Deitch told Jeffrey Ford, in an interview for *Fantastic Metropolis,* that the story took about four years to develop and another five months to fine tune. It grew out of a true story involving a comment made by cartoon pioneer Winsor McKay at a testimonial dinner in the late 1920s. Creator of the classic comic strip *Little Nemo,* McKay told the group that they had taken what he created and "turned it into shit!" through the process of animation.

Boulevard of Broken Dreams follows brothers Ted and Al Mishkin, animators who work for the small Fontaine Talking Fables studio, from their teenage years in the 1920s through Al's death in 1993 in a toy store. It is rich with parodies of well-known figures in the animation and cartoon business, including McKay. Deitch's drawings have been compared to those of the Fleischer brothers, who created the "Betty Boop" comic strip. Ted is Waldo's alcoholic creator, and the cat is driving him to madness, even as he serves as inspiration for the cartoonist.

A *Publishers Weekly* contributor commented on the intricate but clear story line in *Boulevard of Broken Dreams*, saying its "complicated chronology is remarkably engaging, albeit weirdly paced." Ray Olson, in *Booklist*, described the book as "marvelous" and said its main and secondary characters—created in the style of 1920s and 1930s cartoons—are so successfully woven "into what is already a tapestry of flashbacks and flashforwards that the momentum of the whole never flags." Nick Hornby, writing in the *New York Times Book Review*, compared Deitch's drawings to those of Robert Crumb in their "feverish, angry energy." Hornby also said the book "is just as much about the neutering and Disneyfication of animation as it is about the self-destructiveness of genius."

Yakov Chodosh, writing in the *Copacetic Comics Company*, praised Deitch's art, with its bold, black parallel lines used for shading. As Chodosh observed, "Panels can include up to fifteen individual faces, all belonging to characters with their own evident personalities. And his layouts are some of the most innovative that have ever been seen in comics."

Steven Heller, in a review for *Eye*, found that the book "creates emotional tension between those who are fervent about original iconoclastic cartooning versus those who proffer derivative, market-driven pap," but that it is also "a gripping narrative about failure, betrayal, passion, and cruel twists of fate," as well as "a stunning analysis" of the way dementia can take over the mind. Tasha Robinson, in an online review for the *Onion A.V. Club Web site*, commented that the story is "vivid" and "rich," with "many carefully crafted layers" that "cloak reality under fantasy." Ford, in the interview with Deitch, wrote: "Deitch's story blends drama and humor in a non-linear, meta-fictional narrative with black and white pen work that in its complexity of imagery at times achieves the hallucina-

tory. This said, the story never confuses; the characters never fail to elicit the reader's interest or emotional response."

BIOGRAPHICAL AND CRITICAL SOURCES:

BOOKS

Acton, Jay, Alan LeMond, and Parker Hodges, *Mug Shots: Who's Who in the New Earth,* Meridian, 1972.

PERIODICALS

Booklist, April 15, 1992, Gordon Flagg, review of *All Waldo Comics,* p. 1493; November 1, 2002, Ray Olson, review of *Boulevard of Broken Dreams,* p. 465.

Eye, winter, 2002, Steven Heller, review of *Boulevard of Broken Dreams.*

New York Times Book Review, December 22, 2002, Nick Hornby, "Draw What You Know" (review of *Boulevard of Broken Dreams*), pp. 10-11.

Publishers Weekly, October 27, 1989, review of *Beyond the Pale! Krazed Komics and Stories,* p. 61; July 6, 1992, review of *A Shroud for Waldo,* p. 51; December 2, 2002, review of *Boulevard of Broken Dreams,* p. 36.

ONLINE

Copacetic Comics Company Web site, http://home.earthlink.net/ (August 6, 2003), Yakov Chodosh, review of *Boulevard of Broken Dreams.*

Fantastic Metropolis, http://www.fantasticmetropolis.com/ (October 9, 2002), Jeffrey Ford, "An Interview with Kim Deitch."

Lambiek, http://www.lambiek.net/ (August 4, 2003), "Kim Deitch."

Onion A.V. Club Web site, http://www.theonionavclub.com/ (January 29, 2003), Tasha Robinson, review of *Boulevard of Broken Dreams.*

Random House Web site, http://www.randomhouse.com/ (August 6, 2003), "Kim Deitch."*

de KOK, Ingrid 1951-

PERSONAL: Born June 4, 1951, in Johannesburg, South Africa; partner of Tony Morphet; children: one son. *Education:* University of Witwatersrand, B.A., 1972; University of Cape Town, B.A. (with honors), 1974; Queen's University (Kingston, Ontario, Canada), M.A., 1984.

ADDRESSES: Home—Kapstadt, South Africa. *Office*—Centre for Extra Mural Studies, University of Cape Town, Rondebosch, 7701, South Africa.

CAREER: University of Cape Town, Cape Town, South Africa, junior lecturer, 1975-76, associate professor in Center for Extra-Mural Studies, 1988—; Khanya College, Cape Town, South Africa, planning coordinator, 1984-87.

AWARDS, HONORS: Rockefeller Foundation residency fellowship in Bellagio, Italy, 1999; Carpace/Snailpress Poetry Prize, 2000; Dalro Poetry Award, 2002; Civitella Ranieri rellowship, 2003; Herman Charles Bosman Award for English Literature, 2003.

WRITINGS:

POEMS

Familiar Ground, Ravan Press (Johannesburg, South Africa), 1988.
Transfer, Snailpress (Plumstead, South Africa), 1997.
Terrestrial Things, Snailpress (Cape Town, South Africa), 2002.

OTHER

(Editor, with Karen Press) Albie Sachs and others, *Spring Is Rebellious: Arguments about Cultural Freedom,* Buchu Books (Cape Town, South Africa), 1990.
(Compiler, with Gus Ferguson) *City in Words* (poetry anthology), David Philip (Cape Town, South Africa), 2001.

Contributor to literary journals and anthologies, including *Breaking the Silence: A Century of Women's Poetry,* 1990; *Broken Strings: The Politics of Poetry in South Africa,* 1992; and *Book of African Women's Poetry,* 1995. Advisory editor, *World Literature Today: South African Literature in Transition.* Also contributor to numerous academic publications.

Author's works have been translated into Italian, French, Japanese, German, Afrikaans, and Dutch.

SIDELIGHTS: Ingrid de Kok is a poet whose work often focuses on political issues and the history of suffering and discrimination that became part of South Africa's heritage during apartheid. However, when asked by *New Coin Online* interviewer Susan Rich if she is actively concerned with creating a political message in her poems, de Kok replied, "It's not an intentional act or an active project. If it were, given how I work, something would go wrong." The poet also told Rich, "I think the poet's responsibility is to write a good poem. It's a social responsibility as well as an individual responsibility." Expanding on her sense of commitment, de Kok added, "I think that's how you respect your readership, engage with your community, make a contribution—by doing your best piece of work."

De Kok's first volume of poems, *Familiar Ground,* combines intensity with irony by probing political issues and human suffering. Writing in the *Southern African Review of Books,* Malvern van Wyk Smith commented that the poems in this anthology are "more about the appropriation of the terrain, here notably the remembered territory of a South African childhood spent on the edge of the desert." The reviewer also called the middle section of the anthology the "Canadian" section, referring to poems written while de Kok lived in Canada in the late 1970s and early 1980s. These poems, noted van Wyk Smith, are more "self-obsessive" compared with the "power" of the final poems, "presumably unleashed by de Kok's return to South Africa" in 1983. "The poems are largely about other people, not herself," added Smith, "and two delightfully 'found poems' about the tragicomedy of South African life suggest that back home the poems come-tumbling in on her."

It was nearly a decade after *Familiar Ground* before de Kok's next volume of poetry, titled *Transfer,* was published. In an article based on her speech at the launch of *Transfer* and posted on the *Electronic Mail and Guardian* Web site, Antjie Krog noted that these poems contain a "fearlessness, guts to transgress, an unfailing ear for the alternation of consonants on the tongue, a turn of thinking and the ability to capture in the most delicate and individual terms a devastating phenonmenon." Writing in *World Literature Today,* Robert L. Berner noted that the volume of twenty-nine poems can virtually be divided in half: the fourteen poems that make up the first part "deal, usually only by implication, with South African political, social, and environmental conditions." Berner described the poems in the second part of the volume as "private" and more focused on issues like "childbirth and love—and lost love."

De Kok's third volume of poems, *Terrestrial Things,* released in 2002, features recurring themes related to the AIDS pandemic and the Truth and Reconciliation Commission, a courtlike body established by the South African government to hear testimonies from both the victims and the perpetrators of racist violence under the country's former apartheid system. As a result of its hearings, the commission convicted some perpetrators and granted amnesty to others. In the poem "At the Commission," she writes about a police ambush that resulted in a group of young men being shot. The central issue in the resulting trial is whether the police shot the men in cold blood or in self-defense because they were going to be attacked. In an interview with Erica Kelly for the Brock Press Web site, de Kok explained the poem: "The question I raise is does it matter at this point what the exact truth was? No amount of explanation, of cause and effect, can take you away from the fact that they were shot and killed. It's a debate about the nature of truth."

BIOGRAPHICAL AND CRITICAL SOURCES:

BOOKS

Buck, Claire, editor, *The Bloomsbury Guide to Women's Literature,* Prentice-Hall General Reference (New York, NY), 1992.

PERIODICALS

Southern African Review of Books, December, 1988-January, 1989, Malvern van Wyk Smith, review of *Familiar Ground.*
World Literature Today, spring, 1998, Robert L. Berner, review of *Transfer,* p. 443.

ONLINE

Brock Press Web site, http://www.brocku.ca/press/ (May 3, 2002), Erica Kelly, "Interview with a Poet: In Conversation with South African Ingrid de Kok."
Crossing Project, http://www.devon.gov.uk/ (May 3, 2002), "Poetry by Ingrid de Kok."
Electronic Mail and Guardian, http://www.mg.co.za/ (January 19, 1998), Antjie Krog, "Defenceless in the Face of de Kok's Poetry."
H-Net, http://www.h-net.org/ (March 28, 2003), Simon Lewis, review of *Terrestrial Things.*
Ingrid de Kok Home Page, http://www.ems.uct.ac.za/ ingrid (September 24, 2005).
New Coin Online, http://www.ru.ac.za/institutes/isea/ newcoin/ (May 3, 2002), Susan Rich, interview with Ingrid de Kok.

*   *   *

DELGADO, Jane L. 1953-

PERSONAL: Born 1953, in Cuba; immigrated to United States, 1955; daughter of Juan Lorenzo Delgado Borges (a publisher) and Lucila Aurora Navarro Delgado; married Herbert Lustig, 1981 (marriage ended); married; second husband's name Mark; children: Elizabeth. *Education:* State University of New York at New Paltz, B.A., 1972; New York University, M.A., 1975; State University of New York, Stony Brook, M.S., 1985, Ph.D., 1985.

ADDRESSES: Office—National Coalition of Hispanic Health and Human Services Organizations, 1501 16th St. NW, Washington, DC 20036.

CAREER: Clinical psychologist and administrator. *Sesame Street* (television show), New York, NY, children's talent coordinator, 1973-75; New York Experimental and Bilingual Institute, instructor; Board of Cooperative Educational Services, Westbury, NY, staff member, 1977-79; U.S. Department of Health and Human Services, Washington, DC, staff member in Immediate Office of the Secretary, 1979-85; National Coalition of Hispanic Health and Human Services Organizations, president and CEO, 1985—. Kresge Foundation, trustee and chair of Audit and Special Opportunities committees; Patient Safety Institute, secretary and treasurer; Lovelace Respiratory Research Institute, member of executive committee; Ocean Awareness Project, secretary and treasurer. Member of advisory panel on Medicare Education, 2002—member of National Advisory Council for Mrs. Rosalyn Carter's Task Force on Mental Health, Robert Wood Johnson's National Advisory Committee on Hospice and Palliative Care, and Environmental Protection Agency's Clean Air Act Advisory Council; member of honorary board, Alaska Native Heritage Center. Advisor to American Academy of Family Physicians and to March of Dimes.

AWARDS, HONORS: Las Primeras Award, MANA, 1994; Carter-Bumpers Award, 1995; Dr. Harvey Wiley Award/Food & Drug Administration Commissioner's Special Citation, 1995; Community Leadership Award, Puerto Rican Family Institute, 1996; Florence Kelley Consumer Leadership Award, National Consumer League, 2003.

WRITINGS:

(With National Hispanic Women's Health Initiative) *¡Salud! A Latina's Guide to Total Health—Body, Mind, and Spirit,* HarperCollins (New York, NY), 1997, revised edition, Rayo (New York, NY), 2002.

¡Salud! has been published in Spanish.

SIDELIGHTS: A practicing clinical psychologist and head of the largest network of Hispanic health-care providers in the United States, Jane L. Delgado is also the coauthor of *¡Salud! A Latina's Guide to Total Health—Body, Mind, and Spirit.* The book is a medical guide that focuses on the U.S. Latina community, which is often underserved by the health-care system. Delgado divides her book into four sections that discuss the role of family and community in Latina health, specific women's health issues, general Latino community health problems, and lifestyle changes and medicines. Other issues covered include the role of Latina women as caregivers and issues associated with caring for the elderly. The author also pays special attention to sexual issues, such as contraception and the prevention of sexually transmitted diseases that are often culturally taboo topics in the Latina community.

Delgado also addresses how Latinas can be better health-care consumers and provides information on numerous resources from organizations and Web sites to books and pamphlets. Many of the topics addressed are also highlighted by personal histories, as well as a recounting by the author of her own youth and early lack of knowledge about personal health care. Barbara M. Bibel, writing in *Library Journal,* noted that Delgado "honors Hispanic culture throughout by stressing the importance of spirituality, alternative therapies, and family relationships in daily life." In a review in *School Library Journal,* Carmen Ospina called the book "practical, empowering, and engaging" and "the most comprehensive guide by and for Latinas." A *Publishers Weekly* contributor noted that the author "imparts crucial information with a warm, anecdotal, no-nonsense approach."

BIOGRAPHICAL AND CRITICAL SOURCES:

BOOKS

Notable Hispanic American Women, Book 1, Thomson Gale (Detroit, MI), 1993.

PERIODICALS

Library Journal, January, 1998, Maria S. Macias, review of *¡Salud! A Latina's Guide to Total Health—Body, Mind, and Spirit,* p. 82; December, 2001, review of *¡Salud!,* p. 157.
Publishers Weekly, November 19, 2001, review of *¡Salud!,* p. 61.
School Library Journal, August, 2002, Carmen Ospina, review of *¡Salud!,* p. S53.

ONLINE

Patient Safety Institute Web site, http://www.ptsafety. org/ (September 26, 2005), "Jane Delgado, Ph.D., M.S."*

*   *   *

DELIA, Edward M. 1948-

PERSONAL: Born September 23, 1948, in Brooklyn, NY; son of Edward (an executive) and Laura (Chambert) DeLia. *Ethnicity:* "American." *Education:* Brooklyn College of the City University of New York, B.A., 1970; Hofstra University, M.A. (social science),

1978; Fordham University, M.A. (sociology), 1983. *Politics:* Democrat. *Religion:* Lutheran. *Hobbies and other interests:* Philosophy.

ADDRESSES: Office—Five Towns College, 305 N. Service Rd., Dix Hills, NY 11746-5871.

CAREER: Writer. Five Towns College, Dix Hills, NY, professor of sociology, 1987—. Suffolk Community College, adjunct professor, 1990—.

WRITINGS:

The Apocalypse (historical fiction), Vize Publications (Nesconset, NY), 2004.

WORK IN PROGRESS: A work of historical fiction about Pontius Pilate.

SIDELIGHTS: Edward M. DeLia told *CA:* "My major writing interest is in historical fiction as a means of revealing deep structures of meaning about the human condition. Great writing must inspire one to think about philosophical issues; it must motivate in a clear, powerful, and memorable fashion. I write in the first person; men must write from an existential position."

*　　　*　　　*

DELIÈGE, Robert 1953-

PERSONAL: Born June 10, 1953, in Verviers, Belgium; married Vandevelde Lutgart; children: Sumitra, Rahul, Marie, Catherine. *Education:* Attended University of Louvain-la-Neuve, Belgium, 1972-77, and Oxford University, 1977-80.

ADDRESSES: Office—Collège Erasme, Institut Orientaliste, Place B. Pascal, 1, 1348 Louvain-la-Neuve, Belgium. *E-mail*—deliege@acla.ucl.ac.be.

CAREER: Anthropologist, educator, and writer. Institut Orientaliste, College Erasme, Louvain-la-Neuve, Belgium, professor.

WRITINGS:

The Bhils of Western India: Some Empirical and Theoretical Issues in Anthropology in India, National (New Delhi, India), 1985.

Les Paraiyars du Tamil Nadu, Steyler Verlag—Wort und Werk (Nettetal, Germany), 1988, translated by David Phillips as *The World of the "Untouchables": Paraiyars of Tamil Nadu,* Oxford University Press (New York, NY), 1997.

Anthropologie sociale et culturelle (textbook), De Boeck-Université (Brussels, Belgium), 1992.

Les intouchables en Inde: des castes d'exclus, Imago (Paris, France), 1995, translated by Nora Scott as *The Untouchables of India,* Berg Press (New York, NY), 1999.

Anthropologie de la parenté, A. Colin/Masson (Paris, France), 1996.

Gandhi, PUF (Paris, France), 1999.

Introduction à l'anthropologie structurale, Le Seuil (Paris, France), 2001, translated by Nora Scott as *Lévi-Strauss Today: An Introduction to Structural Anthropology,* Berg Press (New York, NY), 2004.

Les castes en Inde aujourd'hui (title means "Today's Castes in India"), Presses Universitaires de France (Paris, France), 2004.

La religion des intouchables de l'Inde (title means "The Religion of the Untouchables of India"), Presses Universitaires du Septentrion (Villeneuve d'Ascq, France), 2004.

Contributor to *Intégration, lien social et citoyenneté,* edited by Gilles Ferréol, Presses Universitaires du Septentrion, 1998.

SIDELIGHTS: Robert Deliège is a Belgian scholar who has written extensively on the Untouchable caste of India. His book *Les intouchables en Inde: des castes d'exclus* gives an overview of the history of this most discriminated-against class of people, a group both reviled by other Hindus as impure and exploited by higher classes due to their willingness to perform jobs no one else wants that are nonetheless indispensable to the function of the Indian economy. The author discusses the views of higher castes on untouchability, as well as the views of the Untouchables themselves. Also covered are recent changes in attitudes toward Untouchables as a result of government-led affirmative-action programs and of socio-religious movements led by the Untouchables themselves. "This excellent book," D.A. Chekki concluded in a *Choice* review, "is highly recommended for those interested in South Asian studies, social stratification, and inequality."

In *Les Paraiyars du Tamil Nadu*—translated as *The World of the "Untouchables": Paraiyars of Tamil Nadu*—Deliège provides an in-depth look at a group of Untouchables, both Hindu and Catholic, living in an isolated village in the south of India. Based on observations made during a two-year stay in this remote region, the author describes the village itself and the daily details of living there. He then discusses the power structure operating within the village. One chapter is devoted to how the Paraiyar make their living, usually as brick makers or occasional laborers. The next chapter relates how this caste of Untouchables is organized and its relations with both higher and lower castes, as well as with other castes of Untouchables. Another chapter covers family relations and marriage; and, in the last chapter, Deliège focuses on what reviewers felt to be the most interesting aspect of the Paraiyar: their religious beliefs and customs. "I particularly enjoyed the chapter on religion," remarked Anthony Good in *MAN*, "which explores the surprisingly slight and subtle differences between Catholics and Hindus." Both Good and Stephen Fuchs, who reviewed the book for *Asian Folklore Studies*, noted that, although Christianity forbids the kind of discrimination Hindus practice, many Tamil Christians still practice untouchability and believe in karma and reincarnation—ideas borrowed from Hinduism—to justify continuing the practice. For Fuchs, *Les Paraiyars du Tamil Nadu* is particularly valuable for its portrait of these Indian Christians: "The author is the first anthropologist to study a Christian Harijan [Untouchable] caste community."

Deliège is also the author of the textbook *Anthropologie sociale et culturelle*. In this book the author casts his net widely, attempting to give an overview of the major developments in social and cultural anthropology, including evolutionism, diffusionism, culturalism, functionalism, and structuralism. There are few textbooks on anthropology available in French, Claude Meillassoux noted in the *Journal of the Royal Anthropological Institute*, and thus Deliège's conventional presentation of his subject, and the candid way he presents viewpoints in opposition to his own, which allows readers to make their own judgments, is exemplary, according to this reviewer. "It would be difficult to ask more of a work covering such a vast field in such a narrow perspective," Meillassoux concluded.

In his book *Les castes en Inde aujourd'hui*, the author further explores the caste system in India, examining both social institutions such as marriage and concepts within anthropology used to study caste. Writing in *Pacific Affairs*, Nicolas Jaoul noted that the author "provides as clear a picture as possible of the multiple developments in the phenomena of caste." Jaoul went on to write: "Rooting himself in the diversity and nuances of local situations, he proposes to study caste as a 'changing institution' . . . whose 'subtle and adaptable nature' . . . clearly comes to the fore once it is conceived of as being in constant evolution." The reviewer also noted that the author provides "a critical examination, one that enables the reader to find his or her way through a vast literature."

BIOGRAPHICAL AND CRITICAL SOURCES:

BOOKS

Deliège, Robert, *Les castes en Inde aujourd'hui*, Presses Universitaires de France (Paris, France), 2004.

PERIODICALS

Asian Folklore Studies, April, 1990, Stephen Fuchs, review of *Les Paraiyars du Tamil Nadu*, p. 174.
Choice, January, 2000, D.A. Chekki, review of *The Untouchables of India*, p. 975.
Contemporary Sociology, March, 2001, Joseph Gusfield, review of *The Untouchables of India*, pp. 119-120.
Ethnic and Racial Studies, September, 1999, Mary Searle-Chatterjee, review of *The World of the "Untouchables": Paraiyars of Tamil Nadu*, p. 938.
Indian Economic and Social History Review, July-September, 2000, Vijay Prashad, review of *The Untouchables of India*, p. 366.
Journal of the Royal Anthropological Institute, March, 1995, Claude Meillassoux, review of *Anthropologie sociale et culturelle*, p. 183.

MAN, March, 1990, Anthony Good, review of *Les Paraiyars du Tamil Nadu,* p. 162.

Pacific Affairs, spring, 2005, Nicolas Jaoul, review of *Les castes en Inde aujourd'hui,* p. 153.*

* * *

DENG, Alephonsion 1984(?)-

PERSONAL: Born c. 1984, in Sudan; immigrated to United States, 2001.

ADDRESSES: Home—San Diego, CA. *Agent*—c/o Author Mail, PublicAffairs, 250 W. 57th St., Ste. 1321, New York, NY 10107.

CAREER: Writer. Ralphs Grocery Store, Hillcrest, CA, employee; former actor.

WRITINGS:

(With Benjamin Ajak, Judy Bernstein, and Benson Deng) *They Poured Fire on Us from the Sky: The True Story of Three Lost Boys from Sudan,* PublicAffairs (New York, NY), 2005.

SIDELIGHTS: For Sidelights, see Deng, Benson.

BIOGRAPHICAL AND CRITICAL SOURCES:

BOOKS

Ajak, Benjamin, Judy Bernstein, Alephonsion Deng, and Benson Deng, *They Poured Fire on Us from the Sky: The True Story of Three Lost Boys from Sudan,* PublicAffairs (New York, NY), 2005.

PERIODICALS

Del Mar Times, May 27, 2005, Erin Spry, "From Death March to New Life on Coast."

Good Times Weekly, July 14, 2005, Christa Martin, review of *They Poured Fire on Us from the Sky.*

Kirkus Reviews, March 1, 2005, review of *They Poured Fire on Us from the Sky,* p. 272.

Library Journal, April 1, 2005, Maria C. Bagshaw, review of *They Poured Fire on Us from the Sky,* p. 107.

Los Angeles Times Magazine, January 5, 2003, David Weddle, "What the Lost Boys of Sudan Found in America."

Publishers Weekly, April 11, 2005, review of *They Poured Fire on Us from the Sky,* p. 40.

San Diego Union-Tribune, June 12, 2005, Wendy L. Smith, review of *They Poured Fire on Us from the Sky.*

ONLINE

BookLoons, http://www.bookloons.com/ (September 29, 2005), Mary Ann Smyth, review of *They Poured Fire on Us from the Sky.*

BookPage, http://www.bookpage.com/ (September 29, 2005), Anne Bartlett, review of *They Poured Fire on Us from the Sky.*

Insight News, http://www.insightnews.com/ (September 29, 2005), Terry Schlichenmeyer, review of *They Poured Fire on Us from the Sky.*

PublicAffairs Web site, http://www.publicaffairsbooks.com/ (September 29, 2005).

They Poured Fire on Us from the Sky Web site, http://www.theypouredfire.com/ (September 29, 2005).*

* * *

DENG, Benson 1984(?)-

PERSONAL: Born c. 1984, in Sudan; immigrated to United States, 2001.

ADDRESSES: Home—San Diego, CA. *Agent*—c/o Author Mail, PublicAffairs, 250 W. 57th St., Ste. 1321, New York, NY 10107.

CAREER: Writer. Ralphs Grocery Store, Hillcrest, CA, employee for two years; Waste Management, El Cajon, CA, overseer of computer and digital photography system.

WRITINGS:

(With Benjamin Ajak, Judy Bernstein, and Alephonsion Deng) *They Poured Fire on Us from the Sky: The True Story of Three Lost Boys from Sudan,* PublicAffairs (New York, NY), 2005.

SIDELIGHTS: Benson Deng, his brother, Alephonsion Deng, and their cousin, Benjamin Ajak, are the authors (with the aid of Judy Bernstein) of *They Poured Fire on Us from the Sky: The True Story of Three Lost Boys from Sudan.* In 1987 Benson and Benjamin fled together from their village in the Sudan following its attack as part of an ongoing war between the Sudan People's Liberation Army and the Sudanese government that began in the 1980s. Two years later, Alephonsion also fled the village. After a decade or so of surviving almost entirely on their own, the three made it to the United States where they wrote their memoir together. Told in a series of essays, the stories recount the boys' many ordeals. For example, when Benson first fled, all he was wearing was his underwear, which remained his only clothing for the next three months as he traveled at night to avoid being found and likely murdered.

Critics were not only moved by the young men's story, but by its eloquence as well. Writing a review of *They Poured Fire on Us from the Sky* for the *BookPage* Web site, Anne Bartlett commented: "In lucid, sometimes lovely writing, the boys tell of hunger, exhaustion, fear and loss—all struggles that no child should have to bear." Writing in *Library Journal,* Maria C. Bagshaw commented that "these men reveal the constancy of human nature: missing a mother, happiness at finding a brother, the thirst for education, and a will to survive." In addition, a *Publishers Weekly* contributor noted that "this collection is moving in its depictions of unbelievable courage."

BIOGRAPHICAL AND CRITICAL SOURCES:

BOOKS

Ajak, Benjamin, Judy Bernstein, Alephonsion Deng, and Benson Deng, *They Poured Fire on Us from the Sky: The True Story of Three Lost Boys from Sudan,* PublicAffairs (New York, NY), 2005.

PERIODICALS

Del Mar Times, May 27, 2005, Erin Spry, "From Death March to New Life on Coast."
Good Times Weekly, July 14, 2005, Christa Martin, review of *They Poured Fire on Us from the Sky.*

Kirkus Reviews, March 1, 2005, review of *They Poured Fire on Us from the Sky,* p. 272.
Library Journal, April 1, 2005, Maria C. Bagshaw, review of *They Poured Fire on Us from the Sky,* p. 107.
Los Angeles Times Magazine, January 5, 2003, David Weddle, "What the Lost Boys of Sudan Found in America."
Publishers Weekly, April 11, 2005, review of *They Poured Fire on Us from the Sky,* p. 40.
San Diego Union-Tribune, June 12, 2005, Wendy L. Smith, review of *They Poured Fire on Us from the Sky.*

ONLINE

BookLoons, http://www.bookloons.com/ (September 29, 2005), Mary Ann Smyth, review of *They Poured Fire on Us from the Sky.*
BookPage, http://www.bookpage.com/ (September 29, 2005), Anne Bartlett, review of *They Poured Fire on Us from the Sky.*
Insight News, http://www.insightnews.com/ (September 29, 2005), Terry Schlichenmeyer, review of *They Poured Fire on Us from the Sky.*
PublicAffairs Web site, http://www.publicaffairsbooks. com/ (September 29, 2005).
They Poured Fire on Us from the Sky Web site, http:// www.theypouredfire.com/ (September 29, 2005).*

*   *   *

DE RIJK, Maarten
See DONKER, Anthonie

*   *   *

DERMANSKY, Marcy

PERSONAL: Married Jurgen Fauth (a writer and critic). *Education:* Attended Haverford College; University of Southern Mississippi, M.A.

ADDRESSES: Home—Astoria, NY. *Agent*—c/o Author Mail, William Morrow and Company, 10 E. 53rd St., 7th Fl., New York, NY 10022.

CAREER: Writer and critic. *About.com,* film critic. Previously worked in temporary jobs and in full-time administrative position.

MEMBER: New York Online Film Critics Society.

AWARDS, HONORS: Carson McCullers Short-Story Prize, Story magazine, 1999; Andre Dubus Novella Award, Smallmouth Press, 2002; MacDowell fellow.

WRITINGS:

Twins (fiction), William Morrow (New York, NY), 2005.

Stories have been published in numerous journals, including *Alaska Quarterly Review, Indiana Review, New Orleans Review, Mississippi Review, Gulf Coast,* and *McSweeney's.* Stories also included in anthology *Love Stories: A Literary Companion to Tennis.*

SIDELIGHTS: Marcy Dermansky's novel, *Twins,* reveals the lives of identical twins Sue and Chloe as each narrate their own story in alternating chapters. Although the sisters form a tight bond, Sue is jealous of Chloe, whom Sue perceives as being perfect in so many ways. The novel primarily focuses on the time between the girls' thirteenth birthday, when they get tattoos as a sign of their devotion to each other, through their eighteenth birthday. Sue is the more devoted of the two and tries to constrain Chloe within her orbit, while Chloe wants to be more independent and experience a normal teenaged life. In addition to this identity struggle between the twins, the trying teen years prove no different for the two, who deal with drug abuse, love, and sex as well as negligent parents. "Her portrayal of the difficulty of growing up and of raising children in today's world rings true," wrote Christine DeZelar-Tiedman in a review in *Library Journal.* A *Publishers Weekly* contributor called the book an "entertaining debut" and also noted there is "an overarching fable-like quality to this moving and well-written story." Writing in *Kirkus Reviews,* a critic commented that the author "gives her misfits real dignity and avoids psycho-social clichés . . . while she neatly captures the girls' suburban high school world with every telling detail." The reviewer went on to write: "Sometimes despairing, sometimes blackly humorous, always engrossing and thoroughly original," *Twins* is "a wonderful debut."

BIOGRAPHICAL AND CRITICAL SOURCES:

PERIODICALS

Kirkus Reviews, June 15, 2005, review of *Twins,* p. 653.
Library Journal, July 1, 2005, Christine DeZelar-Tiedman, review of *Twins,* p. 65.
Publishers Weekly, June 27, 2005, review of *Twins,* p. 40.

ONLINE

About.com, http://worldfilm.about.com/ (September 29, 2005), brief profile of author.
Center for Writers Online, http://centerforwriters.com/ (September 29, 2005), "Dermansky Novel Due in October from William Morrow."
Marcy Dermansky Home Page, http://www.marcy dermansky.com (September 29, 2005).*

*   *   *

DOLAN, Brian

PERSONAL: Male. *Education:* University of Florida, B.A. (magna cum laude), 1992; Cambridge University, Ph.D., 1995.

ADDRESSES: Office—University of California, San Francisco, Department of Anthropology, History, and Social Medicine, 3333 California St., Ste. 485, San Francisco, CA 94143-0850. *E-mail*—dolanb@dahsm. ucsf.edu.

CAREER: Umea University, Umea, Sweden, assistant professor, 1995-96; Cambridge University, Cambridge, England, Wellcome fellow, 1996-97; University of East Anglia, Norwich, England, assistant professor, 1997-2001; University of London, London, England, assistant professor, 2001-02; University of California at San Francisco, associate professor of anthropology, history, and social medicine. Member of advisory committee, University of California Humanities Research Institute.

MEMBER: History of Science Society (chair of committee on education).

WRITINGS:

Science Unbound: Geography, Space, and Discipline, Umea (Umea, Sweden), 1998.

(Editor) *Malthus, Medicine, and Morality: Malthusianism after 1798,* Rodopi (Atlanta, GA), 2000.

Exploring European Frontiers: British Travellers in the Age of Enlightenment, St. Martin's Press (New York, NY), 2000.

Ladies of the Grand Tour: British Women in Pursuit of Enlightenment and Adventure in Eighteenth-Century Europe, HarperCollins (New York, NY), 2001.

Literature and Science: Chemistry, 1650-1850, Pickering & Chatto (London, England), 2004.

Wedgwood: The First Tycoon, Viking (New York, NY), 2004, published as *Josiah Wedgwood: Entrepreneur to the Enlightenment,* HarperCollins (London, England), 2004.

WORK IN PROGRESS: Conducting research for a book on the history of medical perceptions of the lungs.

SIDELIGHTS: Brian Dolan is an historian with research and publishing interests that encompass European cultural and scientific history during the Enlightenment, the history of environmental and occupational health, and the development and impact of medical imaging technologies. He has written books of interest to academic and general audiences, including the widely acclaimed biography *Wedgwood: The First Tycoon.*

Dolan examines the influence of travel narratives in *Exploring European Frontiers: British Travellers in the Age of Enlightenment.* The book is focused on Edward Clarke's *Travels in Various Countries of Europe, Asia, and Africa,* which was published during the years 1810 to 1822. In the role of tutor, Clarke traveled through Scandinavia, Russia, the Holy Lands, North Africa, and Greece during an unusually extensive Grand Tour. His experiences, which included the study of politics, natural science, and archaeology, reflected the British interest in examining the "civilizing process" across Europe and the eastern Mediterranean region.

Reviewers described the book as an informative, perhaps dense contribution to the literature on this historical period. Writing in *The English Historical Review,* Bruce Redford commented, "By adhering so closely to Clarke's itinerary, Dolan makes it difficult to sustain a strong, independent argument." According to *Canadian Journal of History* critic Rob Iliffe, the book is "a useful addition to the growing number of texts devoted to the multifarious ways in which Europeans classified others and thus came to redefine themselves, in and after the process of 'Enlightenment.'"

In the course of writing *Exploring European Frontiers,* Dolan amassed a surprisingly large research file on the bold females who transgressed the customary restrictions on British women to take a grand tour of the European continent. The research resulted in *Ladies of the Grand Tour: British Women in Pursuit of Enlightenment and Adventure in Eighteenth-Century Europe.* Letters, journals, and diaries show how these travelers enjoyed new personal and intellectual freedom. Famous figures, such as Mary Wollstonecraft, and celebrity gossip are featured, as well as more practical issues, such as advice on what to pack.

Ladies of the Grand Tour interested reviewers, some of whom wished for a different style of presentation. The book is "less engaging than one would expect," wrote a *Kirkus Reviews* writer who saw "potentially compelling subject matter." As *Spectator* critic Jane Gardam wrote, "There is such marvellous, shackle-breaking drama that it is a shame Dolan cannot convey it," while in a review for *M2 Best Books,* Darren Ingram called the work "a fascinating and well-researched read that requires a little more patience than the average book." *Booklist* reviewer Mary Carroll described it as "thoroughly researched and gracefully written," and a *Contemporary Review* writer marked *Ladies of the Grand Tour* as "a valuable contribution to the growing number of books about British travellers."

Dolan examines the innovations of British pottery maker Josiah Wedgwood (1730-1795) in the biography *Wedgwood: The First Tycoon.* Born into a family of pottery makers and with resources increased by marriage to a wealthy cousin, he improved how the ceramic wares were made, created better working conditions for his employees, and established the concept that the Wedgwood brand represented "elite taste without social prejudice." His work established Wedgwood as one of the world's finest and most famous potteries; among its products is the blue jasper ware that has been popular for 225 years. While Dolan reveals the ambition that fed Wegwood's efforts, he also shows the philosophical and emotional challenges the man faced. As a rationalist free-thinker and Unitarian, he refused to decorate his china with crests. Threats to the health of his family were also a frequent concern.

The biography was widely reviewed and praised, a *Contemporary Review* contributor calling it "a well balanced account of a remarkable man." In *Publishers Weekly,* a critic noted that the book provides "a magnificent glimpse of life in 18th-century British society." Michael Prodger called Dolan "an exceptionally assured guide" in a review for the London *Telegraph,* and Judy P. Sopronyi commented in *British Heritage* that "The potter's drive seems to permeate the book, impelling the reader on."

BIOGRAPHICAL AND CRITICAL SOURCES:

PERIODICALS

Booklist, November 15, 2001, Mary Carroll, review of *Ladies of the Grand Tour: British Women in Pursuit of Enlightenment and Adventure in Eighteenth-Century Europe,* p. 543; September 15, 2002, Brad Hooper, review of *Ladies of the Grand Tour,* p. 204; October 15, 2004, David Siegfried, review of *Wedgwood: The First Tycoon,* p. 385.

British Heritage, March, 2005, Judy P. Sopronyi, review of *Wedgwood,* p. 60.

Canadian Journal of History, December, 2001, Rob Iliffe, review of *Exploring European Frontiers: British Travellers in the Age of Enlightenment,* p. 542.

Contemporary Review, October, 2001, review of *Ladies of the Grand Tour,* p. 252; April, 2005, review of *Wedgwood,* p. 251.

English Historical Review, April, 2001, Bruce Redford, review of *Exploring European Frontiers,* p. 488.

Kirkus Reviews, September 15, 2001, review of *Ladies of the Grand Tour,* p. 1334; August 15, 2004, review of *Wedgwood,* p. 785.

M2 Best Books, March 13, 2002, Darren Ingram, review of *Ladies of the Grand Tour.*

Publishers Weekly, August 16, 2004, review of *Wedgwood,* p. 53.

Spectator, June 16, 2001, Jane Gardam, review of *Ladies of the Grand Tour,* p. 38.

ONLINE

Telegraph Online, http://arts.telegraph.co.uk/ (November 14, 2004), Michael Prodger, "He Didn't Have Feet of Clay," review of *Wedgwood.**

*   *   *

DOMECQ, Brianda 1942-

PERSONAL: Born August 1, 1942, in New York, NY; immigrated to Mexico, 1951; children: one son, one daughter. *Education:* Universidad Nacional Autónoma de México, graduate, 1979.

ADDRESSES: Home—Madrid, Spain. *Agent*—c/o Author Mail, Texas Christian University Press, Texas Christian University, Box 298300, Fort Worth, TX 76129.

CAREER: Fiction writer and essayist. *Revistas de Bellas Artes,* editor, 1972-73.

MEMBER: Association of Mexican Writers, Mexican Association for Conservation of Nature (member of board; former president).

WRITINGS:

Once días—y algo más (novel), UV Editorial (Xalapa, Mexico), 1979, translation by Kay S. García published as *Eleven Days,* University of New Mexico Press (Albuquerque, NM), 1995.

Bestiario doméstico (stories; also see below), Fondo de Cultura Económica (Mexico City, Mexico), 1982.

Voces y rostros del Bravo (travel essay), photographs by Michael Calderwood, Jilguero (Mexico), 1987.

Acechando el unicornio: La virginidad en la literatura mexicana (collection), Fondo de Cultura Económica (Mexico City, Mexico), 1989.

La insólita historia de la Santa de Cabora (novel), Planeta (Mexico City, Mexico), 1990, translation by Kay S. García published as *The Astonishing Story of the Saint of Cabora,* Bilingual/Review Press (Tempe, AZ), 1998.

De cuerpo entero (autobiography), Universidad Nacional Autónoma de Mexico/Ediciones Corunda (Mexico City, Mexico), 1991.

Mujer que publica—mujer pública (essays), Editorial Diana (Mexico), 1994.

A través de los ojos de ella, two volumes, Ediciones Ariadne (Mexico), 1999.

Un día fui a caballo (stories; also see below), Instituto Seguridad y Servicios Sociales Trabajadores Estado (Mexico City, Mexico), 2000.

When I Was a Horse (includes short stories from *Bestiario doméstico* and *Un día fui a caballo*) translated by Kay S. García, Texas Christian University Press (Fort Worth, TX), 2006.

Contributor to periodicals, including *Excélsior.*

SIDELIGHTS: Journalist and author Brianda Domecq was born in New York City and moved to Mexico with her family as a child. Domecq comes from a mixed background; her Spanish father and American mother had diverse English, Irish, French, Moorish, German, and Jewish ancestries. In her writing she addresses both women's issues and broad human-philosophical questions from a sometimes surprisingly new, woman's point of view.

In Domecq's novel, *Once días—y algo más,* translated and published in English as *Eleven Days,* she draws on her own experiences when she was kidnapped and held for that time period. In *Acechando el unicornio: La virginidad en la literatura mexicana* Domecq explores the question of virginity by examining seventy-five texts from Mexican Literature that address the subject, giving the reader an overview of Mexican literature, culture, and social mores.

The essays in *Mujer que publica—mujer pública,* written over more than a decade, express Domecq's views on gender relations in Mexico and the lack of recognition for female Mexican writers. Charlene Merithew reviewed the volume for the Hope College Web site, noting that the essays "are ingeniously characterized by humor. . . . The author shows her acute ability to

see the humor that lies within the serious situations that affect her and other women, as she gives those situations an unexpected twist of perspective."

Domecq's historical novel *La insólita historia de la Santa de Cabora,* published as *The Astonishing Story of the Saint of Cabora,* is an account of Teresa Urrea, born in Ocorini, Sinaloa, in 1873. The illegitimate, green-eyed daughter of a wealthy landowner and his Yaqui servant, the girl teaches herself to read and write, ride a horse, and play guitar, and when she finally approaches the father she has worshipped from a distance, he accepts her. After falling into a trance, Teresa wakes with miraculous healing powers and is named Saint Teresa of Cabora. Teresa, a pacifist and champion of the poor, is now exploited both for financial and political reasons. She is eventually exiled, with her father, to the United States for her supposed involvement in local uprisings. The first half of the book alternates narratives between a contemporary scholar who is researching Teresa's history and an omniscient narrator who tells Teresa's life. In the middle of the book, the scholar disappears, and the third-person narration takes over the rest of the text.

Melanie Cole, who reviewed the novel in *Hispanic,* wrote that "the surprise ending, which is not really a surprise because the book has been leading to this inevitable conclusion, reminds readers that our lives are forever intertwined with the past. The author leaves us with a wondrous metaphor: that history—and a little sainthood—live within all of us." A *Kirkus Reviews* contributor called the book "an exemplary historical novel."

Domecq told *CA:* "Writing was a survival mechanism from the very beginning. Life was hard to live, but on paper things got worked out and I could at least begin to make some sense of them. I honestly believe that until recently, writing has kept me relatively sane and alive. It has also become my passion. I love to write; I honestly enjoy what I have written and look forward to producing more in the future.

"My passion influences my work. Things need to grip me (or perhaps gripe me) to get me going. After that, it is hard work.

"My writing process is blood, sweat and tears . . . well, most of the time. I basically write in the morning, although when I was a mother with small children, nighttime was my writing time. Since I am through with childraising, I can dedicate my mornings. I just sit down and write—I don't worry about form until it is time. Usually the most difficult part is finding the right structure and narrative voice, once that is discovered, the text writes itself. Then I correct, once, twice, three or four times, sometimes more. Then the text rests, sometimes for quite a while, and then I correct again. This is when I usually share it with someone else, a close friend or an editor, and get the necessary feedback for final corrections.

"The most suprising thing I've learned as a writer is that I can do it. I never really believed that I would be able to, but I just kept doing it and then I realized I was 'one of those.' I have never written commercial books, I have to go into writing with my whole heart and body or it doesn't work. Fortunately, life has given me the opportunity to do this.

"My favorite book is *La insólita historia de la Santa de Cabora*. It is a book that took me seventeen years to write, between research and actual writing. I was convinced that I would never be able to do it, but Teresita (the protagonist) inhabited my mind to such an extent that she didn't let me go ever and finally I wrote it. The book is actually not an historical novel in the real sense of this genre, it can be read on many levels and one of those levels makes Teresa very modern and facing the trials and conflicts of many modern women. Even while I was writing the book, there were entire scenes that the following morning I didn't remember writing, it was gut-writing, unconscious, coming directly from what I call 'The Sediment' which is that miasma of life experience that seems to give birth to creativity."

BIOGRAPHICAL AND CRITICAL SOURCES:

BOOKS

De Beer, Gabriella, editor, *Contemporary Mexican Women Writers: Five Voices,* University of Texas Press (Austin, TX), 1997.
Domecq, Brianda, *De cuerpo entero,* Universidad Nacional Autónoma de Mexico, Ediciones Corunda (Mexico City, Mexico) 1991.
García, Kay S., *Broken Bars: New Perspectives from Mexican Women Writers,* University of New Mexico Press (Albuquerque, NM), 1994.

PERIODICALS

Bilingual Review, September-December, 1998, "Conversation with Brianda Domecq," p. 248.
Booklist, May 15, 1998, Margaret Flanagan, review of *The Astonishing Story of the Saint of Cabora,* p. 46.
Hispanic, July-August, 1998, Melanie Cole, review of *The Astonishing Story of the Saint of Cabora,* p. 94.
Kirkus Reviews, May 15, 1998, review of *The Astonishing Story of the Saint of Cabora,* p. 98.
Library Journal, June 15, 1998, Carolyn Ellis, review of *The Astonishing Story of the Saint of Cabora,* p. 105.
Literatura Mexicana, Volume 10, 1999, Deborah Shaw, review of *La insólita historia de la Santa de Cabora,* pp. 283-312.
Modern Language Review, October, 2001, Nuala Finnegan, "Reproducing the Monstrous Nation: A Note on Pregnancy and Motherhood in the Fiction of Rosario Castellanos, Brianda Domecq, and Angeles Mastretta," p. 1006.
Multicultural Review, March, 1999, review of *The Astonishing Story of the Saint of Cabora,* p. 58.
New York Review of Books, April 20, 1995, review of *Eleven Days,* p. 39.
Publishers Weekly, April 27, 1998, review of *The Astonishing Story of the Saint of Cabora,* p. 46.

ONLINE

Hope College Web site, http://www.hope.edu/ (September 14, 2005), Charlene Merithew, "Brianda Domecq."

*   *   *

DOMINGUE, Ronlyn 1969-

PERSONAL: Born September, 1969, in Baton Rouge, LA; partner of Todd Bourque. *Education:* Louisiana State University, bachelor's degree, 1993, M.F.A., 2003.

ADDRESSES: Agent—Jandy Nelson, Manus & Associates Literary Agency—West, 425 Sherman Ave., Ste. 200, Palo Alto, CA 94306.

CAREER: Writer. Former municipal lobbyist; Gemini Consulting, LA and Dallas, TX, former administrative coordinator; on staff of nonprofit training program for Volunteer Baton Rouge!; Louisiana State University, Shreveport, project manager in School of Social Work Office of Social Service Research and Development; independent consultant for nonprofit organizations; Bertman and Associates (fund development and philanthropy firm), staff member.

AWARDS, HONORS: National Scholastic writing awards, 1985, for short-short story and dramatic script; Evelyn Scott Award for Creative Nonfiction, and Robert Olen Butler Short-Story Award, both Louisiana State University, both 2003.

WRITINGS:

The Mercy of Thin Air, (novel), Atria Books (New York, NY), 2005.

Short stories have appeared in *New England Review, Clackamas Literary Review,* and *New Delta Review.*

WORK IN PROGRESS: Another novel.

SIDELIGHTS: In her novel *The Mercy of Thin Air* Ronlyn Domingue tells the story of Raziela "Razi" Nolan, a young New Orleans woman whose desire for immortality is fulfilled after an accident leaves her a ghost living in what is called "The Between" while waiting to see what comes next. In the meantime, Razi has the ability to influence the lives of those still living. She eventually finds that her wait is longer than expected, and seventy years after she died, she tries to retrace the life of her one true love to see what happened to him. Fortunately, she can trace his life partially through the scents he leaves behind on things he once owned and places he has visited. She soon becomes attached to a young couple who buy an old bookcase her lover once owned. As she looks for clues about her lover, Ronlyn observes the couple's disintegrating marriage as the wife deals with a ghost from her own past. The novel is "filled with vivid descriptions of scents, sounds, and marvelous human sensations," wrote Susanne Wells in a review in the *Library Journal,* adding that the story "gets under one's skin." A *Kirkus Reviews* contributor called the lead character

"the story's compelling narrator" and felt that *The Mercy of Thin Air* contains "sweet, entertaining love stories." Writing in *Publishers Weekly,* a reviewer noted, "A gothically tinged historical take on *The Lovely Bones,* this debut novel manages to carve out some of its own territory."

BIOGRAPHICAL AND CRITICAL SOURCES:

PERIODICALS

Kirkus Reviews, July 1, 2005, review of *The Mercy of Thin Air,* p. 701.
Library Journal, July 1, 2005, Susanne Wells, review of *The Mercy of Thin Air,* p. 65.
Publishers Weekly, July 18, 2005, review of *The Mercy of Thin Air,* p. 180.

ONLINE

Louisiana Book Festival 2005 Web site, http://lbf.state.lib.la.us/ (October 1, 2005), brief profile of author.
Ronlyn Domingue Home Page, http://www.ronlyn domingue.com (October 1, 2005).

*　　*　　*

DONKER, Anthonie 1902-1965
(Nicolaas-Anthonie Donkersloot, Maarten de Rijk, Aart van der Alm)

PERSONAL: Born Nicolaas-Anthonie Donkersloot, October 9, 1902, in Rotterdam, Netherlands; died December 26, 1965, in Amsterdam, Netherlands; married Harmina Tjaardina Dadena, 1945.

CAREER: Poet, critic, and literary historian.

WRITINGS:

Acheron (poetry), Hijman, Stenfort Kroese & Van der Zande Boekverkoopers (Arnhem, Netherlands), 1926.
Grenzen, Hijman, Stenfort Kroese & Van der Zande Boekverkoopers (Arnhem, Netherlands), 1928.

De episode van de vernieuwing onzer poëzie (1880-1894) (essays), De Gemeenschap (Utrecht, Netherlands), 1929.

Kruistochten, De Gemeenschap (Utrecht, Netherlands), 1929.

De draad von Ariadne (poetry), Hijman, Stenfort Kroese & Van der Zande Boekverkoopers (Arnhem, Netherlands), 1930.

Fausten en faunen; beschouwingen over boeken en menschen (criticism), Querido (Amsterdam, Netherlands), 1930.

De schichtige Pegasus: critiek der poëzie, omstreeks (criticism), A.A.M. Stols (Brussels, Belgium), 1932.

Ter zake: beschouwingen over litteratuur en leven (essays), Van Loghum Slaterus (Arnhem, Netherlands), 1932.

Maar wij . . . ? spel van jeugd en arbeid in vier tooneelen (play), Vrijzinnig Christelijke Jeugd Centrale (Utrecht, Netherlands), 1933.

Gebroken licht, Van Loghum Slaterus (Arnhem, Netherlands), 1934.

De Gestalten van tachtig: bloemlezing uit de poëzie der tachtigers, J.M. Meulenhoff (Amsterdam, Netherlands), 1935.

Schaduw der bergen (novel), Querido (Amsterdam, Netherlands), 1935.

Dichter en gemeenschap, Van Loghum Slaterus (Arnhem, Netherlands), 1936.

Gysbrecht van Aemstel, Uitgeversmaatschappij "Joost van den Vondel" (Amsterdam, Netherlands), 1937.

(With Jan Romein and Dirk Coster) *Vondels grootheid* (essays), 1937.

Vondels plaats in de Europese cultuur, Van Loghum Slaterus (Arnhem, Netherlands), 1937.

Penibel journaal, W. de Haan (Utrecht, Netherlands), 1938.

Onvoltooide symphonie, Van Loghum Slaterus (Arnhem, Netherlands), 1938.

Hannibal over de Helicon? En nieuwe dichter generatie en haar werkelijkheid (criticism), Van Loghum Slaterus (Arnhem, Netherlands), 1940.

(Under pseudonym Aart van der Alm) *Marathon,* A.A.M. Stols (Rijswijk, Netherlands), 1941.

Orcus en Orpheus, Van Loghum Slaterus (Arnhem, Netherlands), 1941.

Karaktertrekken der vaderlandsche letterkunde (essays), Van Loghum Slaterus (Arnhem, Netherlands), 1945.

(Under pseudonym Maarten de Rijk) *Orpheus en Euridice,* De Bezige Bij (Utrecht, Netherlands), 1945.

Tralievenster: verzen (poetry), Van Loghum Slaterus (Arnhem, Netherlands), 1945.

De episode van de dichter en de dichterlijke vrijheid, De Gemeenschap (Utrecht, Netherlands), 1946.

Het sterrenbeeld, Van Loghum Slaterus (Arnhem, Netherlands), 1946.

De einder, versamelde gedichten gekozen uit de bundels (collected poems), Van Loghum Slaterus (Arnhem, Netherlands), 1947.

Ik zoek christenen (play), De Haan (Utrecht, Netherlands), 1947.

Tondalus' visoen, De Bezige Bij (Amsterdam, Netherlands), 1947.

De bliksem speelt om den doringboom: verkenning van Zuid-Afrika (travelogue), D.A. Daamen ('s-Gravenhage, Netherlands), 1949.

(With others) *De roman also levensspiegel,* Servire (The Hague, Netherlands), 1950.

De bevreemding: gedichten (poetry), Van Loghum Slaterus (Arnhem, Netherlands), 1953.

Eva en de dichters (essays), Querido (Amsterdam, Netherlands), 1954.

(With others) *Het expressionisme: zes lezingen,* Servire (The Hague, Netherlands), 1954.

Nijhoff, de levensreiziger: een schets van zijn dichtershap (essays), Arbeidspers (Amsterdam, Netherlands), 1954.

(Translator) Samuel Taylor Coleridge, *De ballade van den out matroos* (translation of *The Rime of the Ancient Mariner*), J.M. Meulenhoff (Amsterdam, Netherlands), 1954.

(With A. Querido) *Emanuel Querido: de mens, de schrijver, de uitgever* (biography), Querido (Amsterdam, Netherlands), 1955.

Westwaarts, Wereld-Bibliothek (Amsterdam, Netherlands), 1956.

Het schip dat gij bouwen zult (essays), Querido (Amsterdam, Netherlands), 1959.

Ben ik mijn broeders hoeder? (essays), Querido (Amsterdam, Netherlands), 1960.

De groene wandeling: gedichten (poetry), Querido (Amsterdam, Netherlands), 1962.

V in versvorm: de bezetting en het verzet in verzen op de voet gevolgd, Sijthoff (Amsterdam, Netherlands), 1965, published as *V in vers: de bezetting en het verzet in verzen op de voet gevolgd,* Sijthoff (Leiden, Netherlands).

De grondtoon, een keuze uit de gedichten, Querido (Amsterdam, Netherlands), 1982.

SIDELIGHTS: Anthonie Donker was the most utilized pen name of Dutch poet, critic, and literary historian

Nicolaas-Anthonie Donkersloot. As a poet, Donker was known as a traditionalist writer of verse at a time when many of his peers were much more experimental; and as a literary critic, he had a reputation as a fair and honest evaluator of other authors' works.

BIOGRAPHICAL AND CRITICAL SOURCES:

PERIODICALS

De Nieuwe Stem, March, 1966.
Jaarboek van de Maatschappij der Nederlande Letterkunde te Leiden, 1970, pp. 35-40.
Raam, Tilburg, 1965, pp. 66-70.*

*   *   *

DONKERSLOOT, Nicolaas-Anthonie
    See DONKER, Anthonie

*   *   *

DOONAN, Simon 1952-

PERSONAL: Born 1952, in Reading, England; immigrated to United States in the late 1970s; son of Terry and Betty Noonan; partner of Jonathan Adler (a designer).

ADDRESSES: Agent—c/o Author Mail, Simon & Schuster, 1230 Avenue of the Americas, New York, NY 10020. *E-mail*—sdoonan@observer.com.

CAREER: Designer and writer. Barneys, New York, NY, window display designer, then creative director, 1986—; columnist for *New York Observer.* Actor in film *Beverly Hills Cop,* 1984; appeared as himself on television shows, including *America's Next Top Model.* Formerly worked on Savile Row, London, and at Costume Institute of the Metropolitan Museum of Art, New York, NY.

AWARDS, HONORS: Council of Fashion Designers of America Award; Markopoulos Award, 2003, for outstanding achievement and contributions to the craft of visual merchandising and design.

WRITINGS:

Confessions of a Window Dresser: Tales from a Life in Fashion, Penguin Studio (New York, NY), 1998.
Wacky Chicks: Life Lessons from Fearlessly Inappropriate and Fabulously Eccentric Women, Simon & Schuster (New York, NY), 2003.
Nasty: My Family and Other Glamorous Varmints, Simon & Schuster (New York, NY), 2005.

Contributor to numerous publications, including *Harper's Bazaar* and *Nest.*

ADAPTATIONS: Confessions of a Window Dresser was optioned for film.

SIDELIGHTS: Simon Doonan established a career as a top store-window designer and wrote about his life in the popular memoir, *Confessions of a Window Dresser: Tales from a Life in Fashion.* Writing in *Display and Design Ideas,* Alison Embrey called the book "a witty memoir that takes readers inside the mind of a creative personality." In his book *Wacky Chicks: Life Lessons from Fearlessly Inappropriate and Fabulously Eccentric Women,* Doonan writes about unconventional women and their unusual lifestyles. The book features a wide array of characters, such as the woman who lives in a storage locker with lizards and a tarantula. Other women profiled include a woman who gets her fashion sense from flea markets, a bride who pops out of an egg, and a seller of spandex whose store is in a Florida nudist colony. "Everyone loves an over-the-top woman who is belligerent, resilient, uninhibited, naughty, creative, and hilarious," Doonan told Lori Kaye in an interview for the *Advocate.* As Doonan went on to note, "Wacky chicks are the crowning achievement of women's lib. They are disapproval-immune. They are beacons of uninhibited empowerment."

In a review of *Wacky Chicks* in *Booklist,* Whitney Scott called the effort a "breezy, in-your-face book." Scott also noted that Doonan's style "becomes a character to equal any of the wacky chicks he has interviewed." Jessica Kerwin, writing in *W,* commented: "Brimming with bravura, Doonan's book also provides plenty of tips for those regular gals longing to live la vida loca." Kerwin went on to note, "It's classic Doonan, as fans of his first book and autobiography . . . and avid readers of his weekly column . . . well know."

Doonan focuses on his own life in his book *Nasty: My Family and Other Glamorous Varmints.* "*Nasty* is more of a memoir/montage—I am lucky to have grown up in an insanely wacky family and to have had a complicated sleazy trajectory so I have loads of tawdry anecdotes to share," the author admitted during an interview for the *Conversations about Famous People* Web log. In the book, Doonan delves into his family and his working-class background, as well as expressing his drive to become one of the "beautiful people." The book also features characters every bit as interesting as those profiled in his previous book *Wacky Chicks,* including his wildly unpredictable grandparents and other members of his family. A *Publishers Weekly* contributor noted that "in this colorful memoir, nasty is . . . quite enjoyable." The reviewer also wrote, "This endearing book pays tribute to a madcap childhood and the power of familial love." Nancy R. Ives, writing in *Library Journal,* noted, "While this book is not for the squeamish, its Anglo-Irish humor will delight readers seeking the unusual." A contributor to *Kirkus Reviews* called the book "a kick, a hoot, a truly wonderful read, with loads of down-and-dirty details about characters who are way more interesting than those dull Beautiful People Doonan was so all afire to find."

BIOGRAPHICAL AND CRITICAL SOURCES:

BOOKS

Doonan, Simon, *Confessions of a Window Dresser: Tales from a Life in Fashion,* Penguin Studio (New York, NY), 1998.

Doonan, Simon, *Nasty: My Family and Other Glamorous Varmints,* Simon & Schuster (New York, NY), 2005.

PERIODICALS

Advocate, May 27, 2003, Lori Kaye, "Chick Magnet: Style Maven Simon Doonan Talks about His New Book, *Wacky Chicks,* and the Fabulous Women Who Inspired It," p. 66; June 21, 2005, Sean Kennedy, "The Mod Couple," interview with author, p. 160.

Booklist, May 1, 2003, Whitney Scott, review of *Wacky Chicks: Life Lessons from Fearlessly Inappropriate and Fabulously Eccentric Women,* p. 1559.

Daily News Record, November 19, 2001, "Barney's Elf," profile of author, p. 1.

Display and Design Ideas, March, 2003, Alison Embrey, "Simply Simon: Barneys' Animated Window Dresser Simon Doonan Is Named This Year's Markopoulos Award Winner," p. 20.

Entertainment Weekly, May 27, 2005, Whitney Pastorek, review of *Nasty,* p. 144,

Gifts and Decorative Accessories, May, 2005, Meredith Schwartz, "Simon Doonan Does Windows (like No One Else)," p. 24.

Harper's Bazaar, March, 2002, Philip K. Dick, "What a Gay Man Can Teach You about Fashion," p. 216.

Kirkus Reviews, April 1, 2005, review of *Nasty,* p. 396.

Library Journal, April 15, 2005, Nancy R. Ives, review of *Nasty,* p. 86.

People, June 27, 2005, review of *Nasty,* p. 47.

Publishers Weekly, March 31, 2003, review of *Wacky Chicks,* p. 50; April 18, 2005, review of *Nasty,* p. 52.

W, May, 2003, Jessica Kerwin, review of *Wacky Chicks,* p. 80.

ONLINE

Conversations about Famous People Web log, http://conversationsfamouspeople.blogspot.com/ (October 1, 2005), interview with author.

Gay.com, http://www.gay.com/ (October 1, 2005), Robert Ordona, "Simon Says: An Interview with Style Maven and Author Simon Doonan."

Internet Movie Database, http://www.imdb.com/ (October 1, 2005), information on author's film and television appearances.

Paper Online, http://www.papermag.com/ (October 1, 2005), Patrick McDonald, "The High Brow Interview with Simon Doonan."*

* * *

DOORN, A. van
See GRESHOFF, Jan

* * *

DORIN, Françoise 1928-

PERSONAL: Born January 23, 1928, in Paris, France; married Jean Poiret (a writer and playwright), October 2, 1958 (divorced); children: Sylvie.

ADDRESSES: Home—23 rue Simon-Dereure, Paris 75018, France.

CAREER: Actress, comedienne, singer, and songwriter in Paris, France, c. 1950s-60s.

AWARDS, HONORS: Named chevalier, Ordre National du Mérite; Trophée Dussane, 1973.

WRITINGS:

PLAYS

(Under a pseudonym) *Comme au théâtre* (produced in Paris, France, 1967), published as *Théâtre,* Volume 2, Julliard (Paris, France), 1973.
La facture (four-act comedy), L'Avant-Scène (Paris, France), 1968.
Les Bonshommes (produced in Paris, 1970), L'Avant-Scène (Paris, France), 1970.
Un sale égoiste (four-act comedy), L'Avant-Scène (Paris, France), 1970.
Théâtre, Volume 1: *Le tournant,* Volume 2: *Comme au théâtre,* Julliard (Paris, France), 1973.
Le tube (two-act comedy), Flammarion (Paris, France), 1975.
L'autre valse, L'Avant-Scène (Paris, France), 1976.
L'autre valse and *Si t'es beau . . . t'es con,* R. Laffont (Paris, France), 1978.
(With Loleh Bellon) *Changement à vue* (contains *Le tout pour le tout*), L'Avant-Scène (Paris, France), 1979.
L'intoxe, Flammarion (Paris, France), 1981.
L'étiquette (three acts), Flammarion (Paris, France), 1983.
Les cahiers tango, Flammarion (Paris, France), 1988.
Le retour en Touraine (comedy), Flammarion (Paris, France), 1993.

OTHER

La seconde dans Rome (novel; title means "Second in Rome"), R. Julliard (Paris, France), 1958.
Va voir maman, papa travaille! (novel), R. Laffont (Paris, France), 1976.
Les lits à une place, Flammarion (Paris, France), 1980.
Les miroirs truqués, Flammarion (Paris, France), 1982.
Les jupes-culottes (novel), Flammarion (Paris, France), 1984.

Les corbeaux et les renardes (novel), Flammarion (Paris, France), 1988.
Nini Patte-en l'air, R. Laffont (Paris, France), 1990.
Au nom du père et de la fille (novel), Flammarion (Paris, France), 1992.
Pique et coeur, Flammarion (Paris, France), 1993.
La mouflette (novel), Flammarion (Paris, France), 1994.
Les vendanges tardives, Plon (Paris, France), 1997.
La courte paille (novel), Plon (Paris, France), 1999.
Dorin père et fille (poems), Plon (Paris, France), 1999.
Les julottes (novel), Plon (Paris, France), 2000.
Soins intensifs, Plon (Paris, France), 2001.
La rêve-party (novel), Plon (Paris, France), 2002.
Tout est toujours possible (novel), Plon (Paris, France), 2004.
Et puis après (novel), Plon (Paris, France), 2005.

Author of *Virginie et Paul* (novel; title means "Virginia and Paul"), [Paris, France], c. 1950s; work represented in anthologies, including *Les Plus belles scènes d'amour,* Albin Michel (Paris, France), 1997.

SIDELIGHTS: Françoise Dorin worked as an actress in France for many years, writing a number of songs which she performed with a cabaret group. Still, she was never comfortable on stage. At first, she worked under a pseudonym, and she also wrote her first play, *Comme au théâtre,* under a pen name. Her comedy was a huge hit, and Dorin went on to write many plays and novels. She was once married to Jean Poiret, author of the hit *La cage aux folles.*

Pierre Billard wrote in the *World Press Review* that "there is a fiercely anti-Dorin camp which does not identify with the work of this uncompromisingly Right-Bank author. But she has dramatized the pent-up grudges of the 'silent majority' against 'prophets of permissiveness,' armchair leftists, weak-kneed parents, and sexually liberated women. . . . She rejects the label 'reactionary' along with all others, but a single message underlies her works: To be happy, you must take charge of yourself and avoid all alienating human ties."

BIOGRAPHICAL AND CRITICAL SOURCES:

PERIODICALS

French Review, April, 1981, Nicole Aronson, review of *Les lits à une place,* pp. 758-759.
World Press Review, March, 1981, Pierre Billard, "France's New Boxoffice Queen," p. 62.*

DOUGAN, Andy

PERSONAL: Male.

ADDRESSES: Office—Glasgow Evening Times, 200 Renfield Rd., Glasgow G2 3QB, Scotland.

CAREER: Journalist. Writer for *Glasgow Evening Times,* Glasgow, Scotland.

WRITINGS:

The Actors' Director: Richard Attenborough behind the Camera, introduction by Steven Spielberg, Mainstream (Edinburgh, Scotland), 1994.
Untouchable: A Biography of Robert De Niro, Thunder's Mouth Press (New York, NY), 1996.
The Biography of George Clooney, Boxtree (London, England), 1997.
The Lisbon Lions: Celtic, Virgin (London, England), 1997.
The Glory Glory Bhoys, The Celebration of Celtic's Triumphant 1997-98 Season, Mainstream (Edinburgh, Scotland), 1998.
Martin Scorsese, Thunder's Mouth Press (New York, NY), 1998.
Robin Williams, Thunder's Mouth Press (New York, NY), 1998.
Dynamo: Defending the Honour of Kiev, Fourth Estate (London, England), 2001, published as *Dynamo: Triumph and Tragedy in Nazi-Occupied Kiev,* Lyons Press (Guilford, CT), 2002.
The Hunting of Man: A History of the Sniper, Fourth Estate (London, England), 2004, published as *Through the Crosshairs: A History of Snipers,* Carroll & Graf (New York, NY), 2005.

SIDELIGHTS: Andy Dougan has written books about sports, film directors and actors, as well as a history of snipers. In *The Actors' Director: Richard Attenborough behind the Camera,* Dougan incorporates interviews with Attenborough's colleagues and other actors to provide a biography of the director and discuss his films. "Brief insights are offered, simple and significant stories are told, and individual impressions are revealed," wrote Janet St. John in *Booklist.* In *Robin Williams,* Dougan profiles the comedian and actor, from his time as an overweight child who was bullied through Williams's rise to fame on the television show *Mork and Mindy* and his subsequent success in movies. Rosellen Brewer, writing in *Library Journal,* called the biography "a straightforward account that reveals new facts about a very private celebrity."

Dougan turns his eye toward an historic wartime football, or soccer, game in *Dynamo: Defending the Honour of Kiev,* published in the United States as *Dynamo: Triumph and Tragedy in Nazi-Occupied Kiev.* This true story, as told by Dougan, takes place between 1941 and 1943 in Kiev, Ukraine, which was occupied by the German army during World War II. The author focuses on a group of former star soccer players who headed toward a fateful match on August 9, 1942. The Kiev players, called the Startteam, were on the losing side of the war at the time. As a result they were in terrible physical condition—hungry and exhausted. Their opponents were the Flakelf, a team of soldiers from the German air force, the Luftwaffe, who had been handpicked to make sure the Germans won the game. Further stacking the odds against the Ukrainian players was the fact that an SS officer, a member of an elite group within the German military, was the game's referee. He went into the locker room prior to the match and told the Startteam that they must not win as they had done in two previous matches against the Germans. Dougan recounts the buildup to the match and the terrible aftermath when the Ukrainian players put honor before all.

Writing a review of *Dynamo* in the *Spectator,* Raymond Asquith noted that the book should be "read . . . for the central drama played by ordinary, decent people in extraordinary and evil circumstances." Henry Sheen noted in the *New Statesman* that the author "has . . . managed to find a story that has an inevitable capacity to move and disturb." *Booklist* contributor David Pitt called *Dynamo* "a fascinating, exciting, and, ultimately, deeply unsettling book." Writing in *Military Review,* Michael A. Boden commented: "Dougan recognizes the limits of oral histories and the inconsistencies that pepper the story, and he does not jump to conclusions or connections that are not present. What emerges is a well-told story about a group of men in a difficult situation."

Dougan explores the role of the sniper in twentieth-century wars in his book *The Hunting of Man: A History of the Sniper,* which was published in the United States as *Through the Crosshairs: A History of Snip-*

ers. The author profiles modern military sharpshooters and looks back at past snipers, revealing that American General George Washington was almost the successful target of a British army sniper named Patrick Ferguson. Dougan also explores several assassins and their crimes. In addition, he provides a history of weapons dating back to the bow and arrow and discusses their tactical use. A *Publishers Weekly* contributor called the book a "breezy account of snipers and sniping."

BIOGRAPHICAL AND CRITICAL SOURCES:

PERIODICALS

Booklist, April 15, 1995, Janet St. John, review of *The Actors' Director: Richard Attenborough behind the Camera,* p. 1465; September 15, 2002, review of *Dynamo: Triumph and Tragedy in Nazi-Occupied Kiev,* p. 197.

Kirkus Reviews, April 1, 2005, review of *Through the Crosshairs: A History of Snipers,* p. 396.

Library Journal, December, 1998, Rosellen Brewer, review of *Robin Williams,* p. 108.

Military Review, July-August, 2004, Michael A. Boden, review of *Dynamo,* p. 97.

New Statesman, April 16, 2001, Henry Sheen, review of *Dynamo,* p. 57.

Publishers Weekly, April 4, 2005, review of *Through the Crosshairs,* p. 50.

Spectator, March 24, 2001, Raymond Asquith, review of *Dynamo,* p. 45.*

*   *   *

DUFFY, Gerald G. 1935-

PERSONAL: Born May 14, 1935, in Rome, NY; son of Gerald J. (in sales) and Helen (in sales; maiden name, McLennon) Duffy; married Laura R. Roehler, March 21, 1974 (marriage ended, 1992); married Auleen Olsen (a psychologist), August 13, 1994; children: Michael. *Ethnicity:* "Caucasian." *Education:*

Buffalo State Teachers College, B.S., 1957, M.S., 1964; Northern Illinois University, Ed.D., 1966. *Hobbies and other interests:* Black and white photography.

ADDRESSES: Home—2427 Canter Ln., Deer Park, WA 99006. *Office*—342 Curry Bldg., University of North Carolina at Greensboro, Greensboro, NC 27412-5001. *E-mail*—duffy4edu@aol.com; ggduffy@uncg.edu.

CAREER: Writer. Elementary schoolteacher in Buffalo, NY, 1957-58, and Rome, NY, 1958-60; State University of New York College at Fredonia, teacher at laboratory school, 1960-67; Michigan State University, East Lansing, professor, 1967-92, professor emeritus, 1992—; University of North Carolina at Greensboro, currently Moran Distinguished Professor of Reading. National Reading Conference, past president. *Military service:* Served in military reserves, 1957-63.

AWARDS, HONORS: Member of Reading Hall of Fame.

WRITINGS:

(With G. Sherman) *Systematic Reading Instruction,* Harper & Row (New York, NY), 1969.

(With L. Roehler) *Improving Classroom Reading Instruction,* McGraw Hill (New York, NY), 1985.

Explaining Reading, Guilford Press (New York, NY), 2003.

WORK IN PROGRESS: Research on the effectiveness of reading teachers and on teacher education.

SIDELIGHTS: Gerald G. Duffy told *CA:* "As a former classroom teacher myself, my motivation in writing is rooted in a desire to help practicing teachers deal effectively with the complexities of teaching literacy to twenty-five to thirty diverse children. As such, all my writing and research is designed to make day-to-day classroom teaching of reading more effective, especially for those struggling readers who do not learn to read easily. The enduring principle undergirding all my work is that classroom teaching requires thoughtfully adaptive decision-making, which means that teacher education is the priority issue."

E

EDWARDS-JONES, Imogen

PERSONAL: Born in Birmingham, England.

ADDRESSES: Home—London, England. *Agent*—William Morris Agency, 52/53 Poland St., London W1F 7LX, England.

CAREER: Novelist, journalist, and broadcaster.

WRITINGS:

The Taming of Eagles: Exploring the New Russia, photographs by Joth Shakerley, Weidenfeld & Nicholson (London, England), 1993.
My Canape Hell (novel), Hodder & Stoughton (London, England), 2000.
Shagpile (novel), Flame (London, England), 2002.
(Editor, with Jessica Adams and Maggie Alderson) *Big Night Out,* HarperCollins (New York, NY), 2002.
The Wendy House (novel), Hodder & Stoughton (London, England), 2003.
(Co-author) *Hotel Babylon: Inside the Extravagance and Mayhem of a Luxury Five-Star Hotel* (nonfiction), Blue Hen (New York, NY), 2004.
Tuscany for Beginners (novel), Ballantine Books (New York, NY), 2005.
(With anonymous) *Air Babylon,* Bantam Books (New York, NY), 2005.

ADAPTATIONS: Hotel Babylon is being adapted into an eight-part, prime-time drama for BBC1.

SIDELIGHTS: Imogen Edwards-Jones is a journalist and novelist whose investigations into the inner workings of the hotel and airline industries have revealed often dismaying truths that escape these industries' customers. "Frequent travelers will be fascinated (and maybe a little disturbed)" by *Hotel Babylon: Inside the Extravagance and Mayhem of a Luxury Five-Star Hotel,* observed reviewer Kate Bonamici in *Fortune.* Written with an unnamed coauthor who works as a manager at a luxury hotel in London, the book chronicles, on an hour-by-hour basis, the chaotic, demanding, and sometimes bizarre events in a five-star hotel. Ranging from encounters with celebrities in various chemically altered states to outraged customers who refuse to pay hundreds of dollars in phone sex bills to scheming employees who plot to wring the most money out of their guests, the book is a "no-holds-barred exposé that makes for welcome reading when you're waiting for the next flight or suffering jet lag," stated Margie T. Logarta in *Business Traveller Asia Pacific.* "This book's stories of propositions, sexual exploits and personal hygiene are far more appalling than amusing," remarked a reviewer in the *Economist.* A *Publishers Weekly* contributor called it "an irreverent exposé of the often unimaginable debauchery and dishonesty of the luxury hotel industry."

Air Babylon takes a similar tell-all approach toward the airline industry. Again with the help of an anonymous coauthor with deep insider connections, Edwards-Jones examines an industry rife with "life and death decisions, sex, drugs, money, travel and plenty of people on the make and the take," as she commented in an interview on the *Books at Transworld* Web site. As a result of her experiences writing *Air*

Babylon, Edwards-Jones has become much less optimistic about air travel. "I now realise that there is nothing anyone can do about anything," she said in her interview. "You take your life in your hands every time you fly and it's down to chance if you make [it] to the end of your journey."

Belinda Smith, the protagonist of Edwards-Jones's debut novel, *Tuscany for Beginners,* is a snobbish and thoroughly unpleasant owner of a bed and breakfast in Val di Santa Caterina, Italy. Though she is misanthropic and even deceptive to her guests, the locals look on her as a type of contessa, a lordly figure in the valley whose manners and ways are consummately Italian. When her twenty-year-old daughter, Mary, loses her job in London, Mary comes back to help with the bed and breakfast. Belinda, though, would much rather spend time swilling wine with her expatriate friends. Belinda is outraged when an American buys the neighboring Casa Padronale villa with the intent of turning it into a competing hotel. She schemes and tries every dirty trick she knows to prevent the new bed and breakfast from opening, but her opponent is formidable: Lauren is a former Wall Street executive whose main activity was acquiring companies in hostile takeovers. While she thwarts Belinda at every opportunity, her Yale-educated son strikes up a romance with Mary, which no one but the lovers finds acceptable. "Edwards-Jones has fashioned a near-bloody satirical stab at the sentimental *Under the Tuscan Sun* set, both American and English—with a result quite winning," remarked a *Kirkus Reviews* critic. Edwards-Jones "makes a boisterous American debut with this bawdy, bewitching comedy of ill-manners," commented Carol Haggas in *Booklist.*

BIOGRAPHICAL AND CRITICAL SOURCES:

PERIODICALS

Best Life, January-February, 2005, "Intrepid Traveler," p. 22.

Booklist, March 1, 2005, Carol Haggas, review of *Tuscany for Beginners,* p. 1140.

Business Traveller Asia Pacific, July-August, 2005, Margie T. Logarta, review of *Hotel Babylon: Inside the Extravagance and Mayhem of a Luxury Five-Star Hotel,* p. 18.

Economist, August 14, 2004, "Ever-Revolving Doors: Luxury Hotels," review of *Hotel Babylon,* p. 74.

Fortune, August 8, 2005, Kate Bonamici, review of *Hotel Babylon,* p. 111.

Kirkus Reviews, March 1, 2005, review of *Tuscany for Beginners,* p. 246.

Publishers Weekly, November 8, 2004, review of *Hotel Babylon,* p. 44.

ONLINE

Books at Transworld Web site, http://www.booksat transworld.co.uk/ (October 4, 2005), interview with Imogen Edwards-Jones.

*   *   *

EPIGONOS
   See GJELLERUP, Karl

*   *   *

ERLICK, Nelson

PERSONAL: Born in Philadelphia, PA. *Education:* University of Pennsylvania, B.A.; Drexel University, M.S.; Pennsylvania College of Podiatric Medicine, D.P.M.

ADDRESSES: Home and office—8 Havcrest Cir., Havertown, PA 19083. *E-mail*—nelson@nelsonerlick.com.

CAREER: Physician, novelist, and medical communications specialist. Has worked as a surgeon in private practice, a health technology analyst for a think tank, a writer and information manager for a pharmaceutical company, and medical director for a medical-communications firm.

AWARDS, HONORS: Two William Stickel Gold Medals, one for original research on wound healing, one for original research on diabetes; O'Neal, Jones & Feldman Award, for development of new skeletal radiographic measurement technique.

WRITINGS:

NOVELS

GermLine, Forge (New York, NY), 2003.
The Xeno Solution, Forge (New York, NY), 2005.

WORK IN PROGRESS: A novel about a revolutionary medical technology.

SIDELIGHTS: Nelson Erlick became an author of suspense novels with medical settings after a long career as a surgeon and researcher. "I've always wanted to be a novelist, but it took me 40-plus years to realize it," Erlick said in an interview posted on his home page. His experience in medical practice, research, and communications has given him a knowledge base that allows him "to analyze the intricacies of virtually any field of medicine or technology," he added. In the novels *GermLine* and *The Xeno Solution,* both set largely in his native Philadelphia, he explores medical advances that are groundbreaking yet, to his mind, possible.

The protagonist of *GermLine* is Dr. Kevin Kincaid, a geneticist who is developing a system of gene transplantation that can wipe out congenital defects and diseases. But he is threatened by people who want to control his research because of the power it will bring them, and who plan to set themselves up as tyrannical rulers. Erlick's mix of science and intrigue brought praise from some critics, such as a *Kirkus Reviews* contributor who found the novel "good fun" with its "breathless chase scenes, triple and quadruple crosses, even a bit of romance." *Library Journal* reviewer Jackie Cassada, meanwhile, deemed it a "fast-paced thriller," both "suspenseful" and informative.

The Xeno Solution focuses on another type of transplantation—that of moving organs from pigs to humans. In his career as a researcher, Erlick studied the concept's possibilities, and in the novel, it has become not only possible but common, saving the lives of many people. Retired surgeon Scott Merritt, however, discovers that the transplants have introduced a deadly virus into the organ recipients, and he faces danger from those who want to keep this a secret. Erlick offers "compelling descriptions of the virus's effects," noted a *Publishers Weekly* commentator, who added that the novel is "chilling." In the interview on his Web site, Erlick remarked that the book "is built on realistic potential. . . . I was determined not to put a single word to paper unless *I* believed it was possible."

BIOGRAPHICAL AND CRITICAL SOURCES:

PERIODICALS

Kirkus Reviews, January 1, 2003, review of *GermLine,* p. 1816.

Library Journal, January, 2003, Jackie Cassada, review of *GermLine,* p. 165.
Publishers Weekly, January 13, 2003, review of *GermLine,* p. 42; September 5, 2005, review of *The Xeno Solution,* p. 40.

ONLINE

AllReaders.com, http://www.allreaders.com/ (October 20, 2005), Harriet Klausner, review of *GermLine.*
Curled Up with a Good Book, http://www.curledup.com/ (October 20, 2005), Barbara J. Martin, review of *GermLine.*
Nelson Erlick Home Page, http://www.nelsonerlick.com (October 20, 2005).*

*   *   *

ESCHBACH, Andreas 1959-

PERSONAL: Born September 15, 1959, in Ulm, Germany; married; wife's name Marianne; children: one son. *Education:* Attended Technical University of Stuttgart.

ADDRESSES: Home—France. *Agent*—Tom Doherty Associates, 175 5th Ave., New York, NY 10010. *E-mail*—mail@andreaseschbach.de.

CAREER: Writer. Software developer; founder and managing director of information-technology consulting business, 1993-96.

AWARDS, HONORS: Arno-Schmidt Foundation scholarship, 1994; prize for best novel, Science Fiction Club Deutschland, 1996, for *Die Haarteppichknüpfer;* prize for best novel, Science Fiction Club Deutschland, and Kurd-Laßwitz-Preis for best German novel, both 1997, both for *Solarstation;* prize for best short story, Science Fiction Club Deutschland, 1998, for "Die Wunder des Universums"; prize for best novel, Science Fiction Club Deutschland, Kurd-Laßwitz-Preis, and *Phantastik* award for best novel, all 1999, all for *Das Jesus Video,* and 2004, all for *Der Letzte seiner Art;* Kurd-Laßwitz-Preis, 2000, for *Kelwitts Stern,* and 2002, for *Quest;* Grand Prix de l'Imaginaire for best foreign work, and Prix Bob Morane for best foreign novel, both 2000, both for French translation of *Die Haarteppichknüpfer;* Grand Prix de l'Imaginaire European prize, 2004, for *Eine Trillion Euro.*

WRITINGS:

NOVELS; IN GERMAN UNLESS OTHERWISE NOTED

Die Haarteppichknüpfer, Schneekluth (Munich, Germany), 1995, English translation by Doryl Jensen published as *The Carpet Makers,* foreword by Orson Scott Card, Tor Books (New York, NY), 2005.
Solarstation, Schneekluth (Munich, Germany), 1996.
Das Jesus Video, Schneekluth (Munich, Germany), 1998.
Kelwitts Stern (title means "Kelwitt's Star"), Schneekluth (Munich, Germany), 1999.
Quest, Heyne (Munich, Germany), 2001.
Eine Billion Dollar, Lübbe (Bergisch-Gladbach, Germany), 2001.
Der Letzte seiner Art (title means "The Last of His Kind"), Lübbe (Bergisch-Gladbach, Germany), 2003.
Exponentialdrift, Lübbe (Bergisch-Gladbach, Germany), 2003.
Die Seltene Gabe (title means "The Rare Gift"), Arena (Würzburg, Germany), 2004.
Perfect Copy, Arena (Würzburg, Germany), 2004.
Der Nobelpreis (title means "The Nobel Prize"), Lübbe (Bergisch-Gladbach, Germany), 2005.
Das Marsprojekt: Das Ferne Leuchten (title means "The Mars Project: Far Shining"), Arena (Würzburg, Germany), 2005.
Das Marsprojekt: Die Blauen Türme (title means "The Mars Project: The Blue Towers"), Arena (Würzburg, Germany), 2005.

OTHER

Software after Measure: Planning, Realization and Control of EDP Projects (nonfiction), Pearson Education (Upper Saddle River, NJ), 1992.
(Editor) *Eine Trillion Euro* (short stories), Lübbe (Bergisch-Gladbach, Germany), 2004.
Das Buch von der Zukunft: ein Reiseführer (nonfiction; title means "The Book of the Future: A Travel Guide"), Rowohlt Berlin (Berlin, Germany), 2004.

Short stories published in anthologies, including *Halloween* and *Der Attem Gottes und Anders Visionen 2004* (title means "The Breath of God and Other Visions 2004"), and in magazines, including *Star Vision* and *Science Fiction Media.*

Eschbach's works have been translated into Czech, Dutch, French, Italian, Japanese, Polish, Russian, Spanish, and Turkish.

ADAPTATIONS: Das Jesus Video was adapted by Martin Ritzenhoff and Sebastian Niemann into a film directed by Niemann and produced for German television in 2002. The film is known as *The Hunt for the Hidden Relic* in the United States. Several of Eschbach's works have been released as audiobooks.

SIDELIGHTS: Andreas Eschbach has been writing since his adolescence and had some short stories published in literary magazines in the 1980s, followed by the publication of numerous science-fiction novels, beginning in the 1990s. The reception given his writings eventually encouraged him to abandon his career in information technology and write full time. His work has made him famous in his native Germany and throughout Europe. Although he has won many prizes on that continent, he did not have a novel published in English until 2005. That book was *The Carpet Makers,* Eschbach's first novel, which had been published in Germany ten years earlier as *Die Haarteppichknüpfer.*

The novel is set on a primitive planet where most men work as carpet-weavers, using as raw material the hair of their wives—sometimes more than one wife, all chosen for the appearance of their hair. The carpets, each of which takes one man a lifetime to finish, are exported to the emperor, who lives on another planet. A change in government, however, leads the inhabitants of the carpet-weavers' world to question all they had previously believed.

Some reviewers welcomed Eschbach's English-language debut and found it long overdue. A *Kirkus Reviews* contributor, noting that Eschbach is "one of Germany's leading SF lights," expressed dismay "that such a magnum opus has been allowed to languish in the shadows for ten years." Jackie Cassada, writing in *Library Journal,* called the novel "thoughtful and disturbing," and felt that it would find a wide audience, not limited to science-fiction fans. Eschbach, Cassada added, is "a first-rate storyteller and visionary."

BIOGRAPHICAL AND CRITICAL SOURCES:

PERIODICALS

Kirkus Reviews, February 1, 2005, review of *The Carpet Makers,* p. 155.
Library Journal, March 15, 2005, Jackie Cassada, review of *The Carpet Makers,* p. 74.
Publishers Weekly, March 7, 2005, review of *The Carpet Makers,* p. 54.

ONLINE

Andreas Eschbach Home Page, http://www.andreas eschbach.de (October 20, 2005).*

*   *   *

ESTRADA, Alfredo José 1959-

PERSONAL: Born 1959, in Cuba; married; children: two sons. *Education:* Attended Harvard University; graduated from University of Texas School of Law.

ADDRESSES: Home—Austin, TX. *Agent*—c/o Author Mail, Vista Publishing Corporation, 1201 Brickell Ave., Miami, FL 33131.

CAREER: Writer, editor, and novelist. Worked as a lawyer in New York, NY; *Hispanic* magazine, founder, editor, and publisher, 1988-2000; full-time writer, 2000—.

AWARDS, HONORS: Independent Publisher Book Award for multicultural fiction, 2004, for *Welcome to Havana, Señor Hemingway.*

WRITINGS:

Welcome to Havana, Señor Hemingway (novel), Vista (Miami, FL), 2003.

WORK IN PROGRESS: A novel; a history of Havana, Cuba, expected publication by St. Martin's Press, 2007.

SIDELIGHTS: Writer, editor, and novelist Alfredo José Estrada turned to his own family history to find the kernel of the idea that formed his debut novel, *Welcome to Havana, Señor Hemingway.* When the Cuban-born, Harvard-educated Estrada discovered a photograph of his grandfather, Javier Lopez Angulo, he was astonished to realize that the other person in the picture was legendary American writer Ernest Hemingway. Although it turned out that his grandfather did not know Hemingway personally, Estrada was struck by the idea that his grandfather could have been one of the people who introduced Hemingway to Cuba. Thus, Estrada's novel is constructed around Hemingway's frequently luxurious but often troubled days in Cuba and his fictional relationship with Javier Angulo.

In the book, a Cuban-American writer travels back to Cuba to find out about his grandfather, Javier, who had a close friendship and a subsequent bitter falling-out with Hemingway. When he talks to his grandmother, he discovers she had little affection for Hemingway, but a great deal of love for his grandfather, who had wanted to be a writer himself. The story then segues to 1930s Cuba, where political violence and social unrest make the country a volatile if exciting place to live. Here, Hemingway fishes for marlin, drinks copious amounts of liquor in the taverns, and writes—or tries to write, when writer's block does not plague him. Soon Javier is drawn into the charismatic Hemingway's circle of friends and family. The novel proceeds largely through the actions and interactions of these characters.

One night Hemingway confides in Javier about the sometimes soul-numbing difficulty of being a writer, though he admits that the only thing worse is not writing at all. Eventually, the two have an altercation that leads to the dissolution of their friendship. Javier realizes, tragically, that he will never succeed as a writer. Meanwhile, Hemingway contributes to a bid for freedom during a violent popular revolt and shortly afterward leaves the island.

Library Journal reviewer Jack Shreve called the book a "detailed page-turner of a first novel," while *Miami Herald* critic Fabiola Santiago named it "a smartly executed first novel, notable for gracefully written passages and authentic dialogue." Because of his use of Hemingway as a fictional character, Estrada can speculate at will on the writer's emotions and motivations. This speculation leads to "a credible, remarkably polished story about a troubled writer's relationship with a tropical island and one of its inhabitants," observed David Pitt in *Booklist*. "Fans of Hemingway and Cuban history buffs, especially anyone nostalgic for anything that brings back the grandeur of old Cuba, will love this novel," commented Santiago.

BIOGRAPHICAL AND CRITICAL SOURCES:

PERIODICALS

Booklist, April 1, 2004, David Pitt, review of *Welcome to Havana, Señor Hemingway*, p. 1346.

Hemingway Review, fall, 2004, Steve Paul, review of *Welcome to Havana, Señor Hemingway*, p. 110.

Hispanic, December, 2003, review of *Welcome to Havana, Señor Hemingway*.

Library Journal, May 15, 2005, Jack Shreve, review of *Welcome to Havana, Señor Hemingway*, p. 105.

Miami Herald, June 12, 2005, Fabiola Santiago, "Revisiting Havana and a Family Legend," review of *Welcome to Havana, Señor Hemingway*.

Washington Post, May 29, 2005, Ron Charles, review of *Welcome to Havana, Señor Hemingway*.

ONLINE

Independent Publisher Web site, http://www.independentpublisher.com/ (September 19, 2005), author profile.

*   *   *

ETCHELLS, Olive

PERSONAL: Female.

ADDRESSES: Agent—c/o Author Mail, Constable, 3 the Lanchesters, 162 Fulham Palace Rd., London W6 9ER, England.

CAREER: Writer and novelist.

WRITINGS:

The Jericho Rose (historical novel), Warner (London, England), 1993.

The Jericho Trumpet (historical novel), Warner (London, England), 1996.

No Corners for the Devil (mystery novel), Constable (London, England), 2005.

SIDELIGHTS: English writer and novelist Olive Etchells is the author of a trio of novels. The first two, *The Jericho Rose* and *The Jericho Trumpet,* are historical novels set in England in the period during and following the American Civil War. In *The Jericho Rose,* the war has finally renewed the cotton industry in a Lancashire mill town. As the cotton mills slowly return to action, work remains difficult to find, and Matthew Raike finds that he must travel to Saltley to look for a job, despite looming hardships. By the opening of *The Jericho Trumpet,* Jericho Mills is once again thriving, cotton is readily available, and work is plentiful. The Scofields, owners of the mill, are known to be generous and easy to work with. However, events occur that place a daunting threat in the Scofields' path, endangering the mill and the livelihood of everyone in the area.

No Corners for the Devil finds Manchester suburbanites Rob and Sally Baxter, their daughter, and two sons moving to Cornwall's scenic and idyllic Roseland Peninsula to seek a calmer, safer life than they had in the city. While Rob takes on a part-time teaching assignment, they find temporary peace in a charming round house by the seaside, where there are "no corners for the devil" to dwell in and start mischief. The tranquility starts to unravel when younger son Ben discovers the body of a teenage girl on the beach. The murdered girl, Samantha Trudgeon, had last been seen in the company of the Baxter's older son, Luke, arguing after a party the night before. Deputy Chief Inspector Channon investigates; his brusque and repugnant assistant, Sergeant Bowles, considers Luke the prime suspect. Making things worse is Rob's peculiar reaction to the murder and his unwillingness to offer his family support during the crisis, as well as daughter Tessa's difficult relationship with her mother. Just as Channon begins to doubt the Baxters, another murder abruptly focuses attention away from them. The intuitive and thoughtful Channon must carefully synthesize what he knows and what is not immediately obvious in order to focus on an unlikely killer with a surprising motive.

Etchells "knows how to introduce characters, get straight into the plot and tempt the reader to go on turning the pages," commented reviewer Catherine Hunt on *Shots Online*. Reviewer J.A. Kaszuba Locke, writing on the *Bookloons* Web site, called *No Corners for the Devil* "a beautifully written mystery." Etchells "couples the harrowing ordeal of a likable family with an artful mystery," remarked a *Kirkus Reviews* critic.

BIOGRAPHICAL AND CRITICAL SOURCES:

PERIODICALS

Kirkus Reviews, April 1, 2005, review of *No Corners for the Devil*, p. 387.
Library Journal, June 1, 2005, Rex E. Klett, review of *No Corners for the Devil*, p. 104.
Publishers Weekly, May 9, 2005, review of *No Corners for the Devil*, p. 49.

ONLINE

BookLoons Web site, http://www.bookloons.com/ (October 6, 2005), J.A. Koszuba Locke, review of *No Corners for the Devil*.
Shots: The Crime and Mystery Magazine, http://www.shotsmag.co.uk/ (October 6, 2005), Catherine Hunt, review of *No Corners for the Devil*.*

* * *

EVANS, Diana

PERSONAL: Female. *Education:* University of Sussex, B.A.; University of East Anglia, M.A.

ADDRESSES: Home—London, England. *Agent*—c/o Author Mail, William Morrow & Co., 10 E. 53rd St., 7th Fl., New York, NY 10022.

CAREER: Writer. Has worked as a journalist and arts critic for *Marie Claire, Evening Standard, Source, Independent, Observer, Daily Telegraph, Stage, Dance Theatre Journal*, and *Pride*.

AWARDS, HONORS: Orange Award for New Writers, and Whitbread First Novel Award shortlist, both 2005, and Commonwealth Best First Book Award shortlist, 2006, all for *26A*.

WRITINGS:

26A (novel), William Morrow (New York, NY), 2005.

Author of short fiction published in anthologies. Contributor of articles to newspapers and magazines.

WORK IN PROGRESS: A novel.

SIDELIGHTS: Diana Evans's novel *26A* explores the bond peculiar to twins while also probing other human commonalties and differences. The story, which won Evans the United Kingdom's Orange Award for New Fiction, "was sparked by the death of someone close to me," she related in an interview for the Orange Prize Web site. (Other sources have identified the "someone close" as her twin.) Evans continued, "I had a weirdly comic and mystifying experience of grief and bereavement that had a lot to do with being a twin. The idea of being cut in half but also doubled by the experience stayed with me for a long time before I began writing the book, which eventually became a novel, essentially, about the relationship between twins."

The twins of Evans's novel are Georgia and Bessi Hunter, daughters of a white British father and a black Nigerian mother. They are also the reincarnation of two small animals killed by a motorist; Evans writes in the book, "Before they were born, Georgia and Bessi experienced a moment of indecision. They had been traveling through the undergrowth on a crescent moon night with no fixed destination and no notion of where they were." After their rebirth, they grow up in London with two other siblings, one younger, one older, and witness their father's excessive drinking and their mother's isolation and eccentricity. The twins find shelter from their parents' troubles and the rest of the world with each other in their attic bedroom, which they dub "26A." Initially, the twins are so close that they feel each other's physical pain. On a trip to Nigeria, however, Georgia suffers a sexual assault but does not tell Bessi about it. The assault and the subsequent secrecy begin to undermine the twins' special relationship and start Georgia on a path to mental illness.

Evans's ability to meditate on the nature of twins while at the same time making her story universal, along with the tale's fantastic aspects and her writing style, received praise from numerous reviewers. "Though Evans lost her twin in adulthood, the novel is beyond fictionalised autobiography in its echoing exploration of other 'couples' and doubles, whether spouses, lovers, or parents and children," observed Maya Jaggi in the London *Guardian,* adding that "a novel about being twins grows stealthily, movingly, into one about being human." Sue Wilson, writing in *Scotland on Sunday,* thought Evans had portrayed the "unique and mysterious bond" of the twins with "authenticity" that "is adroitly offset by Evans's magic-realist approach."

In the London *Sunday Times* Christina Koning noted, "The perceptiveness and humour with which Evans describes the pains of growing up is one of the best things about this book; another is the inventiveness of the language." That language also received compliments from *Boston Herald* critic Sarah Rodman, who remarked, "Evans' prose is like stones skipping on the water, hopping in neat rows and occasionally veering dramatically off to one side and back again." A *Publishers Weekly* reviewer deemed *26A* "a funny, haunting, marvelous debut," while a *Kirkus Reviews* commentator described it as "a keen study of home, homelessness and the limits of symbiosis." "At its best," concluded *New Statesman* contributor Sheena Joughin, "this is a poetic, complex and lingering study of forces that can make life sometimes unliveable, wherever you come from, and wherever you live."

Evans told *CA:* "I began writing a journal and poetry in my teens. It came naturally to me, I knew I would write books one day, and once I became a journalist I eventually realised that I wanted, specifically, to write novels. I am inspired by lyrical writers such as Toni Morrison and Arundhati Roy, quirky writers such as Ali Smith, and powerfully sparse writers such as Jean Rhys and Raymond Carver. The most surprising thing I have learned as a novelist who started out as a journalist is that, unlike articles, a novel takes painstaking rewriting and a terrible first draft, it rarely flows off the pen fully formed. My writing process is chaotic, worrysome, overly complex, yearning for a simplicity that might not exist."

BIOGRAPHICAL AND CRITICAL SOURCES:

BOOKS

Evans, Diana, *26A,* William Morrow (New York, NY), 2005.

PERIODICALS

Boston Herald, September 3, 2005, Sarah Rodman, "Author's Twin Tale '26A' Doubly Enticing."
Guardian (London, England), May 28, 2005, Maya Jaggi, "Two into One."
Kirkus Reviews, July 1, 2005, review of *26A,* p. 701.
New Statesman, March 28, 2005, Sheena Joughin, "Secret Self."
Publishers Weekly, July 25, 2005, review of *26A,* p. 41; August 8, 2005, Suzanne Mantell, profile of Diana Evans, p. 104.
Scotland on Sunday, March 27, 2005, Sue Wilson, "Double Trouble and Twin Peaks."
Sunday Times (London, England), April 9, 2005, Christina Koning, "Secrets from the Upper Room."

ONLINE

Orange Prize Web site, http://www.orangeprize.co.uk/ (October 20, 2005), interview with Diana Evans.

F

FAIRCLOTH, Christopher A. 1966-
(Christopher Alan Faircloth)

PERSONAL: Born June 4, 1966, in Tallahassee, FL; son of Charles and Levita Faircloth. *Ethnicity:* "White." *Education:* Earned Ph.D. *Politics:* Democrat.

ADDRESSES: Agent—c/o Author Mail, AltaMira Press, 1630 N. Main St., Ste. 367, Walnut Creek, CA 94596.

CAREER: Writer. Boston University, Boston, MA, research fellow at Gerontology Center; University of Florida, Gainesville, assistant professor of occupational therapy; Veterans Administration Rehabilitation Outcomes Research Center, Gainesville, researcher.

MEMBER: American Sociological Association, Society for the Study of Social Problems, Gerontological Society of America.

WRITINGS:

Aging Bodies, AltaMira Press (Walnut Creek, CA), 2003.
(With Dana Rosenfeld) *Medicalized Masculinities,* Temple University Press (Philadelphia, PA), in press.

WORK IN PROGRESS: Research on everyday experiences of stroke recovery, illness, and the body.

SIDELIGHTS: Christopher A. Faircloth told *CA:* "Many people have asked why I became a sociologist, of all things. My interest in and choice to study the sociology of chronic illness was embedded in the impact that epilepsy had on both my mother and me. Diagnosed at the age of twenty-one, the mental and physical impact on me since then has been significant. My primary way of coping has been my own research and writing on the experiences of chronic illness from a sociological perspective and increasing interest in the relationship between chronic illness and the body.

"If you are looking for me now, you can find me at work or fishing for catfish in a small north central Florida lake."

*   *   *

FAIRCLOTH, Christopher Alan
See FAIRCLOTH, Christopher A.

*   *   *

FELDMAN, Jay 1943-

PERSONAL: Born 1943, in Brooklyn, NY. *Education:* Brooklyn College, B.A., 1963; University of California, Berkeley, M.A., 1965; doctoral study at University of California, Berkeley.

ADDRESSES: Home—Davis, CA. *Agent*—c/o Author Mail, Free Press, 1230 Avenue of the Americas, New York, NY 10020. *E-mail*—jay@jfeldman.com.

CAREER: Novelist, musician, business owner, and playwright. Writer for television, film, and stage. Founder, Baseball for Peace, 1985.

WRITINGS:

Hitting: An Official Major League Baseball Book (nonfiction), Little Simon (New York, NY) 1991.

(And lyricist) *A Loud Noise in a Public Place* (musical play), music by Fred Sokolow, produced in Jackson, MS, at New Stage Theatre, 1994– 95.

When the Mississippi Ran Backwards: Empire, Intrigue, Murder, and the New Madrid Earthquakes (nonfiction), Free Press (New York, NY), 2005.

Suitcase Sefton and the American Dream (fiction), Triumph Books (Chicago, IL), 2006.

Contributor to periodicals, including *Smithsonian, Newsweek, New York Times, Gourmet, New Age Journal, Sports Illustrated,* and *Whole Earth Review.* Writer for Columbia Broadcasting System, Inc. (CBS) television series *Brooklyn Bridge.*

SIDELIGHTS: Writer and playwright Jay Feldman is a frequent contributor to national magazines as well as a writer for television, film, and the theater. With a B.A. in speech and theater and an M.A. in dramatic art, Feldman has worked as a performer, making his living as a musician during the mid-1970s. In addition, Feldman has lived on a commune, owned a music store, and founded Baseball for Peace, a grassroots organization seeking to increase understanding between the United States and Nicaragua through the common medium of baseball. An early work, *Hitting: An Official Major League Baseball Book,* offers comprehensive instruction in the proper ways to hit a baseball for maximum effect.

In *When the Mississippi Ran Backwards: Empire, Intrigue, Murder, and the New Madrid Earthquakes* Feldman presents a history of the awesome physical force and the unexpected social effects of the devastating New Madrid, Missouri, earthquakes that shook the lower Ohio and mid-Mississippi valleys from December 1811 to April 1812. More powerful even than the legendary San Francisco earthquake of 1906, the New Madrid quakes were felt throughout the entire eastern United States. Because they were centered in the more-

sparsely populated Midwest regions, however, fewer lives were lost, but the tremendous power of the quakes still shook towns into rubble, altered the region's geography, and even temporarily reversed the flow of the Mississippi River. Feldman pays particular attention to the geology and seismology (the intensity, direction, and duration) of the quakes as he examines their effects.

Feldman also includes other prominent historical figures and events of the day, including Nicholas Roosevelt, whose steamboat suffered from the effects of the quake on the Mississippi River; Lilburne and Randolph Lewis, slaveowners and nephews of Thomas Jefferson, who were discovered to be murderers when a chimney collapsed during the quake and revealed the remains of a slain ex-slave; George Morgan, New Madrid founder; and legendary Native American chief Tecumseh, who saw in the quakes spiritual disapproval of the whites and the prophecy that the Indians would vanquish the settlers. "Feldman composes a fluent, coherent narrative that culminates in the War of 1812," stated *Booklist* contributor Gilbert Taylor. The author "skillfully presents an exciting narrative based on many primary sources, introducing general readers to frontier life in the 1810s," commented Charles L. Lumpkins in *Library Journal,* while a *Bookwatch* reviewer wrote that Feldman's "lively style" and attention to historical detail "links many seemingly disparate events to provide a uniform history" of the region. A *Publishers Weekly* reviewer called the book "a diverting patchwork of events, with colorful characters, that Feldman's well-paced storytelling turns into a vivid historical panorama."

BIOGRAPHICAL AND CRITICAL SOURCES:

PERIODICALS

Booklist, February 15, 2005, Gilbert Taylor, review of *When the Mississippi Ran Backwards: Empire, Intrigue, Murder, and the New Madrid Earthquakes,* p. 1044.

Bookwatch, August, 2005, review of *When the Mississippi Ran Backwards.*

Library Journal, March 1, 2005, Charles L. Lumpkins, review of *When the Mississippi Ran Backwards,* p. 97.

Publishers Weekly, January 31, 2005, review of *When the Mississippi Ran Backwards,* p. 60.

ONLINE

Jay Feldman Home Page, http://www.jfeldman.com (September 19, 2005).

* * *

FELIX, Werner 1927-

PERSONAL: Born July 30, 1927, in Weissenfels, Germany; son of a tradesman; married Beate Riehmann. *Education:* Weimar Music Academy, completed state exams in music pedagogy, 1951; Halle and Berlin universities, promotion, 1956.

ADDRESSES: Home—Otto-Schmiedt-Strasse 2B, Leipzig, Germany 7033. *Office*—Höchschule für Musik, Grassi-Strasse 8, Leipzig, Germany 7033.

CAREER: Musicologist, educator, and writer. Expert adviser at State Secretariat for Education, 1951-52; College of Music, Weimar, Germany, history of music lecturer, 1952, rector, 1955-65, professor, 1959; Erfürt Conservatory, director, 1953; College of Music, Weimar, professor, 1956, ord. professor, 1974, head of musicology department, beginning 1975; Gewandhaus Orchestra, Leipzig, Germany, manager, 1968-71; National Research and Memory Places of J.S. Bach, Leipzig, general director, 1979—; Music Academy, Leipzig, rector, beginning 1987. Also member of Erfürt District Council, 1958-63; executive council member of GDR Music Council; executive member of board, Neue Bach Gesellschaft (New Bach Society).

MEMBER: East German Chopin Society (president, 1962-87).

AWARDS, HONORS: Fatherland's Merit Order in Bronze, 1977.

WRITINGS:

Die Musik der deutschen Klassik, E.A. Seemann (Leipzig, Germany), 1954.
Franz Liszt: Ein Lebensbild, P. Reclam (Leipzig, Germany), 1961, second edition, 1986.

Christoph Willibald Glück, P. Reclam (Leipzig, Germany), 1965.
(With Armin Schneiderheinze and Winfried Hoffman) *Johann Sebastian Bach: Lebendiges Erbe,* Johann-Sebastian-Back Komitee (Germany), 1973, published in English translation as *Johann Sebastian Bach,* Orbis (London, England), 1985.
Aus der Geschichte des Thomaskantorates zu Leipzig, Breitkopf & Härtel (Wiesbaden, Germany), 1980.
(Editor, with others) *Musikgeschichte: Ein Grundriss,* Deutscher Verlag für Musik (Leipzig, Germany), 1984.

Contributor to numerous professional publications.

SIDELIGHTS: German musicologist Werner Felix has authored several studies on composers such as Johann Sebastian Bach, Franz Liszt, and Christoph Willibald Glück. J.P. Ambrose, who reviewed Felix's *Johann Sebastian Bach: Lebendiges Erbe* for *Choice,* called the book's lavishly illustrated text "beautifully planned and designed" and "highly recommended" the work for "both public and academic libraries at all levels." *Los Angeles Times Book Review* contributor Marc Shulgold called the work a "well-organized survey of Bach's music" that is "peppered with appropriate musical examples."

BIOGRAPHICAL AND CRITICAL SOURCES:

BOOKS

Fuchs, Torsten, and Michael Zock, editors, *Werner Felix zum 70. Geburtstag* (festschrift), Frankfurter Oder Editionen (Frankfurt, Germany), 1997.

PERIODICALS

Choice, April, 1986, J.P. Ambrose, review of *Johann Sebastian Bach: Lebendiges Erbe,* p. 1224.
Los Angeles Times Book Review, December 15, 1985, Marc Shulgold, review of *Johann Sebastian Bach,* p. 8.*

* * *

FENDER, James E.
　See FENDER, J.E.

FENDER, J.E.
(James E. Fender, James Trowbridge)

PERSONAL: Born in Memphis, TN; married; wife's name Ruth. *Education:* University of Alabama, B.A., 1963; Suffolk University Law School, graduated 1981.

ADDRESSES: Agent—c/o Author Mail, University Press of New England, 1 Court St., Ste. 250, Lebanon, NH 03766.

CAREER: Writer, novelist, museum curator, and attorney. Portsmouth Naval Shipyard, Portsmouth, NH, legal counsel. *Military service:* U.S. Air Force, 1960-77; became captain; served in Vietnam.

WRITINGS:

"FROST SAGA"; NOVELS

The Private Revolution of Geoffrey Frost: Being an Account of the Life and Times of Geoffrey Frost, Mariner, of Portsmouth, in New Hampshire, as Faithfully Translated from the Ming Tsun Chronicles, and Diligently Compared with Other Contemporary Histories, University Press of New England (Hanover, NH), 2002.

Audacity, Privateer out of Portsmouth: Continuing the Account of the Life and Times of Geoffrey Frost, Mariner, of Portsmouth, in New Hampshire, as Faithfully Translated from the Ming Tsun Chronicles, and Diligently Compared with Other Contemporary Histories, University Press of New England (Hanover, NH), 2003.

Our Lives, Our Fortunes: Continuing the Account of the Life and Times of Geoffrey Frost, Mariner, of Portsmouth, in New Hampshire, as Faithfully Translated from the Ming Tsun Chronicles, and Diligently Compared with Other Contemporary Histories, University Press of New England (Hanover, NH), 2004.

On the Spur of Speed, University Press of New England (Hanover, NH), 2005.

OTHER

Contributor of poetry, short stories, and articles to periodicals. Also author of the novel *Easy Victories,* under pseudonym James Trowbridge, 1973.

SIDELIGHTS: Writer, novelist, and attorney J.E. Fender is legal counsel for the U.S. Navy's oldest shipyard, the Portsmouth Naval Shipyard in Portsmouth, New Hampshire. He is also curator of the shipyard's museum, tending a perpetually growing set of holdings that include naval artifacts, books, and documents covering the shipyard's entire storied history. An Air Force officer and Vietnam veteran who speaks five languages, Fender spent much of his military career working in operations and intelligence.

As Fender described it in an interview with Gina Carbone in the *Portsmouth Herald,* "I live in the latter part of the eighteenth century from nine p.m. to midnight" as the author of the "Frost" chronicles, a series of books that traces the lives of mariner Geoffrey Frost and his loyal comrade, the mute Ming Tsun. "I feel like I belong in the area of Portsmouth in the time between 1775 and 1800," Fender said in an interview with Cara Lovell for *Foster's Daily Democrat,* "walking the cobblestone streets and the deck of the *Cat,*" Frost's ship.

In the "Frost" novels, Fender describes how he bought an old sea chest and found inside it reams of yellowed paper, with yellowed newspaper clippings, crumbling letters, and extensive writings in Portuguese. Translated into English, the documents tell about seaman Geoffrey Frost, a daring smuggler and sea captain from revolutionary-era America. They also reveal how Ming Tsun, a Mandarin Chinese tortured and rendered mute by having his tongue cut out, was saved by Frost as the captain sailed away from China. In addition, the papers document how Frost and Ming Tsun evolved as mariners and continued their adventures over the years.

In reality, there is no chest full of documents, no Ming Tsun, and no Geoffrey Frost. The entire story was made up by Fender, and, as critics have remarked, the carefully drawn history of the characters and their mysterious backgrounds add a touch of historical realism to the series. "Part of his fun is seeing how long he can keep someone believing the meticulously constructed story is real," Carbone observed.

With a nod to C.S. Forester's Horatio Hornblower, the first book of the series, *The Private Revolution of Geoffrey Frost: Being an Account of the Life and Times of Geoffrey Frost, Mariner, of Portsmouth, in New Hampshire, as Faithfully Translated from the Ming*

Tsun Chronicles, and Diligently Compared with Other Contemporary Histories, details how Frost and Ming Tsun join forces. A seafarer of deep learning and almost superheroic skill, Frost plies the dangerous but lucrative China trade routes, which leads to his association with Ming Tsun. While sailing along the New Hampshire coast, Frost encounters some British ships that nearly destroy him, but he manages to capture a British sloop, which becomes his flagship. When he learns his brother-in-law has been imprisoned in a heavily guarded British fort in Nova Scotia, he mounts a rescue mission, freeing not only his grateful brother-in-law but also dozens of other American prisoners as well. *Library Journal* reviewer Fred Gervat noted that Fender "has made an auspicious start" with the first novel of his series. *Booklist* reviewer Margaret Flanagan commented that the "suspenseful, action-packed tale will appeal to fans of seafaring fiction."

Audacity, Privateer out of Portsmouth: Continuing the Account of the Life and Times of Geoffrey Frost, Mariner, of Portsmouth, in New Hampshire, as Faithfully Translated from the Ming Tsun Chronicles, and Diligently Compared with Other Contemporary Histories continues Frost's story as he works as a licensed privateer along the east coast. The American Revolution continues, and Frost lends his capable hand to the colonies' struggle, capturing several British ships and helping sailors in distress. "Fender offers historical detail . . . plenty of action, and unforgettable characters," remarked George Cohen in *Booklist*.

In *Our Lives, Our Fortunes: Continuing the Account of the Life and Times of Geoffrey Frost, Mariner, of Portsmouth, in New Hampshire, as Faithfully Translated from the Ming Tsun Chronicles, and Diligently Compared with Other Contemporary Histories,* Frost once again strikes against the oppressive British, capturing a large cargo of food and arms. When he learns that American General George Washington and his troops are suffering in Pennsylvania, Frost devises a plan to move his captured goods to aid Washington's beleaguered Continental Army. Avoiding the heavily patrolled waters off the coast, Frost and his crew undertake an overland mission that proves as successful as his seagoing exploits. Frost even has the opportunity to accompany Washington in his crossing of the Delaware River. Margaret Flanagan, writing in *Booklist,* concluded that "fans of seafaring fiction will still enjoy this action-packed tale."

BIOGRAPHICAL AND CRITICAL SOURCES:

PERIODICALS

Booklist, May 15, 2002, Margaret Flanagan, review of *The Private Revolution of Geoffrey Frost: Being an Account of the Life and Times of Geoffrey Frost, Mariner, of Portsmouth, in New Hampshire, as Faithfully Translated from the Ming Tsun Chronicles, and Diligently Compared with Other Contemporary Histories,* p. 1586; May 15, 2003, George Cohen, review of *Audacity, Privateer out of Portsmouth: Continuing the Account of the Life and Times of Geoffrey Frost, Mariner, of Portsmouth, in New Hampshire, as Faithfully Translated from the Ming Tsun Chronicles, and Diligently Compared with Other Contemporary Histories,* p. 1638; April 15, 2004, Flanagan, review of *Our Lives, Our Fortunes: Continuing the Account of the Life and Times of Geoffrey Frost, Mariner, of Portsmouth, in New Hampshire, as Faithfully Translated from the Ming Tsun Chronicles, and Diligently Compared with Other Contemporary Histories,* p. 1423.

Foster's Daily Democrat (New Hampshire), September 1, 2002, Cara Lovell, "Bringing Mariner Tales to Life: Author Weaves History and Fiction in Revolution-Era Book Series."

Kirkus Reviews, March 1, 2005, review of *On the Spur of Speed,* p. 247.

Library Journal, June 1, 2002, Fred Gervat, review of *The Private Revolution of Geoffrey Frost,* p. 194.

Portsmouth Herald (New Hampshire), Gina Carbone, "History with a Hook," profile of J. E. Fender.

ONLINE

Frost Saga Web site, http://www.geoffreyfrost.com/ (September 19, 2005).

New Hampshire Bar Association Web site, http://www.nhbar.org/ (July 4, 2003), Larissa Mulkern, "Telling Tales of the Sea," profile of J.E. Fender.*

*   *   *

FENSTER, Julie M.

PERSONAL: Female.

ADDRESSES: Home—NY. *Agent*—c/o Author Mail, Crown Publishers, 1745 Broadway, New York, NY 10019.

CAREER: Writer and historian.

AWARDS, HONORS: Anesthesia Foundation Book/Multimedia Education Award, 2003, for *Ether Day: The Strange Tale of America's Greatest Medical Discovery and the Haunted Men Who Made It*; Best Book Award, National Automotive Journalism Conference, for *Packard: The Pride*.

WRITINGS:

Boston Guide, Open Road Publishing (New York, NY), 1997.

America's Grand Hotels, Open Road Publishing (New York, NY), 1998.

Ether Day: The Strange Tale of America's Greatest Medical Discovery and the Haunted Men Who Made It, HarperCollins (New York, NY), 2001.

Mavericks, Miracles, and Medicine: The Pioneers Who Risked Their Lives to Bring Medicine into the Modern Age, Carroll & Graf (New York, NY), 2003.

Race of the Century: The Heroic True Story of the 1908 New York to Paris Auto Race, Crown Publishers (New York, NY), 2005.

Packard: The Pride, Automobile Quarterly Publications (New Albany, IN), 2005.

Contributor to periodicals such as *American Heritage, New York Times, Los Angeles Times,* and *American History.* Author of column for *Audacity* (business history magazine). Member of editorial staff, *Automobile Quarterly.*

SIDELIGHTS: Writer and historian Julie M. Fenster is a frequent contributor to magazines and the author of books on business, medical and social history, and automobiles. In *Ether Day: The Strange Tale of America's Greatest Medical Discovery and the Haunted Men Who Made It* Fenster tells the story of the three men who pioneered the use of anesthesia in surgical procedures. The trio includes Charles Jackson, better known as a geologist than a physician; Horace Wells, the first to use nitrous oxide—a gas used as a mild anesthetic—in dentistry; and William Morton, who designed and built the first successful delivery device for administering ether to patients, but who also had a history as a con man. The three were at odds over who actually made the discovery of the highly

flammable ether in the 1840s and who should benefit from it financially. Ultimately, all three died in tragic, diminished circumstances. Fenster also describes how Yale University students used ether as a recreational drug during the early nineteenth century and how firearm maker Samuel Colt raised money at an ether show where attendees could pay to get a whiff of the powerful anesthetic. Fenster "ably renders the three main characters, who typify that common nineteenth-century American combination of brilliance, ambition, and mental instability," remarked a *Publishers Weekly* critic.

Mavericks, Miracles, and Medicine: The Pioneers Who Risked Their Lives to Bring Medicine into the Modern Age is a supplementary volume to a multi-part documentary that aired on television's History Channel. In the book, Fenster provides twenty stories of notable men and women whose work and discoveries significantly advanced medical knowledge. She "provides the necessary context for understanding the significance of her subjects' accomplishments in a readable, undemanding fashion," noted a *Kirkus Reviews* contributor. Among her subjects are Wilhelm Roentgen, who discovered the X-ray and whose name became the term describing the type of ionizing radiation used in X-rays; Ian Wilmer, the man who is credited with cloning Dolly the sheep; Ignaz Semmelweis, who discovered that hand-washing by doctors could help prevent the spread of disease; anatomist Andreas Vesalius, who conducted pioneering work in the sixteenth century; and Werner Forssmann, who developed the process of cardiac catheterization and actually performed the procedure on himself. She arranges the book into five broad categories, including germ theory, understanding the body, magic bullets, the mind, and surgery, and explores the lives and accomplishments of notables whose work falls under each of these groupings. Fenster also profiles Mary Mallon, better known as "Typhoid Mary," who presented one of the most difficult medical challenges in history. "The book includes some vivid storytelling, lively quotations, and nice turns of phrase, with a variety of word derivations and other interesting tidbits," commented Barbara Gastel in the *New England Journal of Medicine.*

Fenster turns to business and social history with *Race of the Century: The Heroic True Story of the 1908 New York to Paris Auto Race.* The story centers on the grand race across twenty-two thousand miles of sometimes unforgiving terrain, harsh weather, dangerous local inhabitants, and enforced isolation. "It's difficult to overstate the audacity of this project," observed a *Publishers Weekly* reviewer. At the time of the race, automobiles were still unreliable and could not be counted on to hold up over such a grueling course. Most roads were unpaved, rivers and ravines were not spanned by bridges, and automotive safety was negligible. Still, according to Fenster, public support ran high—more than fifty thousand spectators were on hand for the race's starting gun—and spectator enthusiasm helped propel the racers on through daunting obstacles. The international competitors all had deep motivations for participating: the French for maintaining their dominance from having won the prior year's race; the Germans for honoring their homeland; and the Americans for proving the strength and versatility of what was then a new industry. A *Kirkus Reviews* contributor commented that "Fenster is a superb storyteller, taking the factual information of the race and investing it with wit and brio."

BIOGRAPHICAL AND CRITICAL SOURCES:

PERIODICALS

American Heritage, June-July, 2005, "Cars, Cards, and Father: A Trio of *American Heritage* Authors Have Expanded Their Articles into Books," includes a brief review of *Race of the Century: The Heroic True Story of the 1908 New York to Paris Auto Race,* p. 16.

Biography, fall, 2001, David F. Musto, review of *Ether Day: The Strange Tale of America's Greatest Medical Discovery and the Haunted Men Who Made It,* p. 999.

Family Practice, October 1, 2001, Joanne M. Berger, review of *Ether Day,* p. 27.

Kirkus Reviews, August 1, 2003, review of *Mavericks, Miracles, and Medicine: The Pioneers Who Risked Their Lives to Bring Medicine into the Modern Age,* p. 1002; April 1, 2005, review of *Race of the Century,* p. 397.

New England Journal of Medicine, January 1, 2004, Barbara Gastel, review of *Mavericks, Miracles, and Medicine.*

Publishers Weekly, June 18, 2001, review of *Ether Day,* p. 69; May 2, 2005, review of *Race of the Century,* p. 191.

ONLINE

American Society of Anesthesiologists Web site, http://www.asahq.org/ (September 19, 2005), biography of Julie M. Fenster.*

FERRANTI, Seth M. 1971-

PERSONAL: Born January 2, 1971, in CA; son of Robert Feeney (an engineer) and Anne Smother Ferranti (a teacher); married Diane K. Schulte (a publisher). *Ethnicity:* "Irish." *Education:* Pennsylvania State University, A.A., 1999; University of Iowa, B.A., 2004. *Religion:* Christian.

ADDRESSES: Home—10015 Commonwealth Blvd., Fairfax, CA 22032.

CAREER: Fiction writer and journalist. Incarcerated in federal prison, Fairfax, VA, 1993-c. 2015.

WRITINGS:

Prison Stories (novel), Gorilla Convict Publications (St. Peters, MO), 2005.

Author of an unproduced screenplay, *The Dope Show.* Contributor to Internet Web sites and to periodicals, including *Don Diva, King, Ave, Vice, Feds,* and *Slam.*

WORK IN PROGRESS: Prison Stories II: The Seven Deadly Sins, a novel about prison life, publication by Gorilla Convict Publications; *White Boyz,* a novel about suburban gangs and the drug trade in and around Washington, DC; *Prison Basketball,* collected nonfiction.

*   *   *

FETTER, Henry D. 1949-

PERSONAL: Born July 18, 1949, in New York, NY. *Education:* Harvard University, A.B., 1971, J.D., 1977; University of California, Berkeley, M.A., 1974.

ADDRESSES: Home—2646 Creston Dr., Los Angeles, CA 90068. *Agent*—Glen Hartley, Writers Representatives, Inc., 116 W. 14th St., New York, NY 10011.

CAREER: Writer. Attorney in private practice, Los Angeles, CA, 1977—.

WRITINGS:

Taking On the Yankees: Winning and Losing in the Business of Baseball, 1903-2003, W.W. Norton (New York, NY), 2003.

Contributor to books, including *Current Developments in Copyright Law,* Practicing Law Institute, 1979; and *Jackie Robinson: Race, Sports, and the American Dream,* edited by Joseph Dorinson and Joram Warmund, M.E. Sharpe (Armonk, NY), 1998; contributor to reference books. Also contributor of articles and reviews to periodicals, including *Journal of Sport History, Public Interest, New York Times, Times Literary Supplement,* and *Heterodoxy.*

BIOGRAPHICAL AND CRITICAL SOURCES:

PERIODICALS

Kirkus Reviews, July 1, 2003, review of *Taking On the Yankees: Winning and Losing in the Business of Baseball, 1903-2003,* p. 892.
Library Journal, August, 2003, Jim Burns, review of *Taking On the Yankees,* p. 93.
New York Sun, September 22, 2003, Tim Marchmon, review of *Taking On the Yankees,* p. 16.
New York Times Book Review, September 28, 2003, Michael Shapiro, review of *Taking On the Yankees,* p. 34.
Publishers Weekly, July 21, 2003, review of *Taking On the Yankees,* p. 186.
Wall Street Journal, October 2, 2003, Chaz Repak, review of *Taking On the Yankees,* p. D10.

*   *   *

FINLAY, Charles Coleman 1964-

PERSONAL: Born July 1, 1964, in New York, NY; divorced; children: two sons. *Education:* Capital University (Columbus, OH), B.A., 1990; attended Ohio State University and Oxford University.

ADDRESSES: Home—Columbus, OH. *Agent*—c/o Author Mail, Pyr, 59 John Glenn Dr., Amherst, NY 14228-2197. *E-mail*—ccfinlay@earthlink.net.

CAREER: Writer, novelist, and historian. Administrator for online writing workshop; consultant in constitutional history. Worked variously for Aviation Safety Institute, Columbus Children's Hospital, and as a studio assistant for a porcelain artist.

AWARDS, HONORS: Nebula Award finalist for best novella, Science Fiction and Fantasy Writers of America, and Hugo Award finalist for best novella, World Science Fiction Society, both 2003, both for "The Political Officer."

WRITINGS:

The Prodigal Troll (fantasy novel), Pyr (Amherst, NY), 2005.
Wild Things (short stories; includes "Footnotes," "The Political Officer," and "We Come Not to Praise Washington"), Subterranean Press (Burton, MI), 2005.

Contributor to anthologies, including: *The Year's Best Science Fiction,* Volume 20, edited by Gardner Dozois, St. Martin's Press (New York, NY), 2003; *One Lamp: Alternate History Stories from the Magazine of Fantasy and Science Fiction,* edited by Gordon Van Gelder, Four Walls Eight Windows (New York, NY), 2003; *Mammoth Book of Best New Horror No. 15,* edited by Stephen Jones, Carroll & Graf (New York, NY), 2004; *Year's Best Fantasy No. 4,* edited by David G. Hartwell and Kathryn Cramer, Eos (New York, NY), 2004; and *In Lands That Never Were: Tales of Sword and Sorcery from the Magazine of Fantasy and Science Fiction,* edited by Gordon Van Gelder, Four Walls Eight Windows, 2004. Contributor of short stories and poetry to periodicals, including *Magazine of Fantasy and Science Fiction, Electric Velocipede, Argosy Quarterly, H.P. Lovecraft's Magazine of Horror, Paradox,* and *On Spec.*

Finlay's works have been translated into Hebrew.

SIDELIGHTS: Novelist and short-story writer Charles Coleman Finlay writes fiction in the genres of science fiction and fantasy. His stories have appeared in a number of periodicals and are widely anthologized in best-of collections. A finalist for the industry's John W. Campbell Award for Best New Writer in 2003, Finlay has also been a finalist for other prominent industry awards, including the Nebula, the Hugo, and the Sidewise awards. An expert in U.S. Constitutional history, Finlay worked as a researcher for historian Saul Cornell's book on anti-federalism and traditions of dissent in America, *The Other Founders,* which won a Society of Cincinnati Prize for history in 2001. He also worked at the Aviation Safety Institute and as a studio assistant for porcelain artist Curtis Benzle. Though he learned from each work experience, he remarked on his home page that "all of it looks much more interesting in retrospect than it did at the time."

As a writer, Finlay debuted in 2001 with his short story "Footnotes," which was published in the *Magazine of Fantasy and Science Fiction,* one of the genre's longest-running fiction magazines and a prestigious venue for short stories, particularly one's first. The story consists entirely of footnotes—some amusing, some frightening, some dramatic—to an article on a future disaster. This storytelling device allows readers to "concoct their own explanations" for what happened and what the story means, remarked a *Kirkus Reviews* critic.

"Footnotes" appears in *Wild Things,* Finlay's collection of short works. Ranging in style from science fiction to heroic fantasy to mainstream, the stories demonstrate Finlay to be "a versatile writer of imaginative fiction," commented a reviewer in *Publishers Weekly.* In "Lucy, in Her Splendor," a vampire learns that her peculiar obsessions have inevitable consequences with which she must contend. The protagonist of "The Smackdown outside Dedham" discovers cosmic Lovecraftian horror to go along with his wrestling mania; "Pervert" meditates on a future society in which men and women are never allowed to meet and mix; and in "Still Life with Action Figure," the collection's closest representative of literary fiction, a cartoonist struggles with the implications of his artist father's debilitating illness. "Solidly told and occasionally memorable, these fourteen tales display an insightful knowledge of human nature," stated the *Publishers Weekly* reviewer. "Finlay displays an astonishing range, an active imagination and a developing assurance and control: a writer to watch," commented a contributor to *Kirkus Reviews.*

Finlay's fantasy novel, *The Prodigal Troll,* is an expansion of his short story "A Democracy of Trolls." While his castle is under siege, Lord Gruethrist sends his infant son, Claye, to a safer haven, accompanied by two loyal retainers, a nursemaid and a knight. When the two retainers are killed, the human child is adopted by a troll female named Windy, who ignores the troll tribe's disapproval and raises Claye as her own. Despised by the brutish trolls, the boy is renamed Maggot and struggles to find a place within a society that is not his own. Smaller and physically weaker than the trolls, Maggot still thrives because of his superior intellect and quick wits. Eventually, he feels the need to rejoin his own kind, particularly in pursuit of the lovely Portia. Unschooled in the ways of man, Maggot finds the world of humans more dangerous and complicated than anything he has ever seen within the world of the trolls. Jackie Cassada, writing in *Library Journal,* commented favorably on the book's "excellent world building and . . . unique and likable hero." A *Kirkus Reviews* critic found "some rough edges" in the work but concluded that the novel is an "unusually intriguing and satisfying work from a writer on the rise."

BIOGRAPHICAL AND CRITICAL SOURCES:

PERIODICALS

Kirkus Reviews, May 1, 2005, review of *The Prodigal Troll,* p. 518; July 15, 2005, review of *Wild Things,* p. 769.

Library Journal, June 15, 2005, Jackie Cassada, review of *The Prodigal Troll,* p. 65.

Locus, April, 2004, "Charles Coleman Finlay: All in the Details," interview with Charles Coleman Finley, p. 68.

Publishers Weekly, April 11, 2005, review of *The Prodigal Troll,* p. 38; July 11, 2005, review of *Wild Things,* p. 67.

ONLINE

Charles Coleman Finlay Home Page, http://home.earthlink.net/~ccfinlay (September 19, 2005).*

*   *   *

FISHER, Jude
See JOHNSON, Jane

FORD-GRABOWSKY, Mary 1947(?)-

PERSONAL: Born c. 1947. *Education:* Princeton Theological Seminary, M.Div., Ph.D.

ADDRESSES: Home and office—P.O. Box 21267, Oakland, CA 94620-1267.

CAREER: Writer, editor, translator, and educator. Regis College, professor in religious studies department; University of Creation Spirituality, Oakland, CA, began as vice president and academic dean, 1995, became member of adjunct faculty and member of board of directors.

AWARDS, HONORS: Award for distinguished service in interfaith work, World Council of Churches, ecumenical branch.

WRITINGS:

Prayers for All People, Doubleday (New York, NY), 1995.
(Author of introductions to selections) *Sacred Poems and Prayers of Love,* selected by Mary Ford-Grabowsky, Doubleday (New York, NY), 1998.
Sacred Voices: Essential Women's Wisdom through the Ages (anthology), HarperSanFrancisco (San Francisco, CA), 2002.
WomanPrayers: Prayers by Women throughout History and around the World, HarperSanFrancisco (San Francisco, CA), 2003.
(Author of annotations) *Spiritual Writings on Mary: Annotated and Explained,* foreword by Andrew Harvey, SkyLight Paths Publishing (Woodstock, VT), 2005.
Stations of the Light: Renewing the Ancient Christian Practice of the Via Lucis as a Spiritual Tool for Today, Doubleday (New York, NY), 2005.

Also author of essays and scholarly articles. Editor of *Fellowship in Prayer,* Princeton Theological Seminary.

SIDELIGHTS: Writer, editor, and educator Mary Ford-Grabowsky focuses on areas related to world religions, prayer, and mystical traditions. As a translator, she specializes in collecting and translating prayers from all over the world. She is a member of the adjunct faculty and board of directors of the University of Creation Spirituality in Oakland, California.

To Ford-Grabowsky, much modern religious instruction is incomplete because it does not take into account the wisdom and contribution of women through the centuries. "There's just no effort to preserve or even publish women's writings," she remarked on the *San Francisco Faith* Web site. For example, evidence indicates that the famed St. Francis of Assisi was married, but little material exists that mentions or includes any writings of his wife, St. Clare of Assisi.

A number of Ford-Grabowsky's works seek to address this imbalance. *Spiritual Writings on Mary: Annotated and Explained* includes a diverse selection of poems, prayers, and stories about the Virgin Mary, the Mother of God, annotated and discussed by Ford-Grabowsky. The book provides numerous "thought-provoking and beautiful selections," noted Graham Christian in *Library Journal. Sacred Voices: Essential Women's Wisdom through the Ages* provides an anthology of writings by more than 150 women. Writers and thinkers represented include Rabia Al-Adawiyya, a Sufi poet; ancient Egyptian Queen Hashepsowe; abolitionist and women's rights advocate Sojourner Truth; athlete Jackie Joyner Kersee; environmental activist Julia Butterfly Hill; poet Emily Dickinson; and novelist Louise Erdrich. The book "maps the entire shimmering continuum of women's spirituality," and the selections are "eloquent, moving, and often stunning," commented Donna Seaman in *Booklist.* This "rich anthology of spiritual writing by women" is "distinguished by its dizzying breadth," observed a *Publishers Weekly* contributor. The book should provide an "interesting introduction to many writers," Christian noted in another *Library Journal* review.

Stations of the Light: Renewing the Ancient Christian Practice of the Via Lucis as a Spiritual Tool for Today is a "courageous book," wrote Christian in a *Library Journal* review. In the volume, Ford-Grabowsky offers a new interpretation of the well-known fourteen Stations of the Cross, which trace the events leading to Jesus's crucifixion and entombment. The version offered by Ford-Grabowsky follows the progress of Jesus's journey after his bodily death, placing considerable focus on the spiritual aspects of Christ's ascension and appearance to his disciples. Ford-Grabowsky provides detailed guidance for each station and offers "a substantive introductory explanation," Christian noted.

BIOGRAPHICAL AND CRITICAL SOURCES:

PERIODICALS

Booklist, March 1, 2002, Donna Seaman, review of *Sacred Voices: Essential Women's Wisdom through the Ages,* p. 1085.

Library Journal, March 1, 2002, Graham Christian, review of *Sacred Voices,* p. 110; March 1, 2005, Graham Christian, review of *Stations of the Light: Renewing the Ancient Christian Practice of the Via Lucis as a Spiritual Tool for Today,* p. 92; July 1, 2005, Graham Christian, review of *Spiritual Writings on Mary: Annotated and Explained,* p. 88.

Publishers Weekly, January 14, 2002, review of *Sacred Voices,* p. 54.

ONLINE

Mary Ford-Grabowsky Home Page, http://www.maryfordgrabowsky.com (September 19, 2005).

San Francisco Faith Web site, http://www.sffaith.com/ (September 19, 2005), commentary on Mary Ford-Grabowsky.*

*   *   *

FRANKEL, Estelle 1953-

PERSONAL: Born January 8, 1953, in New York, NY; daughter of Bernard (a wholesale jeweler) and Phyllis (a homemaker; maiden name, Biezonski) Frankel; married Stephen Goldhart (a psychologist), July 11, 1986; children: Miriam Frankel-Peretz, Elan. *Ethnicity:* "Jewish." *Education:* Attended Michlalah College for Jewish Studies (Jerusalem, Israel), 1970-78; College of Notre Dame, B.S., 1980; California State University, Hayward, M.S., 1982. *Religion:* Jewish. *Hobbies and other interests:* Playing guitar, singing, hiking in natural settings, ocean snorkeling, reading poetry, creating ritual art.

ADDRESSES: Home—902 Curtis St., Albany, CA 94706.

CAREER: Writer and educator. Self-employed psychotherapist in Albany, CA, 1973—. Ordained rabbinic pastor and spiritual guide; teacher in Israel, 1970-78; Lehrhaus Judaica Adult School for Jewish Studies, instructor, 1978—; Chochmat Halev: Wisdom of the Heart Meditation Center, teacher of Jewish mysticism, meditation, and healing, 1994—; chant master; organizer of symposia; public speaker.

MEMBER: Association for Humanistic Psychology, California Association of Marriage and Family Therapists, East Bay California Association of Marriage and Family Therapists.

WRITINGS:

Sacred Therapy: Jewish Spiritual Teachings on Emotional Healing and Inner Wholeness, Shambhala Publications (Boston, MA), 2004.

Work represented in anthologies. Contributor to periodicals, including *Tikkun, Responsive Community, Parabola,* and *Women and Therapy.*

BIOGRAPHICAL AND CRITICAL SOURCES:

PERIODICALS

Library Journal, February 1, 2004, Stephen Joseph, review of *Sacred Therapy: Jewish Spiritual Teachings on Emotional Healing and Inner Wholeness,* p. 93.

Publishers Weekly, October 13, 2003, review of *Sacred Therapy,* p. 74.

ONLINE

Sacred Therapy Web site, http://www.sacredtherapy.com/ (July 26, 2005).

*   *   *

FREEMAN, Walter J.

PERSONAL: Male. *Education:* Yale University, M.D. (cum laude), 1954; attended Massachusetts Institute of Technology, University of Chicago, and Johns Hopkins University; postdoctoral study at University of California, Los Angeles, 1959.

ADDRESSES: Office—University of California, Berkeley, Department of Molecular and Cell Biology, 101 Donner, No. 3206, Berkeley, CA 94720-3200. *E-mail*—drwjfiii@calmail.berkeley.edu.

CAREER: Writer, neurobiologist, and educator. University of California, Berkeley, professor of neurobiology, 1959—.

AWARDS, HONORS: Pioneer Award, Neural Networks Council of the Institute of Electrical and Electronics Engineers (IEEE); A.E. Bennett Award, Society of Biological Psychiatry.

WRITINGS:

Mass Action in the Nervous System: Examination of the Neurophysiological Basis of Adaptive Behavior through the EEG, Academic Press (New York, NY), 1975.
Societies of Brains: A Study in the Neuroscience of Love and Hate, Lawrence Erlbaum Associates (Hillsdale, NJ), 1995.
How Brains Make up Their Minds, Columbia University Press (New York, NY), 2000.
Neurodynamics: An Exploration in Mesoscopic Brain Dynamics, Springer (New York, NY), 2000.

Contributor to scholarly journals and periodicals, including *BioSystems, Journal of Neurophysiology, International Journal of Bifurcation and Chaos, Cognitive Processing,* and *Journal of Physiology.*

SIDELIGHTS: A writer, educator, and neurobiologist, Walter J. Freeman is a noted authority on brain function and related areas of neurobiology. As a researcher at the University of California, Berkeley, Freeman studies complex biological and bioelectrical brain activity. His findings suggest several intriguing ways to look at brain function. Freeman believes that there is a constant background noise in the brain, a chaotic state of electrical activity that "generates a flexible 'I don't know' energy state, from which massive numbers of neurons can be prodded instantaneously to work together and respond to new as well as previously encountered sensory stimuli without getting hopelessly confused," remarked Bruce Bower in *Science News.* This suggests that the brain has available to itself at all times all previously gathered knowledge about the world, which can be instantaneously accessed and processed when an organism encounters a stimulus. Prior knowledge thus does not need to be retrieved from any storage place in the brain. From this charged and ready "I don't know" state, "massive numbers of neurons can instantly generate coordinated responses to sensations," Bower noted. (Neurons are nerve cells in the brain.) Freeman has also found that individual brains are in all ways isolated from other brains; they do not cooperate with any part of the neurological system of other organisms. At first, this finding suggests that there should be great difficulty in forming the types of mutual trust and cooperation among organisms that result in communities, functioning societies, and even successful reproduction and raising of offspring. However, Freeman indicates that "Fortunately, evolution equipped mammals with a biological mechanism for bridging the gap between isolated brains so that pairs of animals in a species can reproduce and raise their offspring," Bower stated.

In *How Brains Make up Their Minds,* Freeman discusses in depth the function of the brain and how it works to satisfy the needs and desires of individual humans. He describes the nature of neurons and how they function. He outlines how structures in the brain change and adapt as humans learn, experience the environment, and interact socially. These changes shape each individual's beliefs and how each person reacts to the world. Freeman also lists the functions of the brain that are absolutely critical to life, including the brain's role in stimulating mitochondria (specialized membrane structures) to activities that prolong life. Though the book does not suffer from a lack of facts, it also contains Freeman's detailed description of his own ideas in theoretical neurobiology. "The talented author writes in a clear and persuasive fashion and his book is organized so as to answer the reader's questions," commented Stewart Wolf in a review for *Integrative Physiological and Behavioral Science.*

Freeman told *CA:* "My favorite book is *Societies of Brains: A Study in the Neuroscience of Love and Hate,* because I wrote it for the sheer pleasure of doing so."

BIOGRAPHICAL AND CRITICAL SOURCES:

PERIODICALS

Integrative Physiological and Behavioral Science, April-June, 2000, Stewart Wolf, review of *How Brains Make up Their Minds,* p. 167.

Quarterly Review of Biology, June, 2002, Bernard J. Baars, review of *How Brains Make up Their Minds,* p. 227.

Science News, January 23, 1988, Bruce Bower, "Chaotic Connections: Do Learning and Memory Spring from Chaos Generated by Brain Cells?," p. 58; November 2, 1996, Bower, "Bridging the Brain Gap: A Scientist Explores the Biology of Isolated Minds and Mutual Trust," profile of Walter J. Freeman, p. 280.

ONLINE

University of California, Berkeley, Department of Molecular and Cell Biology Web site, http://mcb.berkeley.edu/ (September 19, 2005), biography of Walter J. Freeman.

G

GAGE, Otis
See GEIST, Sidney

*   *   *

GAINES, Steven S.

PERSONAL: Male.

ADDRESSES: Home—Wainscott, NY. *Agent*—c/o Author Mail, Little, Brown & Company, 1271 Avenue of the Americas, New York, NY 10020.

CAREER: Writer, biographer, and investigative journalist.

WRITINGS:

Marjoe: The Life of Marjoe Gortner, Harper & Row (New York, NY), 1973.
(With Alice Cooper) *Me, Alice,* Putnam (New York, NY), 1976.
(With Robert Jon Cohen) *The Club,* W. Morrow (New York, NY), 1980.
(With Peter Brown) *The Love You Make: An Insider's Story of the Beatles,* McGraw-Hill (New York, NY), 1983.
Heroes and Villains: The True Story of the Beach Boys, New American Library (New York, NY), 1986.
Simply Halston: The Untold Story, Putnam (New York, NY), 1991.

(With Sharon Churcher) *Obsession: The Lives and Times of Calvin Klein,* Carol Publishing Group (New York, NY), 1994.
Philistines at the Hedgerow: Passion and Property in the Hamptons, Little, Brown (Boston, MA), 1998.
The Sky's the Limit: Passion and Property in Manhattan, Little, Brown (New York, NY), 2005.

SIDELIGHTS: Writer and investigative journalist Steven S. Gaines is also a biographer whose early works consist of biographies of prominent musicians, including the Beatles, Alice Cooper, and the Beach Boys. In *Obsession: The Lives and Times of Calvin Klein,* Gaines and coauthor Sharon Churcher provide a biography of a celebrity from another venue, that of superstar fashion designer Calvin Klein. The coauthors trace Klein's life from his childhood in the Bronx as a boy who would rather sketch fashion designs than play ball; to his drug-fueled days of ascending fame; to his first marriage to Jayne Center, his divorce, and the birth of his adored daughter Marci; and to his more sedate life in his early fifties, married to second wife Kelly Rector.

Obsession did not have an easy path to publication. Neither Klein nor his closest associates would cooperate with Gaines and Churcher, ensuring that the authors had no direct interviews or inside sources to support their reporting. The first publisher, G.P. Putnam's Sons, dropped the book, but did not ask the authors to return the 400,000-dollar advance they had received. Rumors circulated saying that Klein supporter and wealthy entertainment mogul David Geffen had pressured Putnam to drop the book. At the time, Geffen was a major shareholder in MCA, which owns

Putnam, and Gaines and Churcher believe that Geffen was in a position to try to stop the publication of the book. Numerous other high-profile publishers also refused to take on the book; however, it was finally accepted for publication by the privately owned Carol Publishing. The book's troubled genesis characterized what Gaines and Churcher noted was the most difficult obstacle in getting the book published and distributed: "the increasing difficulty of publishing controversial books about powerful people at a time when so many major publishers are owned by multimedia companies," wrote Dana Kennedy in *Entertainment Weekly.*

The authors "have done a thorough job of covering every facet of designer Calvin Klein's hectic career and jittery personality, and, indeed, obsession is the key word here," observed *Booklist* reviewer Donna Seaman. "Vividly told and packed with intimate revelations, *Obsession* dynamites the designer's refined image, exposing a life full of drugs and bisexual escapades," commented reviewer Alex Tresniowski in *People.* "Like most expose writers, the authors hunt down the bad news about their subject," commented Martha Duffy in *Time.* "But on a narrower, parallel track they offer evidence of a driven, sensitive man who has made the most of his considerable talents."

Philistines at the Hedgerow: Passion and Property in the Hamptons focuses on a group of wealthy, eccentric, sometimes obnoxious personalities bound together by their life in the prime real estate and exclusive summer homes of the Hamptons, a rarified "world of privilege, social climbing and serious bad taste" located along the eastern shore of Long Island, stated Michael Neill in *People.* The book contains a wealth of "truly remarkable tales, running the gamut from capsule biographies to historical facts and geographic details," noted *Booklist* reviewer Allen Weakland. Families whose wealth has been in-hand for generations find themselves in constant conflict with the newly rich, whose habits and attitudes sometimes tend toward the more casual and profligate. Among the stories of outrageousness and excess are those of a businessman arrested for putting pumpkins outside his store; a bathing pool for nudes that scandalized older, more conservative residents; a house bought for 35,000 dollars that sold to businessman Ron Perelman for more than twelve million dollars; and a real-estate tycoon who, it turned out, had deceived everyone with whom he came in contact. With his book, Gaines presents "a fascinating description of the eccentricities of the wealthy homeowners and renters" throughout the Hamptons area, noted Alison Hopkins in *Library Journal.*

Gaines shifts his geographic perspective some miles to the east in *The Sky's the Limit: Passion and Property in Manhattan.* He examines the insular, tightly controlled world of high-dollar real estate in New York City, particularly among the "good" buildings on Fifth and Park avenues on Manhattan's Upper East Side. In these locations, social standing is paramount, as the limited pool of individuals who can expect to find housing there are restricted to those listed in the Social Register. Gaines describes the draconian, sometimes neurotic behavior of co-op boards who, for example, turned away music star Madonna the same month nude photographs of her appeared in *Playboy;* found great significance in the fact that a woman carried a knock-off of a designer purse; rejected heirs of Johnson and Johnson who could not even get an apartment for twenty-seven million dollars; and turned down Barbara Streisand on the assumption that the celebrity singer and actress would host too many parties. To find the inside information for his story, Gaines interviewed dozens of people whose lives touch Manhattan real estate every day, including doormen, real-estate brokers, co-op members, building managers, and more. His "profiles of his guides—some of the fanciest real-estate brokers in the city—are charming," observed Benjamin Schwarz in *Atlantic Monthly.* "For the most part these people come off as ironic, skeptical, and very smart—and a lot more interesting, sensible, and humane than their clients." A *Publishers Weekly* contributor remarked that "throughout this addictive narrative, [Gaines] weaves a captivating history of the city and its toniest neighborhoods."

BIOGRAPHICAL AND CRITICAL SOURCES:

PERIODICALS

Atlantic Monthly, May, 2005, Benjamin Schwarz, "Eminent Domains," review of *The Sky's the Limit: Passion and Property in Manhattan,* p. 111.
Booklist, February 1, 1994, Donna Seaman, review of *Obsession: The Lives and Times of Calvin Klein,* p. 978; June 1, 1998, Allen Weakland, review of *Philistines at the Hedgerow: Passion and Property in the Hamptons,* p. 1712.

Entertainment Weekly, May 20, 1994, Dana Kennedy, "Fashion Show and Tell," about the publication of *Obsession,* p. 34; May 19, 1995, review of *Obsession,* p. 57; May 20, 2005, Jessica Shaw, review of *The Sky's the Limit,* p. 79.

Fortune, August 8, 2005, Kate Bonamici, review of *The Sky's the Limit,* p. 111.

Kirkus Reviews, April 1, 2005, review of *The Sky's the Limit,* p. 398.

Library Journal, June 15, 1998, Alison Hopkins, review of *Philistines at the Hedgerow,* p. 97.

People, May 23, 1994, Alex Tresniowski, review of *Obsession,* p. 27; July 6, 1998, Michael Neill, review of *Philistines at the Hedgerow,* p. 47.

Publishers Weekly, March 28, 1994, review of *Obsession,* p. 79; March 14, 2005, review of *The Sky's the Limit,* p. 52.

Time, April 25, 1994, Martha Duffy, review of *Obsession,* p. 80.*

*   *   *

GALLIANO, Luciana 1953-

PERSONAL: Born December 25, 1953, in Turin, Italy; daughter of Francesco and Melina Galliano; married Furio Dutto (marriage ended); married Giuseppe Manzone (an engineer). *Education:* Attended Alessandria Conservatory and Milan Conservatory; University of Turin, laurea (cum laude); Tokyo Ongaku Geijutsu University, M.A. *Politics:* "Left."

ADDRESSES: Home—Via Torquato, Tasso 5, 10122 Turin, Italy. *Office*—Venice University Ca' Foscari, Ca' Bonvicini, 5 Croce 2161, 30135 Venice, Italy. *E-mail*—luciana.galliano@fastwebnet.it.

CAREER: Writer, musicologist, and educator. Milan Conservatory, Milan, Italy, visiting lecturer in history of music, 1985-87; University of Venice, Venice, Italy, assistant professor of music of East Asia, 1996-2002; Venice University Ca' Foscari, Venice, teacher of anthropology of music. University of Turin, visiting lecturer, 1996-99; Turin Conservatory, visiting lecturer, 2001; guest lecturer at other institutions, including Hong Kong Academy of Arts, Takasaki University, Tokyo University of Fine Arts and Music, Palermo Conservatory, and University of Cremona. Conference and concert organizer; seminar participant. Interna-

tional Institute for Advanced Asian Studies, director of music section; International Research Center for Japanese Studies, Kyoto, Japan, fellow researcher; Electronic Music Foundation, member; researcher in Japan, 1987-91.

MEMBER: European Association for Chinese Music Studies, European Association for Japanese Studies, Japanese Musicological Society Ongakugakkai.

WRITINGS:

Yōgaku: Japanese Music in the Twentieth Century, Scarecrow Press (Lanham, MD), 2002.

La sensibilità estetica giapponese, EAM (Turin, Italy), 2004.

Musiche dell'Asia orientale. Un'untroduzione, Carocci (Rome, Italy), 2005.

Power, Beauty, and Music: Eight Studies on Chinese Music, Olschki (Florence, Italy), 2005.

*   *   *

GAOS, Vicente 1919-1980
(Vicente Gaos González-Pola)

PERSONAL: Born March 21, 1919, in Valencia, Spain; died of a heart attack, October 17, 1980, in Valencia, Spain. *Education:* University of Madrid, licentiate (classics), c. 1941; University of Mexico, Ph.D., 1949. *Politics:* Republican.

CAREER: Smith College, Northampton, MA, visiting professor of Spanish, 1948-50; University of Southern California, Los Angeles, instructor, 1950; Fordham University, New York, NY, instructor, 1952; University of Valencia, Valencia, Spain, taught in the study-abroad program sponsored by San Francisco College for Women; taught high school and college-level English in Segovia and Valencia, Spain, beginning 1955.

AWARDS, HONORS: Adonais poetry prize, 1943, for poem "Arcángel de mi noche"; Agora prize, 1963 (only year awarded), for *Mitos para tiempo de incrédulos;* Antonio González de Lama prize, and Spain's national poetry prize, both awarded posthumously, both for *Última Thule.*

WRITINGS:

Arcángel de mi noche: sonetos apasionados, 1939-1943, Hispánica (Madrid, Spain), 1944.

Sobre la tierra, Revista de Occidente (Madrid, Spain), 1945.

Luz desde el sueño, Santarén (Valladolid, Spain), 1947.

La poética de Campoamor, Gredos (Madrid, Spain), 1955, revised and enlarged edition, 1969.

Poesía y técnica poética, Ateneo (Madrid, Spain), 1955.

Profecía del recuerdo, Cantalapiedra (Torrelavega, Spain), 1956.

Temas y problemas de literatura española, Guadarrama (Madrid, Spain), 1959.

Poesías completas (1937-1957), Giner (Madrid, Spain), 1959.

Mitos para tiempo de incrédulos, Agora (Madrid, Spain), 1963.

Concierto en mí y en vosotros, Universidad de Puerto Rico (Rio Piedras, PR), 1965.

Claves de la literatura española, Guadarrama (Madrid, Spain), 1971.

Un montón de sombre, Fomento de Cultura Ediciones (Valencia, Spain), 1972.

Poesías completas II (1958-1973), Provincia (Leóon, Spain), 1974.

Cervantes: novelista, dramaturgo, poeta, Planeta (Barcelona, Spain), 1979.

Última Thule, Provincia (León, Spain), 1980.

Obra poética completa, two volumes, Institución Alfonso el Magnánimo (Valencia, Spain), 1982.

Translation of the Sonnets of Vicente Gaos, translation by Carl W. Cobb, E. Mellen Press (Lewiston, NY), 1997.

Contributor to anthologies, including *Poesía religiosa: antologia (1939-1969),* edited by Leopoldo de Luis, 1969. Also contributor to literary magazines.

EDITOR

Itinerario poético de Dámaso Alonson, two volumes, Escelicer (Madrid, Spain), 1956.

Ramon de Campoamor, *Poesía,* Ebro (Zaragoza, Spain), 1962.

(Also author of introduction and notes) *Antología del grupo poético de 1927,* Anaya (Salamanca, Spain), 1965, revised edition edited by Carlos Sahagún, Cátedra (Madrid, Spain), 1975.

Juan Ramón Jiménez, *Antología poética,* Anaya (Salamanca, Spain), 1965.

Miguel de Cervantes Saavedra, *Don Quijote de la Mancha,* Giner (Madrid, Spain), 1967, published with illustrations by Lorenzo Goñi, RIALP (Madrid, Spain), 1980.

(Also author of introduction and notes) Miguel de Cervantes Saavedra, *Viaje del Parnaso,* Castalia (Madrid, Spain), 1973.

(And author of introduction and notes) Miguel de Cervantes Saavedra, *Poesías completas,* Castalia (Madrid, Spain), 1974.

(Also author of introduction and notes) Pedro de Alarcón, *El sombrero de tres picos,* Espasa-Calpe (Madrid, Spain), 1975.

(And author of introduction) *Diez siglos de poesía castellana,* Alianza (Madrid, Spain), 1975.

Miguel de Cervantes Saavedra, *El ingenioso hidalgo Don Quijote de la Mancha,* three volumes, Gredos (Madrid, Spain), 1987.

TRANSLATOR

Charles Péguy: Poesías, Adonais (Madrid, Spain), 1943.

Arthur Rimbaud, *Poesías. Selección,* Adonais (Madrid, Spain), 1946.

Percy Bysshe Shelley, *Adonais,* Adonais (Madrid, Spain), 1947.

T.S. Eliot, *Cuatro cuartetos,* RIALP (Madrid, Spain), 1951.

Percy Bysshe Shelley, *Adonais y otros poemas breves,* Espasa-Calpe (Buenos Aires, Argentina), 1954.

Especulaciones: ensayos sobre humanismo y filosofía del arte, UNAM (Mexico City, Mexico), 1979.

Traduccines poéticas completas, two volumes, Institución Alfonso el Magnánimo (Valencia, Spain), 1986.

(With Donald Mills) *Los toros: Bullfighting,* Índice (Madrid, Spain), 1987.

SIDELIGHTS: A Spanish poet who lived through the Spanish Civil War and whose verses often express mixed feelings of anguish and joy for life, as well as a questioning of God, Vicente Gaos was also a noted literary critic, translator, and editor of works by such notables as his fellow countryman Miguel de Cervantes. Writing in the *Dictionary of Literary Biography,* essayist Patricia Mason pointed out several themes that run through Gaos's poems: "The search for transcendence, his strained relationship with God, human anguish and solitude, the passing of time, the appreciation of beauty, and the juxtaposition of opposites: life/love and death; God and the void; faith and despair; and light and darkness."

Born to a middle-class family whose members included scholars, poets, politicians, and philosophers, Gaos was a Republican, supporting the Spanish monarchy and opposed to the fascist Generalissimo Francisco Franco. Though many of his family fled Spain when civil war broke out in 1936, Gaos remained behind in his home until the Republican cause was lost and Franco came to power in 1939. He moved from Madrid to Valencia in 1940, where he formed a close friendship with literary critic Dámaso Alonso. It was Alonso who introduced Gaos to the public by arranging a public reading for the poet. Gaos read his sonnets, which were later published in his first collection, *Arcángel de mi noche: sonetos apasionados, 1939-1943.* Most of these verses are love poems, but some also involve the poet's troubled dialogues with God; the title poem of the book earned Gaos the Adonais prize in 1943.

Arcángel de mi noche was soon followed by two more collections: *Sobre la tierra* and *Luz desde el sueño.* The former has been regarded by critics as an expression of the poet's deep anguish, an attitude of despair and pessimism that is the result of the author questioning God's presence in the world. In the latter, Goas continues this questioning, and though the theme of death is prevalent, he also expresses a hope that love can provide moments of happiness.

From 1948 to 1955, Gaos lived abroad, visiting France and Mexico, where he earned a doctoral degree, and teaching at various universities in the United States. During this time, he published no poetry collections, although he did contribute to several American literary magazines. Not long after his return to Spain, Gaos began to publish again, marking a new phase in his career. An interviewer for the publication *Insula* noted at the time that Gaos was a changed person; he was "balder, sharper, more intellectual than ever, but also more human and ironic . . . more fatalistic." Avoiding the literary life of Madrid, the poet took up a career as an English teacher at various high schools and universities while he wrote poetry.

Profecía del recuerdo was published a year after Gaos's return to Spain. Here, the passionate mood of his earlier poems is replaced by a more contemplative tone, and there is not as much emphasis on the theme of love. The poems are composed in free verse, utilizing elements of colloquial language and the natural rhythm of speech. This was a distinct change from the rigid sonnet forms Gaos had originally favored, which he republished in the collection *Poesías completas (1937-1957).* Gaos's later poems continue to offer a blend of despair and hope. Many of these verses are collected in one of his last books, *Poesías completas II (1958-1973).* As one reviewer, Emilio Miró, commented in an *Insula* article translated by Mason, the poems here are "mixed with the experience of life and the passion for life, with the futility of hope and with the impossibility of renouncing it." After Gaos's death, the collection *Última Thule* was published and won both Spain's national poetry prize and the Antonio González de Lama prize.

In the introduction to his poems for the anthology *Poesía religiosa: antologia (1939-1969),* Gaos described his works: "I consider myself to be a religious poet and a good part of my poetry is religious. . . . For poetry to be religious, it does not have to talk about God. No matter what it talks about, it is talking about God, without mentioning him, or, sometimes, mentioning him to deny him."

BIOGRAPHICAL AND CRITICAL SOURCES:

BOOKS

de Luis, Leopoldo, editor, *Poesía religiosa: antologia (1939-1969),* [Spain,] 1969.
Dictionary of Literary Biography, Volume 134: *Twentieth-Century Spanish Poets,* Thomson Gale (Detroit, MI), 1994.

PERIODICALS

Insula, March 15, 1955, interview with Gaos; November, 1974, Emilio Miró, review of *Poesías completas II (1958-1973).**

*   *   *

GAOS GONZÁLEZ-POLA, Vicente
See GAOS, Vicente

GARCÍA TERRÉS, Jaime 1924-1996

PERSONAL: Born May 15, 1924, in Mexico City, Mexico; died April 29, 1996; son of Trinidad and Elisa (Terres) García; married Celia Chavez, May 4, 1960; children: Alonso, Ana Ximena, Ruy Martin. *Education:* Universidad Nacional Autónoma de Mexico, law degree, 1946; degrees from University of Paris and College de France, both 1950.

CAREER: Institute Nacional de Bellas Artes, Mexico City, Mexico, assistant director, 1948-49; Universidad Nacional Autónoma de Mexico, director of cultural affairs and university literary publications, 1953-65; Mexican ambassador to Athens, Greece, 1965-68; Secretaria de Relaciones Exteriores, Mexico City, director of library and archives, 1968-71; La Gaceta, Mexico City, director, 1971-89; Fondo de Cultura Económica, Mexico City, assistant director, 1972-74, director, 1982-89; Public Library of Mexico, Mexico City, director, beginning 1989.

WRITINGS:

Panorama de la critica literaria en Mexico (conference papers), [Mexico,] 1941.
Sobre la responsabilidad del escritor, [Mexico,] 1949.
El hermano menor, [Mexico,] 1953.
Correo nocturno, [Mexico,] 1954.
Las provincias del aire (poems), Fondo de Cultura Económica (Mexico City, Mexico), 1956.
La fuente oscura, Ediciones Mito (Bogota, Colombia), 1961.
Los reinos combatientes (poems), Fondo de Cultura Económica (Mexico City, Mexico), 1961.
La feria de los días: y otros textos políticos y literarios, Universidad Nacional Autónoma de Mexico (Mexico City, Mexico), 1961.
(Editor) *100 imágenes del mar* (poems), Universidad Nacional Autónoma de Mexico (Mexico City, Mexico), 1962, reprinted, Colegio Nacional (Mexico City, Mexico), 1982.
Grecia 60 poesía y verdad (poems), Alacena (Mexico), 1962.
Los infiernos del pensamiento: en torno a Freud, ideología y psicoanálisis, J. Moritz (Mexico City, Mexico), 1967.
Funerales (poems), Universidad Nacional Autónoma de Mexico (Mexico City, Mexico), 1969.

Todo lo más por decir (poems), J. Moritz (Mexico City, Mexico), 1971.
Reloj de Atenas, J. Moritz (Mexico City, Mexico), 1977.
Breve antología, Universidad Nacional Autónoma de Nexuci (Mexico City, Mexico), 1977.
Honores a Francisco de Terrazas, limited edition, Taller Martin Pescador (Tacámbaro, Michoacán, Mexico), 1979.
Corre la voz, J. Moritz (Mexico City, Mexico), 1980.
Poesía y alquimia: los tres mundos de Gilberto Owen, Era (Mexico City, Mexico), 1980.
Letanías profanas: breve antologia, Universidad Nacional Autónoma de Mexico (Mexico City, Mexico), 1981.
(Editor, with Adolfo Castañón) *Los reinos combatientes todavía* (conference papers), 1986.
Ambo, Taller Martin Pescador (Tacámbaro, Michoacán, Mexico), 1987.
Las manchas del sol: poesía, 1956-1987, Alianza (Madrid, Spain), 1988.
Parte de vida, J. Moritz (Mexico City, Mexico), 1988.
El teatro de los acontecimientos, Colegio Nacional (Mexico City, Mexico), 1988.
Baile de máscaras (poetry translations), Ediciones del Equilibrista (Mexico), 1989.
(With José Luis Rivas) *Las provincias del aire,* Consejo Nacional para la Cultura y las Artes (Mexico City, Mexico), 1992.
Obras, compiled by Rafael Vargas, Colegio Nacional, Fondo de Cultura Económica (Mexico City, Mexico), 1995.
Obras I: las manchas del sol: poesía, 1953-1994, compiled by Rafael Vargas, Fondo de Cultura Económica (Mexico City, Mexico), 1996.
Obras II: el teatro de los acontecimientos, compiled by Rafael Vargas, Fondo de Cultura Económica (Mexico City, Mexico), 1997.
Obras III: la feria de los dias, 1953-1994, Fondo de Cultura Económica (Mexico City, Mexico), 2000.

Author of *Carne de dios,* c. 1960s; work represented in anthologies. Translator, from the Greek, of poems by George Seferis.

SIDELIGHTS: Jaime García Terrés, who died in 1996 at the age of seventy-one, was an important Mexican poet, as well as a lawyer, publisher, and diplomat. He was director of Mexico's national art institute and taught at the Universidad Nacional Autónoma de Mexico, where he also was responsible for literary publications. He was director of the Mexican state publishing house Fondo de Cultura Económica during its most relevant period. His post as ambassador to Greece led him to write *Reloj de Atenas,* in which he writes of his life there and in which he makes observations about Greek travel. García Terrés was also a translator of works by others, notably the poems of Greek Nobel laureate George Seferis.

García Terrés wrote many volumes of poetry. In an obituary in the London *Guardian,* Hugo Estenssoro wrote that his "poetic style was very much the man: an elegant limpidity at the service of an intelligence at ease with itself." Estenssoro noted that García Terrés "was also an eclectic, refined essayist." *Corre la voz* is considered to be one of García Terrés's finest poetry collections. M. Durán, writing in *World Literature Today,* described it as "a well-integrated collection in which each part or chapter has a role to play, a voice to add to the chorus; the quality of the poems is unusually high."

Maria José Bas Albertos wrote a study of García Terrés's life and work titled *La poesia civica de Jaime García Terrés,* which was reviewed in *Hispanic Review* by Frank Dauster. Dauster found that, according to Albertos, García Terrés's work "is often direct and deceptively straightforward in technique and reflective in tone. Rather than a flow of images, it is the examination of a thought, the evocation of a feeling, the memory of a voyage or a poem from another time and place, the fascination of the past. . . . The volume is a useful introduction, and one hopes for further studies of a poet who will, lamentably, offer us no further works."

BIOGRAPHICAL AND CRITICAL SOURCES:

BOOKS

Bas Albertos, Marie José, *La poesia civica de Jaime García Terrés,* Universidad de Alicante (Alicante, Mexico), 1996.
Cortés, Eladio, editor, *Dictionary of Mexican Literature,* Greenwood Press (Westport, CT).

PERIODICALS

Hispanic Review, winter, 1998, Frank Dauster, review of *La poesia civica de Jaime García Terrés,* p. 117.

World Literature Today, spring, 1982, M. Durán, review of *Corre la voz,* p. 314; winter, 1990, William Ferguson, review of *Las manchas del sol: poesía, 1956-1987,* p. 81.

OBITUARIES

PERIODICALS

Guardian (London, England), May 1, 1996, Hugo Estenssoro, "Elegant Lines from Mexico," p. 15.*

*   *   *

GARDELL, Jonas 1963-

PERSONAL: Born November 2, 1963, in Täby, Sweden; son of Ingegärd (a psychologist) and Bertil (a psychologist) Gardell; partner of Mark Levengood (a media personality and singer), 1995; children: one (adopted).

ADDRESSES: Agent—c/o Author Mail, P.A. Norstedt & Söner AB, P.O. Box 2052, SE-103 12, Stockholm, Sweden.

CAREER: Writer, comedian, and television director. Director of television movie *Cheek to Cheek,* 1997, and video *Dan Bäckman 2-0,* 2003. Has appeared in Swedish television series and other programs as himself, including episodes of *Først & sist, Bettina S., Sen kväll med Luuk, Adam & Eva,* and *Melodifestivalen 2003.*

WRITINGS:

Den tigande talar/4937 (poetry; title means "The Silent One Speaks"), Författarförlaget (Stockholm, Sweden), 1981.
Passionsspelet (novel; tile means "The Passion Play"), Författarförlaget (Stockholm, Sweden), 1985.
Odjurets tid (novel; title means "The Time of the Beast"), Norstedts (Stockholm, Sweden), 1986.
Präriehundarna (fiction; title means "The Prairie Dogs"), Norstedts (Stockholm, Sweden), 1987.

Vill gå hem? (fiction; title means "Want to Go Home?"), Norstedts (Stockholm, Sweden), 1988.

Fru Björks öden och äventyr (fiction; title means "The Wonderful Adventures of Mrs. Björk"), Norstedts (Stockholm, Sweden), 1990.

En komikers uppväxt (fiction; title means "Growing up a Comedian"), Norstedts (Stockholm, Sweden), 1992.

Mormor gråter och andra texter (essays and other writings; title means "Grandma Is Crying and Other Texts"), Norstedts (Stockholm, Sweden), 1993.

Frestelsernas berg (fiction; title means "Mount of Temptations), Norstedts (Stockholm, Sweden), 1995.

Så går en dag ifrån vårt liv och kommer aldrig åter, Norstedts (Stockholm, Sweden), 1998.

(Author of introduction) Elizabeth Ohlsson, *Ecce homo,* Föreningen Ecce Homo (Malmö, Sweden), 1998.

Oskuld och andra texter, Norstedts (Stockholm, Sweden), 2000.

Ett UFO gör entré (title means "A UFO Makes an Entry"), Norstedts (Stockholm, Sweden), 2001.

Om Gud, Norstedts (Stockholm, Sweden), 2003.

Contributor to books, including *Mellan handslag och samlag: Unga svenska berättare om AIDS: En HIV antologi,* edited by Stig Nordlund, Brevskolan (Stockholm, Sweden), 1987; and *"Ordning, redbarhet och snabb expedition": Svenska bokhandlareföreningen 1893-1993,* edited by Thomas Rönström, Informationsförlaget (Stockholm, Sweden), 1995. Fiction and nonfiction writings have appeared in numerous Swedish periodicals, including *Aftonbladet, Vår bostad, Expressen,* and *Dagens Nyheter.*

Gardell's works have been translated into several languages, including Russian, French, and English.

PLAYS

Good Night, Mr. Moon, produced in Stockholm, Sweden, at Moderna museet, 1987.

Kim å Jonas jubelkavalkad, 1988.

Kim å Jonas går igen, 1989.

Lena och Percy, Präriehund, produced in Göteborg, Sweden, at Stadsteatern, 1989.

En fulings bekännelser, produced in Göteborg, Sweden, at Stadsteatern, 1989.

Isbjörnarna (also see below), produced in Stockholm, Sweden, at Stadsteatern, 1990.

En pall, en mikrofon och Jonas Gardell, produced in Stockholm, Sweden, at Konserthuset, 1991.

Cheek to Cheek (also see below), produced in Stockholm, Sweden, at Stadsteatern, 1992.

En finstämd kväll med Jonas Gardell, produced in Stockholm, Sweden at the Intiman Theater, 1993.

En annan sorts föreställning, Katrineholm (Kosmos, Sweden), 1995.

På besök i Mellanmjölkens land (title means "Visiting the Land of Two Percent"), produced in Göteborg, Sweden, at Lisebergshallen, 1996.

Människor i solen (also see below), produced in Stockholm, Sweden, 1997.

Isbjörnarna; Cheek to Cheek; Människor i solen: tre pjäser, Norstedts (Stockholm, Sweden), 1997.

Komma tillbaka, Konserthuset. produced in Stockholm, Sweden, 1998.

Scheherzad, produced in Stockholm, Sweden, 1999.

Livet (also see below), produced in Göteborg, Sweden, at Lisebergshallen, 2000.

Helvatet är minnet utan makt att förändra, produced in Stockholm, Sweden, 2003.

Väckelsemöte, produced on tour throughout Scandinavia, 2004–06.

SCREENPLAYS

Ömheten, TV-Teatern, 1989.

En komikers uppväxt (produced on Swedish television, 1992), Norstedts (Stockholm, Sweden), 1992.

Pensionat Oskar (title means "Like It Never Was Before"), SVT Kanal 1 Drama, 1995.

(And director) *Cheek to Cheek* (based on Gardell's play of the same title), TV-Teatern, 1997.

Irma och Gerd (six-part television series), 1997.

Livet är en schlager (based on Gardell's play *Livet*), SVT Drama, 2000.

LYRICIST; RECORDINGS

(With Kim Hedås) *Kim å Jonas: Klang och jubelkavalkad,* Nonstop 033-07 (Göteborg, Sweden), 1989.

(Contributor of lyrics) Christer Sandelin, *Till månen runt solen,* Metronome, 1992.

En finstämd kväll med Jonas Gardell: Live på Intiman, Sony Bromma, 1994.

ADAPTATIONS: Fru Björks öden och äventyr has adapted as an opera.

SIDELIGHTS: Jonas Gardell is a Swedish writer and comedian. According to Paul Binding, writing in the London *Guardian,* Gardell has "broken his country's fixation with the norm with his gay sensibility expressed in novels, plays and outrageous one-man shows." Writing in the *Dictionary of Literary Biography,* a contributor noted that "Gardell's award-winning novel and greatest critical success, *En komikers uppväxt* ('Growing up a Comedian,' 1992), has already earned him a place in the contemporary canon of Swedish literature."

Among Gardell's novels are *Passionsspelet* ("The Passion Play"), in which the author tells the homosexual love story of Hampus and Johan in a story that parallels the Biblical account of the relationship between Jesus and Judas Iscariot; and *Odjurets tid* ("The Time of the Beast"), which relates the story of four individuals, including a woman dying of cancer, another woman hiding her past, and a homosexual couple named David and Fredrik. The *Dictionary of Literary Biography* essayist noted that all the characters in the latter title develop "the lies, myths, and illusions that they need in order to endure living." Another novel, *Präriehundarna* ("The Prairie Dogs"), focuses on the morality of a couple named Lena and Percy and their son, Reine, who live in a suburb of Stockholm. Regarding this work, the *Dictionary of Literary Biography* contributor observed, "Critics and reviewers have often claimed that Gardell is present in the book as the prosecutor, a character who occasionally breaks into the narrative to proclaim his own moral premises."

In his fourth novel, *Vill gå hem,* Gardell delves into the lives of the outwardly successful family man Rut and his unhappy sister, Rakel, who is married to an unloving husband. "Just as in *Präriehundarna,* an unknown presence appears in *Vill gå hem* under the guise of the author's remarks, which break up the narrative and comment upon the action in the novel," according to the *Dictionary of Literary Biography* writer. "The comments of this unknown character are often bitterly funny—a satirical retort to both the story at hand and life itself."

Frestelsernas berg ("Mount of Temptations") relates the story of a family falling apart partly due to its tumultuous past, including the abandonment of the father, a drug-abusing son, and another son named Johan who is a homosexual. "The reference to the biblical Temptation on the Mount, however, is most evident in Johan's mother, Maria," commented the essayist in the *Dictionary of Literary Biography.* "She lives among her mementos, which are kept carefully boxed, and grasps for a life that she will never regain. Somehow she knows that her life would be as easy to end as those of the monks who have carved their monastery out of the Mount of Temptation." In his novel *Ett UFO gör entré* ("A UFO Makes an Entry") Gardell tells the story of Juha and Jenny, two unhappy teenagers. Writing a review of *Ett UFO gör entré* in *Publishing Trends,* a critic noted: "Possibly the best of Gardell's 'tender yet cruelly accurate" tales to date, this book is said to dexterously juggle bathos, pathos, and polyester."

BIOGRAPHICAL AND CRITICAL SOURCES:

BOOKS

Dictionary of Literary Biography, Volume 257: *Twentieth-Century Swedish Writers after World War II,* Thomson Gale (Detroit, MI), 2002, pp. 98-105.

PERIODICALS

Guardian (London, England), September 2, 2000, Paul Binding, "All Points North."

Nordic Business Report, September 16, 2002, "Swedish Comedian Becomes a Father, Enters Debate on Adoptions for Homosexual Couples."

Publishing Trends, November, 2001, "The Travolta Generation; Swingin' Sweden's Gardell, Finland's Eager Readers, and Greece's Turk in the Garden."

*   *   *

GARGAGLIANO, Arlen

PERSONAL: Female.

ADDRESSES: Home—New Rochelle, NY. *Agent*—c/o Author Mail, Stewart, Tabori & Chang, 100 5th Ave., New York, NY 10011.

CAREER: Writer.

WRITINGS:

(With Curtis Kelly) *Writing from Within* (textbook), Cambridge University Press (New York, NY), 2001.

(With Rafael Palomino) *Viva la Vida: Festive Recipes for Entertaining Latin-Style,* photographs by Susie Cushner, Chronicle Books (San Francisco, CA), 2002.

(With Rafael Palomino) *Nueva Salsa: Recipes to Spice It Up,* photographs by Miki Duisterhof, Chronicle Books (San Francisco, CA), 2003.

Mambo Mixers: Recipes for Fifty Luscious Latin Cocktails and Twenty Tantalizing Tapas, photographs by Dasha Wright, Stewart, Tabori & Chang (New York, NY), 2005.

SIDELIGHTS: Writer Arlen Gargagliano is a frequent collaborator with New York City restaurateur and chef Rafael Palomino. In *Nueva Salsa: Recipes to Spice It Up,* Gargagliano and Palomino offer sixty-five recipes for a diverse array of different kinds of salsa. Many of the recipes are for salsas that serve as garnishes or side dishes, not merely as substantial dips for chips and snacks. In fact, some of the salsas covered in the book are complete dishes in and of themselves. The authors include serving and presentation suggestions for each salsa as well as detailed ingredient lists and recipes. *Library Journal* reviewer Judith Sutton called it an "attractive little book" with "striking color photographs" of the dishes described within.

In *Viva la Vida: Festive Recipes for Entertaining Latin-Style,* Palomino and Gargagliano concentrate on Nuevo Latino cooking in a book that "open[s] up new territory," observed a *Publishers Weekly* contributor. The recipes offer broad coverage and usage of traditional Latin-American foods and ingredients, including avocados for guacamole and mangos and corn for making a Peruvian-style potato salad. The recipes also offer an "appealing fusion" of ethnic styles and ingredients, noted the *Publishers Weekly* reviewer. Among the culinary hybrids are tuna and chipotle burgers and Asian Ceviche with soy sauce and rice vinegar. The *Publishers Weekly* reviewer noted that the book is easy to use, but also presents a number of recipes with difficult-to-obtain ingredients, which diminishes the volume's overall usefulness. Still, the reviewer found that *Viva la Vida* is "charming all around and should seduce consumers with its attractive packaging."

BIOGRAPHICAL AND CRITICAL SOURCES:

PERIODICALS

Library Journal, April 15, 2003, Judith Sutton, review of *Nueva Salsa: Recipes to Spice It Up,* p. 118.

Publishers Weekly, April 1, 2002, review of *Viva la Vida: Festive Recipes for Entertaining Latin-Style,* p. 74.

ONLINE

McNally Robinson Web site, http://www.mcnally robinson.com/ (September 19, 2005), brief biography of Arlen Gargagliano.*

*   *   *

GEIST, Sidney 1914-2005
(Otis Gage)

OBITUARY NOTICE— See index for *CA* sketch: Born April 11, 1914, in Paterson, NJ; died of complications following a stroke, October 18, 2005, in New York, NY. Artist, educator, and author. Geist was a noted sculptor who also became known as an authority on Romanian sculptor Constantin Brancusi. His education in art was diverse, beginning with studies at St. Stephen's College and continuing with his apprenticeship under Paul Fiene from 1931 to 1937. Geist then studied at the Art Students League for a year and, after serving as a private in the U.S. Army in Europe during World War II, at the Académie de la Grande Chaumière in Paris. While still in Paris in 1950, he participated in a cooperative called the Galerie Huit that was founded by expatriate artists. Returning to Manhattan, he established his own studio and began working on his art in earnest and exhibiting his work. Over the years, Geist became known for his sculptures chiseled and formed out of natural materials such as wood and stone. His style was not easily associated with any particular school or technique, but his art was often distinguished by his bright and bold use of color. Often, the artist found that his use of color caused serious pieces to be viewed by audiences as having a comic effect, and he eventually resigned himself good-humoredly to this interpretation. In addition to his artistic work, Geist was also a teacher. His first such job was as a sculpture instructor for the Pratt Institute in the early 1960s. From 1964 to 1987, he was at the New York Studio School, which he cofounded and which he directed during his first two years there. During the 1980s, he also taught variously at Vassar College, the Vermont Studio School, and the International School of Art. In addition, he would be an instructor at Brooklyn College, the University of California at Berkeley, and Southern Illinois University. As a writer, Geist was particularly well known for his books on Brancusi, including *Brancusi: A Study of the Sculpture* (1967), *Constantin Brancusi, 1876-1957* (1969), and *Brancusi: The Sculpture and the Drawings* (1975), among others. To research these books, he taught himself Romanian so that he could travel to his subject's country and speak with local scholars and translate their texts. Geist was also the author of *Interpreting Cezanne* (1988), and contributed to art journals, sometimes under the pen name Otis Gage.

OBITUARIES AND OTHER SOURCES:

PERIODICALS

Los Angeles Times, October 26, 2005, p. B11.
New York Times, October 21, 2005, p. A23.

*   *   *

GERSHENFELD, Neil
(Neil A. Gershenfeld)

PERSONAL: Married; wife a piano technician; children: Grace, Eli. *Education:* Swarthmore College, B.A.; Cornell University, Ph.D.

ADDRESSES: Office—Massachusetts Institute of Technology, Center for Bits and Atoms, 20 Ames St., Room E15-411, Cambridge, MA 02139. *E-mail*—gersh@cba.mit.edu.

CAREER: Scientist, physicist, educator, and administrator. Massachusetts Institute of Technology, Cambridge, MA, professor and director of Center for Bits and Atoms. Bell Labs, member of research staff; Harvard Society of Fellows, junior fellow.

AWARDS, HONORS: Scientific American Fifty recognition, and Communications Research Leader of the Year recognition, both 2004.

WRITINGS:

(Editor, with Andreas S. Wiegend) *NATO Advanced Research Workshop on Comparative Time-Series Analysis,* Addison-Wesley Publishing Company (Reading, MA), 1994.
The Nature of Mathematical Modeling, Cambridge University Press (New York, NY), 1999.
When Things Start to Think, Henry Holt (New York, NY), 1999.
The Physics of Information Technology, Cambridge University Press (New York, NY), 2000.
Fab: The Coming Revolution on Your Desktop—From Personal Computers to Personal Fabrication, Basic Books (New York, NY), 2005.

Contributor of articles and papers to numerous scientific journals and periodicals. Author's work has been featured in White House and Smithsonian Institution millennium celebrations and in print venues including *New York Times* and *Economist,* and on television networks such as Cable New Network and Public Broadcasting Service.

SIDELIGHTS: Writer, physicist, and educator Neil Gershenfeld is director of the Center for Bits and Atoms at the Massachusetts Institute of Technology (MIT). The center is part of an "interdisciplinary initiative that is broadly exploring how the content of information relates to its physical representation, from atomic nuclei to global networks," noted a writer on the MIT Web site. Gershenfeld's work in studying the most fundamental mechanisms used to manipulate information led to the first complete quantum computation, which is early progress in the development of an entirely new generation of computers based on quantum mechanics and that operate on an atomic scale.

A number of Gershenfeld's books address the complex science and technology behind several broader areas of technological endeavor. In *The Physics of Information Technology* Gershenfeld presents "a synthesis of the fundamental results in selected areas of physics and the information sciences" that shows "how both are used in the technologies of communication, information storage, and computation," noted David G. Goodwin in *Science*. In his book Gershenfeld demonstrates how advances in information technology have relied heavily on advances in physics. The telegraph, for example, could not have been invented until magnetic induction was discovered, Goodwin explained. Transistors would have been impossible without understanding the physics underlying the energy band structure of solids. As both fields advance, "questions regarding the ultimate limits of information technology require an understanding of both physics and the information sciences," Goodwin remarked. Gershenfeld notes that academic programs in information technology rarely offer much exposure to physics, and vice-versa. In his book, he attempts to provide a solid grounding in both concepts of physics and information technology for students and experts in either field. He covers topics such as information theory, electromagnetic theory, tomography, lasers, superconductivity, quantum computing, and more.

When Things Start to Think offers an optimistic overview of future technology and the role it will have in people's lives as it becomes ever-smaller and less obtrusive. Based on Gershenfeld's work at the MIT Media Lab, the book includes discussion of scenarios in which computers are worn as an accessory, work is conducted primarily in virtual reality environments, embedded computers let everyday household objects such as coffee cups and clothing respond to users' needs, and electrically charged "smart paper" can be used and reused again and again. Beyond the enthusiastic review of future technological possibilities, Gershenfeld also provides "reasoned, thoughtful views on information rights and the necessity to cultivate a more scientifically literate society," noted *Library Journal* reviewer Gregg Sapp. As the technology advances, Gershenfeld suggests, improved power and built-in intelligence will allow computer makers to manufacture computing devices usable by anyone, sophisticated machines with their "inherent complexity invisible to users," observed a *Business Week* reviewer. "Especially for technophobes, Gershenfeld's easy style and light use of technical terms makes his book a fun and tantalizing glimpse into the world to come," remarked a *Publishers Weekly* reviewer.

Fab: The Coming Revolution on Your Desktop—From Personal Computers to Personal Fabrication describes a near-future world in which individuals will have the technology at hand to make nearly anything they want with a personal fabricator. Such a device would allow users to make new tools, decorative objects, playthings, even electronic devices. Applications are possible in areas such as energy, electronics, agriculture, medicine, entertainment, and dozens of others. The limitations on the types of items that could be manufactured would constrained mostly by the users' needs and imaginations.

Personal Fabrication Devices, or "fab labs," are "small, inexpensive clusters of tools and software that function as complete job shops," noted *Business Week* reviewer Otis Port. Simple controls will allow almost anyone to operate the machine. Among the tools it will contain will be a milling device for creating precision parts, a cutter for producing circuit boards, and software for installing programming instructions into inexpensive microcontrollers. Gershenfeld believes that in the near future, fab labs could become as ubiquitous as personal computers, and prices could drop from today's 20,000 dollars or more to a more affordable 1,000 dollars or less.

The idea of a personal fabricator is not as far-fetched as it might seem. Rudimentary devices are already in use in several areas throughout the world, where they allow Sami sheepherders in Norway to create customized electronic tracking devices to monitor the whereabouts of their flock; where a farming village in India is creating devices that will tune tractors to run on locally produced organic fuels; where cow-powered generators will bring electricity to a village in Ghana; and where inner-city children in Boston make jewelry to sell and improve their economic condition. Similar technology is already widely used in manufacturing through rapid prototyping machines, devices that essentially "build" a solid object by laying down layer after layer of material in much the same way that an inkjet printer lays down ink.

"Since the author is describing people and projects that actually exist, rather than a fantastical vision of a utopian someday, his central contention is mightily convincing," remarked a *Kirkus Reviews* contributor. "Gershenfeld's account of the technology's evolution is delicious," commented Port, who also noted that "with a knack for technical explanation, he has written an accessible book that even nontechnophiles will love." The "superb" book "heralds a shift in manufacturing as profound as the advent of personal computers," added Port.

BIOGRAPHICAL AND CRITICAL SOURCES:

PERIODICALS

Business Week, February 15, 1999, "Brainy Gizmos," review of *When Things Start to Think,* p. 16E12; May 2, 2005, Otis Port, "Desktop Factories," review of *Fab: The Coming Revolution on Your Desktop—From Personal Computers to Personal Fabrication,* p. 22.

Electronic Engineering Times, May 9, 2005, Chappell Brown, "Prof's Goal: Fabs for the Masses," interview with Neil Gershenfeld, p. 1.

Information Technology and Libraries, September, 1999, Tom Zillner, review of *When Things Start to Think,* p. 169.

Kirkus Reviews, March 1, 2005, review of *Fab,* p. 273.

Library Journal, January, 1999, Gregg Sapp, review of *When Things Start to Think,* p. 145; April 1, 2005, Heather O'Brien, review of *Fab,* p. 117.

Publishers Weekly, December 21, 1998, review of *When Things Start to Think,* p. 40.

Science, September 16, 1994, Andrew R. Solow, "Time-Series Prediction: Forecasting the Future and Understanding the Past," review of *NATO Advanced Research Workshop on Comparative Time-Series Analysis,* p. 1745; August 6, 1999, Brian Sleeman, review of *The Nature of Mathematical Modeling,* p. 842; November 30, 2001, David G. Goodwin, review of *The Physics of Information Technology,* p. 1839.

Science News, May 14, 2005, review of *Fab,* p. 319.

Technology Review, January 1, 1999, Wade Roush, review of *When Things Start to Think,* p. 87.

U.S. News and World Report, January 3, 2000, profile of Neil Gershenfeld, p. 59.

ONLINE

Massachusetts Institute of Technology Web site, http://web.media.mit.edu/ (September 19, 2005), biography of Neil Gershenfeld.

MIT Center for Bits and Atoms Web site, http://cba.mit.edu/ (September 19, 2005).*

*   *   *

GERSHENFELD, Neil A.
See GERSHENFELD, Neil

GILROY, Paul

PERSONAL: Born in London, England. *Education:* Birmingham University, Ph.D., 1986. *Hobbies and other interests:* Listening to, collecting, and critiquing music.

ADDRESSES: Office—Department of Sociology, London School of Economics, Houghton St., London WC2A 2AE, England. *E-mail*—p.gilroy@lse.ac.uk.

CAREER: Goldsmith's College, London, London, England, lecturer in sociology, until c. 1998; Yale University, New Haven, CT, professor of sociology and African-American studies, c. 1998-2005; Anthony Giddens Professor in Social Theory, 2005—. Visiting professor at Birmingham University, South Bank Polytechnic, and Essex University; former guest curator, Tate Gallery and House of World Cultures, Berlin, Germany; former board member, Greater London Council. Has also worked as a disc jockey.

AWARDS, HONORS: American Book Award, Before Columbus Foundation, 1994, for *The Black Atlantic.*

WRITINGS:

There Ain't No Black in the Union Jack: The Cultural Politics of Race and Nation, Hutchinson (London, England), 1987, published with new foreword, University of Chicago Press (Chicago, IL), 1991.

The Black Atlantic: Modernity and Double Consciousness, Harvard University Press (Cambridge, MA), 1993.

Problems in Anti-Racist Strategy, Runnymede Trust, 1987.

Small Acts: Thoughts on the Politics of Black Culture, Serpent's Tail (New York, NY), 1993.

(With Iain Chambers) *Hendrix, Hip-Hop e l'interruzione del pensiero,* Costa & Nolan (Genoa, Italy), 1995.

The Status of Difference: From Epidermalisation to Nano-Politics, Goldsmiths' College Centre for Urban and Community Research (London, England), 1995.

Joined up Politics [and] Post-Colonial Melancholia (lectures), Institute of Contemporary Arts, 1999.

(Editor, with Lawrence Grossberg and Angela McRob-bie) *Without Guarantees: In Honor of Stuart Hall,* Verso (New York, NY), 2000.

Against Race: Imagining Political Culture beyond the Color Line, Belknap Press (Cambridge, MA), 2000, published as *Between Camps: Race, Identity, and Nationalism at the End of the Colour Line,* Allen Lane (London, England), 2000.

After Empire: Melancholia or Convivial Culture?, Routledge (London, England), 2004, published as *Postcolonial Melancholia,* Columbia University Press (New York, NY), 2005.

Contributor to books, including *The Empire Strikes Back: Race and Racism in '70s Britain,* Hutchinson (London, England), 1982; *The Eight Technologies of Otherness,* edited by Sue Golding, Routledge (London, England), 1997; *Becoming National: A Reader,* Oxford University Press (Oxford, England), 1996; and *The Post-Colonial Question,* edited by Iain Chambers and L. Curti, Routledge, 1996. Contributor to journals, including *Third Text, Journal of Black Music Research,* and *Media Education.* Member of editorial board, *New Community, Callaloo,* and *Cultural Studies.*

WORK IN PROGRESS: Real Time, a story of black music in the second half of the twentieth century; a survey of the politics of race in contemporary Britain.

SIDELIGHTS: Sociologist and educator Paul Gilroy is not one to shy away from controversy; his *There Ain't No Black in the Union Jack: The Cultural Politics of Race and Nation* launched him early on into the midst of the controversy over what it means to be black in late-twentieth-century Great Britain. "Gilroy has always been a maverick. His books are difficult in both senses of the word—hard to read (although always rewarding) and highly troublesome," commented Bryan Cheyette in the London *Independent.* "He blends sociology, moral philosophy and cultural theory into a heady brew," wrote Sukhdev Sandhu in the London *Observer.*

In *There Ain't No Black in the Union Jack* Gilroy describes the theories that define and give shape to racism and postulates what could and should be done to overcome racially biased ways of thinking. He examines the movements of the economically disadvantaged and suggests that the avenue to social change may be found on the grassroots level, among local men and women who find their cultural traditions threatened. Reviewer David Edgar, writing in the *Listener,* observed: "For an anti-racist to argue for localism is, in a sense, surprising. It's even stranger to find a socialist emphasising the importance of traditions in the threatened communities he describes. . . . But in his longest chapter—on British black culture in general, and its music in particular—Paul Gilroy demonstrates effectively that cultural traditions are not static, but develop, grow and indeed mutate, as they influence and are influenced by the other changing traditions around them."

Moving away from contemporary culture and expanding his scope, Gilroy turns to a history of what he calls the black diaspora in *The Black Atlantic: Modernity and Double Consciousness.* The black Atlantic is a person of this diaspora—one who was forcibly removed from his home country but never fully assimilated into his new one. It is this displacement that necessitates the "double consciousness" of Gilroy's title. In his view, it is impossible to draw national boundaries to define the thought and experience of this tradition. "Gilroy seeks to rediscover the traditions of the black Atlantic," explained a reviewer for *Sociology Online.* "He does so in the works of [nineteenth-century abolitionist and former slave] Frederick Douglass, [twentieth-century] sociologist W.E.B. Du Bois, and the novelist/critic Richard Wright. Here Gilroy is establishing a set of precepts for the black Atlantic. These three are not just able theorists but personifications of the black Atlantic." Gilroy harnesses the idea of the diaspora to illustrate the similarities between black culture in America, Britain, and the Caribbean in relation to Africa.

Hailed as "a bold and brilliant rethinking of the political geography of race" by Eric Lott in the *Nation, The Black Atlantic* drew praise for its originality and the way in which Gilroy weaves examples ranging from the life of rock musician Jimi Hendrix to the works of novelist Toni Morrison. "Possibly Gilroy's most striking insights come from analyses of black musicians," suggested Stephen Howe in the *New Statesman.* However, some reviewers found that extracting these gems is a bit difficult: "Gilroy's best examples are sometimes buried in passages of forbidding abstraction, but when they appear they light up the sky," wrote Lott, who added, "The whole book is cranked up to a very high philosophical pitch. . . . It drags down Gilroy's flights of brilliance with dull slabs of abstract prose." Simon Critchley, writing in *Sociology,* concluded that the work "is an absolutely stunning book—passionate, profound, readable and relevant—that I cannot recommend too highly. It is a book which has fundamentally changed the way in which I (as philosopher rather than a sociologist) see the inter-linked themes of race, culture and identity. Gilroy's conclusions have challenged and begun to change the way in which I read, think and relate to my discipline—I can think of no higher praise."

Small Acts: Thoughts on the Politics of Black Culture is a collection of essays written by Gilroy between 1988 and 1992. It acts as a companion piece to *The Black Atlantic,* with some of the essays in *Small Acts* giving further depth to topics mentioned in Gilroy's previous book. *Small Acts* includes Gilroy's conversations with Toni Morrison and critic bell hooks, as well as articles he has written and talks he has given. In *Small Acts,* as well as in *Black Atlantic,* Gilroy seeks to find some middle ground between the belief in Afro-centrism and the notion that one's color is irrelevant. "The author skillfully and sensitively examines concepts such as Afrocentrism, ethnic absolutism, or cultural insiderism," wrote E.A. McKinney in *Choice.* "He not only interprets the role they currently play within the black diaspora, but also identifies their limitations in furnishing blacks with a future social/political/cultural survival kit."

In what may be Gilroy's most controversial work, *Against Race: Imagining Political Culture beyond the Color Line,* the author postulates that by thinking of ourselves and dividing on the basis of race, we do a great disservice to humanity and open the doors to future fascist movements. Fascist thought, he contends, is not limited to white people, and he offers proof in the examples of Marcus Garvey, who led a popular Back-to-Africa movement in the 1920s and 1930s, and in the slaughter between the Tutsis and Hutus in Rwanda. Stanley Aronowitz, writing in the *Nation,* explained that *Against Race* is "a powerful, albeit minoritarian defense of the position that racial thinking—not just racism—is a key obstacle to human freedom." Aronowitz added, "Gilroy spares from his critique neither black pride nor black separatism, let alone racism's most virulent forms, fascism and colonialism," adding: "The core of fascism is biological essentialism manifested in the marriage of racial identity with nationalism, ideas that won the admiration of Garvey and some other black nationalists. Moreover,

like many nationalisms, Garvey's was anti-Semitic, and Gilroy shows that he admired Hitler." As Cheyette wrote, "There is so much that is worthwhile in this book that one can forgive almost any eccentricity." Acknowledging the author's somewhat controversial position, Aronowitz concluded: "Gilroy's reach is dazzling, his analysis acute and insightful, but in the end he recognizes that, lacking a political constituency for his planetary humanism, his ideas remain not a program but a utopian hope."

In *Postcolonial Melancholia*—first published as *After Empire: Melancholia or Convivial Culture?*—Gilroy presents four Wellek Library lectures he gave concerning critical theory and in which he discusses such issues as how the historical idea of "race" has hurt democracy. R. Owen Williams, writing in the *Black Issues Book Review,* noted: "The thesis is that multicultural politics are best understood from the perspective and in the context of imperial and colonial history." The reviewer added of Gilroy that, "If his poststructuralist vocabulary doesn't leave you spinning, his big ideas surely will."

BIOGRAPHICAL AND CRITICAL SOURCES:

PERIODICALS

African American Review, fall, 1997, Peter Erickson, review of *The Black Atlantic: Modernity and Double Consciousness,* p. 506.

Art Journal, summer, 2004, Derek Conrad Murray, "Hip-Hop vs. High Art: Notes on Race as Spectacle," p. 4.

Black Issues Book Review, September, 2000, Fred Lindsey, review of *Against Race: Imagining Political Culture beyond the Color Line,* p. 56; May-June, 2005, R. Owen Williams, review of *Postcolonial Melancholia,* p. 63.

Choice, October, 1994, E.A. McKinney, review of *Small Acts: Thoughts on the Politics of Black Culture,* p. 329.

Independent (London, England), May 27, 2000, Bryan Cheyette, "In the Colours of the Future: After the Misery of Ethnic Politics, Can We Imagine a World without 'Race'?," p. 11.

Journal of Black Studies, July, 2001, Molefi Kete Asante, review of *Against Race,* p. 847.

Journal of Literary Studies, June, 2002, Gugu Hlongwane, "What Has Modernity to Do with It?: Camouflaging Race in the 'New" South Africa," p. 111.

Kirkus Reviews, February 15, 1994, review of *Small Acts,* p. 218; February 15, 2000, review of *Against Race,* p. 224.

Library Journal, March 15, 2000, Frank H. Wu, review of *Against Race,* p. 110.

Listener, June 4, 1987, David Edgar, "Racism and Patriotism: Should the Left Be Trying to Recapture the Idea of 'One Nation'?," pp. 44-45.

London Review of Books, March 10, 1994, Adam Lively, "Fisticuffs," p. 16.

MELUS, winter, 1998, Kenneth Mostern, review of *The Black Atlantic,* p. 167.

Nation, May 2, 1994, Eric Lott, "Routes," pp. 602-604; November 6, 2000, Stanley Aronowitz, "Misidentity Politics," p. 28.

New Statesman, December 4, 1987, Jeffrey Weeks, review of *There Ain't No Black in the Union Jack: The Cultural Politics of Race and Nation,* p. 31; November 5, 1993, Stephen Howe, review of *Small Acts* and *The Black Atlantic,* p. 37.

Observer (London, England), June 4, 2000, Sukhdev Sandhu, "Is Snoop Doggy Dogg Really a Race Warrior?," p. 11.

Polity, April, 2004, Joel Oson, review of *Against Race,* p. 529.

Postmodern Culture, September, 1994, Russell A. Potter "Black Modernisms/Black Postmodernisms."

Research in African Literatures, spring, 2002, Isidore Okpewho, "Walcott, Homer, and the 'Black Atlantic,'" p. 27.

Sociology, November, 1994, Simon Critchley, review of *The Black Atlantic,* p. 1008.

Theory, Culture, and Society, Volume 16, number 2, 1999, Vikki Bell, "Historical Memory, Global Movements, and Violence: Paul Gilroy and Arjun Appadurai in Conversation."

Village Voice Literary Supplement, April, 1992, review of *There Ain't No Black in the Union Jack,* p. 19; May 2, 2000, Simon Reynolds, "Hybrid Fidelity," p. 69.

Washington Post Book World, February 6, 1994, Aldon L. Nielsen, "Caught in a Double Bind," p. 7.

ONLINE

Sociology Online, http://www.sociologyonline.co.uk/ (August 29, 2001), "Paul Gilroy: Black Modernism—From Slaveship to Citizenship."

University of Birmingham, London School of Economics Web site, http://www.lse.ac.uk/ (September 27, 2005), faculty profile of Gilroy.

Z Online, http://www.zmag.org/ (April 18, 2006), bell hooks, "Thinking about Capitalism: A Conversation with Cultural Critic Paul Gilroy."*

*   *   *

GJELLERUP, Karl 1857-1919
(Epigonos, Karl Adolf Gjellerup)

PERSONAL: Born June 2, 1857, in Roholte, Denmark; died October 11 (one source says 13), 1919, in Klotzsche, Germany; son of Carl Adolph (a pastor) and Anna Johanne (Fibiger) Gjellerup; married (marriage ended); married Eugenia Anna Caroline Hensinger, 1887. *Education:* University of Copenhagen, B.D. (summa cum laude), 1878. *Hobbies and other interests:* Painting.

CAREER: Poet, dramatist, and novelist.

AWARDS, HONORS: University Gold Medal, for *Arvelighed og moral;* Nobel Prize for Literature (with Henrik Pontoppidan), 1917.

WRITINGS:

(Under pseudonym Epigonos) *En Idealist* (novel), 1878.

(Under pseudonym Epigonos) *Den evige strid,* 1878.

"*Det unge Danmark,*" C.A. Reitzel (Copenhagen, Denmark), 1879.

Rødtjørn (poetry; title means "Hawthorne"), A. Schou (Copenhagen, Denmark), 1881.

Arvelighed og moral (title means "Heredity and Morals"), 1881.

Germanernes Laerling (novel; title means "The Apprentice of the Teutons"), 1882.

Aander og Tider (poems), A. Schou (Copenhagen, Denmark), 1882.

Brynhild (play), 1884.

En klassisk maaned (travel; title means "A Classical Month), 1884.

Vandreaaret (travel; title means "Wander Year"), 1885.

Thamyris (lyric play), 1887.

Minna (novel), 1889, translated into English under same title, W. Heinemann (London, England), 1913.

Wuthhorn (play), first produced in Copenhagen, Denmark, at Dagmar Theatre, 1893.

Kong Hjarne skjald, tragedie i fem handlinger (play; first produced in Copenhagen, Denmark, at Dagmar Theater), Gyldendal (Copenhagen, Denmark), 1893.

Den aeldre Eddas gudesange oversatte samt indledede og forklarede af Karl Gjellerup med tegninger af Lorenz Frølich, P.G. Philipsen (Copenhagen, Denmark), 1895.

Møllen (novel; title means "The Mill"), 1896.

Gift og modgift (play; title means "Toxin and Antitoxin"), first produced in Copenhagen, Denmark, at Dagmar Theatre, 1898.

Offerildene (musical play; title means "The Sacrificial Fires"), 1903.

Der Pilgrimen Kamanita (romance fiction), 1906, translated by John Logie as *The Pilgrim Kamanita: A Legendary Romance,* edited by Amaro Bhikkhu, illustrated by Chuang Muanpinit, A. Bhikkhu (CA), 1999.

Die hügelmühle (novel), five volumes, W. Baensch (Dresden, Germany), 1909.

Verdensvandrerne, romandigtning i tre bøger; omslagstegning af Valdemar Andersen, Gyldendal (Copenhagen, Denmark), 1910.

Der Goldene Zweig (title means "The Golden Bough"), Quelle & Meyer (Leipzig, Germany), 1917.

Das Weib des Vollendeten, ein Legenden-drama von Karl Gjellerup, 2nd edition, Quelle & Meyer (Leipzig, Germany), 1921.

André Gide, Karl Gjellerup, Paul Heyse (includes *Minna*), A. Gregory (New York, NY), 1971.

Also author of tragedy *Scipio Africanus,* drama *Arminius,* and short stories.

SIDELIGHTS: A co-recipient of the 1917 Nobel Prize for Literature, Karl Gjellerup was a novelist and playwright whose works repeatedly explore religious and philosophical issues. His influences ranged from Christian to Darwinist to Buddhist sources, and his fiction consequently explores the issues of the human soul, the nature of existence, and fate. Among his more successful efforts are the play *Brynhild* and the novel *Der Pilgrimen Kamanita.* Though popular in their day, Gjellerup's works are infrequently read today, and the Nobel Prize he won was little noted because at the time the world's attention was focused on World War I.

Born in Denmark, Gjellerup's first major influence was a relative named Johannes Fibiger, a clergyman who raised the boy from the age of three after his father died. From Fibiger, Gjellerup learned to be a scholar, being exposed to music, literature, and philosophy from all around the world. Fibiger's influence also led Gjellerup to study theology at the University of Copenhagen. While he was a student he was greatly influenced by Charles Darwin's *On the Origin of Species,* and by the time he graduated he had become an atheist. In his early works, including *En Idealist* and *Arvelighed og moral,* the author's belief in evolution and science over religion and mysticism is clear. His *Germanernes Laerling,* furthermore, is an obviously fictionalized novel about "a young theologian dealing with a crisis of faith," as an essayist for the *Encyclopedia of World Biography Supplement* observed.

As he matured, Gjellerup became increasingly concerned with the concepts of free will, fate, and the human condition. After moving from his native Denmark to settle in Germany, he fell under the influence of the writers Johann Wolfgang von Goethe and Friedrich von Schiller and began a deeper philosophical exploration of the underlying truths of the universe and existence. Fate comes into play in the romantic tragedies *Brynhild* and *Wuthhorn,* both of which are about lovers who find themselves torn apart from each other by circumstances beyond their control. In another love story, the novel *Minna,* Gjellerup injects his own experience of divorce from his first wife in writing about another doomed relationship. By the 1880s, when these works were being released, Gjellerup had found great popular success; along with this came a government pension, which left him financially comfortable and able to focus on his writing.

In the early 1900s the author began exploring new ground as he studied Buddhist theology. This can be clearly seen in his lyrical novel *Der Pilgrimen Kamanita.* The novel, once again about two lovers who are painfully separated from each other, is set in India. It explores the Buddhist notions of life, death, and rebirth as the lovers become reunited only after they have died. For this and many other contributions, Gjellerup was awarded the Nobel Prize in 1917; two years later he passed away.

BIOGRAPHICAL AND CRITICAL SOURCES:

BOOKS

Encyclopedia of World Biography Supplement, Volume 25, Thomson Gale (Detroit, MI), 2005.

ONLINE

Nobel Prize Web site, http://nobelprize.org/ (January 8, 2005), "Karl Gjellerup—Autobiography."*

*   *   *

GJELLERUP, Karl Adolf
  See GJELLERUP, Karl

*   *   *

GOLDSMITH, Kenneth 1961-
  (Kenneth Paul Goldsmith)

PERSONAL: Born 1961. *Education:* Holds a B.F.A.

ADDRESSES: Home—NJ. *Office*—WFMU, P.O. Box 5101, Hoboken, NJ 07030.

CAREER: Poet and artist. University of Pennsylvania, Philadelphia, fellow in poetics and poetic practice, 2004; WFMU radio, Hoboken, NJ, host.

WRITINGS:

(With Joan La Barbara) *Seventy-three Poems,* Permanent Press (Brooklyn, NY), 1993.
Fidget (nonfiction), Coach House Books (Toronto, Ontario, Canada), 2000.
Soliloquy (nonfiction), Granary Books (New York, NY), 2001.
Day (nonfiction), Figures, 2003.
The Weather (nonfiction), Make Now Press (Los Angeles, CA), 2005.

SIDELIGHTS: Kenneth Goldsmith is a poet and conceptual artist who holds a Bachelor of Fine Arts in sculpture. He served as a fellow of poetics and poetic practice at the University of Pennsylvania's Center for Programs in Contemporary Writing, where he taught an undergraduate class that included creative writing and poetics, and also was part of a series of workshops and readings at the university's Kelly Writers House and the Center for Programs in Contemporary Writing. Goldsmith also works as a host for Hoboken, New Jersey's WFMU radio.

In his writing, Goldsmith takes an unusual approach. *Fidget* is a chronicle of every movement of his body over a thirteen-hour period on Bloomsday, June 16, 1997, and serves as an homage to the work of Irish writer James Joyce, specifically to Joyce's *Ulysses.* A contributor for *Publishers Weekly* called it an "important book from Goldsmith, pointing the way to a rapproachment between poetry and conceptual and performance art—avant-gardists and art lovers of all stripes will want to experience its near-hypnotic pleasures." With *Soliloquy,* Goldsmith records his every word over a period of a week, everything from ordering food at a deli to a conversation with a cab driver. His side only is included, making for a puzzle effect. In a review for *Publishers Weekly,* a contributor remarked that the book "leaves the reader with a convinced sense that language, no matter how un-artful, does the heavy lifting in our lives, and has encoded the entire registry our being."

BIOGRAPHICAL AND CRITICAL SOURCES:

PERIODICALS

Publishers Weekly, June 5, 2000, review of *Fidget,* p. 91; January 21, 2002, review of *Soliloquy,* p. 87; July 21, 2003, review of *Day,* p. 190; June 27, 2005, review of *The Weather,* p. 56.

ONLINE

University of Pennsylvania Web site, http://www.upenn.edu/ (September 20, 2005), "Kenneth Goldsmith."
WFMU Radio Web site, http://www.wfmu.org/ (September 18, 2005), "Kenneth Goldsmith."*

*   *   *

GOLDSMITH, Kenneth Paul
  See GOLDSMITH, Kenneth

GONZÁLEZ GARCÍA, Matías 1866-1938

PERSONAL: Born December 9, 1866, in Naguabo, PR; died March 11, 1938, in Gurabo, PR. *Education:* Earned B.A.; studied medicine for two years at University of Santiago de Compostela, Spain.

CAREER: Journalist and freelance writer. School teacher in San Juan, PR, until 1902; elected to Puerto Rican House of Representatives, 1904; City of Gurabo, PR, town clerk, 1916-20, mayor, 1920-24. Publisher of tabloids, including *El Correo del Este* and *Rocinante,* 1910-14.

AWARDS, HONORS: Gold Medal, 1892, for short story "La primera cría."

WRITINGS:

Cosas de antaño y cosas de orgaño (novel), 1893, reprinted, Caguas (Borinquin, PR), 1922.
El escándelo, Córdova (San Juan, PR), 1894.
Ernesto, El Buscapié (San Juan, PR), 1895.
Cosas, Córdova (San Juan, PR), 1898.
Mis cuentos, 1899.
Carmela (novel), Heraldo Español (San Juan, PR), 1903, third edition, Coquí (San Juan, PR), 1966.
El tesoro de Ausubal, Caguas (Borinquin, PR), 1913.
Morel campos, 1922.
Gritos de Angustina (play), produced in Puerto Rico, 1929.
Amor que vence (play), produced in Puerto Rico, 1929.
Por me tierra y por me dama (play), produced in Puerto Rico, 1929.
Cosas de antaño y cosas de agaño, Editorial Orión (Mexico City, Mexico), 1953.
Cuentos: primera selección (short stories), 2nd edition, compiled and with prologue by Juan Martínez Capó, Instituto de Cultural Puertoriqueña (San Juan, PR), 1992.
(With Nilda González) *Guerra: Una novela sobre la guerra del 1898 en Puerto Rico* (contains novel *Guerra,* originally written, 1899), commentary by Nilda González, Editorial LEA (San Juan, PR), 2000.

Contributor to periodicals, including *El Buscapié, Revista Puertoriqueña de Literatura, Ciencias y Arte, La Illustración Puertoriqueña, La Democracia, El Mundo,* and *Puerto Rico Illustrado.*

SIDELIGHTS: Puerto Rican author Matías González García held various jobs throughout his life, ranging from school teacher to tabloid publisher to local politician. He is often remembered, however, for his many short stories celebrating Puerto Rican language, customs, and culture. Often flavoring his tales with light humor, González García's "work," according to a contributor to *Caribbean Writers,* "is mildly naturalistic, occasionally humorous, even satirical in touches."

BIOGRAPHICAL AND CRITICAL SOURCES:

BOOKS

Herdeck, Donald E., editor, *Caribbean Writers: A Bio-Bibliographical-Critical Encyclopedia,* Three Continents Press (Washington, DC), 1979.
Hill, Marnesba D., and Harold B. Schleifer, *Puerto Rican Authors,* Scarecrow Press (Lanham, MD), 1974.*

*   *   *

GOODMAN, Matthew

PERSONAL: Male.

ADDRESSES: Home—Brooklyn, NY. *Agent*—Henry Dunow, Dunow, Carlson, and Lerner Literary Agency, 27 W. 20th St., Ste. 1003, New York, NY 10011.

CAREER: Writer. *Forward,* New York, NY, author of "Food Maven" food column.

WRITINGS:

Jewish Food: The World at Table, HarperCollins Publishers (New York, NY), 2005.

Contributor to periodicals, including *American Scholar, Harvard Review,* and *Art of Eating.*

SIDELIGHTS: Brooklyn-based author Matthew Goodman writes about a number of subjects, but devotes much of his efforts to writing about food. His column,

"Food Maven," appears regularly in *Forward*, and his writing has also appeared in *American Scholar, Harvard Review*, and *Art of Eating*. Goodman's book *Jewish Food: The World at Table* examines Jewish cuisine from a non-religious viewpoint, focusing on the worldwide nature of the dishes that are used in both secular and religious meals. Recipes range from the expected traditional foods, such as Gefilte fish and cheese blintzes, to more unusual dishes, such as red snapper in coconut milk and a spicy chicken popular in the Jewish neighborhood of Bombay. In a review for *Booklist*, contributor Mark Knoblauch pointed out that "Goodman includes plenty of lively historical and cultural background for his recipes." He went on to call Goodman's effort a "wide-ranging and heterogeneous cookbook that demands a new and deeper definition of Jewish food." *Library Journal* reviewer Judith Sutton called the book "thoroughly researched and the recipes well written" in what she labeled "an increasingly crowded field." A contributor for *Publishers Weekly* remarked that "Goodman deftly tackles his vast subject with these enlightening, engaging essays, which, coupled with the . . . recipes, make for a fine tribute to Jewish cuisine."

BIOGRAPHICAL AND CRITICAL SOURCES:

PERIODICALS

Booklist, March 1, 2005, Mark Knoblauch, review of *Jewish Food: The World at Table*, p. 1125.
Library Journal, February 15, 2005, Judith Sutton, review of *Jewish Food*, p. 152.
Publishers Weekly, January 17, 2005, review of *Jewish Food*, p. 48.

*   *   *

GORDON, Nadia
     See BALMAIN, Julianne

*   *   *

GORTER, Herman 1864-1927

PERSONAL: Born November 26, 1864, in Wormeveer, Netherlands; died September 15, 1927, in Brussels, Belgium; son of Simon (a clergyman) and Johanna (Lugt) Gorter; married Wies Cnoop Koopmans, 1890. *Education:* Attended University of Amsterdam.

CAREER: Poet and writer. Former high-school teacher in Amersfoort, Netherlands.

WRITINGS:

De interpretatione Aeschylimetaphorarum, Lugduni-Batavorum, 1889.
Verzen, W. Versluys (Amsterdam, Netherlands), 1890, published as *Verzen: de editie van 1890*, edited by Enno Endt, Athenaeum-Polak & Van Gennep (Amsterdam, Netherlands), 1987.
Sociaal-demokratie en anarchisme, Brochurenhandel der S.D.A.P. (Amsterdam, Netherlands), 1897.
De school der poëzie, W. Versluys (Amsterdam, Netherlands), 1897, published as *De school der poëzie: verzen*, Van Dishoeck (Bussum, Netherlands), 1925.
Die Klassenkakmpf-Organisation des Proletariats (pamphlets), Kommissions-druckerei der K.A.P.D. (Berlin, Germany), c. 1900, reprinted, 1988.
De grondslagen der Sociaaldemokratie, Brochurenhandel der S.D.A.P. (Amsterdam, Netherlands), 1902.
Mei (poetry; title means "May"), W. Versluys (Amsterdam, Netherlands), 1900, published as *Mei: een gedicht*, introduction by Willem Wilmink, B. Bakker (Amsterdam, Netherlands), 1989.
(With Anton Pannekoek) *Marxisme en revisionise*, J.A. Fortuyn (Amsterdam, Netherlands), 1906.
Een klein heldendicht, W. Versluys (Amsterdam, Netherlands), 1906, reprinted, Pegasus (Amsterdam, Netherlands), 1977.
(With Karl Kautsky) *Ethiek en materialistische geschiedenisbeschouwing*, H.A. Wakker (Rotterdam, Netherlands), 1907.
(With Karl Kautsky) *De we naar de macht* (social history), H.A. Wakker (Rotterdam, Netherlands), 1909.
(Translator) Karl Marx and Friedrich Engels, *Het communistich manifest*, Brochurenhandel der S.D.A.P. (Amsterdam, Netherlands), c. 1910.
Het historisch materialisme: voor arbeiders verklaard, Uitgave der Sociaal-Demokratische Partij (Amsterdam, Netherlands), 1910, published as *Het historisch materialisme: voor arbeiders verklaard: utg.: de tribune: heruitg*, Proletarisch Links (Amsterdam, Netherlands), 1972.
Pan: een gedichte, Pegasus (Amsterdam, Netherlands), 1912.
Het imperialisme de wereldoorlog en de sociaal-democratie, Brochurehandel der S.D.A.P. (Amsterdam, Netherlands), 1914.

De wereldrevolutie (social history), J.J. Bos (Amsterdam, Netherlands), 1919.

De grondslagen v an het communisme, J.J. Bos (Amsterdam, Netherlands), 1920.

Klassenmoraal: een antwoord aan Jhr. de Savornin Lohman en Mr. P.J. Troelstra, J.J. Bos (Amsterdam, Netherlands), 1920.

(Translator) Vladimir Il'ich Lenin, *Staat en revolutie: de leer van het marxisme over den staat en over de taak van het proletariaat in de revolutie,* J.J. Bos (Amsterdam, Netherlands), 1920.

Het opportunisme in de Nederlandsche Communistische Partij, J.J. Bos (Amsterdam, Netherlands), 1921, translated as.

De Algemeene Arbeiders-Bond: revolutionaire bedrijfsorganisaties, Kommunistiche Arbeiders-Partij (Amsterdam, Netherlands), 1921.

Open brief aan partigenoot Lenin, J.J. Bos (Amsterdam, Netherlands), 1921, translated as *The Question of the Unions: A Reply to Lenin,* Oppositionist (London, England), 1973.

De organisaitie voor den klassentstrrijd van het proletariaat, Kommunistische Arbeiders-Partij (Amsterdam, Netherlands), 1922.

Een klein heidendicht, Pegasus (Amsterdam, Netherlands), 1925.

In memoriam, Van Dishoeck (Bussum, Netherlands), 1928.

Liedjes aan de geest der muziek der nieuwe menschheid (poetry), Van Dishoeck (Bussum, Netherlands), 1930.

De arbeidersraad, van Dishoeck (Bussum, Netherlands), 1931.

Sonnetten, van Dishoeck (Bussum, Netherlands), 1934.

De groote dichters: nagelaten studiën over de wereldlitteratuur en haar maatschappilijke grondslagen (poetry history and criticism), Querido (Amsterdam, Netherlands), 1935.

Kenteringssonnetten, Bezige Bij (Amsterdam, Netherlands), 1945, reprinted, Querido (Amsterdam, Netherlands), 1979.

Gedicten; gekozen en ingeleid door J.C. Brandt Corstius, C.A.J. van Dishoeck (Bussum, Netherlands), 1946.

Verzamelde werken, Querido (Amsterdam, Netherlands), 1948.

(With Germt Stuivelling) *De dag gaat open als een gouden roos: een bloemlezing uit zijn poëzie, gekozen en ingeleid,* B. Bakker, 1956.

Twintig gedichten in handschrift, Meulenhoff (Amsterdam, Netherlands), 1964.

Documentatie over de jaren 1866 tot en met 1897, edited by Enno Endt, Polak & van Gennep (Amsterdam, Netherlands), 1964.

Herman Gorter, De Bezige Bij (Amsterdam, Netherlands), 1966.

Verzamelde lyriek tot 1905, Polak & van Gennep (Amsterdam, Netherlands), 1966.

Zie je ik hou van je: romantische dichters over de liefde (poetry), Ominboek (The Hague, Netherlands), 1985.

(With Willem Pijper) *Tweeluik: voor mezzosopraan en altfluit: 1999* (musical score and lyrics based on letter from author), music by Jacques Bank, Donemus (Amsterdam, Netherlands), 2000.

Contributor to journals *De Jonge Gids* and *De Nieuwe Tijd.*

Works translated into several languages, including German, Russian, Polish, Hungarian, Italian, Japanese, Yiddish, and Greek.

ADAPTATIONS: Gorter's poetry was adapted for music by Huub Kerstens as *De stille weg: voor mezzosopraan, bas, viool en piano,* Donemus (Amsterdam, Netherlands), 1985.

SIDELIGHTS: Dutch writer Herman Gorter was a leading figure in the Netherlands' 1880 literary revival. Gorter's poetry, particularly during his earlier years, embodied the aesthetic ideals of the era. As a poet, Gorter is best remembered for *Mei,* an epic-length work that celebrates the Dutch natural landscape through the character of a child, whose name translates to "May." Like the springtime she represents, Mei personifies youth and beauty. Her unrequited love for the blind Balder, "a seeming conflation of the Germanic god and Apollo," according to *Dutch Crossing* contributor J. Timothy Stevens, "represents the absolute self-absorption of the artist."

Authors are often compared to other authors, but in an article for *Dutch Crossing* Judit Gera drew parallels between Gorter's poem "Ik ben alleen in het lemplicht" and Vincent van Gogh's painting "Gaugins stoel." Gera pointed first to the similarities in upbringing between poet and painter: "The fathers of both artists were pastors, although it may be too simplistic to draw the conclusion that their social consciousnesses were due entirely to the role that religion and spirituality played in their families." Both men set their sights early on a theological career, and van Gogh actually became a vicar. Gorter, though he eventually embraced atheism, "continued the literary activities of his father," who wrote for Amsterdam's daily newspaper.

Both Gorter and van Gogh forged strong attachments to the working class. Gorter, notably, joined the Communist party and espoused Marxist ideals, a theme that would emerge many times in his writings. In 1912 he produced the poetry collection *Pan: een gedichte,* which presents a Utopian vision, though such political writings tended to be more openly didactic. Gera declared that both artists, each in his own way, "wanted to achieve something more than their Impressionist contemporaries, who were living under the spell of beauty. They wanted more than . . . [art for art's sake]. Their works are permeated by an inner tension that reveals the broken harmony between the outside world and the interior world of man."

BIOGRAPHICAL AND CRITICAL SOURCES:

BOOKS

Bock, Hans Manfred, *Organisation un Taktik der proletarischen Revolution* (bibliography of the author's political writings), Verl. Neue Kritik (Frankfurt, Germany), 1969.

PERIODICALS

Dutch Crossing, number 22, 1988, Judit Gera, "Artistic Parallels," pp. 127-138; August, 1989, J. Timothy Stevens, "Ganymede, Persephone, and Mei: The Child as Object of Desire," pp. 96-109.*

* * *

GOTTI, Victoria 1963-

PERSONAL: Born 1963, in New York, NY; daughter of John Gotti (a convicted organized crime boss) and Victoria DiGiorgio; married Carmine Agnello (divorced); children: Carmine, John, Frank, Justine (deceased). *Education:* Attended St. John's University.

ADDRESSES: Agent—c/o Author Mail, Crown Publishing Group Publicity, 1745 Broadway, New York, NY 10019.

CAREER: Novelist, editor, columnist, fashion designer, and actor. *New York Post,* columnist; *Star,* columnist. Performer on reality television series *Growing up Gotti,* A&E. Guest on television programs, including *The Big Idea with Donny Deutsch, Passions, Live with Regis and Kathie Lee,* and *Larry King Live.*

WRITINGS:

Women and Mitral Valve Prolapse: A Comprehensive Guide to Living and Coping with M.V.P. and Its Symptoms, Morris Publishing (Kearney, NE), 1995.

NOVELS

The Senator's Daughter, Forge (New York, NY), 1997.
I'll Be Watching You, Crown Publishers (New York, NY), 1998.
Superstar, Crown Publishers (New York, NY), 2000.

Contributor to periodicals, including *Cosmopolitan.*

WORK IN PROGRESS: The Last Socialite, a novel.

SIDELIGHTS: Victoria Gotti is a multifaceted novelist, entrepreneur, actor, and editor. The daughter of convicted murderer and mafia boss John Gotti—known as the charismatic "Dapper Don"—Victoria grew up inside one of history's strongest organized crime families, but remained determined to apply her talents toward making her own way in the world of entertainment and publishing. She is the star of the reality television series *Growing up Gotti,* a show that explores the lives of Victoria and her sons Carmine, John, and Frank, as they live their lives bearing one of the more notorious names of the late twentieth century. While Gotti spent much of the early 2000s trying to repair and reinvent that name, forces beyond her control, especially the media, prevented her from enjoying the respect her accomplishments have earned her. "I just feel like enough already," Gotti stated in an interview with George Wayne in *Vanity Fair.* "I am not a conceited person, but I have done so much with my life. I've written books, I've worked for a major newspaper, I now work for a great magazine, I have a successful TV show. So when are they going to stop—by that I mean those reporters, that media. When are they going to stop? That's my attitude." She observed in an essay in *Cosmopolitan* that "In real life, your family background certainly has some effect on who you are and what you become, but thankfully, it's not a blueprint of your future."

Gotti has been a columnist for major American newspapers, an editor, a fashion designer and entrepreneur with her own clothing line, and a regular guest on a variety of television programs. She has also taken up the cause of women with mitral valve prolapse, a cardiac condition Gotti herself suffers from and which has required her to wear a pacemaker for several years. In *Women and Mitral Valve Prolapse: A Comprehensive Guide to Living and Coping with M.V.P. and Its Symptoms,* Gotti relates her own experiences with the condition and offers inspiration and advice for women who also have it.

She is also a novelist with three books in print. Her early attempts to publish her fiction, however, were hampered by publishers who wanted scandalous insider information on her famous father and his associates. "When I was trying to get my first novel into print, some publishers thought they could entice me to pen something autobiographical by offering me astronomical sums of money," Gotti stated in the *Cosmopolitan* essay. "But I stood firm and turned down those offers. I wanted to write something I was passionate about, not exploit my family's problems."

The Senator's Daughter is a "fast-paced, captivating first novel that engages the reader with a tightly knit plot," commented a *Publishers Weekly* reviewer. When Joe Session, leader of the Boston dock union, is killed, suspicion focuses on nineteen-year-old Tommy Washington. Attorney Taylor Brooke, however, is not convinced Tommy is the hitman, and works to establish that the teen has been framed and to clear his name. Her investigation uncovers possible corruption in the district attorney's office and runs Brooke afoul of many of her colleagues. Michael Sessio, son of the murdered union boss, has sparked Brooke's romantic interest, though she cannot be sure that he was not involved in the elder Sessio's death. Brooke is also

shocked when her estranged father, U.S. Senator Frank Morgan, suddenly reappears in her life. An attempt on Brooke's life convinces her that she is on the right trail, but whose trail it is remains unclear. Gotti "offers shady characters, intrigue, and romance galore with a mystery that keeps one wondering until the end," remarked *Library Journal* reviewer Mary Ellen Elsbernd. *Booklist* critic Kathleen Hughes called the book a "tightly crafted, entertaining suspense novel filled with surprising twists and turns."

I'll Be Watching You, Gotti's second novel, is a "designer-clad thriller," commented a *Publishers Weekly* critic. Author Rose Miller has concentrated her work in the genre of psychological suspense, and her work enjoys considerable popularity and success. Her life seems perfect, with a wealthy, doting husband and a cherished daughter, until darker episodes in Rose's past threaten to return. A stalker has emerged from the shadows, spying on Rose and her family. As her brother-in-law is tried for racketeering and extortion, the stalker begins to move in, threatening Rose and her daughter. Some reviewers, such as Brad Hooper in *Booklist,* stated that the novel does not rise to the same standards as Gotti's debut. However, "The story, like the heroine, keeps afloat on sheer energy and determination," commented a *Publishers Weekly* contributor.

In *Superstar,* Gotti's third novel, two women in their early thirties, Cassidy English and Chelsea Hutton, discover that they were switched at birth for unknown reasons. Cassidy grew up wealthy in Hollywood, while Chelsea endured poverty as the daughter of a single mother. Cassidy saw her actress mother murdered when she was ten years old, and her testimony helped convict her director father of the crime. However, modern DNA evidence has exonerated him, though he still keeps his distance. Chelsea, perhaps deranged, wants revenge on Cassidy for the life she was deprived of but which was rightfully hers. When Cassidy is intimidated into letting powerful producer Jack Cavelli pick the lead in a movie that is intended to save her father's studio, the actress turns out to be Chelsea. When the two women meet, longstanding resentment and hatred trigger events that will leave both of them permanently changed. "The story has all the elements of a satisfying thriller," remarked *People* reviewer Cynthia Sanz, adding that "Gotti isn't a bad writer." A *Publishers Weekly* reviewer called the book a "not-so-amicable princess-and-pauper tale of obsession and deception."

BIOGRAPHICAL AND CRITICAL SOURCES:

PERIODICALS

Allure, November 1, 2004, Judy Bachrach, "Victoria's Secrets," profile of Victoria Gotti, p. 204.

Booklist, March 15, 1997, Kathleen Hughes, review of *The Senator's Daughter,* p. 1225; June 1, 1998, Brad Hooper, review of *I'll Be Watching You,* p. 1668; May 15, 2000, Diana Tixier Herald, review of *Superstar,* p. 1700.

Cosmopolitan, October, 2000, Victoria Gotti, "You Can Battle a Bad Reputation," p. 72.

Entertainment Weekly, March 7, 1997, Matthew Flamm, "Victoria's Secret?," profile of Victoria Gotti, p. 59.

Library Journal, February 15, 1997, Mary Ellen Elsbernd, review of *The Senator's Daughter,* p. 161.

People, March 3, 1997, Patrick Rogers, "Don's Delight," profile of Victoria Gotti, p. 110; September 4, 2000, Cynthia Sanz, review of *Superstar,* p. 59.

Publishers Weekly, January 27, 1997, review of *The Senator's Daughter,* p. 77; June 22, 1998, review of *I'll Be Watching You,* p. 85; June 6, 2000, review of *Superstar,* p. 48.

Vanity Fair, February, 2005, George Wayne, "Victoria Gotti: The Godmother," interview with Victoria Gotti, p. 106.*

*   *   *

GRABIEN, Deborah 1954-

PERSONAL: Born 1954; married Nicholas Grabien, 1983; children: one daughter. *Hobbies and other interests:* Playing guitar and keyboard, rescuing cats and finding them homes.

ADDRESSES: Home—San Francisco, CA. *Agent*—c/o Author Mail, Thomas Dunne Books, 175 5th Ave., New York, NY 10010. *E-mail*—deb@deborahgrabien.com.

CAREER: Novelist.

WRITINGS:

FANTASY NOVELS

Woman of Fire, Piatkus (London, England), 1988, published as *Eyes in the Fire,* St. Martin's Press (New York, NY), 1989.

Fire Queen, Bantam Books (New York, NY), 1990.

Plainsong: A Fable for the Millenium, St. Martin's Press (New York, NY), 1990.

Then Put out the Light, Pan Books (London, England), 1993.

"RINGAN LAINE" MYSTERY SERIES

The Weaver and the Factory Maid, Thomas Dunne Books (New York, NY), 2003.

The Famous Flower of Serving Men, Thomas Dunne Books (New York, NY), 2004.

Matty Groves, Thomas Dunne Books (New York, NY), 2005.

SIDELIGHTS: Writer Deborah Grabien has a love of history, particularly medieval history and Elizabethan drama, that is obvious in her work. Grabien has traveled extensively and lived in various European cities, which helped cement her interest in the past. This, combined with her love of music and her acquaintance with a number of musicians, provides the foundation for much of her writing, which also has strong leanings toward fantasy. Her first novel, *Woman of Fire,* splits the point of view between a modern-day Englishwoman and a woman of the Dumnonii, a tribe that lived during the iron age, approximately two thousand years ago. In another work, *Plainsong: A Fable for the Millenium,* she explores a world where nearly everyone has been killed by a plague, leaving animals, some children, a moron, and a pregnant poetess as the few survivors. In the style of fables, the animals can communicate with the people, and mythological characters also appear throughout the narrative. In a review for *Publishers Weekly,* Sybil Steinberg called the book "an alternative vision of life and remarkable understanding of faith."

Grabien took off ten years from writing in order to learn to cook, but returned to her original passion with a series of mystery novels based on the adventures of Ringan Laine, a British folk musician who also restores houses. The series starts with *The Weaver and the Factory Maid,* in which Ringan finds himself living for free in an eighteenth-century cottage in exchange for restoring it. Of course, the cottage proves to be haunted, and Ringan and his girlfriend, Penny, find themselves involved in a long-buried mystery while they try to determine what happened at the house. Appropriately enough, the story of the ghosts is linked to a haunting folk ballad. A *Publishers Weekly* contributor felt that the book "offers too little plot and a less than engaging protagonist." However, a contributor for *Kirkus Reviews* wrote that, "although unthreatening ghosts produce low-voltage thrills, pastoral warmth and sunny prose from Grabien . . . entertain," and Rex Klett, in a review for *Library Journal,* found Grabien's effort to be "filled with charm, personality, and wit."

In *The Famous Flower of Serving Men* Ringan's girlfriend, Penny, inherits a wonderful old theater from a relative she barely remembers. Believing it to be the perfect home for her acting company, she asks Ringan to take charge of renovating the theater. Unfortunately, a ghost seems intent on chasing away the workmen. Penny and Ringan research the theater's past in hopes of finding a way to set their ghost to rest. Sue O'Brien, in a review for *Booklist,* remarked that "Interesting period details . . . , likable characters, and an absorbing plot distinguish this fast-paced mix of mystery and ghost story," and a contributor for *Publishers Weekly* wrote that "Grabien's grasp of theater, folklore and history provides a feast of enjoyment."

BIOGRAPHICAL AND CRITICAL SOURCES:

PERIODICALS

Booklist, October 1, 2003, Sue O'Brien, review of *The Weaver and the Factory Maid,* p. 304; November 15, 2004, Sue O'Brien, review of *The Famous Flower of Serving Men,* p. 565.

Kirkus Reviews, September 15, 2003, review of *The Weaver and the Factory Maid,* p. 1156; September 1, 2004, review of *The Famous Flower of Serving Men,* p. 838.

Library Journal, October 1, 2003, Rex Klett, review of *The Weaver and the Factory Maid,* p. 120; November 1, 2004, Rex E. Klett, review of *The Famous Flower of Serving Men,* p. 60.

Publishers Weekly, March 9, 1990, Sybil Steinberg, review of *Plainsong: A Fable for the Millennium,* p. 50; November 10, 2003, review of *The Weaver and the Factory Maid,* p. 46; October 11, 2004, review of *The Famous Flower of Serving Men,* p. 59.

ONLINE

All Readers.com, http://www.allreaders.com/ (September 20, 2005), "Deborah Grabien."

All Sci-fi.com, http://www.allscifi.com/ (September 20, 2005), "Deborah Grabien."

Deborah Grabien Home Page, http://www.deborah grabien.com (September 20, 2005).

New Mystery Reader Online, http://www.newmystery reader.com/ (September 20, 2005), "Deborah Grabien."*

*   *   *

GRANT, Amy 1960-
(Amy Lee Grant)

PERSONAL: Born November 25, 1960, in Augusta, GA; daughter of Burton Paine (a radiologist) and Gloria Grant; married Gary Chapman (a songwriter), June 19, 1982 (divorced, June, 1999); married Vince Gill (a country singer), March 10, 2000; children: (first marriage) Matthew Garrison, Gloria Mills, Sarah Cannon; (second marriage) Corrina Grant. *Education:* Attended Furman University and Vanderbilt University.

ADDRESSES: Office—P.O. Box 25330, Nashville, TN 37203. *Agent*—Creative Artists Agency, 3310 West End Ave., 5th Fl., Nashville, TN 37203.

CAREER: Singer, songwriter, and actress. Appeared in films, including *Story, Songs and Stars,* 1984; (as herself) *A Moment in Time,* World Entertainment, 1988; (as Carol) *The Illusion,* 2001; and (as sister of Freya No. 4) *Yorick,* 2002. Appeared as Maryann Lowery in television movie *A Song from the Heart* (also known as *Music from the Heart*), 1999. Appeared in television specials (as herself unless otherwise noted), including *The Patti LaBelle Show,* National Broadcasting Company (NBC), 1985; *Christmas in Washington,* NBC, 1985; *Macy's Thanksgiving Day Parade,* NBC, 1986; *Amy Grant . . . Headin' Home for the Holidays,* NBC, 1986; *An All-Star Celebration Honoring Martin Luther King, Jr.,* NBC, 1986; *ABC Presents a Royal Gala,* American Broadcasting Companies (ABC), 1988; *Walt Disney World Very Merry Christmas Parade,* ABC, 1990; (as narrator) *The Gingham Dog and the Calico Cat,* Showtime, 1990; *The Dream Is Alive: The 20th Anniversary Celebration of Walt Disney World,* Columbia Broadcasting System (CBS), 1991; *Hats off to Minnie Pearl: America Honors Minnie Pearl,* The National Network (TNN; now Spike TV), 1992; *Picture What Women Do,* Lifetime, 1994;

Christmas at Home with the Stars, ABC, 1994; *Tapestry Revisited: A Tribute to Carole King,* Lifetime, 1995; *A Sam's Place Christmas,* TNN (now Spike TV), 1995; *Kathie Lee: Just in Time for Christmas,* CBS, 1996; *Death in Malibu: The Murder of Music Mogul Charlie Minor—The E! True Hollywood Story,* E! Entertainment Television, 1997; (as voice) *Snowden on Ice,* CBS, 1997; *Christopher Reeve: A Celebration of Hope,* ABC, 1998; *When You Believe: Music from "The Prince of Egypt,"* NBC, 1998; (and executive producer) *Amy Grant . . . A Christmas to Remember,* 1999; and *Women Rock! Girls & Guitars,* Lifetime, 2000. Appeared at awards presentations, including *American Music Awards,* ABC, 1986; *20th-Annual Country Music Association Awards,* CBS, 1986; *34th-Annual Grammy Awards,* CBS, 1992; *American Music Awards,* ABC, 1993; *24th-Annual Dove Awards,* The Family Channel, 1993; *25th-Annual Dove Awards,* The Family Channel, 1994; *American Music Awards,* ABC, 1995; *26th-Annual Dove Awards,* The Family Channel, 1995; *30th-Annual Country Music Association Awards,* CBS, 1996; and *TNN Music City News Country Awards,* TNN, 1997. Guest star on television programs, including *Late Show with David Letterman,* 1994, *Who Wants to Be a Millionaire,* 2001; *The View,* 2002; and *Tonight Show with Jay Leno,* 2002. Appeared as herself, *Talk of the Town;* guest host, *CCM-TV,* 1995.

AWARDS, HONORS: Grammy Award for best female gospel performance, contemporary, 1982 for *Age to Age;* Grammy Award for best gospel performance, female, 1983, for "Ageless Melody"; Grammy Award for best gospel performance, female, 1984, for "Angels"; Grammy Award for best gospel performance, female, 1985, for "Find a Way"; Grammy Award for best gospel performance, female, for *Lead Me On;* Dove Awards, Gospel Music Association, 1992, for artist of the year, and for best song for "Place in This World."

WRITINGS:

AUTHOR OF LYRICS, WITH OTHERS; RECORDINGS

Amy Grant, Myrrh/World, 1977.
Fathers Eyes, Myrrh/World, 1979.
Never Alone, Myrrh/World, 1980.
In Concert, Myrrh/World, 1981.
Age to Age, Myrrh/World, 1982.

A Christmas Album, Myrrh/World, 1983.
Straight Ahead, Myrrh/World, 1984.
Unguarded, Myrrh/World, 1985.
The Collection, Myrrh/World, 1986.
Lead Me On, Myrrh/World, 1988.
Heart in Motion, Myrrh/World, 1991.
Home for Christmas, Myrrh/World, 1992.
House of Love, Myrrh/World, 1994.
Behind the Eyes, Myrrh/World, 1997.
A Christmas to Remember, Myrrh/World, 1999.
Legacy . . . Hymns & Faith, Word (Nashville, TN), 2002.
Simple Things, A&M, 2003.

Also released *In Concert, Volume 2.* Songs have been collected on recordings, including *Traveling Light,* 2002.

SIDELIGHTS: Amy Grant was one of the first genuine stars of the world of Christian contemporary music, and she was also one of the first Christian rockers to cross over and find mainstream success. As a teenager in Tennessee, Grant composed and sang youth-oriented praise and worship songs for her church's services. Then at age fifteen she took a job sweeping the floors and doing other menial work in a recording studio, which gave her the opportunity to use the studio to record a tape of her songs as a present to her parents. Unbeknownst to Grant, someone from the studio sent the tape to Word Records, one of the major distributors of Christian contemporary music, and Word was so impressed that they signed her.

Her debut album, *Amy Grant,* was released when she was sixteen, but it was not until five years later, with the release of *Age to Age,* that Grant suddenly found herself to be a star. *Age to Age* was the first Christian contemporary album to go platinum, and Grant's performance at the Grammy Awards that year, dressed in a sexy leopard-print jacket, brought her to the attention of listeners outside the Christian niche. Grant is "better than pretty much anyone else out there at crafting empathetic pop songs that [are] simultaneously personal and universal," Rich Copley wrote in a *Knight Ridder/Tribune News Service* article, citing a fact that quickly endeared Grant to a less-religious audience.

Although Grant had started out with an explicitly Christian message and simple, guitar-based arrangements, as she became more successful she acquired a back-up band, wrote lyrics where the words "God" and "Jesus" are not always used. She also took on more of the trappings of the pop stars with whom she was competing. As *People* contributor Ralph Novak wrote in a review of her 1985 album *Unguarded,* "she has made a smooth transition from rock-tinged gospel to gospel-tinged rock." To Grant, this merely reflected a maturation of her musical style and a chance to communicate a loving message to people who would not necessarily listen to music that was overtly Christian. "I'm not going to throw it in your face, but if you're searching, my songs will really say something to you," Grant told *U.S. News & World Report* interviewer Adam Paul Weisman. However, her religious critics began to accuse her of selling out. Their criticisms became particularly sharp after the release of Grant's 1991 single "Baby Baby," a song which Grant originally wrote for her infant daughter but which could be interpreted as a secular romantic love song, as it was in its music video.

Grant's musical maturation continued into the 1990s, when she began to write music that was less upbeat and inspirational, more personal and introspective. *Behind the Eyes,* her 1997 release, was a completely new thing in Grant's oeuvre: the album does not contain a single explicitly Christian reference. The songs are still spiritual, and in interviews around the times of the album's release Grant was adamant in declaring that she was still a Christian, but she herself could not say if *Behind the Eyes* was a "Christian album" or not. "Being able to label it Christian or non-Christian is not the point for me," she said to William D. Romanowski of *Christianity Today.* "The point was to make available the songs I wrote between 1995 and 1997, and to let them find their own audience."

BIOGRAPHICAL AND CRITICAL SOURCES:

BOOKS

Baker's Biographical Dictionary of Musicians, centennial edition, Schirmer (New York, NY), 2001.

Contemporary Musicians, Volume 7, Thomson Gale (Detroit, MI), 1992.

Contemporary Newsmakers 1985, issue cumulation, Thomson Gale (Detroit, MI), 1986.

Religious Leaders of America, second edition, Thomson Gale (Detroit, MI), 1999.

St. James Encyclopedia of Popular Culture, St. James Press (Detroit, MI), 2000.

PERIODICALS

Amusement Business, December 1, 1997, Cindy Stooksbury Guier, "Amy Grant Taking Holiday Show on the Road for Nineteen-City Tour," pp. 7-8.

Billboard, April 27, 1991, Sean Ross, review of "Baby Baby," pp. 10-11; April 25, 1992, Lisa Collins, "Amy Grant Lands Dove's Top Honor," pp. 10-11; July 30, 1994, Deborah Russell, review of *House of Love,* pp. 1-2; August 9, 1997, Deborah Evans Price, interview with Grant, pp. 12-14; June 12, 1999, Deborah Evans Price, review of "El Shaddai," p. 45; March 31, 2001, Rashaun Hall, review of "Thy Word," p. 35.

Booklist, January 15, 1994, Candace Smith, review of *The Creation,* pp. 943-944.

Business Wire, February 19, 2002, review of *Legacy . . . Hymns & Faith,* p. 2705.

Christianity Today, December 8, 1997, William D. Romanowski, review of *Behind the Eyes,* pp. 44-45.

Entertainment Weekly, August 26, 1994, David Hiltbrand, review of *House of Love,* p. 112; September 19, 1997, Joseph Woodard, review of *Behind the Eyes,* p. 84.

Knight Ridder/Tribune News Service, August 18, 2003, Rich Copley, review of *Simple Things,* p. K3207.

Life, November, 1984, Curt Sanburn, "Amy's World," pp. 186-190.

National Catholic Reporter, December 24, 1999, Robin Taylor, reviews of *A Christmas Album, Home for Christmas,* and *A Christmas to Remember,* p. 6.

People, April 18, 1983, Dolly Carlisle, interview with Grant, pp. 106-107; June 24, 1985, Ralph Novak, review of *Unguarded,* p. 20; July 18, 1988, Ralph Novak, review of *Lead Me On,* p. 23; July 15, 1991, Cynthia Sanz, "Saint Amy Gets Sexy: Pop Goes Christian Music's Amy Grant, with a Secular Single and a Racier Image," pp. 71-72; August 29, 1997, Jeremy Helligar, review of *House of Love,* p. 25; September 15, 1997, Jeremy Helligar, interview with Grant, p. 34; January 18, 1999, "Baby Baby Goodbye," p. 107; November 29, 1999, "Finally a Duet: After Painful Divorces, and Years of Speculation, Vince Gill and Amy Grant Confess They Are in Love," p. 133; March 27, 2000, "Perfect Harmony: With Little Pomp but Just the Right Notes, Vince Gill and Amy Grant Say 'I Do,'" p. 57; March 26, 2001, "In Perfect Harmony: Days after Their First Anniversary,

Vince Gill and Amy Grant Welcome a Baby," p. 129; June 24, 2002, review of *Legacy . . . Hymns & Faith,* p. 35; August 25, 2003, review of *Simple Things,* p. 37; September 1, 2003, Steve Dougherty, interview with Grant, p. 75.

Publishers Weekly, December 20, 1993, review of *The Creation,* p. 36.

Saturday Evening Post, November-December, 1991, Patrick M. Connolly, "Amy Grant: Charting a New Course," pp. 39-42.

Sojourners, May-June, 2002, review of *Traveling Light,* p. 51.

Total Health, February, 1989, "Amy Grant: Total Health Celebrity," pp. 22-23.

USA Today, August 18, 2003, Brian Mansfield, interview with Grant.

US News & World Report, August 25, 1986, Adam Paul Weisman, "Gospel Music Rolls out of the Church, onto the Charts," p. 56.

ONLINE

Amy Grant Home Page, http://www.amygrant.com (August 27, 2003).

Internet Movie Database, http://www.imdb.com/ (August 27, 2003), "Amy Grant."*

*   *   *

GRANT, Amy Lee
See GRANT, Amy

*   *   *

GRAY, Alexandra

PERSONAL: Female.

ADDRESSES: Agent—c/o Author Mail, Grove/ Atlantic, Inc., 841 Broadway, 4th Fl., New York, NY 10003.

WRITINGS:

Ten Men (novel), Atlantic Monthly Press (New York, NY), 2005.

SIDELIGHTS: Alexandra Gray's first novel, *Ten Men,* allows her to address a variety of professions. The jet-setter actress heroine moves from relationship to relationship, each man coming from a different profession. She dubs these men variously as the Schoolmaster, the Lawyer, the Director, as well as the Virgin, and the Lover. Gray uses these relationships to describe the heroine's changing tastes and maturity as she searches for her perfect match. In a review for *Library Journal,* contributor Andrea Y. Griffith found the novel lacking, commenting that "the characters are flimsy caricatures, and the plot drags along." However, Hillary Frey, in a review for *Salon.com,* compared the book to the popular television series *Sex and the City,* calling it "a sort of celebration of singlehood; at the end of the novel, our heroine is an unmarried actress, still trawling the waters. And she's pretty happy, too." Frey concluded that "somewhere, in our heroine, is a little bit of each of us. And somewhere, in all the men she loved, is one we'll recognize."

BIOGRAPHICAL AND CRITICAL SOURCES:

PERIODICALS

Kirkus Reviews, April 1, 2005, review of *Ten Men,* p. 374.

Library Journal, May 1, 2005, Andrea Y. Griffith, review of *Ten Men,* p. 72.

ONLINE

Salon.com, http://www.salon.com/ (June 6, 2005), Hillary Frey, review of *Ten Men.**

*   *   *

GRAYLING, A.C. 1949-
(Anthony Clifford Grayling)

PERSONAL: Born April 3, 1949, in Luanshya, Zambia; son of Henry Clifford and Ursula Adelaide (Burns) Grayling; married Gabrielle Yvonne Smyth, January, 1970; partner of Katie Hickman; children: (with Smyth) Anthony Jolyon Clifford, Georgina Evelyn Ursula; (with Hickman) Madeleine Catherine Jennifer. *Education:* University of London, B.A.; University of Sussex, B.A., M.A.; Magdalen College, Oxford, D.Phil., 1981. *Hobbies and other interests:* Opera, theater, reading, walking, travel.

ADDRESSES: Office—Birkbeck College, University of London, Malet St., Bloomsbury, London WC1 7HX, England. *E-mail*—a.grayling@bbk.ac.uk.

CAREER: Philosopher, radio broadcaster, and educator. St. Anne's College, Oxford, lecturer, 1984-91, senior research fellow, 1997-97, supernumerary fellow, 1997—; Birkbeck College, University of London, London, England, lecturer, 1991-98, reader in philosophy, 1998-2005, professor of philosophy, 2005—. University of Tokyo, Tokyo, Japan, visiting professor, 1997; visiting lecturer, University of Chiba, University of Nagoya, University of Hokkaido, and Lublin University. *Online Review,* editor; *Philosophical Annual of the Chinese Academy of Social Sciences,* contributing editor. Member of editorial board of *Prospect, Reason and Practice,* and *Russell Newsletter. Guardian,* London, England, columnist, 1999-2002; *Times,* London, columnist, 2003—. Booker Prize judge, 2003. Fellow, World Economic Forum and Royal Society of Arts. Radio broadcaster, BBC Radios 4 and 3 and World Service. June Fourth, past chairman. Involved in U.N. Human Rights Initiative. Member, World Economic Forum C-100 Group on relations between the West and the Islamic world.

MEMBER: Aristotelian Society (honorary secretary, 1992-98), Athanaeum Club, Beefsteak Club, Groucho Club.

AWARDS, HONORS: Jan Huss fellowship, 1994, 1996; Leverhulme Trust fellowship, 1999.

WRITINGS:

An Introduction to Philosophical Logic, Barnes & Noble Books (Totowa, NJ), 1982, 3rd edition, Blackwell Publishers (Malden, MA), 1997.

The Refutation of Scepticism, Open Court Publishing Company (LaSalle, IL), 1985.

Berkeley, the Central Arguments, Open Court Publishing Company (LaSalle, IL), 1986.

Wittgenstein, Oxford University Press (New York, NY), 1988, published as *Wittgenstein: A Very Short Introduction,* Oxford University Press (Oxford, England), 2001.

(Editor) *Philosophy: A Guide through the Subject,* Oxford University Press (New York, NY), 1995.

(With Susan Whitfield) *China: A Literary Companion,* Trafalgar Square Publishing (North Pomfret, VT), 1995.

Russell, Oxford University Press (New York, NY), 1996, published as *Russell: A Very Short Introduction,* Oxford University Press (New York, NY), 2002.

Philosophy: Further through the Subject, Oxford University Press (Oxford, NY), 1998.

The Meaning of Things: Applying Philosophy to Life, Weidenfeld & Nicolson (London, England), 2001.

The Reason of Things: Living with Philosophy, Weidenfeld & Nicolson (London, England), 2002.

Meditations for the Humanist: Ethics for a Secular Age, Oxford University Press (New York, NY), 2002.

What Is Good? The Search for the Best Way to Live, Weidenfeld & Nicolson (London, England), 2003.

Life, Sex, and Ideas: The Good Life without God, Oxford University Press (New York, NY), 2003.

The Mystery of Things, Weidenfeld & Nicolson (London, England), 2004.

The Heart of Things: Applying Philosophy to the Twenty-first Century, Weidenfeld & Nicolson (London, England), 2005.

Descartes: The Life of Rene Descartes and Its Place in His Times, Free Press (New York, NY), 2005.

Among the Dead Cities: Was the Allied Bombing of Civilians in WWII a Necessity or a Crime?, Bloomsbury (London, England), 2006.

Contributor to periodicals, including *Literary Review, Observer, Economics, Times Literary Supplement, Independent on Sunday, New Statesman,* and *Financial Times.*

Author of column "Last Word," London *Guardian.*

SIDELIGHTS: Philosopher and educator A.C. Grayling is a professor of philosophy at Birkbeck College, London. He has served on numerous boards and is a past chairman of June Fourth, a human rights group that focuses on China. Other human rights work includes involvement in the U.N. Human Rights Initiative. He also serves in the World Economic Forum's C-100 group on relations between the West and the Islamic world. "The focus of Anthony Grayling's interests in technical academic philosophy is the overlap between theory of knowledge, metaphysics, and philosophical logic," reported a biographer on Grayling's home page. "In summary, they concern the relation between thinking and theorizing about the world, and the knowledge and meaning constraints which govern them."

In a lengthy professional career, Grayling has written both scholarly works and books designed to bring philosophical thought and practice to a general audience. In *Meditations for the Humanist: Ethics for a Secular Age* Grayling provides a "primer designed to stimulate thinking" on the various possibilities, problems, and meanings of being human, remarked *Library Journal* reviewer Terry Skeats. The more than sixty essays cover topics in three broad categories: Virtues and Attributes, Foes and Fallacies, and Amenities and Goods. The works are "balanced, intelligently written, at times caustic, and always (as intended) thought-provoking," added Skeats. Grayling ponders a variety of uniquely human emotions and attributes, including love, community, family, religion, racism, revenge, loyalty, leisure, health, poverty, blasphemy, history, nationalism, and other "abstract terms we experience in a very real way every day," noted a *Publishers Weekly* contributor. Skeats called the collection a "superb little book."

Life, Sex, and Ideas: The Good Life without God contains a collection of short essays on a variety of philosophical subjects stemming from an overarching consideration of religion. These topics include war, capital punishment, politics, fasting, and more. Grayling holds a dim view of religion, noting that it is the primary source of dangerous fanaticism. He contends that religion should be confined to private life and should be strictly excluded from education, public affairs, and other social and political areas. Grayling also comments on terrorism and finds the greater threat to be the diminishment of civil liberties and the inability to practice civilized tolerance. *Library Journal* reviewer David Gordon observed that Grayling is "a fine essayist in action," and that while his viewpoints seem to be stated rather than proved, "readers will benefit from an encounter with his erudite and elegant prose."

In *The Mystery of Things* Grayling offers "a smattering of brief, mildly engaging essays for the lay reader on art, literature, and culture," commented a *Kirkus Reviews* critic. Derived largely from his weekly column in the London *Times,* the essays range widely across subjects related to art, philosophy, and intellectualism. Grayling encourages his readers to develop new ways of considering the world around them and its many physical and nonphysical manifestations. Topics covered include quantum theory, literature, consciousness, genetics, the origin of the universe, and other equally deep, open-ended topics. He ponders the meaning of German chancellor Adolf Hitler as an art collector, the tendency for students to veer away from classical studies, how leftist, left-leaning sentiments correlate with so-called high culture, and the role of genetics in refuting long-held misconceptions about race. "In brisk, pithy, jargon-free prose, Grayling opens issues for ordinary readers, leaving them with something to think about" without providing any definitive answers or premanufactured conclusions, remarked Leslie Armour in *Library Journal.*

The Heart of Things: Applying Philosophy to the Twenty-first Century, Grayling once again approaches philosophy from the viewpoint of the generalist reader, framing significant philosophical issues in terms that can be grasped and used by an intelligent non-specialist. "Eschewing specialist diction, the author provides, in admirably uncomplicated prose, a series of bite-sized reflections on a range of personal and public concerns, together with sketches of some dozen assorted thinkers," commented Chris Arthur, writing in *Contemporary Review.* In a wide-ranging collection of short essays, Grayling returns to the familiar format of brief, pithy musings on problems and topics in modern philosophy, culture, and society. The essays "are not so much applications of philosophy as a collection of thoughtful fragments on diverse topics," Arthur observed. Even though they may not delve deeply into the minutiae of philosophical analysis of a topic, they still provide learned reflections that an educated lay reader can use to form new opinions and new concepts about the world. Arthur concluded that "professional philosophers will probably be as dismissive of this book as the educated person-in-the-street is likely to be of the intricate minutiae with which such philosophers are preoccupied."

BIOGRAPHICAL AND CRITICAL SOURCES:

PERIODICALS

Contemporary Review, July, 2005, Chris Arthur, review of *The Heart of Things: Applying Philosophy to the Twenty-first Century,* p. 49.

Journal of Australian Studies, March, 2003, David Crawford, review of *The Meaning of Things: Applying Philosophy to Life,* p. 143.

Kirkus Reviews, May 1, 2005, review of *The Mystery of Things,* p. 523.

Library Journal, May 15, 2002, Terry Skeats, review of *Meditations for the Humanist: Ethics for a Secular Age,* p. 101; June 1, 2003, David Gordon, review of *Life, Sex, and Ideas: The Good Life without God,* p. 126; June 15, 2005, Leslie Armour, review of *The Mystery of Things,* p. 74.

Publishers Weekly, April 1, 2002, "From the One to the Many," review of *Meditations for the Humanist,* p. 70.

ONLINE

A.C. Grayling Home Page, http://www.acgrayling.com (October 18, 2005).

*   *   *

GRAYLING, Anthony Clifford
See GRAYLING, A.C.

*   *   *

GREB, Gordon 1921-
(Gordon Barry Greb)

PERSONAL: Born August 7, 1921, in Fremont, CA; son of Walter Herman (an engineer) and Irene Agnes (a homemaker; maiden name, Benbow) Greb; married Darlene Alcock (an educator), December 28, 1950; children: Gary Benbow, Darla Jean Greb Mazariegos. *Ethnicity:* "European." *Education:* University of California, Berkeley, A.A., B.A., 1947; University of Minnesota, M.A., 1951.

ADDRESSES: Home—69 Sky Mountain Cir., Chico, CA 95928. *E-mail*—profgreb@cbsglobal.net.

CAREER: Writer, journalist, and educator. *San Leandro News-Observer,* San Leandro, CA, reporter, 1939-43, 1946-47; *San Rafael Daily Independent,* San Rafael, CA, reporter, 1947; San Bernardino Community College, San Bernardino, CA, instructor in English, 1949-50; University of Oregon, Eugene, began as instructor, became assistant professor, 1950-51; Columbia Broadcasting System, Hollywood, CA, news editor, 1951; Stanford University, Stanford, CA, assistant in political science, 1951-54; KSJO-Radio, San Jose, CA, news director, 1954-57; California State University, San Jose, professor of journalism and mass communications, 1956-90. *Military service:* U.S. Army, Infantry, 1943-46; became staff sergeant.

MEMBER: Society of Professional Journalists.

AWARDS, HONORS: Named distinguished broadcast educator, Radio-Television Division, Association for Education in Journalism and Mass Communications, 1996.

WRITINGS:

The Benbow Family: California Pioneers, privately printed, 1994.
Charles Herrold, Inventor of Radio Broadcasting, McFarland and Co. (Jefferson, NC), 2003.

Contributor to periodicals and professional journals.

WORK IN PROGRESS: Gentle People: How It Was before World War II.

SIDELIGHTS: Gordon Greb told *CA:* "Although I've been a news reporter covering current events, the fact that what we do today will become history has always fascinated me. Not only do I desire to record what's happening, but I also want to make a special effort to insure that documents and recordings, whether written, spoken, or mechanically saved on film and tape, are preserved for future generations. Perhaps my chief motivation is best expressed by the philosopher Santayana, who said, 'Those who forget their history are condemned to repeat it.' Civilization and humanity have been built on knowledge. Ignorance is an evil we must try to avoid."

*   *   *

GREB, Gordon Barry
See GREB, Gordon

GREEN, David Geoffrey 1949-

PERSONAL: Born September 21, 1949, in Melbourne, Australia; son of Irvine and Vera (Masters) Green; married Yvonne Briese, July 26, 1980; children: Audrey, Hilary. *Education:* Monash University, B.Sc., 1972, M.Sc., 1974; Dalhousie University, Ph.D., 1977.

ADDRESSES: Home—Australia. *Office*—School of Computer Science and Software Engineering, Monash University, Wellington Rd., Clayton, Victoria 3800, Australia. *E-mail*—david.green@csse.monash.edu.au.

CAREER: LaTrobe University, Melbourne, Victoria, Australia, tutor, 1977-78; Environmental Resources Information Network, Canberra, Australia, associate director, 1990-91; Australian National University, Canberra, Australian Capital Territory, Australia, research fellow, 1989-90, senior fellow, 1991-94; Charles Stuart University, Albury, New South Wales, Australia, professor of environmental information, began 1994; Monash University, Clayton, Victoria, chair of environmental information technology; *Complexity International,* editor.

MEMBER: Ecological Society of Australia, Australian Mathematics Society.

WRITINGS:

(With Terry Bossomier) *Complex Systems: From Biology to Computation,* IOS Press (Amsterdam, Netherlands), 1993, Cambridge University Press (New York, NY), 2000.
(With Terry Bossomier) *Patterns in the Sand: Computers, Complexity, and Everyday Life,* Perseus Books (Reading, MA), 1998.
The Serendipity Machine: A Voyage of Discovery through the Unexpected World of Computers, Allen and Unwin (Crow's Nest, New South Wales, Australia) 2004.

Contributor of articles and scholarly papers to journals, including *Australian Journal of Intelligent Information Processing Systems, Journal of Knowledge-Based Intelligent Engineering Systems, Australian Biologist,* and *Landscape Ecology.* Contributor of chapters to numerous books.

SIDELIGHTS: David Geoffrey Green is an educator and environmental technology expert with a focus on the use of computers to chart ways in which to solve environmental and social issues around the globe. Through his work, he is responsible for the advent of several online information services, including the Guide to Australia and the New South Wales HSC online. He has taught at a number of universities in Australia, including Monash University where he did his undergraduate studies, and is the author of several books.

The Serendipity Machine: A Voyage of Discovery through the Unexpected World of Computers explores the "serendipity effect," a process in which random discoveries in computer science appear to occur in a manner similar to accidental discoveries taking place in the biological sciences. This occurs when one studies vast amounts of computer data for coincidences and patterns. Colleen Cuddy, in a *Library Journal* review, called the book "a fascinating and accessible read." Writing for *Information Today,* Gwen M. Gregory noted that "Green translates technical developments into language that ordinary readers can understand," and "uses his ideas about technological complexity to help us understand the effects of computers on the modern world." She concluded that Green's work "is stimulating, well-written, and easy to read. While not aimed specifically at information specialists, it is nevertheless filled with exciting ideas to challenge your view of computers and how they affect society."

BIOGRAPHICAL AND CRITICAL SOURCES:

PERIODICALS

Information Today, June, 2005, Gwen M. Gregory, "Unexpected Effects of Computers," review of *The Serendipity Machine: A Voyage of Discovery through the Unexpected World of Computers,* p. 48.
Kirkus Reviews, April 1, 2005, review of *The Serendipity Machine,* p. 399.
Library Journal, April 1, 2005, Colleen Cuddy, review of *The Serendipity Machine,* p. 117.

ONLINE

Monash University Web site, http://www.csse.monash.edu.au/ (September 20, 2005), "David Geoffrey Green."*

GREENFIELD, Amy Butler 1968-
(Amy Butler)

PERSONAL: Born 1968, in Philadelphia, PA; married. *Education:* Williams College (summa cum laude); studied at Oxford University, early 1990s.

ADDRESSES: Home—MA. *Agent*—c/o Author Mail, HarperCollins Publishers, 10 E. 53rd St., 7th Fl., New York, NY 10022. *E-mail*—amy@amybutler.com.

CAREER: Writer.

AWARDS, HONORS: Marshall Scholar, Oxford University.

WRITINGS:

(As Amy Butler) *Virginia Bound* (children's fiction), Clarion Books (New York, NY), 2003.
A Perfect Red: Empire, Espionage, and the Quest for the Color of Desire (nonfiction), HarperCollins (New York, NY), 2005.

SIDELIGHTS: Amy Butler Greenfield is descended from a family of dyers and has been interested in the history of color for many years. In her first nonfiction book, *A Perfect Red: Empire, Espionage, and the Quest for the Color of Desire,* the author writes about the red dye cochineal, a vivid, long-lasting, and valuable dye that became the object of intense rivalries beginning in the sixteenth century. In the volume, the author discusses why she wanted to write on the topic, commenting that "I knew . . . that someday I wanted to learn more about cochineal. It was amazing to me that something so precious could have been virtually forgotten by the modern world." The Spaniards first discovered the dye in 1519, when they invaded Mexico, where the cochineal insects from which it is made had been domesticated dating back to the pre-Columbian days. Greenfield reveals how the fashion rage for the color red made this a highly valued commodity that led to the Spaniards trying to keep its source a secret. However, both the English and the Dutch eventually discovered the source, smuggled insects for breeding, and even started largely unsuccessful plantations for breeding. Greenfield also writes about how the dye eventually fell out of favor as other colors became more popular and how its importance has since been reestablished as a safe food and cosmetic coloring agent.

A *Kirkus Reviews* contributor called the book "a smart blend of science and culture." Lisa Klopfer, writing in *Library Journal,* pointed out that "Greenfield packs a dissertation's worth of history into her story without bogging down in the details." Writing in *Publishers Weekly,* a reviewer called the book an "intricate, fully researched and stylishly written history of Europe's centuries-long clamor for cochineal."

Greenfield told *CA:* "Writers can draw stories from any number of places: from dreams, newspaper reports, life crises, even other books. For me, the crucial source of inspiration is history, and that holds true whether I'm writing fiction or nonfiction.

"*Virginia Bound* began with a dusty tome I read in graduate school that included a brief paragraph and footnote about a proclamation from England's King James, ordering that 'idle yonge people' be taken off the streets and shipped to Virginia to provide cheap labor for the new colony in the early 1600s. I had never heard of this before, and I wanted to know what happened to those 'yonge people,' but the scanty records from the time yielded few answers. Still, the thought of those children haunted me for a long time. Eventually I realized it would make a good starting point for a novel.

"*A Perfect Red* had its start in a research trip I made to Spain in the early 1990s, when I was writing a thesis about the introduction of chocolate to Europe. As part of my research, I traveled to Seville's great Archive of the Indies to examine the ancient registers of the Spanish fleets. Chocolate entries were scarce, but what I did see on page after page was *grana,* the Spanish word for cochineal. It soon became clear to me that a mountain of the dark red dyestuff had poured into Seville. I was fascinated that something that was once so precious had been forgotten by the modern world, and in time I decided to write a book about it. For most of human history, the color red was rare and precious, and researching and writing about that time made me see the world differently. I hope *A Perfect Red* will allow readers to see the color with new eyes, too."

BIOGRAPHICAL AND CRITICAL SOURCES:

BOOKS

Greenfield, Amy Butler, *A Perfect Red: Empire, Espionage, and the Quest for the Color of Desire,* HarperCollins (New York, NY), 2005.

PERIODICALS

Booklist, March 1, 2003, review of *Virginia Bound.*
Kirkus Reviews, February 15, 2003, review of *Virginia Bound;* February 15, 2005, review of *A Perfect Red: Empire, Espionage, and the Quest for the Color of Desire,* p. 211.
Library Journal, April 1, 2005, Lisa Klopfer, review of *A Perfect Red,* p. 108.
Publishers Weekly, March 14, 2005, review of *A Perfect Red,* p. 55.

ONLINE

Amy Butler Greenfield Home Page, http://www.amybutlergreenfield.com (June 27, 2005).

*   *   *

GREGSON, James Michael
See GREGSON, J.M.

*   *   *

GREGSON, J.M.
(James Michael Gregson)

PERSONAL: Male.

ADDRESSES: Home—England. *Agent*—Severn House Publishers, 9-15 High Street, Sutton, Surrey SM1 1DF, England.

CAREER: Writer. Taught at high school and university level for twenty-seven years.

WRITINGS:

"LAMBERT AND HOOK" MYSTERY NOVELS

Murder at the Nineteenth, Collins Crime Club (London, England), 1989.
For Sale—With Corpse, Collins Crime Club (London, England), 1990.
Dead on Course, Collins Crime Club (London, England), 1991.
Bring Forth Your Dead, Collins Crime Club (London, England), 1991.
The Fox in the Forest, Collins Crime Club (London, England), 1992.
Stranglehold, Collins Crime Club (London, England), 1993.
Watermarked, Collins Crime Club (London, England), 1994.
Death of a Nobody, HarperCollins (London, England), 1995.
Accident by Design, HarperCollins (London, England), 1996.
Body Politic, Collins Crime Club (London, England), 1997.
Girl Gone Missing, Severn House (Surrey, England), 1998.
Malice Aforethought, Severn House (Surrey, England), 1999.
An Unsuitable Death, Severn House (Surrey, England), 2000.
An Academic Death, Severn House (Surrey, England), 2001.
Death on the Eleventh Hole, Severn House (Surrey, England), 2002.
Mortal Taste, Severn House (Surrey, England), 2003.
Too Much Water, Severn House (Surrey, England), 2005.

"INSPECTOR PEACH" MYSTERY NOVELS

Who Saw Him Die?, Severn House (Surrey, England), 1994.
Missing, Presumed Dead, Severn House (Surrey, England), 1997.
To Kill a Wife, Severn House (Surrey, England), 1999.
A Turbulent Priest, Severn House (Surrey, England), 2000.
The Lancashire Leopard, Severn House (Surrey, England), 2001.

A Little Learning, Severn House (Surrey, England), 2002.

Murder at the Lodge, Severn House (Surrey, England), 2003.

Wages of Sin, Severn House (Surrey, England), 2004.

Dusty Death, Severn House (Surrey, England), 2005.

CRITICAL WRITINGS

Poetry of the First World War, Edward Arnold (London, England), 1976.

Shakespeare: Twelfth Night, Edward Arnold (London, England), 1980.

Public and Private Man in Shakespeare, Croom Helm (London, England), 1984.

OTHER

Golf Rules OK, Black (London, England), 1984.

Sherlock Holmes and the Frightened Golfer (novel), Breese Books (London, England), 2000.

Just Desserts (novel), Severn House (Surrey, England), 2004.

SIDELIGHTS: British author J.M. Gregson taught for twenty-seven years at both the high school and university level before he began writing full time. He has written on diverse subjects, including golf and Shakespeare, but is best known for his mystery novels. Gregson's mysteries fall primarily within the parameters of two series: the Inspector Peach novels, and the Lambert and Hook books. The Lambert and Hook novels follow the adventures of Superintendent John Lambert and Detective Sergeant Bert Hook as they investigate various murders in the English countryside. In *Girl Gone Missing,* Lambert and Hook find themselves changing a missing person case into a murder investigation when the body of Alison Watts is discovered. It soon becomes clear that Watts led a secret life, and that none of her friends, family, or acquaintances can be disregarded in the search for her killer. John Rowen, in a review for *Booklist,* noted the book's straightforward narrative, country settings, and no-nonsense characters," and remarked that the leading characters "combine appealing humanity with dry wit."

In *Malice Aforethought,* Lambert and Hook are torn away from their golf game in order to examine a body that has been discovered in a churchyard. The body is determined to be a man with a past, again providing Lambert and Hook with a long list of potential suspects. *Booklist* reviewer Rowen stated that "the series is recommended for its gritty realism and hard-to-solve mysteries." *An Unsuitable Death* finds the detectives searching for yet another killer, this one having left the corpse on the steps of the town's cathedral. Of this installment in the series, Rowen wrote that "along with a sure sense of police procedure, Gregson offers unsettling insights into drugs, fundamentalist religion, and the delusions that love brings."

With *An Academic Death,* Gregson mines his own background as an educator, setting Lambert and Hook to discover who has murdered a local university professor. A contributor for *Publishers Weekly* commented that "while Gregson develops the characters of Hook and Lambert, he skimps on the unsavory collection of faculty members they investigate, none of whom is sympathetic." However, in another *Booklist* review, Rowen remarked that "the prose and the pace in this latest Lambert and Hook mystery are clipped, clean, and crisp," and called the detectives "an appealing team." In *Mortal Taste,* Lambert and Hook investigate the murder of a school headmaster, and delve into the world of drugs, sex, and possibly pedophilia. A *Kirkus Reviews* contributor found the book "both dependable and inventive—and likely to delight procedural fans on both sides of the pond."

Gregson writes another series of mysteries that focus on Detective Inspector Percy Peach and his associate, Detective Sergeant Lucy Blake. In *To Kill a Wife,* an English accountant is getting ready to kill his spouse, only to have someone else do it before he can get the chance. Rowen, in a review for *Booklist,* reported that "Peach himself makes a memorable hero, as distinctive as Inspector Morse but less brooding." Rex E. Klett, writing for *Library Journal,* found the book "well done, suspenseful, and engaging."

A Turbulent Priest provides Detective Inspector Peach with a corpse when a stream floods and the body rises to the surface. As is typical of Gregson's mysteries, a large number of suspects come to the foreground once the body is identified. *Booklist* reviewer Rowen remarked of this installment in the series that "Gregson combines unsettling insights on contemporary religion with fascinating procedural detail."

In *Murder at the Lodge* Gregson adds internal politics to the situation with the possibility of a promotion for Detective Inspector Peach. Matters are complicated by

Peach's superior, Chief Inspector Thomas Tucker Bullstrode, who finds himself missing valuable information regarding the team's current case. A *Kirkus Reviews* contributor found the novel "another amusing procedural that makes for a lovely evening's entertainment—except, as Peach might observe, for the victim and his killer." By *Wages of Sin,* Bullstrode has banished Peach to the traffic division, but is forced to call him back when he cannot handle a case.

BIOGRAPHICAL AND CRITICAL SOURCES:

PERIODICALS

Booklist, October 1, 1998, John Rowen, review of *Girl Gone Missing,* p. 310; April 15, 1999, John Rowen, review of *To Kill a Wife,* p. 1476; January 1, 2000, John Rowen, review of *Malice Aforethought,* p. 883; March 15, 2000, John Rowen, review of *A Turbulent Priest,* p. 1333; September 1, 2000, John Rowen, review of *An Unsuitable Death,* p. 69; January 1, 2002, John Rowen, review of *An Academic Death,* p. 818; September 15, 2003, Emily Melton, review of *Mortal Taste,* p. 214; April 1, 2004, Emily Melton, review of *Wages of Sin,* p. 1352; October 1, 2004, Emily Melton, review of *Just Desserts,* p. 313.

Kirkus Reviews, May 1, 2002, review of *A Little Learning,* p. 617; October 15, 2002, review of *Death on the Eleventh Hole,* p. 1507; April 1, 2003, review of *Murder at the Lodge,* p. 508; October 15, 2003, review of *Mortal Taste,* p. 1253; March 1, 2004, review of *Wages of Sin,* p. 203; October 14, 2004, review of *Just Desserts,* p. 986; April 1, 2005, review of *Dusty Death,* p. 388.

Library Journal, June 1, 1999, Rex E. Klett, review of *To Kill a Wife,* p. 184; April 1, 2004, Rex Klett, review of *Wages of Sin,* p. 128.

Publishers Weekly, January 21, 2002, review of *An Academic Death,* p. 67; May 20, 2002, p. 51; April 28, 2003, p. 53; November 17, 2003, p. 49.*

*   *   *

GRESHOFF, Jan 1888-1971

(Dirk Bouts, Joh. G. Brands, Paul Buys, A. van Doorn, J. Janszen, Jr., Kees Konyn, A.L. van Kuyck, Ludovicus van Marmerrode, Prikkebeen, Otto P. Reys, Sagetarius en Joost Tak, H.L. Voet, J.J. van Voorne, J. van Zomeren Badius)

PERSONAL: Born December 15, 1888, in Nieuw-Helvoet, Netherlands; died March 19, 1971, in Cape Town, South Africa; married Agatha Christina, 1917.

CAREER: Worked as a journalist. *De witte mier,* founder; editor of Dutch newspapers and literary magazines, including *Forum, Groot Nederland, Nieuwe Arnhemsche Courant,* and *Hollandsch Weekblad; Standpunteand Het Vaderland,* South Africa, editor and literary columnist.

AWARDS, HONORS: Prijs van Amsterdam, 1927; Constantijn Huygensprijs, 1967; since 1978, the Jan Campert Foundation has awarded a biannual literary prize named in Greshoff's honor.

WRITINGS:

POETRY

Aan den verlaten vijver, 1909.
Door mijn open venster, 1910.
(Editor) *Het jaar der dichters: Muzenalmanak voor 1911,* Luctor Emergo (The Hague, Netherlands), 1910.
De ceder (title means "The Cedar"), Hijman, Stenfert Kroese & van der Zande (Arnhem, Netherlands), 1924.
Schaduw, 1924.
Sparsa, 1925.
Vonken van het Vuur, 1925.
Keurdicht, bloemlezing, Boosten & Stols (Maastricht, Netherlands), 1926.
Oud zeer, 1926.
Zeven gedichten, 1926.
Aardsch en Hemelsch, 1926.
Anch'io, 1926.
Lyriek verzameld, Tjeenk Willink (Zwolle, Netherlands), 1928.
Bij feestelijke gelegenheden, 1928.
Confetti, 1928.
Ketelmuziek: Bloemlezing uit Greshoffs poëzie van 1908-1928 (title means "Kettle Music"), edited by E. du Perron, privately published, 1929.
Gedichten, A.A.M. Stols (Maastricht, Netherlands), 1930.
Mirliton, J. Enschedé (Haarlem, Netherlands), 1932.
Janus Bifrons, 1932.
Pro domo, 1933.

Gedichten, 1907-1934, Folemprise (The Hague, Netherlands), 1934.

Ikaros bekeerd (title means "Icarus Converted"), A.A.M. Stols (The Hague, Netherlands), 1938.

Dichters van dezen tijd, P.N. van Kampen (Amsterdam, Netherlands), 1939.

(Editor) *Nieuwe Nederlandse dichtkunst,* J.L. van Schaik (Pretoria, South Africa), 1942.

In de verstrooiing: een verzameling letterkundige bijdragen van schrijvers buiten Nederland, 1940-10 mei 1945, Querido (New York, NY), 1945, translation published as *Harvest of the Lowlands: An Anthology in English Translation of Creative Writing in the Dutch Language, with a Historical Survey of the Literary Development,* Querido (New York, NY), 1945.

Verzameld Werk, P.N. van Kampen (Amsterdam, Netherlands), 1948.

Uitnodiging tot ergernis, bloemlezing, poëzie en proza (title means "Invitation to Irritation"), B. Bakker/Daamen (The Hague, Netherlands), 1957.

De laatste dingen (title means "The Last Things"), A.A.M. Stols (The Hague, Netherlands), 1958.

Wachten op Charon (title means "Waiting for Charon"), Nijgh & van Ditmar (Rotterdam, Netherlands), 1964.

Bloemlezing uit zijn gedichten, compiled by Pierre H. Dubois, Nijgh & van Ditmar (Rotterdam, Netherlands), 1966.

Verzamelde gedichten 1907-1967, Nijgh & van Ditmar (Rotterdam, Netherlands), 1967.

Een eerlijk man heeft niets aan zijn gelaat (title means "An Honest Man's Face Does Him No Good"), compiled by M. Fonse, 1981.

ESSAYS

Latijnsche lente (title means "Latin Spring"), A.W. Sijthoff (Leiden, Netherlands), 1918.

Mengelstoffen op het gebied der Fransche letterkunde (title means "Mixing Substances in the Area of French Literature"), Boosten & Stols, 1924.

Dichters in het koffyhuis, 1924.

(with J. de Vries) *Geschiedenis der Nederlandsche letterkunde* (title means "History of Dutch Literature"), Hijman, Stenfert Kroese & van der Zande, 1925.

Uren (title means "Hours"), Boosten & Stols, 1926.

De wieken van de molen (title means "The Wings of the Windmill"), A.A.M. Stols (Maastricht, Netherlands), 1927.

Currento calamo, 1930.

Spijkers met koppen (title means "Nails with Heads"), A.A.M. Stols (Brussels, Belgium), 1931.

Voetzoekers (title means "Jumping Jacks"), A.A.M. Stols (Brussels, Belgium), 1932.

Arthur van Schendel, J.M. Meulenhoff (Amsterdam, Netherlands), 1934.

Critische vlugschriften (title means "Critical Pamphlets"), 1935.

Rebuten (title means "Rejects"), Querido (Amsterdam, Netherlands), 1936.

In alle ernst (title means "In All Seriousness"), Querido (Amsterdam, Netherlands), 1938.

Steenen voor brood, 1939.

Catrijntje Afrika, H. van Krimpen (The Hague, Netherlands), 1940.

Fabrieksgeheimen (title means "Factory Secrets"), J.L. van Schaik (Pretoria, South Africa), 1941.

Rariteiten, Fakkel-Reeks (Batavia, Indonesia), 1941.

Muze, mijn vriendin (title means "Muse, My Friend"), J.L. van Schaik (Pretoria, South Africa), 1943.

Het spel der spelen (title means "The Game of Games"), Querido (New York, NY), 1944.

Mijn vriend Coster: ter gelegenheid van de zestigste verjaardag van de schrijver (title means "My Friend Coster: On the Occasion of the Writer's Sixtieth Birthday"), Nederlandse Vereeniging voor Druk-en Boekkunst (Haarlem, Netherlands), 1948.

Het boek der vriendschap, memoires, 1950.

(With R. Goris) *Marnix Gijsen,* A.A.M. Stols (The Hague, Netherlands), 1955.

Volière, memoires, A.A.M. Stols (The Hague, Netherlands), 1956.

Bric à brac, 1957.

Menagerie, memoires, A.A.M. Stols (The Hague, Netherlands), 1958.

Pluis en niet pluis, de zes en zeven kruisjes (title means "Something Fishy and Not Fishy, the Six and Seven Crosses"), Heijinis (Zaandijk, Netherlands, 1958.

Afscheid van Europa (title means "Farewell to Europe"), Nijgh & van Ditmar (Rotterdam, Netherlands), 1970.

Also author of other essay collections, including *Het Gefoelied Glas, Lionel des Rieux,* and *Une saison en Enfer.*

APHORISMS

Op de valreep (title means "At the Last Minute"), P.N. van Kampen (Amsterdam, Netherlands), 1939.

Mimosa pudica, 1940.

Kalender zonder dagen (title means "Calendar without Days"), Koninklijke drukkerij de Unie (Batavia, Indonesia), 1941.

Bitterzoet, 1943.

Voor volwassenen (title means "For Adults"), A. Manteau (Brussels, Belgium), 1945.

Als droog zand, 1957.

Janee, De Beuk (Amsterdam, Netherlands), 1958.

Nachtschade, keur uit de aforismen (title means "Nightshade, Pick from the Aphorisms"), A.A.M. Stols (The Hague, Netherlands), 1958.

444 aforismen, keuze uit de aforismen, Nijgh & van Ditmar (Rotterdam, Netherlands), 1969.

265 redenen tot ruzie, keuze uit de aforismen (title means "265 Reasons to Fight, Selections from the Aphorisms"), edited by G. de Ley, 1980.

LETTERS

Sans famille. Die brieven over een hedendaagsch vraagstuk, De Bezige Bij (Amsterdam, Netherlands), 1947.

Leo Vroman, brieven over en weer, briefwisseling met J. Greshoff (title means "Leo Vroman, Letters Back and Forth"), Querido (Amsterdam, Netherlands), 1977.

Beste Sander, Do It Now!: Briefwisseling J. Greshoff/ A.A.M. Stols, (correspondence), three volumes, edited by Salma Chen and S.A.J. van Faassen, Nederlands Letterkundig Museum en Documentatiecentrum (The Hague, Netherlands), 1990–92.

OTHER

Also author of books under pseudonyms Dirk Bouts, Joh. G. Brands, Paul Buys, A. van Doorn, J. Janszen, Jr., Kees Konyn, A.L. van Kuyck, Ludovicus van Marmerrode, Prikkebeen, Otto P. Reys, Sagetarius en Joost Tak, H.L. Voet, J.J. van Voorne, and J. van Zomeren Badius. Editor of *Bram van Velde, 1895-1981,* SDU (The Hague, Netherlands); author of *Zwanen pesten* (title means "Teasing the Swans"), Nijgh & van Ditmar (The Hague, Netherlands); *Cum grano salis,* L. J.C. Boucher (The Hague, Netherlands); *Lyriek, 3;* and *Lyriek, 4.* Coeditor, "Nederlandse Boekerij" series.

SIDELIGHTS: Dutch poet, essayist, and critic Jan Greshoff was a nonconformist thinker. At an early age he began to feel like an outsider because of his yearning for individualism and beauty. Though highly intelligent, Greshoff dropped out of secondary school and went to work as an apprentice journalist. His debut as a poet, *Aan de verlaten vijver,* was published when he was twenty-one. He eventually lived in various countries, including Indonesia, the United States, and South Africa. He discovered and promoted many young writers and brought attention to forgotten ones by publishing their work.

In his first two collections, Greshoff was representative of the "generation of 1910," and wrote romantic, melancholy poems. Between 1910 and 1924 he published no poetry, but his comeback was almost a second debut, because instead of lamenting the baseness of society, he had learned to confront it. He used much simpler, everyday language, and this "poésie parlante" became the genre published in the magazine *Forum,* which he founded. Although he was against engaged literature in principle, much of his work before World War II is obviously influenced by his protest against increasing collectivism. Just before World War II, Greshoff moved his family to South Africa to escape the threat of fascism he saw growing around him. This decision may well have saved his life, because his work was banned by the Nazis soon after they invaded the Netherlands.

After World War II, Greshoff's poetry became more introspective in tone. Because of his extended absence from the Netherlands, he did not witness the development of the experimental "Generation of '50." His more traditional rhymed poems, though still powerful, became dated in the eyes of postwar Dutch readers. In his final two collections, *De laatste dingen* and *Wachten op Charon,* he tried to dispel any remaining illusions and to come to terms with his approaching death.

Greshoff's many collections of aphorisms combine into a sketch of his world view and self-portrait. Together, they paint a picture of an undogmatic man, somewhat conservative yet nonconformist, averse to all slogans and collectivism. He placed great value on friendship, yet cherished a quiet life with his poetry.

BIOGRAPHICAL AND CRITICAL SOURCES:

BOOKS

Cassell's Encyclopedia of World Literature, Morrow (New York, NY), 1973.

PERIODICALS

Nieuw Vlaams Tijdschrift, Volume 25, issue 3, 1973, "De lantaarn en de dissel," pp. 309-310; July-August, 1980, A.G. Christiaens, "Nog over Greshoff te Brussel," pp. 616-620.
Ons erfdeel, January-February, 1980, Pierre H. Dubois, "De Brusselse jaren van Jan Greshoff," pp. 87-95.
Spiegel der Letteren, Volume 20, issue 3, 1978, P. Brachin, "Jan Greshoffs politieke houding, speciaal m.b.t. de 'Action Française,'" pp. 178-186.
Standpunte, Volume 88, 1970, "Kroniek der Nederlandse letteren VII," pp. 56-62; Volume 94, 1971, "Jan Greshoff," pp. 1-3.
Tydskrif vir Letterkunde, Volume 9, issue 1, 1971, "Ten huize van Jan Greshoff," pp. 2-3.*

* * *

GRISTWOOD, Sarah

PERSONAL: Female. *Education:* Attended Oxford University.

ADDRESSES: Agent—c/o Author Mail, Houghton Mifflin Company, Trade Division, Adult Editorial, 8th Fl., 222 Berkeley St., Boston, MA 02116-3764.

CAREER: Freelance journalist.

WRITINGS:

Recording Angels: The Secret World of Women's Diaries, Harrap (London, England), 1988.
Arbella: England's Lost Queen, Houghton Mifflin (Boston, MA), 2005.
Perdita: Royal Mistress, Writer, Romantic, Bantam Books (London, England), 2005.

Contributor to periodicals, including London *Times,* London *Guardian,* and London *Evening Standard.*

SIDELIGHTS: Sarah Gristwood attended Oxford University, after which she went to work as a journalist specializing in women's issues and the arts. Her writing has appeared in various publications, including the London-based *Guardian, Independent, Times,* and *Evening Standard.* In *Arbella: England's Lost Queen,* Gristwood chronicles the life of Arbella Stuart, grandmother of both Beth of Hardwick and Queen Elizabeth I, the niece of Mary Queen of Scots, and a former consideration for the throne in her own right. Gristwood tracks her subject's activities through Queen Elizabeth's lifetime, and also after her death, when Arbella sought to advance her status. Jane Ridley, in a review for *Spectator,* remarked that "Gristwood succeeds triumphantly not only in bringing alive the dead politics of the Jacobean court, but also in making vivid bricks with very little straw—the evidence on Arbella is patchy to say the least. This is an enthralling account of an extraordinary life." A contributor for *Kirkus Reviews* called the book "an intriguing, scholarly look at the short, sad life of Arbella." A *Publishers Weekly* reviewer, noting that Gristwood is sometimes forced to elaborate a bit more than might have been appropriate, given the scarcity of facts available, concluded that "she fully supports the contention that contemporaries took very seriously this now obscure young woman's pretensions to the throne."

BIOGRAPHICAL AND CRITICAL SOURCES:

PERIODICALS

Bookseller, October 18, 2002, Benedicte Page, "The Story of a Contender: Sarah Gristwood Reveals the Surprising Tale of Arbella Stuart, the Woman Who Believed She Could Succeed Elizabeth I to the Throne," p. 28.
History Today, May, 2003, "Elizabethan Era: Elizabeth's London," p. 71; May, 2004, Robert Pearce, review of *Arbella: England's Lost Queen,* p. 86.
Kirkus Reviews, April 1, 2005, review of *Arbella,* p. 399.
Publishers Weekly, April 18, 2005, review of *Arbella,* p. 54.
Spectator, February 22, 2003, Jane Ridley, "The Stuart We Fail to Remember," review of *Arbella,* p. 38; January 22, 2005, Sarah Burton, "Famous for Being Famous," p. 37.

ONLINE

Guardian Online, http://books.guardian.co.uk/ (September 20, 2005), "Sarah Gristwood."

GULLAR, Ferreira 1930-

PERSONAL: Born Joseé Ribamar Ferreira, September 10, 1930, in São do Maranhão, Brazil.

ADDRESSES: Agent—c/o Author Mail, University Press of America, 4501 Forbes Blvd., Ste. 200, Lanham, MD 20706.

CAREER: Poet, playwright, journalist, and artist. Fundação Cultural de Brasilia, president, beginning 1961. Also worked as a disc jockey, c. 1950s.

AWARDS, HONORS: Prince Claus Award, 2002.

WRITINGS:

POETRY

João Boa-Morte, Editôra Universitária 1962.
Ribamar-I, 1965, reprinted, Livaria São José (Rio de Janeiro, Brazil), 1968.
Por você, por mim, Edição Sped (Rio de Janeiro, Brazil), 1967.
Dentro da noite veloz: poemas, Civilização Brasileira (Rio de Janeiro, Brazil), 1975.
A luta corporal: poemas, Civilização Brasileira (Rio de Janeiro, Brazil), 1975, commemorative edition, J. Olympio Editora (Rio de Janeiro, Brazil), 1994.
Poema sujo, Civilização Brasileira (Rio de Janeiro, Brazil), 1976, translated as *Sullied Poem,* Associated Faculty Press (Millwood, NY), 1988, translated by Leland Guyer as *Dirty Poem,* University Press of America (Lanham, MD), 1990.
Antologia poética, Fontana (Rio de Janeiro, Brazil), 1976.
Uma luz do chão, Avenir Editora (Rio de Janeiro, Brazil), 1978.
Na vertigem do dia: poemas, Civilização Brasileira (Rio de Janeiro, Brazil), 1980.
Toda poesia (1950-1980), Civilização Brasileira (Rio de Janeiro, Brazil), 1980, revised and updated edition published as *Toda poesia (1950-1987),* J. Olympio Editora (Rio de Janeiro, Brazil), 1991, second revised and updated edition published as *Toda poesia (1950-1999),* 2000.

Os melhores poemas de Ferreira Gullar, selected by Alfredo Bosi, Global Editora (São Paulo, Brazil), 1983.
Barulhos, 1980-87, J. Olympio Editora (Rio de Janeiro, Brazil), 1987.
Poemas, Tierra Brasileña (Lima, Peru), 1987.
Poemas escolhidos, selected and with a preface by Walmir Ayala, Ediouro Grupo Coquetel (Rio de Janeiro, Brazil), 1989.
O formigueiro, Edição Europa (Rio de Janeiro, Brazil), 1991.
Muitas vozes: poemas, José Olympio (Rio de Janeiro, Brazil), 1999.

Also author of *Poemas,* (Rio de Janeiro, Brazil), 1958.

OTHER

Cultura post em questão, Editôra Civilização Brasileira (Rio de Janeiro, Brazil), 1965.
A luta corporal e novos poemas (biography), J. Alvaro (Rio de Janeiro, Brazil), 1966, fifth edition, J. Olympio Editora (Rio de Janeiro, Brazil), 2000.
(With Antônio Carlos Fontoura and Armando Costa) *A saída? Onde fica a saída?* (play), Grupo Opinião (Rio de Janeiro, Brazil), 1967.
(With Alfredo Dias Gomes) *Dr. Getúlio, sua vida e sua glória* (play), Civilização Brasileira (Rio de Janeiro, Brazil), 1968, published as *Vargas; ou, Dr. Getúlio, sua vida e sua glória,* 1983.
Vanguarda e subdesenvolvimento; ensaios sôbre arte (title means "The Vanguard and Underdevelopment"), Civilização Brasileira (Rio de Janeiro, Brazil), 1969, third edition, 1984.
(With Mário Pedrosa) *Arte basileira hoje; [situação e perspectives],* Paz e Terra (Rio de Janeiro, Brazil), 1973.
(With Augusto dos Anjos) *Toda a poesia,* Paz e Terra (Rio de Janeiro, Brazil), 1976.
(With Bernard Hermann and Vinicius de Moraes) *Rio de Janeiro,* Éditions du Pacifique (Rio de Janeiro, Brazil), 1976.
(With Roberto Pontual) *Visão da terra: arte agora, Antonio Henrique Amaral, Antonio Maia, Emanoel Araujo, Francisco Brennand, Frans Krajcberg, Gilvan Samico, Glauco Rodriques, Humberto Espindola, Ione Saldanha, Márcio Sampaio, Millôr Fernandes, Rubem Valentim,* Atelier de Arte Ediçães (Rio de Janeiro, Brazil), 1977.

Um rubi no umbigo: peça teatral em dois atos (play), Civilização Brasileira (Rio de Janeiro, Brazil), 1978.

(Selector and translator, with Santiago Kovadloff) *Hombre común y otros poemias: antologia bilingüe,* Calicanto Editorial (Buenos Aires, Argentina), 1979.

(With Thomaz Ianelli Olivio Tavares de Araújo, and Roberto Pontual) *Thomaz: oleos e aquarelas: 18 de julho a 14 de agosto 1979* (exhibition catalogue), Museu de Arte Contemporanea do Parana (Parana, Brazil), 1979.

(With Bruno Giorgi, Marcos Antônio Marcondes, and Rômulo Fialdini) *Bruno Giorgi,* Art Editora (São Paulo, Brazil), 1980.

(With Newton Rezende) *Newton Rezende,* Galeria Binino (Rio de Janeiro, Brazil), 1980.

(With Mário Pedrosa and Lygia Clark) *Lygia Clark: textos de Ferreira Bullar, Mário Pedrosa, Lygia Clark,* Edição FunArte (Rio de Janeiro, Brazil), 1980.

(With Beth Brait) *Ferreira Gullar,* Abril Educação (São Paulo, Brazil), 1980.

Sobre arte, Avenir Editora (Rio de Janeiro, Brazil), 1982.

Etapas da arte contemporânea: do cubismo ao neoconcretismo, Nobel (São Paulo, Brazil), 1985.

(With Sérgio Gonzaga and Lucio Stein) *A pintura pintura de Thomaz Ianelli,* Gráficos Brunner (São Paulo, Brazil), 1985.

Crime na flora, ou Ordem e progresso, J. Olympio Editora (Rio de Janeiro, Brazil), 1986.

Indagações de hoje (speech, letters, and diary selections), J. Olympio Editora (Rio de Janeiro, Brazil), 1989.

A estranha vida banal, J. Olympio Editora (Rio de Janeiro), 1989.

(With Louis-Charles Sirjacq) *Le pays des éléphants = O pais dos elefantes,* L'Avant-scène (Paris, France), 1989.

Arumentação contra a morte da arte (essays and criticism), Editora Revan (Rio de Janeiro, Brazil), 1993.

Nise da Silveira: uma psiquiatra rebelde (biography), Relume Dumará (Rio de Janeiro, Brazil), 1996.

(With Denize Torbes) *Punhais e pássaros,* Impressões do Brasil (Rio de Janeiro, Brazil), 1996.

(With Grilo) *Cidades inventadas* (fiction), J. Olympio Editora (Rio de Janeiro, Brazil), 1997.

Rabo de foguete: os años de exílio (memoir), Editora Revan (Rio de Janeiro, Brazil), 1998.

(With Angela Lago) *Um gato chamado gatinho,* Salamandra (São Paulo, Brazil), 2000.

Contributor to periodicals, including *Diogenes.*

Author's works have been published in several languages, including Spanish, German, and English.

SIDELIGHTS: Ferreira Gullar is a one-time political exile and a successful Brazilian poet and playwright. The author first gained widespread notice in South America with his volume of experimental poetry titled *A luta corporal: poemas.* Although Gullar has gone to reach celebrity status in Brazil and South America, he has remained relatively unknown elsewhere. "Gullar's entire life and work constitute important documents of much of the modern social and artistic history of Brazil," wrote Leland Guyer in his introduction to *Dirty Poem,* the English translation of Gullar's most famous work, *Poema sujo.* Guyer also noted that Gullar's one-time exile "contributed greatly to the extensive and elaborately configured recollection that is *Poema sujo,*" adding, "Few works, if any in recent decades have had as much literary impact in Brazil as this work."

According to Guyer, this time writing in *Selecta: Journal of the Pacific Northwest Council on Foreign Languages,* Gullar called *Dirty Poem* his "last will and testament." The poem is an evocation of Gullar's youth in 1940's Brazil and was written by Gullar while the poet was a political exile in Buenos Aires, Argentina. Although the free-verse poem reflects much of the author's impressions from his young days in Brazil, such as his father reading detective novels and the presence of American soldiers in Brazil during World War II, it is also a discourse on Brazilian society in general and on social injustice.

In a review of the English translation, *World Literature Today* contributor Richard A. Preto-Rodas noted that the author "transcends ideology to create a hauntingly sincere remembrance of things past, warts and all." Commenting on the author's ability to evoke his childhood world, Preto-Rodas went on to write, "The reader is enveloped in a sensuous world where bright sunlight gives way to velvety darkness, where the sounds of songbirds rustling in overarching trees meld with the taste of fried cracklings." In a review of the Spanish version of the poem in *World Literature Today,* Klaus Müller-Bergh called the work "the most important lyric statement made in the country during the past ten years." *Modern Language Journal* contributor Larry

D. Miller wrote that the poem "is a very personal statement," but he added, "Yet, this poetry, concerned with the meaning of life, with living it fully and with defining and maintaining a sense of one's origins, has a universal message that speaks across barriers of language and culture."

In his collection of poetry titled *Antologia poética,* Gullar starts with more classically rhymed poems and then moves on to free rhythms and verse. Writing again in *World Literature Today,* Müller-Bergh called the author "one of the most provocative and authentic new voices from Brazil." He went on to comment on a poem in the volume about the sad life of a civil servant and reflected on the poet's approach to writing, noting, "Gullar's concluding esthetic could not be more explicit: in addition to form and artifice, poetry is above all a passionate, revolutionary statement." In a review of the collection of poems titled *Na vertigem do dia: poemas, World Literature Today* contributor Wilson Martins commented the poet's focus on "the poetry of social themes and inspiration, in which he is one of the best, if not the best, in Brazil." Martins also asserted that the author has revealed a "broader understanding of the human condition without giving up his right and duty to be the voice of the voiceless."

BIOGRAPHICAL AND CRITICAL SOURCES:

BOOKS

Gullar, Ferreira, *Dirty Poem,* translated by Leland Guyer, University Press of America (Lanham, MD), 1990.
Gullar, Ferreira, *Rabo de foguete: os años de exílio,* Editora Revan (Rio de Janeiro, Brazil), 1998.

PERIODICALS

Modern Language Journal, November, 1978, Larry D. Miller, review of *Poema sujo,* pp. 358-359.
Revista Canadiene de Estudios Hispanico, fall, 1989, Ricardo da Silveira Lobo Sternberg, "Memory and History in Ferreira Gullar's *Poema sujo,*" pp. 131-143.
Selecta: Journal of the Pacific Northwest Council on Foreign Languages, Volume 8, 1987, Leland R. Guyer, "*Poema sujo;* Last Will and Testament."

Texto Critico Xalapa, Volume 11, 1978, Richard Roux, "Um Cara Cara a Cara," pp. 220-239.
World Literature Today, autumn, 1977, Klaus Müller-Bergh, review of *Poema sujo,* pp. 605-606; summer, 1978, Klaus Müller-Bergh, review of *Antologia poética,* pp. 449-450; summer, 1981, Wilson Martins, review of *Na vertigem do dia,* p. 443; autumn, 1991, Richard A. Preto-Rodas, review of *Dirty Poem,* pp. 685-686.

ONLINE

Prince Claus Fund Web site, http://www.princeclausfund.org/ (September 27, 2005), brief profile of author.*

*   *   *

GUNST, Laurie

PERSONAL: Born in Richmond, VA; married. *Education:* Graduated from University of New Hampshire; Harvard University, Ph.D.

ADDRESSES: Home—New York, NY; WY. *Agent*—c/o Author Mail, Soho Press, Inc., 853 Broadway, New York, NY 10003.

CAREER: Writer, memoirist, and educator. New School University, New York, NY, educator.

AWARDS, HONORS: Harry Guggenheim Foundation grant.

WRITINGS:

Born Fi' Dead: A Journey through the Jamaican Posse Underworld, Holt (New York, NY), 1995.
Off-White: A Memoir, Soho Press (New York, NY), 2005.

Contributor to periodicals, including *Nation* and *Spin.* Contributor to books, including *The Stories That Shape Us: Twenty Women Write about the West,* edited by Teresa Jordan and James R. Hepworth, Norton (New York, NY), 1995.

SIDELIGHTS: Author and memoirist Laurie Gunst, the daughter of a wealthy southern Jewish family, grew up in Virginia during the racially tense days of Jim Crow and segregation. She was raised, in all practical terms, by Rhoda Lloyd, a black woman who had been her grandmother's maid. Gunst relates her childhood experiences and intensely close relationship with Lloyd, and the evolution of her own attitudes toward race, in *Off-White: A Memoir.* Gunst's childhood was troubled, and she came to view Lloyd as more than a mother, finding in her the one source of unshakable stability Gunst needed during her childhood and early adulthood.

In her book Gunst relates the barely functional relationship she had with her parents while growing up. She was overweight as a child, and was treated unkindly by her mother, whose insults included discouraging Gunst from attending the college she desired by saying she wasn't "Radcliffe material." Her philandering father drank too much and dwelled on her physical imperfections. Her grandparents' and great-grandparents' lives included a variety of scandals. While studying at Harvard University, Gunst herself became a cocaine addict. Further troubling was the racial hatred in her family's past. Some of her ancestors had been involved in racially divisive acts, including helping the Klan encourage a race riot. Despite her troubles past and present, Gunst found a kinship beyond race with Lloyd. Lloyd remained her closest ally, advisor, and confidante, transcending the role of nurse and nanny to become a thoroughly loved, genuinely cherished family member. Even after Lloyd died in 1986, Gunst still felt her presence, and reported that she frequently conversed with her ghost.

In *Off-White,* Gunst "has a compelling story, especially for readers willing to suspend disbelief from a high, high branch," commented a *Kirkus Reviews* critic. *Library Journal* contributor Janet Ingraham remarked that "Gunst's soul-baring scrutiny of a complicated interracial relationship is compelling, and the coda, in which she searches out Rhoda's kin, is deeply satisfying." Reviewer Deborah Aubespin, writing in the Louisville, Kentucky *Courier-Journal,* observed that "Like all of us, Gunst is a product of her time; however, she is able to grow and learn from her experiences." Aubespin concluded that the book is "is a triumph of the spirit."

An historian with a Ph.D. in history from Harvard University, Gunst is also an expert on Jamaican pos-

ses, or violent drug gangs. These groups have had a devastating effect on the Caribbean island since the early 1980s and are the subject of her book *Born Fi' Dead: A Journey through the Jamaican Posse Underworld.* Originally, the posses existed as groups of mercenary street fighters converted to serve as political enforcers and intimidators. However, in the early 1980s, many posse members came to the United States where they put their efforts into developing and expanding a crack cocaine trade between the United States and Jamaica. The posses then became emblematic of the drug-related activities that have driven cities such as Kingston, Jamaica, into poverty and violence.

Gunst's book is based on first-hand interviews with the people she met while conducting her research in Kingston, people who refer to themselves as "sufferers," victims of decades of political turmoil as well as of the violence and poverty that follow the posses and their drug trade. Gunst's tale "is a bitter one, full of blameless death, misery and wasted opportunity," remarked reviewer Chris Martin in *Geographical.*

Brought up on violent American Western films, kung-fu movies, and action thrillers, the posse members often derive their attitudes from unrealistic media sources. The book's title refers to the credo of the posse members, that they are "born to die," probably early in life, most likely violently, and that survival depends on following the rule of kill or be killed. A preference for state-of-the-art military weaponry have sealed the posses' pact with violence and death.

Martin called *Born Fi' Dead* "a chilling read; a savage incantation of a people without hope." Gunst's bleak analysis of the prevalent culture of drugs and violence in Jamaica, noted a *Publishers Weekly* reviewer, "shows just how ill-fated the island has become."

BIOGRAPHICAL AND CRITICAL SOURCES:

BOOKS

Gunst, Laurie, *Off-White: A Memoir,* Soho Press (New York, NY), 2005.

PERIODICALS

Courier-Journal (Louisville, KY), August 21, 2005, Deborah Aubespin, "Very Special Kinship Explored in *Off-White.*"

Geographical, September, 1999, Chris Martin, review of *Born Fi' Dead: A Journey through the Jamaican Posse Underworld,* p. 71.

Kirkus Reviews, May 15, 2005, review of *Off-White,* p. 575.

Library Journal, July 1, 2005, Janet Ingraham, review of *Off-White,* p. 94.

Publishers Weekly, January 23, 1995, review of *Born Fi' Dead,* p. 53.*

* * *

GUZMAN, Sandra
(Sandra Guzmán)

PERSONAL: Born in Puerto Rico; daughter of Lydia (a wet nurse). *Ethnicity:* Hispanic American *Education:* Rutgers University, New Brunswick, NJ, B.A.

ADDRESSES: Agent—c/o Author Mail, Three Rivers Press, 1745 Broadway, New York, NY 10019. *E-mail*—Sandra@thelatinasbible.com.

CAREER: El Diario/La Prensa, reporter; senior spokeswoman to New York City controller Elizabeth Holtzman; WNJU-TV, New York, NY, assignment manager, public affairs producer for news, and public affairs producer for *Enfoque 47*; *Good Day, New York,* New York, NY, segment producer; *Latina* magazine, New York, NY, editor-in-chief; Soloella.com (bilingual Web site), content director and editor-in-chief. Serves on Smithsonian Institution's National Board for Latino Initiatives.

AWARDS, HONORS: New York Chapter of the National Academy of Television Arts and Sciences, Emmy Award, 1995, for *Embargo Contra Cuba.*

WRITINGS:

The Latina's Bible: The Nueva Latina's Guide to Love, Sex, Spirituality, and La Vida, Three Rivers Press (New York, NY), 2002.

SIDELIGHTS: Sandra Guzman has served the Hispanic-American audience through print, television, and electronic forms. When she wrote *The Latina's Bible: The Nueva Latina's Guide to Love, Sex, Spirituality, and La Vida,* Guzman wanted to supply a source of guidance she had once looked for herself but never found. Her book addresses the conflicts and contradictions young Latinas struggle with in the United States, suggesting ways that they can embrace their culture and develop satisfying relationships and careers. The author recalls conflicts she experienced with her mother and religion, and the feeling that she was being denied the freedom to live like her non-Hispanic friends. Her advice touches on subjects ranging from food, dating, and beauty to sexuality, college, and networking.

The book provides an engaging presentation on important subjects, according to several reviewers. A *Publishers Weekly* contributor called *The Latina's Bible* "a valuable resource" and noted that it is "guided by a sense of community-oriented feminism." Writing in *Library Journal,* Lisa Wise called it "a clear and readable guide" that included sensitive issues avoided in other works. Sheila Shoup described the book as "humorous, serious, and fun" in *School Library Journal,* and concluded that "this book will speak to young Hispanics." In the *Journal of Adolescent & Adult Literacy,* Susan Carlile recommended the book to women ages seventeen to twenty-five and remarked that Guzman's style suggests a "good friend offering intimate advice on life."

BIOGRAPHICAL AND CRITICAL SOURCES:

BOOKS

Notable Hispanic American Women, Book Two, Thomson Gale (Detroit, MI), 1998.

PERIODICALS

Journal of Adolescent & Adult Literacy, April, 2003, Susan Carlile, review of *The Latina's Bible: The Nueva Latina's Guide to Love, Sex, Spirituality, and La Vida,* p. 610.

Library Journal, March 1, 2002, Lisa Wise, review of *The Latina's Bible,* p. 122.

Publishers Weekly, December 6, 1999, John F. Baker, "Calling Latin Women," p. 17; February 25, 2002, review of *The Latina's Bible,* p. 55.

School Library Journal, June, 2002, Sheila Shoup, review of *The Latina's Bible,* p. 174.*

GUZMÁN, Sandra
See GUZMAN, Sandra

H

HABIBI, Emile
See HABIBY, Emile

* * *

HABIBI, Imil
See HABIBY, Emile

* * *

HABIBY, Emile 1919(?)-1996
(Emile Habibi, Imil Habibi)

PERSONAL: First name sometimes transliterated Imil or Hamil; born 1919 (some sources say 1921 or 1922), in Haifa, Palestine (now Israel); died 1996, in Haifa, Israel.

CAREER: Politician, writer, and editor. Israeli Communist Party, founding member; elected to Israeli Knesset three times; Al-Ittihad ("Unity," bi-weekly periodical), editor-in-chief.

AWARDS, HONORS: Israeli Literary Prize, 1992, for *Al-Waqa'I al-gharibah fi ikhtifa Sa'id abi al-nahs al-Mutasha'il* ("The Secret Life of Saeed, the Ill-Fated Pessoptimist"); State of Palestine Certificate of Merit; Medal of Jerusalem for Culture, Literature, and Art.

WRITINGS:

Sudasiyat al-ayyam al-sittah (short stories; title means "Sextet of the Six Days"), Dar al-'Awday (Beirut, Lebanon), 1969.

Kafr Qasim: fi al-dhikrá al-20 li-majzarat Kafr Qasim: al-majzarah, al-siyasah, Manshurat 'Arab-sak (Haifa, Israel), 1976.

Luka' ibn Luka': thalath jalasat amama sunduq al-'ajab: hikaya masrahiyah, Dar al-Farabi (Beirut, Lebanon), 1980.

Al-Waqa'I al-gharibah fi ikhtifa Sa'id abi al-nahs al-Mutasha'il (fiction), 1974, translated from the Arabic by Salma Khadra Jayyusi and Trevor Le Gassick as *The Secret Life of Saeed, the Ill-Fated Pessoptimist: A Palestinian Who Became a Citizen of Israel,* Vantage Press (New York, NY), 1982, reprinted, Interlink Books (New York, NY), 2002.

Ikhtiyah (novel), Mu'assasat Bisan Bris (Nicosia, Cypress), 1985.

Khurafiyat saraya bint al-ghul (novel), Dar 'Arabisk (Haifa, Israel), 1991.

Nahwa 'alam bi-la aqfas (title means "Toward a World without Ages"), Maktab wa-Maktabat Kull Shay' (Haifa, Israel), 1993.

Writings have been translated into several languages, including French and English.

SIDELIGHTS: When Israel was created in 1948 and took over Haifa many Palestinians emigrated, but Emile Habiby decided to stay. He began writing fiction in 1967 in response to a comment by an Israeli education minister who said that Palestinians would have produced a national literature if they truly existed as a people. Habiby answered this challenge with *Sudasiyat al-ayyam al-sittah,* which means "Sextet of the Six Days." The book is a collection of short stories describing the impact of the Six-Day War on Palestinians. "Unlike most short-story cycles which are linked through a character, place, or event, the link generating the structural unity of the Sextet is that of impact, shock, and irony," wrote Sabry Hafez in *Contemporary World Writers.*

Habiby followed up with his most famous work, *Al-Waqa'I al-gharibah fi ikhtifa Sa'id abi al-nahs al-Mutasha'il,* which has been published in English as *The Secret Life of Saeed, the Ill-Fated Pessoptimist: A Palestinian Who Became a Citizen of Israel.* Like Habiby, the protagonist, Saeed, is a Palestinian who decides to stay in Israel in 1948. Saeed, however, becomes an informer for the new Israeli state. After an affair with a woman named Yuaad (meaning "Return"), he marries Baqiya ("Staying"). Their son grows up to join the Palestinian resistance, while Saeed soon finds himself imprisoned by the Israeli government. In addition to these political themes the novel also introduces mystical elements when Saeed contacts extra-terrestrials in tunnels first dug by Crusaders.

In a review of *The Secret Life of Saeed, the Ill-Fated Pessoptimist, Times Literary Supplement* contributor Robert Irwin noted, "Much of the novel . . . is wild farce, and it is full of irony, slapstick, proverbs, puns and alliteration, historical, literary and mystical allusions." Beth Warrell, writing in *Booklist,* commented that "even readers who disagree with him will find this strange novel to be thought-provoking on a number of levels. Helpful translators' notes serve as a primer on Middle Eastern history and culture." In a review of a 2002 English edition of the book, Fred Rhodes commented in *Middle East* that the book "achieves the impossible: A comic novel on the crisis in Palestine . . . yet remains hilarious throughout." A *Kirkus Reviews* contributor noted the author's "incisive satiric characterizations of true believers and extremists of all persuasions."

When the novel was first published in 1974, it created a sensation in the Arab world, as well as in Israeli society in its Hebrew translation. Habiby's decision to accept the Israeli Prize for Literature for his novel set off a firestorm of protest among Arab intellectuals, many of whom condemned his acceptance as an act of treachery to the Palestinian cause. For Habiby, however, survival in the face of Israeli oppression and a determination to foster a Palestinian literary tradition in the face of these obstacles was true loyalty. "The merit, he tells his detractors—among whom, incidentally, there are many Palestinians who left Israel—does

not lie in running away, but in staying and coping with the situation," noted *Israel Studies* contributor Rachel Felday Brenner.

In 1996, Habiby secured permission for one of those Palestinian émigrés, famed poet Mahmoud Darwish, to visit him in Haifa. News cameras were set to record the historic meeting between the two literary giants, but Habiby died the night before Darwish's arrival. According to an article in the *New York Times,* Darwish gave a eulogy for Habiby and noted: "Emile is leaving the stage and cracking his last joke."

BIOGRAPHICAL AND CRITICAL SOURCES:

BOOKS

Contemporary World Writers, edited by Tracy Chevalier, 2nd edition, St. James Press (Detroit, MI), 1993.

PERIODICALS

American Book Review, March, 1985, review of *The Secret Life of Saeed, the Ill-Fated Pessoptimist: A Palestinian Who Became a Citizen of Israel,* p. 4.
Booklist, January 1, 2002, Beth Warrell, review of *The Secret Life of Saeed, the Ill-Fated Pessoptimist,* p. 806.
Books & Bookmen, August, 1985, review of *The Secret Life of Saeed, the Ill-Fated Pessoptimist,* p. 31.
Christian Science Monitor, September 14, 1989, review of *The Secret Life of Saeed, the Ill-Fated Pessoptimist,* p. 13.
Guardian (London, England), August 16, 2003, David Jays and Isobel Montgomery, review of *The Secret Life of Saeed, the Ill-Fated Pessoptimist,* p. 24.
Israel Studies, fall, 2001, Rachel Felday Brenner, "The Search for Identity in Israeli Arab Fiction: Atallah Mansour, Emile Habiby, and Anton Shammas," p. 91.
Kirkus Reviews, January 15, 2002, review of *The Secret Life of Saeed, the Ill-Fated Pessoptimist,* p. 73.
Listener, July 4, 1985, review of *The Secret Life of Saeed, the Ill-Fated Pessoptimist,* p. 31.

Middle East, October, 2003, Fred Rhodes, review of *The Secret Life of Saeed, the Ill-Fated Pessoptimist*, p. 65.

Nation, September 17, 1990, review of *The Secret Life of Saeed, the Ill-Fated Pessoptimist*, p. 280.

New Statesman, May 24, 1985, review of *The Secret Life of Saeed, the Ill-Fated Pessoptimist*, p. 29.

New York Times, December 30, 2001, "A Poet's Palestine as a Metaphor."

Spectator, December 6, 1986, review of *The Secret Life of Saeed, the Ill-Fated Pessoptimist*, p. 33.

Times Literary Supplement, July 18, 1986, Robert Irwin, "Stay or Return," p. 793.

World Press Review, December, 1991, Tahar Ben Jelloun, "Palestinians Turn to Lethal Humor," pp. 27-28.

ONLINE

Levantine Center Web site, http://www.levantinecenter.org/ (May 8, 2002), review of *The Secret Life of Saeed, the Ill-Fated Pessoptimist*.

Middle East News Online, http://www.middleeastwire.com/ (November 9, 2001), Hada Sarhan "The Intertwined World of Occupation and the Knesset."*

* * *

HAISMA, Nyckle 1907-1943

PERSONAL: Born May 18, 1907, in Ie, Netherlands; died of diphtheria, February 22, 1943, in Tjilatjap, Bandoeng, Indonesia; married Etsje van der Veen, 1929; children: one son, one daughter. *Education:* Earned teaching certificate.

CAREER: Taught in Dutch Indies.

AWARDS, HONORS: Gysbert Japicxprijs, 1946, for body of work.

WRITINGS:

Simmerdagen (for children), 1933.
De kar (for children), 1936.
Paed oer 't hiem, Osinga (Bolsward, Netherlands), 1937.
Suderkrús, 1938.
Paed nei eigen hoarnleger, 1940.
Peke Donia, de koloniaal (novel), Osinga (Bolsward, Netherlands), 1943.
Simmer, 1948.
Wrotters fan de Froskepôlle, In ferhaal ut Sumatra, translation by D.A. Tammings, Brandenburgh (Sneek, Netherlands), 1949.
It lân forline, Brandenburgh (Snits, Netherland), 1951.
Samle fersen, 1981.

SIDELIGHTS: Nyckle Haisma came from a farming background, but rather than join his father on the farm after elementary school, he insisted on getting a secondary education. He received a scholarship for a teachers' training college on the condition that he would spend time teaching in the Dutch Indies (now Indonesia). Shortly after their wedding in 1929, he and his wife traveled to Medan, Indonesia, in fulfillment of this obligation. During World War II, like most colonialists, Haisma was interred in a Japanese prison camp after the Dutch capitulation in 1942. There he contracted diphtheria and died in 1943.

Haisma wrote novels, children's books, and poetry. His double novel, *Peke Donia, de koloniaal*, captures the atmosphere of the Indonesian experience through the eyes of an immigrant. Haisma crafted his restless protagonist's character and the atmosphere surrounding him in a romantic work that captured the spirit of the time.*

* * *

HALLDÉN, Ruth 1927-

PERSONAL: Born 1927.

ADDRESSES: Agent—c/o Author Mail, Bokforlaget Prisma, Tryckerigatan 4, SE-103, Stockholm 12, Sweden.

CAREER: Uppsala Nya Tidning (newspaper), Uppsala, Sweden, freelance journalist; *Dagens Nyheter*, literary critic, 1967—.

WRITINGS:

Hus utan trädgård (poems), Bonnier (Stockholm, Sweden), 1959.

Landskap i gult och guld (poems), Norstedt (Stockholm, Sweden), 1963.

Esaias Tegnér och kritiken (essays), 1982.

En bra bok (essays), 1991.

Vid romanens rötter (essays), Bonnier (Stockholm, Sweden), 1997.

Tanker om kultur (essays), Prisma (Stockholm, Sweden), 1999.

SIDELIGHTS: Ruth Halldén has written two poetry collections, the second of which, *Landskap i gult och guld,* received a positive review from Margit Abenius in *Svensk litteraturtidsskrift.* Abenius found the tension in the poems to be interesting and compelling; she praised the poems' composition and style, particularly the works "Kuperat landskap" and "Erfarenhet," where themes of loneliness, bleakness, and loss of values are balanced against obstinate rebelliousness.

Halldén, a journalist and literary critic, has also published several essay collections. In *Tanker om kultur,* she criticizes late-twentieth-century popular culture and discusses why people should read Swedish literature. She bemoans the fact that reading books has become a status symbol, and that the pleasure of reading a good book is no longer in and of itself the object of reading. According to Maja Lundgren in *Aftonbladet,* Halldén mainly blames the readers, the "literary correct" who do not trust themselves enough to decide for themselves what constitutes quality writing. Halldén argues that the boundary between high and low literature, entertainment and avant garde must be opened.

BIOGRAPHICAL AND CRITICAL SOURCES:

PERIODICALS

Svensk Litteraturtidsskrift, Volume 27, number 1, 1964, Margit Abenius, "Tre lyriker," pp. 11-16.

ONLINE

Aftonbladet, http://www.aftonbladet.se/ (August 10, 2001), Maja Lundgren, review of *Tanker om kultur.**

HAMMOND, Diane
(Diane Coplin Hammond)

PERSONAL: Born in NY; married; husband's name Nolan; children: Kerry.

ADDRESSES: Agent—c/o Author Mail, Doubleday, 1745 Broadway, New York, NY 10019.

CAREER: Writer and editor. Has served as spokesperson for the Oregon Coast Aquarium and the Free Willy Keiko Foundation.

AWARDS, HONORS: Oregon Arts Commission, literary fellowship.

WRITINGS:

Keiko's Story: The Real-Life Tale of the World's Most Famous Killer Whale (juvenile biography), Peduncle Press (Waldport, OR), 1998.

Going to Bend (novel), Doubleday (New York, NY), 2004.

Homesick Creek (novel), Doubleday (New York, NY), 2005.

Has published work in *Yankee, Mademoiselle,* and *Washington Review.*

ADAPTATIONS: Going to Bend was adapted for audio cassette, read by Hillary Huber, Blackstone Audiobooks, 2004.

SIDELIGHTS: Novelist Diane Hammond has written two novels steeped in what she called the "insular culture of coastal Oregon" in an interview for *Book Browse.* A native New Yorker, Hammond adjusted to a dramatically different lifestyle when she moved to Oregon, which included isolation and weather that dominated everything. Her first novel, *Going to Bend,* tells the story of two women in their early thirties who have grown up together in the small fishing village of Hubbard, Oregon. Petie Coolbaugh is a gruff, cynical woman who is trying to survive economic and emotional hard times. Her husband, with whom she has two young children, is often unemployed and their relationship is troubled. Her friend Rose Bundy is a single mother who has a sunnier outlook on life, but faces an equal dose of hardship. When a brother and sister from California move to town and open a café, Petie temporarily finds work making soup and Rose becomes involved in producing a cookbook with the café owners.

Reviewers commended the author for her skilled handling of the story. *Booklist* reviewer Bill Ott explained that while he feared the book would be "a working-class weeper," Hammond has created "something considerably more subtle." Kate Ayers commented in a *Bookreporter.com* review that "the glimpse into the lives of Rose Bundy and Petie Coolbaugh is so authentic . . . I could smell the soup." Hammond's writing was appraised by a reviewer in *Publishers Weekly* as "clean, sharp prose, idiosyncratic dialogue and deep insight into relationships" Similarly, *Library Journal* contributor Rebecca Sturm Kelm praised the novel's "earthy dialog, precise narrative," and "well-placed humor." Writing for *Pop Matters* online, Teri A. McIntyre welcomed the work as ranking among "similar tales that seek to honestly portray the lives of mature, life-addled women."

Homesick Creek is also set in Hubbard, but shares only one minor character with its predecessor. The story again revolves around two female friends and contrasts the problems they find in marriage. Bunny is a waitress married to car salesman Hack. They are financially comfortable, but Bunny is concerned that her charming mate is having an affair with a new co-worker. Her friend Anita has more faith in husband Bob, despite his problems keeping a job and his dependence on alcohol. When Bob begins having unexplained absences, Anita suspects that his drinking is getting worse, yet fails to see a new crisis in the making.

Critics echoed the kind of commentary Hammond received for her first novel. In a *Bookreporter.com* review, Kate Ayers wrote that, "ultimately it weighs in as a story of genuine friendship, love gone wrong, and families in crises." A *Kirkus Reviews* writer commented that "Hammond is deft at balancing the subtle tensions that make for complex characters," and a *Publishers Weekly* critic cited the book's "spare language and good humor that easily encompasses rich commentary on marital physics."

BIOGRAPHICAL AND CRITICAL SOURCES:

PERIODICALS

Booklist, November 15, 2003, Bill Ott, review of *Going to Bend,* p. 574.

Kirkus Reviews, November 15, 2003, review of *Going to Bend,* p. 1329; May 1, 2005, review of *Homesick Creek,* p. 496.

Library Journal, December, 2003, Rebecca Sturm Kelm, review of *Going to Bend,* p. 166.

Publishers Weekly, December 1, 2003, review of *Going to Bend,* p. 42; May 2, 2005, review of *Homesick Creek,* p. 173.

ONLINE

Book Browse, http://www.bookbrowse.com/ (September 29, 2005), "A Conversation with Diane Hammond."

Bookreporter.com http://www.bookreporter.com/ (September 29, 2005), Kate Ayers, review of *Going to Bend*; (September 25, 2005) Kate Ayers, review of *Homesick Creek.*

Curled Up with a Good Book, http://www.curledup.com/ (October 8, 2005), Amanda Cuda, review of *Going to Bend.*

Pop Matters, http://www.popmatters.com/ (August 25, 2004) Teri A McIntyre, review of *Going to Bend.*

Romantic Times Online, http://www.romantictimes.com/ (September 29, 2005), Sheri Melnick, review of *Homesick Creek.**

*   *   *

HAMMOND, Diane Coplin
   See HAMMOND, Diane

*   *   *

HANKS, Tom 1956-

PERSONAL: Born Thomas Jeffrey Hanks, July 9, 1956, in Concord, CA; son of Amos Hanks (an itinerant cook) and Janet Turner (a hospital worker); married Samantha Lewes (an actress and producer; also known as Susan Dillingham), 1978 (divorced, 1985); married Rita Wilson (an actress and producer), April, 1988; children: (first marriage) Colin, Elizabeth; (second marriage) Chester, Truman Theodore. *Education:* Attended Chabot College and California State University, Sacramento.

ADDRESSES: Agent—Creative Artists Agency, 9830 Wilshire Blvd., Beverly Hills, CA 90212; PMK, 955 S. Carillo Dr., Ste. 200, Los Angeles, CA 90048.

CAREER: Actor, director, producer, and screenwriter. Actor in films, including *Elliot, He Knows You're Alone* (also known as *Blood Wedding*), United Artists, 1980; (as Allen Bauer) *Splash,* Touchstone, 1984; (as Rick Gassko) *Bachelor Party,* Twentieth Century-Fox, 1984; (as Lawrence Bourne III) *Volunteers,* Columbia, 1985; (as Richard) *The Man with One Red Shoe,* Twentieth Century-Fox, 1985; (as Walter Fielding) *The Money Pit,* Universal, 1986; (as David Basner) *Nothing in Common,* TriStar, 1986; (as David) *Every Time We Say Goodbye,* TriStar, 1986; (as Pep Streebek) *Dragnet,* Universal, 1987; (as Josh Baskin) *Big,* Twentieth Century-Fox, 1988; (as Steven Gold) *Punchline,* Columbia, 1988; (as Ray Peterson) *The 'Burbs,* Universal, 1989; (as Scott Turner) *Turner and Hooch,* Buena Vista, 1989; (as Joe Banks) *Joe versus the Volcano,* Warner Bros., 1990; (as Sherman McCoy) *The Bonfire of the Vanities,* Warner Bros., 1990; (as Jimmy Dugan) *A League of Their Own,* Columbia, 1992; (as narrator and the adult Mike) *Radio Flyer,* Columbia, 1992; (as Sam Baldwin) *Sleepless in Seattle,* TriStar, 1993; (as Andrew Beckett) *Philadelphia,* TriStar, 1993; (as Forrest Gump) *Forrest Gump,* Paramount, 1994; (as Jim Lovell) *Apollo 13,* Universal, 1995; (as himself) *The Celluloid Closet,* Sony Pictures Classics, 1995; (as the voice of Sheriff Woody) *Toy Story* (animated), Buena Vista, 1995; (as Mr. White) *That Thing You Do!,* Twentieth Century-Fox, 1996; (as Captain John Miller) *Saving Private Ryan,* Paramount/DreamWorks, 1998; (as Joe Fox) *You've Got Mail,* Warner Bros., 1998; (as the voice of Sheriff Woody) *Toy Story 2* (animated), Buena Vista/Walt Disney, 1999; (as Paul Edgecomb) *The Green Mile* (also known as *Stephen King's the Green Mile*), Warner Bros., 1999; (as Chuck Noland) *Cast Away,* DreamWorks/Twentieth Century-Fox, 2000; (as Michael Sullivan) *Road to Perdition,* DreamWorks, 2002; (as Carl Hanratty) *Catch Me If You Can,* DreamWorks, 2002; (as the conductor/hero boy) *The Polar Express,* 2004; (as Professor Goldthwait Higginson Dorr) *The Ladykillers,* 2004; (as Victor) *The Terminal,* 2004; (as Andy Rosenzweig) *A Cold Case,* 2006; and (as Robert Langdon) *The Da Vinci Code,* 2006. Also actor in television movies, including (as Robbie Wheeling) *Rona Jaffe's Mazes and Monsters,* Columbia Broadcasting System (CBS), 1982. Director of film *That Thing You Do!,* Twentieth Century-Fox, 1996. Producer of films, including *Cast Away,* DreamWorks/Twentieth Century-Fox, 2000; *My Big Fat Greek Wedding* IFC Films, 2001; *The Polar Express,* 2004; *Connie and Carla,* 2004; *NASCAR: The IMAX Experience 3D,* 2004; *The Spider and the Fly,* 2004; and *A Cold Case,* 2004. Appeared in television specials, including

59th-Annual Academy Awards Presentation, American Broadcasting Companies (ABC), 1987; *Just the Facts,* syndicated, 1987; *3rd-Annual Hollywood Insider Academy Awards Special,* USA Network, 1989; *The Barbara Walters Special,* ABC, 1989; *Saturday Night Live 15th-Anniversary,* National Broadcasting Company (NBC), 1989; *62nd-Annual Academy Awards,* ABC, 1990; *64th-Annual Academy Awards,* ABC, 1992; *6th-Annual American Comedy Awards,* ABC, 1992; *Hollywood Hotshots,* Fox, 1992; *65th-Annual Academy Awards,* ABC, 1993; *Through the Eyes of Forrest Gump,* 1994; *67th-Annual Academy Awards,* ABC, 1995; *23rd American Film Institute Life Achievement Award: A Salute to Steven Spielberg,* NBC, 1995; (as himself) *I Am Your Child,* ABC, 1997; *Saturday Night Live 25th Anniversary,* NBC, 1999; (as the narrator) *Shooting War,* ABC, 2000; (as himself) *America: A Tribute to Heroes,* 2001; *Orange British Academy Film Awards,* 2001; *73rd-Annual Academy Awards,* ABC, 2001; *74th-Annual Academy Awards,* ABC, 2002; *The Making of "Road to Perdition,"* 2002; *AFI Lifetime Achievement Award: A Tribute to Tom Hanks,* 2002; *54th-Annual Primetime Emmy Awards,* 2002; *Hollywood Celebrates Denzel Washington: An American Cinematheque Tribute,* 2003; *75th-Annual Academy Awards,* 2003; and *Celebrity Profile.* Actor in television miniseries, including (as Jean-Luc Despont) *From the Earth to the Moon,* HBO, 1998; and (as a British officer) *Band of Brothers,* HBO, 2001. Actor in television series, including (as Kip Wilson and Buffy Wilson) *Bosom Buddies,* ABC, 1980-82. Appeared in episodes of television series, including (as Rick Martin) "Friends and Lovers," *The Love Boat,* ABC, 1980; (as Gordon) "The Road Not Taken: Part 1," *Taxi,* ABC, 1982; (as Dwayne) "A Little Case of Revenge," *Happy Days,* ABC, 1982; (as Ned Donnelly) "The Fugitive: Parts 1 & 2," *Family Ties,* NBC, 1983; (as Ned Donnelly) "Say Uncle," *Family Ties* NBC, 1984; *Saturday Night Live,* NBC, 1985; *The Dick Cavett Show,* ABC, 1986; "Sally Field and Tom Hanks' Punchline Party," *HBO Comedy Hour,* Home Box Office (HBO), 1988; *Saturday Night Live,* NBC, 1988; "None but the Lonely Heart," *Tales from the Crypt,* HBO, 1992; "I'll Be Waiting," *Sydney Pollak's Fallen Angels,* Showtime, 1993; (as himself) "Bald Star in Hot Oil Fest!," *The Naked Truth,* NBC, 1995; *Ruby Wax Meets,* British Broadcasting Corporation (BBC), 1997; (as himself) "Tom Hanks and Rita Wilson: That Thing They Do," *Famous Families,* Fox Family, 1998; and *Inside the Actors Studio,* Bravo, 1999; *Breakfast,* BBC, 2001; and others. Guest on television programs, including *The Tonight Show, The Dennis Miller Show,* and *Late Night with David Let-*

terman. Executive producer of television miniseries, including (and director of part one) *From the Earth to the Moon,* HBO, 1998; (and director of "Crossroads," *Band of Brothers,* HBO, 2001; and *We Stand Alone Together,* 2001. Executive producer of television series *My Big Fat Greek Life,* CBS, 2003—. Director of episodes of television series, including "None But the Lonely Heart" (also known as "This'll Kill Ya'" and "On a Dead Man's Chest"), *Tales from the Crypt,* HBO, 1992; "The Monkey's Curse," *A League of Their Own,* 1993; and "I'll Be Waiting," *Sydney Pollak's Fallen Angels,* Showtime, 1993. Appeared in stage productions, including (as Proteus) *Two Gentlemen of Verona,* Great Lakes Shakespeare Festival, Lakewood, OH, 1978; (as Grumio) *The Taming of the Shrew,* and (as Cassius) *Othello,* both Great Lakes Shakespeare Festival; and in *Mandrake,* Riverside Theatre, New York City. Appeared in videos, including (as Barry Algar) *Saturday Night Live: The Best of Mike Myers,* 1998; (as Mr. Short-Term-Memory Jeff Morrow) *Saturday Night Live: Game Show Parodies,* 1998; (as himself) *Return to Normandy* (also known as *The Making of "Saving Private Ryan"*), 1998; (as himself) *"Captain Miller," Into the Breach: "Saving Private Ryan,"* 1998; (as himself) *Behind the Scenes: Cast Away,* 2000; (as himself) *Rescued from the Closet,* Columbia TriStar Home Video, 2001; and (as himself) *People Like Us: Making "Philadelphia,"* 2003.

AWARDS, HONORS: Academy Award for best actor, Academy of Motion Picture Arts and Sciences, 1993, for *Philadelphia,* 1994, for *Forrest Gump*; Distinguished Public Service Award, U.S. Navy, 1999, for *Saving Private Ryan*; Life Achievement Award, American Film Institute, 2002.

WRITINGS:

That Thing You Do! (screenplay) Twentieth Century-Fox, 1996.
From the Earth to the Moon (television miniseries, segments six, seven, eleven, and twelve) Home Box Office (HBO), 1998.
Band of Brothers (television minseries, part one) HBO, 2001.

Author of foreword, *Virtual Apollo: A Pictorial Essay of the Engineering and Construction of the Apollo Command and Service Modules, the Historic Spacecraft that Took Man to the Moon,* by Scott P. Sullivan, Collector's Guide Publishers, 2002.

SIDELIGHTS: Tom Hanks was considered one of the most popular and most successful actors in Hollywood during the late 1980s and 1990s. "In this age of the outlaw, [Hanks] defines the ideal norm: he is our best us on our worst day, soldiering on through heartbreak," Richard Corliss and Cathy Booth wrote in *Time* magazine. His back-to-back Oscar-winning roles of the 1990s, as an AIDS-afflicted lawyer in *Philadelphia* and as the simple-minded hero of *Forrest Gump,* began this theme in Hanks's work, which continued in his similarly highly-praised roles as the commander of a doomed space mission in *Apollo 13* and the commander of a World War II unit in *Saving Private Ryan.*

When Hanks was at the top of his acting game, immediately after *Forrest Gump,* he abandoned acting for a time to write and direct a film, *That Thing You Do!.* "In the midst of the second go-around of the Academy Award attention, it just became a very unhealthy place for me to be," he explained to *Newsweek* interviewer David Ansen. "It should have been a celebratory thing, but because it has just been going on so long I was tired and falling into the traps of narcissism in a way that just isn't good for you. So I started writing this to see how far I could write it."

That Thing You Do! "is a modest ode to joy, a celebration of youthful high spirits in the year 1964," Ansen wrote. The film follows four boys who form a rock-and-roll band in the innocent early years of the genre and go on to be one-hit wonders. It's "an intentionally modest maiden effort," Leah Rozen noted in *People,* but it is "a pleasingly bouncy movie" that is "fundamentally nice." In addition to writing and directing the film, Hanks cast it himself and played a small part as the band's manager. He also took charge of the film's soundtrack, declaring that no real rock songs would be used; instead, they had to write new songs that sounded like authentic relics of that era. Hanks even wrote four of those songs himself.

Once Hanks had convinced the studios of his skill behind the camera, he became involved in writing and directing two epic nonfiction miniseries for the cable channel Home Box Office (HBO). The miniseries were in part inspired by buzz from two of Hanks's more notable films: *From the Earth to the Moon,* about the U.S. space program, by *Apollo 13,* and *Band of Brothers,* based on Stephen Ambrose's book about a company of paratroopers fighting in Europe in the closing days of World War II, by *Saving Private Ryan.*

"I just get to pursue things that I think are fascinating, and I get to do it on a pretty big level without a lot of constraints," Hanks explained to *Esquire* interviewer Bill Zehme. "I may be the only person alive who is fascinated by this stuff, but I have found myself another way to explore the material further. I view it almost as my ongoing education."

BIOGRAPHICAL AND CRITICAL SOURCES:

BOOKS

International Directory of Films and Filmmakers, Volume 3: *Actors and Actresses,* St. James Press (Detroit, MI), 1996.
Newsmakers 2000, Issue 2, Gale (Detroit, MI), 2000.
St. James Encyclopedia of Popular Culture, five volumes, St. James Press (Detroit, MI), 2000.

PERIODICALS

Daily Variety, June 12, 2002, Christopher Grove, "From Twilight to Primetime: Hanks Tribute Reflects Org's Aim to Honor Careers in Full Bloom," pp. A1-A2, Deirdre Mendoza, "Hanks Gets behind the Camera in Some of His Biggest Roles," pp. A5-A6.
Entertainment Weekly, July 9, 1993, "The Nice Man Cometh: Tom Hanks," pp. 14-20; August 16, 1996, David Poland, interview with Hanks, p. 12; October 11, 1996, Jeff Gordinier, review of *That Thing You Do!,* pp. 24-29; March 7, 1997, Casey Kasem, review of *That Thing You Do!,* p. 73.
Esquire, September, 2001, Bill Zehme, "Tom Hanks Acts like a Man: The True Story of a True American Optimist Whose Life Began When He Decided to Stop Being Such a Weenie," pp. 140-146.
Film Comment, March-April, 1997, Armond White, review of *That Thing You Do!,* pp. 43-45.
Knight Ridder/Tribune News Service, October 9, 1996, Mal Vincent, interview with Hanks, p. 1009K-5194.
Maclean's, October 14, 1996, Brian D. Johnson, review of *That Thing You Do!,* pp. 89-90, interview with Hanks, p. 90.
Newsweek, October 7, 1996, David Ansen, review of *That Thing You Do!,* pp. 76-77.

People, October 7, 1996, Leah Rozen, review of *That Thing You Do!,* p. 19; December 9, 1996, Johnny Dodd, interview with Hanks, p. 34.
Sarasota Herald Tribune, October 4, 1996, George Meyer, review of *That Thing You Do!,* p. T9.
Time, May 27, 1996, Brenda Luscombe, review of *That Thing You Do!,* p. 87; October 7, 1996, Richard Corliss, review of *That Thing You Do!,* pp. 92-93; December 21, 1998, Richard Corliss and Cathy Booth, "The Film of the Year. A Perky New Comedy. These Are High Times for Our Most Versatile Star," p. 70; May 15, 2000, "Saving Tom Hanks: Shedding Pounds and Pounding the Surf to Film an Island Survival Tale," p. 78.

ONLINE

Internet Movie Database, http://www.imdb.com/ (July 8, 2003), "Tom Hanks."*

*   *   *

HARRINGTON, Joyce 1931-

PERSONAL: Born 1931, in Jersey City, NY; children: two sons. *Education:* Studied at Pasadena Playhouse.

ADDRESSES: Agent—Scott Meredith Literary Agency, Inc., 845 3rd Ave., New York, NY 10022.

CAREER: Foote, Cone & Belding (advertising agency), New York, NY, director of public relations; publicity writer for American Association of Advertising Agencies.

AWARDS, HONORS: Edgar Allan Poe award, Mystery Writers of America, 1973, for "The Purple Shroud."

WRITINGS:

No One Knows My Name (novel), St. Martin's (New York, NY), 1980.
Family Reunion (novel), St. Martin's (New York, NY), 1982.
Dreemz of the Night (novel), St. Martin's (New York, NY), 1987.

Contributor to anthologies, including *Ellery Queen's Crookbook,* Random House (New York, NY), 1974; *Ellery Queen's Crime Wave,* Putnam (New York, NY), 1976; *Ellery Queen's Searches and Seizures,* Davis (New York, NY), 1977; *Ellery Queen's A Multitude of Sins,* Davis, 1978; *Best Detective Stories of the Year 1978,* edited by Edward D. Hoch, Dutton (New York, NY), 1978; *Ellery Queen's Scenes of the Crimes,* Davis, 1979; *Ellery Queen's Crime Cruise Round the World,* Davis, 1981; *The Year's Best Mystery and Suspense Stories 1982,* edited by Hoch, Walker (New York, NY), 1982; *The Year's Best Mystery and Suspense Stories 1983,* edited by Hoch, Walker, 1983; *The Year's Best Mystery and Suspense Stories 1986,* edited by Hoch, Walker, 1986; *The Year's Best Mystery and Suspense Stories 1988,* edited by Hoch, Walker, 1988; *The Year's Best Mystery and Suspense Stories 1991,* edited by Hoch, Walker, 1991; and *Murder in the Family,* Berkley Publishing Group (New York, NY), 2002. Contributor of stories to magazines, including *Ellery Queen's Mystery Magazine* and *Antaeus.*

SIDELIGHTS: Even before publication of her first novel in 1980, Joyce Harrington had already established herself as a crime and suspense writer of short stories. Her first story, the Edgar-winning "The Purple Shroud," is a quiet tale of a summer art instructor and the wife he has betrayed, building into a murder story of understated terror. Harrington followed this with "The Plastic Jungle," a macabre tale of a girl and her mother living in today's plastic society.

Two of her 1974 stories, "My Neighbor, Ay" and "The Cabin in the Hollow," offer settings as different as Brooklyn and rural West Virginia. "Night Crawlers" presents a memorable portrait of a woman worm farmer and a hidden treasure. "Blue Monday" offers a study of a murderer and his victim. Three Harrington stories published during 1977 illustrate her many moods well. "Grass" is a domestic drama of conflict between a husband and wife; "The Old Gray Cat" is a mood piece full of surprises for the unwary reader; and "The Thirteenth Victim" is a horror story about a man who constructs art works around the bodies of the dead.

Harrington's short-story output diminished as she began to work on her novels, but she still continued to write a few stories in the 1980s. For example, "A Place of Her Own" is a penetrating study of a New York bag lady; other notable pieces that reflect her sometimes bizarre portrayals of the human condition include "Sweet Baby Jenny" and "Address Unknown."

Harrington's first novel, *No One Knows My Name,* is a more conventional murder mystery. The psychotic killer stalking cast members of a summer theater at the Duck Creek Playhouse makes for a suspenseful debut. Her second novel, *Family Reunion,* features Jenny Holland, who returns from New York City to the reunion at River House in what becomes a blend of gothic novel and psychological thriller. And while the question in *No One Knows My Name* is basically one of whodunit, *Family Reunion* goes deeper, asking the reader to discover what shocking deed the characters committed so long ago. After her third novel, 1987's *Dreemz of the Night,* Harrington's output diminished considerably, and since then she has only contributed a few short stories to anthologies.

BIOGRAPHICAL AND CRITICAL SOURCES:

BOOKS

St. James Guide to Crime and Mystery Writers, 4th edition, St. James Press (Detroit, MI), 1996.

PERIODICALS

Publishers Weekly, May 8, 1987, Sybil Steinberg, review of *Dreemz of the Night,* p. 64.*

*   *   *

HARRISON, Nora Vitz 1955-

PERSONAL: Born July 7, 1955, in Tucson, AZ; daughter of Martin G. and Eleanor B. Vitz. *Education:* University of Redlands, B.A.; University of Sydney, M.A.

ADDRESSES: Agent—c/o Author Mail, Capital Books, 22841 Quicksilver Dr., Sterling, VA 20167.

CAREER: Writer.

MEMBER: Phi Beta Kappa.

AWARDS, HONORS: Rotary Foundation fellow in Australia.

WRITINGS:

Dear Kilroy: A Dog to Guide Us (nonfiction), Capital Books (Sterling, VA), 2003.

BIOGRAPHICAL AND CRITICAL SOURCES:

ONLINE

Dear Kilroy: A Dog to Guide Us Web site, http://www.dearkilroy.com/ (July 3, 2005).

*   *   *

HATHORN, Elizabeth
  See HATHORN, Libby

*   *   *

HATHORN, Elizabeth Helen
  See HATHORN, Libby

*   *   *

HATHORN, Libby 1943-
  (Elizabeth Hathorn, Elizabeth Helen Hathorn)

PERSONAL: Full name, Elizabeth Helen Hathorn; surname is pronounced "hay-thorn"; born September 26, 1943, in Newcastle, New South Wales, Australia; children: Lisa, Keiran.

ADDRESSES: Agent—Fran Moore, Curtis Brown, Level 1/2 Boundary Street, Paddington 2021 Australia; fax: 612-93616161.

CAREER: Teacher and librarian in schools in Sydney, New South Wales, Australia, 1965-81; worked as a deputy principal, 1977; consultant and senior educa-

Libby Hathorn

tion officer for government adult education programs, 1981-86; full-time writer, 1987—; writer-in-residence at University of Technology, Sydney, 1990, Woollahra Library, 1992, and at Edith Cowan University, 1992. Consultant to Dorothea Mackellar National Poetry Competition/Festival for children; speaker for student, teacher, and parent groups; Australia Day Amabassador, 1992—.

AWARDS, HONORS: The Tram to Bondi Beach was highly commended by the Children's Book Council of Australia (CBCA), 1982; *Paolo's Secret* was shortlisted for Children's Book of the Year Award and for New South Wales Premier's Literary awards, both 1986; Honour Award, CBCA, 1987, Kids Own Australian Literary Award (KOALA) shortlist, 1988, and Young Australians Best Book Award (YABBA) shortlist, 1989, 1990, all for *All about Anna*; Literature Board of the Australia Council fellowships, 1987, 1988; Honour Award, CBCA, 1988, for *Looking out for Sampson*; Children's Book of the Year Award short-list, 1990, for *The Extraordinary Magics of Emma McDade*; Society of Women Writers honors, 1990, for the body of her work during 1987-89; Honour Book of the Year for older readers, CBCA, 1990, American Library Association Best Book for Young Adults citation, 1991, Canberra's Own Outstanding List shortlist, all 1991, and translation award from Stichting Collectieve Propaganda van het Nederlands Boek, 1992, all for *Thunderwith*; CBCA Notable Book ciations, 1991, for *So Who Needs Lotto?* and *Jezza Says;* New South Wales Children's Week Medal for literature, 1992; Kate Greenaway Award, 1995, for *Way Home;* Australian Violence Prevention Certificate Award, 1995, for *Feral Kid* and *Way Home;* Parent's Choice Award, and Society of Women Writers (New South Wales, Australia) award, both for *Way Home;* Society of Women Writers award, 1995, for *Feral Kid* and *The Climb,* 1997, for *Rift,* 2001, for *Grandma's Shoes,* and 2003, for *The River;* CBCA Notable Book citations, 1993, 1996, 1997, 2003; White Raven citation, Bologna Children's Book Fair, 2001, for *The Gift;* best adaptation citation, Australian Writers' Guild, 2001, for libretto of *Grandma's Shoes*; Australian Interactive Media Industry Award for Best New Children's Product, for *Weirdstop 2003;* Prime Minister's Centenary Medal, 2003.

WRITINGS:

FOR CHILDREN AND YOUNG ADULTS

(Under name Elizabeth Hathorn; with John Hathorn) *Go Lightly: Creative Writing through Poetry,* illustrated by Joan Saint, Boden (Sydney, New South Wales, Australia), 1974.

Stephen's Tree (storybook), illustrated by Sandra Laroche, Methuen (Sydney, New South Wales, Australia), 1979.

Lachlan's Walk (picture book), illustrated by Sandra Laroche, Heinemann (London, England), 1980.

The Tram to Bondi Beach (picture book), illustrated by Julie Vivas, Collins (London, England), 1981, Kane/Miller (Brooklyn, NY), 1989.

Paolo's Secret (novella), illustrated by Lorraine Hannay, Heinemann (London, England), 1985.

All about Anna (novel), Heinemann (London, England), 1986.

Looking out for Sampson (storybook), Oxford University Press (Oxford, England), 1987.

Freya's Fantastic Surprise (picture book), illustrated by Sharon Thompson, Scholastic (New York, NY), 1988.

The Extraordinary Magics of Emma McDade (storybook), illustrated by Maya, Oxford University Press (New York, NY), 1989.

Stuntumble Monday (picture book), illustrated by Melissa Web, Collins Dove, 1989.

The Garden of the World (picture book), illustrated by Tricia Oktober, Margaret Hamilton Books, 1989.

Thunderwith (novel), Heinemann (Melbourne, Victoria, Australia), 1989, Little, Brown (Boston, MA), 1991.

Jezza Says (novel), illustrated by Donna Rawlins, Angus & Robertson (Melbourne, Victoria, Australia), 1990.

So Who Needs Lotto? (novella), illustrated by Simon Kneebone, Penguin (Camberwell, Victoria, Australia), 1990.

Talks with My Skateboard (poetry), Australian Broadcasting Corp., 1991.

(Editor) *The Blue Dress* (stories), Heinemann (Melbourne, Victoria, Australia), 1991.

Help for Young Writers (nonfiction), Nelson (Melbourne, Victoria, Australia), 1991.

Good to Read (textbook), Nelson (Melbourne, Victoria, Australia), 1991.

Who? (stories), Heinemann (Melbourne, Victoria, Australia), 1992.

Love Me Tender (novel), Oxford University Press (New York, NY), 1992, published as *Juke-box Jive,* Hodder (Sydney, New South Wales, Australia), 1996.

The Lenski Kids and Dracula (novella), Penguin (Camberwell, Victoria, Australia), 1992.

Valley under the Rock (novel), Reed Heinemann (Melbourne, Victoria, Australia), 1993.

Way Home (picture book), illustrated by Greg Rogers, Crown (New York), 1993.

There and Back (poetry), Macmillan/McGraw Hill (Santa Rosa, CA), 1993.

The Surprise Box, illustrated by Priscilla Cutter, SRA School Group (Santa Rosa, CA), 1994.

Feral Kid (novel), Hodder & Stoughton (Sydney, New South Wales, Australia), 1994.

Looking for Felix, illustrated by Ned Culio, SRA School Group (Santa Rosa, CA), 1994.

Grandma's Shoes (picture book), illustrated by Elivia Savadier, Little, Brown (Boston, MA), 1994, illustrated by Caroline Magerl, Hodder (Sydney, New South Wales, Australia), 2000.

What a Star (novel), HarperCollins, 1994.

The Wonder Thing (picture book), illustrated by Peter Gouldthorpe, Penguin (Camberwell, Victoria, Australia), 1995.

The Climb (novel), Penguin (Camberwell, Victoria, Australia), 1996.

Chrysalis (novel), Reed (Melbourne, Victoria, Australia), 1997.

Rift (novel), Hodder Headline (Sydney, New South Wales, Australia), 1998.

Sky Sash So Blue (picture book), illustrated by Benny Andrews, Simon & Schuster (New York, NY), 1998.

Magical Ride, Hodder Headline (Sydney, New South Wales, Australia), 1999.

(With Gary Crew) *Dear Venny, Dear Saffron* (novel), Lothian, 1999.

Ghostop Book 1: Double Sorrow (novel), Hodder Headline (Sydney, New South Wales, Australia), 1999.

Ghostop Book 2: Twice the Ring of Fire (novel), Hodder Headline (Sydney, New South Wales, Australia), 1999.

Ghostop Book 3: For Love to Conquer All (novel), Hodder Headline (Sydney, New South Wales, Australia), 1999.

The Gift, illustrated by Greg Rogers, Random House (New York, NY), 2000.

(Author of libretto) *Grandma's Shoes* (children's opera, based on her novel), music by Grahame Koehne, produced in Sydney, New South Wales, Australia, 2000.

A Face in the Water, illustrated by Uma Krishnaswamy, Goodbooks, 2000.

The River (picture book), Curriculum Corporation (Shanghai, China), 2001.

Okra-Acacia: The Story of the Wattle Pattern Plate (picture book), Curriculum Corporation (Shanghai, China), 2001.

The Painter (novel), Hodder Headline (Sydney, New South Wales, Australia), 2001.

Volcano Boy (verse novel), Lothian (South Melbourne, Victoria, Australia), 2002.

Over the Moon (picture book), illustrated Caroline Magerl, Lothian (South Melbourne, Victoria, Australia), 2003.

The Great Big Animal Ask (picture book), illustrated Anna Pignato, Lothian (South Melbourne, Victoria, Australia), 2004.

(Author of libretto) *Sky Sash So Blue,* (children's opera), music by Phillip Ratlifee, produced at Miles College, AL, 2004.

Author of poetry anthology *Heard Singing,* Out of India Press, 1998. Writer and producer for interactive storytelling series *Weirdstop 2003, Coolstop 2004,* and *Wonderstop 2005.*

FOR ADULTS

(With G. Bates) *Half-Time: Perspectives on Mid-life,* Fontana Collins, 1987.

Better Strangers (stories), Millennium Books, 1989.

Damascus, a Rooming House (libretto), performed by Australian Opera at Performance Space, Sydney, New South Wales, Australia, 1990.

The Maroubra Cycle: A Journey around Childhood (performance poetry), University of Technology, Sydney, New South Wales, Australia, 1990.

(And director) *The Blue Dress Suite* (music theater piece), produced at Melbourne International Festival, Melbourne, Victoria, Australia, 1991.

Author of series *On Course!: Today's English for Young Writers,* Macmillan, and *Help for Young Writers,* Nelson.

Some of Hathorn's works have been translated into Greek, Italian, Dutch, German, French, Norwegian, Danish, Swedish, Portuguese, and Korean.

ADAPTATIONS: Thunderwith was produced as the *Hallmark Hall of Fame* television movie *The Echo of Thunder; Songs with My Skateboard* was adapted for music by Stephen Lalor.

SIDELIGHTS: Libby Hathorn is an Australian writer who produces poetry, picture books, drama, novels, short stories, and nonfiction for children, young adults, and adults. Best known in the United States for her critically acclaimed novel *Thunderwith,* Hathorn has created works ranging from serious stories of troubled youth to lighthearted, fast-paced comedies. She writes of powerful female characters in her novels for junior readers, such as the protagonists in *All about Anna* and *The Extraordinary Magics of Emma McDade;* or of lonely, misunderstood teenagers in novels such as

Feral Kid, Love Me Tender, and *Valley under the Rock.* As Maurice Saxby noted in *St. James Guide to Children's Writers,* "In her novels for teenagers especially, Hathorn exposes, with compassion, sensitivity, and poetry the universal and ongoing struggle of humanity to heal hurts, establish meaningful relationships, and to learn to accept one's self—and ultimately—those who have wronged us."

"I must have been very young indeed when I decided to become a writer," Hathorn once commented. "My grandmother always kept my stories in her best black handbag and read them out loud to long-suffering relatives and told me over and over that I'd be a writer when I grew up." Though Hathorn started her career as a teacher and librarian, she did eventually become a writer. "Libby Hathorn knows exactly how today's children think and feel," observed Saxby in *The Proof of the Puddin': Australian Children's Literature, 1970-1990.* "She has an uncanny ear for the speech nuances of the classroom, playground and home. . . . [She] is always able to penetrate the facade of her characters and with skill and subtlety reveal what they are really like inside."

Hathorn grew up near Sydney, Australia, and recalled that at the time her parents did not own a car. "In fact, not many people on the street where I lived in the early 1950s owned cars. We had no television, either. We amused ourselves with storytelling and reading out loud and lots of games." Hathorn often read and told stories to her sisters and brother; she was encouraged by her parents, who "loved books" and had bookcases crammed with them. "Books were pretty central in our lives," she stated. "My father in particular read to us at night when he could get home in time. He was a detective and had long shifts at night that often kept him late. When he read we didn't interrupt, in fact we'd never dream of it as his voice filled the room because it seemed so obviously important to him—the ebb and flow of the language. My mother—who was very proud of her Irish ancestry—told us lots of true stories about the history of our family and also about her own girlhood."

As a child, Hathorn read "adventure books set in the Australian bush, like *Seven Little Australians,* as well as classics like *Black Beauty, The Secret Garden, Little Women,* and books by Emily and Charlotte Brontë," she once explained. She also read works by Australian authors "with considerable delight at finding Australian

settings and people in print." Later, Hathorn would lend her own work an Australian flavor after noticing "the need for more books that told Australian kids about themselves."

Hathorn began writing her own stories and poems when she was still a girl. Though she was often shy and quiet, Hathorn once noted that she could keep company "entertained with strings of stories that I made up as I went along." Her family encouraged her, and Hathorn "loved being at center stage—so I couldn't have been altogether a shy little buttercup." At school, she enjoyed reading and creative writing, and was disappointed in later years when "we had to write essays and commentaries but never, never stories or poems. I was extremely bored in my final years at school." Hathorn has also acknowledged that her high school years weren't all bad: "After all, I was introduced to the works of William Shakespeare, and particularly in my later years the poetic nature of his work touched me deeply. And best of all we studied the Romantic poets and I fell in love with John Keats and Samuel Coleridge as well as Percy Bysshe Shelley, Lord Byron, and William Wordsworth."

After graduating from high school, Hathorn worked in a laboratory and studied at night for a year before attending college full-time. Despite her parents' objections, she contemplated a career in journalism, hoping that she could learn "the art and craft of novel writing." "Anyway, my parents thought it important that I have a profession where I could earn a reasonable living—writers being notoriously underpaid," Hathorn remarked. "I was drawn to teaching; so after a year of broken specimen flasks and test tubes and discovering that my science courses did not enthrall me, I left the laboratory."

Hathorn attended Balmain Teacher's College (now the University of Technology, Sydney). "I must admit that I found the regulations of the place quite hard," she recalled. "Many of the lectures of those days seemed so dull to me that I wondered whether indeed I would last as a teacher for very long." Hathorn did enjoy her literature classes and was surprised to find that "when I came out of the rather dull years at college, I not only liked classroom teaching, but I also discovered that it was the most thrilling, absorbing, rewarding, and wonderful job anyone could have!"

After teaching for several years in Sydney, Hathorn applied for a position as a school librarian. "Although I was sorry to leave the intimacy of family that a classroom teacher has with her own class, the library was a new and exciting chapter for me," Hathorn once commented. "I had books, books, and more books to explore and the amazingly enjoyable job of bringing stories to every child in the school!" Her job as a librarian, the author added, "had a major influence on my decision to seriously try to publish my stories."

Hathorn's first book for children was *Stephen's Tree,* which was published in 1979. She followed this with two picture books: *Lachlan's Walk* and *The Tram to Bondi Beach.* In the genre of children's picture books, Hathorn discovered, as she explained, "such a scarcity of Australian material! I wanted to talk about our place, here and now, and have pictures that Australian children would instantly recognize. *Stephen's Tree* was a breakthrough in publishing. I had to fight with my publisher to have a gumtree on the cover. They wanted an ash or elm or oak so it would sell in England and Europe! Similarly, I was told *The Tram to Bondi Beach* should not mention Bondi. I won those fights and I must say *The Tram to Bondi Beach* has made its way onto the American market and American children didn't seem to have much trouble at all."

The Tram to Bondi Beach tells the story of Keiran, a nine-year-old boy who longs for a job selling newspapers to passengers on the trams that travel through Sydney. Keiran wants to be like Saxon, an older boy, who is an experienced newspaper seller. Reviewers commented on the nostalgic quality of the story, which is set in the 1930s. Marianne Pilla, in the *School Library Journal* complimented its "smooth" narrative and "vivid" passages. *Times Literary Supplement* contributor Ann Martin called it "a simple but appealing tale," and Karen Jameyson wrote in *Horn Book* that the book "will undoubtedly hold readers' interest."

Hathorn followed *The Tram to Bondi Beach* with *Paolo's Secret, All about Anna,* and *Looking out for Sampson.* As Hathorn once noted, *All about Anna,* her first novel, "is based on a wild, naughty cousin I had who drove her mother's car down the road at ten years of age and did other wild deeds—a perfect subject to write about." The book details the comic adventures of Lizzie, Harriet, Christopher, and their energetic, imaginative cousin, Anna. Lizzie, the narrator, explains that "I like being with Anna because somehow things always seem fast and furious and funny when she's around—and well, she's just a very unusual person."

Like *All about Anna, Looking out for Sampson* touches on family themes. Bronwyn wishes that her younger brother, Sampson, were older so that she could have a friend instead of someone to babysit. And when Cheryl and her mother come to stay with Bronwyn's family, Bronwyn's situation worsens. A disagreeable girl, Cheryl hints that Bronwyn's parents must care more about Sampson, since they give the toddler so much attention. After Sampson is lost briefly at the beach, however, Cheryl and Bronwyn reconcile and Bronwyn's parents express their appreciation of her.

Around the time *All about Anna* was published in 1986, Hathorn decided to give up her job and become a full-time writer. "I wanted to be a full-time writer secretly all my life but when I began my working life as a teacher this dream seemed to recede," the author once explained. "And once I was married and with two children I felt I had to keep up my contribution to our lifestyle. My husband is also a teacher and I thought it would be unfair if he had to work every day while I was home writing. It was as if in the eyes of the world writing was not work! And I'm to blame for allowing myself to think like that too.

"I've changed my mind now and I wish I had had the courage to do so much sooner. While I loved teaching, after some years of it I was ready for change. I was already writing short stories but I was aching to tell longer stories, to produce a novel for older readers. This was very hard when I was working full-time and had young children—so the stories I chose to write at that time were for younger children and were either picture books or junior novels like *All about Anna* and *Looking out for Sampson.*"

Among Hathorn's other books for young readers is *The Extraordinary Magics of Emma McDade.* The story describes the adventures of the title character, whose superhuman powers include incredible strength, the ability to call thousands of birds by whistling, and control over the weather. Another of Hathorn's books geared toward beginning readers is *Freya's Fantastic Surprise.* In it Miriam tells the class at news time that her parents bought her a tent, a surprise that Freya attempts to top by making up fantastic stories that her classmates realize are false. Freya eventually has a real surprise to share, however, when her mother announces that Freya will soon have a new sister. Published in the United States as well as Australia, *Freya's Fantastic Surprise* was praised by critics. Louise L. Sherman noted in *School Library Journal* that "Freya's concern about impressing her classmates . . . is on target." In a *Horn Book* review, Elizabeth S. Watson called the book "a winner" and commented that "the text and pictures combine to produce a tale that proves truth is best."

Hathorn began writing her first novel for young adults, *Thunderwith,* after receiving an Australia Council grant in 1987. "At home writing for a year, I realized that this was to be my job for the rest of my life," Hathorn once remarked. "And since I have been able to give full-time attention to my writing it has certainly flowered in many new directions. I have begun writing longer novels for young adults and I have been able to take on more ambitious projects like libretti and music theatre pieces, which I enjoy tremendously."

Thunderwith, published in 1989, is the story of fourteen-year-old Lara, who begins living with the father she barely knows after her mother dies of cancer. Lara's new home is in the remote Wallingat Forest in New South Wales, Australia. Though Lara's relationship with her father develops smoothly, he is often away on business and Lara's stepmother is openly antagonistic towards her. Lonely and grief-stricken, Lara finds solace in her bond with a mysterious dog that appears during a storm. She names the dog Thunderwith and keeps his existence a secret; she only tells the aboriginal storyteller she has befriended at school. Eventually, Lara realizes that Thunderwith has filled the space that her mother's death created, enabling her to come to terms with her loss. Lara is also able to slowly win over her stepmother and to adjust to her new home and family life.

The setting of *Thunderwith* is one with which Hathorn is intimately acquainted. As a child, she had relatives who lived in the Australian bush, and she spent many holidays in the country. "This was to prove very important to me," Hathorn once stated. "The bush weaves its own magic and it's something you cannot experience from a book or television show in a suburban setting. My holidays, especially those on my grandmother's farm in the Blue Mountains, created in me an enduring love for the Australian bush. As a writer, however, up until a few years ago the settings I chose to write about were in the hub of the family and quite often in suburbia."

Hathorn came upon the idea for *Thunderwith* after her brother bought land in Wallingat Forest. "During the first holiday there a huge storm blew up at about midnight and such was the noise and intensity of it we all rose from our beds to watch it," Hathorn once said. "You can imagine how vulnerable you'd feel way out in the bush with thunder booming and lightning raging and trees whipping and bending . . . and in the midst of this fury suddenly I saw a dog. A huge dark dog dashed across the place where some hours earlier we'd had a campfire and eaten our evening meal under the stars—a lovely looking half-dingo creature.

"When I lay down again I had the image of the dog in my mind, against the landscape of the bush and storm. Again and again I saw the dog and a line of a poem seemed to fall into my head from the storm clouds above. 'With thunder you'll come—and with thunder you'll go.' What did it mean? What could it mean? By morning I had unraveled the mystery of the lines of poetry and I had a story about a girl called Lara whose mother dies in the first chapter and who comes to live on the farm in a forest with her dad and a new family."

The dog that Hathorn had seen became *Thunderwith,* "Lara's friend, her escape, and her link to her mother," as Hathorn explained. Lara's mother was modeled after Hathorn's friend Cheryl, who died of cancer before the book was finished. "I feel that Cheryl's spirit leaps and bounds all through it," the author once noted. "So you see for me there are many emotions through many experiences that weave themselves into my stories and into this story in particular—happiness in being together, the joy one feels in being surrounded by natural beauty, a dark sadness at loss, and the pain in hardships that must be endured. And the way people can change and grow even through dark and mystifyingly sad experiences. But you may be pleased to know that love and hope win out in *Thunderwith*. They have to—as I believe eventually they have to in life itself."

Thunderwith garnered praise as a sensitive and realistic young adult novel. A *Publishers Weekly* reviewer commented that "Hathorn deftly injects a sense of wonderment into this intense, very real story." According to *Horn Book* contributor Watson, *Thunderwith* possesses "a believable plot featuring a shattering climax and a satisfyingly realistic resolution." Robert Strang, writing in *Bulletin of the Center for Children's Books,* commended Hathorn's "especially expert weaving of story and setting." Similarly, *Magpies* contributor Jameyson noted that Hathorn's "control over her complex subject is admirable; her insight into character sure and true; her ear for dialogue keen." Jameyson added that the author's "nimble detour from the usual route will leave readers surprised, even breathless."

Hathorn has also published poems for children and a story collection for young adults. Her poetry book *Talks with My Skateboard* is divided into several sections and includes poems about outdoor activities, school, family life, cats, and nature. The poem "Skateboard" is written from a child's perspective: "My sister has a skateboard / and you should see her go . . . She can jump and twirl / Do a twist and turn, / What I want to know / Is why I can't learn?" *Who?*, published in 1992, contains stories about ghosts, love and friendship, and mysteries, some of which are based on tales that Hathorn's mother told her. The collection includes "Who?," in which a pitiful ghost awakens a family from their beds; "An Act of Kindness," in which a family mysteriously loses their ability to remember the names of objects; and "Jethro Was My Friend," where a young girl attempts to save her beloved bird from rapidly rising floodwaters.

Hathorn published more novels, including the young-adult book *Love Me Tender* and a comic work for junior readers, *The Lenski Kids and Dracula.* Hathorn once commented that "*Love Me Tender* was a story I circled for a few years. It drew on my girlhood experiences although it's about a boy called Alan. It's a gentle story set in the days of rock and roll." In the novel, Alan and his sister and brothers are abandoned by their mother and sent to live with various relatives. Alan is taken in by his bossy, unsmiling Aunt Jessie, and the story chronicles his "interior journey as hope fades that he will ever see his Mum and his family again," Hathorn explained. "Alan changes but more importantly he causes people around him—including his old aunt—to change too. Self-growth is a very important message for young people today—looking inside and finding that strength to go on." *Love Me Tender* is among Hathorn's favorite creations; the book "has a place in my heart," she once commented, because it captures the atmosphere of the author's girlhood in the 1950s. Reviewing the book, which was reprinted in 1996 as *Juke-box Jive, School Librarian* critic Mary Hoffman commented that "this could so easily have been just a collection of cliches [but] what raises it is Libby Hathorn's honesty about Alan's feelings for his mother and his aching realization that the family will never all live together again."

A common thread in several of Hathorn's works is the author's belief in love, hope, and the resiliency of the human spirit. "With all the faults in the world, the injustices, the suffering, and the sheer violence that I am forced to acknowledge though not accept, I still have a great sense of hope," Hathorn once noted. "Human beings never cease to surprise me with their unexpectedness, their kindness, their cheerfulness, their will to go on against the odds. That's inspiring. And I feel a sense of hope should be nurtured in young people, for they are the hope of the world. My stories may sometimes have sad endings but they are never without some hope for the future."

In several books Hathorn has combined her interest in young people with her concerns about the environment, poverty, and homelessness. "My picture book *The Wonder Thing,* written after a visit to a rainforest to 'sing' about the beauty of the place, is also a plea for the survival of the earth's riches—trees, forests, mountains, and rivers," the author once explained. "There are only four to five words per page and it is a prose poem; I try to make those words the most delicately beautiful and evocative that I can." Both her picture book, *Way Home,* and her novel, *Feral Kid,* take up the theme of the homelessness of young people. "I feel strongly that we should never accept the fact of homeless children on our streets. A society that allows this sort of thing is not a responsible and caring society to my mind; I very much want people to look closely at stories like mine and begin asking questions about something that is becoming all too common a sight in all cities of the world."

An abandoned adolescent figures in the 1998 novel, *Rift.* Vaughan Jasper Roberts is stuck with his grandmother in an isolated coastal town when his parents take off. "At times ponderous and confusing, this is a complex novel in which Hathorn explores human fragility and courage, manipulation and madness and the comfort of habit and ritual," noted Jane Connolly in a *Magpies* review.

Hathorn also teamed up with writer Gary Crew to produce an epistolary novel between two teenagers in *Dear Venny, Dear Saffron,* and has experimented with online storytelling on her Web site, adapting the novel *Ghostop* from that format. Despite the diversity of publications, Hathorn has not neglected her interest in picture books. Her 1998 *Sky Sash So Blue* tells the story of a young slave, Susannah, who is willing to give up her one bit of ornament—her sky-blue sash, to ensure that her sister has a lovely wedding dress. A writer for *Children's Book Review Service* called this book a "lovely story of hardship, perseverance and love," while reviewer Carol Ann Wilson pointed out in *School Library Journal* that Hathorn employs an article of clothing, as she did in *Grandma's Shoes,* "to symbolize the indomitable spirit of family." Wilson concluded that "Susannah's narrative makes human and accessible the poignant struggles of a people, a family, and one little girl." Hathorn collaborated with American composer Phillip Ratliffe to adapt *Sky Sash So Blue* as a children's opera, which was produced at Miles College in Birmingham, Alabama in 2004 and 2005.

Hathorn acknowledged that although her writings often contain messages, "I don't ever want to write didactic books that berate people, young or old, with messages. I don't think you can really write a successful book by setting out with a 'do-good' or any other kind of message in mind. I can only write what moves me in some way to laugh or to cry or to wonder. I don't know what I'll be writing about a few years hence. There is a great sense of adventure in this—and a sense of mystery about what will find me."

As for advice to aspiring young writers, Hathorn has said: "The more you write the better you write. It's as simple and as difficult as that. To write well you must develop an ease with the pen and paper or the word processor or whatever—but most of all an ease with words. To do this you must be immersed in words; they should be your friends and your playthings as well as your tools. So, young writers, write a lot and love what you write so much that you work over it and shine it up to be the best you can possibly do—and then SHARE IT WITH SOMEONE."

AUTOBIOGRAPHICAL ESSAY: Libby Hathorn contributed the following autobiographical essay to *CA:*

I wish I could say I was born abroad, in far off Africa or deep in Papua New Guinea, and it was my exotic, isolated childhood that fed my imagination so that I was destined to be a writer. Or that I was raised on a remote, sprawling cattle station in the outback of Australia, where books and radio were my only friends. But no! Mine was a suburban childhood, busy with two sisters and a brother for company, spent in

Young Libby, ready for Sunday school, c. 1950s

Sydney, Australia. And this is where I have spent most of my life, despite traveling widely as an adult, and is a place that has had its significance in all my writing life.

In fact, I was born in the city of Newcastle, some two hours north of Sydney, where my father had been posted for two years during the Second World War. However, most of my early childhood was in the eastern suburbs of Sydney, at Maroubra where we lived, a little too far from Maroubra Beach; and my adolescence was spent at Tamarama, a more picturesque suburb. Our house, in a tiny but verdant valley park, was a stone's throw from the small (and later to become highly fashionable), treacherous and yet quite lovely city beach. We could look out the kitchen window and see the breakers of the Pacific Ocean crash onto the fine yellow sand of Tamarama Beach any time of day, and I remember going to sleep strangely calmed by the rhythm and roar of that surf. And we could take the walk along rugged cliffs to the much loved expanse of nearby Bondi Beach. One of my early books, *The Tram to Bondi Beach,* celebrates this beach, albeit as it was way back in the 1930s. Even now I don't like to be inland, to be too far from the edge that's been part and parcel of my whole life.

And yet how I longed for Europe and England during my adolescent years, a desire fed by the books and movies I'd seen, that perpetuated the idea that "real life" was elsewhere. I was to discover much later certain riches were to be discovered "in my own backyard," so to speak, when I began writing stories. In fact, I'd written poetry since my early childhood, completing a rhyming alphabet when I was in second grade—a first remembered "publication" because of the praise my grandmother, in particular, gave it. I'd read every book I could lay my hands on in our house, many of them with English backgrounds, and many way beyond my years, so that I felt I knew England, country and city, as if it were my place. But at the same time, I was listening to many a story by different members of our large, extended family, set firmly in an Aussie setting.

Despite a lack of romantic origins, my childhood was rich—filled with the busy-ness of being part of a largish family of four children and countless aunts and uncles, some of whom came and went. It wasn't without its trials of course—a small house, too many people and certain tensions between family members at times, but it was a household that shared stories and poetry, and valued books, all the stuff of feeding the imagination. From our parents, who—especially my mother—quoted long tracts of poetry, to a father fond of recounting gritty tales of his country boyhood, to a fabulist story-telling uncle, to a grandmother who read poetry aloud, our childhood was immersed and flavoured by story and poem. Another grandmother lived in the Blue Mountains, running tearooms there, and this was a marvelous contrast to city living. Megalong Valley was the setting for many of my early "rapturous" nature poems. To wake to the smell of the eucalyptus with overtones of last night's open fire, to hear the raucous song of the kookaburra and other native birds, and to look out onto the green and more green and rugged, yellowy brown steep cliffs lit by morning sun . . . no wonder my sisters and I delighted in our holidays there.

It was a life to which books and story were intrinsic. Our father, a young detective at the time, told bedtime stories of his boyhood whenever he was home on time to do so, but also and, maybe even more importantly for me, he was fond of reading from our old grey-covered, much loved *A Treasury of Verse*. In those days kids went to bed early, with the ritual of being dosed with something called Fry's Emulsion which,

we were told—though we didn't believe a word of it—"was good for your system," whatever that meant. The poetry did far more good than the ghastly tasting medicine. Who would not thrill to strange, entrancing, yet incomprehensible to a small child, words like Coleridge's?

In Xanadu did Kubla Khan

A stately pleasure-dome decree

Or the opening lines of the famous Australian ballad by Henry Kendall,

By channels of coolness the echoes are calling,

And down the dim gorges I hear the creek falling

My father's readings booked no interruption and we listened intently. We would shed a tear sometimes for the dog that drowned in *The Ballad of the Drover*, hugely enjoyed his more light-hearted reading of a poems such as *The Jackdaw of Rheims* and we wondered at the mysterious story of *Abou Ben Adhem*. But we never spoke a word when he gave forth those heartfelt readings.

I think my love affair with words began right there, if it didn't with mother's recitation, word perfect, of "Slip rails and the Spur." And of course, her singing—the truly melancholy rendition of "Come to Me My Melancholy Baby" or the more light-hearted "Little Mister Baggy Britches" when our baby brother was a bit fractious. I loved this quiet time in our house but best of all I loved to hear the poetry that seemed so natural to her or so important to my dad. Something was "lit up" so that the words seemed alive and singing and powerful or playful, like the surf of Maroubra Beach or Bondi that beat out a rhythm that dramatically pounded in my bones and in my blood. Even a disliked teacher, primly reading the famous Australian ballad by Banjo Patterson, "The Man From Snowy River" (later to become a movie), had its own inexorable charm. It all lay in the poetry itself! The power of words to evoke images, to make music and to make you feel so many emotions just by their saying, the way it did, was extraordinary to me. And still is. And the particular cadence and "truth" a good poem seems to hold in some magical way.

During my lifetime—as a child of the forties, an adolescent of the fifties and sixties—I was lucky to see Australian children's literature come into full flower. In fact, the seventies and eighties, as our publishing houses began publishing local voices, is a time described as the "Golden Age" of Australian children's literature by critic and revered elder in the field, Maurie Saxby. My library teacher at Maroubra Junction Girl's School in Sydney in the early 1950s would never have dreamed of such a thing, ever tidying those shelves of largely English adventure stories such as Enid Blyton's Famous Five. Classics like *Black Beauty, Anne of Green Gables,* and *The Secret Garden* rubbed spines with only a few Australian children's texts, among them such memorable names as Patricia Wrightson, Joan Phipson, and Nan Chauncy.

But it was really the well-worn "Billabong" series by Mary Grant Bruce and the equally well-worn work of Ethel Turner's series that I read over and over, attracted by serial narratives in an Australian setting. Television was something that had happened in America and had no bearing on our lives yet. So the characters of those books peopled our childhood. Reading was all-important and we could simply never have enough books. To this day I have several books on my bedside table and always travel "heavy," taking old friends that I might need near me and a clutch of new to some far-off city or country town that may not sport a bookshop.

But harking back, we lived in a small two bedroom house in Maroubra during my early childhood, a family of four children: Margaret, Elizabeth, Suzanne and Stephen. Everything was done at the old oak kitchen table, from homework to ironing to shelling peas. It wasn't until my older sister Margi went to high school that my mother bought us our first desk, which was to be communally owned, of course, and which fitted miraculously in the verandah sleep-out my sister and I shared. To me, it was luxury to have a place set apart specially for writing, not to mention the added pleasure of a set of drawers in the desk to be filled just with the accoutrements of writing. I loved touching the packet of envelopes, the writing pads (loose sheets of paper were a rarity), the floral stationery set I had been lucky enough to get for Christmas, the HB pencils, and opening the special spotted black-and-white case that housed my precious Conway Stewart fountain pen and matching propelling pencil.

When we reached high school, each child was given a 'good' pen-and-pencil set, instructed that it had been expensive to purchase and was expected to last us through all our high school days. My father owned a treasured maroon and silver Parker pen and I don't remember ever seeing him with another writing implement. We never shared pens, as we understood it could damage the unique way the user had shaped the nib. But I remember practising his distinctive signature and wishing I could use his fine pen to replicate the downstroke. "Light on the upstroke and heavy on the downstroke," our teachers endlessly instructed us, endeavouring for each and every child to achieve a "copperplate" writing style.

We were all readers in that house, though I was the only writer. That is, the only child that crept away to write her own stories or poems, finding a private though darkish space behind the big tapestry lounge chair in the lounge room, in our busy and noisy household.

In infants school, we were supplied readers, each child with the same one. I'd wrestled in Grade 1 with the boredom of Fay and Don, walking down English-style streets in English-type clothes and living in smart English-type bungalows with never a gum tree in sight. However, my Grade 2 Reader remains in mind as a pleasurable compilation of poems and stories, well-thumbed and well-loved. Dramatic stories about girls like Grace Darling, whose daring rescue of shipwrecked souls intrigued me, especially the idea that a girl could ride a horse into the surf and save people! And then the poems that were read aloud and "performed" in what was known as Verse Speaking—a lesson I found thrilling. Fragments of verse, and the particular intonation of my Grade 2 teacher Miss Hinder, have stayed with me a lifetime. "I shall lie in the reeds and hoooowl for your green glass bead, I love them so . . . give them me," and so on.

The readers were exhausted after a term and yet we were obliged to re-read around the class on a regular basis. And often the teacher requested we keep to the place, "finger on the word please" of the poor stumbling child selected to read aloud.

The introduction at home to Australian storybooks such as *Blinky Bill* and *Snugglepot and Cuddlepie* and the beloved Gumnutland host of characters was significant. Books that speak to children about the place they themselves know well, as Dorothy Wall and

May Gibbs did for me as young child, must have a lasting impression, and a lifelong significance. Here among Peter Rabbit and friends, Pooh Bear and friends and a host of Disney characters in far-flung settings, which were loved too, were stories of our own land, our bush, our city, our animals and our flora, very much our place.

I distinctly remember the thrill of pleasure at May Gibbs' gentle and environmentally friendly Gumnut-land stories, coupled with her charming Australian artwork of our own bottlebrush and gum trees and bush creatures. British books and British influence were still so strong in the 1950s, though things were slowly beginning to change in that regard, and the arts were reflecting this change, our burgeoning literature at the forefront in the naming (and thus the possessing) of things in our own landscape. This was a gradual process of relinquishing Britain and Europe as the centre of our world, and recognising our own country as an entity in itself, and Asian countries as our closest neighbours.

Having said that, much later in the 1990s it was still not easy to have children's books with an Asian theme published. I'd made plans to write a series I'd called Asiastory—six stories set in various Asian countries close to home—as a kind of interesting challenge. But it was to be more difficult than I'd imagined. The first one, a picture storybook set in Vietnam, *The Wishing Cupboard,* which was the first published story to go online in Australia, took six or seven years to find a publisher at Lothian. And it was only in 1999 that I had my book *The River,* which is set in China, launched in Shanghai through an educational publishing house, Curriculum Corporation. I've had four of the stories published to date, and am currently determinedly working on a Korean story.

*

In high school, we were steeped in English literature— from John Donne to the Romantics, our Shakespeare texts studied thoroughly over a whole year, so thoroughly we could quote whole tracts of it. There was not much modern poetry taught at school so I had to find that elsewhere. It was years later I was to discover the charms of other cultures. Translations of Spanish Lorca and Pablo Neruda, American poets like William Carlos Williams, Monica Dickens, and Hugh Langston, the Welsh poet Dylan Thomas, to mention a few.

Teachers had an enormous impact on my life right through my schooling. The shy and beautiful Miss Miller in Grade 1 (who, incidentally, I remember to this day never returned the book on China that my German grandfather gave the family and I proudly took to school, a beautiful book with the unusual treat of coloured pictures). It was important to actually own books but they were a rare treat as gifts. The ample and warm Mrs. Tanner (Grade 3) who always delayed to chat and laugh when my handsome father called to pick us up from school (a really unusual event) and who relentlessly encouraged the use of "good words." A memorable lesson was writing the words "got" and "said "on a piece of paper, going into the school garden which the kids attended to in Nature study lessons, and burying the words. "You can think of a better one to use in your compositions, girls!"

Then there was the principal, the chaotic Miss Swain (Grade 6) who loved to see the whole school march from assembly—where we saluted the flag and swore allegiance to the King of England and later the Queen—to military style music like "Colonel Bogey's March." She was generally a good-natured teacher, despite having the dual role of running the whole school. But she made what she called 'a terrible mistake' that we kids all paid for.

Every week we had to write a tightly structured two-page composition: opening paragraph, two more paragraphs using adverbial or adjectival phrases that were listed on the blackboard, and a closing paragraph that "tied off" all ends neatly. One memorable day, when she obviously hadn't had time to prepare the "strait-jacket," we were told, "Today girls, you may write an adventure story!" It was music to our ears. She did not mention any length at all, let alone an adverbial phrase.

Forty-five twelve-year-old girls, well schooled on Enid Blyton and her Famous Five adventure books and Ethel Turner's heart-rending *Seven Little Australians,* went to town. It was a black afternoon when our work was handed back to the class with cold and disapproving comments for each and every one of us.

At least half of us, wild with freedom, had written six or eight or even ten pages of story! She told us she refused to read beyond page three of any of them, that they were generally poor, undisciplined and imitative—well, yes! But then followed a diatribe when poor, hapless, overweight, unpopular, super-bright classmate Judith Meakin was made to stand up and explain why her "disgusting" story had featured something as horrific as murder. And not just one, this vile child had included three murders on board a launch in Sydney Harbour. She laboured the girl's inappropriate subject matter in a rage of disapproval, so humiliating that I'd have been reduced to tears. But Judith stood there, clutching the desk red-faced and, I'm certain, not understanding what all the fuss was about.

It seems laughable in this day and age of violence and death depicted on film and TV, including the news of the day, that a child writing a murder story could be so castigated. But the 1950s were the days before television in Australia, and straightlaced was the way you would describe suburban Maroubra. In any case, there was censorship about what books were allowed into the country (for example, D.H. Lawrence's *Lady Chatterly's Lover* could be read only by university professors even in my adolescence) and the press of the day could not refer directly to things such as a pregnancy. Poor Judith had no doubt read a diet of cheap thrillers and, in reflecting them in her own way, took the full fury of our teacher's annoyance at the outpourings of frustrated writers. I remember thinking then that Judith had been daring and that there was surely a power in a story that could make an adult so mad!

Endorsements for budding writers must have been important. I was in Year 4 when I received my first award, a purplish certificate for my penned (this was a dip pen and ink-penned story) from a large department store, Farmer's, that for some mysterious reason encouraged young Sydney writers. I believe I still have that certificate. But it was not for certificates I wrote the poems and stories that seemed to come from some mysterious source, poured out into precious exercise books where every page was covered, paper being in short supply and thus prized.

In the incredible paper affluence of my adulthood it's almost unimaginable to think how paper and pencils and pens were prized possessions. It was a luxury to have a Woolworth's Jumbo-sized writing pad. Single sheets such as our fax and computer paper were simply not available.

I knew more of British history at ten, twelve, fourteen years of age than I did of Australian history. Aboriginal history was for the most part shamefully ignored or, what little there was, often quite inaccurately presented. This was all to change dramatically when I reached college. But I must say I'm grateful to this day for that rich literary background afforded by our schools, which set up a continual love affair with writers of the stature of William Shakespeare and the Romantic poets, to mention but a few.

My sisters and I haunted libraries like the one in Maroubra with the unlikely and agreeable name of Quandong, where one paid, say, a shilling to borrow two books for a week. Later we traveled by bus a few suburbs away to the Randwick Public Library to take out our precious one book each. I was ten or eleven before Maroubra had a public library in the guise of the Mobile Library—a wondrous caravan of books that traveled some of the library-less suburbs of our area, hooking into the powerline to light up its intriguing interior and the eager knot of readers—and thus bring the demise of private libraries.

The brightness of some of those childhood memories may be somewhat enhanced by time, but images of us just being around books and readers are especially clear. Lying on the beds, long sunny afternoons totally immersed in Mary Grant Bruce's Billabong series, my big sister, head in a book, occasionally making a comment about the outback world and the characters we knew and loved. "I think I have a bit of crush on Wally," she might say.

"Well, I think I'm in love with Jim and I want to be Norah," I'd reflect.

"But they're brother and sister!" she'd tell me, usually having the last word.

I know as a big sister to Suzanne, three years my junior, I'd often read aloud to her. She always attests to my improving her reading comprehension, as I'd read some of our school-set novels (not my choice of fiction) such as *Black Arrow* or *The Hill,* and then each three pages or so I'd quiz her on what I'd read. "You really have to listen!" I'd threaten, "or I won't read to you anymore." Thus improving her concentration.

I love that idea of sharing other worlds and I believe that the act of reading allows us to share the dream. We can enter into another's thoughts and another's world as if it were our own.

Libby (center), with her sisters Margaret (left) and Suzanne

It's strange how certain memories of a less-happy kind remain imprinted. There was a procession of pets who had a great impact on the family. Though we longed to own a dog and my little sister Suzanne arrived home occasionally with a stray, we had cats and kittens! A series of cats were called variously Tiddles if male, or Skinny Minny if female. There was no commercially prepared petfood at the time, and the pets always ate the scraps from the family table and were generally more on the lean side compared to the cats I've owned since the advent of tinned petfood. With the birth of several batches of kittens, we ran out of willing recipients. Vets were not plentiful and the drowning of kittens was not unusual in our street, and was by far more merciful than dumping those hapless kittens in back lanes. But somehow neither of our parents could bring themselves to do the deed when we'd done our best but had clearly run our of prospective owners.

My mother's brother, Uncle Allen, was called to do the job. Not a particularly aggressive or bold man, he must nonetheless have had the requisite skills for kitten-drowning. It was done on the back step where all

the children gathered and I remember watching with a certain amount of fear mixed with an awful curiosity. We knew it was inevitable the kittens must go or became strays, uncared for, but how could you actually kill something that was alive and soft and warm? The dark, the cluster of children, the metal bucket, the tiny squirming still blind soft little creatures, Uncle Allen grim but resolute. The hapless mother, Skinny Minny, being cuddled somewhere else, the thought of death in the air, the realization of utter powerlessness. That's a vivid memory for me.

Another stark memory was being locked in. This was a holiday with my older sister Margaret, on a farm on the Nepean River at the foot of the Blue Mountains, where boy cousins were good company for most of the time. It was a dairy farm and magical to us city girls. I didn't realize the grind of 200 cows having to be milked morning and night and the effort this must have cost my uncle and his older son. We loved to come here as the days were long and filled with fun. We learned boys' sports, bows and arrows, the wonder of an air rifle and the game of mice trapping in a recently ploughed field. Then there was riding a tractor to the Nepean River and discovering the wonder of the fact that potatoes didn't grow on bushes but were grown under the ground.

The milking sheds were fascinating and to be visited most afternoons. The cows were always docile, there was a certain exciting smell, milky in the shed and overlain with the cow manure in the yard, the sound of the milking machines sucking away at so many cows' teats—probably thirty cows milked at a time. There was the added wonder of the separation room, and then the cold room, where huge metal milk drums were stored, waiting for pickup. Bruce, my cousin, was a good-natured boy, a year or so older, but he seized the opportunity one afternoon as we two visited the cold room to experience the shiveriness once again, to heave closed the thick metal door and leave us not only shivering in the cold, but marooned in the terror of utter darkness.

Screams were to no avail it seemed, and the few minutes we were incarcerated there seared some memory of terror forever. When he gleefully opened the door and we emerged, I was changed. I was shaking and couldn't speak and remained so, despite the sun on my arms and that comforting ordinary odour of cow manure, for some time. Once again it was the notion of facing death and knowing you were powerless. And worse still, not brave. Not in the least brave. Ever since then, I have felt a kind of panic at the idea of being closed in, and like at least a sliver of light at night when asleep.

*

My first year in high school I made a very special friend in Pat who had laughing eyes, a mop of black curly hair and an outrageous sense of humour. She also just happened to live not far around the corner from my house in Maroubra—a wonderful accident of fate. Some fifty years later we are still friends and still discussing some of the same issues about the arts, despite both having brought up our families separately. Ten years ago I tried to set down something of the preciousness of this relationship in my poem "Childhood Friend" from *Maroubra Cycle*. (*Maroubra Cycle* has been set to music by composer Stephen Lalor and was later performed under the direction of Paul Weingott at University of Technology—Sydney (UTS) as a musical, when I was writer-in-residence there).

> You were farewelling me,
>
> I saw you there
>
> Standing by the gate
>
> And heard your laughter
>
> Down the midnight road
>
> And thought
>
> A poem is there in you
>
> Standing, laughing
>
> Talking, delaying, beside
>
> The darkened paling fence
>
> So reminiscent of our childhood. . . .
>
> —"Childhood Friend"

Pat was "artistic" and dreamed of becoming a painter and our conversations over the adolescent years were always of the arts: debates, musings wondering as we fledgling artists tested our own theories in painting and writing in a world not much interested in two Maroubra lasses and their dreams. Pat illustrated my first picture storybook *Kyo,* which was the story of a much-loved dog of my mother's. Kyo, who gained this name from the New South Wales country town Kyogle, was a wonderful black-and-white terrier my mother swore could smile—at her, of course. She was picked up by the RSPCA when she wandered off one day from Tamarama Beach; we never saw Kyo again. My mother was inconsolable and in fact never had another dog, so Pat and I wrote a story about Kyo's wandering with a very happy ending. She was found! It wasn't even published but I have the original artwork to this day among my treasures.

I attended Teachers' College after an unsuccessful stint as a laboratory assistant in the Medical School at the University of Sydney. Two lecturers at Balmain Teachers' College—as it was then called before becoming part of UTS—greatly influenced my writing: Ray Cattell who moved to University of New South Wales as I arrived) and the principal, a tall, forbidding-looking gentlemen, Mr. Greenhalgh. It was the English lecturer at Balmain who introduced me to Ray Cattell after my poem won the College Poetry Prize. Ray in turn introduced me to the works of W.B. Yeats when I unwittingly cautioned him to "tread softly" on his criticisms of my own poetry. "Tread softly for you tread on my dreams" he quoted immediately and there began a love affair with works of Yeats. Visits to his home gave timely insight to my passionate but sometimes rambling first poetry, and he insisting I could make poetry my life's work. If only I didn't have to earn a living, I thought, though poetry I knew even then would remain central to my life and inform all my writing.

The other lecturer, the principal of the college, also stands out in my mind impressing me with his far-too-short series of lectures on philosophy and imploring us, the young students about to embark on our teaching lives, not to "walk through the fields with our gloves on," referring to a famous poem whose name eludes me. I remember buying Will Durant's *The Story of Philosophy* and a whole world opening up to me.

This was intensified by the advent of a soulful and totally engaging person in my life. It's true he was a man, several years older and much more sophisticated than I, but this seemed incredibly attractive to me in

As a young teacher, 1965

itself. With him I could discuss poetry and philosophy and many an evening we sat in the rose garden in Hyde Park; he was too poor to take me to dinner and I was but a poor college student. I listened to the wisdom of John C. It didn't occur to me that when we did go out to the movies or even to coffee that it was I who paid, and it was only years later that I understood why John became attracted to a woman closer to his age who had a smart apartment and a high-paying job. Still, I never regretted his flair for romance and his rather Oscar Wildish take on life.

My school friend Pat and I had discussed classical music but were introduced to the joys of ownership through a friend's dad who'd joined something called The World Record Club. *Brahms' Hungarian Dances* was the first 45 classical record that I ever purchased. Dad was mad about *The Student Prince,* as we all were, and I played it along with Beethoven symphonies. Later came admiration for Bach—I even purchased a small harmonium from a friend, Wendy's dad, who worked at the music shop Paling's, so I could learn to play Bach's Toccata and Fugue.

Saturday mornings, the three girls were expected to do the housework which consisted of vacuuming the house, scrubbing, polishing and—as custom had it in summertime—giving the whole house a good spray of Mortein Plus, which had just come onto the market, with a bright red large pump flyspray. Our work was made lighter by the stereogram, a large polished-wood affair with a lid that was raised to reveal the turntable, a side compartment for 33's and another for 78's and the smaller 45's. We'd put on the long-playing 33's (LP's) of which our parents had such delights as *Oklahoma, Carousel, South Pacific,* and *Showboat.* A favourite was an LP called *The Merry Widow,* considered classical music.

This didn't mean I wasn't in love with Elvis Presley or didn't dance to the new rock and roll. My novel,

Love Me Tender, reflects this time through the eyes of a young woman.

Round the corner at Pat's house, her mother had secured a real treasure of an LP, sent all the way from England, of Emlyn Williams reading Charles Dickens. Though I'd read *A Tale of Two Cities,* I was delighted by excerpts from *Pickwick Papers* and *Oliver Twist* read aloud to us gathered in the lounge room as we were to listen round the precious record player, before the advent of television in Australia of course.

The bookcase in the small lounge room of our house at Maroubra was cram-packed. My parents had sets of books alongside the novels, encyclopedias and dictionary (Webster's), a huge tome. Sets of science, philosophy (The Living Thoughts Library: of Thoreau, Descarts, Spinoza, etc.) alongside *Readers' Digest* series books and World War II books. These I remember were large clothbound with firm spines: *Soldiering On,* Army, Navy and Air Force accounts of the returned men, anxious to somehow tell something of their disquieting stories.

Arthur Mees' *Book of Everlasting Things* seems such a quaint idea in a world of computers with knowledge at your fingertips. Bu it was a much-loved tome, a book of wonder, despite its rather smudgy black-and-white photographs of sights such as the pyramids, or the Amazon River.

An aunt of mine was housekeeper for a very-well-off family in nearby Dover Heights and this was rather fortunate for us. The Rusten girls were readers, and we only imagined their life, as we never met them. But in a way I thought we had, for their names were often inscribed in the books that came our way. The Rustens gave our aunt the entire set of "Billabong" books by Mary Grant Bruce, doled out on birthdays and Christmases to eager recipients; twelve or fourteen of them that were published in Great Britain by Ward Lock. Some rather trashy love stories such as *Broken Wings* by F.J. Thwaites found their way onto our shelves, made all the more meaningful because of the fact that our mother admitted she had once or twice gone out with him as a young man.

Shy the Platypus by Lesley Reece was another treasure. I was to later meet Lesley at the Fremantle Children's Literary Centre in 1997, and to learn that as a young journalist he'd actually interviewed James Joyce in Paris.

My story *The Day TV Came* was published by the Museum of Contemporary Art when it opened to an exhibition celebrating the coming of television to Australia in the 1950s; though fictional, it tried to capture some of the wonder of film on tap in one's own house. Our television, like our record player, was a substantial piece of furniture—two wooden doors in a cabinet with fake gold handles, opening to reveal a screen below which giant knobs conveyed us to worlds beyond our world, albeit in black and white. When our family bought a television in 1959, we were transfixed by any and every program. Sunday nights were family occasions when we gathered for a TV dinner generally, toasted tomato and cheese on specially designed TV plates, either made in a waffle iron or in our dad's new-fangled griller. Bought from a door-to-door salesman, the Spaceship, so named for its shape, could grill anything to a crisp, from sausages to sandwiches. One of the features of Sunday evening viewing was *Wonderful World of Disney* and eating toasted "samos" as our dad called them, toasted to perfection on the Spaceship. Or during the week watching exciting American shows like *77 Sunset Strip, The Fugitive, Maverick, I Love Lucy,* or *Father Knows Best.* There were very few Australian shows. *Homicide,* the first cop show, comes to mind as well as a copycat Saturday afternoon *Bandstand* where you could watch people your own age rock and rolling—and even get a ticket to go out to Gore Hill and become part of the audience that was filmed! If you were brave enough.

*

As a young woman I began writing poetry, hesitatingly at first given the models of such accomplishment I'd had. I was drawn to write about what I knew, events and landscapes and people and all the strange yet somehow "ordinary" miracles that Walt Whitman so cleverly describes in his poem of that name. Poetry writing was a major pastime but I began keeping notebooks, fragments of conversation, dreams, reflections. I remember a line of poetry I wrote when I was eighteen years old that said though I, too, longed for Europe, I wanted to know my own country and that henceforth I was "stepping out into Australian times."

In a lustful search for a diversity of texts after my school years and whilst at college, I began consciously exploring Australian literature, particularly poetry. The work of Judith Wright, David Campbell, John Shaw Neilsen, Christopher Brennan. I still keep a raggedy copy of that very first *Penguin Anthology of Australian Verse* that introduced to me to the wealth of Australian voices. Later at college I began to explore more contemporary voices, the likes of Les Murray, Gwen Harwood, Elizabeth Riddell and Peter Porter. The wonderful old bookshop on Pitt Street in Sydney, Angus & Robertson's with its polished linoleum covered basement where poetry and plays resided, became a place of miraculous discoveries. As did the magical little Rowe Street with its first coffee shops and book shops and records imported from overseas for which you'd have to save to buy.

Translations by Arthur Waley and Ezra Pound of Chinese poetry, and that extreme jewel of verse, the Japanese haiku, were discovered in Rome Street. This largesse, along with the newly translated novels of European authors such as André Gide and Thomas Mann, Albert Camus and a whole range of Russian novelists from Tolstoy to Chekhov and Dostoyevsky. My head was hardly ever out of a book and it was a wonder I graduated from college at all. When I did I was to discover the real joys of teaching and must say that my first year at Bankstown Primary School was a year of wonders. Despite the rigours of the timetable imposed then (thirty minutes for this and twenty-five for that, and woe betide you if you didn't teach the said subject at the said hour) I found I could encourage poetry writing with my nine year olds—45 of them in a room designed to take up to fifty pupils! This was 1964 and classes were large.

I remember distinctly the exciting drives to Bankstown Public School (a long train and bus ride from my home at Tamarama Beach) with my new friend Wendy Stites. She was a young teacher at Bankstown Infants who was lucky enough to own a car, a VW Beetle, with whom I shared petrol money and long conversations. We talked of life and love at length being young women at the time, alongside the joys of art and poetry, and how we could influence the kids we taught. She was later to marry Australian filmmaker Peter Weir and devote all her creative passion to design and wardrobe for movies.

At this time I was going out with a young medical student, Ron Gray, of Polish parentage (his mother had promptly changed their name on arrival as a migrant to Australia) who shared this love of the arts and especially of poetry, and gave into my hands some treasure tomes from his own bookcase. I still have the

poetical works Rainer Maria Rilke he parted with somewhat reluctantly, because I'd told him the book was not to be had in any Sydney bookshop and I loved the work so much. Forbidden movies in Trade Union Hall (*Quiet Flows the Don*) or "continental movies" as we called them, like *Virgin Spring* or *La dolce vita* at the the Savoy, Lido or the Paris Theatre, where at interval there was the luxury of buying Italian coffee, were part and parcel of the discovery of "other times."

Ron was an extraordinarily clever fellow academically, but I remember his frustration at not being able to paint or write poetry and sometime a flash of annoyance when I'd produce some writing about a place we'd visited together—the fir forest where we'd camped or the Blue Mountains where we'd taken long bracing walks. He was a loving person to me and I am glad to have had such a strong and tender relationship over three or four years of growing up time. But it was through him I realised that understanding and loving poetry or fiction was not enough, that there was another dimension that has nothing to do with the will, and that perhaps in some miraculous and inexplicable way, writing had chosen me!

I broke my medical student's heart when after four years and with our inevitable marriage in sight, I met John Hathorn, a teacher seven years my senior, dashing, romantic, and persuasive. But there was grief for me too, in that break, as I felt Ron was part of my most formative years and intoxicated though I was with John's energy and excitement, there were moments of real longing to see Ron again.

My own writing in that time consisted of largely unpublished poetry. I remember the thrill of first acceptance in *The Poetry Journal,* then managed by poet Grace Perry, of my first poem. This coincided with meeting John, my husband to be, at the school I'd been transferred to, Bellevue Hill Primary School. In those first heady days of our relationship I expressed my desire to be a writer—and a published writer at that!—and explained that it was central to my life. After we were married in 1968, John Hathorn, being a practical soul, suggested that I begin my foray into publishing by writing textbooks. We worked together on the first little books for infants and then I decided I'd write up all the marvellous work the children were capable of in poetry, and *Go Lightly,* my first substantial book, was published. As I was not fully confident to "go it alone," John was actually listed as coauthor. He had,

Engaged to John Hathorn, 1966

after all, I reasoned, trialled all the poetry techniques written up in the book.

The birth of my children, daughter Lisa in 1970 and then Keiran in 1973, changed our lives once again. I could not think about writing, especially children's books, in the same way. Bringing up children enlivens your perceptions and memories of your own childhood, feeding the fires.

The seventies saw a new confidence in the arts that we all responded to. We'd left behind to some extent the "outback image" that had been promulgated through books and movies, and began to record our urban and indeed our multicultural experiences as wave after wave of migrants settled into the cities, impacting on the Australian way of life. It seemed to young artists unburdened by the weight of a long European history

that we were free to go in any direction. But Australian children were still largely invisible in the body of literature available to them and I think myself lucky to have been writing at the time that publishers acknowledged that "gap."

I had been a classroom teacher but moved into the role of librarian in the primary school where I worked now at Drummoyne, a significant move on my part. Librarianship suited my addiction to books and story and gave me an up-to-the-minute overview of what children were reading. I was very much aware that we needed books about our place, the city as well as the country. I read hundreds of books and was delighted by some Australian novels by Colin Thiele and Ivan Southall, some early Australian picture storybooks like Lydia Pender's *Barnaby's Rocket,* and the Aboriginal tales *The Rainbow Serpent* by Dick Roughsey.

Looking back, there were two particular writers I discovered in well-stacked shelves who I think deeply influenced my own writing. A series of readers by the English writer Leila Berg, which told hilarious stories of working class kids and their parents, opened my eyes to the way ordinary folk could be written about and also to the fact that ordinary folk were not really well represented in Australian children's literature. And then the work of the Dutch writer Meindert de Jong with his wonderful novel, *Journey from Peppermint Street,* and for younger readers *Nobody Plays with a Cabbage.* These were sensitive stories written in spare and beautiful prose and they truly inspired me. I also noticed at this time some very "cool" paperbacks books for struggling readers by a certain Paul Jennings were being very well borrowed from the library, Paul to become a legend in his own lifetime with a series of hilarious novels some years later.

*

It all happened at a party, whose I don't recall, but I was introduced to a young man who worked for an English publishing company, Methuen, who had an office in Sydney. And yes, he'd talk to the children's editor there about a book I was writing.

Stephen's Tree was my first picture storybook. It was set at my brother's then garden market in Waverley, a veritable rainforest of ferns and trees and Australian plants right in the heart of the suburbs. I was thrilled to have a work of fiction underway but I had to debate long and hard with Methuen about having a gum tree central to the story. They strongly advised a beech, ash or elm so the work would sell better in England! It was important for me to have the gum tree but it was equally important to be published.

My first children's book editor, the gentle but resolute Liz Fulton, must have argued well, for a gum tree it was! The book was launched at our local Waverley Library by Peter Weir, who'd already begun to make his name with his first movie, *Picnic at Hanging Rock,* and all Sandra Laroche's delicate depictions of gum trees and kids were exhibited. The book attracted much media attention not only because it was about an Australian tree but also because *Stephen's Tree* was a publishing experiment. The publisher, responsive to our multicultural society of largely Greek and Italian migrants, published *Stephen's Tree* in dual text ver-

sions, both Greek and Italian! This experiment was repeated with *Lachlan's Walk.* Though the books sold well in the English version, the dual language was not a great seller and sad to say, the idea of dual texts was canned!

This connection to Waverley Library for my first-ever book launch was auspicious. Sanrda illustrated my next children's picture storybook *Lachlan's Walk,* set at Watson's Bay and based on a true story about my sister's son Lachlan wandering away from home towards a dangerous cliffside park. It too, was launched at Waverley Library by cartoonist Bruce Petty. And it was to be there at the library that I became aware of the outstanding work of illustrator Julie Vivas through enthusiastic children's librarian, Roniet Myerthal. Julie had an exhibition of her watercolours and after I'd seen her work, Roniet arranged a meeting where I invited Julie to illustrate my next book *The Tram to Bondi Beach,* to be set in the 1930s, the time of paperboys and trams in Sydney.

Julie assured me that her art was not suitable for children's literature, but I thought differently and asked to show some of her work to my Methuen publishers, who immediately agreed with me that she would make a fine partner for the text. Julie had a tough time of it family-wise the year she undertook her superb illustrations for the story, her first picture book, for her husband was away in Spain and she had two small children to look after. We visited the Loftus, the Tram Museum south of Sydney, to get reference photographs because by that time, in 1980s, trams had disappeared from the Sydney streets. Here the children Ana and Kate, along with my children Lisa and Keiran, acted as models for paperboys and passengers. *The Tram to Bondi Beach,* launched by Maurie Saxby, was highly commended by the Children's Book Council of Australia (CBCA), and Julie's new career was begun. The then NSW Film and Television group wanted to make a movie of *Tram* with its setting in the Depression in Bondi. I wrote the first filmscript filled with hope about the possibility of Julie's marvellous artwork and my story, but it was to be one of those many movie projects that only "almost" came off.

During this time in the seventies with two children and a teacher-librarian career, I was fortunate on the home front to have the help of a wonderful woman my mother's age who came to stay for three weeks and stayed instead over a period of twenty years. Without

The author's children, Christmas, 1979: (front) Lisa and (back right) Keiran, with their friend Isabelle

Paddy's help, her organisation of household matters, her sense of humour and her winning ways with little children, I could not have given such time to my own writing. She became a treasured family member at our house and though elderly now, is still interested to hear every scrap of information about our children, Lisa and Keiran.

Back in the eighties as my own children were growing older—though it's true I'm forever interested in picture storybooks—I began to write "chapter books," or what we called junior novels, for young readers. *All about Anna,* which recalled my Maroubra childhood and was where I consciously placed a girl as an adventurous main character, won honours in the CBCA awards. This was followed by a fantasy, *The Extraordinary Magics of Emma McDade,* the first of my short novels to be translated into Korean, and was similarly short-listed for awards. *Paolo's Secret* in 1985 was written to portray the loneliness of some children in the school

yard when limited by language. As a teacher-librarian in an inner city school I was very much aware of this situation for shy children who found the prospect of the playground daunting. But the novel that was to change my life in the late eighties, and indeed take me all the way to Hollywood, was written for young adult readers and was strongly inspired by the bushland setting of the central coast of New South Wales.

Thunderwith was written in 1988 on my brother's farm in the Wallingat Forest, which is north of Sydney. This is the story of the loss and alienation of a young girl named Lara, as she has to come to terms not only with the death of a beloved mother, but with her dad's new family and a hostile new stepmother. Its setting is uniquely Australian and when my agents Curtis Brown offered it for publication, in 1988, the 10,000-dollar advance paid by the publisher Heinneman was then considered the largest ever given in Australia for a children's book.

Immediately there were offers for movie options from three Australian companies and it was finally optioned Southern Star Xanadu. Sandra Levy (currently the head of the Australian Broadcasting Company) was the producer of Xanadu then, and I would have been more than happy to work with her as she had such a sensitivity to the story, but there was to be a lull in movie-making which meant it was difficult to get finances together. In the meantime, *Thunderwith* the novel travelled well into Europe, being bought in Holland and Denmark, Sweden and Great Britain, then was also published in the United States and was serialized in India. It went into reprint several times in its first year, picking up honours in the CBCA awards, too. But it was the offer by Hallmark Hall of Fame in the United States in the late nineties to make a television movie, and to have me as the writer, that was the most exciting news for this story. Several meetings in Hollywood with producer Dick Welsh indicated that they wanted me to write a treatment for the movie placing Gladwyn, the mother, central to the story. This was because their demographic was largely adult females, they told me, and for family viewing.

Armed with some how-to-write-movies guidebooks back home, I took off to Seal Rocks and the Wallingat and began the arduous task of writing a movie script to please my producers. Later, American writers were brought on to finish the script and though I was disappointed, I knew I'd reached a time when I simply couldn't make any more changes and still feel it was my story.

Simon Wincer, as director, had chosen Victoria, his home state, rather than New South Wales where the story is actually set. My husband John, who had become ill with leukaemia, had been under heavy treatment and though in remission, had little energy at this time. He encouraged me to take our daughter Lisa and visit the set. It was amazing to go on the set at Mt. Beauty in Victoria to see a whole property changed, roads built, a farmhouse and outhouses constructed, palms planted to create a plantation, a dam built, to mention just a few of the wonders that happened. Judy Davis played a marvelous Gladwyn and was nominated for an Emmy for her performance in *The Echo of Thunder,* as it was called. Lauren Hewitt made a strong Lara and Emily Browning (later starring in *Lemony Snicket*) made her film debut as an engaging young Opal. *Thunderwith* today is still one of my best-selling novels and is a set text in many schools across Australia.

*

In the mid-nineties John had retired from school and we traveled widely, including living in a loft in Mulberry Street in New York, whilst I made better contact with my then agent Laura Blake at Curtis Brown. During that time I met Little Brown's Maria Modugno who had taken both *Thunderwith* and *Grandma's Shoes,* and later Simon and Schuster's Virginia Duncan who had taken *Sky Sash So Blue.* Virginia, moving to Greenwillow, was to hand over to Stephanie Owens Lurie but told me in a farewell letter that *Sky Sash* was the best children's story she'd ever worked on! Stephanie was incredibly enthused and put Benny Andrew's wonderful artwork for the cover of *Sky Sash* on their S&S catalogue. Whilst in New York I also visited the office of the legendary Margaret McElderry who told me how she'd enjoyed reading *Thunderwith.* It was a great visit, at the end of which came the American offers for the movie of *Thunderwith.*

Another book that had a huge impact was my picture storybook *Way Home.* It was inspired by the sight of a boy in the underground in London who was begging at the bottom of the giant escalators. He seemed incredibly young to be there alone. I boarded the train and began thinking of my own children safe and sound in a Midland farmhouse, and wrote a poem about a boy called Shane that was to become the basis of the text of *Way Home.* Mark McLeod, who was a publisher with Random House then, loved the text and magically brought the illustrator Gregory Rogers and me together. We traversed the streets of Sydney taking photographs as source material and then Greg returned to Brisbane, where he worked over his amazing artwork that was to win the much-coveted Kate Greenaway Medal in the United Kingdom.

That it was an Australian artist illustrating and Australian text has always amazed and pleased me. It also won a Parents' Choice in America. Praise for the book in Britain and the United States, where it was also published, was high. Luminaries such as Jeremy Briggs and Anthony Browne had positive things to say about it, and after meeting Anthony at an Australian conference, he invited me to send a text I might think suitable for his work. The reviews for *Way Home* in Australia were not generally good, and it garnered no honours here in any award. But the book has remained in print ever since and is a set text in many schools. The theatre company Barking Gecko produced a play I'd written based on the book with music by a composer Stephen Lalor, whom I'd worked with over the years and who has set much of my children's poetry to music. It remains one of my favourites.

At the same time, taken up with the reports I was reading on homeless kids around the world, and surprised at the number in Australia, I wrote *Feral Kid.* This is a young-adult novel about an older boy who is homeless, and it was to be optioned by Hallmark Hall of Fame, as well.

On our travels, John and I lived in Holland for a few months in a wonderful apartment on the Prinsengracht found by my Dutch publishers at Ploegsma. There we met the delightful Nanny Brinkman, at this time still the head of the company, and her husband Paul, who gave us much of his time in showing us Holland. Nanny had taken my novels *Thunderwith* and *Feral Kid* and later *The Climb.* Their own house on the Kaisergracht, a huge former merchant's home, was a wonder to us with its ample, beautifully furnished rooms and its rooftop garden with views of Amsterdam all around.

I was inspired at the Vincent van Gogh Museum in Amsterdam to write my novel *The Painter,* based on the imagined life of an adolescent would-be painter, Bernard, who meets Vincent in Arles and whose life is changed by this encounter. Every morning I'd get on

Writing Thunderwith *in the Wallingat Forest, 1998*

the tram to the Museum whilst John hunted antiques and, in the library there, undertake the delightful task of reading Vincent's letters, and then viewing letters that the offspring of his models had written and so on. John and I felt we could have stayed in Amsterdam forever. I had previously signed a six-book contract with publishers Hodder Headline in Australia, and my novels were in the hands of a wonderful children's publisher, Belinda Bolliger. I still consult with Belinda on all my work and trust her judgment particularly when it comes to editing.

Picture storybook texts are the closest thing to poetry for me and I'll always want to write them. But it is a pretty amazing thing when they move from picture storybook to opera. *Grandma's Shoes,* which was published in Great Britain and the United States and has been published twice in Australia with two different artists (one of Belinda's choice), was to become the first children's opera performed in Australia in the new millennium. This is the story of a young girl's search for her grandmother, wearing her precious shoes, and deals with the loss of a beloved family member in a consoling way. There is even an air of triumph for the little girl as she pledges to take up her grandma's storytelling skills.

Not only did I approach Opera Australia with the story text and the idea for an opera, but through my editor at Oxford University Press, Rita Scharf, I had an auspicious meeting with Kim Carpenter, director of Theatre of Image. Kim loved the text and encouraged me to write the libretto. He introduced me to Graeme Koehne, an Adelaide composer whose work is known world-wide. We gained support from Opera Australia by way of musicians and singers, rehearsal spaces and advertising. *Grandma's Shoes* had a Kim Carpenter setting of a giant book out of which stepped all the characters, and his puppets and backdrop of animations made it a truly wonderful performance. It played to full houses and later I was thrilled to receive an AWGIE award from the Australian Writers Guild for this libretto. And later to receive a Prime Minister's Millennium Award for 2000.

The author with her husband, John, in Monet's garden, Giverny, 1996

Opera is expensive and difficult to mount so it was with some delight in 2003 that I received an invitation from Alabama to have my text for my picture story-book *Sky Sash So Blue,* published by Simon & Schuster in 1999 in the States, used as libretto. This picture storybook, embellished so lovingly by the artwork of Benny Andrews, is a celebration of freedom; it was inspired by reading Toni Morrison's powerful novel *Beloved* and is set in the same period of slavery in the deep south. The invitation was from a music lecturer at Miles, an all-black college, in Birmingham, Alabama. Phillip Ratliffe had plans for a children's opera using the text already written in verse.

We undertook a long correspondence by e-mail and eventually Philip announced that not only had he almost completed the opera but that he'd secured the funds for its performance in November, 2004. The visit, which enabled me to see the rehearsals and the calibre of opera singers and chamber orchestra, was an exciting one, for it was my first experience of the south. But I must admit that on first hearing Philip's

startling atonal music I wondered how young people—some as young as Grade 2—would respond. However, a group of teachers using Maxine Green's music, of the Lincoln Centre reputation, as an inspirational aesthetic education model had fully prepared their students.

So on the day of performance around 700 African-American students enjoyed the opera with its sparse set and accomplished singers and the use of a long, trailing sky sash of deep blue. In 2005, I had more correspondence from Phillip, to indicate *Sky Sash So Blue* will be performed again. This has been made possible by the Cultural Alliance and the Division of Humanities at Miles College, with in-kind donations from the Birmingham Museum of Art, UAB, Midfield Schools, and the Alabama School of Fine Arts. Miracles do happen!

*

I have been fortunate over the years in invitations to speak in other countries and often am asked if this is the stuff of inspiration. If it's true that settings do have a huge impact, you never know whether you are going to be found by a story no matter how dramatic or how different the landscape. My initial visit to Papua New Guinea visit was to launch the region's first ever PNG Children's Book Fair in 1994. After a tour of some of the schools in Port Moresby, accompanied by an Australian journalist who lived there, I was taken to various island schools and touched by the enthusiasm with which a writer was greeted in schools that often lacked libraries and were even sometimes short of notepaper.

On the volcanic island of Rabaul, viewing the terrifying outcome of the 1993 eruption and talking to the locals, I was inspired for my verse novel *Volcano Boy,* though it wasn't to be written until many years later. The following year in 1995, I was invited to run a writing course on the marvelous island of Madang in Papua, New Guinea, and had my first experience of snorkeling in a truly tropical place. I couldn't wait for my workshops to be over, to run helter skelter to my cabin change into swimming gear and spend hours, head in the water, in a world that was dramatically lovely strange and inspirational. At home, my son, who had undertaken a scuba diving course, had enthused about the underwater world being a great subject for a novel. And it was strange that after a cult leader in California had enticed a group of his followers, some of them quite young, to commit suicide together, and I'd seen a video of his "explanation" to them, that all these things came together in the novel *Rift.*

An author tour organized by the Australia Council in 1997 took revered Australian writer David Malouf and Gillian Mears and me to India for a marvelous three weeks. Visiting bookshops and universities, we had speaking engagements in New Delhi, Bangalore, Madras (now Chennai), and Bombay (now Mumbai). We were met by writers in each of these places and had two each of our own books launched there by Senator Alston, the then minister for the arts. The impact of India on the tourist has been attested to many times. Suffice to say we were enthralled by the diversity, delighted by our hosts, upset by the poverty that was so apparent and yet charmed by the generosity of those we met. However, we were so programmed as to never get to see the Taj Mahal, something I'd always dreamt of visiting, and where I was sure a story would be lurking.

One fortunate connection I'd made was with a printer at an ashram at Pondicherry famous for the quality of

With authors David Malouf and Gillian Mears, Chennai, India, 1997

the paper it produced. To and fro communication indicated they'd do a limited edition of a book of my poems on especially chosen paper of a generous thickness, with petal impressed endpapers and a handmade binding in Hablik cloth.

Invited to speak at the prestigious International Board of Books for Young People (IBBY) Conference, which was to be held in New Delhi, India, I returned the next year, 1998, this time with my friend Pat and my two sisters Margaret and Suzanne, who had heard my enthusiastic descriptions of this exotic culture. This time, after IBBY, I determined to make the journey to Agra as well as one to the equally famed Lake Palace. India simply seduced us as we moved from place to place, dazzled by all we saw and especially the Taj Mahal which was all and more than I'd expected.

I'd met a charming publisher at IBBY and was invited to present my text set at the Taj Mahal to her small, brave children's publishing house, Tulika Books, just getting underway in Chennai. *A Face in the Water* is a timeslip story which takes an historic view of the building of the Taj and stars the daughter of the

Hathorn with her son, Kieran, and daughter, Lisa (holding baby Ruby Rose), Dorrigo, New South Wales, 2004

emperor Shah Jahan and two present-day Australian kids.It was illustrated by a young Indian artist Uma Krishnaswamy and published in India in 2000.

We visited Pondicherry and the ashram where *Heard Singing* was to be printed on hand-made paper. Australian paper-cutting artist Brigitte Stoddard's delicate work in Australian wildflowers graced this limited edition. Brigitte eventually illustrated my junior novel, *Okra and Acacia; The Story of the Wattle Pattern Plate,* based on the Chinese legend "The Story of the Willow Patter Plate," which was published by Hodder Headline. A wonderful hand-sewn hessain wrapped bundle of poetry books eventually arrived in Sydney from India and it gave me a great deal of pleasure to have seen the whole process and to know that I had been able to influence the look and feel of *Heard Singing.* Gifts were made of the book, some were sold and it remains a favourite book on my own shelves.

My husband John died in 1998 when leukaemia he'd contracted in 1996 re-occurred. He had been fighting it for two years and his bravery in the face of a bone marrow transplant was amazing, though so difficult to witness, as he remained positive in the face of all his trials. I've tried to write a book about our last overseas journey together in 1997 between his treatments, where we lived for a short time in a magical chateau in Normandy, John collecting antiques whilst I wrote a filmscript; but somehow that book is still unfinished.

There have been some big life changes in that time both at home and in my work. Both my children are with partners and in fact I'm grandmother to a baby girl, Ruby Rose (inspiration for storybooks of course). My son Keiran working in Information Technology has inspired me to work on interactive stories. Our small company has released two CD-ROMs thus far. The first one, *Weirdstop,* which comprises stories of the weird variety for ten-to fourteen-year-olds, immediately won the Australian Interactive Media Industry Award for Best New Children's Product in 2003. *Coolstop* which links sport and literacy was launched by an Olympic medallist in late 2004, and we're currently working on a game and story for younger readers we've called *Wonderstop*, which is environmental in approach. A whole new world of writing and producing has opened up.

This does not mean that I'm not writing story books. My historic novel *Georgiana* is still underway, as is a new picture storybook; whilst last year saw the launch of children's picture storybook *The Great Big Animal Ask* by film producer Rebel Penfold Russell. I'm also working on a poetry Web site, which is a long overdue project with notes for parents and teachers as to how to "turn kids on to poetry!" You see, poetry has rewarded me in every possible way. Writer Shirley Hazzard has attested that poetry changes things. And there's no doubt in my mind that those early poetry sessions with our parents, the reading and the reciting, always having poetry books to hand that illuminated my world, and taking on poetry as a significant companion has been the greatest influence on my writing, and indeed on all of my life.

BIOGRAPHICAL AND CRITICAL SOURCES:

BOOKS

Hathorn, Libby, *Talks with My Skateboard,* Australian Broadcasting Corp., 1991.
St. James Guide to Children's Writers, 5th edition, edited by Sara Pendergast and Tom Pendergast, St. James Press (Detroit, MI), 1999, pp. 482-483.
Saxby, Maurice, *The Proof of the Puddin': Australian Children's Literature, 1970-1990,* Ashton Scholastic, 1993, pp. 219-221.

PERIODICALS

Australian Bookseller and Publisher, March, 1992, p. 26.
Booklist, February 15, 1998, p. 1019.
Books for Keeps, November, 1996, p. 10.
Bulletin of the Center for Children's Books, April, 1991, Robert Strang, review of *Thunderwith,* p. 194; May, 1998, pp. 322-323.

Children's Book Review Service, August, 1998, review of *Sky Sash So Blue,* pp. 164-165.
Horn Book, March-April, 1989, Elizabeth S. Watson, review of *Freya's Fantastic Surprise,* p. 199; July, 1989, Karen Jameyson, review of *The Tram to Bondi Beach,* p. 474; July, 1991, Elizabeth S. Watson, review of *Thunderwith,* p. 462; July-August, 1998, p. 472.
Junior Bookshelf, October, 1990, p. 232.
Magpies, March, 1990, Karen Jameyson, review of *Thunderwith,* p. 4; March, 1993, p. 31; July, 1998, Jane Connolly, review of *Rift,* p. 38; November, 1999, p. 38; November, 1999, Annette Dale Meiklejohn, "Know the Author: Libby Hathorn," pp. 10-13.
Publishers Weekly, May 17, 1991, review of *Thunderwith,* p. 65; August 1, 1994, p. 79; December 18, 1995, p. 53; June 22, 1998, p. 91.
School Librarian, August, 1996, Mary Hoffman, review of *Juke-box Jive,* p. 105.
School Library Journal, July, 1989, Marianne Pilla, review of *The Tram to Bondi Beach,* p. 66; August, 1989, Louise L. Sherman, review of *Freya's Fantastic Surprise,* p. 120; May, 1991, p. 111; October, 1994, p. 123; March, 1996, p. 189; June, 1998, Carol Ann Wilson, review of *Sky Sash So Blue,* p. 108.
Times Literary Supplement, July 23, 1982, Ann Martin, "Encouraging the Excellent," p. 792.
Voice of Youth Advocates, June, 1991.

OTHER

Libby Hathorn Web site, http://www.libbyhathorn.com (January 26, 2005).

*   *   *

HATZFELD, Jean 1949-

PERSONAL: Born 1949, in Madagascar.

ADDRESSES: *Home*—Paris, France. *Agent*—c/o Author Mail, Farrar, Straus and Giroux, 19 Union Square West, New York, NY 10003.

CAREER: Journalist. *Libération* (daily newspaper), France, journalist, beginning 1977; left daily journalism, c. 1994. Directed four television documentaries.

AWARDS, HONORS: Prix Culture 2000, Prix Pierre Mille, and Prix France Culture, all for *Dans le nu de la vie,* 2000; Prix Femina, essay category, 2003, and Prix Jossef Kessel, 2004, both for *Une saison de machettes.*

WRITINGS:

L'air de la guerre: sur les routes de Croatie et de Bosnie-Herzégovine, Editions de L'Olivier (Paris, France), 1994.

La guerre au bord du fleuve (novel), Editions de L'Olivier (Paris, France), 1999.

Dans le nu de la vie: récits des marais rwandais, Seuil (Paris, France), 2000, translated as *Into the Quick of Life: The Rwandan Genocide—The Survivors Speak,* Trans-Atlantic Publications, 2005.

Une saison de machettes: récits, Seuil (Paris, France), 2003, translated as *Machete Season: The Killers in Rwanda Speak: A Report,* Farrar, Straus & Giroux (New York, NY), 2005.

Contributor to *L'Autre Journal, Géo, Actuel, Rolling Stone,* and *Autrement.*

SIDELIGHTS: Jean Hatzfeld was born in Madagascar but later moved with his family when they returned to the Auvergne region of France. He worked as a journalist for the French daily *Libération* from 1977 until sometime in the 1990s, and covered political upheavals in Poland, the former Czechoslovakia, and Romania. He also served as a war correspondent in the Middle East and the former Yugoslavia, where he was injured in a Kalashnikov attack. His first two books are set in the former Yugoslavia: *L'air de la guerre: sur les routes de Croatie et de Bosnie-Herzégovine,* and the novel *La guerre au bord du fleuve.* Other work have taken Hatzfeld to Haiti, Congo, Algeria, Burundi, and Iran. In 1994 Hatzfeld reported on the genocide taking place in Rwanda. He later decided to concentrate all of his work on this subject and quit his job as a daily reporter. In the award-winning book *Dans le nu de la vie: récits des marais rwandais,* which was translated as *Into the Quick of Life: The Rwandan Genocide—The Survivors Speak,* he collects stories from Tutsi survivors. The book was followed by *Une saison de machettes: récits,* which also won awards in France. This publication offers the perspective of ten Hutu men who killed their Tutsi neighbors.

Une saison de machettes was translated as *Machete Season: The Killers in Rwanda Speak: A Report.* The title refers to the speed of the slaughter and a common method of killing. During the course of three months, about 800,000 Rwandans from the Tutsi tribe were killed by fellow citizens from the Hutu tribe. Because many of the murderers were poor farmers, they were skilled with machetes and often used them to cut down their victims. Hatzfeld interviewed ten Hutu men from the village of Nyamata who had taken part in the killing, these discussions taking place while they were serving sentences in prison. The men reveal how propaganda on talk radio and financial incentives were perhaps more important than coercion in turning Hutus against Tutsis. They also show a shocking lack of guilt, as well as a surprising expectation of being forgiven upon their release.

In reviews, the translation was described as an important, unusual, and frightening book. "Hatzfeld has a remarkable ability to pry into the killer's memory and conscience," a *Publishers Weekly* critic remarked. In *Kirkus Reviews* a critic called the book "a trove for future historians and ethnographers . . . and eye-opening, sobering reading for the rest of us." *Washington Post* writer Alison Des Forges commented that "this imperfect but devastating book tells us more about the how of genocide than the why. It lets us listen to the bean farmers but tells us too little about their fears to make us understand why these ordinary people committed extraordinary crimes." According to *Salon.com* reviewer Suzy Hansen, "*Machete Season* is realistic and, above all else, terrifying; Hatzfeld brilliantly organises his subjects' stories for maximum effect. His method captures the rhythm of a genocide—the cold, workmanlike, fierce nature of its repetition."

Hatzfeld told *CA:* "I don't know what first got me interested in writing because I've written since adolescence. It was probably because I didn't like to speak; probably also to feel less alone or to try to charm the girls. Now, it's a wonderful job for me; I am unable to do anything else. As a journalist, my main influence is the American tradition of writer/novelist/reporter in the last century; as novelist, I don't know—so many writers. There are two surprising things I've learned as a writer: First, the ideas come often when writing, not before; and secondly, the writer never knows how his book, or his report, will be read."

BIOGRAPHICAL AND CRITICAL SOURCES:

PERIODICALS

Kirkus Reviews, April 1, 2005, review of *Machete Season: The Killers in Rwanda Speak: A Report,* p. 399.
Publishers Weekly, April 4, 2005, review of *Machete Season,* p. 50.
San Francisco Chronicle, June 26, 2005, Austin Merrill, "The Rwandan Story in the Words of the Killers," review of *Machete Season.*
Washington Post Book World, August 21, 2005, Alison Des Forges, review of *Machete Season,* p. 3.

ONLINE

Bookslut, http://www.bookslut.com/ (October 8, 2005), Sarah Statz, review of *Machete Season.*
Salon.com, http://www.salon.com/ (July 20, 2005), Suzy Hansen, "Conversations with Mass Murderers," review of *Machete Season.*

*   *   *

HAZLEGROVE, Cary 1960(?)-

PERSONAL: Born c. 1960; married Andy Bullington (a guitarist); children: Virginia Page. *Education:* Hollins University, graduated, 1978.

ADDRESSES: Home—Nantucket Island, MA. *Office*—Cary Hazlegrove Photography, P.O. Box 442, Nantucket, MA 02554-0442. *E-mail*—cary@hazlegrove.com.

CAREER: Photographer.

MEMBER: Nantucket Preservation Trust (member of board).

WRITINGS:

(And photographer) *Nantucket: Seasons on the Island,* introduction by David Halberstam, Chronicle Books (San Francisco, CA), 1995.

(And photographer) *Nantucket: The Quiet Season,* foreword by Nathaniel Philbrick, Chronicle Books (San Francisco, CA), 2005.

PHOTOGRAPHER

Bill Gleeson, *Weekends for Two in the New England: Fifty Romantic Getaways,* Chronicle Books (San Francisco, CA), 1996.
Bill Gleeson, *Weekends for Two in the Southwest: Fifty Romantic Getaways,* Chronicle Books (San Francisco, CA), 1997.
Bill Gleeson, *Weekends for Two in the Mid-Atlantic States: Fifty Romantic Getaways,* Chronicle Books (San Francisco, CA), 1998.
Melissa Clark and Samara Farbar Mormar, *The Nantucket Restaurants Cookbook: Menus and Recipes from the Faraway Isle,* Random House (New York, NY), 2001.

Photography published in newspapers and periodicals, including *New York Times, Boston Globe, Chicago Tribune, Condé Nast Traveler, House and Garden, Food and Wine, Southern Accents,* and *Parade.*

SIDELIGHTS: Photographer Cary Hazlegrove first arrived on Nantucket Island not long after graduating from Virginia's Hollins University in 1978, and immediately began her life-long love affair with the region. "I fell in love with the island the second my feet hit the ground," she shared in a profile for the Nantucket Preservation Trust. In 1980 she began producing slide shows of her photographs, an annual tradition that endured for twenty-three years. Several compilations of Hazlegrove's works have been published in book form, including *Nantucket: Seasons on the Island, The Nantucket Restaurants Cookbook: Menus and Recipes from the Faraway Isle,* and *Nantucket: The Quiet Season.*

The photographs in *Nantucket: Seasons on the Island* depict the popular tourist destination during its peak travel seasons in addition to its blustery winters. *Booklist* reviewer Gilbert Taylor commented, "These pretty colorplates celebrate . . . sandy, windswept Nantucket. Hazlegrove focused on Nantucket from a native's perspective in *Nantucket: The Quiet Season,* which includes quotes from island inhabitants in addition to photos taken during the off-season. Alison Hopkins wrote in a review for *Library Journal*, "Hazlegrove's love and understanding of the area shine throughout this well-planned book, which will be savored by many." Hazlegrove also contributed photographs to Melissa Clark and Samara Farbar Mormar's *The Nantucket Restaurants Cookbook*, which *Library Journal* reviewer Tom Cooper called "as much travel book as it is cookbook. Hazlegrove's pictures dwell equally on Nantucket Island scenery as on the food presented."

BIOGRAPHICAL AND CRITICAL SOURCES:

PERIODICALS

Booklist, April 1, 1995, Gilbert Taylor, review of *Nantucket: Seasons on the Island*, p. 1374.
Library Journal, March 15, 2001, Tom Cooper, review of *The Nantucket Restaurants Cookbook: Menus and Recipes from the Faraway Isle*, p. 101; March 1, 2005, Alison Hopkins, review of *Nantucket: The Quiet Season*, p. 102.

ONLINE

Cary Hazlegrove Home Page, http://www.hazlegrove.com (September 27, 2005).
Nantucket Preservation Trust Web site, http://www.nantucketpreservation.org/ (September 27, 2005), profile of author.*

*   *   *

HENNINGSEN, Agnes 1868-1962
(Agnes Kathinka Malling Henningsen, Helga Maynert)

PERSONAL: Born November 18, 1868, in Skovsbo (one source says Ullerslev), Denmark; died 1962; daughter of Peter (a tenant farmer) and Ophelia Petra Amalia Cathinca (Malling) Andersen; married Mads Henningsen, c. 1887 (divorced, 1907); married Simon Koch (a writer and civil servant), 1919 (died, 1935); children: (first marriage) four.

CAREER: Novelist and playwright.

AWARDS, HONORS: Otto Benson author's prize, 1938; Herman Bang prize, Gyldendal publisher, 1946; Holger Drachmann prize, 1953; Jeanne and Henir Nathansen merit award, 1960.

WRITINGS:

Glansbilledet: En Historie om Damer (novel; title means "The Paper Saint: A Story for Ladies"), Nordiske (Copenhagen, Denmark), 1899.
Strømmen (novel; title means "The Current"), Nordiske (Copenhagen, Denmark), 1899.
Polens Døtre (novel; title means "Daughters of Poland"), Nordiske (Copenhagen, Denmark), 1901.
De Spedalske (novel), Nordiske (Copenhagen, Denmark), 1903.
Moralen (play), first produced at the Folketeatret, Copenhagen, Denmark, 1903.
Den uovervindelige: Skuespil i fire Akter (five-act play; title means "The Invincible"; first produced at Dagmarteatret, Copenhagen, Denmark, 1908), Gyldendal (Copenhagen, Denmark), 1905.
Lykken: En Elskovhistorie, Gyldendal (Copenhagen, Denmark), 1905.
Elskerinden (play; first produced at Dagmarteatret, Copenhagen, Denmark, 1906), Gyldendal (Copenhagen, Denmark), 1906.
Den elskede Eva (novel; title means "The Beloved Eva"), Gyldendal (Copenhagen, Denmark), 1911.
Hævnen (play), first produced at Dagmarteatret, Copenhagen, Denmark, 1912.
Den rige Fugl (play), first produced at Royal Theatre, 1916.
Den store Kærlighed (novel; title means "The Great Love"), Gyldendal (Copenhagen, Denmark), 1917.
Den Guderne elsker (novel), Gyldendal (Copenhagen, Denmark), 1921.
Troense (play), first produced at Royal Theatre, 1922.
Barnets Magt (novel), Gyldendal (Copenhagen, Denmark), 1923.
Den fuldendte Kvinde (novel), Gyldendal (Copenhagen, Denmark), 1925.
Das vollkommene weiß, G. Kieipenheuer (Potsdam, Germany), 1926.
Kærlighedens Aarstider (novel; title means "Seasons of Love"), Gyldendal (Copenhagen, Denmark), 1927.
Det rige Efteraar (novel; title means "Rich Autumn"), Gyldendal (Copenhagen, Denmark), 1928.

Den sidste Aften (novel; title means "Last Evening"), Gyldendal (Copenhagen, Denmark), 1930.

Le kun, Gyldendal (Copenhagen, Denmark), 1935.

Det rigtige Menneske (novel; title means "The True Person"), Gyldendal (Copenhagen, Denmark), 1938.

Let Gang på Jorden: Erindringer (memoir; title means "Take the Carefree Path"), Gyldendal (Copenhagen, Denmark), 1941.

Letsindighedens Gave: Erindringer (memoir; title means "The Gift of Recklessness"), Gyldendal (Copenhagen, Denmark), 1943.

Byen erobret: Erindringer (memoir; title means "The Conquered City"), Gyldendal (Copenhagen, Denmark), 1945.

Kærlighedssynder: Erindringer (memoir), Gyldendal (Copenhagen, Denmark), 1947.

Dødsfjende—hjertenskær, Gyldendal (Copenhagen, Denmark), 1949.

Jeg er levemand, Gyldendal (Copenhagen, Denmark), 1951.

Den rige fugl: Erindringer (memoir), Gyldendal (Copenhagen, Denmark), 1953.

Skygger over vejen: Erindringer (memoir; title means "Shadows on the Path"), Gyldendal (Copenhagen, Denmark), 1955.

Vi ses i Arizona (novel; title means "See You in Arizona"), Gyldendal (Copenhagen, Denmark), 1956.

Den lidenskabelige pige (novel; title means "The Passionate Girl"), Gyldendal (Copenhagen, Denmark), 1958.

Bølgeslag (novel; title means "Breaking Waves"), Gyldendal (Copenhagen, Denmark), 1959.

Contributor, sometimes under pseudonym Helga Maynert, to periodicals, including *København.*

SIDELIGHTS: Agnes Henningsen was a significant Danish writer whose publications include both fiction and autobiographical accounts. She was born in 1868 in Skovsbo, Denmark, where her father worked as a tenant farmer. A self-avowed libertine, Henningsen became engaged, when she was only fifteen years old, to an uncle, and was thereupon sent away to continue her schooling. Four years later, she married a tutor who shared her belief in sexual freedom. In the early 1890s, when her husband, who had begun working as a schoolteacher, proved to be financially irresponsible, Henningsen commenced earning an income by writing for various periodicals, and in the following years she maintained her literary career while raising four children, the youngest of whom was conceived outside her marriage.

As Henningsen became an increasingly familiar figure in Copenhagen's literary society, her husband entered into a relationship with one of his female students. The ensuing scandal compelled him to flee Denmark and travel to the United States, where he eventually achieved prominence as a Danish diplomat. After her marriage ended in 1907, Henningsen divided her family, sending two children to live with her husband's parents and moving the other two with her into her married lover's home. While living in this unusual arrangement, Henningsen wrote about the negative ramifications of female sexuality in *Glansbilledet: En Historie om Damer* and *Strømmen,* two novels described by Lise Præstgaard Andersen in the *Dictionary of Literary Biography* as "somewhat depressing." Henningsen fared better with her next tale, *Polens Døtre,* which concerns a pair of complicated relationships maintained by an engaging lecturer who espouses freedom of erotic expression. Despite its focus on the sordid consequences of sexual recklessness, *Polens Døtre* found favor with Danish liberals who championed the book as a compelling representation of liberated eroticism.

Henningsen continued to probe the emotional repercussions of eroticism in novels such as *Den elskede Eva* and *Den store Kærlighed.* In both novels, Andersen noted, Henningsen provides "descriptions of the sexual affairs of so-called liberating people [that] are anything but positive." As Andersen added, "The erotic scenes in these novels would probably not offend most modern readers, and it is clear that the author is much more concerned with depicting subtle emotions than with sexuality."

In the late 1920s, eight years after she remarried, Henningsen commenced work on a series of three autobiographical novels: *Kærlighedens Aarstider, Det rige Efteraar,* and *Den sidste Aften,* charting a young woman's development as a writer and lover. The series begins with the heroine mired in a stifling marriage, and it continues with her ending that relationship for life with another man. But even as she realizes a measure of prominence as a writer, the heroine continues to suffer in her personal relationships, including a second marriage. The trilogy ends with the heroine vying with a young woman for the company of a gigolo. After completing *Den sidste Aften,* the end of the trilogy, Henningsen failed to produce a new publication for five years, and in the last years of the 1930s she issued only one further work, *Det rigtige Menneske,* which she wrote in honor of her late husband, Simon Koch.

In 1941, with World War II raging across Europe, Henningsen revived her literary career with *Let Gang på Jorden: Erindringer,* the first of several autobiographical volumes. "The memoirs begin with the author's birth and come to an end sometime in the 1930s, before the death of Koch," wrote Andersen. "Each volume is written in a gripping, impressionistic style and ends in an exciting climatic point." The series also includes *Byen erobret: Erindringer,* in which Henningsen recalls the scandal of her first husband's involvement with a student, and *Skygger over vejen: Erindringer,* the final memoir, in which she relates an infidelity undertaken while her husband lay dying. Andersen summarized Henningsen's series of memoirs as "the largest autobiographical work in Danish literature," and she praised it as "one of the best written and most entertaining works in this genre." Writing about the memoirs in *Scandinavian Studies,* Marina Allemano noted, "In her long autobiographical narrative . . . Henningsen shows that the idea of the fully emancipated, creative, feminine, and maternal woman cannot be embodied by a single person within the existing discourses and socio-political realities of her lifetime, and for that reason alone, she tells the stories of a multitude of other women."

Upon completion of *Skygger over vejen,* Henningsen returned to fiction, producing a trilogy comprised of *Vi ses i Arizona, Den lidenskabelige pige,* and *Bølgeslag,* which is described by Andersen as "a variation on her theme of a women's right to freedom in love and her duty of absolute honesty toward herself and others." Henningsen was in her late eighties when she commenced work on this series, and she was in her early nineties when she completed it in 1959.

BIOGRAPHICAL AND CRITICAL SOURCES:

BOOKS

Dictionary of Literary Biography, Volume 214: *Twentieth-Century Danish Writers,* Thomson Gale (Detroit, MI), 1999.

Henningsen, Agnes, *Let Gang på Jorden: Erindringer,* Gyldendal (Copenhagen, Denmark), 1941.
Henningsen, Agnes, *Letsindighedens Gave: Erindringer,* Gyldendal (Copenhagen, Denmark), 1943.
Henningsen, Agnes, *Byen erobret: Erindringer,* Gyldendal (Copenhagen, Denmark), 1945.
Henningsen, Agnes, *Den rige fugl: Erindringer,* Gyldendal (Copenhagen, Denmark), 1953.
Henningsen, Agnes, *Skygger over vejen: Erindringer,* Gyldendal (Copenhagen, Denmark), 1955.

PERIODICALS

Scandinavian Studies, summer, 2004, Marina Allemano, "Somatic Gaps and Embodied Voices in Agnes Henningsen's Memoirs," p. 155.*

* * *

HENNINGSEN, Agnes Kathinka Malling
   See HENNINGSEN, Agnes

* * *

HERBSTEIN, Manu 1936(?)-

PERSONAL: Born c. 1936, in Muizenberg, South Africa; married; wife's name Akua (owner and operator of a furniture factory and a housing development company); children: two sons.

ADDRESSES: Home—Accra, Ghana.

CAREER: Civil and structural engineer, primarily in Ghana. Also worked in England, Scotland, India, Nigeria, and Zambia. Supporter of African National Congress of South Africa, beginning c. 1950s.

MEMBER: British Institution of Structural Engineers (fellow), Ghana Institution of Engineers (fellow; past member of council).

AWARDS, HONORS: Best First Book Prize, Commonwealth Writers, 2002, for *Ama: A Story of the Atlantic Slave Trade.*

WRITINGS:

Ama: A Story of the Atlantic Slave Trade (novel; e-book), http://www.ama.africatoday.com, 2000.

BIOGRAPHICAL AND CRITICAL SOURCES:

ONLINE

African Postcolonial Literature in English in the Post-colonial Web, http://www.scholars.nus.edu.sg/ (December 3, 2002), Tamara S. Wagner, review of *Ama: A Story of the Atlantic Slave Trade.*

AuthorsDen.com, http://www.authorsden.com/ (January 3, 2003), "Manu Herbstein."*

*   *   *

HERRICK, Rebecca 1960-
   (Rebecca L. Herrick)

PERSONAL: Born November 10, 1960, in Lincoln, NE; daughter of Maurice (a chemist) and Eloise (a teacher; maiden name, Dickerson) Herrick; companion of Lori Franklin; children: Neal Franklin. *Ethnicity:* "Northern European." *Education:* Tufts University, M.A., 1986; University of Nebraska, Ph.D., 1991.

ADDRESSES: *Office*—Department of Political Science, 513 MS, Oklahoma State University, Stillwater, OK 74078. *E-mail*—herrick@okstate.edu.

CAREER: Writer. Oklahoma State University, Stillwater, assistant professor, 1991-96, associate professor of American government and women and politics, 1996—.

AWARDS, HONORS: Grants from American Political Science Association, 1992, and Dirksen Center, 1999; award from C-SPAN cable television network, 1993; named Oklahoma political scientist of the year, Oklahoma Political Science Association, 2002.

WRITINGS:

Fashioning a More Ethical Representative, Praeger Publishers (Westport, CT), 2003.

Contributor to books, including *United States Electoral Systems: Their Impact on Women and Minorities,* edited by Wilma Rule and Joseph F. Zimmerman, Greenwood Press (Westport, CT), 1992; *Gays and Lesbians in the Democratic Process: Public Policy, Public Opinion, and Political Representation,* edited by Ellen D. Riggle and Barry Tadlock, Columbia University Press (New York, NY), 1999; and *Women Transforming Congress,* edited by Cindy Simon Rosenthal, University of Oklahoma Press (Norman, OK), 2003. Contributor of articles and reviews to academic journals, including *Politics and Policy, Legislative Studies Quarterly, Women and Politics, Oklahoma Politics, Social Science Journal, Journal of Homosexuality, American Review of Politics, Journal of Political and Military Sociology, National Political Science Review,* and *American Politics Research.*

WORK IN PROGRESS: An examination of the differences between citizen and professional legislators in the House of Representatives.

*   *   *

HERRICK, Rebecca L.
   See HERRICK, Rebecca

*   *   *

HIND, Archie

PERSONAL: Male.

ADDRESSES: *Agent*—c/o Author Mail, Birlinn, West Newington House, 10 Newington Rd., Edinburgh EH9 1QS, Scotland.

AWARDS, HONORS: Manchester *Guardian* Fiction Award, 1966, for *The Dear Green Place.*

WRITINGS:

The Dear Green Place, New Authors (London, England), 1966, reprinted, Birlinn (Edinburgh, Scotland), 2002.

SIDELIGHTS: Scottish writer Archie Hind is primarily known for *The Dear Green Place,* a largely autobiographical novel about a working-class writer, Mat Craig, who discovers the true beauty to be found in the industrial city of Glasgow. The title of the book is actually a translation of Glasgow's original Celtic name. For Mat, divided against himself, "writers are always other people," until he surprises himself by becoming a writer. The book was awarded the Manchester *Guardian* Fiction Prize in the year it was published, and since that time, it has been embraced as one of the seminal books in the city's literary history.

"On its own it stands as a fine evocation of Glasgow—places, people, ethos—with scene after scene where description and emotions blend," wrote Moira Burgess on *West Coast* online. Neil Philip mentioned the book in a piece for *British Book News,* commenting that the novel goes "to the heart" of contemporary Glasgow. Since the publication of *The Dear Green Place,* a number of other working-class novels about Glasgow have been written, confronting the social dislocations and upheavals endemic to the thriving, industrial city. Like Hind, many still manage to find the "dear green place" behind the steel and the grime and the busy lives of city inhabitants.

BIOGRAPHICAL AND CRITICAL SOURCES:

BOOKS

Burgess, Moira, *Imagine a City—Glasgow in Fiction,* Argyle Publishing, 1998.

PERIODICALS

British Book News, July, 1984, Neil Philip, review of *The Dear Green Place,* pp. 389-390.*

*   *   *

HOFFER, Peter Charles 1944-

PERSONAL: Born August 3, 1944, in Brooklyn, NY; married, 1970; children: one. *Education:* University of Rochester, A.B., 1965; Harvard University, M.A., 1966, Ph.D., 1970.

ADDRESSES: Home—GA. *Office*—Department of History, University of Georgia, Rm. 220, LeConte Hall, Athens, GA 30602. *E-mail*—pchoffer@arches.uga.edu.

CAREER: Professor of history and researcher. Ohio State University, Columbus, assistant professor of history, 1970-77; University of Notre Dame, South Bend, IN, visiting assistant professor of history, 1977-78; University of Georgia, Athens, assistant professor, 1978-82, associate professor, 1982-86, professor, 1986-93, research professor, 1993-2001, distinguished research professor of history, 2001—. Wolfe Lecturer, Brooklyn College, 1994; Rorshach Lecturer, Rice University, 1994.

MEMBER: American Historical Association, Organization of American Historians, Institute of Early American History and Culture, American Society of Legal History.

AWARDS, HONORS: National Endowment for the Humanities research grant, 1973-74, 1975; American Philosophical Society research grant, 1977, 1983; Colonial Williamsburg Foundation research grant, 1978; Project '87 research grant, 1979; American Bar Foundation research fellowship, 1980-81; National Endowment for the Humanities fellowship, 1986, 1989-90; University of Georgia Humanities Center fellowship, 1989; Golieb fellow, New York University Law School, 1991-92, 1995, 1997; Outstanding Book Award, *Choice,* 1992; Albert Christ-Janer Award for Creative Research, University of Georgia, 1993; University of Georgia research grant, 1996; Best of the Best Book Award, American Library Association, 1998-99.

WRITINGS:

(With N.E.H. Hull) *Murdering Mothers: Infanticide in England and New England, 1558-1803,* New York University Press (New York, NY), 1981.

Revolution and Regeneration: Life Cycle and the Historical Vision of the Generation of 1776, University of Georgia Press (Athens, GA), 1983.

(With N.E.H. Hull) *Impeachment in America, 1635-1805,* Yale University Press (New Haven, CT), 1984.

Liberty or Order: Two Views of American History from the Revolutionary Crisis to the Early Works of George Bancroft and Wendell Phillips, Garland Publishing (New York, NY), 1988.

The Law's Conscience: Equitable Constitutionalism in America, University of North Carolina Press (Chapel Hill, NC), 1990.

Law and People in Colonial America, Johns Hopkins University Press (Baltimore, MD), 1992.

(With William W. Stueck) *Reading and Writing American History: An Introduction to the Historian's Craft,* D.C. Heath (Lexington, MA), 1994.

The Devil's Disciples: Makers of the Salem Witchcraft Trials, Johns Hopkins University Press (Baltimore, MD), 1996.

The Salem Witchcraft Trials: A Legal History, University Press of Kansas (Lawrence, KS), 1997.

The Brave New World: A History of Early America, Houghton Mifflin (Boston, MA), 2000.

(With N.E.H. Hull) *Roe v. Wade: The Abortion Rights Controversy in American History,* University Press of Kansas (Lawrence, KS), 2001.

American History: Early Colonizations to 1877, College Network (Indianapolis, IN), 2002.

American History I: Study Guide, College Network (Indianapolis, IN), 2002.

The Great New York Conspiracy of 1741: Slavery, Crime, and Colonial Law, University Press of Kansas (Lawrence, KS), 2003.

Sensory Worlds in Early America, Johns Hopkins University Press (Baltimore, MD), 2003.

Past Imperfect: Facts, Fictions, and Fraud in the Writing of American History, PublicAffairs (New York, NY), 2004.

EDITOR

(With Bradley Chapin and William W. Beck) *Modern Strategies for Teaching the American Revolution,* Ohio Historical Society (Columbus, OH), 1976.

(With William B. Scott) *Criminal Proceedings in Colonial Virginia: Fines, Examinations of Criminals, Trials of Slaves, etc. from March 1710 (1711) to (1754),* University of Georgia Press (Athens, GA), 1984.

A Rage for Liberty: Selected Articles on the Immediate Causes of the American Revolution, Garland Publishing (New York, NY), 1988.

The Stresses of Empire: Selected Articles on the British Empire in the Eighteenth Century, Garland Publishing (New York, NY), 1988.

Africans Become Afro-Americans: Selected Articles on Slavery in the American Colonies, Garland Publishing (New York, NY), 1988.

An American Enlightenment: Selected Articles on Colonial Intellectual History, Garland Publishing (New York, NY), 1988.

American Patterns of Life: Selected Articles on the Provincial Period of American History, Garland Publishing (New York, NY), 1988.

Colonial Women and Domesticity: Selected Articles on Gender in Early America, Garland Publishing (New York, NY), 1988.

Commerce and Community: Selected Articles on the Middle Atlantic Colonies, Garland Publishing (New York, NY), 1988.

The Context of Colonization: Selected Articles on Britain in the Era of American Colonization, Garland Publishing (New York, NY), 1988.

Homage to New England: Selected Articles on Early New England History, 1937 to 1963, Garland Publishing (New York, NY), 1988.

Indians and Europeans: Selected Articles on Indian-White Relations in Colonial North America, Garland Publishing (New York, NY), 1988.

An Empire Takes Shape: Selected Articles on the Origins of the Old English Colonial System, Garland Publishing (New York, NY), 1988.

The Marrow of American Divinity: Selected Articles on Colonial Religion, Garland Publishing (New York, NY), 1988.

A Nation in the Womb of Time: Selected Articles on the Long-Term Causes of the American Revolution, Garland Publishing (New York, NY), 1988.

New England Rediscovered: Selected Articles on New England Colonial History, 1965 to 1973, Garland Publishing (New York, NY), 1988.

The Pace of Change: Selected Articles on Politics and Society in Pre-revolutionary America, Garland Publishing (New York, NY), 1988.

The Peopling of a World: Selected Articles on Immigration and Settlement Patterns in British North America, Garland Publishing (New York, NY), 1988.

Planters and Yeoman: Selected Articles on the Southern Colonies, Garland Publishing (New York, NY), 1988.

Puritans and Yankees: Selected Articles on New England Colonial History, 1974 to 1984, Garland Publishing (New York, NY), 1988.

(Editor with N.E.H. Hull and William James Hoffer) *The Abortion Rights Controversy in America: A Legal Reader,* University of North Carolina Press (Chapel Hill, NC), 2004.

OTHER

Contributor to books, including *Oxford Companion to American Law, Oxford Companion to the Supreme Court, Encyclopedia of the British North American Colonies,* and *Encyclopedia of the American Legislative System.* Contributor to periodicals, including *William and Mary Quarterly, Rutgers Law Journal, American Journal of Legal History,* and *Cardozo Law Review.*

SIDELIGHTS: Peter Charles Hoffer's writings often focus on early American history, but he has also written on contemporary issues facing historians and educators. Modern-day plagiarism and professional misconduct among historians is the subject of his book *Past Imperfect: Facts, Fictions, and Fraud in the Writing of American History.* Hoffer specifically addresses incidents of dishonesty that were revealed in the early 2000s, including overt plagiarism in books by Stephen Ambrose and Doris Kearns Goodwin and fabrication of data by Michael Bellesiles in his controversial work *Arming America.* David J. Garrow, writing for the *Wilson Quarterly,* commented that *Past Imperfect* "offers the most comprehensive and erudite analysis of the Bellesiles scandal to date, and his [Hoffer's] thoughtful and wide-ranging review of the full raft of recent plagiarism cases and other transgressions leaves no doubt that Bellesiles's were 'the most egregious of our era.' . . . *Past Imperfect* offers an exceptionally astute survey of recent trends in the history profession." A *Publishers Weekly* reviewer remarked: "Those concerned with the integrity and future of the field will find this analysis illuminating." A contributor to *Kirkus Reviews* suggested that "what emerges in this well-researched assessment of a nasty problem are both the author's love for his discipline and his grief for the losses it has sustained."

Published in 2003, Hoffer's *Sensory Worlds in Early America* was released, documenting how the five senses were utilized and appreciated by early colonists. *English Historical Review* contributor Mark Jenner wrote that the book "promises to be a pioneering study which explores the interplay of the senses in practice." Robert Flatley, writing in *Library Journal,* called *Sensory Worlds in Early America* "well written and researched" and "an innovative and unusual work."

Hoffer first tackles the history of abortion rights in the United States in 2001's *Roe v. Wade: The Abortion Rights Controversy in American History. Library Jour-*

nal reviewer Mary Jane Brustman noted that the book "does an unusually good job of covering the full legal history from Colonial times to 2001. It is crammed with information but remains very readable." Mary Carroll commented in a *Booklist* review that the book "exposes teens to nuanced discussion of often overly simplified controversial and emotional issues." A *Publishers Weekly* reviewer regarded *Roe v. Wade* as a "page-turner" and a "remarkable volume" that should be "popular with law students and lay readers alike." In 2004, Hoffer coedited *The Abortion Rights Controversy in America: A Legal Reader* with N.E.H. Hull and William James Hoffer. Ted G. Jelen described the book in a *Perspectives on Political Science* review as "an essential resource for anyone seeking to understanding the legal ramifications of the abortion issue."

Hoffer has also published two books centering on the Salem Witch Trials, which occurred in Salem, Massachusetts in the seventeenth century: the scholarly *The Devil's Disciples: Makers of the Salem Witchcraft Trials* and *The Salem Witchcraft Trials: A Legal History,* both of which are aimed at the general reader. In *Review of Politics,* Timothy J. McMillan wrote that *The Devil's Disciples* is "a well-documented and well-argued analysis of the roles of psychology and culture in producing the hysteria and trials." He also added that "the structure of *The Salem Witchcraft Trials* is useful and compelling" and that the book serves as "a useful introduction to this important aspect of colonial American history."

BIOGRAPHICAL AND CRITICAL SOURCES:

PERIODICALS

Booklist, October 1, 2001, Mary Carroll, review of *Roe v. Wade: The Abortion Rights Controversy in American History,* p. 297.

English Historical Review, June, 2004, Mark Jenner, review of *Sensory Worlds in Early America,* p. 804.

Kirkus Reviews, August 15, 2004, review of *Past Imperfect: Facts, Fictions, and Fraud in the Writing of American History,* p. 788.

Library Journal, November 15, 2001, Mary Jane Brustman, review of *Roe v. Wade,* p. 80; November 1, 2003, Robert Flatley, review of *Sensory Worlds in Early America,* p. 98.

Perspectives on Political Science, winter, 2005, Ted G. Jelen, review of *The Abortion Rights Controversy in America: A Legal Reader,* p. 49.

Publishers Weekly, September 10, 2001, review of *Roe v. Wade,* p. 79; September 13, 2004, review of *Past Imperfect,* p. 70.

Review of Politics, summer, 1998, Timothy J. Mc-Millan, review of *The Salem Witchcraft Trials: A Legal History,* p. 595.

Wilson Quarterly, winter, 2005, David J. Garrow, review of *Past Imperfect,* p. 112.

ONLINE

University of Georgia Department of History Web site, http://www.uga.edu/history/ (October 18, 2005), author profile.*

*   *   *

HOFMO, Gunvor 1921-1995

PERSONAL: Born 1921, in Oslo, Norway; died 1995.

WRITINGS:

POETRY

Jeg vil hjem til menneskene (title means "I Want to Go Home to People") Gyldendal (Oslo, Norway), 1946.

Fra en annen virkelighet (title means "From Another Reality"), Gyldendal (Oslo, Norway), 1948.

Blinde nattergaler (title means "Blind Nightingale"), Gyldendal (Oslo, Norway), 1951.

I en våkenatt, Gyldendal (Oslo, Norway), 1954.

Testamente til evighet, Gyldendal (Oslo, Norway), 1955.

Samlede dikt, Gyldendal (Oslo, Norway), 1968.

Gjest på jorden, Gyldendal (Oslo, Norway), 1971.

November, Gyldendal (Oslo, Norway), 1972.

Veisperringer, Gyldendal (Oslo, Norway), 1973.

Mellomspill, Gyldendal (Oslo, Norway), 1974.

Hva fanger natter, Gyldendal (Oslo, Norway), 1976.

Det er ingen hverdag mer: dikt i utvalg, edited by Odd Solumsmoen, Den norske bokklubben (Stabekk, Norway), 1976.

Det er sent, Gyldendal (Oslo, Norway), 1978.

Stjernene og barndommen, Gyldendal (Oslo, Norway), 1986.

Nabot, Gyldendal (Oslo, Norway), 1987.

Ord til bilder, Gyldendal (Oslo, Norway), 1989.

Fuglen, Gyldendal (Oslo, Norway), 1990.

Navnløst er alt i nalten, Gyldendal (Oslo, Norway), 1991.

Tiden, Gyldendal (Oslo, Norway), 1992.

Epilog, Gyldendal (Oslo, Norway), 1994.

Samlede dikt, Gyldendal (Oslo, Norway), 1996.

Etterlatte, Gyldendal (Oslo, Norway), 1997.

Jeg glemmer ingen, Gyldendal (Oslo, Norway), 1999.

SIDELIGHTS: Poet Gunvor Hofmo was profoundly influenced by the destruction she witnessed during World War II. A sense of loneliness and despair pervades her poetry. Hofmo repeatedly presents the idea that each person is alone in the world, and although one might long for a sense of home, of connection to others, this is rarely, if ever, attainable. Her first book of poems, *Jeg vil hjem til menneskene,* introduces these themes, which would be repeated throughout the body of her work. This initial collection of poems was written according to strict metric forms, but all her subsequent work used freer verse forms.

Tiden is a collection of deceptively simple and traditional nature poems, according to Walter D. Morris in *World Literature Today.* "Soon, however, the mood changes," Morris wrote, "and we see that the subject under discussion is the end of life, death, darkness, and the beyond." Images of the dead recur throughout the collection, making the small problems of ordinary life seem even smaller. The narrator, who hears the voices of the dead, becomes a mystical interface between the two realms. Morris praised Hofmo's clear language and her ability to create a sustained mood throughout the collection.

In 1997, two years after Hofmo died, Morris reviewed *Samlede dikt,* a collection planned to celebrate Hofmo's seventy-fifth birthday. In her fifty years of writing, she had completed twenty volumes containing approximately 700 poems about such recurring themes as the mystery of human existence, faith, and justice. The anniversary volume contains all of her previously published volumes, some of which had long been out of print. Morris noted that, "in some ways, the latter poems show more resignation and acceptance of things, as well as the certainty of God's presence. . . . Like many other Norwegian poets, Hofmo turns often to images of nature—trees, flowers, fields, and the sea—but always with the idea of something deep and mysterious in the background: God and eternity."

BIOGRAPHICAL AND CRITICAL SOURCES:

PERIODICALS

World Literature Today, spring, 1992, Walter D. Morris, review of *Navnløst er alt i nalten,* p. 355; spring, 1993, Walter D. Morris, review of *Tiden,* p. 400; spring, 1995, Walter D. Morris, review of *Epilog,* p. 386; summer, 1997, Walter D. Morris, review of *Samlede dikt,* p. 608.*

*   *   *

HOGG, Tracy 1960-2004

PERSONAL: Born August 6, 1960, in Doncaster, England; died of melanoma, November 25, 2004, in Doncaster, England; married twice; second husband's name Tom; children: two. *Education:* Doncaster School of Nursing, Doncaster, England, R.N.M.H.

CAREER: Child care consultant and writer. St. Catherine's Hospital for the Mentally Handicapped, Doncaster, England, nurse; Baby Techniques (retail store and childcare consulting service), Encino, CA, founder.

WRITINGS:

(With Melinda Blau) *Secrets of the Baby Whisperer: How to Calm, Connect, and Communicate with Your Baby,* Ballantine Books (New York, NY), 2001.
(With Melinda Blau) *Secrets of the Baby Whisperer for Toddlers,* Ballantine Books (New York, NY), 2002.
(With Melinda Blau) *The Baby Whisperer Solves All Your Problems (by Teaching You How to Ask the Right Questions),* Atria Books (New York, NY), 2005.

SIDELIGHTS: Trained as a mental-health nurse in her native England, Tracy Hogg made a name for herself in the United States as a nanny and childcare consultant to Hollywood's elite. Her experience working with special-needs children and as an advisor to parents of newborns imparted a special talent for being able to interpret the cries and body language of infants. Hogg moved to Los Angeles, California, in 1992, and after establishing a clientele that included numerous movie and television stars, she opened a retail store and consulting service called Baby Technique. Her uncanny ability to soothe newborn babies—and their parents—led to her earning the nickname "the baby whisperer."

Hogg worked with freelance writer Melinda Blau to compose the popular three-part "Baby Whisperer" series. Hogg was encouraged to pen the first book in the series, *Secrets of the Baby Whisperer: How to Calm, Connect, and Communicate with Your Baby,* by her clients after her pamphlet "How to Hire a Nanny—Not a Ninny" became widely circulated. *Secrets of the Baby Whisperer* was released in 2001 and provides advice on easing the transition from the hospital to the home, relying on acronyms such as EASY (eating, activity, sleeping, your time) and SLOW (stop, listen, observe, what's up). At the core of Hogg's child-rearing philosophies is a balance between the extremes of "attachment parenting" (including cosleeping and on-cue feeding) and the "cry-it-out" method, with a focus on treating the infant with respect and establishing a structured routine from the outset. Nancy Spillman, a contributor to *Booklist,* wrote that the first book "bubbles with unbridled enthusiasm." A *Publishers Weekly* reviewer described Hogg as writing with "spunky British humor" and "compassion." Annette V. Janes, writing for *Library Journal,* described the book as possessing "unusual tenderness and heart. . . . This is the perfect gift for a new mom and family."

Hogg and Blau moved onto the toddler stage in *Secrets of the Baby Whisperer for Toddlers,* published in 2002. With a format similar to the original book, Hogg introduces the acronym HELP, which stands for hold yourself back, encourage exploration and experimentation, limit, and praise. A reviewer for *Publishers Weekly* remarked, "Hogg offers basic advice on most aspects of childrearing, including toilet training, protecting newly ambulatory toddlers, sibling rivalry and tantrums. Her suggestions are occasionally humorous and always practical." *Booklist* contributor Mary

Frances Wilkens commented that the book is "a welcome addition to childcare guides, an area that is crowded but lacking in substance. Its focus on just those few years between infancy and preschool makes it a real treasure."

The final book in Hogg's series is titled *The Baby Whisperer Solves All Your Problems (by Teaching You How to Ask the Right Questions)* and addresses many of the questions parents raised after reading the earlier "Baby Whisperer" books, in addition to offering several new techniques for preventing chronic sleeping and eating problems. A reviewer for *Library Bookwatch* described it as "an outstanding final book which explores how [Hogg] arrived at her solutions—and how parents can, too." A *Publishers Weekly* contributor wrote, "The high-spirited Hogg is humorous yet relentless in her quest to help parents find out why their baby acts a certain way and how to manage and respond to various behaviors." Saddly, Hogg died at the age of forty-four of melanoma, just over a month before her last book was released.

BIOGRAPHICAL AND CRITICAL SOURCES:

PERIODICALS

Booklist, June 1, 2001, Nancy Spillman, review of *Secrets of the Baby Whisperer: How to Calm, Connect, and Communicate with Your Baby*, p. 1908; December 15, 2001, Mary Frances Wilkens, review of *Secrets of the Baby Whisperer for Toddlers*, p. 682.

Library Bookwatch, April, 2005, review of *The Baby Whisperer Solves All Your Problems (by Teaching You How to Ask the Right Questions)*.

Library Journal, January 1, 2001, Annette V. Janes, review of *Secrets of the Baby Whisperer*, p. 146.

Publishers Weekly, December 18, 2000, review of *Secrets of the Baby Whisperer*, p. 75; December 24, 2001, review of *Secrets of the Baby Whisperer for Toddlers*, p. 61; January 17, 2005, review of *The Baby Whisperer Solves All Your Problems*, p. 49.

ONLINE

Baby Whisperer Web site, http://www.babywhisperer.com/ (September 29, 2005).

OBITUARIES

PERIODICALS

America's Intelligence Wire, December 8, 2004.

ONLINE

Telegraph Online, http://www.telegraph.co.uk/ (October 12, 2004).*

*   *   *

HUNSICKER, Harry 1963(?)- (Harry Hunsicker, Jr.)

PERSONAL: Born c. 1963, in Dallas, TX; son of Harry (a real-estate appraiser) and Foree Hunsicker; married.

ADDRESSES: Home—Dallas, TX. *Office*—Hunsicker Appraisal Company, Inc., 4901 Cole Ave., Dallas, TX 75205-3401. *E-mail*—harry@harryhunsicker.com.

CAREER: Commercial real-estate appraiser and novelist. Hunsicker Appraisal Company, Inc., Dallas, TX, real estate appraiser, 1991—, president, 2004—.

WRITINGS:

Still River: A Lee Henry Oswald Mystery, Thomas Dunne Books/St. Martin's Minotaur (New York, NY), 2005.

SIDELIGHTS: Harry Hunsicker had an established career as a commercial real-estate appraiser—a job he kidded to *Dallas Morning News* writer Cheryl Hall is for people who find accounting too exciting—when his passion for creative writing led him to try his hand at writing a novel. *Still River: A Lee Henry Oswald Mystery* was the result of six months of writing and eighteen months of canvassing literary agents. The book is set in Dallas, Texas, and is the first in an intended series about private investigator Lee Henry Oswald, who in his first outing becomes entangled in a world of corrupt real-estate deals and drug trafficking after taking on a missing person's case.

Rex E. Klett wrote in a *Library Journal* review that "deft prose, wry observation, and a cleverly manipulated plot bode well for this new series." *Dallas Morning News* contributor Nancy Keil commented: "Hunsicker's clever writing and intriguing plot keep the pages of *Still River* turning quickly right up to the slam-bang ending." A reviewer for *Publishers Weekly* remarked that "Hunsicker introduces enough fresh notes to make this a solid debut." "This is a strong urban noir starring an intriguing character," wrote Harriet Klausner for *MBR Bookwatch,* the critic adding that "sub-genre readers will welcome Harry Hunsicker into the fold."

Hunsicker has noted that the process of writing a novel reinvigorated his commitment to his family's business, of which he became president in 2004. As he shared in his interview with Hall, "I've had so much fun, this should have been illegal."

BIOGRAPHICAL AND CRITICAL SOURCES:

PERIODICALS

Dallas Morning News, July 11, 2004, Cheryl Hall, "Doing It by the Book: Career Again Intrigues Businessman," p. A22; May 11, 2005, Nancy Keil, "Harry Hunsicker's Lively Whodunit Turns Dallas into a Shooting Gallery."

Library Journal, June 1, 2005, Rex E. Klett, review of *Still River: A Lee Henry Oswald Mystery,* p. 107.

MBR Bookwatch, May, 2005, Harriet Klausner, review of *Still River.*

Publishers Weekly, April 25, 2005, review of *Still River,* p. 43.

ONLINE

Harry Hunsicker Home Page, http://www.harry hunsicker.com (September 26, 2005).*

*   *   *

HUNSICKER, Harry, Jr.
See HUNSICKER, Harry

I-J

IZOARD, Jacques 1936-

PERSONAL: Born 1936, in Liége, Belgium.

ADDRESSES: Agent—c/o Author Mail, Éditions de La Difference, 30 Rue Ramponeau, Paris 75020, France.

AWARDS, HONORS: Prix Mallarmé, 1978, for *Vêtu, dévetu, libre.*

WRITINGS:

Les sources de feu brûlent le feu contraire (poems), Societe des Ecrivains (Brussels, Belgium), 1964.

Aveuglément (poems), H. Fagne (Brussels, Belgium), 1967.

Un chemin de sel pur (poems), G. Chambelland (Paris, France), 1969.

Des laitiers, des scélérats (poems), Éditions Saint-Germain-des-Pres (Paris, France), 1971.

Voix vêtements saccages, B. Grassett (Paris, France), 1971.

Six poèmes, [Liége, Belgium], 1972.

La patrie empaillée (poems; also see below), B. Grasset (Paris, France), 1973.

(Editor) *Oodradek,* [Liége, Belgium], 1973.

(With Eugène Savitzkaya) *Rue obscure* (prose poems), Atelier de l'Agneau (Liége, Belgium), 1975.

La chamber d'iris, Fond de la Ville (Belgium), 1976.

Andrée Chedid, Seghers (Paris, France), 1977.

Vêtu, dévetu, libre (poems; also see below), P. Belfond (Paris, France), 1978.

(With Bertrand Bracaval) *Voyage sous la peau,* Prenian (France), 1983.

Corps, maisons, tumultes (poems and prose), P. Belfond (Paris, France), 1990.

La patrie empaillée: Vêtu, dévêtu, libre, Labor (Brussels, Belgium), 1992.

(With Eugéne Savitzkaya) *Ketelslegers,* Labor (Brussels, Belgium), 1997.

Le bleu et la poussière: poèmes, Éditions de la Différence (Paris, France), 1998.

Bègue, bogue, borgne, Atelier de l'Agneau (Liége, Belgium), 1999.

Pièges d'air, illustrations by Selçuk Mutlu, Fram (Liége, Belgium), 2000.

Dormir sept ans (poems), illustrations by Selçuk Mutlu, Éditions de la Différence (Paris, France), 2001.

Les girafes du sud, illustrations by Selçuk Mutlu, Éditions de la Différence (Paris, France), 2003.

SIDELIGHTS: Belgian poet and author Jacques Izoard began publishing his work in the early 1960s with *Les sources de feu brûlent le feu contraire.* Since that time, Izoard has been recognized as a leading literary voice in his native land. In 1979 he was awarded the prestigious Prix Mallarmé for *Vêtu, dévêtu, libre.* Although he was most prolific in the 1970s and early 1980s, Izoard continued to publish into the 1990s and beyond, beginning that decade with a collection of poems, prose poems, and aphorisms titled *Corps, maisons, tumultes.* That volume earned the praise of critics and prompted Mechthild Cranston to call Izoard a "visual poet" in *World Literature Today.*

Izoard was born in the Belgian city of Liége, and the majority of the pieces in *Corps, maisons, tumultes* are set there. Most of the book's other poems and aphorisms are set elsewhere in Belgium, in the Walloon countryside, along the banks of the Meuse River or in the Ardennes region. Rather than portray Belgium as a rainy and dreary country, which is the way many foreigners perceive it, Izoard instead creates colorful scenes of green grasses, blooming poppies, and sunshine. Cranston commented on Izoard's optimistic book, saying that "he delights in the . . . tactile, muscular universe of palpable energy, where elves and dwarfs and fairies and dolls and puppets and flying kites move with ease." Izoard's other important works include *Voix vêtements saccages* and *Des laitiers, des scélérats.*

BIOGRAPHICAL AND CRITICAL SOURCES:

PERIODICALS

World Literature Today, spring, 1991, Mechthild Cranston, review of *Corps, maisons, tumultes,* p. 267.*

*   *   *

JACKSON, Joshilyn

PERSONAL: Born in FL; married; husband's name Scott; children: two. *Education:* Georgia State University, Atlanta, B.A.; University of Illinois, Chicago, M.A.

ADDRESSES: Home and office—3705 New Macland Rd., Ste. 200-111, Powder Springs, GA 30127. *E-mail*—joshilyn@joshilynjackson.com.

CAREER: Writer. The Players (children's theatre group), Atlanta, GA, writer and actor; University of Illinois, Chicago, instructor in English. Worked variously as a dinner-theatre actor, staff writer and editor for *Postfeminist Playground,* writing consultant, ghost writer, and essayist.

WRITINGS:

Gods in Alabama (novel), Warner Books (New York, NY), 2005.
Between, Georgia (novel), Warner Books (New York, NY), 2006.

Short fiction published in numerous publications, including *TriQuarterly,* and *Calyx.*

SIDELIGHTS: Despite dropping out of college to embark on an early career as an actor, Joshilyn Jackson knew from an early age that writing was in her blood. "I always had a story going in my head. And I had imaginary friends much longer than I want to admit," Jackson shared in an interview with *Publishers Weekly* contributor Lucinda Dyer. After several years of acting in regional theatre productions and with a traveling dinner-theatre troupe, Jackson began writing her own plays. She returned to college to earn bachelor's and master's degrees in English, and soon began work on her first novel. *Gods in Alabama* was published in 2005 and tells the story of Arlene Fleet, a young Southerner who has fled her small town for Chicago as part of a pact with God—she vows to lead a moral life in exchange for keeping her secret murder of the local high school quarterback under wraps. She is forced to face her demons—and her racist family—when her secret threatens to be revealed. Said Jackson of her protagonist to *Bookpage* contributor Jay MacDonald, "She wants honesty, she wants goodness, she's yearning for goodness. I think that ultimately makes her a really likable person, because we all do crappy things. It's the people who keep trying to choose what is right that you like. We all screw up."

Kaite Mediatore wrote in a review for *Booklist,* "Cleverly disguised as a leisurely paced southern novel, this debut rockets to the end, even as the plot turns back on itself, surprising characters and readers alike." *Library Journal* contributor Rebecca Kelm remarked, "Forget steel magnolias—meet titanium blossoms in Jackson's debut novel, a potent mix of humor, murder, and a dysfunctional Southern family." A *Publishers Weekly* reviewer described *Gods in Alabama* as a "frank, appealing debut," commending Jackson's "genuine affection for the people and places of Dixie." Bernadette Adams Davis commented in a *Bookreporter.com* review that "among Jackson's shining accomplishments is the strength of her characters' voices. . . . This is a promising debut, and Jackson has the potential to become an important southern author."

Jackson's sophomore release, *Between, Georgia,* is also set in the Deep South and follows two feuding families over fifty years. When asked to describe her second novel by a *Southern Literary Review* interviewer, Jackson remarked, "People ask me if it is 'like' *Gods in Alabama,* and I don't know how to answer that. The plot, the characters are nothing like *Gods in Alabama.* It's a different book, but at the same time, I think it's pretty obvious I wrote it. It's that same odd blend of humor and violence."

BIOGRAPHICAL AND CRITICAL SOURCES:

PERIODICALS

Booklist, March 15, 2005, Kaite Mediatore, review of *Gods in Alabama,* p. 14.
Library Journal, March 1, 2005, Rebecca Kelm, review of *Gods in Alabama,* p. 78.
Publishers Weekly, January 24, 2005, Lucinda Dyer, "Joshilyn Jackson: Gods in Alabama," p. 119; February 28, 2005, review of *Gods in Alabama,* p. 41.

ONLINE

BookPage, http://www.bookpage.com/ (September 28, 2005), Jay MacDonald, "Get over it! Joshilyn Jackson's Debut Novel Is Forthright, Frank, and Funny" (author interview).
Bookreporter.com, http://www.bookreporter.com/ (September 28, 2005), Bernadette Adams Davis, review of *Gods in Alabama.*
Southern Literary Review Online, http://www. southernlitreview.com/ (September 28, 2005), author profile and interview.

*   *   *

JAFFE, Michael Grant

PERSONAL: Male.

ADDRESSES: Home—Cleveland, OH. *Agent*—W.W. Norton and Company, 500 5th Ave., New York, NY 10110.

CAREER: Writer. Formerly worked as sports journalist, *Sports Illustrated.*

WRITINGS:

Dance Real Slow (novel), Farrar, Straus & Giroux (New York, NY), 1996.
Skateaway (novel), Farrar, Straus & Giroux (New York, NY), 1999.
Whirlwind (novel), Norton (New York, NY), 2004.

ADAPTATIONS: Dance Real Slow was adapted as film *A Cool, Dry Place,* featuring actor Vince Vaughn.

SIDELIGHTS: A former sports writer, Michael Grant Jaffe turned his attention to fiction with his first novel, *Dance Real Slow.* The novel traces the experiences of Gordon Nash, a young attorney living in Kansas and trying to raise his four-year-old son Calvin on his own after his wife leaves him. Gordon's days are filled with small-time cases and divorces, and his nights with coaching the local high-school basketball team. His quiet life and a new relationship are threatened when his wife suddenly wants to return to him. Joanne Wilkinson, writing for *Booklist,* called the book "gracefully written," and remarked that the "winning characterization of four-year-old Calvin . . . is right on the mark." In a review for the *Financial Post,* Stephen Smith commented that "it's an impressive, assured performance for a debut, fiction that feels like useful, enlightening truth, unadorned and yet lyrical in the writing."

Jaffe's follow-up novel, *Skateaway,* tells the story of the Boone family, whose lives are far too controversial for their blue-collar town of Lukin, Ohio. The family's three children are affected by their mother's work as an OB/GYN who performs abortions despite protests from the local residents; meanwhile, their artist father descends into mental illness. Beth E. Andersen, in a review for *Library Journal,* wrote that "Jaffe's likable cast of characters lures the reader on . . . with language so piercingly on target it feels poetic." A contributor for *Publishers Weekly* remarked that, "although sometimes Jaffe's turns of phrase twist self-consciously, his finely tuned prose reclaims mundane, Midwestern America from flat eighties minimalism," and GraceAnne A. DeCandido called it a "brilliantly imagined and gorgeously written story, with . . . precise emotional tone and tempo."

Whirlwind, Jaffe's next book, tells the story of divorced North Carolina weatherman Lucas Prouty, and what happens when he goes missing while covering Hurricane Isabel. Presumed dead, Prouty causes a media frenzy when he turns up more than a week later. In a review for *Library Journal,* contributor Andrea Tarr commented that Jaffe "ably illustrates callous media manipulations and paparazzi ploys." A contributor for *Publishers Weekly* opined that "Jaffe's sharp, ironic satire of the TV news industry is lively and funny," while Carol Haggas, writing for *Booklist,* remarked that "Jaffe avoids painting Prouty as just another goofy weather guy in a bad sports coat. Instead, Lucas is everyman ever caught in a moral dilemma."

BIOGRAPHICAL AND CRITICAL SOURCES:

PERIODICALS

Booklist, April 1, 1996, Joanne Wilkinson, review of *Dance Real Slow,* p. 1343; September 15, 1999, GraceAnne A. DeCandido, review of *Skateaway,* p. 233; January 1, 2000, review of *Skateaway,* p. 817; September 1, 2004, Carol Haggas, review of *Whirlwind,* p. 61.
Entertainment Weekly, April 26, 1996, review of *Dance Real Slow,* p. 49; March 12, 1999, Michael Grant Jaffe, "Dry Spell: A Novel Experience," p. 16; October 22, 2004, Leah Greenblatt, review of *Whirlwind,* p. 101.
Financial Post, September 21, 1996, Stephen Smith, review of *Dance Real Slow,* p. 29.
Library Journal, October 15, 1999, Beth E. Andersen, review of *Skateaway,* p. 106; September 1, 2004, Andrea Tarr, review of *Whirlwind,* p. 140.
New York Times, February 6, 2000, Patrice Clark Koelsch, review of *Skateaway.*
People, November 29, 2004, Debby Waldman, review of *Whirlwind,* p. 57.
Publishers Weekly, April 24, 1995, "Agency Expands," p. 19; January 22, 1996, review of *Dance Real Slow,* p. 57; May 6, 1996, Paul Nathan, review of *Dance Real Slow,* p. 25; August 23, 1999, review of *Skateaway,* p. 47; October 4, 2004, review of *Whirlwind,* p. 69.

ONLINE

Austin Chronicle Online, http://www.austinchronicle. com/ (November 19, 1999), Ada Calhoun, review of *Skateaway.*

Capital Times (Madison, WI), http://www.madison. com/ (October 15, 2005), Rob Thomas, review of *Whirlwind.*
Curled Up with a Good Book, http://www.curledup. com/ (October 15, 2005), Luan Gaines, review of *Whirlwind.*

*   *   *

JANSZEN, J., Jr.
See GRESHOFF, Jan

*   *   *

JASKI, Bart 1964-

PERSONAL: Born October 15, 1964, in Zuidlaren, Netherlands; son of Walter (a teacher) and Wil (van den Berge) Jaski; married Katharina Lanting, September 5, 1998; children: Louisa, Valerie. *Education:* Attended University of Gröningen, 1983-87; National University of Ireland, University College, Cork, M.Phil. (first-class honors), 1989; Trinity College, Dublin, Ph.D., 1994. *Hobbies and other interests:* Music, reading, skiing, field hockey.

ADDRESSES: Office—Department of Celtic, University of Utrecht, Trans 10, 3512 JK Utrecht, Netherlands. *E-mail*—bart.jaski@1et.uu.nl.

CAREER: Writer, historian, and educator. Royal Irish Academy, Dublin, editorial assistant for *Thesaurus Linguarum Hiberniae,* 1992-94; National Archives, The Hague, Netherlands, research assistant, 1996-98; Dutch Organization for Scientific Research, The Hague, researcher at University of Utrecht, 1998-2002; University of Utrecht, Utrecht, Netherlands, lecturer in Celtic studies, 2002—. Van Hamel Foundation for Celtic Studies, chair, 1997-2004. Exchange scholar in Ireland, Netherlands Organization for International Cooperation in Higher Education, 1988.

WRITINGS:

Early Irish Kingship and Succession, Four Courts Press (Dublin, Ireland), 2000.

(Editor, with I. Genee and B. Smelik) *Arthur, Brigit, Conn, Deirdre . . . Verhaal, taal en recht in de Keltische wereld: Liber amicorum voor Leni van Strien-Gerritsen,* De Keltische Draak (Nijmegen, Netherlands), 2003.

Contributor to books, including *The Fragility of Her Sex? Medieval Irish Women in Their European Context,* edited by C.E. Meek and K. Simms, Blackrock, 1996; and *The Propagation of Power in the Medieval West,* edited by Martin Gosman, Arjo Vanderjagt, and Jan Veenstra, [Groningen, Netherlands], 1997. Contributor to scholarly journals, including *Early Medieval Europe, Ériu, Peritia,* and *Cambrian Medieval Celtic Studies.* Coeditor, *Kelten,* 2004—.

WORK IN PROGRESS: Research on the Irish origin legends and the transmission of texts in manuscripts.

SIDELIGHTS: Bart Jaski told *CA:* "When I studied history at the University of Gröningen, I attended a class by Richard Vaughan on the Vikings. The story about the battle of Clontarf in 1014 caught my imagination, and I became interested in the Vikings in Ireland, especially after reading books by Alfred P. Smyth, Edmund Curtis, and Donnchadh Ó Corráin. The last became my supervisor when I went to Ireland for a year after being awarded an exchange scholarship. At the University College in Cork I wrote an M.Phil. thesis about the political role of the Vikings in Ireland. The results were encouraging, so after a year in the Netherlands I enrolled for a Ph.D. in medieval history at Trinity College, Dublin. My supervisor, Katharine Simms, told me that I had to look for a more challenging topic than political history, so I chose Irish regnal succession, as I found that the current theories about that were not fitting the evidence. My doctoral thesis, rewritten and with three chapters added, was published as *Early Irish Kingship and Succession.*

"I like writing about early Irish history because it is complex and challenging. There is still much important work to be done, so it is a very rich field of study. My interest in it is not focused on one or two topics, but covers almost all aspects of the whole period and more, and it extends to ties between Ireland and the rest of Europe. Ireland often followed the same trends as its neighbors, but because of the different sort of evidence, this is often not immediately visible. As a non-Irishman and a trained historian, I tend to look at certain matters from a different perspective than Irish scholars do."

JENSEN, Bill

PERSONAL: Male. *Education:* Rochester Institute of Technology, B.F.A., 1977, M.S., 1995.

ADDRESSES: Home—Tacoma, WA. *Office*—The Jensen Group, 1 Franklin Place, Morristown, NJ 07960. *E-mail*—bill@simplerwork.com.

CAREER: Business consultant, public speaker, and writer. The Jensen Group (business consulting firm), Morristown, NJ, president and CEO, 1985—.

WRITINGS:

Simplicity: The New Competitive Advantage in a World of More, Better, Faster, Perseus Books (New York, NY), 2001.
Work 2.0: Rewriting the Contract, Perseus Books (New York, NY), 2002.
The Simplicity Survival Handbook: 32 Ways to Do Less and Accomplish More, Perseus Books (New York, NY), 2003.
What Is Your Life's Work?: Answer the Big Question about What Really Matters . . . And Reawaken the Passion for What You Do, HarperCollins Publishing (New York, NY), 2005.

Contributor to publications, including *Harvard Business Review, Strategy and Leadership, Knowledge Management Journal, Focus on Change Management, Human Resource Planning Society Journal, Employee Relations Today, National Productivity, Internal Communications, Communication World,* and *Strategic Communication Management.*

SIDELIGHTS: Bill Jensen has worked since 1985 as a consultant to businesses interested in simplifying their workplace and inspiring employees to improved productivity. His ongoing research in the areas of change management, behavioral communications, and leadership development have led to the publication of numerous books designed, as he mentions on his company Web site, to "make it easier for people to get stuff done."

Jensen's first book, *Simplicity: The New Competitive Advantage in a World of More, Better, Faster,* offers advice to both employers and employees on minimizing wasted time and maximizing efficiency. University of California, Davis's *IT Times* onlin writer Nancy Harrington remarked, "the tools and examples Jensen includes in the book could be useful to any newcomer or old-timer in the workforce, to any employee or manager who believes that achieving clarity provides a workplace advantage. It's a pretty accessible read and offers some tactics an individual can put to work immediately." Mark Schindele wrote in a review for the *Take Back Your Time* Web site that "this engaging book offers solutions to today's hectic work place with humor, insight and common sense."

In *Work 2.0: Rewriting the Contract,* Jensen presents company leaders with strategies for improving employee productivity and morale. A *MyBusiness* magazine reviewer described it as a "well-written book containing practical advice for managers and business owners." Walt Boyes, a contributor to *Automation.com,* commented: "Like a Zen master, Jensen is one of a few thinkers on organizations and the way we work who also practices what he preaches." *Work 2.0: Rewriting the Contract* "is an extremely important book for both employers, employees, and jobseekers."

The Simplicity Survival Handbook: 32 Ways to Do Less and Accomplish More builds on Jensen's beliefs about simplifying the work environment by providing a guide to improving time management and reducing workplace complexity. Christopher T. Ernst, writing for *Personnel Psychology,* described *The Simplicity Survival Handbook* as "one of the best books I have read for dealing with the challenges of work in these hyperturbulent times. . . . The value of this book is both in the simple presentation of the tools, and the way in which they are grounded in a number of daily workplace rituals." As Ernst concluded, "The positive ratio of good ideas to time spent reading serves to strongly endorse the value of this book. Reading *The Simplicity Survival Handbook* is time and attention well spent. And that is the ultimate yardstick in a world of finite time and infinite choice." A reviewer for *Publishers Weekly* remarked that Jensen's "concise presentation . . . lays everything out perfectly the first time."

Jensen focuses on the personal impact of career priorities in *What Is Your Life's Work?: Answer the Big Question about What Really Matters . . . And Reawaken the Passion for What You Do,* in which he compiles letters and journal entries addressing what matters most in people's lives. A *Publishers Weekly* contributor commented: "Jensen does a wonderful job of pulling together meaningful, often moving letters gathered in the course of his consulting work," further adding that the book has "an abundance of meaningful philosophy, insight and advice."

BIOGRAPHICAL AND CRITICAL SOURCES:

PERIODICALS

Personnel Psychology, spring, 2005, Christopher T. Ernst, review of *The Simplicity Survival Handbook: 32 Ways to Do Less and Accomplish More,* p. 257.
Publishers Weekly, November 3, 2003, review of *The Simplicity Survival Handbook,* p. 70; April 11, 2005, review of *What Is Your Life's Work?: Answer the Big Question about What Really Matters . . . And Reawaken the Passion for What You Do,* p. 46.

ONLINE

Automation.com, http://www.automation.com/ (September 26, 2005), Walt Boyes, review of *Work 2.0: Rewriting the Contract.*
IT Times Online, http://ittimes.ucdavis.edu/ (October 8, 2005), Nancy Harrington, review of *Simplicity: The New Competitive Advantage in a World of More, Better, Faster.*
MyBusiness Online, http://www.nfib.com/ (June 2, 2004), review of *Work 2.0.*
Simpler Work Web Site, http://www.simplerwork.com/ (September 26, 2005), company information and author biography.
Take Back Your Time Web site, http://www.simpleliving.net/timeday/ (September 26, 2005), Mark Schindele, review of *Simplicity.**

*　　*　　*

JHUNG, Paula

PERSONAL: Married; children: two.

ADDRESSES: Home and office—P.O. Box 1658, Rancho Santa Fe, CA 92067. *E-mail*—life@paulajhung.com.

CAREER: Writer and decorating consultant. Clean Design (decorating consulting service), Rancho Santa Fe, CA, founder.

WRITINGS:

How to Avoid Housework: Tips, Hints, and Secrets on How to Have a Spotless Home, Simon & Schuster (New York, NY), 1995.
Guests without Grief: Entertaining Made Easy for the Hesitant Host, Simon & Schuster (New York, NY), 1997.
Cleaning and the Meaning of Life: Simple Solutions to Declutter Your Home and Beautify Your Life, Health Communications (Deerfield Beach, FL), 2005.

Contributor to periodicals, including *Family Circle, Woman's Day, Cosmopolitan, House Beautiful, Home, Bridal Guide, Woman's World, Boston Herald, Dallas Morning News, Los Angeles Times,* and *Washington Post.*

SIDELIGHTS: Decorating consultant Paula Jhung was influenced at an early age by the clutter and disarray of her childhood home. Lamenting the disorder that persisted despite her mother's nonstop efforts, Jhung shared in an interview posted on her home page: "I wanted a different life. I found it by creating surroundings that boosted my mood, yet demanded little from me." She further specified her mission as an interior designer: "Through my own trial and error I've found the easiest ways to pare down, lighten up, and make a home more comfortable, convenient and reflective of who we are." Jhung presents these hard-won methods in several books designed to minimize stress and maximize order. Her first book, *How to Avoid Housework: Tips, Hints, and Secrets on How to Have a Spotless Home,* was commended for its "down-to-earth advice" by *Booklist* reviewer Mike Tribby. A contributor to *Publishers Weekly* remarked, "This breezy, upbeat book will gladden slatterns everywhere."

Jhung followed *How to Avoid Housework* with *Guests without Grief: Entertaining Made Easy for the Hesitant Host* and *Cleaning and the Meaning of Life: Simple Solutions to Declutter Your Home and Beautify Your Life.* She shared in an interview with *North County Times* staff writer Agnes Diggs the philosophy behind *Cleaning and the Meaning of Life*: "Once we get a handle on how our homes nurture and support us, we're better able to manage and relate to the world around us. It just makes life a lot more serene, going into a house that doesn't demand a lot of you." A *Publishers Weekly* reviewer commented of the book, "Jhung's strategies for 'taking the mess out of domestic and the irk out of work' are fun to read and easy to implement."

Jhung told *CA:* "As to what influences my work? I'd say it's a passion for the psychology of our surroundings—how they can uplift, stress, or depress us. My writing process? I first find a working title, then throw everything I know, think I know, or want to know about the topic on paper. It's usually ninety-five percent garbage, but out of that garbage I usually glean a few fertile seeds. The most surprising thing I've learned as a writer? That someone with such a short attention span could stick it out for over twenty years. Which of my books is my favorite? That's like asking which of my kids I like best. I love them each equally for their particular quirks and qualities. What kind of effect I hope my books will have? To make life a little easier, a little richer, and a lot more fun."

BIOGRAPHICAL AND CRITICAL SOURCES:

PERIODICALS

Booklist, May 1, 1995, Mike Tribby, review of *How to Avoid Housework: Tips, Hints, and Secrets on How to Have a Spotless Home,* p. 1542.
Publishers Weekly, April 3, 1995, review of *How to Avoid Housework,* p. 60; April 11, 2005, review of *Cleaning and the Meaning of Life: Simple Solutions to Declutter Your Home and Beautify Your Life,* p. 48.

ONLINE

North County Times Online, http://www.nctimes.com/ (May 13, 2005), Agnes Diggs, "Local Author Sees Link between Clean and Serene."
Paula Jhung Home Page, http://www.paulajhung.com (September 27, 2005).

*   *   *

JOHNSON, Helen Jane
See JOHNSON, Jane

JOHNSON, Jane 1960-
(Jude Fisher, Helen Jane Johnson, Gabriel King, a joint pseudonym)

PERSONAL: Born 1960, in Cornwall, England; daughter of Donald and Brenda Mary Johnson. *Education:* Goldsmiths College, London, B.A.; University College, M.A. *Hobbies and other interests:* Rock climbing, cinema, writing.

ADDRESSES: Home—Coleshill, Buckinghamshire, England. *Office*—HarperCollins Publishers, 77-85 Fulham Palace Rd., London W6 8JB, England. *E-mail*—jane.johnson@harpercollins.co.uk.

CAREER: Editor and writer. George Allen & Unwin Publishers, London, England, editor, 1984-90; Harper-Collins Publishers, London, editor, 1990—, Voyager imprint, publishing director, 1996—.

WRITINGS:

FOR CHILDREN

The Secret Country, Simon & Schuster (New York, NY), 2005.
Shadow World, Simon & Schuster (New York, NY), in press.

AS JUDE FISHER

The Lord of the Rings: The Fellowship of the Ring: Visual Companion, Houghton Mifflin (Boston, MA), 2001.
The Lord of the Rings: The Two Towers: Visual Companion, Houghton Mifflin (Boston, MA), 2002.
The Lord of the Rings: The Return of the King: Visual Companion, Houghton Mifflin (Boston, MA), 2003.
The Lord of the Rings: Complete Visual Companion, Houghton Mifflin (Boston, MA), 2004.

"FOOL'S GOLD TRILOGY"; AS JUDE FISHER

Sorcery Rising, DAW (New York, NY), 2002.
Wild Magic, DAW (New York, NY), 2003.
The Rose of the World, DAW (New York, NY), 2005.

WITH M. JOHN HARRISON; UNDER JOINT PSEUDONYM GABRIEL KING

The Wild Road, Arrow (London, England), 1997, Ballantine (New York, NY), 1998.
The Golden Cat, Ballantine (New York, NY), 1999.
The Knot Garden, [England] 2000.
Nonesuch, Century, 2001.

WORK IN PROGRESS: An historical novel set in Britain and Morocco in the seventeenth century involving pirates.

SIDELIGHTS: Jane Johnson began her career as an editor of fantasy and science fiction. She had long been devoted to the works of J.R.R. Tolkien, and a stroke of luck led her to a position at Allen & Unwin Publishers, which had originally published Tolkien's works. Within six months of being hired, Johnson was working as an editor on Unwin's Tolkien titles and their new fantasy list. Part of her work with the Tolkien list involved finding illustrators for new editions of Tolkien's work, including John Howe and Alan Lee, whose work served as an inspiration for Peter Jackson's movie trilogy of Tolkien's work. She has worked with such well-known fantasy and science-fiction writers as Arthur C. Clarke, David Eddings, Raymond Feist, Robin Hobb, Steven King, George R.R. Martin, Kim Stanley Robinson, and M. John Harrison, the last with whom she began writing her first fantasy series.

When she began editing the work of Harrison, the pair hit it off and began a personal relationship that lasted until 1995. Though this relationship ended, their professional work had just begun, and the pair, under the joint pseudonym Gabriel King, published four titles together. *The Wild Road* was the first of a series about Tag, the cat. Johnson explained to an interviewer for *Eternal Night Web site, The Wild Road* was "submitted under the Gabriel King pseudonym, so that the work would be judged on its own merits and not for who either of us were."

The Wild Road is the story of Tag, a young cat with the destiny to rescue the king and queen of the cats. Tag is pursued by a human known only as the Alchemist, who wishes to travel the Wild Roads that cats guard. "This is a story about the overwhelming instinct to survive against insurmountable odds," noted

S. Kay Elmore in *SFSite.com,* the critic continuing: "It reads like a forgotten mythology, including all the elements of a classic hero story, but it is by no means formulaic." Georges T. Dodds, also writing for *SFSite.-com,* commented that *The Wild Road* "strikes an excellent balance between an animalistic and anthropomorphic treatment. . . . [The characters] are rich and complex, each having their own histories, personalities, and hurdles to overcome."

Tag's story continues in *The Golden Cat,* and the tale grows darker as animals are dying at the entrances and exits of the Wild Roads. The royal cats have three golden kittens, but all three of the young ones disappear, and Tag must solve the mystery. In the final book of the series, *The Knot Garden,* a human, Anna Prescott, becomes a central figure. She settles in the town of Ashmore, a place that intersects the Wild Roads, and Anna herself becomes the cause of chaos unleashed on both the village and the Wild Roads. Again, cats must come to the rescue. After completing the series, Johnson and Harrison created the stand-alone novel *Nonesuch,* which again features the village of Ashmore.

While her writing work had just begun, Johnson's work with Tolkien's "Lord of the Rings" series reached a new level when Peter Jackson's movie trilogy of the series made its way to theaters. To accompany the movies, Johnson, as Jude Fisher, created a number of "Visual Companions." While working on the books, she traveled to New Zealand where the movies were being filmed. "It was the most amazing time," she told an interviewer for *Eternal Night Web site.* "As a Tolkien fan since the age of twelve, and Tolkien publisher for over ten years . . . it was a very emotional experience to see the world coming to life just as I had envisaged it." Of her work on the "Visual Companions," Susan Salpini wrote in *School Library Journal,* "The informative, interesting text is supplemented by many gorgeous pictures," and Patricia White-Williams, in the same publication, found the "Visual Companions" to be "an entertaining read."

In 2002, Johnson tried her hand at writing her own series and produced the "Fool's Gold Trilogy," published under her pen name Jude Fisher. She commented to the *Eternal Night Web site* interviewer that the sale of her first series as Gabriel King "was pretty exciting; but not as scary as selling the solo fantasy series in 2000, which was terrifying beyond belief."

Sorcery Rising, which begins the series, takes place at Allfair, a festival during which a truce is called among the nations of Elda. Katla Aranson comes to sell her metalwork; Virelai, a mage's apprentice, comes to escape. He has stolen Rosa Eldi, his master's mistress who has no memory of her life, and a black cat, which contains his master's magic. The characters simply mean to go about their lives, but their fates are intertwined, and much more rests on their decisions than they are aware. "This is a complex novel, with a dense plot and an intricate interweaving of many different viewpoints and storylines. It's clear, however, that it's only the opening to a much larger saga," claimed Victoria Strauss, writing for *SFSite.com.* Jackie Cassada of *Library Journal* considered *Sorcery Rising* to be a "fast-paced introduction" to a new world, and recommended, readers "of epic fantasy should enjoy this tale."

Wild Magic follows Virelai into the service of Lord Tycho Issian, who is obsessed with Rosa Eldi, who has married the Eyran king Rayn Asharson. Issian will stop at nothing to take Rosa Eldi from the Eyran king. Katla, who escaped death at the end of the previous novel, wishes to accompany her father on a dangerous journey, even though she has been told her destiny is elsewhere. Commenting on the number of characters and subplots, Victoria Strauss wrote in *SFSite.com* that "It's not just a narrative, but a technical challenge to juggle so many stories and players without dropping or shortchanging at least a few of them, but Fisher manages this with great skill." Cassada, writing again for *Library Journal,* noted the combination of "large-scale intrigues with personal accounts of struggle and courage," while *Booklist* reviewer Paula Luedtke gave the novel a "thumbs-up." Johnson herself called the novel "Lord of the Rings meets Bridget Jones," reported Benedicte Page in *Bookseller.*

The series concludes with *The Rose of the World,* which explains that Rosa Eldi is actually one of the three original gods of Elda, and the cat Virelai stole is the second. As she remembers who she is, Rosa Eldi realizes she must be united with the third god, Sirio, the Man, or chaos will come to all of Elda and the world will be destroyed by magic. Luedtke, in *Booklist,* considered the novel "the nerve-wracking, intoxicating conclusion" of the series, and commented on its "fabulous, multilayered poetic story of a world, full of complex, painfully real, endearingly vulnerable characters." Harriet Klausner, writing for *MBR Book-*

watch, commented that the novel "ties up all the loose ends, answering all questions satisfactorily while rewarding readers with a fantastic climax."

Although many of her novels and her work on the *Lord of the Rings* movie companion books appeal to a young-adult audience, it was not until 2005 that her first novel specifically written for children was published. As she explained to Adam Volk in *SFSite.com,* "I wrote *The Secret Country* as a sort of secret, selfish project when I should have been working on something else, and never designed it for a market or a readership, but for the 9-year-old in me who's still alive and kicking." *The Secret Country* tells the story of Ben, a boy who, though he does not realize it, is from the magical world of Eidolon. On a visit to a local pet shop run by Mr. Dodds, Ben encounters a cat who speaks to him, explaining that Dodds is bringing magical creatures from Eidolon into the world, where they are dying without magic. The cat, Iggy, begs Ben to help him and the other creatures of Eidolon to return home, thwarting Mr. Dodds's plan. Dodds's "bigger plan, though, we find in the second book is to take over Eidolon," explained Johnson in an interview with Sandy Auden of *Alien Online.* The second book, *Shadow World,* additionally reveals that Mr. Dodds is also known as Dodman, and can transform himself into an eight-foot-tall monster with a dog's head.

Asked by Adam Volk of *SFSite.com* whether she preferred writing or editing, Johnson replied, "They really are very different jobs, so it's hard to compare: one is all about teamwork, talking, persuasion and compromise (that'll be publishing for those who are still guessing); the other is most of the time solitary, selfish and a bit mad. I think the combination is a good one, at least for staying sane, since there's not much room for creativity in the publishing industry now and writing gives me an outlet for that energy which I need."

BIOGRAPHICAL AND CRITICAL SOURCES:

PERIODICALS

Booklist, June 1, 2002, Paula Luedtke, review of *Sorcery Rising,* p. 1696; July, 2003, Paula Luedtke, review of *Wild Magic,* p. 1877; February 1, 2005, Paula Luedtke, review of *The Rose of the World,* p. 950.

Bookseller, May 9, 2003, Benedicte Page, "A World of Her Own: Writing as Jude Fisher, Voyager Publisher Jane Johnson Creates Fantasy Novels Which Feature a Powerful, Rock-Climbing Heroine," p. 25.

Cartography and Geographic Information Science, October, 2004, Denis Wood, "The Maps of Tolkien's Middle-Earth," p. 255.

Kirkus Reviews, May 1, 2002, review of *Sorcery Rising,* p. 624.

Library Journal, July, 2002, Jackie Cassada, review of *Sorcery Rising,* p. 127; July, 2003, Jackie Cassada, review of *Wild Magic,* p. 132; March 15, 2004, Michael Rogers, "Go to the Movies—Off Screen," p. 80.

MBR Bookwatch, February, 2005, Harriet Klausner, review of *The Rose of the World.*

Publishers Weekly, June 17, 2002, pp. 48-49; June 23, 2003, review of *Wild Magic,* p. 51; January 17, 2005, review of *The Rose of the World,* p. 39.

School Library Journal, April, 2002, Patricia White-Williams, review of *The Lord of the Rings: The Fellowship of the Ring: Visual Companion,* p. 189; March, 2004, Susan Salpini, review of *The Lord of the Rings: The Return of the King: Visual Companion,* p. 252.

ONLINE

Alien Online, http://www.thealienonline.net/ (September 28, 2005), Sandy Auden, "Fantasy/Horror Book Deals: Barclay, Johnson, Gallagher."

Eternal Night Web site, http://www.eternalnight.co.uk/ (October 10, 2005), interview with Johnson.

Jude Fisher Home Page, http://www.judefisher.co.uk (September 28, 2005).

SFSite.com, http://www.sfsite.com/ (October 10, 2005), S. Kay Elmore, review of *The Wild Road;* Georges T. Dodds, review of *The Wild Road* and *The Golden Cat;* Victoria Strauss, review of *Sorcery Rising* and *Wild Magic;* Adam Volk, "An Interview with Jane Johnson."*

*   *   *

JONES, Jami Biles
See JONES, Jami Lynn

JONES, Jami Lynn 1951-
(Jami Biles Jones)

PERSONAL: Born December 14, 1951, in Dayton, OH; daughter of Martin Broomall (a nuclear engineer) and Lee (a homemaker; maiden name, Kennedy) Biles; married John W. Jones (a librarian), April 3, 1993 (died June 10, 2004); children: Joshua. *Ethnicity:* "Caucasian." *Education:* Mills College, B.A., 1970; University of Maryland, M.L.S., 1974; Nova Southeastern, Ph.D., 1994. *Religion:* Protestant.

ADDRESSES: Home—202 Berkshire Rd., Greenville, NC 27858. *Office*—Department of Library Science, Joyner 1106, East Carolina University, Greenville, NC 27858. *E-mail*—jami@askdrjami.org; jonesj@mail. ecu.edu.

CAREER: Pennsville Public Library, Pennsville, NJ, director, 1983-87; high school media specialist in Middletown, DE, 1987-91; Arizona State Library, Phoenix, consultant, 1991-92; Sampson County Public Library, Clinton, NC, director, 1992-93; media specialist for public school district of Naples, FL, 1994-2004; East Carolina University, Greenville, NC, assistant professor, 2004—. Presenter of workshops on resiliency and teen issues. Originator of the Amanda Award, Florida Association of Media in Education.

MEMBER: American Library Association, Society of Children's Book Writers and Illustrators, Florida Association of Media in Education, North Carolina Library Association, North Carolina School Media Association.

WRITINGS:

UNDER NAME JAMI BILES JONES

Helping Teens Cope: Resources for School Library Media Specialists and Other Youth Workers, Linworth Publishing (Worthington, OH), 2003.
Resiliency, Franklin Watts (New York, NY), 2006.

Author of "Teen Talk," a column in *School Library Journal,* 2004-05; Contributor to periodicals, including *Newsweek.*

WORK IN PROGRESS: The Power of Media Specialists to Raise Academic Achievement and Strengthen At-Risk Youth, for Linworth Publishing; a work of fiction, expected, 2008.

SIDELIGHTS: Jami Lynn Jones told *CA:* "I was not born a writer, and I certainly did not set out to become one, but when my son's girlfriend died, my first response was to pick up a pen and commit my thoughts and grief to paper. Since Amanda's death in 2001, I have spent hours reading about, talking to, and observing teens in hopes that my writing will speak to two groups: adolescents who are growing up in a society that is not teen-friendly and adults who allow this situation to exist. I do not think of myself as a writer, but rather as an advocate for teens whose philosophy is best summed up by the late great English essayist and social commentator J.B. Priestly, who wrote that 'society gets the teenagers it deserves.'

"When I started advocating for teens, I was living in Florida. I became more and more disturbed by the actions of some retirees who firmly believed that because they had raised their own children, their social responsibility to educate and support youth had been fulfilled. Since then I have read that as the population ages and baby-boomers retire, much of America will have Florida's demographics. If this comes to pass, it does not bode well for teens. What are my writing goals? I want to motivate teens to petition for the support they need. I want to influence adults to embrace youth. I want to one day live in a society that has the teens it deserves."

BIOGRAPHICAL AND CRITICAL SOURCES:

PERIODICALS

School Library Journal, May, 2004, Dana McDougald, review of *Helping Teens Cope: Resources for School Library Media Specialists and Other Youth Workers,* p. 181.

ONLINE

Ask Dr. Jami Web site, http://askdrjami.org (November 24, 2005).

JORGENSON, Olaf

PERSONAL: Male. *Education:* Arizona State University, Ed.D.

ADDRESSES: Agent—c/o Author Mail, NSTA Press, 1840 Wilson Blvd., Arlington, VA 22201-3000.

CAREER: Educator, administrator, and writer. Mesa Unified School District, Mesa, AZ, former director of K-12 science, social studies, and world languages; American School, Tegucigalpa, Honduras, former principal; Hawaii Preparatory Academy, Kamuela, HI, headmaster; formerly a teacher and administrator in various American and foreign schools. Leadership Assistance for Science Education Reform (LASER) strategic planning institute, National Science Resources Center, faculty member.

MEMBER: Association of Science Materials Centers (president-elect).

WRITINGS:

(With Jackie Cleveland and Rick Vanosdall) *Doing Good Science in Middle School: A Practical Guide to Inquiry-Based Instruction,* NSTA Press (Arlington, VA), 2004.

SIDELIGHTS: Although he is now an educational administrator, Olaf Jorgenson spent several years as a classroom science teacher. In *Doing Good Science in Middle School: A Practical Guide to Inquiry-Based Instruction,* Jorgenson and two other experienced teachers—Jackie Cleveland, a former Presidential Award for Excellence in Science Teaching winner, and Rick Vanosdall, who, like Jorgenson, once oversaw science instruction for the Mesa, Arizona school district—explain an innovative method for teaching science to sixth-, seventh-, and eighth-grade students. Jorgenson, Cleveland, and Vandosall advocate an active pedagogy, where students formulate hypotheses and test them experimentally, rather than the common, passive, reading-based science instruction. The book includes ten specific suggestions for hands-on scientific experiments, described by a *School Library Journal* contributor as "developmentally appropriate and engaging," around which teachers can build lesson plans that encourage students to do science rather than merely read about it in a textbook. *Doing Good Science in Middle School* also features explanations of how middle-school students think and learn, explains why teaching students how to ask and answer questions scientifically is at the heart of teaching good science, and presents suggestions for integrating other subjects, including literacy and mathematics, into science classrooms. The result, wrote a *Journal of College Science Teaching* contributor, is "a comprehensive practitioner's guide."

BIOGRAPHICAL AND CRITICAL SOURCES:

PERIODICALS

Journal of College Science Teaching, July-August, 2005, review of *Doing Good Science in Middle School: A Practical Guide to Inquiry-Based Instruction,* p. S5.
NEA Today, March, 2005, "Making Science Class Count," p. 60.
School Library Journal, April, 2005, review of *Doing Good Science in Middle School,* p. S77.

ONLINE

National Science Teachers Association Web site, http://www.nsta.org/ (September 28, 2005), "New Book from NTSA Press Addresses Challenges of Keeping Middle Schoolers Tuned in to Science."*

*   *   *

JOSEPHY, Alvin M., Jr. 1915-2005

OBITUARY NOTICE— See index for *CA* sketch: Born May 18, 1915, in Woodmere, NY; died October 16, 2005, in Greenwich, CT. Historian, editor, and author. Josephy was an authority on the history of Native Americans in the West, especially the Nez Percé tribe. He came from a family of publishers; he was the grandson of Samuel Knopf and nephew of Alfred A. Knopf. Josephy's college hopes were dashed during his second year at Harvard University in 1934, when his family's money ran out because of the Great Depression. Contacting an uncle who worked in Hollywood, he got a job as a junior writer for Metro-Gold-wyn-Mayer. He found the work not to his liking, however, and followed this with jobs at a Wall Street brokerage firm and then as a foreign correspondent in Mexico. Here he notably had an opportunity to interview Leon Trotsky, the exiled Russian revolutionary. During World War II, Josephy continued his correspondent work as a reporter covering the Marine Corps in the Pacific theater. He returned to Hollywood after the war and took up script writing again, finding some success with the film *The Captive City* (1952). Josephy became involved in publishing and editing when he joined the staff of *Time* magazine in New York City as an associate editor during the 1950s. It was while here that he started to become interested in Native American history, primarily because he found existing resources at the time to be so scant. He began taking trips out West to do research, and was shocked by the deplorable conditions in which tribes were living, thanks to policies of the Eisenhower administration that took away the Native Americans' autonomy. Josephy interviewed these people and became particularly interested in the Nez Percé and their famous leader Chief Joseph. He began writing about Indian history with such publications as *The Patriot Chiefs: A Chronicle of American Indian Leadership* (1961) and *Chief Joseph's People and Their War* (1964). In 1960, Josephy left *Time* to take a job as vice president and senior editor of American Heritage books. He did this for sixteen years, then served as editor and editor in chief of *American Heritage* magazine until 1979. During the late 1960s, he also became active in preserving Native American culture as commissioner of Indian Arts and Crafts Board for the U.S. Department of the Interior. Beginning in 1977, he became a trustee for the Museum of the American Indian, as well as for the Natural Resources Defense Council, an environmental group. As a founding board chairman of the National Museum of the American Indian, one of his last public appearances was at the opening ceremony for the museum in 2004. Among his many other books, Josephy was the author of *The Indian Heritage of America* (1968), *Black Hills, White Sky* (1979), *Now that the Buffalo's Gone: A Study of Today's American Indians* (1982), and *Five-Hundred Nations* (1994). At the time of his death, he had completed editing the anthology *Lewis and Clark through Indian Eyes* (2006).

OBITUARIES AND OTHER SOURCES:

BOOKS

Josephy, Alvin M., Jr., *A Walk toward Oregon: A Memoir,* Knopf (New York, NY), 2000.

PERIODICALS

Chicago Tribune, October 18, 2005, section 3, p. 8.
Los Angeles Times, October 21, 2005, p. B9.
New York Times, October 18, 2005, p. C19.
Washington Post, October 18, 2005, p. B6.

*   *   *

JUDSON, Daniel
(Rabbi Daniel Judson)

PERSONAL: Married Sandy Falk (an obstetrician). *Religion:* Jewish.

ADDRESSES: Agent—c/o Author Mail, Jewish Lights Publishing, Sunset Farm Offices, Route 4, P.O. Box 237, Woodstock, VT 05091.

CAREER: Temple Beth David of the South Shore, Canton, MA, rabbi.

WRITINGS:

(Editor, with Kerry M. Olitzky) *The Rituals and Practices of a Jewish Life: A Handbook for Personal and Spiritual Renewal,* with a foreword by Vanessa L. Ochs, illustrated by Joel Moskowitz, Jewish Lights Publishing (Woodstock, VT), 2002.

(With Nancy H. Wiener) *Meeting at the Well: A Jewish Spiritual Guide to Being Engaged,* with a foreword by Lawrence A. Hoffman, UAHC Press (New York, NY), 2002.

(With wife, Sandy Falk, and Steven A. Rapp) *The Jewish Pregnancy Book: A Resource for the Soul, Body, and Mind during Pregnancy, Birth, and the First Three Months,* Jewish Lights Publishing (Woodstock, VT), 2004.

(With Kerry M. Olitzky) *Jewish Ritual: A Brief Introduction for Christians,* Jewish Lights Publishing (Woodstock, VT), 2005.

SIDELIGHTS: Daniel Judson is a rabbi and the author of several books on Judaism. Some of his books, including *Meeting at the Well: A Jewish Spiritual*

Guide to Being Engaged (with coauthor Nancy H. Wiener) and *The Jewish Pregnancy Book: A Resource for the Soul, Body, and Mind during Pregnancy, Birth, and the First Three Months* (written in collaboration with his wife, obstetrician Sandy Falk, and yoga practitioner Steven A. Rapp), help Jews to use their religion for support during times of change in their life. In *The Jewish Pregnancy Book,* the three authors draw on their specialties to provide a guide that "supports and acknowledges the whole being of the expectant Jewish mother," wrote a *Jewish Woman* contributor. Falk explains the medical side of pregnancy and birth, tracing the development of the fetus and discussing prenatal tests that doctors might recommend. Rapp suggests the use of the aleph-bet form of yoga, which uses poses that mimic the letters of the Hebrew alphabet, to help stay in physical shape during pregnancy. Judson, meanwhile, provides a Jewish spiritual perspective on the process, including prayers, rituals, and discussions of such religious questions as at what point in development a baby receives his or her soul. The resulting book is "a delightful and spiritual celebration of life's beginnings," concluded a *Publishers Weekly* critic.

In *Jewish Ritual: A Brief Introduction for Christians* Judson and Rabbi Kerry M. Olitzky discuss the histories of various Jewish traditions, including wearing kippahs and tefillin, keeping the Shabbat and studying the Torah. The two authors examine the scriptural bases for each ritual, its history, and its parallel rituals in Christianity. "The format is easy to follow," George Cohen wrote in *Booklist,* "and the language quite accessible." "Given today's permeable religious boundaries and the cross-fertilization between traditions," wrote a *Publishers Weekly* contributor, "this handbook should be warmly welcomed on the religious bookshelf."

BIOGRAPHICAL AND CRITICAL SOURCES:

PERIODICALS

Booklist, January 1, 2005, George Cohen, review of *Jewish Ritual: A Brief Introduction for Christians,* p. 789.

Jewish Woman, spring, 2004, review of *The Jewish Pregnancy Book: A Resource for the Soul, Body, and Mind during Pregnancy, Birth, and the First Three Months.*

Publishers Weekly, November 24, 2003, review of *The Jewish Pregnancy Book,* p. 61; January 17, 2005, review of *Jewish Ritual,* p. 51.*

K

KARR, Clarence 1941-

PERSONAL: Born October 27, 1941, in Petrolia, Ontario, Canada; son of Frederick (a farmer and carpenter) and Adeline Irene (a homemaker) Karr; married Kathryn Ann Nolting (a teacher), January 29, 1971; children: Jennifer, Kristin Karr Thurston, Ryan. *Ethnicity:* "Canadian/British." *Education:* University of Western Ontario, B.A. (honors), 1964, M.A., 1966; University of New South Wales, Ph.D., 1970. *Religion:* Lutheran.

ADDRESSES: Home—1395 Graham Cr., Nanaimo, British Columbia V9S 2E2, Canada. Office—Malaspina University College, Nanaimo, British Columbia V9R 5S5, Canada. E-mail—ckarr@shaw.ca.

CAREER: Writer and educator. Bishops University, Lennoxville, Quebec, Canada, assistant professor, 1971-74; University of Winnipeg, Winnipeg, Manitoba, Canada, assistant professor, 1974-75; Malaspina University College, Nanaimo, British Columbia, Canada, professor, 1975—. Nanaimo District Museum, chair, 1993-98; Nanaimo Community Archives, chair, 1999-2004.

MEMBER: Bibliographical Society of Canada, Canadian Historical Association, Society for the History of Authorship, Reading, and Publishing.

WRITINGS:

Authors and Audiences: Popular Canadian Fiction in the Early Twentieth Century, McGill-Queen's University Press (Montreal, Quebec, Canada), 2000.

WORK IN PROGRESS: *L.M. Montgomery as Reader,* completion expected in 2007.

*   *   *

KERN, Edith 1912-2005

OBITUARY NOTICE— See index for *CA* sketch: Born February 7, 1912, in Düsseldorf, Germany; died September 29, 2005, in New York, NY. Educator and author. A professor emerita at Smith College, Kern was a teacher of Romance languages and comparative literature who was one of the first people to write a scholarly article on Samuel Beckett. She emigrated from Germany in 1938 and later became a U.S. citizen. A 1942 graduate of Bridgewater College, she earned her M.A. in 1944 and her Ph.D. in 1946, both from Johns Hopkins University. She then taught briefly at the University of Maryland before moving on to the University of Kansas, where she was on the faculty from 1947 to 1952. The rest of the 1950s were spent at the University of Pennsylvania, where she was director of the television teaching project. During the 1950s, she also became notable for writing the first scholarly article on Beckett published in the United States (it appeared in *Yale French Studies*). Kern joined St. John's University as professor of French in 1960, and from 1965 to 1972 she taught comparative literature and Romance literature at the University of Washington. Continuing her peripatetic career, she was next Silbert Professor of Humanities and chair of the comparative literature department at Smith, and from 1977 to 1981 was John Cranford Adams Professor at Hofstra University. She left teaching for a time to direct a number of seminars for the National Endowment for the Humanities, as well as serving as president of the Modern Language Association from 1976 to 1977. Kern's last teaching job was with the New School in New York City, which she joined in 1986. Her scholarly articles were widely published and translated, and she was the author or editor of several books, including *Sartre: A Collection of Critical Essays* (1962), *Existential Thought and Fictional Technique: Kierkegaard, Sartre, Beckett* (1970), and *Tradition and Innovation in Comedy: A Contribution to the History of Laughter* (1984). In addition to these accomplishments, Kern was also founding editor of the journal *Dada/Surrealism.*

OBITUARIES AND OTHER SOURCES:

PERIODICALS

Chronicle of Higher Education, December 2, 2005, p. A38.
New York Times, October 9, 2005, p. A44.

*   *   *

KHASHOGGI, Soheir 1947(?)-

PERSONAL: Born c. 1947, in Alexandria, Egypt; daughter of Mohammed (a physician) and Samiha Khashoggi; married a Lebanese doctor, c. 1972 (marriage ended); married a Lebanese businessman, c. 1979 (divorced, 1989); children: (first marriage) Samiha (daughter); (second marriage) three daughters. *Education:* Attended San Jose State University and American University of Beirut; Interior Design Center of Beirut, degree. *Religion:* Muslim.

ADDRESSES: Home—Greenwich, CT. *Agent*—c/o Author Mail, Forge, 175 5th Ave., New York, NY 10010.

CAREER: Artist, interior designer, and writer. Women for Women, member of the board.

WRITINGS:

NOVELS

Mirage, Forge (New York, NY), 1996.
Mosaic, Forge (New York, NY), 2004.
Nadia's Song, Forge (New York, NY), 2005.

SIDELIGHTS: Novelist Soheir Khashoggi was born into one of the richest families in Saudi Arabia; her brother, Adnan Khashoggi, is a famous billionaire businessman, and her nephew, the late Dodi al Fayed, was the boyfriend of Britain's Princess Diana. She spent much of her childhood in relatively liberal Egypt (where she was born) and attended Western schools, so when she returned to Saudi Arabia and entered into an arranged marriage she sharply felt the strictures that the conservative Islam of Saudi Arabia put on her life. At age twenty-six, she convinced one of her brothers to give permission for her to leave the country (a woman cannot leave Saudi Arabia without the permission of her husband or a male relative), took her daughter, and started a newer, freer life.

Khashoggi's first career was painting, but in 1996 she began publishing novels about the experiences of Muslim women. Her first book, *Mirage,* is set in a fictional country called al-Remal that bears striking similarities to Saudi Arabia. The book's protagonist, Amira Badir, is thrilled at first when her parents arrange a marriage to Prince Ali Ashad for her, but she quickly discovers that the prince is not a perfect husband. He beats her, drinks heavily, and lusts after boys. With the help of a French doctor Amira escapes al-Remal, changes her identity, and moves to the United States, but she still lives in fear of Ali and his "security" forces. "Khashoggi paints in glamorous and startling colors the segregated 'women's world' of traditional upper-class Islamic culture," wrote a *Publishers Weekly* critic, and *Booklist* reviewer Emily Melton praised her as "a natural-born storyteller who quickly engages her reader in a tale that is stylish, suspenseful, and entertaining."

Khashoggi's second novel, *Mosaic,* is about a Muslim woman already settled in the United States. Dina Ahmed runs a floral-design shop in New York City, where she lives with her husband, Karim, and three children: teenage son Jordy and eight-year-old twins Ali and Suzanne. Karim is originally from Jordan but has lived in the United States, generally contentedly, for many years. However, after the September 11 terrorist attacks he feels like Americans are becoming prejudiced against Arabs. He also worries about the effects that permissive American society is having on his children, particularly after he finds out that Jordy is gay. Karim estranges himself from Jordy and, seeking to save his two younger children, takes them to Jordan without Dina's permission or knowledge.

Although Dina goes to great lengths to try to bring her children home, "the author wisely avoids both thriller cliches and post-9/11 politics to engage in a series of believable, thought-provoking compromises," noted a *Publishers Weekly* critic. Writing in *Booklist,* Misha Stone particularly praised "the combination of savvy writing and three-dimensional characters," while a *Kirkus Reviews* contributor deemed *Mosaic* "another page-turning tale with a topical theme."

"My books are banned in Saudi Arabia," Khashoggi told *Scotsman* interviewer Susan Mansfield,"because I'm an Arab woman, I'm not supposed to talk about the culture, not supposed to talk about love. It's not something to be ashamed of to express your feelings, to say what's on your mind, and work to help others."

BIOGRAPHICAL AND CRITICAL SOURCES:

PERIODICALS

Booklist, December 1, 1995, Emily Melton, review of *Mirage,* p. 587; September 15, 2004, Misha Stone, review of *Mosaic,* p. 208.
Kirkus Reviews, August 1, 2004, review of *Mosaic,* p. 706; May 1, 2005, review of *Nadia's Song,* p. 498.
People, April 29, 1996, Joanne Kaufman, "Banned in Her Homeland, Supported in Her Home," p. 41.
Publishers Weekly, September 11, 1995, "Spanning Two Worlds," p. 16; November 20, 1995, review of *Mirage,* p. 65; October 4, 2004, review of *Mosaic,* p. 69.
Scotsman, November 18, 2003, Susan Mansfield, interview with Khashoggi.*

*　　*　　*

KIHN, Martin

PERSONAL: Married Julia Douglass (a singer/songwriter). *Education:* Yale University, B.A.; Columbia University, M.B.A. (with honors), 2001.

ADDRESSES: Home—New York, NY. *Agent*—c/o Author Mail, Warner Books, 1271 Avenue of the Americas, New York, NY 10020. *E-mail*—elvis@martinkihn.com.

CAREER: Writer. Previously worked for large management consulting firm; MTV Networks, New York, NY, "Pop-up Video," head writer; *Fast Company,* member of consulting debunking unit.

WRITINGS:

House of Lies: How Management Consultants Steal Your Watch and Then Tell You the Time: A True Story, Warner Books (New York, NY), 2005.

Contributor to periodicals, including *New York Times, Forbes, New York, Gentleman's Quarterly, Details, Cosmopolitan,* and *Spy.*

SIDELIGHTS: Martin Kihn combines his love of writing with his business prowess in his book *House of Lies: How Management Consultants Steal Your Watch and Then Tell You the Time: A True Story.* In this comedic look at the business world and the people who inhabit it, Kihn sheds light on the truth behind the myths concerning the high-rate management consulting profession, using examples from his own experiences as an employee at a large management consulting firm. A contributor for *Publishers Weekly* called Kihn's book a "highly intelligent and deeply funny debut memoir," and added that "his reconstructed dialogue from within his (unnamed) firm . . . is alone worth the price of admission." Farhad Manjoo, writing for *Salon.com,* stated that "the real story here focuses on the damnable daily life of the modern management consultant. Kihn's breezy, Jay McInerney-inspired writing style renders this drudgery precisely, often hilariously."

BIOGRAPHICAL AND CRITICAL SOURCES:

PERIODICALS

Booklist, February 15, 2005, Mary Whaley, review of *House of Lies: How Management Consultants Steal Your Watch and Then Tell You the Time: A True Story,* p. 1042.
Publishers Weekly, January 17, 2005, review of *House of Lies,* p. 42.
Training, August, 2005, Skip Corsini, review of *House of Lies,* p. 38.

ONLINE

Martin Kihn Home Page, http://www.martinkihn.com (April 18, 2006).

Salon.com, http://www.salon.com./ (October 16, 2005), Farhad Manjoo, review of *House of Lies.**

*   *   *

KILIAN, Michael D. 1939-2005
(Rex Dancer, Michael David Killian)

OBITUARY NOTICE— See index for *CA* sketch: Born July 16, 1939, in Toledo, OH; died of liver failure, October 26, 2005, in Falls Church, VA. Journalist and author. Kilian was a writer and editor for the *Chicago Tribune* who also wrote novels and, in the 1990s, took over as the writer of the *Dick Tracy* comic strip. After attending the New School for Social Research, he worked as a writer for station KNTV in San Jose, California, in the early 1960s and served in the U.S. Army in Korea from 1963 to 1965. Returning to school, he attended the University of Maryland and then found work with the City News Bureau in Chicago in 1965. The next year, he joined the staff at the Chicago *Tribune* as a reporter and assistant political editor. From 1971 to 1978, Kilian was an editorial writer and editorial-page columnist; he then became a columnist based in Washington, DC. Kilian became known for his writings about the conflict in Northern Ireland, as well as for covering presidential campaigns and for his occasional satirical looks at politics, the media, and high society. Kilian began publishing novels in the 1980s, beginning with the thriller *The Valkyrie Project* (1981). Preferring fast-paced thrillers and mysteries, he produced series titles in the "Harrison Raines Civil War Mystery Series" and "Jazz Age Mystery Series" books. In addition, he wrote historical novels, such as the popular *Major Washington* (1998), political nonfiction, such as *Who Runs Washington?* (1982), a series of suspense books under the pen name Rex Dancer, and the humorous title *Flying Can Be Fun* (1985), which drew on his experience as a glider pilot. In 1993, Kilian paired up with illustrator Dick Locher to become the latest in a series of cartoonists who had taken up the *Dick Tracy* comic strip since creator Chester Gould retired in 1977. Working to keep the strip contemporary and relevant, Kilian wrote stories about such modern-day crimes as child kidnapping and electronic piracy; he also created a story line in which Tracy's wife, Tess Trueheart, files for divorce. A recipient of the Tribune Jones-Beck writing award in 1986, Kilian was also a CBS Radio commentator from 1973 to 1982, as well as for National Public Radio from 1978 to 1979.

OBITUARIES AND OTHER SOURCES:

PERIODICALS

Chicago Tribune, October 27, 2005, section 2, p. 13.
Los Angeles Times, October 29, 2005, p. B16.
Washington Post, October 27, 2005, p. B6.

*   *   *

KILLIAN, Michael David
See KILIAN, Michael D.

*   *   *

KING, Gabriel
See JOHNSON, Jane

*   *   *

KING, Melissa 1967(?)-

PERSONAL: Born c. 1967, in AR; children: Jackson. *Hobbies and other interests:* Basketball.

ADDRESSES: Home—Fayetteville, AR. *Agent*—c/o Author Mail, Houghton Mifflin, 215 Park Ave. S., New York, NY 10003.

CAREER: Writer; formerly affiliated with natural foods company, Chicago, IL.

WRITINGS:

She's Got Next: A Story of Getting in, Staying open, and Taking a Shot (memoir), Houghton Mifflin (Boston, MA), 2005.

Contributor to *Sports Illustrated, Chicago Reader, Sport Literate,* and *Arkansas Times.* Contributor to *The Best American Sports Writing 1999,* edited by Richard Ford, Houghton Mifflin (Boston, MA), 1999.

SIDELIGHTS: In *She's Got Next: A Story of Getting in, Staying open, and Taking a Shot,* Melissa King traces the way that basketball shaped her life. She first learned the game while living in her native Arkansas, but it was when she moved to Chicago at age twenty-seven that basketball became an integral part of her existence. Bored, lonely, and unhappy with her job, King joined an organized amateur league, but she soon found more satisfaction playing in pickup games throughout the city. King writes about how basketball helped her to get through, noted a *Publishers Weekly* contributor, "but she's equally engaged by the character and psychology of her fellow players." *She's Got Next* mixes vignettes of these other athletes with King's reflections on life and her chosen game. The result is "a pleasant, conversational book—part sports memoir, part chick lit, and part amateur philosophy," Whitney Pastorek commented in *Entertainment Weekly.* Despite the book's wide range, King's "poetic prose, as rhythmic as a dribble, will carry readers wherever she goes," concluded a *Kirkus Reviews* critic.

She's Got Next is nominally a memoir, but, as King explained in an interview on the Houghton Mifflin Web site, "one does have to remember, with writing like this, that the writer is choosing what to write about, and she's working from memory. . . . What we remember and what stands out at the end of the day is that small thing that happened and made us feel something, and feelings aren't journalism."

BIOGRAPHICAL AND CRITICAL SOURCES:

BOOKS

King, Melissa, *She's Got Next: A Story of Getting in, Staying open, and Taking a Shot,* Houghton Mifflin (Boston, MA), 2005.

PERIODICALS

Entertainment Weekly, June 10, 2005, Whitney Pastorek, "She Hoops to Conquer," p. 113.

Kirkus Reviews, April 1, 2005, review of *She's Got Next,* p. 402.
Publishers Weekly, May 2, 2005, review of *She's Got Next,* p. 189.

ONLINE

Houghton Mifflin Web site, http://www.houghton mifflinbooks.com/ (September 23, 2005), "A Conversation with Melissa King."
Melissa King Home Page, http://www.melissaking.net (September 23, 2005).*

* * *

KITTEL, Frederick August
See WILSON, August

* * *

KLIMLEY, Abbott Peter
See KLIMLEY, A. Peter

* * *

KLIMLEY, A. Peter 1947-
(Abbott Peter Klimley)

PERSONAL: Born March 7, 1947, in White Plains, NY; son of Stanley P. (a commercial artist) and Dorothy (a fashion artist; maiden name, Abbott) Klimley; married April 7, 1971; wife's name Patricia M. (in biotechnology business). *Ethnicity:* "Caucasian." *Education:* State University of New York at Stony Brook, B.S., 1970; University of Miami, Coral Gables, M.S., 1976; University of California, San Diego, Ph.D., 1982.

ADDRESSES: Home—2870 Eastman Ln., Petaluma, CA 94952. *Office*—Department of Fish, Wildlife, and Conservation Biology, 1334 Academic Surge Bldg., Biotelemetry Laboratory, University of California, Davis, Davis, CA 95616; fax: 707-752-4154. *Agent*—Ed Knapman, New England Publishing Association, P.O. Box 5, Chester, CT 06412. *E-mail*—apklimley@ucdavis.edu.

CAREER: Writer, scientist, and educator. Chemistry teacher at a preparatory school in Tarrytown, NY, 1971-72; teacher of marine biology and oceanography at other schools in New York, 1972-73; University of California, San Diego, postdoctoral researcher at Scripps Institution of Oceanography, 1982-84, assistant research scientist, 1984-87; University of California, Davis, assistant research behaviorist at Bodega Marine Laboratory, 1987-95, associate research behaviorist, 1996-2001, adjunct associate professor of wildlife, fish, and conservation biology, 1999—.

H.T. Harvey and Associates, senior fisheries ecologist, 2001-02; chief scientist for sea cruises related to the study of sharks and other marine wildlife. Point Reyes Bird Observatory, research associate, 1991—; Centro de Investigaciones de Biologicas, La Paz, Mexico, adjunct faculty member, 1993—; University of California, Santa Cruz, research associate at Institute of Marine Science, 1997—; guest speaker at other institutions, including Southampton College, San Francisco State University, University of South Florida, University of Washington, Seattle, Oregon State University, University of California, Berkeley, and Woods Hole Oceanographic Institution; symposium organizer; conference and seminar participant throughout the world. Consultant to Marine Acoustics, Inc. Affiliated with production of documentary films, some broadcast on Discovery Channel and programs *Nova* and *Wild Kingdom,* including: *Hammerheads of Sea of Cortez,* Don Meir Productions, 1982; *Profiles of Ocean Pioneers,* Public Broadcasting Service, 1983; *World of Sharks,* Turner Broadcasting Network and Public Broadcasting Service, 1988; *Hammerhead Science in the Gulf of California,* KTV-Television, 1989; *The World of White Sharks,* Osford Film Productions, 1993; *Sharks,* Audubon Films, 1994; *The Red Triangle,* Tom Horton Films, 1995; *The Science of Shark Attacks,* Turner Broadcasting Network, 1996; *Hammerheads: Nomads of the Sea,* Thomas Lucas Productions, 1998; *Megahai,* Beyond Productions Limited, 1998; *Sharks of Cocos Islands,* Howard Hall Productions, 1999; *Tracking White Sharks at Año Nuevo Island,* National Geographic Films, 1999; *Megashark,* Turner Broadcasting Network, 2000; and *Sharks at the Farallones,* KGO-TV Television, 2001. Guest on television and radio programs; public speaker.

MEMBER: American Association for the Advancement of Science, American Elasmobranch Society, American Society of Ichthyologists and Herpetologists, Association for the Study of Animal Behavior, Sigma Xi.

AWARDS, HONORS: Scientific Achievement Award, Southern California Academy of Science, 1981; SNAP EXCEL Silver award, *American Scientist,* 1995, for article "The Predatory Behavior of the White Shark"; certificate of excellence, Bookbuilders West Book Show, 1998, for *Great White Sharks: The Biology of Carcharodon carcharias;* grants from institutions, organizations, and agencies, including Foundation for Ocean Research, Sea World-San Diego, National Science Foundation, U.S. Department of Defense, National Undersea Research Program, National Geographic Society, Morris Animal Foundation, Bodega Marine Laboratory, California Department of Boating and Waterways, Discovery Channel, Gulf of the Farallones National Marine Sanctuary, Monterey Bay National Marine Sanctuary, Natal Sharks Board, National Audubon Society, Shark Research Institute, National Marine Fisheries Service, National Parks Service, and David and Lucile Packard Foundation.

WRITINGS:

(Editor, with D. G. Ainley, and contributor) *Great White Sharks: The Biology of Carcharodon carcharias,* Academic Press (San Diego, CA), 1996.
The Secret Life of Sharks: A Leading Biologist Reveals the Mysteries of Shark Behavior, Simon & Schuster (New York, NY), 2003.

Contributor to scientific journals and other periodicals, including *California Fish and Game, Oceanus, Sea Frontiers, Marine Aquarist, Environmental Biology of Fishes, Fisheries Bulletin, Marine Biology, Marine Technology Journal, Natural History,* and *Journal of Comparative Psychology.* Consulting editor, *American Scientist,* 1995—; "off-board" editor, *Oecologia,* 1997—.

WORK IN PROGRESS: Research on animal behavior and behavioral ecology of marine vertebrates; conservation; marine fisheries biology, ecology, and oceanography; and the development of behavioral and environmental sensors, computer-decoded telemetry, automated data logging, and archival tags.

SIDELIGHTS: A. Peter Klimley told *CA:* "I wrote *The Secret Life of Sharks: A Leading Biologist Reveals the Mysteries of Shark Behavior* for two reasons. First, I wanted to communicate to non-scientists the excitement, manner, and fulfillment of scientific exploration. Second, I wanted to provide the public with a more-accurate and less-sensational image of the shark—debunking the myth that sharks are simply feeding machines. My approach was to start each chapter with a real-life experience and complete it with information that I learned from my scientific studies about sharks."

BIOGRAPHICAL AND CRITICAL SOURCES:

PERIODICALS

American Scientist, January-February, 1998, Jose I. Castro, review of *Great White Sharks: The Biology of Carcharodon carcharias,* p. 89.
Booklist, July, 2003, Nancy Bent, review of *The Secret Life of Sharks: A Leading Biologist Reveals the Mysteries of Shark Behavior,* p. 1853.
Library Journal, June 1, 2003, Margaret Rioux, review of *The Secret Life of Sharks,* p. 158.
Publishers Weekly, June 9, 2003, review of *The Secret Life of Sharks,* p. 49
Quarterly Review of Biology, March, 1998, Robert H. Huetter, review of *Great White Sharks,* p. 82; December, 2003, David A. Ebert, review of *The Secret Life of Sharks,* p. 511.
Science News, July 12, 2003, review of *The Secret Life of Sharks,* p. 31.

*   *   *

KNOPF, Chris

PERSONAL: Male.

ADDRESSES: *Agent*—c/o Author Mail, Permanent Press Publishing Company, 4170 Noyac Rd., Sag Harbor, NY 11963.

CAREER: Writer.

WRITINGS:

The Last Refuge (mystery novel), Permanent Press (Sag Harbor, NY), 2005.

SIDELIGHTS: Chris Knopf's debut novel, *The Last Refuge,* centers on Sam Acquillo, a man whose life has fallen apart. Once a high-powered executive with a wife and child, Sam punches the chairman of his company's board after the chairman tried to sell Sam's division. His wife divorces him, and he and his daughter are not on good terms. Sam has nothing to do but drink and putter around his parents' Long Island cottage until he discovers his neighbor, Regina Broadbent, dead in her bathtub. Regina is an elderly woman and others assume that the death is an accident, but Sam suspects foul play—he was once an industrial designer, and he knows that bathtub plugs do not hold water for the multiple days that Regina's body appeared to have been lying in the tub. He convinces Regina's unfriendly nephew to let him be the administrator of Regina's estate, which allows him to carry out his investigation. It also gives him license to look into Regina's financial affairs, where, with the help of his friend and banker Amanda Battison, he makes some interesting discoveries. The tale is "arresting," wrote a *Publishers Weekly* reviewer, with "snappy dialogue and . . . colorful, oddball characters, including a gay billionaire." A *Kirkus Reviews* critic commented that "Knopf turns a mean sentence," allowing the author "to make Sam's charged flashbacks more interesting than the main event."

BIOGRAPHICAL AND CRITICAL SOURCES:

PERIODICALS

Kirkus Reviews, April 1, 2005, review of *The Last Refuge,* p. 389.
Publishers Weekly, April 25, 2005, review of *The Last Refuge,* p. 43.*

*   *   *

KOENIG, Andrea

PERSONAL: Female. *Education:* Syracuse University, M.F.A.

ADDRESSES: *Office*—English Department, College of Arts and Sciences, Oklahoma State University, 205 Morrill Hall, Stillwater, OK 74078. *E-mail*—koeniga@okstate.edu.

CAREER: Writer and educator. Oklahoma State University, Stillwater and Tulsa, assistant professor of English and creative writing, c. 1999—. Johns Hopkins Summer Seminar in Creative Nonfiction, Center for Talented Youth, instructor, 2004; *Cimarron Review,* fiction coeditor, 2004.

AWARDS, HONORS: Fulbright scholarship, 1996; Arts and Sciences Research Award, Oklahoma State University, 2004.

WRITINGS:

Thumbelina (novel), Scribner (New York, NY), 1999.
Hello Life (novel), Soho Press (New York, NY), 2005.

Contributor to *NUA: Studies in Contemporary Irish Writing* and *Tulsa World.*

WORK IN PROGRESS: New fiction.

SIDELIGHTS: Andrea Koenig is the author of *Thumbelina* and *Hello Life,* two novels about teenage girls trying to cope with almost unbelievable hardship. The narrator of the first, whose name is supremely ironic because of her six-foot height, is a fourteen year old whose mother has just committed suicide and who is pregnant by her late mother's abusive, HIV-positive, bisexual lover. In foster care Thumbelina meets another pregnant teen named Myrna, and the two run away together. "Their tragicomic attempts to fashion a life make up the main plot action," Starr E. Smith wrote in *Library Journal.* They try living with Myrna's sister and on the streets, they make an attempt at becoming strippers, and they ponder adoption versus keeping their children. "In less nimble hands, such subject matter could have turned this novel into a preachy disaster," Eric Lorberer commented in Wassau, Wisconsin's *City Pages,* "but Koenig's finger wisely stays on the pulse of her main character."

Sixteen-year-old Gwen Perez, the protagonist of *Hello Life,* finds herself in foster care following the death of her mother in a car accident. Gwen could not be more different from her housemate, fellow foster child Lila Abernathy, an aspiring ballerina who has recently overcome leukemia. Gwen has been the subject of town gossip since before she was born: her mother, a talented musician who could have made a career of it, instead gave up on music to become involved with a Mexican man, Gustavo Perez, who left town after she became pregnant. "The story is really the portrayal of an attempt at reconciliation—between these two young women of different social classes brought together through hardship, and between the girls and their town's recognition of their rich individual talents," explained a *Kirkus Reviews* critic.

"It's hard to say what exactly inspires my material," Koenig told Oklahoma State University Web site contributor Alanna Bradley. "I only hope readers will be able to relate to these girls, pity them, and perhaps see themselves in their fear and toughness."

BIOGRAPHICAL AND CRITICAL SOURCES:

PERIODICALS

Booklist, January 1, 1999, Grace Fill, review of *Thumbelina,* p. 832.
City Pages (Wassau, WI), March 17, 1999, Eric Lorberer, review of *Thumbelina.*
Dallas Morning News, July 2, 2005, Si Dunn, review of *Hello Life.*
Kirkus Reviews, May 1, 2005, review of *Hello Life,* p. 498.
Library Journal, December, 1998, Starr E. Smith, review of *Thumbelina,* p. 156.
Publishers Weekly, November 9, 1998, review of *Thumbelina,* p. 54; April 11, 2005, review of *Hello Life,* p. 36.

ONLINE

Oklahoma State University Department of English Web site, http://english.okstate.edu/ (October 10, 2005).
Oklahoma State University Web site, http://www.okstate.edu/ (September 23, 2005), Alanna Bradley, "Say Hello to Life: OSU Author to Release Highly Anticipated Second Novel."
University of Illinois at Urbana Champaign Department of English Web site, http://www.english.uiuc.edu/ (September 23, 2005), "Robert J. and Katharin Carr Visiting Authors Series, 2002-2003."*

KOIKE, Kazuo 1936-

PERSONAL: Born 1936, in Japan. *Hobbies and other interests:* Golfing, Kendo, archery.

ADDRESSES: Agent—c/o Author Mail, Dark Horse Comics, 10956 SE Main St., Milwaukie, OR 97222.

CAREER: Manga writer, poet, and fiction writer. Host of television programs; movie producer and screenwriter; founder of a golf magazine; Gekiga-Sonjuku school for writers and artists, founder.

AWARDS, HONORS: Eisner awards; Harvey awards for Best Presentation of Foreign Material, 2001, and for Best Graphic Album of Previously Published Work, and for Best Presentation of Foreign Material, both 2002, all for *Lone Wolf and Cub.*

WRITINGS:

"CRYING FREEMAN" SERIES MANGA COLLECTIONS; TRANSLATED FROM THE JAPANESE

Crying Freeman, illustrated by Ryoichi Ikegami, Viz Communications (San Francisco, CA), 1990.

Shades of Death, illustrated by Ryoichi Ikegami, Viz Communications (San Francisco, CA), 1992.

Portrait of a Killer, Part 1 illustrated by Ryoichi Ikegami, Viz Communications (San Francisco, CA), 1992.

Portrait of a Killer, Part 2 illustrated by Ryoichi Ikegami, Viz Communications (San Francisco, CA), 1992.

Journey to Freedom, Volume 1, illustrated by Ryoichi Ikegami, Viz Communications (San Francisco, CA), 1995.

Journey to Freedom, Volume 2, illustrated by Ryoichi Ikegami, Viz Communications (San Francisco, CA), 1995.

Abduction in Chinatown, illustrated by Ryoichi Ikegami, Viz Communications (San Francisco, CA), 1996.

A Taste of Revenge, illustrated by Ryoichi Ikegami, Viz Communications (San Francisco, CA), 1996.

The Killing Ring, illustrated by Ryoichi Ikegami, Viz Communications (San Francisco, CA), 1996.

"LONE WOLF AND CUB" SERIES MANGA COLLECTIONS; ORIGINALLY PUBLISHED AS "KOZURE OAMI"

The Assassin's Road (originally published in *Manga Action,* 1970-76), translated by Dana Lewis, illustrated by Goseki Kojima, Dark Horse Comics (Milwaukie, OR), 2000.

The Gateless Barrier (originally published in *Manga Action,* 1970-76), translated by Dana Lewis, illustrated by Goseki Kojima, Dark Horse Comics (Milwaukie, OR), 2000.

The Flute of the Fallen Tiger (originally published in *Manga Action,* 1970-76), translated by Dana Lewis, illustrated by Goseki Kojima, Dark Horse Comics (Milwaukie, OR), 2000.

The Bell Warden (originally published in *Manga Action,* 1970-76), translated by Dana Lewis, illustrated by Goseki Kojima, Dark Horse Comics (Milwaukie, OR), 2000.

Black Wind (originally published in *Manga Action,* 1970-76), translated by Dana Lewis, illustrated by Goseki Kojima, Dark Horse Comics (Milwaukie, OR), 2001.

Lanterns for the Dead (originally published in *Manga Action,* 1970-76), translated by Dana Lewis, illustrated by Goseki Kojima, Dark Horse Comics (Milwaukie, OR), 2001.

Cloud Dragon, Wind Tiger (originally published in *Manga Action,* 1970-76), translated by Dana Lewis, illustrated by Goseki Kojima, Dark Horse Comics (Milwaukie, OR), 2001.

Chains of Death (originally published in *Manga Action,* 1970-76), translated by Dana Lewis, illustrated by Goseki Kojima, Dark Horse Comics (Milwaukie, OR), 2001.

Echo of the Assassin (originally published in *Manga Action,* 1970-76), translated by Dana Lewis, illustrated by Goseki Kojima, Dark Horse Comics (Milwaukie, OR), 2001.

Hostage Child (originally published in *Manga Action,* 1970-76), translated by Dana Lewis, illustrated by Goseki Kojima, Dark Horse Comics (Milwaukie, OR), 2001.

Talisman of Hades (originally published in *Manga Action,* 1970-76), translated by Dana Lewis, illustrated by Goseki Kojima, Dark Horse Comics (Milwaukie, OR), 2001.

Shattered Stones (originally published in *Manga Action,* 1970-76), translated by Dana Lewis, illustrated by Goseki Kojima, Dark Horse Comics (Milwaukie, OR), 2001.

The Moon in the East, the Sun in the West (originally published in *Manga Action,* 1970-76), translated by Dana Lewis, illustrated by Goseki Kojima, Dark Horse Comics (Milwaukie, OR), 2001.

Day of the Demons (originally published in *Manga Action,* 1970-76), translated by Dana Lewis, illustrated by Goseki Kojima, Dark Horse Comics (Milwaukie, OR), 2001.

Brothers of the Grass (originally published in *Manga Action,* 1970-76), translated by Dana Lewis, illustrated by Goseki Kojima, Dark Horse Comics (Milwaukie, OR), 2001.

The Gateway into Winter (originally published in *Manga Action,* 1970-76), translated by Dana Lewis, illustrated by Goseki Kojima, Dark Horse Comics (Milwaukie, OR), 2001.

The Will of the Fang (originally published in *Manga Action,* 1970-76), translated by Dana Lewis, illustrated by Goseki Kojima, Dark Horse Comics (Milwaukie, OR), 2002.

Twilight of the Kurokuwa (originally published in *Manga Action,* 1970-76), translated by Dana Lewis, illustrated by Goseki Kojima, Dark Horse Comics (Milwaukie, OR), 2002.

The Moon in Our Hearts (originally published in *Manga Action,* 1970-76), translated by Dana Lewis, illustrated by Goseki Kojima, Dark Horse Comics (Milwaukie, OR), 2002.

A Taste of Poison (originally published in *Manga Action,* 1970-76), translated by Dana Lewis, illustrated by Goseki Kojima, Dark Horse Comics (Milwaukie, OR), 2002.

Fragrance of Death (originally published in *Manga Action,* 1970-76), translated by Dana Lewis, illustrated by Goseki Kojima, Dark Horse Comics (Milwaukie, OR), 2002.

Heaven and Earth (originally published in *Manga Action,* 1970-76), translated by Dana Lewis, illustrated by Goseki Kojima, Dark Horse Comics (Milwaukie, OR), 2002.

Tears of Ice (originally published in *Manga Action,* 1970-76), translated by Dana Lewis, illustrated by Goseki Kojima, Dark Horse Comics (Milwaukie, OR), 2002.

In These Small Hands (originally published in *Manga Action,* 1970-76), translated by Dana Lewis, illustrated by Goseki Kojima, Dark Horse Comics (Milwaukie, OR), 2002.

Perhaps in Death (originally published in *Manga Action,* 1970-76), translated by Dana Lewis, illustrated by Goseki Kojima, Dark Horse Comics (Milwaukie, OR), 2002.

Struggle in the Dark (originally published in *Manga Action,* 1970-76), translated by Dana Lewis, illustrated by Goseki Kojima, Dark Horse Comics (Milwaukie, OR), 2002.

Battle's Eve (originally published in *Manga Action,* 1970-76), translated by Dana Lewis, illustrated by Goseki Kojima, Dark Horse Comics (Milwaukie, OR), 2002.

The Lotus Throne (originally published in *Manga Action,* 1970-76), translated by Dana Lewis, illustrated by Goseki Kojima, Dark Horse Comics (Milwaukie, OR), 2002.

Contributor to *Manga chō shinkaron* (title means "Comic Evolution"), Kawade Shobo Shinsha (Tokyo, Japan), 1989. Adapted *Lone Wolf and Cub* series for film as *Baby Cart Assassin,* produced in Japan, c. 1972.

ADAPTATIONS: The *Lone Wolf and Cub* series was adapted for U.S. television, 2002; the *Crying Freeman* series was adapted for film in France, 1995; *Lone Wolf and Cub* was adapted as four stage plays and five recordings.

SIDELIGHTS: The work of versatile Japanese graphic novelist Kazuo Koike has seen a renewal of interest on an international scale in the *manga* (Japanese comic book; translated as "irresponsible pictures") series he created with illustrator Goseki Kojima, who died in 2000. *Lone Wolf and Cub*—set in seventeenth-century feudal Japan—was first serialized in Japan beginning in 1970, and by the late 1980s it had sold some eight million copies there. Published in the United States as a series of twenty-eight book-length collections in 2000-2002, *Lone Wolf and Cub* has also been adapted for television. In addition, Koike's *Crying Freeman* series attained popularity during the 1990s. Koike has also written screenplays, poetry, and fiction; hosted television programs; and mentored young Japanese artists and writers—including Rumiko Takahashi, of *Ranma 1/2* fame—at his Gekiga Sonjuku school.

Koike was born before World War II into a family steeped in the Japanese tradition of bushido, the Way of the Warrior. "So, it was natural for me to understand Hagakure Bushido, based on the idea of Buddhism and Confucianism," he said in an interview with Frank Miller for *Comics Interview* magazine.

Japanese manga are pocket-sized—usually about four by six inches—black-and-white comic books with about 300 pages. The most popular print medium in

Japan, they are as popular as television with people of both genders and all ages. Each of the twenty-eight volumes of the English version of *Lone Wolf* is some 300 pages long, with glossaries and notations.

Koike's main character in *Lone Wolf and Cub* is Ogami Itto, a former samurai warrior and the Shogun's executioner, assigned to help samurai and their lords commit *seppuku,* ritual suicide. Executioners used an extremely sharp sword to cut off the head, leaving a flap of skin at the neck to prevent the head from falling from the body after the samurai had disemboweled himself. Bushido, the Warrior's Way, dictated that each samurai be as sharp in spirit as his sword was sharp, and each type of sword stroke had a mystical significance.

When Tokugawa unites the Japanese provinces under his dictatorship and brings an end to the provincial wars, thousands of samurai are left without employment, becoming *ronin,* or masterless warriors. Itto is one of these, and he wanders the countryside on the "road to damnation" (*Meifumado*) with his three-year-old son, Daigoro, whose mother has been killed. Itto becomes an assassin for hire as he vows revenge against Retsudo Yagyû and his clan, who killed Itto's wife and accused him of plotting to overthrow the Shogun, destroying his good name. He becomes known as the Baby Cart Assassin, and Daigoro grows up with the constant violence of his father's way of life, often becoming involved in the fights in some small way and even seeming to help his father. Father and son form a bond that is apparent in the wordless frames of the series, when just a look tells the whole story as the two tense for battle.

Roger Sabin, in a review of *Lone Wolf and Cub* for the London *Observer,* noted that the art resembles Japanese scroll paintings and said the series "deserves its reputation as a classic." Marc Bernardin, in a review for *Entertainment Weekly* commented, "You're just as liable to come across . . . black-and-white tone poems . . . as you are an action sequence that fully realizes the chaos of combat." In a review of Volume 1, *The Assassin's Road,* Warren Ellis, for *Artbomb,* described the series as changing the comics medium "the way Kurosawa changed film" and said it should be compared to "a Criterion DVD release of something central to its artform." In a review of Volume 2, *The Gateless Barrier,* Peter Siegel praised Koike's painstaking research of the historical period

and called the series "a highly addictive read." The second volume explores the plight of women in seventeenth-century Japan and brings Itto face to face with his ability to kill even the Buddha. In a review of Volumes 22-25, Steve Raiteri, in *Library Journal,* said Koike's writing "has amazing depth and power" and called the story "riveting, sometimes shocking." He called Kojima's drawings "some of the most impressive realistic Japanese artwork yet seen in America." In these later volumes, Itto arrives in Edo (Tokyo) to face Retsudo in a duel, but an insane food taster who wants to kill them both intervenes.

In his *Dark Horse Comics Web site* biography, Koike was quoted as saying, "Comics are carried by characters. If a character is well created, the comic becomes a hit." He has certainly proved this theory with his work.

Koike and illustrator Ryiochi Ikegami's *Crying Freeman* has also achieved international acclaim, although it is even more violent than *Lone Wolf and Cub* and has more adult themes. It is the story of a young Japanese boy who is indoctrinated into a Chinese cult of master assassins. The boy is marked as a killer by a huge and colorful dragon tattoo that covers most of his body. Sex and violence abound in this series, which Eddy von Mueller, in the *Bloomsbury Review,* called brutal, horrifying, and gruesome. "One of the principal paradoxes that confront Westerners when viewing the Japanese is that their scrupulous politeness can coexist with pervasive images of violence and savagery," von Mueller commented. Although *Crying Freeman* has been well received in the United States, some comic book stores have banned it because it carries violence, especially against women, to such an extreme.

In the interview with Miller, Koike spoke about his role as a mentor to new Japanese talent. "You can't teach comics," he said. "You have to pull one's talent out, that's all. If you teach, you are just imposing your style on a person. In my school, we help a person to recognize his own talent, what he is the best at."

BIOGRAPHICAL AND CRITICAL SOURCES:

PERIODICALS

Bloomsbury Review, September, 1992, Eddy von Mueller, "Children of the Floating World: Manga and Popular Culture in Japan," p. 23.

Entertainment Weekly, July 19, 2002, Marc Bernardin, "Father Knows Best: A Boy and His Dad Walk a Bloody Path to Redemption in the Epic Japanese Comic *Lone Wolf and Cub,*" p. 68.

Library Journal, March 15, 1990, Keith R.A. DeCandido, review of *Lone Wolf and Cub,* p. 55; January, 2003, Steve Raiteri, review of *Lone Wolf and Cub: Heaven and Earth, Tears of Ice, In These Small Hands,* and *Perhaps in Death,* p. 84.

Observer (London, England), September 2, 2001, Roger Sabin, "Side by Side in the Fantasy League" (review of *Lone Wolf and Cub*), p. 16.

ONLINE

Artbomb, http://www.artbomb.net/ (August 12, 2003), "Creator Profile: Kazuo Koike, Biography"; Warren Ellis, review of *Lone Wolf and Cub: The Assassin's Road;* and Peter Siegel, review of *Lone Wolf and Cub: The Gateless Barrier.*

Comics Interview, http://www.mightyblowhole.com/ (April 12, 2006), David Anthony Kraft and Frank Miller, "Interview with Kazuo Koike and Goseki Kojima."

Dark Horse Comics Web site, http://www.darkhorse.com/ (August 12, 2003), "Harvey Awards."

Internet Movie Database, http://www.imdb.com/ (December 16, 2003), "Kazuo Koike."

Mangamaniacs, http://www.mangamaniacs.org/ (August 12, 2003), review of *Lone Wolf and Cub.**

*   *   *

KONYN, Kees
See GRESHOFF, Jan

*   *   *

KRONENWETTER, Michael 1943-

PERSONAL: Born February 12, 1943, in West Palm Beach, FL; son of Lanore Kronenwetter (founder of a trucking company); married Catherine Patricia Patterson (a laboratory information systems supervisor) December 16, 1971; children: Catherine, Jay. *Education:* Attended Northwestern University, 1961, Senior Dramatic Workshop, 1962, and University of Wisconsin, 1963-68. *Religion:* Roman Catholic. *Hobbies and other interests:* Traveling, theater, going to movies, "watching the Green Bay Packers play football and my now-adult children accomplish all the things they do."

ADDRESSES: Home and office—117 Sturgeon Eddy Rd., Wausau, WI 54401.

CAREER: Freelance writer. Nonesuch Bookstore, Kingston, Ontario, Canada, owner and operater, early 1970s; *Whig-Standard,* Kingston, television critic, late 1970s; *City Pages,* Wausau, WI, columnist.

MEMBER: Amnesty International, Mystery Writers of America, Crime Writers of Canada, Murder Must Advertise, Authors Guild, Central Wisconsin Children's Theater (board member), Children's Reading Roundtable of Chicago.

AWARDS, HONORS: National Educational Film Festival Award, 1983, for filmstrip "America's Power and Prestige since Vietnam"; certificate of merit, Wisconsin Public Radio, 1986, for unproduced radio play *A Death in Richland Center;* Private Eye Writers of America/St. Martin's Minotaur Best First Private Eye writing competition winner, 2004.

WRITINGS:

JUVENILE LITERATURE

Are You a Liberal? Are You a Conservative?, F. Watts (New York, NY), 1984.

The Threat from Within: Unethical Politics and Politicians, F. Watts (New York, NY), 1986.

Free Press vs. Fair Trial: Television and Other Media in the Courtroom, F. Watts (New York, NY), 1986.

Politics and the Press, F. Watts (New York, NY), 1987.

Journalism Ethics, F. Watts (New York, NY), 1988.

The Military Power of the President, F. Watts (New York, NY), 1988.

The War on Terrorism, J. Messner (Englewood Cliffs, NJ), 1989.

Managing Toxic Wastes, J. Messner (Englewood Cliffs, NJ), 1989.

Northern Ireland, F. Watts (New York, NY), 1990.

Drugs in America: The Users, the Suppliers, the War on Drugs, J. Messner (Englewood Cliffs, NJ), 1990.

Taking a Stand against Human Rights Abuses, F. Watts (New York, NY), 1990.

The New Eastern Europe, F. Watts (New York, NY), 1991.

Covert Action, F. Watts (New York, NY), 1991.

London, New Discovery Books (New York, NY), 1992.

United They Hate: White Supremacist Groups in America, Walker & Co. (New York, NY), 1992.

Under Eighteen: Knowing Your Rights, Enslow Publishers (Hillside, NJ, 1993.

Prejudice in America: Causes and Cures, F. Watts (New York, NY), 1993.

The Congress of the United States, Enslow Publishers (Springfield, NJ), 1996.

The Supreme Court of the United States, Enslow Publishers (Springfield, NJ), 1996.

Political Parties of the United States, Enslow Publishers (Springfield, NJ), 1996.

The FBI and Law Enforcement Agencies of the United States, Enslow Publishers (Springfield, NJ), 1997.

America in the 1960s, Lucent Books (San Diego, CA), 1998.

OTHER

America's Power and Prestige since Vietnam (filmstrip), Human Relations Media, 1982.

Capitalism vs. Socialism: Economic Policies of the U.S. and the USSR, F. Watts (New York, NY), 1986.

Welfare State America: Safety Net or Social Contract?, F. Watts (New York, NY), 1993.

Capital Punishment: A Reference Handbook, ABC-CLIO (Santa Barbara, CA), 1993.

How Democratic Is the United States?, F. Watts (New York, NY), 1994.

The Peace Commandos: Nonviolent Heroes in the Struggle against War and Injustice, New Discovery Books (New York, NY), 1994.

How to Write a News Article, F. Watts (New York, NY), 1995.

Protest!, Twenty-first Century Books (New York, NY), 1996.

Encyclopedia of Modern American Social Issues, ABC-CLIO (Santa Barbara, CA), 1997.

Terrorism: A Guide to Events and Documents, Greenwood Press (Westport, CT), 2004.

First Kill (mystery novel), St. Martin's Minotaur (New York, NY), 2005.

Also author of an unproduced radio play, *A Death in Richland Center.* Contributor to periodicals.

SIDELIGHTS: The majority of Michael Kronenwetter's books are about politics and history, and most are geared toward young adult readers. Titles such as *Political Parties of the United States* and *Prejudice in America: Causes and Cures* provide a broad overview of their subject matter and serve as an introduction for younger readers. The first book discusses the differences between the political parties, chronicling how their disagreements have often helped to fuel the country's progress. Writing for *Booklist,* Ilene Cooper commented that Kronenwetter's book "shows how parties have influenced every aspect of the country's political life." In his volume on prejudice, Kronenwetter is thorough in his discussion of how people are singled out by color, race, and religion, providing primarily modern-day examples of racist behavior and circumstances. Hazel Rochman, in a review for *Booklist,* reflected that Kronenwetter "is candid that things are not fair, that many have to overcome extra barriers of discrimination and poverty, that individuals have to fight the despair of seeing themselves only as victims."

Kronenwetter also writes on the subjects of politics and history for adults, with a particular concentration on current events. *Terrorism: A Guide to Events and Documents* provides an overview of extremist groups and terrorist factions that have become most visible over the past few decades. Among other incidents, he looks at the massacre of Israeli athletes at the 1972 Olympics, the rise of the Ku Klux Klan in the twentieth century, and the terrorist attacks of September 11, 2001. Arthur Meyers, writing for *Booklist,* remarked that "the writing is lively and clear."

With *First Kill,* Kronenwetter turned to fiction. The novel is a soft-boiled murder mystery, following private investigator Hank Berlin as he investigates the murder of his high school friend. A contributor for *Publishers Weekly* called the book "a solid fiction debut," while a contributor for *Kirkus Reviews* noted that there were "people to care about in a briskly paced debut novel."

Kronenwetter told *CA:* "My favorite books range from such an individually inspired nonfiction book as *Let Us Now Praise Famous Men* (written by James Agee with photographs by Walker Evans) to the relatively serious mystery or thriller stories written by such masterful authors as Graham Greene, James Lee Burke, and Reginald Hill. The books I like the most of my own are *Taking a Stand against Human Rights Abuses* and *The Peace Commandos: Nonviolent Heroes in the Struggle Against War and Injustice* (both of which are intended primarily for young adults); *Terrorism,* which is intended for adults of any age; and, my very first detective novel, *First Kill,* which is intended for the fans of mystery stories."

BIOGRAPHICAL AND CRITICAL SOURCES:

PERIODICALS

Booklist, February 1, 1994, Janice Del Negro, review of *Under Eighteen: Knowing Your Rights,* p. 1001; February 15, 1994, Hazel Rochman, review of *Prejudice in America: Causes and Cures,* p. 1069; June 1, 1996, Ilene Cooper, review of *Political Parties of the United States,* p. 1690; January 1, 1997, Debbie Carton, review of *Protest!,* p. 838; April, 1998, Mary Ellen Quinn, review of *Encyclopedia of Modern American Social Issues,* p. 1345; November 15, 2004, Arthur Meyers, review of *Terrorism: A Guide to Events and Documents,* p. 615.

Chicago Tribune, October 23, 2005, Dick Adler, review of *First Kill.*

January, September-October, 2005, J. Kingston Pierce, review of *First Kill.*

Kirkus Reviews, July 15, 2005, review of *First Kill,* p. 767.

Library Journal, May 1, 1998, Mary Jane Brustman, review of *Encyclopedia of Modern American Social Issues,* p. 94.

Publishers Weekly, July 18, 2005, review of *First Kill,* p. 187.

School Library Journal, October, 2004, Mary N. Oluonye, review of *America in the 1960s,* p. 67.

Washington Times, September 25, 2005, Lloyd Smith, review of *First Kill.*

ONLINE

Wausau Daily Herald Online, http://www.wausau dailyherald.com/ (August 31, 2005), Gary Gisselman, review of *First Kill.*

KRUM, Sharon

PERSONAL: Born in Australia; immigrated to United States.

ADDRESSES: Agent—Robert Kirby, PFD, Drury House, 34-43 Russell St., London WC2B 5HA, England.

CAREER: Writer. Freelance journalist for fashion and news magazines.

WRITINGS:

Walk of Fame (novel), St. Martin's Press (New York, NY), 2001.
The Thing about Jane Spring (novel), Viking (New York, NY), 2005.

Contributor to periodicals.

ADAPTATIONS: Walk of Fame was adapted as a screenplay.

SIDELIGHTS: Sharon Krum is an Australian-born journalist whose first novel, *Walk of Fame,* reflects her view of the state of celebrity in the United States. Narrator Tom Webster is a native Texan who is now a business writer living in New York City. A year earlier, Tom's wife left him for his best friend. Fortysomething Tom, a history buff, now takes on the challenge to become famous in one month. A glossy magazine has offered him 100,000 dollars to do so and then to expose himself as a fraud. He is aided by B-film actress Alexandra West, and their relationship advances his fame in the tabloids, which, in turn, motivates him to tell more lies.

In an interview with Kiersten Marek for *Pif* online, Krum noted that although her agent was able to sell her book in Australia, England, Japan, and Germany, U.S. publishers were not interested in an unknown author. "One editor said to my agent, if Jay Leno had written this, I would have it on the shelves yesterday. . . . So we couldn't find a publisher because I wasn't famous, and that is exactly what I was saying in the book. Fame sells things, and often they are junk. . . . That's the world we live in today. Fame is the currency, and I didn't have enough of it to move my book." Krum said that with Tom Webster, "I wanted to create a hero who would look with a jaundiced eye at the process yet ultimately become a convert."

Krum's debut was eventually published in the United States. *Booklist* reviewer Michelle Kaske felt that "Krum's sharp, funny dialogue and good characters keep readers wondering what will happen next." A *Publishers Weekly* contributor wrote that "there are no stunning revelations, but the end result is an agreeably smart and amusing story about what most sensible people already know: fame in America is not necessarily based on merit."

The protagonist of Krum's second novel, *The Thing about Jane Spring* is an aggressive prosecuting attorney who was raised by her general father and whose demeanor frightens off juries and judges and the men who never come back after a first date. Jane observes 1950s icon Doris Day in a classic-movie marathon and decides to borrow from the bouncy blonde who always landed her man. Jane trades her business suits for her grandmother's vintage pastels and her no-nonsense attitude for a fetching smile. Her new persona meets the approval of her secretary, a tough detective, and juries, among others, and may be a weapon as she faces a handsome defense attorney during a trial that is important to her career.

A *Kirkus Reviews* contributor wrote that "this is a winning fable about the seemingly lost art of being a lady. Smart and bracingly funny."

BIOGRAPHICAL AND CRITICAL SOURCES:

PERIODICALS

Booklist, May 15, 2001, Michelle Kaske, review of *Walk of Fame,* p. 1732.

Entertainment Weekly, July 15, 2005, Jennifer Armstrong, Clarissa Cruz, review of *The Thing about Jane Spring,* p. 76.

Hollywood Reporter, June 13, 2005, Chris Barsanti, review of *The Thing about Jane Spring,* p. 12.

Kirkus Reviews, May 1, 2005, review of *The Thing about Jane Spring,* p. 499.

Library Journal, May 15, 2005, Loralyn Whitney, review of *The Thing about Jane Spring,* p. 106.

Orlando Sentinel, July 20, 2005, Rebecca Swain Vadnie, review of *The Thing about Jane Spring.*

Publishers Weekly, April 9, 2001, review of *Walk of Fame,* p. 52; June 6, 2005, review of *The Thing about Jane Spring,* p. 39.

ONLINE

Pif, http://www.pifmagazine.com/ (September 8, 2005), Kiersten Marek, "Interview with Sharon Krum."*

* * *

KUGLER, Eileen Gale 1950-

PERSONAL: Born May 3, 1950, in Elizabeth, NJ; daughter of Milton J. (a hardware retailer) and Edith (a teacher; maiden name, Allen) Gale; married Larry B. Kugler (an educational consultant), June 13, 1971; children: Sara R., Alexander. *Education:* George Washington University, B.A. (with special honors), 1972. *Religion:* Jewish.

ADDRESSES: Home and office—Embrace Diverse Schools, 6807 Bluecurl Cir., Springfield, VA 22152. *E-mail*—EKugler@EmbraceDiverseSchools.com.

CAREER: Writer and consultant. *Food Chemical News,* assistant editor, 1974-77; U.S. Department of Agriculture, director of information for Food Safety and Inspection Service, 1979-81, member of communications staff, 1982-87; Public Voice for Food and Health Policy, director of communications, 1988-90; Institute for Science in Society, deputy director, 1991-92; Kugler Communications, Springfield, VA, founder, principal, trainer, speaker, and consultant, 1992—. Embrace Diverse Schools, founder, 2002.

MEMBER: National Association for Multicultural Education, Association for Supervision and Curriculum Development, National Speakers Association, Teachers against Prejudice.

AWARDS, HONORS: Superior Service Award, U.S. Department of Agriculture, 1983; Book of the Year designation, Delta Kappa Gamma International, and

Multicultural Book of the Year designation, National Association for Multicultural Education, both 2003, and *Choice* citation in outstanding academic title category, all for *Debunking the Middle-Class Myth: Why Diverse Schools Are Good for All Kids;* named Virginia Education Advocate of the Year, American Association of University Women, 2004.

WRITINGS:

Debunking the Middle-Class Myth: Why Diverse Schools Are Good for All Kids, Scarecrow Press (Lanham, MD), 2002.

Contributor to periodicals, including *Technos Journal, Catalyst, Educational Leadership, Washington Post,* and *USA Today.*

SIDELIGHTS: Eileen Gale Kugler told *CA:* "My writing champions the benefits that diversity brings to education. As I contemplated writing my book, I feared that I—a middle-class white woman—did not have standing to write a book about diversity. But, after long conversations and much soul-searching, I came to realize that my perspective is not only valid, it's critical.

"My two children attended one of the most diverse public high schools in the country—Annandale High in Fairfax County, Virginia—and I am deeply grateful that they had the opportunity to be educated in this remarkable school. I watched parents of younger children move out of our school district as they fell victim to negative myths about schools with a broad mix of racial, ethnic, and socio-economic backgrounds. At the same time, I watched my children flourish both academically and socially. Both went on to excel at top national colleges and in challenging careers, and both feel 'privileged' (their word) to have been a part of their multi-cultural public high school. Today, my children are comfortable in any environment, talking to just about anyone. And they know how to listen and how to respect opinions that are different from their own, growing from the exposure.

"My passion for the benefits of an education in a diverse school has led me to write and speak about the strengths of these schools and to work with communities to develop strategies that build support for them.

I've talked with many parents, students, and educators, and I have heard the same passion about the learning environment expressed over and over again. There is overwhelming enthusiasm for what these schools have to offer, and there is overwhelming frustration at the misinformation that abounds among those who don't have first-hand experience with a diverse school.

"This story needs to be told. We need to share the lessons learned from these remarkable places. We need to spread the information so that middle-class parents—parents who have the luxury to choose their neighborhoods—stop falling for the negative myths that lead them to move into neighborhoods where the majority of students look and think alike. We need to encourage these parents to seek out schools where children of various backgrounds enrich academics and social interactions by bringing a range of experiences and knowledge to the classroom, because that is simply the best way to educate all children.

"As enriching as diverse schools can be, they can only reach their potential with leadership who enthusiastically take on the challenges that make them successful. The courageous and dedicated educational leaders and teachers who daily accept this challenge need the support of all the stakeholders in the community—students, parents, and community members of all backgrounds. A diverse school that is well run and supported by the community is an academic and social gold mine. It provides just the type of education that our students and our greater society need."

"My goal is to encourage parents of every economic status and every race or culture to seek out well-run diverse public schools, enjoy their benefits, and help to make them work. I hope my writing inspires competent educators to flock to the diverse schools and work to provide all students with what they need to achieve. And I hope entire communities will rally around these previous gems in their midst. When it all comes together, the results are extraordinary.

"The experience of being part of a school like Annandale High School can't be bought or measured on standardized tests. It is beyond value or measurement, and it will be in your heart for a lifetime. Through my writing I hope to share that gift with others."

BIOGRAPHICAL AND CRITICAL SOURCES:

ONLINE

Embrace Diverse Schools Web site, http://www. embracediverseschools.com/ (July 4, 2005).
Kugler Communications Web site, http://www.kugler com.com/ (July 4, 2005).

*   *   *

KÜHN, Dieter 1935-

PERSONAL: Born February 1, 1935, in Cologne, Germany.

ADDRESSES: *Office*—c/o Duncker & Humbolt, Postfach 410329, Berlin, Germany.

CAREER: Playwright, novelist, biographer, essayist, and children's writer.

MEMBER: PEN.

AWARDS, HONORS: Förderpreis, 1973; Georg Mackensen-Preis, and Hörspeilpreis, Kriegsblinden, both 1974, both for *Goldberg-Variationen: Hörspieltexte mit Materialien;* Herman Hesse prize, 1977, for *Ich Wolkenstein: eine Biographie;* Stadtschreiber von Bergen-Enkheim, 1980-81; Förderpreis, Lüneburger Autorenschmiede, 1982; Großer Literaturpreis, Bayerischen Akademie der schönen Künste, 1989; Stiftungsgastdozentur, Johann Wolfgang Goethe-Universität, 1992-93; Stadtschreiber in Mainz, 1993.

WRITINGS:

Analogie und Variation: zur Analyse von Robert Musils Roman "Der Mann ohne Eigenschaften," Bouvier (Bonn, Germany), 1965.
N., Suhrkamp (Frankfurt, Germany), 1970.
Ausflüge im Fesselballon (novel), Suhrkamp (Frankfurt, Germany), 1971.
Musik und Gessellschaft (essays), Tsamas (Hamburg, Germany), 1971.

Grenzen es Widerstandes (essays), Suhrkamp (Frankfurt, Germany), 1972.
Siam-Siam: ein Abenteuerbuch, Suhrkamp (Frankfurt, Germany), 1972.
Mit dem Zauberpferd nach London (children's novel), Luchterhand (Darmstadt, Germany), 1973.
Die Präsidentin, Suhrkamp (Frankfurt, Germany), 1973.
Festspiel für Rothäute, Suhrkamp (Frankfurt, Germany), 1974.
Unternehmen Rammbock: Planspielstudie z. Wirkung Gesellschaftskrit (criticism), Suhrkamp (Frankfurt, Germany), 1974.
Johan Most: ein Sozialist in Deutschland, Hanser (Munich, Germany), 1974.
(With Ludwig Harig) *Netzer Kam aus der Tiefe des Raumes: notwendige Beitrage zur Fussball-Weltmeisterschaft,* Hanser (Munich, Germany), 1974.
Stanislaw der Schweiger (novel), Suhrkamp (Frankfurt, Germany), 1975.
Luftkrieg als Abenteuer, Hanser (Munich, Germany), 1975.
(Translator) Eduard Pöppig, *In der Nähe des ewigen Schnees,* Insel (Frankfurt, Germany), 1975.
Josephine: aus der öffentlichen Biografie der Josephine Baker (biography), Suhrkamp (Frankfurt, Germany), 1976.
Achmeds Geheimsprache (children's book), 1976.
Goldberg-Variationen: Hörspieltexte mit Materialien, Suhrkamp (Frankfurt, Germany), 1976.
Op der Parkbank (three radio plays; includes *Op der Parkbank, Jesang op der Walz,* and *Stervenswötche,* originally broadcast 1969-72), Greven (Cologne, Germany), 1976.
Ich Wolkenstein: eine Biographie, Insel (Frankfurt, Germany), 1977.
Ludwigslust, Suhrkamp (Frankfurt, Germany), 1977.
Die Geisterhand (children's book), Insel (Frankfurt, Germany), 1978.
Löwenmusik (essays), Suhrkamp (Frankfurt, Germany), 1979.
Der Herr der fliegenden Fische, Insel (Frankfurt, Germany), 1979.
Und der sultan von Oman, Suhrkamp (Frankfurt, Germany), 1979.
Auf der Zeitachse: vier Konzepte, Suhrkamp (Frankfurt, Germany), 1980.
Galaktisches Rauschen: Sechs Hörspiele, Fischer-Taschenbuch (Frankfurt, Germany), 1980.
Herr Neidhart (biography), Insel (Frankfurt, Germany), 1981.

Liederbuch für Neidhart (criticism), Insel (Frankfurt, Germany), 1981.

Schnee und Schwefel: Gedichte (poems), Suhrkamp (Frankfurt, Germany), 1982.

Der wilde Gesang der Kaiserin Elisabeth, Fischer (Frankfurt, Germany), 1982.

Das Missverständnis: polemische Überlegungenzum politischen Standort Arno Schmidts, Edition Text + Kritik (Munich, Germany), 1982.

Die Kammer des schwarzen Lichts (novel), Suhrkamp (Frankfurt, Germany), 1984.

Der Himalaya im Wintergarten, Suhrkamp (Frankfurt, Germany), 1984.

Erläuterungen zu Arno Schmidts "Alexander, oder, Was ist die Wahrheit," Edition Text + Kritik (Munich, Germany), 1984.

Der König von Grönland (novel; title means "The King of Greenland"), Janus Presse (Cologne, Germany), 1985.

Flaschenpost für Goethe, Insel (Frankfurt, Germany), 1985.

Bettines letzte Liebschaften, Insel (Frankfurt, Germany), 1986.

(Translator and contributor of introductory material) Wolfram von Eschenbach, *Der Parzival de Wolfram von Eschenbach,* edited by Eberhard Nellmann, Insel (Frankfurt, Germany), 1986.

Kommentierendes Handbuch zu Arno Schmidts Roman "Aus dem leben eiens Fauns," Edition Text + Kritik (Munich, Germany), 1986.

Neidhart aus dem Reuental (biography), Insel (Frankfurt, Germany), 1988.

Auf der Zeitachse: Biographische Skizzen, Kritische Konzepte, Suhrkamp (Frankfurt, Germany), 1989.

Beethoven und der schwarze Geiger (novel), Insel (Frankfurt, Germany), 1990.

(Translator) Gottfried von Strassburg, *Tristan und Isolde,* Insel (Frankfurt, Germany), 1991, revised edition, Fischer (Frankfurt, Germany), 2003.

Die Minute eines Segelfalters: Erzählung, Insel (Frankfurt, Germany), 1992.

Das Heu, die Frau, das Messer (novella), Insel (Frankfurt, Germany), 1993.

Varnhagen und sein später Schmäher: über einige Vorurteile Arno Schmidts (biography), Aisthesis (Bielefeld, Germany), 1994.

(With Marcus Rosenstein) *Rugby: Kampf in Gasse und Gedränge,* Weinmann (Berlin, Germany), 1995.

Clara Schumann, Klavier: ein Lebensbuch (biography), Fischer (Frankfurt, Germany), 1996.

Goethe zieht in den Krieg: eine biographische Skizze, Fischer (Frankfurt, Germany), 1999.

Auf dem Weg zu Annemarie Böll (biography), Heinrich-Böll-Stiftung (Berlin, Germany), 2000.

Frau Merian!: eine Lebensgeschichte (biography), Fischer (Frankfurt, Germany), 2002.

Mit Flügelohren: mein Hörspielbuch, Fischer (Frankfurt, Germany), 2003.

Schillers Schreibtisch in Buchenwald: Bericht, Fischer (Frankfurt, Germany), 2005.

Contributor of commentary to *Aus meinem Leben,* by Bettina von Arnim, 1982; plays are included in *Spectaculum: 27, Neun moderne Theaterstücke,* 1977.

SIDELIGHTS: German writer Dieter Kühn, winner of several literary prizes, has distinguished himself in various literary forms, including radio plays, novels, biographies, essays, and children's books. He studied German and English literature, writing his Ph.D. thesis on Robert Musil's masterwork, *The Man without Qualities.* Kühn's prolific output began in 1970, when his first work, *N.,* was published. This volume was followed by a steady stream of novels, essay collections, and other books—more than twenty titles before the end of the decade, followed by an only-slightly less-copious number through the 1980s and 1990s.

Art and culture are among Kühn's favored themes. He has written biographies of pianist Clara Schumann and American dancer Josephine Baker. In addition, he has published *Beethoven und der schwarze Geiger,* a novel about Ludwig van Beethoven (1770-1827) that focuses on the German composer's relationship with the violinist Bridgetower, son of a Polish mother and an escaped slave from Barbados. Bridgetower was an historical figure; in fact, he is the dedicatee of Beethoven's "sonata mulattica," better known as the Kreutzer Sonata. In the novel, Kühn imagines the composer on a ship bound for Africa in 1813, along with Bridgetower; a masked traveler; Johanna; and the young Charlotte, with whom Beethoven falls in love and who is based on the historical figure of Josephine von Brunswick. In a *World Literature Today* review of the novel *Beethoven und der schwarze Geiger,* Ulf Zimmermann commented that an "excess of contemporary baggage" weakens the book, with the composer expressing enlightened twentieth-century views on race and gender relationships. However, the critic credited Kühn with "faithful" realism regarding Beethoven's difficult personality.

Another novel that attracted critical notice is *Der König von Grönland,* the story of a man who had served as a weather reporter on a ship from Greenland during World War II and, fifty years later, plans a work of "sky art" that will use technology and folk magic to bring the Arctic northern lights to Cologne. Zimmermann, in *World Literature Today,* read the novel as an exploration of the theme of art's ability to transcend politics.

Among Kühn's biographical works, *Varnhagen und sein später Schmäher: über einige Vorurteile Arno Schmidts* is noted for its strong views about its subject, Berlin diplomat and journalist Karl August Ludwig Philipp Varnhagen (1785-1858). Unlike other critics who have looked more favorably on Varnhagen, Kühn sides with critic Arno Schmidt, who dismissed Varnhagen as an opportunist. Indeed, Liliane Weissberg pointed out in her *German Quarterly* review of *Varnhagen und sein später Schmäher* that the book is more a discussion of Schmidt than of its titular subject. Though she acknowledged Kühn's extensive research for this project, Weissberg found the "mixture of gossip, speculation, and vitriolic language" in his book a significant flaw. Kühn received the Hermann Hesse Prize for an earlier biography, *Ich Wolkenstein: eine Biographie,* on Middle High German poet Oswald von Wolkenstein (1377-1445).

Kühn has also written a respected translation of Wolfram von Eschenbach's *Der Parzival,* which critic David Yeandle, in *Medium Aevum,* praised for its readability. Yeandle noted that this translation, to which Kühn also contributed introductory material, "is an ideal edition for students . . . [that] will add to the ever-increasing body of secondary literature on *Parzival* in the most positive and pleasing way, in that it fulfills an essentially consolidatory role and sifts the wheat from the chaff." Kühn's body of criticism also includes works on German poet Johann Wolfgang von Goethe (1749-1832), Bavarian knight and Middle High German lyric poet Neidhart von Reuenthal, and Schmidt.

BIOGRAPHICAL AND CRITICAL SOURCES:

BOOKS

Stollberg, Jochen, editor, *Dieter Kühn,* Begleitheft zur Ausstellung der Stadt-und Universitätsbibliothek (Frankfurt, Germany), 1993.

PERIODICALS

German Quarterly, spring, 1997, Liliane Weissberg, review of *Varnhagen und sein später Schmäher: über einige Vorurteile Arno Schmidts,* pp. 199-200.

Medium Aevum, spring, 1996, David Yeandle, review of *Der Parzival de Wolfram von Eschenbach,* p. 165.

World Literature Today, spring, 1991, Ulf Zimmermann, review of *Beethoven und der schwarze Geiger,* p. 293; summer, 1998, Ulf Zimmermann, review of *Der König von Grönland,* p. 604.*

*   *   *

KUNKEL, Benjamin

PERSONAL: Male.

ADDRESSES: Home—New York, NY. *Agent*—c/o Author Mail, Random House, 1745 Broadway, New York, NY 10019.

CAREER: Writer.

WRITINGS:

Indecision (novel), Random House (New York, NY), 2005.

Contributor to periodicals, including *Dissent, Nation,* and *New York Review of Books.* Founding editor, *n+1.*

SIDELIGHTS: Benjamin Kunkel's debut novel *Indecision* is the story of Dwight Wilmerding, a bright, well-to-do, but unambitious man who is nearing the age of thirty. Dwight seems content to go through the motions at his low-level job at the Pfizer pharmaceutical company, relax in his apartment, and reflect on his unnatural attraction to his psychiatrist sister, Alice. After losing his job, he diagnoses himself as suffering from abulia, or an inability to make decisions. Dwight enters a clinical trial for a new drug being developed for the treatment of abulia, and soon begins to make dramatic changes in his life. He moves to South America, in search of his high-school love, and his adventures eventually land him deep in the jungles of Ecuador. A *Kirkus Reviews* writer commented that *Indecision* "isn't high art, but it's full of high spirits" and is "well-paced." Prudence Peiffer, a reviewer for *Library Journal,* vacillated between finding Dwight "annoying or appealing," and remarked that the author himself seems undecided as to whether the book as a whole should be a commentary on American mores or simply "a lighthearted romp." Nevertheless, Peiffer recommended *Indecision* as "a promising first work."

BIOGRAPHICAL AND CRITICAL SOURCES:

PERIODICALS

Kirkus Reviews, June 15, 2005, review of *Indecision,* p. 657.

Library Journal, July 1, 2005, Prudence Peiffer, review of *Indecision,* p. 68.

Publishers Weekly, July 18, 2005, review of *Indecision,* p. 180.

Vogue, August, 2005, Megan O'Grady, review of *Indecision,* p. 164.*

*   *   *

KUPER, Daniela

PERSONAL: Born in Chicago, IL. *Religion:* Jewish.

ADDRESSES: Home—Brooksville, ME. *Agent*—c/o Author's Mail, St. Martin's Press, 175 5th Ave., New York, NY 10010.

CAREER: Writer.

AWARDS, HONORS: Harold U. Ribalow Prize nomination, *Hadassah* magazine, 2005, for fiction with a Jewish theme; Pushcart Prize nomination; five literary fellowships.

WRITINGS:

Hunger and Thirst, St. Martin's Press (New York, NY), 2004.

Contributor of short stories to periodicals.

WORK IN PROGRESS: A novel, *Holy Ghost.*

SIDELIGHTS: Daniela Kuper was born and raised on the North Side of Chicago, the setting for her first novel, *Hunger and Thirst.* The story is set in a predominantly lower-middle class Jewish area called East Rogers Park during the 1950s. In a time when Nazi Germany is a fresh memory and the next generation is the hope for every family to elevate their status, the Trout family undergo the stress that can take place behind the quest for the American dream. Daughter Joan suffers from being caught in the middle between her father's loyalty to the old neighborhood and her mother's attempts to join the modern world. Whitney Scott, in a review for *Booklist,* remarked that "Kuper conjures a vividly textured culture as the backdrop for the poignant, funny story of the Trouts."

BIOGRAPHICAL AND CRITICAL SOURCES:

PERIODICALS

Booklist, September 1, 2004, Whitney Scott, review of *Hunger and Thirst,* p. 62.

Kirkus Reviews, August 15, 2004, review of *Hunger and Thirst,* p. 768.

ONLINE

Chicago Sun Times Online, http://www.suntimes.com/ (April 24, 2005), Tom McNamee, "Chicago Rich in Formidable Scribes."

Daniela Kuper Hope Page, http://www.danielakuper. com (October 18, 2005).*

*   *   *

KUYCK, A.L. van
See GRESHOFF, Jan

L

LANE, Vicki

PERSONAL: Born in FL; married; children: two sons. *Hobbies and other interests:* Quilting, painting, reading, gardening.

ADDRESSES: Home—NC. *Agent*—Ann Collette, Helen Rees Literary Agency, 376 North St., Boston, MA 02113-2103. *E-mail*—vicki_lane@mtnarea.net.

CAREER: Former English teacher in Florida.

WRITINGS:

Signs in the Blood, Bantam Dell (New York, NY), 2005.

Co-author of two books about quilting.

WORK IN PROGRESS: Another "Elizabeth Goodweather" mystery.

SIDELIGHTS: After teaching English for nine years in Florida, Vicki Lane and her husband decided it was time to move from an increasingly congested state. They settled on a farm in North Carolina, where they have since homesteaded and raised their two sons. Among Lane's hobbies is quilting, and after coauthoring two quilting books, she decided in 2000 to take a fiction-writing class taught by novelist Bill Brooks, which was offered at a local community college. Lane had always been an avid reader, citing Tony Hiller-man's "Leaphorn and Chee" series as a favorite among the many mysteries she reads. So at the end of the class when Brooks challenged her by saying she would never write a novel, she decided to prove him wrong. After a year of writing, she had penned a mystery about an Appalachian sleuth named Elizabeth Goodweather. Yet, when she sent the manuscript to agents, they rejected it. Finally, one agent told Lane that she needed to write the first novel set in Elizabeth Goodweather's home area—rather than a vacation locale—so that readers could fall in love with not only the sleuth, but the setting as well. So, saving her initial attempt for a later book in her projected series, Lane penned the debut novel, *Signs in the Blood,* which a *Publishers Weekly* reviewer called a "well-crafted, dramatic tale of murder, miracles and midlife romance." Set in Ridley Branch, North Carolina, Goodweather, a middle-aged widow and owner of a flower and herb farm, investigates the death of a longtime friend's son. Among the novel's enthusiasts number *Romantic Times* reviewer Sheri Melnick, who praised Lane's "evocative descriptions" of the mountain setting, and *Book Loons* online reviewer Pat Elliott, who found "all the characters who people this land . . . engrossing." For her part, Lane wrote at her home page: "I think that, as an outsider, I sometimes see more clearly the wonderful things that people who grew up here take for granted."

BIOGRAPHICAL AND CRITICAL SOURCES:

PERIODICALS

Publishers Weekly, April 11, 2005, review of *Signs in the Blood,* p. 39.

ONLINE

Book Loons, http://www.bookloons.com/ (October, 2005), Pat Elliott, review of *Signs in the Blood.*

Romantic Times Online, http://www.romantictimes. com/ (October, 2005), Sheri Melnick, review of *Signs in the Blood,*

Vicki Lane Home Page, http://www.vickilane mysteries.com.*

*   *   *

LARSEN, Deborah
(M. Deborah Larsen Cowan)

PERSONAL: Born in St. Paul, MN. *Religion:* Roman Catholic.

ADDRESSES: Home—Gettysburg, PA. *Office*—Department of English, Breidenbaugh Hall, Campus Box 0397, 300 N. Washington St., Gettysburg, PA 17325. *E-mail*—mdcowan@gettysburg.edu.

CAREER: Gettysburg College, Gettysburg, PA, associate professor of English and M.S. Boyer chair in poetry.

WRITINGS:

Stitching Porcelain: After Mateo Ricci in Sixteenth-Century China (poetry), New Directions (New York, NY), 1991.

The White (novel), Knopf, (New York, NY), 2002.

The Tulip and the Pope: A Nun's Story (memoir), Knopf (New York, NY), 2005.

Contributor to periodicals, including *New Yorker.*

SIDELIGHTS: Deborah Larsen's books include *Stitching Porcelain: After Mateo Ricci in Sixteenth-Century China,* a volume of poetry; *The Tulip and the Pope: A Nun's Story,* a personal memoir; and *The White,* a novel based on the true story of a young white woman who was captured by Indians and chose to remain a part of their culture even when she had chances to leave it.

Larsen, who serves as a professor of writing and poetry at Gettysburg College, won praise for her poetry collection *Stitching Porcelain.* This series of poems is based on the life of Matteo Ricci, an Italian Jesuit who lived in China from 1583 until he died in 1610. While the poetry in this volume is inspired by Ricci's work and the work of other writers, it nevertheless has "an undeniable originality," noted Jessica Greenbaum in a *Nation* review. Praising the author's skill, she further stated: "It is a rare volume that can make someone else's life feel heartfelt and necessary, but this is the magnificent balance offered by Deborah Larsen's first collection."

Larsen drew from another real life story for her novel *The White,* published in 2003. The central character is Mary Jemison, who in 1758 was captured by members of the Shawnee tribe. Her family, also captured, was scalped before her eyes, but her life was spared because she bore a resemblance to a young Shawnee who had been killed, and whose family wanted to adopt her. *The White,* recreates Jemison's descent into emotional numbness and the gradual reawakening of her soul into a completely different type of life. Reviewing the book for *Kliatt,* Nola Theiss noted that the style is full of abrupt transitions, just as Jemison's life was. By recreating the captive's thoughts, the book is a reading experience that is, like the life that inspired it, "sometimes confusing and disorienting," according to Theiss. *Library Journal* reviewer Starr E. Smith praised the author for writing in "elegant, poetic language that evokes time, place, and character with feeling and conviction," and a *Publishers Weekly* reviewer stated: "Larsen's lyricism and imagery are haunting, and her poet's sensibility is omnipresent."

The story of Larsen's own early life is recounted in her memoir *The Tulip and the Pope.* The author spent some time in a Roman Catholic convent as a young woman, and although she ultimately decided against taking her vows, her description of her time with the sisters in the Iowa convent "is loving and respectful," stated a *Kirkus Reviews* writer. A *Publishers Weekly* writer also recommended *The Tulip and the Pope* as "affectionate rather than bitter . . . a richly detailed reminiscence of convent life and a sensitive evocation of a young Catholic woman's coming-of-age."

BIOGRAPHICAL AND CRITICAL SOURCES:

BOOKS

Larsen, Deborah, *The Tulip and the Pope: A Nun's Story,* Knopf (New York, NY), 2005.

PERIODICALS

Booklist, June 1, 2002, Kristine Huntley, review of *The White,* p. 1686.

Hollins Critic, February, 2000, review of *The Tulip and the Pope,* p. 24.

Kirkus Reviews, May 15, 2002, review of *The White,* p. 688; July 1, 2005, review of *The Tulip and the Pope,* p. 720.

Kliatt, November, 2003, Nola Theiss, review of *The White,* p. 16.

Library Journal, June 15, 2002, Starr E. Smith, review of *The White,* p. 94.

Minneapolis Star Tribune, July 21, 2002, review of *The White.*

Nation, October 12, 1002, Jessica Greenbaum, review of *Stitching Porcelain: After Mateo Ricci in Sixteenth-Century China,* p. 406.

Publishers Weekly, June 3, 2002, review of *The White,* p. 61; June 27, 2005, review of *The Tulip and the Pope,* p. 57.

Rocky Mountain News, September 6, 2002, William Dieter, review of *The White.*

San Francisco Chronicle, July 21, 2002, Alan Cheuse, review of *The White.*

Washington Post Book World, August 4, 2002, Michael Kernan, review of *The White,* p. 13.*

*   *   *

LASTIMADO, Benedict 1950-

PERSONAL: Born June 12, 1950, in Ewa, HI; son of Zac, Sr. (in social services) and Rita (Tecson) Lastimado; married Jutta Metzler (in community services), September 12, 1973. *Ethnicity:* "Pacific Islander/Asian." *Education:* University of Maryland, B.S., 1982; Boston University, M.B.A., 1986; Seattle University, Ed.D., 1996. *Hobbies and other interests:* Jogging, weightlifting.

ADDRESSES: Office—Grossmont-Cuyamaca Community College District, 8800 Grossmont College Dr., El Cajon, CA 92020-1799. *E-mail*—ben.lastimado@gcccd.net.

CAREER: Writer and consultant. U.S. Army, career officer in human resources, 1970-90, retiring as chief warrant officer second class; Green River Community College, Auburn, WA, director for human resources and labor relations, 1990-95; Federal Way School District, Federal Way, WA, director for human resources and labor relations, 1995-2000; Clover Park Technical College, Lakewood, WA, vice president for human resources and labor relations, 2000-04; Grossmont-Cuyamaca Community College District, El Cajon, CA, vice chancellor for human resources and labor relations, 2004—. Also adjunct professor, workshop presenter, and private consultant.

MEMBER: Society for Human Resources Managers, Rotary International.

AWARDS, HONORS: Military awards include Meritorious Service Medal with three oak leaf clusters.

WRITINGS:

Increasing Your Human Resources Profession's Value, University Press of America (Lanham, MD), 2003.

Contributor to *Training and Development.*

WORK IN PROGRESS: The Four Pillars of Human Resources Leadership.

*   *   *

LATIFI, Afschineh 1969-

PERSONAL: Born 1969, in Tehran, Iran; daughter of Mohammad Bagher (an engineer and a colonel in the Iranian army) and Fatemeh (a schoolteacher) Latifi. *Education:* Old Dominion University, graduated, 1989; Wake Forest School of Law, law degree, 1992. *Religion:* Muslim.

ADDRESSES: Home—New York, NY. *Agent*—c/o Author Mail, Regan Books, 10 E. 53rd St., 7th Fl., New York, NY 10022.

CAREER: Tucker and Latifi (law firm), New York, NY, partner.

WRITINGS:

(With Pablo F. Fenjves) *Even after All This Time: A Story of Love, Revolution, and Leaving Iran* (autobiography), Regan Books (New York, NY), 2005.

SIDELIGHTS: Afschineh Latifi was ten years old when her father, a colonel in the army of the Shah of Iran, was arrested and executed following the rise to power of the Ayatollah Khomeini. Until then, the family had lived in comfort and security; after the execution, Latifi, her mother, her sister and two brothers lived in fear of the increasingly repressive regime of the Ayatollah. Eventually Latifi's mother became determined to get the two girls out of the country, to a place they could grow up outside the fundamentalist regime that had taken power in Iran. They went first to a European boarding school, and eventually to the home of an uncle who lived in the United States. The girls were young at the time, and although their mother had promised that the family would be reunited some day, they had to become unusually self-reliant at an early age. Several years after their escape from Iran, the girls were joined by their mother, and after several more years passed, the author made a return visit to her homeland. Latifi tells her family's story in her book *Even after All This Time: A Story of Love, Revolution, and Leaving Iran.*

Latifi's story is a highly dramatic one, yet she told an interviewer for the HarperCollins Web site that one of her aims in writing the book was to help readers understand that "at the heart of it all, even though we were Iranians, did not speak much of the language, had funny clothes, unshaved legs, and many other 'un-American' teenage characterstics, we were still really just teenagers—Teenagers, who enjoyed going to the Friday night football game and tried out for the cheerleading squad. I also wanted to show that we were going through the same awkward transitions that teenagers go through no matter which continent they live on and what language they speak. Our issues were just compounded by unfortunate external factors." She has also stated that she wrote the book as a tribute to her mother's strength and courage.

Reviewing the book for *Women's Wear Daily,* Vanessa Lawrence noted that the author "narrates the tale with a mixture of distance and honesty." Maria C. Bagshaw,

a contributor to *Library Journal,* credited Latifi with "poignantly" telling "both the good and the bad, the comical and the dramatic" aspects of her story. The Latifi family's courage and endurance in the face of great loss and hardship should stand as a "compelling testament to the dauntless nature of the human spirit," even in the face of great adversity, according to *Booklist* writer Margaret Flanagan. While a *Kirkus Reviews* contributor cited the book's "flat" quality, a *Publishers Weekly* reviewer recommended *Even after All This Time* as a "remarkable, resonating tale."

BIOGRAPHICAL AND CRITICAL SOURCES:

BOOKS

Latifi, Afschineh, and Pablo F. Fenjves, *Even after All This Time: A Story of Love, Revolution, and Leaving Iran,* Regan Books (New York, NY), 2005.

PERIODICALS

Booklist, February 15, 2005, Margaret Flanagan, review of *Even after All This Time,* p. 1056.
Entertainment Weekly, March 25, 2005, Gilbert Cruz, review of *Even after All This Time,* p. 78.
Kirkus Reviews, January 15, 2005, review of *Even after All This Time,* p. 103.
Library Journal, March 1, 2005, Maria C. Bagshaw, review of *Even after All This Time,* p. 96.
Publishers Weekly, January 17, 2005, review of *Even after All This Time,* p. 42.
Women's Wear Daily, April 19, 2005, Vanessa Lawrence, review of *Even after All This Time,* p. 4.

ONLINE

BookLoons, http://www.bookloons.com/ (September 20, 2005), Hilary Williamson, review of *Even after All This Time.*
HarperCollins Web site, http://www.harpercollins.com/ (September 17, 2005), biographical information about Afschineh Latifi.*

*   *   *

LEFF, Laurel 1957-

PERSONAL: Born 1957. *Education:* Princeton University, undergraduate degree; University of Miami, M.A.; Yale University, Master's in law.

ADDRESSES: Office—School of Journalism, College of Arts and Sciences, Northeastern University, 360 Huntington Ave., Boston, MA 02115. *E-mail*—l.leff@neu.edu.

CAREER: Northeastern University, Boston, MA, assistant professor of journalism. Formerly reporter for *Wall Street Journal* and *Miami Herald,* and editor for *American Lawyer, Media,* and *Hartford Courant.*

WRITINGS:

Buried by the Times: The Holocaust and America's Most Important Newspaper (nonfiction), Cambridge University Press (New York, NY), 2005.

SIDELIGHTS: Laurel Leff examines a unique point in the history of World War II in her book *Buried by the Times: The Holocaust and America's Most Important Newspaper.* Leff contends that the *New York Times* never allowed its coverage of the Nazi's genocidal war against European Jews to be seen on the front page. The newspaper's publisher, Arthur Hays Sulzberger, was himself Jewish and helped many European relatives reach safety when the Nazis began to round up and exterminate Jewish citizens. Yet Sulzberger was also very much opposed to the idea of a Jewish state and did not want the *New York Times* to be identified as a Jewish newspaper. Leff's analysis of Sulzberger's inner conflicts and editorial decisions forms "a brilliant history, one whose insights offer much for editors to think about today when a new war is under way in which an Islamist foe seeks the destruction of the state in which the remnant of European Jewry found redemption," stated Seth Lipsky in *Columbia Journalism Review.* Lipsky concluded: "The importance of Leff's book is in helping us to understand what happened so that we can be faster on our feet and avoid the same mistakes now that a new war against the Jews is under way and a new generation of newspaper men and women are on the story."

Reviewing the book for the *Weekly Standard,* Jack Fischel noted that Sulzberger's position was by no means unique. Many prominent American Jews believed, as he did, that identifying Judaism as a nation only played into the racist beliefs of Hitler and his followers. Still, their eagerness to avoid being seen as a race apart from the rest of America led to a tragically muted response to the genocide in Europe. "In documenting how the Times contributed to a political environment that led to inaction, Leff also reveals much about the insecurity of American Jews at that time," commented Fischel.

BIOGRAPHICAL AND CRITICAL SOURCES:

PERIODICALS

Columbia Journalism Review, May-June, 2005, Seth Lipsky, review of *Buried by the Times: The Holocaust and America's Most Important Newspaper,* p. 70.
Weekly Standard, April 11, 2005, Jack Fischel, review of *Buried by the Times,* p. 38.

ONLINE

Northeastern University Web site, http://www.neu.edu/ (September 20, 2005), personal information about Laurel Leff.*

*   *   *

LEIGH, Danny 1972-

PERSONAL: Born 1972, in Edinburgh, Scotland.

ADDRESSES: Home—Brighton, England. *Agent*—c/o Author Mail, Bloomsbury Publishing, 38 Soho Square, London W1D 3HB, England.

CAREER: Writer. Has worked as a musician and journalist.

AWARDS, HONORS: Dazed/Egg creative bursary for emerging novelists.

WRITINGS:

NOVELS

The Greatest Gift, Faber & Faber (London, England), 2004.
The Monsters of Gramercy Park, Bloomsbury (New York, NY), 2005.

SIDELIGHTS: Danny Leigh's first novel to be published in the United States was *The Monsters of Gramercy Park,* a suspenseful story featuring a frustrated writer who hopes to pick up material for a bestselling book by interviewing a hardened criminal, who is also the author of a children's book. The writer, Lizbeth, began her writing career with a bestselling account of her near-fatal encounter with a serial killer. She was able to sustain her writing success for a while with a mystery series; but Lizbeth has grown bored, her sales are slumping, and she is tempted to escape into the heroin addiction she previously defeated. Wilson Velez is a prison inmate serving a life sentence for his leadership of the Sacred Incan Royals, an extremely violent street gang. By interviewing him and analyzing his life of crime—and his literary leanings—Lizbeth hopes to recreate the success of her first book. "The bulk of Leigh's chilly, finely etched narrative shows Wilson and Lizbeth trying to outmaneuver each other," commented a *Kirkus Reviews* contributor, who found Leigh's story "powerful." A *Publishers Weekly* reviewer found that while the story's elements are not particularly original, the author's "depictions of prison life are unusually intense" and deemed the book as a whole to be "a taut psychological thriller."

BIOGRAPHICAL AND CRITICAL SOURCES:

PERIODICALS

Kirkus Reviews, July 1, 2005, review of *The Monsters of Gramercy Park,* p. 703.
Publishers Weekly, June 27, 2005, review of *The Monsters of Gramercy Park,* p. 39.*

                    *   *   *

LELAND, John 1959-

PERSONAL: Born 1959; married; wife's name Risa; children: Jordan. *Education:* Attended Columbia University.

ADDRESSES: Home—New York, NY. *Agent*—c/o Author Mail, Ecco Press, 10 E. 53rd St., 7th Fl., New York, NY 10022.

CAREER: Journalist. *Spin* magazine, columnist, until 1989; *Newsday,* journalist, beginning 1989; *Newsweek,* lifestyle section editor, beginning 1993; *Details,* former editor-in-chief; *New York Times,* currently reporter.

WRITINGS:

Hip: The History, Ecco Press (New York, NY), 2004.

SIDELIGHTS: John Leland is a well-known entertainment writer whose work has appeared in major periodicals for over two decades. When his literary agent suggested he write a book defining and tracing the origins of the term "hip," Leland was at first reluctant. Yet as he began researching, he found it to be a fascinating topic. "As I learned more, especially about the West African roots of the word hip, I began to see hip as a story we create about ourselves to get around the official racial narratives that we have thrust on us," Leland told *RockCritics.com* reporter Joe Estes, adding, "In this sense, I saw hip as ahead of—and in some cases a remedy to—the limited views of race that infuse government, school, church and the workplace. It seemed very central to who we think we are as Americans. And so, important." With this piqued interest, Leland approached the project seriously, first defining in *Hip: The History,* the term's African origin (from the Wolof "hipi"). Thus Leland writes, "Hip is an awareness or enlightenment across cultural lines. It means that you know more than you're supposed to about the other guy's game," whoever that "other guy" might be. Leland further defined the book this way: "To a great extent it's a book about race and pop culture, and about a paradox that seems to shape so much of America: Even as the nation's history has been defined by racial division and antipathy, in our pop culture, which we invent to tell stories about ourselves, we are at our best wildly hybrid. I question the popular assumption that what we call black culture and white culture are really separate." Indeed, Leland proposes that Blacks and whites have long been borrowing facets of each other's cultures and transforming what has been taken. This back-and-forth action is "the heat of hip." He continued, "The book's thesis is that hip emerges originally as an awareness that bridges binary polarities: black and white mainstream and margins, insider and outsider, conformist and rebel, etc. The binaries no longer shape our lives. We're much more complicated ethnically, and the forces that once lined up against hip behavior—church, capital, parents, role models—now all want to see themselves as hip."

In the work, Leland discusses such topics as slavery's effect on the blues; Emerson, Thoreau, and Whitman as the original gangsters (read individualists); the Harlem Renaissance; bebop; tricksters; the criminally hip (outlaws, gangsters, players, and hustlers); hip ladies; the drug connection; digital hipness. The work caught the attention of many reviewers, including *Booklist* reviewer Mike Tribby, who praised it as "a highly readable, provocative resource," *Library Journal* commentator Carol J. Binkowski, who called it "absorbing analysis," and *Boston Globe* reviewer Renee Graham, who dubbed it "entertaining and enlightening." In the *Washington Post Book World* John Strausbaugh elaborated, calling *Hip* "an impressive achievement— thorough, exhaustively researched and eventually a bit exhausting," and added that Leland "seems to know everything there is to know about hip. He's read all the books, listened to all the music, seen all the movies. He manages to lay it all out with a detached authority that's just a hair shy of the know-it-all smugness implied by the book's title." Yet not all reviewers were so laudatory. For instance, a *Kirkus Reviews* critic described the work as "comprehensive but overwrought." Even so, *School Library Journal* reviewer Emily Lloyd predicted that *Hip* will be "a surefire way to excite teens about the forces at work in American history."

BIOGRAPHICAL AND CRITICAL SOURCES:

PERIODICALS

Booklist, October 1, 2004, Mike Tribby, review of *Hip: The History,* p. 87.

Boston Globe, November 12, 2004, Renée Graham, "Either You Is or You Ain't: John Leland Riffs on What It Is to Be Hip,"

Kirkus Reviews, August 15, 2004, review of *Hip: The History,* p. 791.

Library Journal, September 1, 2004, Carol J. Binkowski, review of *Hip: The History,* p. 173.

Newsweek, October 4, 2004, Devin Gordon, "Fast Chat: Writing from the 'Hip,'" p. 12.

Publishers Weekly, August 16, 2004, review of *Hip: The History,* p. 51.

School Library Journal, March, 2005, Emily Lloyd, review of *Hip: The History,* p. 245.

Time, October 18, 2004, Richard Lacayo, "Hip's History: Two Cool Books Decode Its Passions and Put-ons," p. 88.

U.S. News & World Report, November 1, 2004, Thomas Hayden, "Of Hepcats and Cool Dudes," p. 64.

ONLINE

RockCritics.com, http://rockcritics.com/ (April 18, 2006), Joe Estes, "History of a Hipster: Interview with John Leland."

Washington Post Book World Online, http://www. washingtonpost.com/ (April 18, 2006), John Strausbaugh, review of *Hip: The History.**

*   *   *

LENARD, Lisa
    See LENARD-COOK, Lisa

*   *   *

LENARD-COOK, Lisa 1952-
    (Lisa Lenard)

PERSONAL: Born June 23, 1952, in Buffalo, NY; daughter of Baryl (a company president) and Donna (a homemaker; maiden name, Krohn; later surnames Goldman and Fliegler) Lenard; married Michael E. Kushner (an attorney), April 8, 1978 (divorced April 9, 1984); married Bob Cook (a musician, composer, and project manager), May 1, 1995; children: (first marriage) Kaitlin. *Education:* State University of New York at Buffalo, B.A. (with honors), 1974; Vermont College, M.F.A., 1993. *Politics:* Independent. *Religion:* Jewish. *Hobbies and other interests:* Reading, travel, hiking, music, art, science.

ADDRESSES: Agent—Anne Hawkins, JHA Literary, 71 W. 23rd St., Ste. 1600, New York, NY 10010. *E-mail*—lisa@lisalenardcook.com.

CAREER: Novelist and editor. Fort Lewis College, Durango, CO, visiting professor of English, 1992-97; teacher of private writing classes. Chamber Music Albuquerque, board member; Friends of Corrales Library, member.

MEMBER: Modern Language Association of America, Associated Writing Programs, Corrales Historical Society, PEN New Mexico, New Mexico CultureNet.

AWARDS, HONORS: Fellow, Colorado Council on the Arts, 1995; New Millennium Award; Jim Sagel Prize for the novel, 2003, for *Dissonance;* citations for Southwest Book of the Year, Tucson-Pima County Library, 2003, for *Dissonance,* and 2004, for *Coyote Morning.*

WRITINGS:

(As Lisa Lenard) *K.I.S.S. Guide to Dreams,* DK Publishing (New York, NY), 2002.

(As Lisa Lenard; with Arlene Tognetti) *The Intuitive Arts on Love,* Alpha Books (Indianapolis, IN), 2003.

Dissonance (literary fiction), University of New Mexico Press (Albuquerque, NM), 2003.

Coyote Morning (literary fiction), University of New Mexico Press (Albuquerque, NM), 2004.

UNDER NAME LISA LENARD; "COMPLETE IDIOT'S GUIDE" SERIES

(With Madeline Gerwick-Brodeur) *The Complete Idiot's Guide to Astrology,* Alpha Books (New York, NY), 1997, 3rd edition, 2003.

(With Arlene Tognetti) *The Complete Idiot's Guide to Tarot and Fortune Telling,* Alpha Books (New York, NY), 1998, 2nd edition, 2003.

(Coauthor) *The Complete Idiot's Guide to New Millennium Predictions,* Alpha Books (New York, NY), 1999.

(With Kay Lagerquist) *The Complete Idiot's Guide to Numerology,* Alpha Books (Indianapolis, IN), 1999, 2nd edition, 2004.

(With David Hammerman) *The Complete Idiot's Guide to Reincarnation,* Alpha Books (Indianapolis, IN), 2000.

The Complete Idiot's Guide to Drawing, illustrated by Lauren Jarrett, Alpha Books (Indianapolis, IN), 2000, 2nd edition, 2000.

(With Carolyn Flynn) *The Complete Idiot's Guide to Palmistry,* revised edition, Alpha Books (Indianapolis, IN), 2004.

Author of column "Art of Fiction," for *Authorlink.com.*

WORK IN PROGRESS: Novels *Best Girl, Men in White Horses, Long Division* and *Mercy;* a stage adaptation of *Dissonance;* and the short-story collection *After the Fire.*

SIDELIGHTS: Lisa Lenard-Cook told *CA:* "Where does fiction come from? My favorite definition is from McCauley and Lanning's *Technique in Fiction:* 'Fiction originates in direct personal impression linked by imagination with the writer's resources of experience.' When I think about my own writing process, I like to begin with the first part of this equation, *direct personal impression.* For example, you might be walking down the street one day when you see a striking woman, beautifully dressed, striding purposefully toward you. Let's say that woman suddenly stops short and turns, and you realize that the hastily dressed, runny-nosed child a few steps behind in fact belongs with her. Let's say the woman yanks the child's hand (let's say the child is a girl), spits a few stern words, and then marches resolutely past you, child in tow.

"If you're a fiction writer, scenes like this will get stuck in your head. That's my term, and maybe there's a better one, but that's precisely what happens: The scene gets 'stuck,' and plays over and over again. I call this a *fictional seed,* and it forms one axis of that 'direct personal impression.' But I can't begin to write. Not yet. It's only one seed.

"That's because, for me, it takes at least three seemingly unrelated seeds to start writing. I never know what three seeds will come together to grow a story. I only know that when the moment happens, when the third seed is planted, I am compelled to write. After I've illustrated the other two axes of this equation, I'll come back and show you how this works with a story of my own.

"The second part of the equation is *linked by imagination.* Chances are, when I painted that fictional woman, you began to imagine a history for her even if you aren't a fiction writer. We can't help it. Humans are, above all, creatures of imagination, and when we see something we can't explain, we imagine an explanation.

"You might imagine, for example, that the woman is not what she seems, a fact that's revealed by the child. Perhaps she doesn't know how she'll pay for their lunch, even where they'll get lunch, and is on her way to an appointment that could change not only that, but the direction of her life. But she's saddled with this child, and she doesn't have a babysitter, and—Well, you can see my direction. It's only one possible scenario amongst many, of course.

"The last part of the equation is the *writer's resources of experience*. If you've ever laughed or cried, been angry or overjoyed, loved, hated, or anything in between, you have your own resources of experience. In the best fiction, you use these resources to translate this emotion onto the page for the particular fiction you're writing.

"Now here's that example I promised you. About ten years ago, both a friend's mother and a neighbor in the remote corner of southwest Colorado where I then lived were diagnosed with Alzheimer's. I noticed a number of parallels in the two women's behavior: how polite they were; how both seemed to find joy in simple things they could no longer name. As I drove back and forth to Durango every day, I often found my thoughts turning to something one or the other had said or done. I knew this obsession was a seed. But I wasn't ready to write—not yet. It was only one seed.

"Meanwhile, in that drought summer, the fires burned. In the evening, my daughter and I would sit on our porch and watch the planes shuttle back and forth to Grand Junction. When a plane dropped its slurry, the sky would flare pink. My daughter, an artist, and I, a writer, would sit entranced, night after night after night. This direct personal impression too became a fictional seed. But it still wasn't enough.

"Then, late that summer, I read a story in the *Rocky Mountain News* about wild horses that were starving on BLM land in New Mexico. BLM management believed their only choice was to kill the horses before they became a nuisance to nearby ranchers. This brief news item became the third seed. I know this because as soon as I read it I sat down and wrote the first line of my short story, 'Wild Horses.'

"'Wild Horses' is told from the point of view of a rancher in southwest Colorado whose wife has Alzheimer's. He oscillates between his memories of the woman he married and the daily reality of the woman she's become. In the evenings, they sit on their porch and watch planes ferry slurry to nearby fires. Then a BLM functionary announces that the wild horses that live in the canyon beyond their ranch are going to be shot. Throughout this story, we see the wife only through the husband's eyes, and yet, because the husband has the use of my imagination and my direct resources of experience about things like bewilder-

ment, anger, and most of all, love, in this story's few pages we are able to connect deeply with these characters and their particular predicament.

"Let's review how the three axes work for this story: *Direct personal impressions:* the Alzheimer's, the fires, the wild horses; *Imagination:* this couple—who they were and who they are now; *The writer's resources of experience:* bewilderment, anger, love. Fictional seeds can take years to germinate, but ultimately, it really is this simple. The key is to trust your instincts enough to allow the magic to happen."

BIOGRAPHICAL AND CRITICAL SOURCES:

PERIODICALS

Library Journal, September 1, 2003, Lisa Rohrbaugh, review of *Dissonance,* p. 208; October 1, 2004, Christine DeZelar-Tiedman, review of *Coyote Morning,* p. 70.

ONLINE

Lisa Lenard-Cook Home Page, http://www.lisalenard cook.com (July 4, 2005).

*   *   *

LENNON, Maria T.

PERSONAL: Born in CA; married; children: three. *Education:* London School of Economics, degree (with honors), 1990.

ADDRESSES: Home—Los Angeles, CA. *Agent*—Marly Rusoff & Associates, P.O. Box 524, Bronxville, NY 10708. *E-mail*—info@mariatlennon.com.

CAREER: Writer. International School, Genoa, Italy, teacher of creative writing and English; writer for a travel magazine; associate editor for a travel Web site.

WRITINGS:

Making It Up as I Go Along (novel), Shave Areheart Books (New York, NY), 2005.

SIDELIGHTS: Maria T. Lennon drew from her own life while writing her debut novel *Making It Up as I Go Along.* Like her protagonist, Saffron Roch, Lennon came from an upper-class background in California and traveled widely until becoming pregnant. In the novel, the father of Saffron's child is her unfaithful lover. She must leave her work as a journalist in war-torn Sierra Leone to head to London, and then California, where she unexpectedly inherits a multi-million-dollar estate from her adoptive mother. Her half-brother, disinherited by his birth mother, seems strangely unruffled about being cut out of the will, but as time passes, it becomes clear that he is not as passive as he seems. Saffron finds that reporting on civil war is easier to cope with than the demands of single motherhood in Malibu, but she does get support from an unlikely group of friends, including some "trophy wives" of wealthy older men, all of whom are also new to motherhood. Her story becomes more complicated when she learns that a mysterious African man she loved is in danger of execution.

A *Publishers Weekly* reviewer judged *Making It Up as I Go Along* "a winning mix of humor and suspense." Elizabeth Blakesley Lindsay, reviewing the book for *Library Journal,* called it "deeper than many typical chick-lit novels." The pressures of new motherhood have been examined in many other books, as Mia Geiger pointed out in her *Denver Post* online review, but "thanks to a thoroughly likable, witty-yet-insecure heroine desperately trying to make the best decisions, along with an absence of sentimental mush in the storytelling, the author makes a familiar topic feel fresh."

BIOGRAPHICAL AND CRITICAL SOURCES:

PERIODICALS

Kirkus Reviews, April 1, 2005, review of *Making It Up as I Go Along,* p. 377.
Library Journal, March 1, 2005, Elizabeth Blakesley Lindsay, review of *Making It Up as I Go Along,* p. 79.
Publishers Weekly, May 16, 2005, review of *Making It Up as I Go Along,* p. 37.

ONLINE

Denver Post Online, http://www.denverpost.com/ (September 20, 2005), Mia Geiger, review of *Making It Up as I Go Along.*

LI, Yiyun 1972-

PERSONAL: Born 1972, in Beijing, China; immigrated to United States, 1996; married; children: two sons. *Education:* Peking University, B.A.; University of Iowa, M.F.A., M.S.

ADDRESSES: Home—Oakland, CA. *Office*—Mills College, 5000 MacArthur Blvd., Oakland, CA 94613. *E-mail*—yiyun.write@gmail.com.

CAREER: University of Iowa, Ames, teaching fellow; Mills College, Oakland, CA, assistant professor of English, 2005—.

AWARDS, HONORS: Plimpton Prize for New Writers, *Paris Review,* 2005, for short story "Immortality"; Pushcart Prize, 2005.

WRITINGS:

A Thousand Years of Good Prayers (short stories), Random House (New York, NY), 2005.

Contributor of fiction and memoir to periodicals, including *New Yorker, Ploughshares,* and *Paris Review.*

WORK IN PROGRESS: A novel about a Chinese community in the 1970s.

SIDELIGHTS: Yiyun Li was born in China and came to the United States in 1996, having only a limited command of English at that time. By 1998, however, she began writing in English, and soon was enrolled in two writing programs at the University of Iowa. An essay she wrote about the massacre of students by Chinese forces in Tiananmen Square was published and brought her some attention, and soon her fiction and nonfiction was appearing in such prestigious publications as the *New Yorker, Paris Review,* and *Ploughshares.* The ten stories in Li's first book, *A Thousand Years of Good Prayers,* explore the effects of the Cultural Revolution on modern Chinese people, both those living in their homeland and those who have moved to America. In one story, a pair of immigrants are watching a Christmas parade in Chicago, envying all those around them who have been untouched by tragic historical events. In another story, a Chinese peasant is called to account by the Office of Birth Control for having too many children. Later, when his son is drowned by a government official, the man goes on a killing spree. According to a *Kirkus Reviews* writer, there is some "ungainly plotting but the author is one to watch." A *Publishers Weekly* reviewer stated: "These are powerful stories that encapsulate tidily epic grief and longing."

BIOGRAPHICAL AND CRITICAL SOURCES:

PERIODICALS

Kirkus Reviews, July 1, 2005, review of *A Thousand Years of Good Prayers,* p. 704.
M2 Best Books, February 19, 2004, "First Plimpton Prize Winner Announced,"
Publishers Weekly, June 27, 2005, review of *A Thousand Years of Good Prayers,* p. 39.

ONLINE

University of Iowa Web site, http://www.grad.uiowa.edu/ (September 20, 2005).*

*   *   *

LI Fei-kan
   See BA Jin

*   *   *

LINNANE, Fergus

PERSONAL: Male.

ADDRESSES: *Home*—Chelsfield, Kent, England. *Agent*—c/o Author Mail, Sutton Publishing, Phoenix Mill, Thrupp, Stroud, Gloucestershire, GL5 2BU, UK.

CAREER: Author and journalist. Former executive editor of the *European.*

WRITINGS:

London's Underworld: Three Centuries of Vice and Crime, Robson (London, England), 2002.
The Encyclopedia of London Crime and Vice, Sutton (Stroud, Gloucestershire, England) 2003.
London: The Wicked City: A Thousand Years of Vice in the Capital, Robson (London, England), 2003.

SIDELIGHTS: Retired journalist and editor Fergus Linnane has published books on the history of crime and vice in London. The first, *London's Underworld: Three Centuries of Vice and Crime,* is a chronological account that encompasses the notorious personalities, political climate, and cultural context that accompanies the rise and fall of criminal activity in the British city. Linnane begins his account in the eighteenth century, exploring the city's nearly lawless streets. During this era, bounty hunters called "thief takers" were relied on to bring criminals to justice. The most untrustworthy of these figures was Jonathan Wild, a man who took payments in exchange for protection and ended his days on the scaffold. Linnane then shows the difficulty of establishing an effective and respected police force, which finally took hold at the dawn of the twentieth century.

Critical response to the book revealed it to be a vast but interesting work. Ian Thomson noted in the *Spectator* that it is "fun to read but ultimately it cloys. . . . one longs for a bit of civility." A *Kirkus Reviews* writer commented that the author "carefully places each event and character in context, leading to some redundancy, but . . . it's a forgivable fault." According to an *M2 Best Books* critic, the work offers "a fairly impartial look at crime and related society." *New Statesman* critic Razor Smith, who wrote from prison, remarked that the book would be "fascinating to those who like their 'true crime' to have an informative and historical flavour." He concluded that *London's Underworld* is "shocking, sometimes amusing, but never boring."

In *London: The Wicked City: A Thousand Years of Vice in the Capital,* the author narrows his focus to the sex trade in London. Across the span of a thousand years, he highlights famous prostitutes and notorious gentlemen, and he charts changing tastes and laws. Victorians, for example, had a fascination with flagellation, while twenty-first-century sex clubs in Soho are described as relatively bland. In a review for the *Spectator,* Ian Thomson advised that the book "consists largely of (rather prurient) sketches of commercial sex and swiveling in red-light London from Chaucer's day to the present. The subject can hardly fail to interest."

BIOGRAPHICAL AND CRITICAL SOURCES:

PERIODICALS

Contemporary Review, September, 2003, review of *London's Underworld: Three Centuries of Vice and Crime,* p. 187.

Kirkus Reviews, May 1, 2005, review of *London's Underworld,* p. 526.

M2 Best Books, April 29, 2003, review of *London's Underworld.*

New Statesman, April 21, 2003, Razor Smith, review of *London's Underworld,* p. 51.

Spectator, June 7, 2003, Ian Thomson, "From Gin Craze to Twin Krays," review of *London's Underworld,* p. 40; December 27, 2003, Ian Thomson, "All the Sad Variety of Hell," review of *London: The Wicked City: A Thousand Years of Vice in the Capital,* p. 32.*

*   *   *

LIPTON, Peggy 1947-

PERSONAL: Born August 30, 1947, in New York, NY; daughter of Harold (a corporate lawyer) and Rita (an artist) Lipton; married Quincy Jones (a producer, composer, actor, music conductor and arranger, and executive), September 14, 1974 (divorced, c. 1987); children: Kidada, Rashida (daughters).

ADDRESSES: Home—New York, NY; and Los Angeles, CA. *Agent*—c/o Author Mail, St. Martin's Press, 175 5th Ave., New York, NY 10010.

CAREER: Actress in films and television, including television series *The John Forsythe Show,* 1965, *The Mod Squad,* American Broadcast Companies, Inc. (ABC), 1968-73, *Twin Peaks,* ABC, 1990, and *Angel Falls,* Columbia Broadcasting System, 1993. Actress in films, including *Purple People Eater,* 1988, *I'm*

Gonna Git You Sucka', 1988, *True Identity,* 1991, *The Postman,* 1997, and *Jackpot,* 2001. Actress on stage, including roles in *The Guys* and *The Vagina Monologues.* Worked as a model in New York, NY, c. early 1960s. Singer on album, *Peggy Lipton.*

MEMBER: Break the Cycle.

AWARDS, HONORS: Golden Globe Award for best actress in a leading role, 1970, for *The Mod Squad.*

WRITINGS:

(With David and Coco Dalton) *Breathing Out* (autobiography), St. Martin's Press (New York, NY), 2005.

Author of song "L.A. Is My Lady."

SIDELIGHTS: Peggy Lipton was a successful model when she was still a teenager, and was only twenty-one years old when she landed the part that would make her an icon of the 1960s—that of undercover detective Julie Barnes in the television series *The Mod Squad.* Created by Aaron Spelling, the show featured three hip, young people who were working for the police after getting in trouble with the law. It took on topical subjects of the time, such as campus unrest and war protestors. Lipton's character, Julie, was the runaway daughter of a San Francisco prostitute; her waiflike beauty quickly made her a celebrity. Although she has often been described as the quintessential "California girl," Lipton was actually born and raised in New York City, the daughter of a well-to-do family. *The Mod Squad* catapulted her into the fast-paced world of Hollywood, a work in which Lipton was ill-prepared to cope.

Lipton relates the story of her life in her autobiography, *Breathing Out,* cowritten with David and Coco Dalton. Behind the golden-girl façade, Lipton was a survivor of sexual abuse, someone who had to overcome a stutter to move forward with an acting career, and a woman who made numerous sexual conquests among the celebrities of the day. Elvis Presley, Paul McCartney, and Sammy Davis, Jr. were just a few of the men with whom she was linked; the actress eventually married musician and record producer Quincy Jones, with whom she had two children. Her marriage to an African American several years her senior provoked an angry response from some, but the marriage lasted for many years, while Lipton took a break from acting to concentrate on raising her two daughters. After the girls left home, the marriage dissolved, in part due to Lipton's struggle with depression. A *Publishers Weekly* writer called Lipton's story "cliched" and her writing "clunky," but predicted that readers will still enjoy the portrait of the wild life of the 1960s and 1970s. A *Kirkus Reviews* writer found that, somewhat surprisingly, the sections on Lipton's later life are the most compelling: "Her descriptions of the post-marriage, post-*Mod Squad* phase of her career are the strongest sections here. The chapter on *Twin Peaks*, the David Lynch television show with Lipton playing Norma Jennings, is fascinating and passionate." John Smyntek, in a review for the *Detroit Free Press,* found that the memoir lacks depth, but is nevertheless enjoyable. He wrote: "There is minimal hot air and you get a real sense of the shallowness of her existence. It is a guilty pleasure for any connoisseur of gossip. . . . Let us give her credit for linking up with the right storytellers and creating something out of what might seem only a pile of personal dust."

BIOGRAPHICAL AND CRITICAL SOURCES:

BOOKS

Contemporary Theatre, Film, and Television, Thomson Gale (Detroit, MI), 2001.
Lipton, Peggy, with David Dalton and Coco Dalton, *Breathing Out,* St. Martin's Press (New York, NY), 2005.

PERIODICALS

Detroit Free Press, June 26, 2005, John Smyntek, review of *Breathing Out.*
Entertainment Weekly, May 13, 2005, Margeaux Watson, review of *Breathing Out,* p. 94.
In Style, May 1, 2001, Monica Corcoran, "The Mom Squad: A Force of One, Peggy Lipton Uses Straight Talk and Motherly Advice to Teach Teens to Break the Cycle of Domestic Violence," p. 375.
Kirkus Reviews, March 15, 2005, review of *Breathing Out,* p. 338.

People, September 8, 1986; April 4, 1988; May 12, 1997, p. 180.
Publishers Weekly, April 11, 2005, review of *Breathing Out,* p. 41.
Women's Wear Daily, May 26, 2005, "Star Wars," p. 4; July 21, 2005, Molly Prior, "The Mod Squad," p. 22S.

ONLINE

Books in Review, http://www.geocities.com/pett projects/ (September 20, 2005), Adrienne Petterson, review of *Breathing Out.*
Ear Candy, http://www.earcandymag.com/ (September 20, 2005), review of *Breathing Out.*
Internet Movie Database, http://www.imdb.com/ (April 18, 2006), biographical information about Peggy Lipton.
TV.com, http://www.tv.com/ (September 20, 2005), biographical information about Peggy Lipton.*

*   *   *

LISICK, Beth 1968-

PERSONAL: Born 1968; married; children: Gus.

ADDRESSES: Agent—c/o Author Mail, Regan Books, 10 E. 53rd St., 7th Fl., New York, NY 10022. *E-mail*—blisick@hotmail.com.

CAREER: Poet, fiction writer, and musician. Columnist for *SFGate.com;* member of comedy troupe *White Noise Radio Theater.*

AWARDS, HONORS: Firecracker Award for fiction, 2002, for *This Too Can Be Yours*; Best of the Fest award, NewFest Film Festival, for *Diving for Pearls.*

WRITINGS:

Monkey Girl: Swingin' Tales (poetry), Manic D Press (San Francisco, CA), 1997.
This Too Can Be Yours (short stories), Manic D Press (San Francisco, CA), 2001.
Everybody into the Pool: True Tales (autobiography), Regan Books (New York, NY), 2005.

OTHER

Also author of screenplays *Diving for Pearls, Compulsory Breathing, Fumbling towards Rock,* and *Rusty Citation.* Author of column, "Buzz Town," for *SFGate.com.*

SIDELIGHTS: Beth Lisick grew up in a stable, middle-class family in Saratoga, New York, but broke out of that well-ordered world to make a name for herself as an avant-garde performer in the underground arts, working with music, theater, literature, spoken word, and film. In addition, she writes a gossip column about the San Francisco art scene for *SFGate.com,* the on-line version of the *San Francisco Chronicle.* Lisick got her start reading at open-mic poetry readings, through which she eventually attracted the attention of Jennifer Joseph, the publisher in charge of Manic D Press, and also the host of a poetry-reading series at the Paradise Lounge. Lisick read at the lounge regularly for some time, and then Joseph asked her to compile some of her work into manuscript form. The result was the poetry collection *Monkey Girl: Swingin' Tales.*

Lisick's next book, *This Too Can Be Yours,* is a collection of short stories. In her third, *Everybody into the Pool: True Tales,* Lisick recalls her varied life experiences, from attending society luncheons and being crowned homecoming princess in Saratoga, New York, to taking a job dressing as a banana, living in an apartment that had been sprayed by leaking sewage, and trying to unlock the latent lesbianism she felt she should have while touring with a lesbian band. Commenting on the book to Becca Costello in the *Sacramento News and Review,* she said: "I was this upper-middle-class teen. I was a cheerleader and a homecoming princess, and I just turned into this weird-ball artist person who has lived a different life than I was raised to live. The essays go from me growing up to me being a mom myself and driving a station wagon with a car seat in the back. The book is also about what I see as the death of alternative culture."

Discussing *Everybody into the Pool* with Todd Inoue for *MetroActive.com,* Lisick mused, "I didn't write it for any other reason than to write funny stories." Jennifer Reese, in *Entertainment Weekly,* believed Lisick achieves this goal, calling the sketches in the book "fizzy and delightful." The author's fondness for contrasting her mainstream upbringing with her colorful later life was noted by Audrey Snowden in *Library Journal.* Snowden wrote that while there are many loose ends and some abrupt transitions in *Everybody into the Pool,* the stories "most definitely entertain." The author's "sharp observations and self-deprecation" are evident in this collection, and they prove her to be "an accomplished storyteller," according to a *Kirkus Reviews* contributor. *Book Slut* online reviewer Laura Lee Mattingly credited Lisick with taking on "topics such as adolescence, sexuality, race, and socio-economic class with ease, wit, and a sparkling sense of humor," but added that the author can also be "clever and poignant," as she is in the book's final piece, concerning her new son and the experience of motherhood.

BIOGRAPHICAL AND CRITICAL SOURCES:

PERIODICALS

Entertainment Weekly, July 8, 2005, Jennifer Reese, review of *Everybody into the Pool: True Tales,* p. 75.

Kirkus Reviews, May 15, 2005, review of *Everybody into the Pool,* p. 577.

Library Journal, June 1, 2005, Audrey Snowden, review of *Everybody into the Pool,* p. 128.

People, July 18, 2005, Jonathan Durbin, review of *Everybody into the Pool,* p. 49.

Portland Tribune (Portland, OR), August 26, 2005, Eric Bartels, "Out of a 'Dark Place' and into the Country."

Sacramento News and Review, November 13, 2003, Becca Costello, "Beth Lisick Does It All."

ONLINE

Beth Lisick Home Page, http://www.bethlisick.com (October 15, 2005).

Book Slut, http://www.bookslut.com/ (October 15, 2005), Laura Lee Mattingly, review of *Everybody into the Pool.*

MetroActive.com, http://www.metroactive.com/ (July 6, 2005), Todd Inoue, "Making a Splash."*

LIU Xinwu 1942-

PERSONAL: Born June 4, 1942, in Chengdu, Sichuan Province, China; son of Liu Tianyan and Wang Yuntao; married Lu Xiaoge, 1970; children: one son. *Education:* Beijing Normal University, graduated 1961.

ADDRESSES: Office—8th Fl., No. 1404, Anding Menwai Dongheyan, Beijing 100011, China.

CAREER: Writer. High school teacher, 1961-76; Beijing Publishing House, Beijing, China, editor, 1976-80; *People's Literature* (journal), Beijing, chief editor, 1987-90.

MEMBER: Chinese Writers' Association (member of council).

AWARDS, HONORS: National short-story competition first prize, 1978, for "Banzhuren," and 1979; national prize for children's writing, 1979, 1988; Mao Dun literature prize, 1985, for *Zhong gu lou.*

WRITINGS:

(With others) *Yazhou zhi di yu ren,* Taibei shang wu yin shu guan (Taibei, China), 1975.

Zheng da ni di yan jing (fiction), Beijing ren min chu ban she (Beijing, China), 1976.

Mu xiao liu nian (stories), Zhongguo shao nian er tong chu ban she (Beijing, China), 1978.

Shang hen: duan pian xiao shuo he ju ben (stories), Sheng huo, du shu, xin zhi san lian shu dian (Xianggang, China), 1978.

Lian ai, hun yin, jia ting, Zhongguo quing nian chu ban she (Beijing, China), 1979.

Rang wo men lai tao lun ai quing, Shanghai ren min chu ban she (Shanghai, China), 1979.

Ban zhu ren, Zhongguo quing nian chu ban she (Beijing, China), 1979.

Zhe li you huang jin: zhong duan pian xiao shuo ji (stories), Guangdong ren min chu ban she (Canton, China), 1980.

Liu Xinwu duan pian xiao shuo xuan (stories), Beijing chu ban she (Beijing, China), 1980.

Lü ye yu huang jin: duan pian xiao shuo ji (stories), Guangdong ren min chu ban she (Canton, China), 1980.

Da yan mao (stories), Zhejiang ren min chu ban she (Hangzhou, China), 1981.

Ru yi (stories), Beijing shu ban she (Beijing, China), 1982.

(With others) *Heihai di fan: fang Luo shi ge san wen ji,* Chun feng wen yi chu ban she (Shanyang, China), 1983.

Tong wen xue qing nian dui hua, Wen hua yi shu chu ban she (Beijing, China), 1983.

As You Wish (screenplay), China Video Movies (Palo Alto, CA), 1983.

Dao yuan chu qu fa xin (stories; title means "Posting Letters from Distant Places"), Sichuan ren min chu ban she (Chengdu, China), 1984.

Ri cheng jin bo (fiction; title means "Tight Schedule"), Qun zhong chu ban she (Beijing, China), 1984.

(With others) *Xin shi qi huo jiang xiao shuo chuang zuo jing yan tan* (criticism), Hunan ren min chu ban she (Changsha, China), 1985.

Zhong gu lou (novel; title means "Bell and Drum Towers"), Ren min wen xue chu ban she (Beijing, China), 1985.

Jialing jiang liu jin xue guan (stories; title means "Jialing River Runs in the Veins"), Shanxi ren min chu ban she (Xi'an, China), 1985.

Ri cheng jin po (stories), Qun zhong chu ban she (Beijing, China) 1985.

Wo ke bu pa shi san sui (fiction), Xin shi ji chu ban she (Canton, China), 1985.

Bali yu jin xiang (travel), Qun zhong chu ban she (Beijing, China), 1986.

Mu bian shi jie zhi (stories; title means "A Fossilized Ring"), Qinghai ren min chu ban she (Xining, China), 1986.

Chui liu ji (essays), Shanxi ren min chu ban she (Xi'an, China), 1986.

Du hui yong tan diao (stories), Zuo jia chu ban she (Beijing, China), 1986.

Li ti jiao cha qiao (fiction; title means "Overpass"), Ren min wen xue chu ban she (Beijing, China), 1986.

Zhongguo da lu xian dai xiao shuo xuan (stories), two vols. Yuan shen chu ban she (Taibei Shi, China), 1987.

Xie po wen tan (criticism), Shanghai wen yi chu ban she (Shanghai, China), 1987.

5.19 chang jing tou: Liu Hsin-wu hsiao shuo hs'uan (fiction; title means "Zooming in on 19 May

1985"), Sichuan wen yi chu ban she (Chengdu, China), 1987.

Wang fu jing wan hua dong, Hunan wen yi chu ban she (Changsha, China), 1987.

Ta you yi tou pi jian fa (stories), Lin bai chu ban she you xian gong si (Taipei, China), 1988.

Si ren zhao xiang bu (photographs), Nan Yue chu ban she (Xianggang, China), 1988.

(With others) *Liu Xinwu dai biao zuo* (fiction), Huanghe wen yi chu ban she (Zhengzhou, China), 1988.

Xiao yuan xiao shuo (stories), Shanghai jiao yu chu ban she (Shanghai, China), 1988.

Yi pian lü ye dui ni shuo (essays; title means "Talking to You about a Green Leaf"), Hebei jiao yu chu ban she (Shijiazhuang, China), 1989.

Black Walls and Other Stories, edited by Don J. Cohn, introduction by Geremie Barme, Chinese University of Hong Kong (Hong Kong, China), 1990.

Yi chuang deng huo (fiction), Hua yi chu ban she (Beijing, China), 1991.

Feng guo er (fiction; title means "Overheard"), Zhongguo qing nian chu ban she (Beijing, China), 1992.

Xian gei ming yun di zi luo lan: Liu Xinwu tan sheng cun zhi hui, Shanghai ren min chu ban she (Shanghai, China), 1992.

Lan ye cha (fiction), Qin + yuan chu ban she (Xianggang, China), 1992.

You jia ke gui (fiction), Guangdong lü yu chu ban she (Guangzhou, China), 1992.

Wei ni zi ji gao xing, Nei Menggu ren min chu ban she (Huhehaote, China), 1992.

Dafenqi (biography), Jiangsu jiao yu chu ban she (Nanjing, China), 1992.

Sha xing, Qin + yuan chu ban she (Xianggang, China), 1993.

Si pai lou (fiction), Shanghei wen yi chu ban she (Shanghai, China), 1993.

Chen mo jiao liu, Zhongguo hua qiao chu ban she (Beijing, China), 1993.

Wo shi zen yang di yi ge ping zi, Chengdu chu ban she (Chengdu, China), 1993.

Liu Xinwu wen ji, eight volumes, Hua yi chu ban she (Beijing, China), 1993.

Zhongguo dang dai ming ren sui bi (essays), Shanxi ren min chu ban she (Xi'an, China), 1993.

Fu xin you shu, Qun zhong chu ban she (Beijing, China), 1993.

Yang wang cang tian: Liu Xinwu sui bi (essays), Zhi shi chu ban she (Shanghai, China), 1994.

Nan ban nü zhuang yu nü ban nan zhuang, Zhong yuan nong min chu ban she (Zhengzhou, China), 1994.

Qin Keqing zhi si, Hua yi chu ban she (Beijing, China), 1994.

(With others) *Min jian zong jiao yu jie she* (religion), Guo ji wen hua chu ban gong si (Beijing, China), 1994.

Xiao jiao yu bian zi, Guo ji wen hua chu ban gong si (Beijing, China), 1994.

Jin ji yu duo xing, Guo ji wen hua chu ban gong si (Beijing, China), 1994.

Wei da ren mo mo xu yuan (essays), You shi wen hua shi ye gong si (Taipei, China), 1994.

Yi xue yu zhan gua, Guo ji wen hua chu ban gong si (Beijing, China), 1994.

Jiao xue mei ti (teaching aids), Xin li chu ban she you xian gong si (Taipei, China), 1994.

Liu Xinwu juan (stories), Hai xia wen yi chu ban she (Fuzhou, China), 1994.

(With others) *Huang hou yu pin fei,* Guo ji wen hua chu ban gong si (Beijing, China), 1994.

Wèi ta rén mò mò xu yuàn, You shi wen hua (Taipei, China), 1994.

(With others) *Xiang dui yi xiao,* Zhong gong zhong yang dang xiao chu ban she (Beijing, China), 1994.

Ren sheng fei meng zong nan xing (diary excerpt), Shanghai ren min chu ban she (Shanghai, China), 1995.

Liu Xinwu hai wai you ji (travel), Hua wen chu ban she (Beijing, China), 1995.

Xian ren cheng lu pan (stories), Hua yi chu ban she (Beijing, China), 1995.

Nü xing yu cheng shi, Zhongguo cheng shi chu ban she (Beijing, China), 1995.

Liu Xinwu xiao shuo jing xuan (short stories), Tai bai wen yi chu ban she (Xi'an, China), 1996.

Kai fa xin da lu, Jilin ren min chu ban she (Changchun, China), 1996.

Liu Xinwu guai dan xiao shuo zi xuan ji, Lijiang chu ban she (Guilin, China), 1996.

Wo shi Liu Xinwu, Tuan jie chu ban she (Beijing, China), 1996.

Bian yuan you guang (criticism), Han yu da ci dian chu ban she (Shanghai, China), 1996.

Qi feng lou (fiction), Ren min wen xue chu ban she (Beijing, China), 1996.

Liu Xinwu za wen zi xuan ji (essays), Bai hua wen yi chu ban she (Tianjin, China), 1996.

Ni heng di shen mo ge (essays), Hunan wen yi chu ban she (Changsha, China), 1996.

(With others) *San wei: du shu he pin shu di sui bi* (criticism), Shan dong hua bao chu ban she (Jinan, China), 1996.

(With Zhang Yiwu) *Liu Xinwu Zhang Yiwu dui hua lu: "hou shi ji" di wen hua liao wang* (criticism), Lijiang chu ban she (Guilin, China), 1996.

Dian shi jiao yu jie mu di qi hua yu zhi bo, Li ming wen hua shi yan gu fen you xian gong si (Taipei, China), 1997.

Si ren zhao xiang bu (photographs), Shanghai yuan dong chu ban she (Shanghai, China), 1997.

Ba zui zhang yuan, Shanghai yuan dong chu ban she (Shanghai, China), 1997.

(With others) *Duo nan di zu qiu: Zhongguo zu qiu yu qiu mi di xue lei zheng cheng* (nonfiction), 1997.

Wo yan zhong di jian zhu yu huan jing, Zhongguo jian zhu gong ye chu ban she (Beijing, China), 1998.

Xian shang yi pian an ning, Qun zhong chu ban she (Beijing, China), 1998.

Awen di shi dai (fiction), Zhuhai chu ban she (Zhuhai, China), 1998.

Shu yu lin tong zai, Shandong hua bao chu ban she (Jinan, China), 1999.

Hong lou san chai zhi mi: Liu Xinwu Hong xue tan yi jing pin, Hua yi chu ban she (Beijing, China), 1999.

Guo sui dao di xin qing (essays), Hua dong shi fan da xue chu ban she (Shanghai, China), 1999.

Lan mei gui (fiction), Zhongguo hua qiao chu ban she (Beijing, China), 1999.

Ba shi liu ke xing xing (children's stories), Xi wang chu ban she (Taiyuan, China), 1999.

Yi qie dou hai lai de ji, Zhongguo qing nian chu ban she (Beijing, China), 2000.

Wo ai chi ku gua (essays), Guangzhou chu ban she (Guangzhou, China), 2000.

Lou qian bai yu lan: Liu Xinwu zui xin xiao xiao shuo ji (stories), Zhongguo guang bo dian shi chu ban she (Beijing, China), 2000.

Liu Xinwu kan Beijing, Shanghai wen yi chu ban she (Shanghai, China), 2000.

Liao jie Gao Xingjian, Kai yi chu ban she (Xiang-gang, China), 2000.

(With others) *Ke wai yu wen: Xiao xue yi nian ji* (primary-school textbook), Liaoning ren min chu ban she (Shenyang, China), 2000.

(With others) *Ke wai yu wen: Xiao xue er nian ji* (primary-school textbook), Liaoning ren min chu ban she (Shenyang, China), 2000.

(With others) *Ke wai yu wen: Xiao xue san nian ji* (primary-school textbook), Liaoning ren min chu ban she (Shenyang, China), 2000.

(With others) *Ke wai yu wen: Chu zhong yi nian ji* (primary-and middle-school textbook), Liaoning ren min chu ban she (Shenyang, China), 2000.

(With others) *Ke wai yu wen: Chu zhong er nian ji* (primary-and middle-school textbook), Liaoning ren min chu ban she (Shenyang, China), 2000.

(With others) *Ke wai yu wen: Chu zhong san nian ji* (primary-and middle-school textbook), Liaoning ren min chu ban she (Shenyang, China), 2000.

(With others) *Ke wai yu wen: Gao zhong yi nian ji* (senior high-school textbook), Liaoning ren min chu ban she (Shenyang, China), 2000.

(With others) *Ke wai yu wen: Gao zhong er nian ji* (senior high-school textbook), Liaoning ren min chu ban she (Shenyang, China), 2000.

(With others) *Ke wai yu wen: Gao zhong san nian ji* (senior high-school textbook), Liaoning ren min chu ban she (Shenyang, China), 2000.

(With others) *Ke wai yu wen: Xiao xue si nian ji* (primary-school textbook), Liaoning ren min chu ban she (Shenyang, China), 2000.

(With others) *Ke wai yu wen: Xiao xue wu nian ji* (primary-school textbook), Liaoning ren min chu ban she (Shenyang, China), 2000.

Cong you yu zhong sheng hua, Wen hui chu ban she (Shanghai, China), 2001.

Ren zai feng zhong, Zuo jia chu ban she (Beijing, China), 2001.

Qin jin cang mang (travel), Zhongguo lü you chu ban she (Beijing, China), 2001.

Zou bian ming cheng (travel), Xin shi jie chu ban she (Beijing, China), 2002.

SIDELIGHTS: With "Banzhuren" ("Class Teacher"), a short story published in 1977, Liu Xinwu launched a movement in Chinese fiction known as "wound" or "scar" literature. The stories in this genre focus on the wounds caused by China's Cultural Revolution (1966-1976). Drawing on Liu's own experiences as a middle-school teacher, "Banzhuren" tells of the travails of a teacher trying to reach out to a group of students scarred in one way or another by the Cultural Revolution. "The style is marred by jargon and a rather wooden style," wrote David Jiang and Li Ruru in *Contemporary World Writers.* "The story owed its considerable success less to literary merit than to the timing of its publication. . . . Liu Xinwu said what everyone wanted to say but had not quite dared."

Despite this rather courageous event, Liu has been considered a loyal Communist Party writer by various critics. Writing in *Westerly,* Kam Louie found that, "of the writers in China now who write about social issues, Liu Xinwu adheres more closely to the Party line than almost anyone else." Other literary critics have found more complexity in his relationship with the government. Liu "has taken some highly controversial stands, going so far as to support the 1989 democracy movement in Beijing," wrote Mary Banas in *Booklist*. Twice, he was removed from editing the prestigious *People's Literature* for overstepping the bounds.

In 1990, the Chinese University of Hong Kong put out an English-language edition of Liu's works titled *Black Walls and Other Stories*. "Liu's stories are more social vignettes than innovative and artistic pieces of literature and so perhaps the reader is to see them as a key to recent history," wrote Gregory Lee in *China Quarterly*. Lee added that, "even eight years later, the title story 'Black Walls' still seems impressive and well-crafted, as does 'The Wish.'" According to Frances LeFleur in *World Literature Today*, the stories "illustrate his evolution from a rather naïve originator of post-Cultural Revolution 'wound literature' to a middle-aged observer of a world wherein the lines between black and white modernization and 'bourgeois pollution' are much less clearly drawn."

BIOGRAPHICAL AND CRITICAL SOURCES:

BOOKS

Contemporary World Writers, St. James Press (Detroit, MI), 1993, pp. 329-330.
Liu Xinwu (bibliography), Ren min wen xue chu ban she (Beijing, China), 1996.

PERIODICALS

Booklist, August, 1990, Mary Banas, review of *Black Walls and Other Stories,* p. 2156.
China Quarterly, December, 1990, Gregory Lee, review of *Black Walls and Other Stories,* pp. 746-748.
Westerly, September, 1981, Kam Louie, "Youth and Education in the Short Stories of Liu Xinwu," pp. 115-119.
World Literature Today, autumn, 1991, Frances LaFleur, review of *Black Walls and Other Stories,* p. 766.*

LI Yaotang
　　See BA Jin

*　　*　　*

LYNCH, Jim 1961-

PERSONAL: Born 1961, in WA; married; children: one daughter.

ADDRESSES: Home—Olympia, WA. *Agent*—c/o Author Mail, Bloomsbury USA, 175 5th Ave., Ste. 300, New York, NY 10010.

CAREER: Writer.

AWARDS, HONORS: National journalism awards.

WRITINGS:

The Highest Tide (novel), Bloomsbury (New York, NY), 2005.

Contributor of short fiction to literary magazines.

SIDELIGHTS: Jim Lynch's novel *The Highest Tide* tells the story of a pivotal summer in a young boy's life. The boy, Miles O'Malley, finds a giant squid beached near his home. He is the first person to see the creature alive, and this event is especially significant to him because he has long been fascinated by environmental issues. Soon thereafter, Miles finds a rare fish near his home and saves a dog, two incidents that lead people to believe he is some kind of prophet. The media converges on him, even as the coastline prepares for the highest tide seen in fifty years. Through it all, Miles struggles to understand his place in the adult world. A *Publishers Weekly* reviewer praised Lynch for his skill in using marine life as "a subtly executed metaphor for the bewilderments of adolescence." *Library Journal* reviewer Lisa Rohrbaugh called Lynch's writing "eloquent," particularly when the subject was the ocean; but found that when Miles's sexual awakening becomes the focus, the story "declines into juvenile mediocrity." A writer for *Kirkus Reviews* also found *The Highest Tide* at its best when the focus is on the water; at such times it becomes "a stunning light show, both literal, during phosphorescent plankton blooms, and metaphorical, in the poetic fireworks."

BIOGRAPHICAL AND CRITICAL SOURCES:

PERIODICALS

Kirkus Reviews, June 15, 2005, review of *The Highest Tide,* p. 658.

Library Journal, July 1, 2005, Lisa Rohrbaugh, review of *The Highest Tide,* p. 69.

Publishers Weekly, July 18, 2005, review of *The Highest Tide,* p. 183.

ONLINE

Bookreporter.com, http://www.bookreporter.com/ (September 20, 2005), review of *The Highest Tide.**

M

MALANGA, Steven

PERSONAL: Born in Newark, NJ. *Education:* St. Vincent's College, B.A.; University of Maryland, M.A.

ADDRESSES: Office—Manhattan Institute, 52 Vanderbilt Ave., New York, NY 10017.

CAREER: Journalist. Manhattan Institute, New York, NY, senior fellow. *Crain's New York Business,* formerly executive editor, managing editor, and columnist; master teacher at University of Maryland; guest on television and radio programs.

AWARDS, HONORS: Award for best investigative story of the year, Association of Area Business Publications, 1998, for series of articles about the influence of trial lawyers in New York State.

WRITINGS:

The New New Left: How American Politics Works Today (nonfiction), Ivan R. Dee (Chicago, IL), 2005.

Contributing editor, *City Journal.* Contributor to periodicals.

SIDELIGHTS: Steven Malanga is a politically conservative writer and editor whose book *The New New Left: How American Politics Works Today* examines the growth of public-assistance and social service programs sponsored by the U.S. government, and the industries that have grown up around them. Discussing his book in an interview on the *Brothers Judd* Web site, Malanga stated that urban aid programs and other programs created as part of the War on Poverty declared by former U.S. president Lyndon B. Johnson were begun with good intentions, but were soon taken over by the "New New Left," which Malanga defined as a "new brand of social service professional just starting to come out of our college and university social service departments at a time in the late 1960s and early 1970s when they were becoming radicalized. These folks were intellectually at war with our free market system and wanted to use the War on Poverty as a means of ramping up government spending which would force taxes higher, thereby helping redistribute income in our country, they believed." In his book, Malanga explains that, while welfare was conceived as a form of temporary assistance, social-service professionals began to frame it an ongoing necessity for many people. Malanga continued, "They introduced the notion that the poor in our cities were not only suffering economically but that our system had robbed them of their sense of community and inner worth, which could only be revived with the help of government social service programs." Malanga believes that these shifts in attitude are responsible for the creation of "a new kind of urban, inter-generational dependency," as well as "a whole economy of people whose profession revolved around government funding to fix social problems."

A *Kirkus Reviews* writer was skeptical about the book's worth, calling *The New New Left* a "right-wing nostrum" in which the author warns readers about "a shadowy world of academics, laborites, students, environmentalists and minorities opposes all that is good and just in American life." A very different opinion was expressed by a reviewer for *Brothers Judd,* who stated: "In this collection of his very fine essays, Mr. Malanga traces the outlines of this infernal contraption that the New New Left has erected, looks at the ill effects it has had, especially on our cities, and warns us of its future plans. . . . The basic case Mr. Malanga has to make is quite compelling."

BIOGRAPHICAL AND CRITICAL SOURCES:

PERIODICALS

Kirkus Reviews, March 1, 2005, review of *The New New Left: How American Politics Works Today,* p. 277.

ONLINE

Brothers Judd Web site, http://www.brothersjudd.com/ (September 26, 2005), interview with Steven Malanga; (June 20, 2005) review of *The New New Left.**

*   *   *

MALONE, David M. 1954-

PERSONAL: Born February 7, 1954, in Ottawa, Ontario, Canada; son of Thomas Paul (a journalist and diplomat) and Deirdre Lavalette Ingram (a journalist) Malone. *Education:* University of Montreal, graduated, 1954; also graduate of American University in Cairo and Harvard University; Oxford University, D.Phil.

ADDRESSES: Office—Canadian Department of Foreign Affairs, 125 Sussex Dr., Ottawa, Ontario K1A 0G2, Canada. *E-mail*—david.malone@internation.gc.ca.

CAREER: Diplomat and educator. Canadian Foreign Service, Ottawa, Ontario, assignments in Egypt, Kuwait, and Jordan, member of United Nations Economic and Social Council, 1990-92, ambassador and deputy permanent representative to United Nations, 1992-94, successive director general of policy, international organizations, and global issues bureaus, 1994-98; International Peace Academy, president, 1998-2004; Canadian Department of Foreign Affairs, Ottawa, assistant deputy minister for Africa and the Middle East, 2004—. Brookings Institute, former guest scholar in economic studies program; University of Toronto, visiting professor, 1988-89; Columbia University, adjunct professor of international relations, 1991-94; University of Toronto, senior fellow of Massey College, 1994—; Carleton University, Ottawa, adjunct research professor at Norman Paterson School of International Affairs, 1998; New York University, adjunct professor at School of Law, 1999-2004; Institut d'Études Politiques, Paris, France, visiting professor, 2002-04.

WRITINGS:

Decision-Making in the UN Security Council: The Case of Haiti, Oxford University Press (Oxford, England), 1999.
(Editor, with Mats Berdal) *Greed and Grievance: Economic Agendas in Civil Wars,* Lynne Rienner Publishers (Boulder, CO), 1999.
(Editor, with Fen Osler Hampson) *From Reaction to Conflict Prevention: Opportunities for the UN System,* Lynne Rienner Publishers (Boulder, CO), 2002.
(Editor, with Yuen Foong Khong) *Unilateralism and U.S. Foreign Policy: International Perspectives,* Lynne Rienner Publishers (Boulder, CO), 2002.
(Editor) *The UN Security Council: From the Cold War to the Twenty-first Century,* Lynne Rienner Publishers (Boulder, CO), 2004.

Contributor to periodicals, including *International Herald Tribune* and Toronto *Globe & Mail.*

WORK IN PROGRESS: The UN Security Council and Iraq, 1980-2005: Boom and Bust, for Oxford University Press.

*   *   *

MANZUR, Meher 1953-

PERSONAL: Born March 15, 1953. *Education:* Dhaka University, B.A. (with honors), 1973, M.A., 1974; University of Western Australia, M.Econ., 1983, Ph.D., 1990.

ADDRESSES: Office—School of Economics and Finance, Curtin University of Technology, GPO Box U1987, Perth, Western Australia 6845, Australia; fax: 61-8-9266-3026. *E-mail*—manzurm@cbs.curtin.edu.au.

CAREER: Economist and educator. Bangladesh Bank, Dhaka, deputy director of foreign exchange, 1983-85; University of Western Australia, Perth, Western Australia, Australia, lecturer in economics, 1990-91; National University of Singapore, fellow in economics and statistics, 1991-93, senior fellow, 1997; Curtin University of Technology, Perth, senior lecturer, 1993-2003, associate professor of finance and banking, 2003—. Visiting scholar at Wakayama University, 1998, International Monetary Fund, Washington, DC, 2000, University of Chicago, 2000, University of Western Australia, 2000-01, and Bangladesh Bank, 2001; presenter at conferences.

MEMBER: Financial Management Association International, European Financial Management Association, Economic Society of Australia.

AWARDS, HONORS: Colombo Plan fellow, Australian Development Assistance Bureau, 1980-82; Book of the Year award, Curtin University of Technology, 2002.

WRITINGS:

Exchange Rates, Prices, and World Trade: New Methods, Evidence, and Implications, Routledge, Chapman & Hall (New York, NY), 1993.
(Editor and contributor) *Exchange Rates, Interest Rates, and Commodity Prices,* Edward Elgar (Northampton, MA), 2002.

Contributor to books. Contributor to academic journals, including *Journal of Applied Economics, Asia Pacific Journal of Economics and Business, Journal of Economic Integration, Singapore Economic Review, Journal of International Money and Finance,* and *Australian Journal of Management.*

WORK IN PROGRESS: Research on exchange rate dynamics, financial engineering, capital structure, and initial public offerings based on empirical evidence from China.

MARCUS, Gary F.
(Gary Fred Marcus)

PERSONAL: Male. *Education:* Hampshire College, B.A., 1989; Massachusetts Institute of Technology, Ph. D., 1993.

ADDRESSES:

CAREER: University of Massachusetts, Amherst, instructor, 1993-97; New York University, New York, NY, associate professor of psychology and director of Infant Language Center.

AWARDS, HONORS: Robert L. Fantz award for new investigators in cognitive development.

WRITINGS:

NONFICTION

The Algebraic Mind: Integrating Connectionism and Cognitive Science, MIT Press (Cambridge, MA), 2001.
The Birth of the Mind: How a Tiny Number of Genes Create the Complexity of Human Thought, Basic Books (New York, NY), 2004.
(Compiler) *The Norton Psychology Reader,* Norton (New York, NY), 2005.

Contributor to periodicals, including *Cognition, Cognitive Psychology,* and *Journal of Child Language.*

WORK IN PROGRESS: A book synthesizing developmental biology and cognitive development.

SIDELIGHTS: Gary F. Marcus takes a scientific look at the workings of human consciousness in his book *The Birth of the Mind: How a Tiny Number of Genes Create the Complexity of Human Thought. Library Journal* reviewer Laurie Bartolini praised his "lively text," which delves into the ways that various genes interact to produce a mind that is further modified by experiences and environment. The author supports his ideas with research from the fields of psychology and biology, and points out the important role that learning plays in stimulating the proper development of the brain cells. Marcus takes the reader all the way to the molecular level, explaining brain function in terms of strings of chemical reactions. He further includes his own theories on the ways human mental genes may have evolved to their current state. A reviewer for *Publishers Weekly* stated that Marcus "strikes a rare and delicate balance of scientific detail and layperson accessibility," presenting his story in "compelling" style. *The Birth of the Mind* was also recommended as a "lucid, pleasing chronicle" of genetics and the mind by *Booklist* reviewer Gilbert Taylor.

BIOGRAPHICAL AND CRITICAL SOURCES:

PERIODICALS

Booklist, November 15, 2003, Gilbert Taylor, review of *The Birth of the Mind: How a Tiny Number of Genes Create the Complexity of Human Thought,* p. 550.
Library Journal, January, 2004, Laurie Bartolini, review of *The Birth of the Mind,* p. 150.
Publishers Weekly, November 17, 2003, review of *The Birth of the Mind,* p. 58.

ONLINE

New York University Web site, http://www.psych.nyu.edu/ (October 12, 2005), biographical information about Gary Marcus.*

*   *   *

MARCUS, Gary Fred
    See MARCUS, Gary F.

*   *   *

MARMERRODE, Ludovicus van
    See GRESHOFF, Jan

*   *   *

MARTIN, Waldo E., Jr. 1951-

PERSONAL: Born 1951. *Education:* Duke University, B.A.; University of California, Berkeley, Ph.D.

ADDRESSES: Office—Department of History, University of California, Berkeley, 3229 Dwinelle Hall, Berkeley, CA 94720-2550. *E-mail*—wmartin@berkeley.edu.

CAREER: University of California, Berkeley, professor of history. Distinguished Lecturer, Organization of American Historians, 2005-06.

MEMBER: Organization of American Historians.

WRITINGS:

NONFICTION

The Mind of Frederick Douglass, University of North Carolina Press (Chapel Hill, NC), 1984.
(Editor) *Brown v. Board of Education: A Brief History with Documents,* Bedford/St. Martin's Press (Boston, MA), 1998.
(Editor, with Patricia A. Sullivan) *Civil Rights in the United States,* Macmillan Reference USA (New York, NY), 2000.
No Coward Soldiers: Black Cultural Politics and Postwar America, Harvard University Press (Cambridge, MA), 2005.

Contributor to *Making America: The Society and Culture of the United States,* edited by Luther S. Luedtke, University of North Carolina Press (Chapel Hill, NC), 1992; and *Struggles in the Promised Land: Toward a History of Black-Jewish Relations in the United States,* Oxford University Press (New York, NY), 1997.

WORK IN PROGRESS: A book on the culture of the civil rights-Black Power movement.

SIDELIGHTS: Waldo E. Martin, Jr., is an educator whose research and writing covers many aspects of modern social movements and especially the civil rights movement. His book *No Coward Soldiers: Black Cultural Politics and Postwar America* was developed from a series of lectures the author delivered at Harvard University, and focuses on the civil rights and Black Power movements in American history, covering the period from 1945 to 1975. During this time, the author contends, there was a profound shift in the way African Americans looked at themselves, and this shift was reflected particularly in the music of the era. *Library Journal* reviewer Thomas J. Davis noted that Martin's treatment of this "pivotal" subject matter includes links to other important writers about the African-American experience.

Civil Rights in the United States, a reference book coedited by Martin, is relevant to the social struggles of not only African Americans, but also women, prisoners, the disabled and other groups. *School Library Journal* reviewer Dana McDougald called it a "clearly written, accessible" resource, and *Library Journal* contributor Anthony O. Edmonds deemed *Civil Rights in the United States* "a very important reference work because of its enormous reach; it should be in all sizable academic and public libraries."

BIOGRAPHICAL AND CRITICAL SOURCES:

PERIODICALS

Booklist, August, 2000, review of *Civil Rights in the United States,* p. 2195.
Library Journal, September 1, 2000, Anthony O. Edmonds, review of *Civil Rights in the United States,* p. 192; March 1, 2005, Thomas J. Davis, review of *No Coward Soldiers: Black Cultural Politics and Postwar America,* p. 98.
School Library Journal, November, 2000, Dana McDougald, review of *Civil Rights in the United States,* p. 94.

ONLINE

Organization of American Historians Web site, http://www.oah.org/ (September 27, 2005), personal information about Waldo E. Martin, Jr.
University of California, Berkeley Web site, http://history.berkeley.edu/ (September 27, 2005), personal information about Waldo E. Martin, Jr.*

*   *   *

MATTURRO, Claire Hamner 1954-

PERSONAL: Born 1954, in AL; married; husband's name Bill. *Education:* University of Alabama, M.A., and J.D. (with honors).

ADDRESSES: *Home*—FL; South GA. *Agent*—c/o Author Mail, William Morrow, 10 E. 53rd St., 7th Fl., New York, NY 10022. *E-mail*—skinnydipping04@yahoo.com.

CAREER: Attorney, educator, and novelist. Journalist in Alabama; Alabama Court of Civil Appeals, former staff attorney; Dickinson & Gibbons (law firm), Sarasota, FL, partner for nine years; Florida State University College of Law, faculty member for six years; former reference librarian and college instructor in Tallahassee, FL.

AWARDS, HONORS: First prize, SEAK Inc. legal fiction writing contest; Best First Mystery, *Romantic Times,* 2005, for *Skinny-Dipping.*

WRITINGS:

Skinny-Dipping (novel), William Morrow (New York, NY), 2004.
Wildcat Wine (novel), William Morrow (New York, NY), 2005.
Bone Valley (novel), William Morrow (New York, NY), 2006.

Editor, *Trial Advocate Quarterly.*

WORK IN PROGRESS: Another "Lilly Cleary" novel tentatively titled *Bugfest, Georgia.*

SIDELIGHTS: Claire Hamner Matturro drew on her own experience as an attorney and a resident of Florida to create her mystery series featuring Lilly Belle Cleary, an eccentric, six-foot-tall female lawyer from the Deep South. Lilly is an attorney, and an obsessive health-food devotee who defends doctors, professionals, and hospitals in medical malpractice cases. She first appears in *Skinny-Dipping,* which a *Publishers Weekly* reviewer called a "witty, intelligent novel of suspense." In this story, Lilly finds herself the subject of a choking attack, has one of her clients die mysteriously, and is shot at. Furthermore, she is saddled with an odious client in a tricky malpractice trial. The suspenseful plot is also peppered with humor, for as Matturro explained in a *Publishers Weekly* interview, "With the trial attorneys I knew, they were all funny; humor was very important to them to balance the stress." She also knew that she wanted her book to be "legalistic without being boring, which is very tricky." Cheryle M. Dodd, a reviewer for *Florida Bar Journal,* wrote that, thanks to Lilly's "cheeky" personality and an eccentric cast of secondary characters, the author "succeeds in entertaining the reader." A *Kirkus Reviews* contributor felt that the plot of *Skinny-Dipping* is a bit thin, but maintained that the book is "funny, sharp, savvy both as to the courtroom and the human condition."

In *Wildcat Wine,* Matturro's second novel featuring the vegetarian attorney, Lilly finds herself involved in a strange episode involving her first love, a man known as Farmer Dave, who turns up at her house with a truck full of stolen organic wine. On a trip to a local park to look for wildlife, Dave happens upon a bag of cash and a dead body. Soon he is under suspicion of murder. Lilly still cares for Dave, though she is not in love with him, and she sets everything else aside to clear his name. Reviewing the book for the *Miami Herald,* Wanda Demarzo noted approvingly that "Matturro devises a unique and complex plot with a lot of high-energy juice. She is a welcome addition to the growing list of notable crime writing novelists inspired by the beauty and insanity of Florida." A *Kirkus Reviews* commentator found Matturro's plot to be somewhat light, but called Lilly an "authentic charmer." Harriet Klausner, reviewing the novel for *MBR Bookwatch,* called it "a light hearted chick lit mystery."

Matturro told *CA:* "Reading *To Kill a Mockingbird* in fifth grade hooked me. I wanted to be both a lawyer and a writer after reading that book, which is the best legal thriller ever in my opinion.

"I read a lot of mysteries so it's hard to way what influences my work; I probably am influenced in ways I don't really know by these books. But I know I owe a great deal to Barry Hannah, an extraordinary writer who was also my creative-writing professor at the University of Alabama. I write everything first in my head, mostly at three a.m. or during long walks in the woods or the country side. Then it's just a matter of typing. I work in the afternoons, and do a great many revisions and edits and rewrites.

"Perhaps the most humbling thing I've learned as a writer was what I learned from my copyeditor, to whit, I really didn't know my grammar nearly as well as I thought I did.

"*Bone Valley* is my favorite book, because it deals with two important subjects near and dear to my heart: wildlife and animal rehabilitation and stopping the phosphate mines' destruction of central Florida. And yet, despite these serious topics, it's still a funny book.

"Primarily my books are to entertain. I hope my readers will laugh. But each book also has a serious message in it that I hope the readers will learn and act upon."

BIOGRAPHICAL AND CRITICAL SOURCES:

PERIODICALS

Detroit Free Press, October 27, 2004, Carol O'Connell, review of *Skinny-Dipping.*

Florida Bar Journal, January, 2005, Cheryle M. Dodd, review of *Skinny-Dipping,* p. 59.

Kirkus Reviews, August 15, 2004, review of *Skinny-Dipping,* p. 782; April 1, 2005, review of *Wildcat Wine,* p. 390.

MBR Bookwatch, May, 2005, Harriet Klausner, review of *Wildcat Wine.*

Miami Herald, June 8, 2005, Wanda Demarzo, review of *Wildcat Wine.*

Publishers Weekly, May 17, 2004, John F. Baker, "Four Novels Signed before Debut," p. 12; September 20, 2004, review of *Skinny-Dipping,* p. 44; Alia Akkam, interview with Claire Hamner Maturro, p. 44.

South Florida Sun-Sentinel, May 11, 2005, John Goodger, review of *Wildcat Wine.*

ONLINE

Claire Hamner Matturro Home Page, http://www.clairematturro.com (September 27, 2005).

WMNF Radio Web site, http://www.wmnf.org/ (September 26, 2005), biographical information on Claire Hamner Matturro.

*   *   *

MAYNERT, Helga
See HENNINGSEN, Agnes

McDERMOTT, Terry

PERSONAL: Male.

ADDRESSES: Agent—c/o Author Mail, HarperCollins Publishers, 10 E. 53rd St., 7th Fl., New York, NY 10022.

CAREER: Journalist, beginning c. 1980; *Los Angeles Times,* Los Angeles, CA, currently national correspondent.

AWARDS, HONORS: Several journalism awards.

WRITINGS:

Perfect Soldiers: The Hijackers: Who They Were, Why They Did It, HarperCollins (New York, NY), 2005.

SIDELIGHTS: After the tragedy of the September 11, 2001, terrorist attacks on the United States, many people wondered who the airline hijackers were and what motivated them to kill themselves and so many other people. Journalist Terry McDermott attempts to answer these questions in his first book, *Perfect Soldiers: The Hijackers: Who They Were, Why They Did It.* Because much of the information about the attacks gathered by federal agencies is classified, the author faced considerable roadblocks in discovering who the hijackers were. Nevertheless, he discovered some revealing facts. In all, nineteen people were involved in the hijackings, coming from various Arabic nations, including Saudi Arabia, Lebanon, the United Arab Emirates, Egypt, and Yemen. Conducting research in Egypt, Germany, and elsewhere, McDermott focuses on the individuals about whom he discovered the most, including Muhammad el-Amir Atta, one of the leaders of the orchestrated crime. Drawing on recorded testimony from the 9/11 Commission, Federal Bureau of Investigation files, and interviews with those who knew the hijackers, he learned that they were not uneducated, easily deceived, poor, politically radical young men; rather, many received a good education and came from families who were well off. They met at a mosque in Germany, where they began to discuss Islam and their jihadist philosophy took shape.

As he explains the story behind the hijacking, McDermott also provides some background history, including the origins of Al Qaeda during the Soviet invasion of Afghanistan in the 1980s, and notes the lapses in both U.S. and German intelligence and security agencies that allowed the hijacks to occur. "McDermott did not learn everything he had hoped," noted Steve Weinberg in the *Houston Chronicle.* "Thirteen of the 19 hijackers remain ciphers despite the 300-plus pages of narrative. . . . But the six whose existences could be documented nearly leap off the pages." Although McDermott "never really fulfills the promise of his subtitle to explain why they did it," according to a *Kirkus Reviews* critic, *Perfect Soldiers* still offers lessons for the reader. Aside from problems within governmental agencies that may have allowed the terrorist strikes to occur, what is chilling about McDermott's contentions, commented several reviewers, is the theme that ordinary people could be become suicidal killers. As David J. Garrow put it in his *Wilson Quarterly* review, "it's the life stories McDermott recounts, rather than the conclusions he draws from them, that make *Perfect Soldiers* such a memorable book." Reviewers also complimented McDermott for his objectivity regarding Islam and its radical elements. The author "neither idicts Islam nor excuses the terrorists' crimes," observed Francine Prose in *O,* "but draws a chilling, clear, and cautionary map of the small, fateful steps with which ordinary men cross the dangerous line between faith and fanaticism."

BIOGRAPHICAL AND CRITICAL SOURCES:

PERIODICALS

Houston Chronicle, April 29, 2005, Steve Weinberg, "Ordinary Monsters the Scariest," review of *Perfect Soldiers: The Hijackers: Who They Were, Why They Did It.*

Kirkus Reviews, March 1, 2005, review of *Perfect Soldiers,* p. 278.

Library Journal, April 1, 2005, Sarah Jent, review of *Perfect Soldiers,* p. 111.

O, May, 2005, Francine Prose, "The Heart of a Destroyer: Why Did They Do It?," review of *Perfect Soldiers,* p. 240.

Publishers Weekly, February 14, 2005, review of *Perfect Soldiers,* p. 60.

Washington Post Book World, May 1, 2005, Jonathan Yardley, "The 9/11 Hijackers," review of *Perfect Soldiers,* p. 2.

Wilson Quarterly, summer, 2005, David J. Garrow, review of *Perfect Soldiers,* p. 119.*

McMANUS, John 1977-

PERSONAL: Born 1977, in Blount County, TN. *Education:* Goucher College, graduated, 1999; graduate study at Hollins University.

ADDRESSES: Home—Austin, TX. *Agent*—c/o Publicity Department, Picador, 175 5th Ave., New York, NY 10010.

CAREER: Fiction writer.

AWARDS, HONORS: Whiting Writers Award, 2000, for *Stop Breakin Down.*

WRITINGS:

Stop Breakin' Down (short stories), Picador (New York, NY), 2000.
Born on a Train (short stories), Picador (New York, NY), 2003.
Bitter Milk (novel), Picador (New York, NY), 2005.

Contributor to periodicals, including *Ploughshares* and *Oxford American.*

SIDELIGHTS: Tennessee author John McManus is the author of the award-winning short-story collection *Stop Breakin' Down.* Along with his second collection, *Born on a Train,* and his first novel, *Bitter Milk,* the author has quickly established a reputation for creating intriguing, colorful characters "rebelling against an indifferent and often brutal world," as Martha Kinney commented in *Artforum International.* Because his stories often feature young narrators, McManus has sometimes been considered an author of young-adult fiction, despite the fact that his tales often contain violent scenes.

Stop Breakin' Down, which won the 2000 Whiting Writers Award, includes several stories featuring young, sensitive teenagers or boys living through tragic situations, such as poverty, or in urban settings where their peers engage in drug abuse or other reckless behavior. "All the characters here seem to rush and tumble toward disaster," wrote a *Publishers Weekly* critic, who described the book as a "rambunctious

debut." *Booklist* contributor James Klise labeled the collection "impressive" and praised the author's "young, fresh voice." Some reviewers did not view McManus's follow-up collection, *Born on a Train,* to be quite as accomplished. Noting that the tales here "strive for authenticity and occasionally achieve it," a *Kirkus Reviews* writer felt that "McManus seems enamored of trapping his characters in hillbilly hell and stranding both them and readers there—for an inordinate amount of time."

McManus's first effort at novel writing, *Bitter Milk,* is an atmospheric tale of a Southern teenager troubled by obesity, an imaginary companion, and a dysfunctional family. Without a father, Loren Garland finds himself completely alone when his mother also abandons him to go to a clinic for a sex-change operation. Seeking refuge in family, Loren goes to several relatives for help before finding Papaw, his quirky grandfather who also recently suffered a loss. He also finds friendship with his cousin Eli. Interestingly, the novel is narrated by Luther, a character whose identity is never clearly explained, though he might be the ghost of Loren's twin brother, who died during childbirth. Kinney, in her review of *Bitter Milk,* found this narrative ploy to be ineffective because it "does not advance the narrative in any meaningful way." Otherwise, the critic claimed that "McManus's intricate passages of dialogue and sympathetic narration make for compelling reading." A *Publishers Weekly* writer called *Bitter Milk* an "affecting but uneven first novel." A *Kirkus Reviews* contributor, however, concluded that the novel is clearly "the work of a young writer still seeking his own voice," and "when McManus finds it, the results may be spectacular."

BIOGRAPHICAL AND CRITICAL SOURCES:

PERIODICALS

Artforum International, summer, 2005, Martha Kinney, review of *Bitter Milk,* p. 52.
Booklist, May 15, 2000, James Klise, review of *Stop Breakin' Down,* p. 1728.
Kirkus Reviews, December 1, 2002, review of *Born on a Train,* p. 1723; April 1, 2005, review of *Bitter Milk,* p. 378.
Library Journal, August, 2000, Christine DeZelar-Tiedman, review of *Stop Breakin' Down,* p. 164.

Publishers Weekly, April 10, 2000, review of *Stop Breakin' Down,* p. 72; April 25, 2005, review of *Bitter Milk,* p. 37.

Texas Monthly, June, 2005, Mike Shea, review of *Bitter Milk,* p. 64.

ONLINE

CollectedStories.com, http://www.collectedstories.com/ (September 19, 2005), "A Word with the Writer," interview with John McManus.

Emerging Writers Forum Online, http://www.breaktech.net/EmergingWritersForum/ (May 19, 2005), Dan Wickett, "Interview with John McManus."*

* * *

McMONEAGLE, Joseph 1946-
(Joseph W. McMoneagle)

PERSONAL: Born January 10, 1946, in Miami, FL; son of Joseph (a stockman) and Lorine (a homemaker; maiden name, Muns) McMoneagle; married Margaret M. Murphy (divorced); married Nancy Lea Honeycutt (a company vice president), November 22, 1985; children: Scott. *Education:* City Colleges of Chicago, associate degree. *Politics:* "Independent." *Hobbies and other interests:* Motorcycle riding, fishing, hiking, reading.

ADDRESSES: Home—VA. *Office*—Intuitive Intelligence Applications, Inc., P.O. Box 100, Nellysford, VA 22958. *E-mail*—jmceagle@cstone.net.

CAREER: U.S. Army, 1964-84, attained rank of chief warrant officer; U.S. Army Security Agency, operations specialist, 1964-75; counterintelligence and physical security officer, Augsburg, Germany, 1975-77; Office for Emitter Location and Identification, U.S. Army Intelligence and Security Command, Arlington, VA, officer in charge, 1977-78; special intelligence projects officer, Fort Meade, MD, 1978-84. Intuitive Intelligence Applications, Inc., Nellysford, VA, owner and executive director, 1984—. J.B. Rhine Center, Durham, NC, research associate; Laboratories for Fundamental Research, Palo Alto, CA, research associate, 1995—. Appeared on television programs, including in *Put to*

the *Test,* American Broadcasting Companies; *Mysteries of the Mind* (*Reader's Digest* special), and *Paranormal World of Paul McKenna,* BBC Channel Four. Anomalous Phenomena Research Center, New York, NY, member of board of directors. *Military service:* U.S. Army, 1964-84.

MEMBER: Disabled Veterans, Parapsychological Association, American Federation of Television and Radio Artists.

AWARDS, HONORS: Named knight commander, Order of Saint Stanislas, 2002, for charitable contributions to surviving children of Chernobyl. *Military:* Army Service Ribbon; Overseas Service Ribbon (three awards); Noncommissioned Officers Professional Development Ribbon; Meritorious Service Medal (two awards); Army Commendation Medal (three awards); Meritorious Unit Commendation (three awards); Vietnam Campaign Medal; Vietnam Service Medal; National Defense Service Medal; Good Conduct Medal (five awards); Vietnam Gallantry Cross (with palm); named to Legion of Merit; two Overseas Bars; Expert Rifleman Badge; Marksman Pistol Badge; Expert Bayonet Badge.

WRITINGS:

Mind Trek: Exploring Consciousness, Time, and Space through Remote Viewing, Hampton Roads (Norfolk, VA), 1993, revised edition, 1997.

The Ultimate Time Machine: A Remote Viewer's Perception of Time and Predictions for the New Millennium, Hampton Roads (Charlottesville, VA), 1998.

Remote Viewing Secrets: A Handbook, Hampton Roads (Charlottesville, VA), 2000.

The Stargate Chronicles: Memoirs of a Psychic Spy, Hampton Roads (Charlottesville, VA), 2002.

Contributor to *Captain of My Ship, Master of My Soul: Living with Guidance,* Hampton Roads (Charlottesville, VA), 2001; contributor to periodicals, including *Journal of Parapsychology;* author of unpublished novels, screenplays, and plays.

SIDELIGHTS: Joseph McMoneagle is a U.S. Army veteran who worked at several security agencies of the U.S. government as a psychic, or remote viewer. Mc-

Moneagle saw duty in many countries, and he suffered severe injuries as the result of a helicopter accident in Vietnam, before being assigned to psychic viewing units. In 1970, while stationed in Germany, he had a near-death experience in which he saw his body from another perspective. That event was his initiation into the world of remote viewing. After leaving the military, McMoneagle worked at several labs as a researcher in remote viewing. He has appeared live and on camera in broadcasts from the United States and England, demonstrating his expertise in understanding the paranormal.

McMoneagle describes his first remote viewing experiences in *Mind Trek: Exploring Consciousness, Time, and Space through Remote Viewing.* He writes of his work with parapsychologists Russell Targ, Harold Puthoff, and Edward May, beginning in 1972, at the Stanford Research Institute (now SRI International) in Palo Alto, California. SRI was commissioned by the Defense Intelligence Agency and the U.S. Army in the early 1980s to teach soldiers the process of remote viewing and the Controlled Remote Viewing (CRV) protocol, which is based on the mental ability to achieve stages of access. Beginning in 1978 McMoneagle worked at Fort Meade, Maryland, as a member of the Stargate program. There he participated in experiments that increased his understanding of the nature of his gift, using CRV and extended remote viewing. He notes that psychic perceptions are very different from those experienced through the five senses and that the things and places perceived in the remote-viewing world are called "targets." While he was with Stargate, Mcmoneagle was awarded the Legion of Merit for his participation in various "psychic spy" programs.

In *The Ultimate Time Machine: A Remote Viewer's Perception of Time and Predictions for the New Millennium* McMoneagle offers 150 predictions for the future. His next book, *Remote Viewing Secrets: A Handbook,* offers advice for those who would like to learn about remote viewing, noting that success depends in nearly equal amounts on desire and focus, training, and natural talent. He notes that training cannot make a psychic, but that remote viewing can be taught. He uses martial-arts metaphors in discussing his approaches and the stages of ability. The volume also includes a bibliography for students who would like to learn the history of remote viewing.

In an interview with *Washington Post* contributor Linton Weeks, McMoneagle related that he was often given a photograph of a person and asked for the subject's location. He said that this was the way in which he helped locate hostages held in Iran. He also said that he predicted the site where Skylab would fall, nearly a year before it returned to Earth in 1979. All told, he was involved in approximately 450 missions involving remote viewing.

Drawing on such experiences, McMoneagle's *The Stargate Chronicles: Memoirs of a Psychic Spy* "is part autobiography, part history, part soul-searching, with a bit of railing against the system," wrote Richard S. Broughton in the *Journal of Parapsychology.* In the first half, McMoneagle writes of his childhood and decision to join the army, saying that because of his test results, he was assigned to intelligence work. He writes of his career in remote viewing from its beginnings to its decline, which resulted from a heavy workload and lack of replacements. Broughton wrote that McMoneagle's "accounts, along with the more evidential professional publications, leave one with the impression that remote viewing as psychic spying can work, and for a brief period of time it did serve the U.S. intelligence operations quite well as an adjunct to conventional intelligence gathering. Given the current state of the world, one cannot help but wonder why governments are not rushing to develop this technology." Broughton further commented, "Most analysts agree that the real key to fighting terrorism is excellent intelligence. Certainly remote viewing is not a panacea, but if it were used as it was in the past— simply as one component of many in the task of developing actionable intelligence—should it not be in use today? McMoneagle raises that question as well, but has no real answer for why it is not." Through his company, Intuitive Intelligence Applications, Inc., McMoneagle now uses his skills for clients who include drillers who want to know where to find oil.

McMoneagle told *CA:* "I love to write. Hemmingway is my favorite author. My writing process is hard work every day. My experiences have driven what I write. I'm subject to change in the next three to five minutes."

BIOGRAPHICAL AND CRITICAL SOURCES:

BOOKS

McMoneagle, Joseph, *The Stargate Chronicles: Memoirs of a Psychic Spy,* Hampton Roads (Charlottesville, VA), 2002.

PERIODICALS

Journal of Parapsychology, June, 2001, Angela Thompson Smith, review of *Remote Viewing Secrets: A Handbook,* p. 179; fall, 2003, Richard S. Broughton, review of *The Stargate Chronicles,* p. 389.

Library Journal, February 1, 2000, Kimberly A. Bateman, review of *Remote Viewing Secrets,* p. 103.

Publishers Weekly, October 14, 2002, review of *The Stargate Chronicles,* p. 79.

Washington Post, December 4, 1995, Linton Weeks, "Up Close and Personal with a Remote Viewer," interview with Joseph McMoneagle, p. B1.

ONLINE

Joseph McMoneagle Home Page, http://www.mcmoneagle.com (April 15, 2006).

Parapsychological Association Web site, http://www.parapsych.org/ (September 20, 2005), profile of Joseph McMoneagle.*

* * *

McMONEAGLE, Joseph W.
See McMONEAGLE, Joseph

* * *

McPHERSON, Edward

PERSONAL: Male.

ADDRESSES: Home—Brooklyn, NY. *Agent*—c/o Author Mail, Newmarket Press, 18 E. 48th St., New York, NY 10017.

CAREER: Writer.

WRITINGS:

Buster Keaton: Tempest in a Flat Hat, Newmarket Press (New York, NY), 2005.

Contributor to periodicals, including *Talk, New York Observer, New York Times Style, I.D.,* and *Esopus.*

SIDELIGHTS: In *Buster Keaton: Tempest in a Flat Hat,* Edward McPherson readdresses the life of silent film comedian Buster Keaton. A number of biographies have already been written about Keaton, but while many biographers have discussed the actor's troubled childhood in depth, McPherson is more interested in the genius of Keaton as a filmmaker. As Muriel Zagha commented in her *Times Literary Supplement* review, "McPherson distances himself from other biographers and film scholars who have variously interpreted Keaton's impassivity as the tragic mask of an abused child." Instead, the author asserts that the stony-faced expression Keaton assumed in his on-screen persona was worn purely for comedic effect. As a young stage performer, he had discovered that he got more laughs when he grossly understated his reaction to the pratfalls and other amusing stunts he performed. McPherson goes on to describe in detail Keaton's creative brilliance, his attention to factual detail, and the ups and downs of his career.

Library Journal writer Roy Liebman was disappointed that McPherson largely neglects Keaton's work in movies that had sound, adding that the author's attempts at "analyzing Keaton's genius" are "often trite and unconvincing." On the other hand, a *Publishers Weekly* reviewer asserted that McPherson "adroitly describe[s] the extraordinary visual lunacy Keaton produced on screen to achieve cinema art." As Zagha similarly wrote: "One particularly enjoyable part of McPherson's narrative is his vivid, often hilarious evocation of Keaton's early years" in what she concluded is an "informative new biography."

BIOGRAPHICAL AND CRITICAL SOURCES:

PERIODICALS

Library Journal, May 15, 2005, Roy Liebman, review of *Buster Keaton: Tempest in a Flat Hat,* p. 119.

Publishers Weekly, April 11, 2005, review of *Buster Keaton,* p. 44.

Times Literary Supplement, October 28, 2004, Muriel Zagha, "Buster Keaton's Great Stone Face."*

* * *

MELDRUM, Andrew 1951-
(Andrew Barclay Meldrum, Jr.)

PERSONAL: Born November 19, 1951, in Cleveland, OH; son of Andrew Barclay and Mary (Burrell) Mel-

drum; married Dolores Maria Cortes, November 25, 1988. *Education:* Middlebury College, B.A., 1974; Columbia University, M.J., 1977.

ADDRESSES: Home—24 Princess Dr., Highlands, Harare, Zimbabwe. *Agent*—c/o Author Mail, Atlantic Monthly Press, 841 Broadway, New York, NY 10003.

CAREER: Hudson Times, Hudson, OH, editor, 1974-76; *Lorain Journal,* Lorain, OH, education reporter, 1977-78; *Riverside Press Enterprise,* Riverside, CA, general assignment reporter, 1978-80; Agence France-Presse, Harare, Zimbabwe, deputy bureau chief, 1982-89; reporter in Zimbabwe until 2003; *Guardian,* London, England, South African correspondent, beginning 1986; *Economist,* London, South African correspondent, beginning 1989.

MEMBER: Zimbabwe Foreign Correspondent Association (vice chair, 1989-95).

AWARDS, HONORS: Best Educational Reporter award, Ohio School Boards, 1978.

WRITINGS:

Where We Have Hope: A Memoir of Zimbabwe, Atlantic Monthly Press (New York, NY), 2005.

Contributing editor, *Africa Report,* 1986-95, and *African Business,* 1994.

SIDELIGHTS: As a young, idealistic journalist, Andrew Meldrum traveled to the nation of Zimbabwe in 1980 to report on the birth of an African country newly independent from Great Britain. Zimbabwe, which had been called Rhodesia when it was under British rule, had been fighting for freedom for years, and the leader of that rebellion, Robert Mugabe, was named president of the new country. When Meldrum first met Mugabe, it was as someone who admired the political leader and who hoped the president would bring freedom and prosperity to Zimbabwe. Unfortunately, it was soon made clear that Mugabe would become an oppressor and tyrant, ruining life for the majority of Zimbabweans, often murdering them so that he could maintain power and wealth for himself, his family, and his few allies. Despite the obvious

decay of civilization in Zimbabwe, Meldrum remained in the country, appreciating the generous and kind citizens there even as he grew to despise President Mugabe. He worked as a foreign correspondent for British newspapers and the Agence France-Presse, regularly sending back reports about the political and social changes in Zimbabwe. Eventually, Mugabe had Meldrum arrested. The reporter was put on trial, and even though two courts in Zimbabwe found him not guilty of violating the Access to Information and Protection of Privacy Act, a law tailored to oust foreign reporters, Mugabe sent his police to physically detain Meldrum and, in 2003, he was deported. The last foreign correspondent to be expelled from Zimbabwe, Meldrum nevertheless stayed in Africa. He moved to Pretoria, South Africa, and has since then continued his work.

In *Where We Have Hope: A Memoir of Zimbabwe* Meldrum relates his decades-long sojourn in Zimbabwe in what *Contemporary Review* critic Jason Mosley described as "very much a memoir—a personal account of his experiences—but stylistically it feels like a collection of feature stories." Because of this organization, Mosley felt the book "suffers somewhat from the lack of an overall structure," but added that it is still "an excellent introduction to Zimbabwe's crisis." Reviewers especially noted that, despite everything he witnessed, Meldrum maintains a feeling of hope for the young nation. The reporter actually places much of the blame on the current status of politics in Zimbabwe on European imperialism. As he explained to *Bookseller* contributor Benedicte Page, "I've tried to make the point that I still hold [former British colonial leader] Ian Smith guilty, ultimately, and the Rhodesian system, which used force to deny people their basic civil rights. It meant the people had to use violence to obtain their civil rights." But, he added, "I have been around long enough to know that Africa is paying a terrible price for colonisation, for being backwards in industrialization, but that there are many fine people who stand up for the same principles that we uphold in the Western world, and they are being strengthened by this struggle."

A *Kirkus Reviews* contributor described *Where We Have Hope* as a "harrowing and deeply disturbing record of that country's downward spiral" and praised Meldrum for his "crisp narrative [that] is remarkably free of rancor." A *Publishers Weekly* reviewer also complimented the author for remaining "hopeful, and this frank account is the better for it."

BIOGRAPHICAL AND CRITICAL SOURCES:

BOOKS

Meldrum, Andrew, *Where We Have Hope: A Memoir of Zimbabwe,* Atlantic Monthly Press (New York, NY), 2005.

PERIODICALS

African Business, November, 2004, review of *Where We Have Hope: A Memoir of Zimbabwe,* p. 64.

Africa News Service, June 12, 2002, "Trial of Journalist Andrew Meldrum"; May 17, 2003, "*Guardian* Reporter Andrew Meldrum Ordered to Leave Zimbabwe."

Asia Africa Intelligence Wire, May 20, 2003, "Zimbabwe: Regional Media Body Protests against Andrew Meldrum's Deportation."

Bookseller, April 2, 2004, Benedicte Page, "What Zimbabwe Taught Me: Journalist Andrew Meldrum Reported on the Regime of Robert Mugabe for More than Two Decades, before Being Expelled from the Country Last Year," p. 29.

Contemporary Review, February, 2005, Jason Mosley, "Disappointment and Disillusionment in Zimbabwe," review of *Where We Have Hope,* p. 111.

Economist, July 20, 2002, "Booting out the Messenger"; May 24, 2003, "Good News Only, from Now One," p. 12.

IPR Strategic Business Information Database, May 18, 2003, "Zimbabwe: IPI Condemns Deportation of *Guardian* Correspondent from Zimbabwe.".

Kirkus Reviews, April 1, 2005, review of *Where We Have Hope,* p. 404.

Publishers Weekly, May 2, 2005, review of *Where We Have Hope,* p. 188.

Time International, August 23, 2004, Gerd Behrens, "A Revolution Betrayed: A Memoir of Zimbabwe Chronicles the Sad Descent of This Troubled Land, but Radiates Love—and Even Hope," p. 57.

Weekly Standard, March 14, 2005, Roger Bate, "Kingdom of Mugabe: Three Volumes Chronicle Zimbabwe's Descent into the Heart of Darkness," p. 38.

ONLINE

Guardian Online, http://www.guardian.co.uk/ (January 11, 2002), "Defying Mugabe."

Mother Jones Online, http://motherjones.com/ (September 19, 2005), Dave Gilson, "Hoping against Hope: An Interview with Andrew Meldrum."*

*   *   *

MELDRUM, Andrew Barclay, Jr.
    See MELDRUM, Andrew

*   *   *

MENZER, Joe

PERSONAL: Born in OH; married; children: four.

ADDRESSES: Office—Winston-Salem Journal, 418 N. Marshall St., Winston-Salem, NC 27101. *Agent*—c/o Author Mail, Simon & Schuster, 1230 Avenue of the Americas, New York, NY 10020. *E-mail*—jmenzer@ wsjournal.com.

CAREER: Winston-Salem Journal, Winston-Salem, NC, sportswriter, 1995—.

WRITINGS:

(With Burt Graeff) *History of the Cleveland Cavaliers,* Sagamore Publishing (Champaigne, IL), 1994.

(With Bob Condor) *The Carolina Panthers: The First Season of the Most Successful Expansion Team in NFL History,* Macmillan (New York, NY), 1996.

Four Corners: How UNC, N.C. State, Duke, and Wake Forest Made North Carolina the Center of the Basketball Universe, Simon & Schuster (New York, NY), 1999.

The Wildest Ride: A History of NASCAR; or, How a Bunch of Good Ol' Boys Built a Billion-Dollar Industry out of Wrecking Cars, Simon & Schuster (New York, NY), 2001.

Buckeye Madness: The Glorious, Tumultuous, Behind-the-Scenes Story of Ohio State Football, Simon & Schuster (New York, NY), 2005.

Contributor to periodicals, including *Sporting News, Inside Sports, Hoop,* and *Basketball Weekly.*

SIDELIGHTS: Sportswriter Joe Menzer has written a number of books on a variety of sports. His *Four Corners: How UNC, N.C. State, Duke, and Wake Forest Made North Carolina the Center of the Basketball Universe* is a fifty-year history of North Carolina college basketball beginning in the 1950s and 1960s, when college basketball first attracted national attention through television coverage. Menzer profiles some of the most memorable coaches of that period, including North Carolina State's Everett Case, Norm Sloan, and Jim Valvano; Duke's Mike Krzyzewski; Wake Forest's Bones McKinney; and the University of North Carolina's Dean Smith and Frank McGuire. Case, nicknamed the "Old Gray Fox," was the first to install an applause meter and make a production of pregame introductions. McGuire ensured his 1957 championship by recruiting players from his native New York. McKinney relied on cola and barbiturates to contain the pressure as the competition grew. *Booklist* contributor Wes Lukowsky felt that this book will bring back memories for older fans "and provide younger ones with a context in which to understand one of sports's most impassioned rivalries."

The Wildest Ride: A History of NASCAR; or, How a Bunch of Good Ol' Boys Built a Billion-Dollar Industry out of Wrecking Cars is Menzer's study of the National Association of Stock Car Auto Racing. NASCAR began when Southern moonshiners souped up cars to evade federal agents from the Internal Revenue Service during the 1940s. Today, stock-car auto racing is the fastest-growing sport in the country. Menzer interviews prominent figures and profiles the superstars of NASCAR, including Junior Johnson, Darrell Waltrip, and Richard Petty. "Menzer tells dozens of great stories . . . , stopping to linger over several key moments and personalities that shaped the sport over the years," noted David Pool in the *Charlotte Observer.* Rob Cline commented in *Bookreporter.com* that "the strength of Menzer's book is his storytelling ability. . . . Menzer's casual, talky style makes for exciting and easy reading." Eric C. Shoaf noted in *Library Journal* that the book is "highly entertaining and full of facts rather than fluff." A *Book* reviewer wrote that Menzer "is critical where he should be, but his affection for the only sport that still lets you bring your own beer shines through."

Menzer, who was born in Ohio, writes about his home team in *Buckeye Madness: The Glorious, Tumultuous, Behind-the-Scenes Story of Ohio State Football.* The book opens as the Buckeyes win the 2003 Fiesta Bowl and then goes back in time five decades to when coach Woody Hayes joined the team. Hayes was notable for his volatility, for physically abusing his players during practice, and for encouraging the team to employ dangerous tackling maneuvers. He was eventually fired for attacking an opposing player. A *Kirkus Reviews* contributor wrote that "you don't have to be a Buckeye to like Menzer's tale, one of the more readable football books of recent years."

BIOGRAPHICAL AND CRITICAL SOURCES:

PERIODICALS

Book, July, 2001, review of *The Wildest Ride: A History of NASCAR; or, How a Bunch of Good Ol' Boys Built a Billion-Dollar Industry out of Wrecking Cars,* p. 27.

Booklist, January 1, 1999, Wes Lukowsky, review of *Four Corners: How UNC, N.C. State, Duke, and Wake Forest Made North Carolina the Center of the Basketball Universe,* p. 819; July, 2001, David Rouse, review of *The Wildest Ride,* p. 1968.

Charlotte Observer, July 17, 2001, David Poole, review of *The Wildest Ride.*

Kirkus Reviews, May 15, 2005, review of *Buckeye Madness: The Glorious, Tumultuous, Behind-the-Scenes Story of Ohio State Football,* p. 578.

Library Journal, February 1, 1999, Terry Jo Madden, review of *Four Corners,* p. 100; June 15, 2001, Eric C. Shoaf, review of *The Wildest Ride,* p. 80.

Publishers Weekly, December 21, 1998, review of *Four Corners,* p. 45; June 11, 2001, review of *The Wildest Ride,* p. 76; May 30, 2005, review of *Buckeye Madness,* p. 50.

ONLINE

Bookreporter.com, http://www.bookreporter.com/ (September 28, 2001), Rob Cline, review of *The Wildest Ride.**

*   *   *

MENZIES, Gavin 1937-

PERSONAL: Born August 14, 1937, in England; married; wife's name Marcella (owner of a real estate business); children: two daughters. *Education:* Attended Royal Naval College (Dartmouth, England).

ADDRESSES: *Home*—London, England. *Agent*—c/o Author Mail, HarperCollins, 10 E. 53rd St., 7th Floor, New York, NY 10022.

CAREER: Royal Navy, 1953-70, served in submarines, 1959-70, commander of HMS *Rorqual,* 1968-70; freelance writer and traveling researcher, 1970—.

MEMBER: Association of Zheng He Studies.

WRITINGS:

1421: The Year China Discovered America, Bantam (London, England), 2002, William Morrow (New York, NY), 2003, revised international edition published as *1421: The Year China Discovered the World,* 2003, William Morrow, 2004.

Contributor to periodicals, including *History Today.*

ADAPTATIONS: *1421: The Year China Discovered America,* was adapted as a television documentary by Paladin Invision/Pearson Broadband, 2004.

SIDELIGHTS: In 1989 retired British naval officer Gavin Menzies took a wedding anniversary trip with his wife to China. There Menzies became fascinated with the works of the greatest Ming Dynasty Emperor Zhu Di, who built the Forbidden City, moved the Chinese capital to Beijing, and repaired the Great Wall, in addition to amassing a fleet of treasure ships commanded by eunuch admirals that he sent out to sail around the world and trade with "barbarians" in distant lands. Menzies's interest spurred him to begin research for a book about Zhu, Zhu's Mongolian rival, and world events in the year 1421.

However, partway through the manuscript Menzies learned of a Venetian map dating from 1424 that charted islands in the Caribbean not believed to have been discovered, except by indigenous peoples, until Columbus sailed sixty-eight years later. Knowing that only the Ming Dynasty had the fleet to make such voyages at the time, Menzies began new research into the sea voyages of medieval China. What he found caused him to change the course of his research to show that the Chinese—not the Europeans—were the first non-native peoples to discover the Americas, Australia and

New Zealand, even Antarctica and the Arctic. After a total of fourteen years of research, during which time Menzies visited 120 countries, 900 museums, and nearly every port that was actively trading in the fifteenth century, his book *1421: The Year China Discovered America* was completed. An international best-seller, it set off a firestorm of both interest and controversy worldwide with its potential to rewrite world history.

Since his book was first published in 2002, Menzies has given talks around the world, including in Malaysia, Singapore, Taiwan, Hong Kong, and Japan. He has been named a visiting professor at Yunan University in China. Correspondence began pouring in from readers after the book's release, some seventy-five percent of it containing evidence of Chinese settlement and exploration in the Americas and elsewhere. A Web site created for the book provides regular updates on new evidence and research. A four-part television documentary based on the book aired in 2004. An updated paperback edition, *1421: The Year China Discovered the World,* was published worldwide in 2003.

Menzies's theory has a basis in thoroughly documented history. Emperor Zhu Di dispatched his Grand Eunuch, Zheng He—who later became known as Sin Bao, or Sinbad the Sailor—as admiral of a Chinese armada that was to explore the ends of the earth. Although the consensus among scholars is that the fleet only sailed as far as Madagascar, Menzies contends that, during a two-and-a-half-year period, Chinese ships sailed around Africa's Cape of Good Hope, reached the Caribbean and the Americas, sailed north to the Arctic, reached Australia and New Zealand, and sailed south to Antarctica, mapping the new territories along the way. The map that first sparked Menzies's interest, the author believes, was copied from one procured from the Chinese by a Venetian trader in India. Menzies says that by the time Columbus and others sailed, they had maps of the New World to travel by.

By the time Zheng He and his surviving fleet arrived home, however, tragedy had struck the emperor—his palace had burned, his favorite concubine had been killed, and he had abdicated the throne. The contry's new isolationist rulers destroyed the returning explorers' maps and charts and stopped China's expansionist programs, stranding, says Menzies, thousands of Chinese colonists in the new lands. Among the evidence of this early Chinese exploration, according to Menzies, are Chinese-introduced species of chickens and certain plants, porcelain and jade, sunken junks, and accounts of Chinese-speaking peoples found by the first Europeans to explore the Americas. Physical evidence includes a tower in Rhode Island that resembles a Chinese lighthouse, and the so-called Bimini Road, off Florida's coast, which Menzies claims the Chinese built to repair their junks after a hurricane.

Menzies traced the Chinese fleet's probable routes around the globe, predicting where ocean currents would have taken them, and he found a number of shore marker stones carved in Asian languages. He also used his navigational experience gained in the Royal Navy to predict how the Chinese navigated by the North Star and by the star Canopus.

Reviewers had mixed reactions to Menzies's book. A number of mainstream scholars disputed his evidence as circumstantial, navigationally impossible, and poorly documented. Others argue that small groups of Asians, rather than the large Ming fleet, were more likely to have traveled to the Americas over time. Still, most reviewers agree that Menzies's theory is fascinating and worth further investigation. Steven U. Levine, in *Library Journal,* called the book "an exciting and eminently readable work that both the armchair traveler and the amateur historian are certain to enjoy." William B. Cassidy, in *Traffic World,* praised Menzies for bringing greater readership to the known maritime accomplishments of the Ming Dynasty. He concluded that *1421* "offers an often entertaining challenge to our beliefs about the past and reason to reflect on the way we construct history."

In contrast to such positive reviews, a *Publishers Weekly* contributor said that Menzies's evidence "ranges from reasonable to ridiculous." Jonathan Mirsky, in the *Spectator,* described the author's technique thusly: "stir together some facts and supposition and present the mixture as a big fact." Julia Lovell, in the *Times Literary Supplement,* commented that "one does sometimes wonder . . . whether Menzies first looked at the facts and then made up his mind, or vice versa." John Noble Wilford, in the *New York Times Book Review,* observed, "One must read with care how Menzies describes and interprets the archaeological material. . . . Nor is Menzies' use of maps reassuring." Although agreeing that it is possible the Chinese

did make landfalls in parts of the world well before Europeans and that records of these voyages may have been destroyed, Wilford concluded: "Menzies has yet to make a compelling case. . . . It is unlikely that all the emperor's ships and all the emperor's admirals, for all their vaunted capabilities, could have put together concerted expeditions of the scope ascribed to them." Tom Holman, in the *Bookseller,* on the other hand, wrote: "*1421* is written in an accessible style that bears the wealth of knowledge behind the claims extremely lightly, though it is backed up by a mass of supporting notes and appendices."

Menzies himself has no doubts. As he told Holman: "I've had thousands of letters from all over the world, but not a single one saying that what I've found is rubbish. . . . Every single explorer who set sail after 1421 had charts. And it was they who said so in their logs—not me." He told a *People* contributor: "There's not one chance in a hundred million that I'm wrong."

BIOGRAPHICAL AND CRITICAL SOURCES:

PERIODICALS

Booklist, March 15, 2003, Margaret Flanagan, review of *1421: The Year China Discovered America,* p. 1271.

Bookseller, March 29, 2002, Tom Holman, "Behind the Headlines," p. 13; August 16, 2002, Tom Holman, "Exploring Uncharted Waters: Gavin Menzies Is Making Waves with His Claim that Early Chinese Explorers Pre-dated the Discoveries of Christopher Columbus and Captain Cook," p. 32.

Geographical, June, 2002, Chris Amodeo, "Ancient Mariner," p. 8; January, 2003, Christian Amodeo, "Gavin Menzies (In Conversation)," p. 98.

History Today, May, 2002, "A Former Submarine Officer Believes Explorers from China Were the First to Circumnavigate the Globe," p. 10.

M2 Best Books, January 8, 2003, "Author Claims Chinese Discovered America before Columbus."

Maclean's, December 30, 2002, "Sailing the Ocean Blue Long before Columbus," p. 87.

New York Times Book Review, February 2, 2003, John Noble Wilford, "Pacific Overtures," p. 9.

People, February 24, 2003, "Bye, Columbus? One of the Seven Voyages of Sinbad Took Him to the New World in 1421, Says Author Gavin Menzies," p. 88.

Publishers Weekly, November 25, 2002, Natalie Danford, "Navigating Controversy: A New Book Claims That the Chinese Explored the Americas Long before Columbus Did," p. 20; January 6, 2003, review of *1421,* p. 52; February 10, 2003, Daisy Maryles, "1492? 1421? Whatever . . . ," p. 60.

Science News, February 1, 2003, review of *1421,* p. 79.

Spectator, November 2, 2002, Jonathan Mirsky, "How the Ming Fleets Missed Manhattan," p. 68.

Times Literary Supplement, December 13, 2002, Julia Lovell, "The Grand Eunuch's Voyage," p. 32.

Traffic World, February 24, 2003, William B. Cassidy, "Ancient Mariners: If China's 'Sinbad' Visited America before Columbus, Transpacific Trade Is Very Old, Indeed," p. 32.

ONLINE

1421 Web site, http://www.1421.tv/ (August 14, 2003).

CNN Online, http://www.cnn.com/ (January 13, 2003), Adam Dunn, "Did the Chinese Discover America?"

RPG Net, http://www.rpg.net/ (August 14, 2003), Robert Scott Sullivan, review of *1421.**

*   *   *

MERZEL, Dennis Genpo 1944-
(Genpo Roshi)

PERSONAL: Born June 3, 1944, in New York, NY; son of Ben (a tool-and-die maker) and Lillian Merzel; married Brenda Liu, December 22, 1974 (divorced, 1990); married Stephanie Young (an administrator), July 4, 1995; children: Tai B., Nicole L. *Education:* California State University, Long Beach, B.A., 1966; University of Southern California, M.S., 1968.

ADDRESSES: Home—723 9th Ave., Salt Lake City, UT 84103. *Office*—Kanzeon Zen Center International, 1268 E. South Temple, Salt Lake City, UT 84102. *E-mail*—genporoshi@aol.com.

CAREER: Writer and priest. Zen Buddhist priest, sometimes addressed as Genpo Roshi; Kanzeon Zen Center International, Salt Lake City, UT, president, Zen master, head teacher, and abbot, 1984—; White Plum Asanga, president and head teacher, 1996—.

WRITINGS:

The Eye Never Sleeps: Striking to the Heart of Zen, Shambhala Publications (Boston, MA), 1991.

Beyond Sanity and Madness: The Way of Zen Master Dogen, introduction and calligraphy by Hakuyu Taizan Maezumi, Charles E. Tuttle (Boston, MA), 1994.

24/7 Dharma: Impermanence, No-Self, Nirvana, Journey Editions (Boston, MA), 2001.

The Path of the Human Being: Zen Teachings on the Bodhisattva Way, Shambhala Publications (Boston, MA), 2003.

WORK IN PROGRESS: The Dharma Game; Big Mind-Great Heart, completion expected in 2007.

BIOGRAPHICAL AND CRITICAL SOURCES:

PERIODICALS

Library Journal, August, 2003, Mark Woodhouse, review of *The Path of the Human Being: Zen Teachings on the Bodhisattva Way,* p. 91.

*   *   *

MILLER, Zell 1932-
(Zell Bryan Miller)

PERSONAL: Born February 24, 1932 in Young Harris, GA; son of Stephen Grady and Birdie (an art teacher and mayor) Miller; married Shirley Carver, 1954; children: Murphy, Matthew. *Education:* University of Georgia, graduated, 1957, M.A., 1958. *Hobbies and other interests:* Baseball, country music.

ADDRESSES: Agent—c/o Author Mail, Stroud & Hall Publishers, P.O. Box 27210, Macon, GA 31221.

CAREER: Civil servant and educator. Young Harris, GA, mayor, 1959-60; elected to Georgia senate, 1960-64; State of Georgia, lieutenant governor, 1974-91, elected governor, 1991-99; elected to U.S. Senate, 2000-04. McKenna Long & Aldridge (law firm), member of staff, 2005—. Fox News Channel, commentator, 2004—. Has taught at Young Harris College, Emory University, and University of Georgia. Director emeritus, United Community Banks. Member of board of directors, Gray Television. *Military service:* U.S. Marine Corps, 1953-56, became sergeant.

AWARDS, HONORS: Governor of the Year designation, *Governing* magazine, 1998.

WRITINGS:

The Mountains within Me, Cherokee Publishing Company (Atlanta, GA), 1985.
Corps Values: Everything You Need to Know I Learned in the Marines, Longstreet Press (Atlanta, GA), 1996.
They Heard Georgia Singing, Mercer University Press (Macon, GA), 1996.
Listen to This Voice: Selected Speeches of Governor Zell Miller, Mercer University Press (Macon, GA), 1998.
A National Party No More: The Conscience of a Conservative Democrat, Stroud & Hall Publishers (Macon, GA), 2003.
A Deficit of Decency, Stroud & Hall Publishers (Macon, GA), 2005.

SIDELIGHTS: A former U.S. senator and governor of Georgia, Zell Miller is a controversial but stalwart figure in American politics. His mother, Birdie Miller, raised him after his father died when he was seventeen days old. As an art teacher and one of Georgia's earliest female members, Birdie Miller gave her son an example to follow of hard work and public dedication. After graduating from the University of Georgia, Miller became a history professor at Young Harris College. He entered politics in 1959, starting as the mayor of Young Harris, Georgia, and was elected to the state senate in 1960. Characterized as a conservative democrat, Miller held a number of key posts throughout his more-than-forty-five years in public office. From 1975 to 1991 he was lieutenant governor of Georgia. From 1991 to 1999 he served two terms as Georgia governor, where his contributions include the creation of the HOPE scholarship program that allowed high-school and continuing-education students greater opportunity to acquire a secondary education. The HOPE program was and continues to be financed entirely by the Georgia state lottery, which Miller also

introduced in 1992. He also increased state education spending to new highs, funding vital educational programs for students at all levels, including a voluntary pre-kindergarten program for four year olds. Education continued to be a prime force behind his governorship. After his tenure in state government, Miller returned to teaching in a college setting in 1999, teaching at Emory University, Young Harris College, and the University of Georgia. He also served on a number of corporate boards.

In 2000, Miller was elected to the U.S. Senate to fill the position left by the late Paul Coverdell. A longtime democrat, Miller sparked controversy when he diverged from his party to support George W. Bush over John Kerry in the 2004 U.S. presidential election. Miller also became known for fiery speeches and blunt criticism aimed at what he perceived as problems within the Democratic Party. After one such speech, given at the 2004 Republican National Convention and in which he accused the Democratic Party of moving too far to the political left, he received a scathing letter from former president Jimmy Carter. The former president called Miller's speech "rabid and mean-spirited," and accused him of "historically unprecedented disloyalty" that betrayed the Democratic Party's trust, noted a *UPI Newstrack* writer. In 2004, after leaving the senate, Miller became a commentator for Fox News, where he frequently appears on television programs such as *Hannity and Colmes.*

Miller has also been the author of several successful books. In *Corps Values: Everything You Need to Know I Learned in the Marines,* Miller describes how he used his enlistment in the Marine Corps to turn his life around when it hit a low point. A college dropout who felt inferior because of his rural background, Miller ended up in jail after getting drunk and crashing his car into a ditch. Desperate for a direction, he signed up for the Marines, and he credits his ninety days of boot camp on Parris Island with instilling in him the values and discipline necessary to succeed. Discipline, punctuality, and loyalty not only form the foundation of the Corps, they also underlie all human interaction in civilized society, Miller believes. In addition, individual goals can be pursued even as a person makes a contribution to the greater good of society.

A National Party No More: The Conscience of a Conservative Democrat is "part political memoir, part polemic, and all a rousing good read," noted a reviewer on the *Brothers Judd* Web site. Miller pulls no punches in his sharp criticism of the Democratic Party. To Miller, the Democratic Party has stopped being a national party—a party of the people—because it can no longer compete in the American south with candidates who are not southerners and not conservatives. He explains how he believes democrats' "views will cause the party to lose even more influence if they do not change their ways, and recognize what is good for the majority of Americans instead of supporting [the] special interest groups" that have exerted an increasing effect on the party, commented Ryan Thompson on the *Rant* Web site. He "examines every Democratic stereotype and declares them all true with a sharp, biting wit and a trademark southern charm," stated Matthew T. Joe on *Townhall.com*. Miller advocates that Democrats reduce their pandering to special-interest groups, become more in-tune with the average American and the American south, and move their politics more toward the centrist viewpoint. "*A National Party No More* should be read by political pundits on both side of the political debate, for Miller presents his case in a respectful, civil matter," remarked Tom Donelson for *Blogcritics.org*.

BIOGRAPHICAL AND CRITICAL SOURCES:

PERIODICALS

Atlanta Business Chronicle, January 22, 2001.

Education Week, March 29, 2001, "Bio of Zell Miller."

M2 Best Books, December 12, 2003, review of *A National Party No More: The Conscience of a Conservative Democrat.*

Reason, December, 2004, Cathy Young, "Martial Vices: Zell Miller's Un-American View of the Armed Forces," p. 17.

UPI Newstrack, September 8, 2004, "Jimmy Carter Lashes out at Miller Speech."

ONLINE

Biographical Directory of the United States Congress Online, http://bioguide.congress.gov/ (September 3, 2005), biography of Zell Miller.

Blogcritics.org, http://www.blogcritics.org/ (October 12, 2004), Tom Donelson, review of *A National Party No More.*

Brothers Judd.com, http://www.brothersjudd.com/ (September 3, 2005), review of *A National Party No More.*

Carl Vinson Institute of Government Web Site, http://www.cviog.uga.edu/ (September 3, 2005), "A Brief Biography of Georgia Governor Zell Miller."

Rant.us, http://www.therant.us/ (January 25, 2004), Ryan Thompson, review of *A National Party No More.*

TownHall.com, http://www.townhall.com/ (September 3, 2005), Matthew T. Joe, review of *A National Party No More*; Roger Banks, review of *A National Party No More.*

U.S. Senate Web site, http://www.senate.gov/ (September 3, 2005), biography of Senator Zell Miller.*

* * *

MILLER, Zell Bryan
See MILLER, Zell

* * *

MITCHELL, Paulette

PERSONAL: Female. *Education:* University of Iowa, graduated, 1971; attended La Varenne Cooking School (Paris, France).

ADDRESSES: Home—Minneapolis, MN. *Agent*—c/o Author Mail, Rodale, 33 E. Minor St., Emmaus, PA 18098. *E-mail*—food@ibsys.com.

CAREER: Educator and writer. Taught at cooking schools, including Kitchen Window Cooking School and Byerly's School of Culinary Arts. Restaurant consultant and lecturer.

WRITINGS:

The New American Vegetarian Menu Cookbook: From Everyday Dining to Elegant Entertaining, Rodale (Emmaus, PA), 1984.

The Fifteen-Minute Vegetarian Gourmet, Macmillan (New York, NY), 1987, published as *The Fifteen-Minute Gourmet: Vegetarian,* IDG Books (Foster City, CA), 1999.

The Fifteen-Minute Single Gourmet, Macmillan (New York, NY), 1994.

The Complete Book of Dressings, Macmillan (New York, NY), 1995.

The Fifteen-Minute Chicken Gourmet, Macmillan (New York, NY), 1997, published as *The Fifteen-Minute Gourmet: Chicken,* IDG Books (Foster City, CA), 1999.

The Complete Soy Cookbook, Macmillan (New York, NY), 1998.

Noodles, IDG Books (Foster City, CA), 1999.

Vegetarian Sandwiches: Fresh Fillings for Slices, Pockets, Wraps, and Rolls, Chronicle Books (San Francisco, CA), 2000.

Vegetarian Appetizers: Simply Delicious Recipes for Easy Entertaining, Chronicle Books (San Francisco, CA), 2001.

A Beautiful Bowl of Soup: The Best Vegetarian Recipes, Chronicle Books (San Francisco, CA), 2004.

The Spirited Vegetarian: Over 100 Recipes Made Lively with Wine and Spirits, Rodale (Emmaus, PA), 2005.

SIDELIGHTS: Paulette Mitchell has worked in the culinary field for a number of years, as a lecturer, consultant, and cooking instructor. She is also a celebrated food writer, specializing in creating recipes that are quick to prepare; she has written extensively about vegetarian cooking as well. Mitchell is a popular instructor, having taught many different cooking classes at the Kitchen Window Cooking School and Byerly's School of Culinary Arts. Mitchell is the author of more than ten cookbooks, including 1984's *The New American Vegetarian Menu Cookbook: From Everyday Dining to Elegant Entertaining,* 1987's *The Fifteen-Minute Vegetarian Gourmet,* and 2000's *Vegetarian Sandwiches: Fresh Fillings for Slices, Pockets, Wraps, and Rolls.*

In 2004 Mitchell wrote and published *A Beautiful Bowl of Soup: The Best Vegetarian Recipes.* In it the author highlights a variety of vegetarian soup recipes, including classics such as black bean soup and minestrone soup, along with more unique varieties like chestnut soup and wild rice-cranberry soup. Accompanying each recipe is a host of colorful photographs, simple instructions, and practical tips for cooking and managing a home kitchen. Mitchell also includes nineteen vegan soup recipes.

Readers and reviewers responded positively to *A Beautiful Bowl of Soup* overall. Her "helpful hints on how-tos and ingredients add to the overall excellence," wrote Sybil Pratt in a review for *BookPage.* "This book makes a convincing argument for soup as the star course of any meal," observed a *Publishers Weekly* contributor.

The following year, Mitchell published *The Spirited Vegetarian: Over 100 Recipes Made Lively with Wine and Spirits.* Here the author has showcased vegetarian recipes that include various spirits: wine, beer, and liquors. Dishes include Yukon gold potato-leek soup, red wine ratatouille, and broiled bananas with rum-raisin sauce. All courses, from appetizers to desserts, are featured. Mitchell also includes a chart that outlines various wine types and their characteristics. Again, reviewers praised Mitchell's work in *The Spirited Vegetarian.* The book "fills one of the last untapped niches in the ever-burgeoning vegetarian cookbook market," wrote a *Publishers Weekly* contributor. This work "is a testament to the fact that a vegetarian life-style can be gourmet and fun," observed a reviewer for *Wisconsin Bookwatch.*

BIOGRAPHICAL AND CRITICAL SOURCES:

PERIODICALS

AFAA's American Fitness, April, 1988, review of *The Fifteen-Minute Vegetarian Gourmet,* p. 48.

E, July-August, 2005, Stephanie White, review of *Vegetarian Appetizers: Simply Delicious Recipes for Easy Entertaining,* p. 61.

MPLS-St. Paul Magazine, January, 1995, Sylvia Paine, "The Great Minnesota Food Guide," p. 26; August, 1995, Gael Fashingbauer Cooper, "Fast Food," p. 39.

Publishers Weekly, June 5, 2000, review of *Vegetarian Sandwiches: Fresh Fillings for Slices, Pockets, Wraps, and Rolls,* p. 89; December 1, 2003, review of *A Beautiful Bowl of Soup: The Best Vegetarian Recipes,* p. 53; January 17, 2005, review of *The Spirited Vegetarian: Over 100 Recipes Made Lively with Wine and Spirits,* p. 48.

Whole Earth, summer, 1999, Daphne Derven, review of *The Complete Soy Cookbook,* p. 102.

Wisconsin Bookwatch, April, 2005, review of *The Spirited Vegetarian.*

ONLINE

BookPage, http://www.bookpage.com/ (September 27, 2005), Sybil Pratt, "Soup's On!"

Global Gourmet Online, http://www.globalgourmet. com/ (September 27, 2005), "The Fifteen-Minute Gourmet."*

* * *

MOEHRINGER, J.R. 1964-

PERSONAL: Born December 7, 1964, in New York, NY. *Education:* Yale University, B.A., 1986.

ADDRESSES: Office—Los Angeles Times, National Bureau, Denver, 202 W. 1st St., Los Angeles, CA 90012.

CAREER: Journalist and writer. *New York Times,* New York, NY, news assistant, 1986-90; *Rocky Mountain News,* Denver, CO, reporter, 1990-94; *Los Angeles Times,* Los Angeles, CA, reporter, 1994-97, Atlanta bureau chief, 1997—.

AWARDS, HONORS: Niemann fellow to Harvard University; Livingston Award for Young Journalists, 1997; feature writing award, Associated Press News Executives Council, 1997; Pulitzer Prize for feature writing, finalist, 1998, winner, 2000.

WRITINGS:

The Tender Bar: A Memoir, Hyperion (New York, NY), 2005.

SIDELIGHTS: American journalist J.R. Moehringer has written for newspapers across the United States, including the *New York Times, Los Angeles Times,* and *Rocky Mountain News.* His work has won numerous awards, including the 2000 Pulitzer Prize for feature writing.

In 2005, Moehringer published his first book, *The Tender Bar: A Memoir.* The story recounts the author's childhood and early adulthood growing up in Manhasset, New York, where he lived with his single mother in his grandfather's house. As a boy, eagerly searching for a father figure, Moehringer accompanies his bartender uncle to the local town bar. There he meets a cast of characters—Bob the Cop, Cager, Stinky, Colt, Smelly, Jimbo, Fast Eddy, and Bobo—who take him under their wing and adopt him into their family of sorts. The memoir follows Moehringer into college at Yale University and through unsuccessful romantic relationships as well as the beginning of his career as a journalist.

Overall, critics lauded Moehringer's work in *The Tender Bar.* Many found the book to be a strong addition to the coming-of-age genre, one that carries with it a range of emotions for readers. The book is "a straight-up account of masculinity, maturity and memory that leaves a smile on the face and an ache in the heart," wrote a *Kirkus Reviews* contributor. Others found the memoir to be full of entertaining anecdotes that make for an engrossing read. "Moehringer has hours and hours of stories that any bar hound worth his stool would bend both ears to drink in," observed Gregory Kirschling in a review for *Entertainment Weekly.*

BIOGRAPHICAL AND CRITICAL SOURCES:

BOOKS

Moehringer, J.R., *The Tender Bar: A Memoir,* Hyperion (New York, NY), 2005.

PERIODICALS

Denver Post, July 24, 2005, Bill Husted, review of *The Tender Bar.*

Entertainment Weekly, September 2, 2005, Gregory Kirschling, review of *The Tender Bar,* p. 82.

Kirkus Reviews, July 15, 2005, review of *The Tender Bar,* p. 779.

Publishers Weekly, June 27, 2005, review of *The Tender Bar,* p. 50.

ONLINE

Pulitzer Prize Web site, http://www.pulitzer.org/ (September 20, 2005), biography of J.R. Moehringer.*

MOHSIN, Amena 1958-

PERSONAL: Born January 22, 1958, in East Pakistan (now Bangladesh); daughter of Mohammad (a physician) and Zebunessa (a homemaker) Mohsin; married Anisur Rahman (a surgeon), January 14, 1983; children: Mufrad Nabeel (son). *Ethnicity:* "Bangali." *Politics:* "Humanism." *Religion:* Muslim. *Hobbies and other interests:* Music.

ADDRESSES: Office—Department of International Relations, University of Dhaka, Dhaka, Bangladesh.

CAREER: Writer and educator. University of Dhaka, Dhaka, Bangladesh, professor of international relations, 1984—. East-West Center, Honolulu, HI, scholar, 1984-86.

AWARDS, HONORS: CIDA fellow, 1989-90; Commonwealth scholar in England, 1992-95.

WRITINGS:

The Politics of Nationalism: The Case of the Chittagong Hill Tracts, Bangladesh, University Press (Dhaka, Bangladesh), 1997.
The Chittagong Hill Tracts, Bangladesh: On the Difficult Road to Peace, Lynne Rienner Publishers (Boulder, CO), 2003.

Also author of essays "The State of 'Minority' Rights in Bangladesh,rdquo; International Centre for Ethnic Studies (Colombo, Sri Lanka), 2001; editor of "Ethnic Minorities of Bangladesh: Some Reflections, the Saontals and the Rakhaines,rdquo; Grameen Trust (Dhaka, Bangladesh), 2002.

WORK IN PROGRESS: Futures of Democracy in Bangladesh; research on civil society and conflict resolution in Bangladesh.

SIDELIGHTS: Amena Mohsin told *CA:* "Primarily I want to raise awareness about the issues. I believe I am privileged to have acquired an education in a country where people strive to have two meals a day.

Education is a luxury, not a right in a country like Bangladesh, so I have a responsibility and obligation to my people at large.

"The level of violence and intolerance prevailing today makes me think about what kind of a world we are living in, what we are leaving for our children, and these thoughts inspire me to write.

"I go out to the field, observe, and talk to people. I think a lot, and what I think and believe to be right and just: I write. Basically, I think and write."

*   *   *

MONAGAN, John S. 1911-2005
(John Stephen Monagan)

OBITUARY NOTICE— See index for *CA* sketch: Born December 23, 1911, in Waterbury, CT; died of heart disease, October 23, 2005, in Washington, DC. Politician, lawyer, and author. Monagan was a former Democratic U.S. Congressman for the state of Connecticut. A bright student who excelled at swimming in high school, he attended Dartmouth College, where he edited the school's humor magazine and graduated in 1933. He then earned his law degree from Harvard University in 1937. Joining his uncle's law practice in Waterbury, he worked there for two years and became interested in politics. An operation to treat colon cancer in 1941 made him ineligible for military service during the war. Instead, he pursued politics as a finance commissioner for his home town and served as Waterbury's mayor from 1942 to 1948. He then returned to private practice for about a decade before running for the U.S. House of Representatives. He won the election and served as a congressman from 1959 until 1973. During this time, Monagan played several important roles. As chair of the House Government Operations subcommittee, for example, he helped expose problems at the Federal Housing Administration concerning the Housing Renewal program; his fluency in several languages also made him a natural candidate for the Committee on Foreign Affairs, and he worked on political and trade relations with countries in Europe and South America. Losing a bid for reelection in 1972, Monagan returned to law, joining Whitman & Ransom in New York City as a senior resident partner until retiring in 1980. Afterward, he kept busy by serving as president of the U.S. Association of Former Members of Congress, lecturing, contributing articles to publications such as the *New York Times,* and publishing the biographies *Horace, Priest of the Poor* (1985) and *The Grand Panjandrum: Mellow Years of Justice Holmes* (1988). Named to the Waterbury, Connecticut, Hall of Fame in 1997, Monagan's last book was the autobiography *Pleasant Institution: Key—C Major* (2001).

OBITUARIES AND OTHER SOURCES:

BOOKS

Monagan, John S., *Pleasant Institution: Key—C Major,* University Press of America (Lanham, MD), 2001.

PERIODICALS

Los Angeles Times, October 26, 2005, p. B11.
Washington Post, October 25, 2005, p. B6.

*   *   *

MONAGAN, John Stephen
    See MONAGAN, John S.

*   *   *

MOORE, Barrington, Jr. 1913-2005

OBITUARY NOTICE— See index for *CA* sketch: Born May 12, 1913, in Washington, DC; died October 16, 2005, in Cambridge, MA. Sociologist, political theorist, educator, and author. An important political sociologist by all accounts, Moore was a retired senior research fellow at Harvard University's Russian Research Center, where he studied how history, economics, sociology, and other factors influence the political course of nations. A 1936 graduate of Williams College, he went on to earn a Ph.D. from Yale University in 1941. He then was hired as a research analyst for the U.S. Justice Department, and, not long after the United States entered World War II, was assigned to work for the Office of Strategic Services—

forerunner of the CIA. After the war, Moore was on the faculty of the University of Chicago for three years. In 1948, he joined the Russian Research Center, remaining there until his retirement in 1979. Not surprisingly, his first publications focused on the Soviet Union, including *Soviet Politics: The Dilemma of Power* (1950) and *The Strengths and Weaknesses of the Soviet System* (1952). Moore believed that to understand the politics of a nation, one had to take a multidisciplinary approach; politics, he felt, did not exist in isolation from history, economics, and other factors. He laid down his ideas in what is considered to be his most groundbreaking and highly influential work, *Social Origins of Dictatorship and Democracy: Lord and Peasant in the Making of the Modern World* (1966), which has become a standard college text and is still in print. Many other highly praised works followed, including *Injustice: The Social Bases of Obedience and Revolt* (1978), *Authority and Inequality under Capitalism and Socialism* (1987), and *Moral Purity and Persecution in History* (2000).

OBITUARIES AND OTHER SOURCES:

PERIODICALS

Independent (London, England), November 17, 2005, p. 59.
New York Times, October 22, 2005, p. B14.

*   *   *

MORETTI, Luigi 1907-1973
    (Luigi Walter Moretti)

PERSONAL: Born January 2, 1907, in Rome, Italy; died July 14, 1973, in Isola di Capraia Italy; son of Giuseppe and Giuseppina (Palmerini) Moretti; married Maria Teresa Albani, July 3, 1968. *Education:* University of Rome, diploma in architecture (with honors), c. 1930.

CAREER: Owner and director of architectural and town planning firms in Rome and Milan, Italy, and in Algiers, Algeria, 1932-73. University of Rome, member of architecture faculty, 1931-34; National Institute for Mathematical Research and Urban Planning, founder, 1957. Architect; designer of dozens of buildings, including fencing school and Empire Square in Rome, apartment houses in Milan, Villa la Saracena, Montreal Stock-Exchange Tower, Fonti de Bonifacio VIII, Watergate building in Washington, DC, and houses in Alexandria, VA. City of Rome, member of committee for territorial planning, 1959-60, and town planning committee, 1964-73; member, Pontificia Commissione di Arte Sacra, 1960-73.

MEMBER: Accademia del Disegno, Accademia Nazionale di San Luca (national academician), American Institute of Architects (fellow).

AWARDS, HONORS: Valadier prize, 1930; first prize, Triennale Competition for Roman Studies, 1931; Italian national architecture prize, 1957; Vallombrosa prize, 1959; Gold Medal of the Professional Arts, 1960; Gold Medal for Sciences and Fine Arts, Italian Ministry of Public Information, c. 1964; national architecture prize, Accademia Nazionale dei Lincei, 1968; winner of numerous building competitions.

WRITINGS:

(With Michel Tapié and Friedrich Leo Bayerthal) *Musee-manifeste: structures et styles autres,* Edizioni d'Arte F. Pozzo (Turin, Italy), 1963.
(With P. Pascal) *Apocalisse,* [Rome, Italy], 1964.
Structures in Michelangelo, 1964.
Generalized Structures in Borromini, 1967.

Contributor to architecture journals. Editor, *Spazio,* beginning 1952.

BIOGRAPHICAL AND CRITICAL SOURCES:

BOOKS

Contemporary Architects, 3rd edition, St. James Press (Detroit, MI), 1994, pp. 665-668.*

* * *

MORETTI, Luigi Walter
See MORETTI, Luigi

MORI, Toshio 1910-1980

PERSONAL: Born March 20, 1910, in Oakland, CA; died 1980.

CAREER: Writer and botanist. Worked in family-owned horticultural nursery.

AWARDS, HONORS: American Book Award, Before Columbus Foundation, 1985, for *Yokohama, California.*

WRITINGS:

Doitsugo yonshukan: Deutsche sprache in vier wochen (German textbook for Japanese speakers), Daigaku Shorin (Tokyo, Japan), 1938.
Yokohama, California (stories), introduction by William Saroyan, Caxton Printers (Caldwell, ID), 1949, with introduction by Lawson Fusao Inada, University of Washington Press (Seattle, WA), 1985.
Woman from Hiroshima, Isthmus Press (San Francisco, CA), 1978.
The Chauvinist, and Other Stories, introduction by Hisaye Yamamoto, Asian-American Studies Center, University of California (Los Angeles, CA), 1979.
Unfinished Message: Selected Works of Toshio Mori, introduction by Lawson Fusao Inada, foreword by Steven Y. Mori, Heyday Books (Berkeley, CA), 2000.

Contributor of stories to periodicals; editor of *Trek* (newspaper), Topaz Relocation Center, Topaz, UT, c. 1940s.

SIDELIGHTS: Toshio Mori, a second-generation Japanese immigrant or "nisei," was one of the first Japanese Americans to make a mark on the American writing scene. His first novel, *Yokohama, California,* was scheduled to be published in 1942, but World War II intervened. After the Japanese attack on Pearl Harbor, Hawaii, Mori and 100,000 other Japanese immigrants and Japanese Americans were sent to internment camps. Mori continued to write while in the Topaz Relocation Center in Topaz, Utah, and edited a newspaper for his fellow internees. One of his novellas, *The Brothers Murata,* also makes use of Topaz as a setting. After the war, *Yokohama, California* eventually found its way to print, although not until 1949.

Many of Mori's numerous short stories also draw on events in his own life, including the decades he spent working in his family's horticultural nursery business. In "Through Anger and Love," the protagonist is a nine-year-old boy, the son of a flower-seller, who, angry at his father, sets off to sell flowers by himself. Another story, "The Chessmen," "is a prize, a heart-rending tale of an old nurseryman-gardener who is about to be put out to pasture," Akira Tofina wrote in *Review of Arts, Literature, Philosophy, and the Humanities* online.

Unfinished Message: Selected Works of Toshio Mori collects more than a dozen of Mori's stories. Lonny Kaneko, who reviewed the volume in the *International Examiner,* noted that "there are three or four traditional conflict-based stories in the collection, but many others demonstrate a touch that is unique and off-the-beaten path." Kaneko called *Unfinished Message* "a delightful read."

BIOGRAPHICAL AND CRITICAL SOURCES:

PERIODICALS

International Examiner (Seattle, WA), April 30, 2001, Lonny Kaneko, review of *Unfinished Message: Selected Works of Toshio Mori,* p. 12.
MELUS, summer, 1988, Margaret Bedrosian, "Toshio Mori's California Koans," p. 46; winter, 1999, Benzi Zhang, "Mapping Carnivalistic Discourse in Japanese-American Writing," p. 19.

ONLINE

Heyday Books Web site, http://www.heydaybooks.com/ (August 16, 2005).
Review of Arts, Literature, Philosophy, and the Humanities Online, http://www.ralphmag.org/ (August 16, 2005), Akira Tofina, review of *Unfinished Message.**

*   *   *

MOYAL, Ann 1926-
(Ann Mozley Moyal)

PERSONAL: Born 1926. *Education:* Educated at University of Sydney.

ADDRESSES: Home—Canberra, Australia. *Agent*—c/o Author Mail, Australian Scholarly Publishing, P.O. Box 299, Kew, 3101 Victoria, Australia.

CAREER: Historian and writer. Griffith University, Queensland, Australia, former director of Science Policy Research Centre; held research and teaching positions at Australian Academy of Science, Australian National University, University of Sydney, and New South Wales Institute of Technology.

MEMBER: Australian Science History Club, Independent Scholars Association of Australia (founder and past president).

WRITINGS:

A Guide to the Manuscript Records of Australian Science, Australian National University Press (Canberra, Australian Capital Territory, Australia), 1966.
(Editor) *Scientists in Nineteenth-Century Australia: A Documentary History,* Cassell Australia (Melbourne, Victoria, Australia), 1976.
Science Technology, and Society in Australia: A Bibliography, Griffith University (Brisbane, Queensland, Australia), 1978.
Clear across Australia: A History of Telecommunications, Nelson (Melbourne, Victoria, Australia), 1984.
A Bright and Savage Land: Scientists in Colonial Australia, Collins (Sydney, New South Wales, Australia), 1986, Penguin (New York, NY), 1993.
(Editor) *Portraits in Science,* National Library of Australia (Canberra, Australian Capital Territory, Australia), 1994.
Breakfast with Beaverbrook: Memoirs of an Independent Woman, Hale & Iremonger (Sydney, New South Wales, Australia), 1995.
Platypus: The Extraordinary Story of How a Curious Creature Baffled the World, Smithsonian Institution Press (Washington, DC), 2001.
(Editor) *The Web of Science: The Scientific Correspondence of the Rev. W.B. Clarke, Australia's Pioneer Geologist,* Australian Scholarly Publishing (Melbourne, Victoria, Australia), 2003.

SIDELIGHTS: Australian author Ann Moyal has worked as an historian for a number of years, specializing in Australian science, technology, and telecommunications. She has also worked for many years as a researcher and academic at Australian universities. Moyal is the author and editor of numerous books regarding the history of science, including 1984's *Clear across Australia: A History of Telecommunications*, 1986's *A Bright and Savage Land: Scientists in Colonial Australia*, and 1995's *Breakfast with Beaverbrook: Memoirs of an Independent Woman*, which is Moyal's autobiography. Moyal is also the founder and past president of the Independent Scholars Association of Australia, and has served as an honorary editor of *Search* and *Prometheus*.

One of Moyal's best-known works is 2001's *Platypus: The Extraordinary Story of How a Curious Creature Baffled the World*. This work examines the scientific history of the platypus, from its introduction to the scientific community in the late eighteenth century through the late nineteenth century. As the author explains, many important scientists of that time were baffled by the unique and uncharted platypus, namely Charles Darwin and George Bennett. Moyal follows a chronological sequence and intertwines the change in scientific theories about the platypus with the change in evolutionary theory. The book also contains black-and-white illustrations, color plates, stories, and poems related to the platypus. With this work, "The reader will learn not only about the platypus, but also the history of science in categorizing living beings," observed Nola Theiss in a review for *Kliatt*.

Overall, critics had much to praise in *Platypus*. *Antipodes* contributor Wendy Varney considered Moyal's work to have a widespread appeal that a variety of readers could embrace. "It is a book that will appeal to those interested in the history and philosophy of science, those wishing to know a little more of the history of colonial relations between Britain and Australia and those who are simply after a 'good read,'" wrote Varney. Frank E. Fish, in a review for the *Quarterly Review of Biology*, found the book to be a significant contribution to literature regarding this enigmatic animal. "From an historical perspective, Moyal has done a exceptional job in documenting the impact of the platypus," commented Fish.

BIOGRAPHICAL AND CRITICAL SOURCES:

BOOKS

Moyal, Ann, *Breakfast with Beaverbrook: Memoirs of an Independent Woman*, Hale & Iremonger (Sydney, New South Wales, Australia), 1995.

PERIODICALS

Antipodes, June 2002, Wendy Varney, review of *Platypus: The Extraordinary Story of How a Curious Creature Baffled the World,* p. 92.
Booklist, August 2001, Nancy Bent, review of *Platypus,* p. 2066.
Journal of Australian Studies, March 2002, Pia van Ravenstein, review of *Platypus,* p. 213.
Kliatt, May 2005, Nola Theiss, review of *Platypus,* p. 47.
Library Journal, September 1, 2001, Marianne Stowell, review of *Platypus,* p. 220.
Natural History, November 2001, review of *Platypus,* p. 86.
Publishers Weekly, July 16, 2001, review of *Platypus,* p. 170.
Quarterly Review of Biology, September 2002, Frank E. Fish, review of *Platypus,* p. 310.

ONLINE

University of Melbourne's Australian Science Archives Project Web site, http://www.asap.unimelb.edu.au/ (September 21, 2005), biographical information on Ann Moyal.*

*   *   *

MOYAL, Ann Mozley
See MOYAL, Ann

*   *   *

MOYNIHAN, Maura 1957-
(Maya Smith)

PERSONAL: Born July 25, 1957, in Albany, NY; daughter of Daniel Patrick (a politician and diplomat) and Elizabeth (a writer) Moynihan; children: Michael Avedon. *Ethnicity:* "Irish." *Education:* Harvard University, B.A., 1980. *Politics:* Liberal Democrat. *Religion:* Hindu. *Hobbies and other interests:* Music, dance, languages.

ADDRESSES: Home—3 Peter Cooper Rd., Apt. 3G, New York, NY 10010. *E-mail*—mmoynihan108@aol.com.

CAREER: Writer. Founder of a multilingual radio program; cocreator of a comedy duo; also worked as a journalist, rock musician, and clothing designer. Moynihan Station Citizen's Group, director; consultant on refugee issues, especially regarding India, Nepal, and Tibet.

MEMBER: Asia Society, Alliance Français.

WRITINGS:

Yoga Hotel (short stories; with musical compact disc), Regan Books (New York, NY), 2003.

Some writings appear under pseudonym Maya Smith.

WORK IN PROGRESS: Covergirl.

SIDELIGHTS: Maura Moynihan told *CA:* "I wanted to be a poet from the time I could speak, move, and think. I wrote my first poems when I was five and left them at my parents' bedside. Of course, when you grow up and discover that there really is no place, no role, no status for a poet in modern American life, you have to find ways to survive and keep writing. We don't have royal patrons in America, just agents and publishers.

"I write because that is the only way I can make sense of living, and because in writing I elevate my own life from a random, banal series of events, hazards, rituals, and transform it into a pilgrimage, a quest for purpose. I still think writing fiction is important, even though the American public doesn't read new fiction—fiction feeds Hollywood, which is now the purveyor of what is supposed to be culture. There's no sense in complaining about it; that's just how it is. Writers have always had to struggle against convention and apathy.

"I write fiction because fiction is the only way to tell the whole truth. In fiction I can examine people's motives, not merely their actions. I can be humorous, which allows me to show a character's hubris and pretense and cunning while feeling immense compassion. I love all my characters, especially the villains. At some point, all villains end up miserable and alone.

"I've been influenced by the Victorian novelists (who hasn't?) and by F. Scott Fitzgerald, Mary McCarthy, Ruth Prowler Jhabvala.

"I always write my first drafts in longhand. Sometimes these are the sharpest, clearest drafts, but I have to rewrite and rewrite. A writer has to write all the time. There is no such thing as writer's block if you allow yourself to write badly and throw it out. Just move your hand across the page, or the keyboard, and try to know when to stop. Sometimes you can write a piece to death. Make sure the characters tell you what to do. Don't impose a story line on them—they should reveal to you what will happen. If you know your characters well enough, they will write the story for you. It's sheer magic when that happens, and we writers live for those moments.

"I write about the years I spent in India, about westerners in India and the ancient conflict of cultures. I love to write about conflict, people in conflict, whether it involves class, sex, money, religion, or race—as long as it clashes. Then the story line is going to follow the qualities of the characters, whether they are brave or cowardly, weak or stubborn, kind or selfish. A writer can test the characters, put them in unpredictable situations, and let them tell you what they will do. It doesn't always work. Some characters never develop; in that case, you can let them go and find new ones.

"Other professions may rise and die. Other jobs may pay a lot more money, but writers will always be working."

BIOGRAPHICAL AND CRITICAL SOURCES:

PERIODICALS

Kirkus Reviews, August 1, 2003, review of *Yoga Hotel,* p. 984.
Library Journal, June 15, 2003, Lisa Rohrbaugh, review of *Yoga Hotel,* p. 103.
People, September 22, 2003, review of *Yoga Hotel,* p. 58.
Publishers Weekly, July 7, 2003, review of *Yoga Hotel,* p. 51.

*   *   *

MUGGLESTONE, Lynda
(Lynda C. Mugglestone)

PERSONAL: Female.

ADDRESSES: Office—Pembroke College, Oxford University, Oxford OX1 1DW, England. *E-mail*—lynda.mugglestone@pmb.ox.ac.uk

CAREER: Educator and writer. Pembroke College, Oxford, Oxford, England, dean and fellow in English language. Contributor to British Broadcasting Corporation Radio; lecturer.

MEMBER: Dictionary Society of North America, English Dictionary Forum.

WRITINGS:

(Editor) George Eliot, *Felix Holt, the Radical,* Penguin (New York, NY), 1995.

Talking Proper: The Rise of Accent as Social Symbol, Oxford University Press (New York, NY), 1995.

(Editor) *Lexicography and the OED: Pioneers in the Untrodden Forest,* Oxford University Press (New York, NY), 2000.

Lost for Words: The Hidden History of the Oxford English Dictionary, Yale University Press (New Haven, CT), 2005.

WORK IN PROGRESS: A book on World War I dealing with the cultural interface of language, lexicography, and social change.

SIDELIGHTS: Lynda Mugglestone has worked as an educator for a number of years; she has served as a dean of Pembroke College, Oxford, as well as a fellow in English language and literature at that same university. Her teaching specialties include the standardization and history of English, dialect in literature, and the language used by specific authors, including Geoffrey Chaucer and Charles Dickens. Her research interests follow a similar vein, and include the history of the English language in the nineteenth century and the cultural, social, and linguistic history of dictionaries. Mugglestone is a frequent lecturer at universities around England, and a regular contributor to British Broadcasting Corporation radio programming.

In 1995, Mugglestone published *Talking Proper: The Rise of Accent as Social Symbol.* Drawing from eighteenth-and nineteenth-century source materials regarding British society, the author analyzes the change in attitude toward speech accents, and how that change coincided with the standardization of written and spoken English. Mugglestone illustrates how accent, once a neutral ornament to speech, became increasingly symbolic of one's social class and status; she also documents reactions and challenges to this change in thought toward accent.

Overall, *Talking Proper* was greeted positively by reviewers and readers. Many found the work to be a thorough history of a topic that still influences British society today. "This book . . . dramatically and appropriately illustrates what amounts to a 'national obsession,' . . . a preoccupation of countless pundits from the eighteenth century onwards," wrote Katie Wales in the *Review of English Studies.* Other reviewers enjoyed the author's insightful interpretations and fresh take on a popular subject. "While many literary texts reinforce prevailing linguistic stereotypes, Mugglestone's readings of writers like [T.S.] Eliot and [Charles] Dickens underline how those authors subtly subvert sociolinguistic stereotypes by dissociating manners from morals," observed *Notes and Queries* contributor Carol Percy.

Mugglestone's next major work was 2005's *Lost for Words: The Hidden History of the Oxford English Dictionary.* With this book the author documents the making of the *Oxford English Dictionary* (OED); Mugglestone used newly discovered documents from Bodleian Library's Murray Papers and the OED archives to provide new insight into the tome's creation. The author also shows the distinct difference between editor James A.H. Murray's original, idealized concept for the OED and the reference work that was finally published in 1928.

Again, reviewers has much to praise in *Lost for Words.* Many lauded Mugglestone's tireless research and thorough documentation of the dictionary's history. "Through archival evidence Mugglestone illuminates the thousands of decisions regarding inclusion/exclusion, labeling, etymology, definitions, social and political biases, and limitations of money, space, and nine that went into making the OED," wrote Paul D'Alessandro in a review for the *Library Journal.* Others appreciated Mugglestone's keen interest in her subject, one that shines through in her writing and style. "She writes with obvious admiration for the aging clan of editors who struggled at what was generally acknowledged to be a Sisyphean task," observed *American Scholar* contributor Caroline Preston.

BIOGRAPHICAL AND CRITICAL SOURCES:

PERIODICALS

American Scholar, summer, 2005, Caroline Preston, review of *Lost for Words: The Hidden History of the Oxford English Dictionary,* p. 138.

Language, March, 2005, Dick Bailey, review of *Talking Proper: The Rise of Accent as Social Symbol,* pp. 269-271.

Library Journal, May 15, 2005, Paul D'Alessandro, review of *Lost for Words,* p. 118.

Notes and Queries, December, 1996, Carol Percy, review of *Talking Proper,* p. 491.

Review of English Studies, November, 1996, Katie Wales, review of *Talking Proper,* p. 550.

Virginia Quarterly Review, fall, 2005, Peter Walpole, review of *Lost for Words,* p. 295.

Weekly Standard, May 23, 2005, Paul Dean, review of *Lost for Words,* p. 34.

ONLINE

Pembroke College Web site, http://www.pmb.ox.ac.uk/ (September 25, 2005), information on Lynda Mugglestone.

*   *   *

MUGGLESTONE, Lynda C.
    See MUGGLESTONE, Lynda

MULLER, Mancow 1969-

PERSONAL: Born June 21, 1969, in PA; son of John (a seller of kitchen cabinets) and Dawn (a homemaker; maiden name, Smith) Muller; married Sandy Ferrando (in public relations), February 14, 2003. *Ethnicity:* "Mixed." *Education:* Studied public relations. *Politics:* Libertarian. *Religion:* "Blue Domer."

ADDRESSES: Home and office—1155 W. Armitage, No. 605, Chicago, IL 60614. *E-mail*—mancow@mancow.com.

CAREER: Writer and radio host. Host of nationally syndicated radio show; guest on television programs, including *Fox and Friends* news program, Fox Broadcasting Co.

WRITINGS:

(With John Calkins) *Dad, Dames, Demons, and a Dwarf: My Trip down Freedom Road* (nonfiction), Regan Books (New York, NY), 2003.

WORK IN PROGRESS: Monkeys in People Clothes, a sequel to *Dad, Dames, Demons, and a Dwarf.*

SIDELIGHTS: Mancow Muller told *CA* that his primary motivation for writing is "to express my soul." Muller added that his writing has been inspired by "the death of my father and [having to go] into the world alone without the man who had been my guide, rudder, and best friend."

N-O

NATHAN, Micah

PERSONAL: Born in Los Angeles, CA; married. *Education:* State University of New York, Buffalo, graduated.

ADDRESSES: Home—Brookline, MA. *Agent*—Marly Rusoff & Associates, Inc., P.O. Box 524, Bronxville, NY 10708. *E-mail*—goa@micahnathan.com

CAREER: Novelist. Worked variously as a radio talk-show host, filmmaker, and motivational speaker.

WRITINGS:

Gods of Aberdeen (novel), Simon & Schuster (New York, NY), 2005.

SIDELIGHTS: Author Micah Nathan was born in Hollywood, grew up in rural New York state, and attended the State University of New York at Buffalo. He has worked in a number of fields, including radio, film, and public speaking. Nathan has also enjoyed time spent as an amateur kickboxer.

In 2005, Nathan published his first novel, *Gods of Aberdeen.* The story follows sixteen-year-old scholarship student Eric Dunne, who leaves his New Jersey foster family behind to attend wealthy Aberdeen College in New England. There he finds himself involved with a research project meant to find the philosopher's stone, which is believed to hold the key to immortality. Eric's journey involves an awkward romance, dabblings in drugs, and a pursuit of the occult.

Overall, reviews of *Gods of Aberdeen* were positive. Readers found the novel's plotline to be exciting and fast-paced, making for an interesting story. Nathan's book is a "malevolently thrilling coming-of-ager wrapped in a philosophical detective tale," wrote a *Kirkus Reviews* contributor. Other critics thought the author's voice honestly reflects his college-aged subjects, and will attract readers interested in coming-of-age novels. "Nathan perfectly captures the angst and pretension of adolescents taking themselves very seriously," commented a reviewer for *Publishers Weekly.*

BIOGRAPHICAL AND CRITICAL SOURCES:

PERIODICALS

Hollywood Reporter, June 13, 2005, Chris Barsanti, review of *Gods of Aberdeen,* p. 12.
Kirkus Reviews, April 1, 2005, review of *Gods of Aberdeen,* p. 380.
Library Journal, June 1, 2005, Barbara Hoffert, review of *Gods of Aberdeen,* p. 119.
Publishers Weekly, April 11, 2005, review of *Gods of Aberdeen,* p. 31.

ONLINE

Micah Nathan Home Page, http://www.micahnathan. com (September 25, 2005).*

NAYLOR, Sharon

PERSONAL: Female.

ADDRESSES: Home—Madison, NJ. *Agent*—c/o Author Mail, Sourcebooks, Inc., 1935 Brookdale Rd., Ste. 139, Naperville, IL 60563. *E-mail*—slnaylor@optonline.net.

CAREER: Wedding consultant and writer.

MEMBER: International Special Events Society, Association of Bridal Consultants, American Society of Journalists and Authors.

WRITINGS:

1,001 Ways to Save Money—and Still Have a Dazzling Wedding, Contemporary Books (Chicago, IL), 1994, revised edition, 2001.
100 Reasons to Keep Him, 100 Reasons to Dump Him, Three Rivers Press (New York, NY), 1997.
Learning the Ropes, Ferguson (Chicago, IL), 1998, revised edition, 2004.
The Unofficial Guide to Divorce, Macmillan (New York, NY), 1998.
How to Plan an Elegant Wedding in Six Months or Less: Achieving Your Dream Wedding When Time Is of the Essence, Prima Home (Roseville, CA), 2000.
1,001 Ways to Have a Dazzling Second Wedding, New Page Books (Franklin Lakes, NJ), 2001.
The Complete Outdoor Wedding Planner: From Rustic Settings to Elegant Garden Parties, Everything You Need to Know to Make Your Day Special, Prima (Roseville, CA), 2001.
The Mother-of-the-Bride Book: Giving Your Daughter a Wonderful Wedding, Citadel Press (Secaucus, NJ), 2001.
The New Honeymoon Planner: Selecting the Ideal Location and Planning the Trip of a Lifetime, Prima (Roseville, CA), 2002.
How to Have a Fabulous Wedding for $10,000 or Less: Creating Your Dream Day with Romance, Grace, and Style, Prima (Roseville, CA), 2002.
The Ultimate Bridal Shower Idea Book: How to Have a Fun, Fabulous, and Memorable Party, Prima (Roseville, CA), 2003.

(With Michelle Roth and Henry Roth) *Your Day, Your Way: The Essential Handbook for the 21st-Century Bride,* Three Rivers Press (New York, NY), 2003.
Your Special Wedding Vows, Sourcebooks (Naperville, IL), 2004.
Your Special Wedding Toasts, Sourcebooks (Naperville, IL), 2004.
The Groom's Guide: A Wedding Planner for Today's Marrying Man, Citadel Press (New York, NY), 2004.
1,000 Best Wedding Bargains, Sourcebooks (Naperville, IL), 2004.
1,000 Best Secrets for Your Perfect Wedding, Sourcebooks (Naperville, IL), 2004.
The Busy Bride's Essential Wedding Checklists, Sourcebooks (Naperville, IL), 2005.
The Bridesmaid Handbook, Sourcebooks (Naperville, IL), 2005.
Essential Guide to Wedding Etiquette, Sourcebooks (Naperville, IL), 2005.

Contributor to Web sites, and to periodicals, including *Bridal Guide, Bride Again, Shape, Health, Woman's Day,* and *Cosmopolitan.*

SIDELIGHTS: Sharon Naylor has written extensively on the subjects of marriage and weddings. She has served as a consultant and specialist to wedding-related Web sites NJWedding.com and SheKnows.com, and is a contributor to bridal magazines including *Bridal Guide, Bride Again,* and *Bride's,* as well as to women's magazines such as *Women's Day, Shape,* and *Cosmopolitan.* Naylor has spoken frequently on talk shows and news television programs, and is a member of the American Society of Journalists and Authors and the International Special Events Society.

The author of more than twenty-five books, Naylor has written about throwing an economical wedding in 1994's *1,001 Ways to Save Money—and Still Have a Dazzling Wedding;* on planning outdoor weddings in 2001's *The Complete Outdoor Wedding Planner: From Rustic Settings to Elegant Garden Parties, Everything You Need to Know to Make Your Day Special;* and on organizing a wedding from the groom's perspective in 2004's *The Groom's Guide: A Wedding Planner for Today's Marrying Man.*

Naylor addresses couples looking to plan weddings under time constraints in her book *How to Plan an Elegant Wedding in Six Months or Less: Achieving*

Your Dream Wedding When Time Is of the Essence. The author writes that most couples do much of the planning in a short time-period anyway, and spend much of the rest of their engagement worrying about the plans. So Naylor outlines a quick and efficient timeline for planning a wedding six months out, and includes helpful tips, shortcuts, and anecdotes. Readers found Naylor's book to be helpful and timely overall, and useful to a wide range of brides-and grooms-to-be. *How to Plan an Elegant Wedding in Six Months or Less* contains "practical, organized advice applicable to many couples," wrote Bonnie Poquette in a review for *Library Journal.*

Naylor addresses couples approaching their second marriage with her book *1,001 Ways to Have a Dazzling Second Wedding.* With this work she offers practical tips regarding a wide variety of topics, including beauty, dress, family dynamics, and honeymoons. She also discusses the special challenges and etiquette issues that arise with second weddings. Again, critics praised Naylor for her work, with many acknowledging the author's considerable expertise as an asset to literature on this subject. "Naylor's experience with the wedding industry shines through," observed Poquette in another *Library Journal* review.

The Bridesmaid Handbook is a guide to all wedding-related events that a bridesmaid is involved in. Naylor focuses on the role and duties a bridesmaid is expected to perform, as well as the commitments—both time-wise and financial—that come along with the honor of being a bridesmaid. The book addresses specific topics such as picking bridal shower venues, addressing invitations, and arranging for catering. Naylor again was lauded for her work on this book; readers found this detailed guidebook to be useful for all sorts of bridesmaids and maids of honor. *The Bridesmaid Handbook* is "useful for the first timer or the old hand who needs a quick refresher course," commented Poquette in a *Library Journal* review.

BIOGRAPHICAL AND CRITICAL SOURCES:

PERIODICALS

Library Journal, April 1, 2001, Bonnie Poquette, reviews of *How to Plan an Elegant Wedding in Six Months or Less: Achieving Your Dream Wed-*
ding *When Time Is of the Essence* and *1,001 Ways to Have a Dazzling Second Wedding,* p. 127; May 15, 2005, Bonnie Poquette, review of *The Bridesmaid Handbook,* p. 140.
Newsweek International, May 12, 2003, John Sparks, "A Clean Getaway," p. 66.

ONLINE

AbsoluteWrite.com, http://www.absolutewrite.com/ (September 27, 2005), Jenna Glatzer, interview with Sharon Naylor.
Sharon Naylor Home Page, http://www.sharonnaylor. net (September 27, 2005).*

*   *   *

O'CONNELL, Tyne

PERSONAL: Children: Cordelia, two sons.

ADDRESSES: Home—London, England. *Agent*—c/o Author Mail, Bloomsbury USA, 175 5th Ave., Ste. 315, New York, NY 10010. *E-mail*—askcalypso@ca-lypsochronicles.com.

CAREER: Writer.

WRITINGS:

NOVELS

Sex, Lies, and Litigation, Trafalger Square (London, England), 1998.
What's a Girl to Do?, Headline (London, England), 1998.
Making the A-List, Headline (London, England), 1999.
That Girl-Boy Thing, Headline (London, England), 2001.
The Sex Was Great But . . . , Red Dress Ink (Toronto, Ontario, Canada), 2004.
Sex with the Ex, Red Dress Ink (Toronto, Ontario, Canada), 2005.

"CALYPSO CHRONICLES"; FOR CHILDREN

Pulling Princes, Bloomsbury (New York, NY), 2004.
Dueling Princes, Bloomsbury (New York, NY), 2005.
Stealing Princes, Bloomsbury (New York, NY), 2005.

OTHER

Author for television sitcoms. Contributor to periodicals, including *Vogue UK, Ms., Journal UK, Marie Claire Australia, Elle, Cosmopolitan,* and *Vogue Australia.*

O'Connell's books have been translated into French, German, Czech, Slovak, and Estonian.

ADAPTATIONS: Pulling Princes was adapted as an audio book, Bolinda Audio, 2005.

SIDELIGHTS: Tyne O'Connell writes for both adults and young readers and has claimed that all of her novels are autobiographical in that they are based on her own life and on the experiences of her children. In her adult novel *The Sex Was Great But . . .* the author tells the story of the relationship between Holly Klein, host of the reality-based *MakeMeOver* television show, and the underachieving Leo. Holly meets Leo when he is out panhandling and recovers Holly's stolen purse. When Leo gets hurt tracking down the purse, Holly takes him back to her house so he can clean up, and the two soon find that they are attracted to each other. When Holly's producer meets Leo, she gets the idea of putting him on the show, which features celebrity makeovers, leading many in Hollywood to believe that Leo is a person of importance. Despite their mutual attraction, however, Holly refuses to be seen in public with Leo, and their relationship is soon in trouble. Writing in *Booklist,* Kristine Huntley called the novel a "delightful, lighthearted romp."

In *Sex with the Ex* public-relations professional Lola is a beautiful woman with many friends and a great job representing a successful private club called Posh House. Nevertheless, when her ex-husband and two old boyfriends attend a party at the club, Lola comes to the realization that she lacks one important thing to make her life complete: a man. She finds that she is still attracted to her ex-husband, Richard, despite his many problems, which include cocaine abuse, little money, and a girlfriend he has no qualms about deceiving. Despite her better judgment and against the advice of her friends, Lola begins to see Richard again. "Devout chick-lit lovers could do worse than this breezy romance," remarked a *Kirkus Reviews* critic.

The author has also written a series of novels for the younger set featuring the teenager Calypso Kelly. The first book in the series, *Pulling Princes,* finds the American-born Calypso in a British boarding school and striving to leave her outsider status behind and become part of the popular set. Her goal seems to be in reach until classmate Holly becomes jealous when Calypso garners the attention of Prince Freddie, who is second in line to the British throne. A *Publishers Weekly* contributor called the effort "frothy and fast-paced," while Claire Rosser, writing in *Kliatt,* commented that the story is "outrageously funny." In *Stealing Princes,* O'Connell continues the adventures of Calypso, who this time must deal with a new roommate who may be out to steal her boyfriend, Prince Freddie. *Booklist* contributor Cindy Welch observed that the "boarding school setup provides some fun."

O'Connell_told *CA:* "When I was seven, I was consumed by the bittersweet hilarity of Nancy Mitford's fictional works. When I discovered that the fictional worlds she created were actually referencing her own life, I was completely captivated. I knew that was what I wanted to do: make my life fictional and my fiction alive. As I travelled the world as a professional gambler, my only outlet was writing. Then, when my first book was published by Headline UK, I folded on my last poker hand and focused on the writing.

"My life experiences and my children inform and influence all my work. Wherever I am in the world, I wake up, sit at my laptop with four double espressos and sit at my laptop and write. My family wanders in and out as I work and I carry on conversations. Around ten or twelve of an evening I like to go out, mostly to private members clubs where I meet with friends. I am usually in bed with an improving book by three or four in the morning. I don't sleep more than five hours in a twenty-four-hour period. When I was a gambler I seemed to need to sleep all the time.

"The most surprising thing I have learned as a writer is that it is almost possible to live in a parallel world while writing a book—without completely losing your mind. It also surprises me that other people are interested in what is, essentially, a very solitary and lonely art. I do like my 'Calypso Chronicle' series, which are a genuflection to my three children as well as my own childhood. But am also madly fond of *Sex with the Ex* because the story is based on the most painful time of my own life and yet it makes me laugh whenever I read it.

"All my books deal with the darkest, most awful, most embarrassing aspects of my own life, but somehow when I write them down, they come out as comedy, which I suppose is a bit worrying. It's rather cathartic to find yourself laughing at someone else's embarrassing shambolic life and I hope that's what my writing offers to the reader."

BIOGRAPHICAL AND CRITICAL SOURCES:

PERIODICALS

Booklist, August, 2004, Kristine Huntley, review of *The Sex Was Great But . . . ,* p. 1910; September 1, 2005, Cindy Welch, review of *Stealing Princes,* p. 112.

Girls' Life, February-March, 2005, review of *Pulling Princes,* p. 40.

Kirkus Reviews, October 15, 2004, review of *Pulling Princes,* p. 1012; September 1, 2005, review of *Sex with the Ex,* p. 938.

Kliatt, November, 2004, Claire Rosser, review of *Pulling Princes,* p. 11.

Publishers Weekly, October 4, 2004, review of *Pulling Princes,* p. 88; June 6, 2005, review of *Stealing Princes,* p. 67.

School Library Journal, December, 2004, Angela J. Reynolds, review of *Pulling Princes,* p. 152.

USA Today, January 12, 2005, review of *Sex with the Ex.*

ONLINE

Calypso Chronicles Web site, http://www.calypso chronicles.com/ (November 15, 2005).

Tyne O'Connell Home Page, http://www.tyneoconnell. com (November 15, 2005).

*   *   *

ORIZET, Jean 1937-

PERSONAL: Born March 5, 1937, in Saint-Henry, France; married Isabelle Constantin (an administrator), June 22, 1968; children: Juliette, Anne. *Education:* Attended universities and colleges in United States; Madrid, Spain; Paris, France; and Geneva, Switzerland.

ADDRESSES: Office—Le Cherche Midi, 23, rue du Cherche-Midi, 75006 Paris, France. *E-mail*—jorizet@ cherche-midi.com.

CAREER: Poet, publisher, and vintner. *Poésie 1* (quarterly), Paris, France, founding editor, 1960s; Cherche Midi (publishing firm), Paris, founding director, 1960s; international representative for various arts groups, including Alliance Française. Pernod Ricard (wine and spirits firm), Paris, attaché, 1963. Worked in family vineyard and winery, 1960s; worked variously as a gas station attendant, warehouseman, and for wine merchants. Taught at French military academy, Paris. *Military service:* Served in French military; became second lieutenant;

MEMBER: Académie Mallarmé, French PEN, European Academy of Poetry (founding member, 1996), Association of the Friends of Alain Bosquet (founding member, 1998).

AWARDS, HONORS: Charles Vildrac prize, 1972, for *Silencieuse entrave au temps;* Max Jacob prize, 1975, for *En soi le chaos: poésie 1960-1974;.* Apollinaire prize, 1982, for *Le voyageur absent;* Grand Prix de poésie, Académie Français, 1990, for *Poems;* Gustave Gasser prize, 1995; named chevalier, French Legion of Honor, 1995.

WRITINGS:

POEMS

Errance, Éditions de la Grisière, 1962, reprinted Melis editions (Nice, France), 2001

L'horloge de vie, Gard, G. Chambelland (La Bastide-d'Orniol, France), 1966.

Miroir oblique, Librairie Saint-Germain-des-Prés (Paris, France), 1969.

Silencieuse entrave au temps, illustrated by Max Papart, Librairie Saint-Germain-des-Prés (Paris, France), 1972.

Les grandes baleines bleues, Librairie Saint-Germain-des-Prés (Paris, France), 1973.

Adventuriers, RMQS (Méry/Oise, France), 1974.

En soi le chaos: poésie 1960-1974, Éditions Saint-Germain-des-Prés (Paris, France), 1975.

Solaire apocalypse; Homme année zéro, Éditions de la Grisière (Mâcon, France), 1975.

Niveaux de survie, P. Belfond (Paris, France), 1978.

Poèmes cueillis dans la prairie, Éditions Saint-Germain-des-Prés (Paris, France), 1978.

Le voyageur absent, B. Grasset (Paris, France), 1982.

Poèmes, 1974-1989, Cherche Midi (Paris, France), 1990.

L'homme et ses masques: Man and His Masks (bilingual collection), translations by Pat Boran, Dedalus (Dublin, Ireland), 1998.

La cendre et l'étoile, poèmes, 1978-2004, Cherche Midi (Paris, France), 2005.

EDITOR

Cent poètes pour jeunes d'aujourd'hui (anthology; French poetry), Cherche Midi (Paris, France), 1980.

L'humour des poètes (anthology), Cherche Midi (Paris, France), 1981.

Les plus beaux poèmes pour les enfants (anthology; poetry for children), Éditions Saint-Germain-des-Prés, (Paris, France), 1982.

(With others) *La nouvelle poésie française* (anthology; poems from *Poésie 1,* number 107), Librairie A. Colin (Paris, France), 1983.

Tiers of Survival: Selected Poems (French and English), translations by Aletha Reed DeWees, Mundus Artium Press (Dallas, TX), 1984.

Gérard Schneider, *Schneider: peintures* (art collection), L'Autre Musée/La Différence (Paris, France), 1984.

(With Louis Orizet) *Les cent plus beaux textes sur le vin,* (essays), Cherche Midi (Paris, France) 1984.

(With others) *La poésie comique, des origines à nos jours,* (anthology), 1986.

(With others) *La nouvelle poésie française,* (anthology), Poésie 1 (Paris, France), 1987.

Les cent plus beaux poèmes de la langue française (anthology), Cherche Midi (Paris, France), 1987.

(With others) *Anthologie de la poésie française: les poètes et les œuvres, les mouvements et les écoles,* Larousse (Paris, France), 1988, revised edition, 1998.

Jules Renard, *Les pensées* (poetry), Cherche Midi (Paris, France), 1990.

Françoise Lison-Leroy, *Pays géomètre,* L'Age d'homme (Lausanne, Switzerland), 1991.

La bibliothèque de poésie France Loisirs, sixteen volumes, France Loisirs (Paris, France), 1992.

(With Marcel Jullian) *L'amour de François Villon à Frédérick Tristan: l'information poétique,* Cherche Midi (Paris, France), 1995.

Une anthologie de la poésie amoureuse en France: Xlle-XXe siècle, Bartillat (Etrepilly, France), 1997.

Les poètes et le rire (anthology), Cherche Midi (Paris, France), 1998.

Les plus beaux sonnets de la langue française, Cherche Midi (Paris, France), 1999.

Les aventures du regard (literary criticism; French poetry), J.P. Huguet (Loire, France), 1999.

Alphonse Allais, *Pensées, textes et anecdotes,* 2000.

Jean Joubert (literary criticism), Autres Temps (Marseille, France), 2000.

(With Marcel Jullian) *Dossier: poésie et dandysme* (anthology), Cherche Midi (Paris, France), 2001.

Lettre à Claude Erignac: l'ami assassiné, Cherche Midi (Paris, France), 2003.

L'entretemps, brèves histories de l'art, Table Ronde (Paris, France), 2005.

OTHER

(With others) *Blaise Cendrars* (literary criticism), Poésie (Paris, France), 1981.

Dits d'un monde en miettes, Éditions Saint-Germain-des-Prés (Paris, France), 1982.

Histoire de l'entretemps: la rame d'Ulysse, Table Ronde (Paris, France), 1985.

La peau du monde, P. Belfond (Paris, France), 1987.

L'épaule du cavalier: histoire de l'entretemps (novel), Cherche Midi (Paris, France), 1991.

Hommes continuels, Belfond (Paris, France), 1994.

Le miroir de Méduse (fiction), Cherche Midi (Paris, France), 1994.

La poussière d'Adam: histoire de l'entretemps (fiction) Cherche Midi (Paris, France), 1997.

La vie autrement: à l'ombre douce du temps, Cherche Midi (Paris, France), 1999.

Jean Orizet, Autres temps (Marseille, France), 1999.

L'homme fragile, Castor Astral (Bordeaux, France), 2002.

Jean-Marc Brunet, Fragments Editions (Paris, France), 2003.

SIDELIGHTS: Jean Orizet has been a prominent figure in French poetry since the 1960s, when he founded the publishing house Cherche Midi and cofounded the quarterly *Poésie 1.* In addition to his many volumes of poetry and prose, Orizet, through Cherche Midi, has also published the work of other poets.

Orizet was born in a small village near Marseille, where his mother was a mathematics professor and his father a vintner. Orizet enjoyed growing grapes and creating wines, and he worked in the family business during the 1960s. The young Orizet began writing at an early age, and he visited the United States through a grant at the age of fifteen. He continued his education in Spain and Switzerland, and he soon became an internationalist who represented France not in public office but as an ambassador of the arts with cultural groups. His friends included the great French poets of the period and, through his work abroad, the poets of many other countries as well. His travels took him throughout Europe, Asia, Africa, South America, and the United States.

Nicholas Catanoy, in a review of *Niveaux de survie* for *World Literature Today,* commented that the poems in the collection honor the pretechnology era and the delicacy of nature. Catanoy noted the poems' "elegant line and clear sound" and added, "Some of the poems are, by turns, roughly realistic. Yet there is an Orizet touch, a world of self-disciplined candor that binds the words in a magnificent tempo."

Le voyageur absent is a collection of prose poems in which Orizet chronicles his travels and describes his various modes of transportation, from a Rolls Royce to a rickshaw. Adelaide M. Russo noted in *French Review* that "the scenes he transcribes, having all passed through the prism of Orizet's sensibility, share its equal measures of irony, ethical concern, and a sense of history perceived in terms of the political realities of our times and the cultural heritage of the past." Catanoy observed that the most distinctive characteristic of Orizet's work "is not so much its originality as its mixture of openness and cleverness, even the way it sometimes stumbles over its own reality."

L'homme et ses masques: Man and His Masks is a collection of translated poems from five collections that were published from 1978 through 1989. "His themes remain the same throughout," remarked a *Kirkus Reviews* contributor, listing them as "the confrontation with emptiness, the persistence of memory, the triumph of irrationality." Mechthild Cranston wrote in *World Literature Today* that "though often cataclysmic, Orizet's world is not without hope. However, he puts his faith not in the technocrats who crack computer codes, but in the poets who attempt to decipher in the nucleus from which we have scattered like atoms of clay the name and the message of plausible new geneses."

Orizet told *CA:* "After reading hundreds of books as a young boy, I began to feel the urge of writing poetry when I was twelve. I felt it as necessary as breathing and eating. It has not stopped ever since. Nerval, Rimbaud, Verlaine, Mallarme, Michaux, Borges, Burzetti, Hemingway were some of my first heroes in writing. To describe a writing process is practically impossible, in my view!

"As a writer, and above all, as a poet, I have discovered how the words put together in a certain way could produce a magic emotion and some sort of a mysterious power on human mind and human sensibility. Among the books I wrote, I am particularly attached to *Lettre à Claude Erignac: l'ami assassiné.* He was like a brother to me, and I will never recover from his assassination by Corsican nationalists in Ajac'cio. I wrote this letter book to keep on being with him beyond death and sorrow.

"If only one or two of my poems could survive me and bring a small spark of joy, hope or pleasure to a few readers, my existence as a poet would be justified. I like very much these lines of Jorge Luis Borges: 'Why do you write? I write for myself, for a few friends, and to soften the course of time.' This is the way I feel myself."

BIOGRAPHICAL AND CRITICAL SOURCES:

PERIODICALS

French Review, October, 1983, Adelaide M. Russo, review of *Le voyageur absent,* pp. 139-140.

Kirkus Reviews, November 15, 1999, review of *L'homme et ses masques: Man and His Masks,* p. 1775.

World Literature Today, autumn, 1979, Nicholas Catanoy, review of *Niveaux de survie* p. 646; spring, 1983, Nicholas Catanoy, review of *Le voyageur absent,* pp. 250-251; spring, 2000, Mechthild Cranston, review of *L'homme et ses masques,* p. 393.

ONLINE

Cherche Midi Web site, http://cherche-midi.com/ (September 23, 2005), profile of Jean Orizet.

Cordite Poetry Review Online, http://www.cordite.org.au/ (September 23, 2005), "James Stuart Interviews Jean Orizet."

* * *

OZ, Mehmet C. 1960-
(Mehmet Cengiz Oz)

PERSONAL: Born June 11, 1960, in Cleveland, OH; son of Mustafa and Suna (Atabay) Oz; married; wife's name Lisa; children: four. *Education:* Harvard University, B.A., 1982; University of Pennsylvania, M.D., M.B.A., 1986.

ADDRESSES: Office—New York-Presbyterian Hospital/Columbia, Milstein Hospital Bldg., Room 7 GN 435, 177 Fort Washington Ave., New York, NY 10032.

CAREER: Cardiac surgeon and writer. Columbia-Presbyterian Medical Center, New York, NY, chief resident of general surgery, 1990-91, cardiothoracic surgery resident, 1991-93; Columbia University Medical Center, New York, NY, attending surgeon, 1993—, Cardiovascular Institute director, 2001—, vice chairman of cardiovascular services, 2001—; Columbia University College of Physicians & Surgeons, New York, NY, professor of surgery, 2001—.

MEMBER: American Association of Thoracic Surgeons, American College of Surgeons, American College of Cardiology, American College of Cardiology, American Society for Artificial Internal Organs, Association for Academic Surgery, International Society for Heart & Lung Transplantation, Turkish-American Physicians Association, American Heart Association, 21st Century Cardiac Surgical Society, Association of Turkish American Scientists, International Society for Optical Engineering, American Society for Laser Medicine and Surgery, American College of Angiology.

AWARDS, HONORS: Blakemore Research Prize, Columbia University College of Physicians & Surgeons, 1988-91; research award, American Society of Laser Medicine and Surgery, 1991; named Turkish-American of the Year, Assembly of Turkish-American

Associations, 1996; named Global Leader of Tomorrow, World Economic Forum, 1999; Books for a Better America Award, 1999, for *Healing from the Heart.*

WRITINGS:

(With Ron Arias and wife, Lisa Oz) *Healing from the Heart: A Leading Heart Surgeon Explores the Power of Complementary Medicine,* Dutton (New York, NY), 1998.
(Editor, with Daniel J. Goldstein) *Minimally Invasive Cardiac Surgery,* Humana Press (Totowa, NJ), 1999, 2nd edition, 2004.
(Editor, with Daniel J. Goldstein) *Cardiac Assist Devices,* Futura Publishing (Armonk, NY), 2000.
(Editor, with Richard A. Stein) *Complementary and Alternative Cardiovascular Medicine,* Humana Press (Totowa, NJ), 2004.
(With Michael F. Roizen) *You—The Owner's Manual: An Insider's Guide to the Body That Will Make You Healthier and Younger,* HarperCollins (New York, NY), 2005.

Contributor of over 350 articles to numerous professional journals and periodicals, including the *New England Journal of Medicine, Journal of the American Medical Association, Newsweek, Time,* and *O.*

SIDELIGHTS: Mehmet C. Oz has worked as a cardiac surgeon for a number of years; he has held the positions of professor of surgery for the Columbia University College of Physicians & Surgeons, director of the Cardiovascular Institute at Columbia University Medical Center, and attending surgeon at New York-Presbyterian Hospital. His clinical specialties include minimally invasive heart surgery and adult cardiac transplant, while his research interests include complementary medicine and heart replacement. Oz is also a prolific writer, publishing more than 350 articles and serving as a regular contributor to a number of professional and general-interest periodicals. He frequently speaks on health-related topics with network news programs and other media, and is an active member of several professional organizations.

Oz is also the author, coauthor, and editor of several books related to medicine and overall personal health. His first book, 1998's *Healing from the Heart: A Leading Heart Surgeon Explores the Power of Complemen-*

tary Medicine, was cowritten with Ron Arias and Oz's wife, Lisa Oz; the book discusses the benefits of combining traditional and alternative forms of medicine in order to better serve patients. Oz also coedited two cardiac-related titles, *Minimally Invasive Cardiac Surgery* and *Cardiac Assist Devices,* the latter with Daniel J. Goldstein. The author's work has been popular with a large mainstream audience. Oz's writing is "reader-friendly and amusing," wrote *Library Journal* contributor Barbara M. Bibel.

In 2005, Oz published the popular work *You—The Owner's Manual: An Insider's Guide to the Body That Will Make You Healthier and Younger* with coauthor and fellow physician Michael F. Roizen. Their book begins with a quiz that helps readers determine how much they actually know about the human body and how it works. Following chapters focus on specific body parts and systems, including the heart, brain, digestive system, and reproductive system. Helpful information, such as healthy habits and related diseases, augment each section. The book's tone is humorous, with colorful illustrations and cartoon figures accompanying the text. Also included is a food plan with recipes and an exercise plan outline.

Overall, reviewers and readers lauded the authors' work on *You—The Owner's Manual.* Many found the book's refreshing approach to medicine through humor to be an asset to the work. "This lighthearted book will be most useful to those who like their health lessons served with a side of humor," wrote a *Publishers Weekly* contributor. Other readers enjoyed the usefulness of the book's information and the down-to-earth language used throughout. *You—The Owner's Manual* is a "user-friendly medical guide that's not only crammed with practical advice, but also fun to read," observed a critic for the *Saturday Evening Post.*

BIOGRAPHICAL AND CRITICAL SOURCES:

PERIODICALS

America's Intelligence Wire, June 12, 2005, "Doctors Mehmet Oz, Michael Roizen Give Tips on Living Healthy."

Esquire, May, 2005, review of *You—The Owner's Manual: An Insider's Guide to the Body That Will Make You Healthier and Younger,* p. 77; June, 2005, Mehmet C. Oz, "Ask Dr. Oz," p. 80.

Library Journal, June 15, 2005, Barbara M. Bibel, review of *You—The Owner's Manual,* p. 92.

Publishers Weekly, April 11, 2005, review of *You—The Owner's Manual,* p. 47; August 1, 2005, Steven Zeitchik, "Them: The Shopping-It-Around Manual?," p. 10.

Saturday Evening Post, July-August, 2005, review of *You—The Owner's Manual,* p. 72.

Turkish Times, May, 2003, Erin M. Rada, "Dr. Mehmet Oz, Heart Surgeon with a Big Heart."

ONLINE

Columbia University Department of Surgery Web site, http://www.cumc.columbia.edu/ (September 27, 2005), professional information about Mehmet C. Oz.

*   *   *

OZ, Mehmet Cengiz
    See OZ, Mehmet C.

P

PA Chin
   See BA Jin

       *   *   *

PALMER, Michael A.

PERSONAL: Married; children: two. *Education:* Temple University, Ph.D, 1981.

ADDRESSES: Home—Greenville, NC. *Office*—Department of History Program in Maritime Studies, Brewster A-315, East Carolina University, Greenville, NC 27858. *E-mail*—palmerm@mail.ecu.edu.

CAREER: Naval Historical Center, Washington, DC, assistant editor, 1983-86, assistant head of contemporary history, 1986—; East Carolina University, Greenville, NC, professor of history, 1991—, chair of department, 1999—. *Military service:* U.S. Navy, Office of the Chief of Naval Operations, worked in Strategic Concepts Group.

AWARDS, HONORS: Meritorious Civilian Service medal, U.S. Department of the Navy, 1991; Samuel Eliot Morison Award for naval literature, and Book of the Year Award, American Revolutionary War Round Table of New York, both for *Stoddert's War: Naval Operations during the Quasi-War with France, 1798-1801;* Moncado Prize, Society for Military History.

WRITINGS:

Stoddert's War: Naval Operations during the Quasi-War with France, 1798-1801, University of South Carolina Press (Columbia, SC), 1987, with new introduction, Naval Institute Press (Annapolis, MD), 2000.

Origins of Maritime Strategy: American Naval Strategy in the First Postwar Decade, Naval Historical Center (Washington, DC), 1988, 2nd edition published as *Origins of the Martime Strategy: The Development of American Naval Strategy, 1945-1955,* Naval Institute Press (Annapolis, MD), 1990.

Arctic Strike!: A Visual Novel of the War of Tomorrow, Avon Books (New York, NY), 1991.

Guardians of the Gulf: A History of America's Expanding Role in the Persian Gulf, 1833-1992, Free Press (New York, NY), 1992.

On Course to Desert Storm: The United States Navy and the Persian Gulf, Naval Historical Center (Washington, DC), 1992.

The War That Never Was, Vandamere Press (Arlington, VA), 1994.

Lee Moves North: Robert E. Lee on the Offensive, John Wiley (New York, NY), 1998.

Command at Sea: Naval Command and Control since the Sixteenth Century, Harvard University Press (Cambridge, MA), 2005.

Also author of novel *An American Eagle.* Assistant editor, "Naval War of 1812: A Documentary History" series, Naval Historical Center, 1983-86. Contributor to periodicals, including *American Neptune, Mariner's Mirror, Armed Forces Journal International, American Historical Review,* and *International Journal of Middle East Studies.*

SIDELIGHTS: Michael A. Palmer is a military historian who has written on subjects ranging from the

U.S. Civil War to the Gulf War. His particular areas of expertise are maritime history and military power at sea. Palmer's knowledge is evident in his history *Command at Sea: Naval Command and Control since the Sixteenth Century*. In this study, Palmer points out the changes in shipbuilding and firepower that made military power at sea not only possible, but vital for the defense of any nation. He studies the challenges of leading a fleet into battle, and suggests that the philosophy of naval command has swung back and forth between allowing operatives independence and insisting on a more-centralized authority. The author also takes a look at the way key battles in history might have played out with a few changes in strategy. According to *Booklist* reviewer Frieda Murray, Palmer "unabashedly propounds looser command structure." A *Publishers Weekly* reviewer called *Command at Sea* "dense and demanding," adding that it "requires some background in naval history but will be a feast for qualified readers."

BIOGRAPHICAL AND CRITICAL SOURCES:

PERIODICALS

Booklist, March 15, 2005, Frieda Murray, review of *Command at Sea: Naval Command and Control since the Sixteenth Century*, p. 1250.
Publishers Weekly, January 17, 2005, review of *Command at Sea*, p. 45.

ONLINE

East Carolina University Web site, http://www.ecu.edu/ (October 20, 2005), biographical information about Michael A. Palmer.*

*   *   *

PANKHURST, Estelle Sylvia
See PANKHURST, Sylvia

*   *   *

PANKHURST, Sylvia 1882-1960
(Estelle Sylvia Pankhurst)

PERSONAL: Born May 5, 1882, in Manchester, England; died September 27, 1960, in Addis Ababa, Ethiopia; daughter of Richard Marsden (an attorney) and Emmeline Pankhurst (a suffragist); common-law wife of Silvio Ersmus Corio; children: Richard Pankhurst. *Education:* Attended art school in Vienna, Austria, and at Royal College of Art.

CAREER: Political activist and author. Founder of East London Federation of Suffragettes; founder, *Women's Dreadnought* (socialist journal; renamed *Worker's Dreadnought*, 1917); cofounder, with Charlotte Despard, Women's Peace Army; founder, *New Times and Ethiopian News;* editor, *Ethiopian Observer.*

AWARDS, HONORS: Decoration of the Queen of Sheba.

WRITINGS:

The Suffragette: The History of the Women's Militant Suffrage Movement, 1905-10, Sturgis & Walton (New York, NY), 1911.
Housing and the Worker's Revolution: Housing in Capitalist Britain and Bolshevik Russia, Workers' Socialist Federation (London, England), 1917.
Lloyd George Takes the Mask Off, Workers' Socialist Federation (London, England), 1920.
Rebel Ireland: Thoughts on Easter Week, 1916. Workers' Socialist Federation (London, England), c. 1920.
Soviet Russia as I Saw It, Workers' Dreadnought (London, England), 1921.
Writ on Cold Slate, Workers' Dreadnought (London, England), 1922.
Education of the Masses, Dreadnought (London, England), 1924.
India and the Earthly Paradise, Sunshine Publishing House (Bombay, India), 1926.
Delphos: The Future of International Language, Dutton (New York, NY), 1927.
Save the Mothers: A Plea for Measures to Prevent the Annual Loss of about 3,000 Child-Bearing Mothers and 20,000 Infant Lives in England and Wales, and a Similar Grievous Wastage in Other Countries, Knopf (London, England), 1930.
The Suffragette Movement: An Intimate Account of Persons and Ideals (autobiography), Longmans (New York, NY), 1931.
The Home Front: A Mirror to Life in England during the World War, Hutchinson (London, England), 1932.

The Life of Emmeline Pankhurst: The Suffragette Struggle for Women's Citizenship, T.W. Laurie (London, England), 1935, Houghton Mifflin (Boston, MA), 1936.

British Policy in Eastern Ethiopia, the Ogaden, and the Reserved Area, privately printed (Woodford Green, Essex, England), 1946.

British Policy in Eritrea and Northern Ethiopia, privately printed (Woodford Green, Essex, England), 1946.

The Ethiopian People: Their Rights and Progress, New Times & Ethiopian News Book Department (Woodford Green, Essex, England), 1946.

Eritrea on the Eve: The Past and Future of Italy's "First-Born" Colony, Ethiopia's Ancient Sea Province, New Times and Ethiopian News Book Department (Woodford Green, Essex, England), 1951.

(With Richard Pankhurst) *Ethiopia and Eritrea: The Last Phase of the Reunion Struggle, 1941-52,* Lalibela House (Woodford Green, Essex, England), 1953.

Ethiopia: A Cultural History, Lalibela House (Woodford Green, Essex, England), 1955.

Also author of *The Truth about the Oil War,* Dreadnought (London, England), and *A Sylvia Pankhurst Reader,* edited by Kathryn Dodd, Manchester University Press (Manchester, England).

ADAPTATIONS: Shoulder to Shoulder, a television play, was adapted from Pankhurst's life and writings, 1974.

SIDELIGHTS: Sylvia Pankhurst, along with her mother, Emmeline Pankhurst, and older sister, Christabel Pankhurst, was a prominent suffragist in England during the early 1900s. Unlike her mother and sister, however, she was a more fervent supporter of the lower classes, a pacifist who opposed England's entry into World War I, and a supporter of the Russian Revolution and independence for Ethiopia (then called Abyssinia). She was also a talented artist who studied painting in Venice and London. Although Christabel and Emmeline Pankhurst became more prominent in the women's suffrage movement, it was Sylvia Pankhurst who first led them to more radical means of drawing attention to their cause.

After her father's death in 1898, Pankhurst was asked by the Independent Labour Party (ILP) to help decorate its hall in his memory. However, when the newly decorated hall was opened to the public, neither she nor her mother—nor any woman—was allowed to enter. This outrage led Sylvia to radical actions that were soon emulated by her sister and mother. Her pro-suffrage activities got her imprisoned for the first of several times in 1906. However, she soon began to split with Christabel and Emmeline on several points. Unlike them, Pankhurst remained a member of the ILP, and she also believed that social and political equality must run hand in hand with the women's suffrage issue. Christabel and her mother, in contrast, abandoned the ILP to form the Women's Social and Political Union (WSPU) and focused solely on voting rights, which they believed would, when obtained, lead to other social improvements in England.

In 1914 Sylvia broke with the WSPU and concentrated her energies on the working-class East London Federation. She established a newspaper, the *Women's Dreadnought,* which was renamed the *Worker's Dreadnought* in 1917; this reflected her decreased support for feminism and her increased socialist sympathies. With the outbreak of war in 1914 the WSPU ceased its militancy and directed all of its energies toward supporting the war cause. The union's open support of the war widened the gulf between Sylvia and her sister and mother. Christabel's *The Suffragette* became the pro-war *Britannia;* Sylvia, on the other hand, cofounded the Women's Peace Army with Charlotte Despard and attended the International Congress of Women for Peace at the Hague. In 1917 she welcomed the Bolshevik revolution, and at the end of the war she visited Russia. She also joined the British Communist Party, but eventually her demands for freedom of expression resulted in her expulsion.

At the end of the war Pankhurst became involved with left-wing exile Silvio Erasmus Corio, with whom she had a child in 1927. She never married Corio, nor did her son, Richard, take Corio's surname. The birth of this child out of wedlock further strained the relationship between mother and daughter, as did her mother's decision to become a conservative candidate for Parliament in the general election of 1929. Pankhurst became even more left wing over time. She opposed fascism and, in protest over Italy's invasion of Ethiopia, founded the *New Times & Ethiopia News,* which she edited for twenty years. She also wrote a number of books on Ethiopia and moved there in 1956, where she helped to establish a Social Service Society and edited the *Ethiopia Observer.* For her services to

Ethiopia, she received the decoration of the Queen of Sheba and died in Addis Ababa on September 27, 1960.

BIOGRAPHICAL AND CRITICAL SOURCES:

BOOKS

Castle, Barbara, *Sylvia and Christabel Pankhurst,* Penguin (Harmondsworth, England), 1987.

Mitchell, David, *The Fighting Pankhursts: A Study in Tenacity,* J. Cape (London, England), 1967.

Noble, Iris, *Emmeline and Her Daughters: The Pankhurst Suffragettes,* Messner (New York, NY), 1971.

Pankhurst, Richard, *Sylvia Pankhurst, Artist and Crusader: An Intimate Portrait,* Paddington Press (New York, NY), 1979.

Romero, Patricia, *E. Sylvia Pankhurst: Portrait of a Radical,* Yale University Press (New Haven, CT), 1987.*

*   *   *

PARISI, Barbara 1954-

PERSONAL: Born March 31, 1954, in New York, NY; daughter of William and Gloria (Simon) Parisi; married Michael Pasternack. *Ethnicity:* "White." *Education:* New York University, Ph.D., 1991.

ADDRESSES: Agent—c/o Author Mail, Scarecrow Press, Inc., 4501 Forbes Blvd., Ste. 200, Lanham, MD 20706. *E-mail*—ryanrep@verizon.net.

CAREER: Writer and educator. Theatrical director and practitioner; college professor.

WRITINGS:

Empowerment through Communication, Kendall-Hunt (Dubuque, IA), 1994.

(With Robert Singer) *The History of Brooklyn's Three Major Performing Arts Institutions,* Scarecrow Press (Lanham, MD), 2003.

WORK IN PROGRESS: Rewriting *Empowerment through Communication.*

*   *   *

PARKHURST, Carolyn 1971-

PERSONAL: Born 1971; married; children: one son. *Education:* American University, M.F.A. (creative writing). *Hobbies and other interests:* Collecting masks, traveling, cooking.

ADDRESSES: Home—Washington, DC. *Agent*—c/o Author Mail, Warner Books, Inc., 1271 Avenue of the Americas, New York, NY 10020.

CAREER: Writer. National Endowment for the Arts, summer internship.

WRITINGS:

The Dogs of Babel (novel), Little, Brown (Boston, MA), 2003.

ADAPTATIONS: The Dogs of Babel was adapted as an audiobook read by Erik Singer, Time Warner Audio-Books, 2003.

WORK IN PROGRESS: A second novel, short stories.

SIDELIGHTS: American writer Carolyn Parkhurst has won acclaim for her first novel, *The Dogs of Babel,* in which grieving widower and linguistics professor Paul Iverson attempts to teach his dog, Lorelei, to talk in hopes of learning whether his wife, Lexy's, death, in a fall from a backyard apple tree, was accident or suicide. As Paul researches the possibility that dogs can acquire language and attempts to teach Lorelei to use a typewriter, he mourns Lexy and recalls the tenderness of their all-too-short romance and marriage. Meeting with little success in getting a word from Lorelei, he finally turns to a gruesome criminal who once conducted facial and palate surgery on dogs to give them an ability to form words. He also meets with the Cerberus Society, which has a similar mission. In the end, he learns that some things should never be done and comes to terms with Lexy's memory.

The mysterious Lexy, a maker of festive papier-mâché masks, lover of the mystical, and childlike in her attraction to Disneyland and puzzles, is based loosely on the author herself, a collector of masks and lover of puzzles. Parkhurst said in an online interview with Matt Borondy for *Identity Theory* that both of her characters' feelings about having children were also inspired by her own feelings; she was pregnant with her son while writing the novel and gave birth to him just after midnight on the day she finished it. "When Paul fantasizes about setting his baby down on a blanket on the grass or pushing her through the neighborhood in a carriage, those images reflect the great excitement I felt about having a child of my own," she told Borondy. "And when Lexy wonders if she's cut out to be a mother, that reflects the kind of fears I had about becoming a parent."

Parkhurst was also inspired by her dog Chelsea, which died while she was writing the book. "I think that the experience of living with such a sweet dog is probably what made me want to write about dogs in the first place," she told Borondy. "He helped me with my research, too. When Paul was doing intelligence tests with Lorelei, I did the same thing with Chelsea, and it gave me some interesting material." Parkhurst also did research on service dogs and on the intelligence they show in sensing when an owner is ill or on the verge of, for example, having a heart attack or an epileptic seizure.

Parkhurst's story received a lot of attention from reviewers for a first novel. A *People* contributor praised the author, saying she "illuminates the emotional landscape that faces a surviving spouse who is trying to decide how much of life is about the past and how much is about the future." A *Kirkus Reviews* contributor, however, found it "a simple love story without the gumption to go in more unsettling directions" and thought the "compelling idea" weakened by "anticlimactic detail." Lev Grossman, in a review for *Time*, deemed it "a neatly, almost perfectly constructed novel," but said it "feels smaller than life" and lacks "raw, sobbing rage."

A *New Yorker* contributor cited the mysticism as overdone and Paul's experiments with Lorelei rushed, resulting in the book's "developing neither verisimilitude nor artful absurdity." A *Publishers Weekly* contributor found the novel's execution flawed and concluded: "Parkhurst is a fluid stylist, and there are memorable moments here, as well as some terrific characters . . . , but one get the sense of an author trying to stuff every notion she's ever had into her first book, with less than splendid results." Beth Kephart, in *Book*, wrote that *The Dogs of Babel* "has love, it has grief, it has mourning, it has forgiveness, but it also has a preponderance of flaws. . . . What rescues this book, from time to time, is the lyrical quality of the prose."

Barbara Hoffert, in *Library Journal*, wrote that "Parkhurst delivers a remarkable debut in quiet, authoritative prose." Viva Hardigg, in *Entertainment Weekly*, observed: "Parkhurst tells her tale with considerable skill. She can slice and dice a character in a couple of well-chosen strokes." However, Hardigg noted that Parkhurst's dialog sometimes gives way to cliché. In conclusion, though, she maintained that the author "packs a serious literary arsenal" in her prose and called *The Dogs of Babel* "a humanistic parable of the heart's confusions."

In an interview for *Barnes & Noble.com*, Parkhurst said she wrote her first story at age three. Some of the authors who have influenced and inspired her are Toni Morrison, Kazuo Ishiguro, Virginia Woolf, Michael Chabon, Robert Olen Butler, Margaret Atwood, and Patrick McGrath.

BIOGRAPHICAL AND CRITICAL SOURCES:

PERIODICALS

Book, January-February, 2003, David Bowman, "The New Virginia Woolf: Carolyn Parkhurst," p. 47; May-June, 2003, Beth Kephart, "Animal Magnetism" (review of *The Dogs of Babel*), p. 74.

Entertainment Weekly, June 13, 2003, Viva Hardigg, "Top of the Pups: A Widower Tries to Teach His Canine to Talk in Carolyn Parkhurst's Moving *The Dogs of Babel*," p. 98.

Kirkus Reviews, April 1, 2003, review of *The Dogs of Babel*, p. 502.

Library Journal, March 15, 2003, Barbara Hoffert, review of *The Dogs of Babel*, p. 116.

New Yorker, June 16, 2003, review of *The Dogs of Babel*, p. 197.

People, June 16, 2003, review of *The Dogs of Babel*, p. 53.

Publishers Weekly, March 17, 2003, review of *The Dogs of Babel,* p. 50.

Time, June 16, 2003, Lev Grossman, "They Called It Puppy Love," p. 68.

ONLINE

Barnes & Noble.com, http://www.barnesandnoble.com/ (October 3, 2003), "Meet the Writers: Carolyn Parkhurst."

Identity Theory, http://www.identitytheory.com/ (May 29, 2003), Matt Borondy, "Interview: Carolyn Parkhurst."*

*   *   *

PARKS, Rosa 1913-2005
(Rosa Louise Lee Parks)

OBITUARY NOTICE— See index for *CA* sketch: Born February 4, 1913, in Tuskegee, AL; died October 24, 2005, in Detroit, MI. Activist and author. Widely hailed as the mother of the African-American anti-segregation movement, Parks became famous in 1955 when her refusal to give up her bus seat to a white man in Montgomery, Alabama, sparked the bus strike and the civil rights movement led by the Reverend Martin Luther King, Jr. Growing up in Tuskegee, Alabama, she developed a finely honed sense of right and wrong even as a little girl. In her 1990 autobiography, *The Autobiography of Rosa Parks,* which was later released as *Rosa Parks: My Story* (1992), she recalled an early incident when a white boy threatened her with racial slurs. The young Parks picked up a brick and dared him to come after her, but he retreated. Alabama in the 1920s was a dangerous place for many blacks, and Parks also recalled how her father kept a gun in the house in case the Ku Klux Klan threatened them. Educated at home by her mother until she was eleven, Parks later attended the Montgomery Industrial School, an institution run by white people for the education of blacks where the staff was also subjected to attacks by racists. When she was of college age, she attended what is now Alabama State University, but she had to leave school before graduating in order to take care of her ailing grandmother and, later, her mother. Parks took on a number of jobs, including domestic servant and aide in a hospital; she also married Raymond Parks, a member of the Nationa Association for the Advancement of Colored People (NAACP) and a man she respected for showing no fear of white people. Living in Montgomery, Parks endured the entrenched racism and segregationist policies of the area for many years. One of the laws there restricted black people to sitting in the back rows of a bus; the front rows were reserved for white people, and even if those seats were empty black people were not allowed to use them. Finally, on December 1, 1955, Parks had had enough. Getting on a bus driven by James Blake, a man with whom she had had an unpleasant encounter years before, she sat in one of the middle rows. When the front rows filled up with white passengers, a white man demanded that she move so he could sit down. When Blake gave her an ultimatum to either move or be arrested, she told him to go ahead and call the police. He did so, and what followed would go down in history. Parks, actually, had not been the first black woman in Montgomery to refuse to such demands; two other women had acted similarly. However, because of her exemplary personal history, Parks was chosen by the local NAACP as a rallying point; at the time, she was secretary of the Montgomery NAACP branch, and a working, married woman who regularly attended church. When Parks's case went to the courts, the city's black population organized a bus strike. Since two-thirds of the bus passengers in Montgomery were black, the city's public transportation system was soon in a financial crisis. Parks helped work on the strike by serving as a dispatcher, organizing ways for blacks with cars to carpool with others. The young Reverend King was selected to lead the strike. By the end of 1956, the U.S. Supreme Court had ruled Alabama's bus law unconstitutional. The bus strike in Montgomery ended, but it soon spread through other cities in the South. White reaction to the protests was violent and often bloody, and Parks and her husband faced repeated threats against their lives. Afraid for the worst, they decided to leave Alabama in 1957 and move to Detroit, Michigan, where some of Parks's relatives lived. In Detroit, Parks continued to work for the movement, and, among other activities, was present at the 1963 march led by King in Washington, DC. In 1975, she was hired by U.S. Representative John Conyers, Jr. to work on his staff, which she did until retiring in 1988. By this time, she had long been recognized as an icon in the civil rights movement. Many honors were bestowed upon her, including a Martin Luther King, Jr. Leadership Award in 1987, the Medal of Freedom in 1996, and the Congressional Gold Medal in 1999. In 2000, a museum and library were dedicated in her name in Montgomery, and the bus where she made her famous stand is now housed at the Henry Ford Museum in Detroit. Parks continued to work on worthy causes until her health began to fail. During the 1990s, she also coauthored several books, including *Quiet Strength: The Faith, the Hope, and the Heart of a Woman Who Changed a Nation* (1994), *Dear Mrs. Parks: A Dialogue with Today's Youth* (1996), and *I Am Rosa Parks* (1997). Among her important causes later in life was the founding of the Rosa and Raymond Parks Institute, which helped young blacks in the areas of education and improving self-esteem. At her death Parks became the first black woman to lie in state at the rotunda of the Lincoln Memorial.

OBITUARIES AND OTHER SOURCES:

BOOKS

Parks, Rosa, and Jim Haskins, *Rosa Parks: My Story,* Dial Books (New York, NY), 1992.
Parks, Rosa, and Gregory J. Reed, *Quiet Strength: The Faith, the Hope, and the Heart of a Woman Who Changed a Nation,* Zondervan (Grand Rapids, MI), 1994.
Parks, Rosa, and Jim Haskins, *I Am Rosa Parks,* Dial Books for Young Readers (New York, NY), 1997.

PERIODICALS

Chicago Tribune, October 25, 2005, section 1, pp. 1, 16.
Los Angeles Times, October 25, 2005, pp. A1, A12-13.
New York Times, October 26, 2005, p. C24.
Times (London, England), October 26, 2005, p. 70.

*　　*　　*

PARKS, Rosa Louise Lee
　　See PARKS, Rosa

*　　*　　*

PARKYN, Neil 1943-

PERSONAL: Born 1943.

ADDRESSES: Agent—c/o Author Mail, Merrell Publishers Limited, 81 Southwark St., London SE1 0HX, England.

CAREER: Architect and journalist.

WRITINGS:

(Editor) *The Seventy Wonders of the Modern World,* Thames & Hudson (New York, NY), 2002.
SuperStructures: The World's Greatest Modern Structures, Merrell (London, England), 2004.

SIDELIGHTS: British author Neil Parkyn works as an architect and a city planner. In 2002, Parkyn edited *The Seventy Wonders of the Modern World,* which highlights structures from around the world, providing information about each structure's dimensions, reason for construction, and history. The structures are arranged by category, and include religious buildings, castles, state buildings, skyscrapers, bridges, canals, and colossal statues. The text for each structure is augmented by a number of photographs and illustrations. Donna Seaman, in a review for *Booklist,* described the book as an "efficiently designed, photo-rich, mind-expanding volume," while *School Library Journal* contributor Judy McAloon called the book a "beautifully executed, well-organized work."

Parkyn is also the author of *SuperStructures: The World's Greatest Modern Structures,* which features fifty-seven important structures from the last one hundred years, including bridges, tunnels, airports, hydroelectric dams, observatories, and sports stadiums.

BIOGRAPHICAL AND CRITICAL SOURCES:

PERIODICALS

Booklist, December 1, 2002, Donna Seaman, review of *The Seventy Wonders of the Modern World,* p. 639.
Geographical, December, 2002, review of *The Seventy Wonders of the Modern World,* p. 69.
Library Journal, October 15, 2002, Russell T. Clement, review of *The Seventy Wonders of the Modern World,* p. 70; March 1, 2005, David R. Conn, review of *SuperStructures: The World's Greatest Modern Structures,* p. 83.
School Library Journal, May, 2003, Judy McAloon, review of *The Seventy Wonders of the Modern World,* p. 181.
Science News, December 21, 2002, review of *The Seventy Wonders of the Modern World,* p. 401.*

PEARCE, David W. 1941-2005
(David William Pearce)

OBITUARY NOTICE— See index for *CA* sketch: Born October 11, 1941, in Harrow, England; died September 8, 2005. Economist, educator, and author. Pearce was a retired University College London professor who specialized in the study of environmental economics in which the establishment of environmental protections are weighed against their economic costs. His educational background included a B.A. and M.A. from Lincoln College, Oxford, in 1963 and 1967, followed by a Ph.D. from the University of East Anglia. During the mid-1960s, Pearce taught at the University of Lancaster, Bailrigg. He subsequently was on the faculty of the University of Southampton and the University of Leicester, and at the latter was director of the Public Sector Economics Research Centre from 1974 to 1977. That year, he moved on to the University of Aberdeen, where he was professor of political economy and, from 1981 to 1983, head of his department. Pearce's longest academic association with University College London began in 1983. Here, he headed the department of economics from 1984 to 1988 and was director of the London Environmental Economics Centre from 1988 to 1990, and associate director the next two years. He also became director of the school's Centre for Social and Economic Research on the Global Environment in 1991, and retired as a professor emeritus in 2004. As an economist, Pearce was renowned for spearheading the discipline of environmental economics. His scientific, sensible approach to the controversial issue of the importance of a clean environment versus the economic costs swayed government policy in the United Kingdom. Pearce created highly detailed cost-benefit analyses of environmental protection and proposed ways to balance business and the environment, such as the creation of green taxes and tradable development permits. A prolific author, coauthor, and editor, he published over forty books on economics and the environment, including *Environmental Economics* (1976), *Blueprint for a Green Economy* (1989), *The Social Costs of Energy* (1992), and *Economics and Environment: Essays on Ecological Economics and Sustainable Development* (1998). For his many contributions, he was named to the Order of the British Empire in 2000.

OBITUARIES AND OTHER SOURCES:

PERIODICALS

Times (London, England), November 16, 2005, p. 64.

PEARCE, David William
See PEARCE, David W.

*   *   *

PEARLMAN, Edith 1936-

PERSONAL: Born 1936; married; children: two. *Hobbies and other interests:* Reading, walking, matchmaking.

ADDRESSES: Home—Brookline, MA. *Agent*—c/o Jill Kneerim, Kneerim & Williams, 225 Franklin St., Boston, MA 02110-2804. *E-mail*—info@edith pearlman.com.

CAREER: Writer.

AWARDS, HONORS: Spokane Annual Fiction Prize for *Love among the Greats and Other Stories,*; syndicated fiction awards, 1987, 1991; Drue Heinz Prize for Literature, 1996; *Antioch Review* Distinguished Fiction Award, 1999; Mary McCarthy Prize in Short Fiction, 2003, for *How to Fall: Stories.*

WRITINGS:

FICTION

Vaquita and Other Stories, University of Pittsburgh Press (Pittsburgh, PA), 1996.
Love among the Greats and Other Stories, Eastern Washington University Press (Spokane, WA), 2002.
How to Fall: Stories, Sarabande Books (Louisville, KY), 2005.

Contributor of stories to literary journals, including *Atlantic Monthly, Smithsonian, Preservation, Yankee,* and *New York Times.* Stories have appeared in anthologies, including *Best American Short Stories, O. Henry Prize Collection, Best Short Stories from the South,* and *The Pushcart Prize Collection.*

SIDELIGHTS: Edith Pearlman is an accomplished fiction writer, having published more than 150 stories in a number of literary journals and general-interest magazines. Her work has also appeared in anthologies, including *Best American Short Stories, Best Short Stories from the South,* and *The Pushcart Prize Collection.* She is also a travel writer, and has written about her travels to Budapest, Jerusalem, and Tokyo for the *New York Times* and other national publications. The author noted on her home page that her inspiration comes from the works of such noted authors as A.S. Byatt, Charles Dickens, and Sylvia Townsend Warner.

In 2002, Pearlman published the short-story collection *Love among the Greats and Other Stories,* for which she won the Spokane Annual Fiction Prize. This collection brings together stories revolving around unusual characters and their complicated relationships. In "Toyfolk," a toy manufacturing executive is transferred to a small town in Czechoslovakia, where he befriends some toy collectors who are not who they seem. In "Fidelity," three characters in their sixties become involved in a complicated love triangle, one that lasts for the next twenty years.

Love among the Greats and Other Stories was met with positive reviews. "Pearlman's characters are interesting and real, the writing elegant and concise," wrote *Booklist* contributor Marta Segal Block. Other readers found the author's stories to be, not overly dramatic, but powerful in their simplicity and realism. "She tells wonderfully well-drawn stories about people who live uneventfully, but with great richness and contentment," observed Mary Ann Gwinn in a review for the *Seattle Times.*

In 2005, Pearlman published her third book, *How to Fall: Stories,* for which she won the Mary McCarthy Prize. With this work the author again brings together the tales of a strange cast of characters in one volume, including a public television anchor, a comedian's silent sidekick, and a seventeen-year-old girl. Many of the stories take place in the fictional Boston suburb of Godolphin, a place of monotony and seeming normalcy. "The Large Lady" involves an unattractive woman's fundraising efforts in suburbia; "Rules" follows a stoic mother and her home-schooled daughter volunteering in a soup kitchen; "Home Schooling" tells the story of twin sisters Willy and Harry and their unusual childhood. Reviewers again praised Pearlman for her work in *How to Fall,* especially the author's delicate and clever style of storytelling. "Pearlman's light touch and wry tone give the stories a pleasant buoyancy," wrote a *Publishers Weekly* contributor.

BIOGRAPHICAL AND CRITICAL SOURCES:

PERIODICALS

Booklist, November 15, 1996, Jim O'Laughlin, review of *Vaquita and Other Stories,* p. 572; October 15, 2002, Marta Segal Block, review of *Love among the Greats and Other Stories,* p. 388.
Kirkus Reviews, August 15, 2002, review of *Love among the Greats and Other Stories,* p. 1170.
Publishers Weekly, September 30, 1996, review of *Vaquita and Other Stories,* p. 60; October 28, 2002, review of *Love among the Greats and Other Stories,* p. 49; January 17, 2005, review of *How to Fall: Stories,* p. 34.
Seattle Times, January 30, 2003, Mary Ann Gwinn, review of *Love among the Greats and Other Stories.*

ONLINE

Edith Pearlman Home Page, http://www.edithpearlman.com (September 27, 2005).
Salon.com, http://www.salon.com/ (February 22, 2005), Andrew O'Hehir, review of *How to Fall.*

*   *   *

PEKELIS, Coco
    See DALTON, Coco

*   *   *

PERLMAN, Elliot 1964-

PERSONAL: Born 1964.

ADDRESSES: Agent—c/o Author Mail, Riverhead Books, 375 Hudson St., New York, NY 10014.

CAREER: Writer and lawyer.

AWARDS, HONORS: Best Book of the Year, *Age* newspaper (Melbourne, Victoria, Australia), 1998, and Best Book of the Year, Fellowship of Australian Writers, both for *Three Dollars.*

WRITINGS:

FICTION

Three Dollars, MacMurray & Beck (Denver, CO), 1999.

Seven Types of Ambiguity, Riverhead Books (New York, NY), 2004.

The Reasons I Won't Be Coming (short stories), Riverhead Books (New York, NY), 2005.

(With Robert Connolly) *Three Dollars* (screenplay; based on Perlman's novel), Film Finance (Australia), 2005.

SIDELIGHTS: Before becoming a novelist, Elliot Perlman was a lawyer based in Melbourne, Victoria, Australia. In his first book, *Three Dollars*, Perlman presents readers with narrator Eddie Harnovey, who feels constrained by his conservative, middle-class surroundings. All around him he sees life falling apart, from his depressed wife and sick child to his divorcing friends. Eddie recounts his life story starting with his boyhood. He becomes a chemical engineer working for a government agency when he suddenly loses his job and finds that his total cash-on-hand assets amount to three dollars. His struggle to survive and make sense of both his own situation and the world around him drive the narrative. A *Publishers Weekly* contributor noted the narrator's "self-deprecating wit, caustic social comment, spirited sensitivity and big heart." The reviewer added, "Perlman's sheer storytelling virtuosity gives this essentially domestic tale the narrative drive of a thriller and the unforgettable radiance of a novel that accurately reflects essential human values." Carolyn Kubisz, writing in *Booklist,* remarked that the author "deftly and confidently explores a world that can be harsh and unforgiving but also full of hope." Calling the book "an intelligent and humorous recollection of disaster," *Antipodes* contributor Lars Ahlstrom added, "The story mirrors our time, and asks questions that are relevant today."

Seven Types of Ambiguity features separate narrations by seven characters in the novel, including a prostitute in love with Simon and Simon's psychiatrist. They all tell the story of a love affair gone wrong and its consequences. When Simon is dumped by Anna he cannot let go to the point that ten years later he is still following her life, even though she has married and has a child. When he determines that Anna's son is suffering as a result of Anna's failing marriage, Simon kidnaps the boy, leading to a series of disasters that affect the various narrators' lives. "Constant love in the face of terrible odds—such is the old-fashioned but deeply satisfying theme in a thoroughly modern Australian import," wrote a *Kirkus Reviews* contributor. A *Publishers Weekly* reviewer noted that, "by copping the title of William Empson's classic of literary criticism, . . . Perlman . . . sets a high bar for himself, but he justifies his theft with a relentlessly driven story." Marc Kloszewski, writing in *Library Journal,* commented that "Perlman reaches for the brass ring, and he successfully shapes this heady material into an all too-rare literary page-turner." In a review in *Newsweek,* Malcolm Jones wrote: "Within a chapter or so, you're bound to relax, happy in the knowledge that while this novel has been packaged as an ambitious literary event, it is, far more importantly, a page turner, a psychological thriller that is, in short, dangerous, beguiling fun."

BIOGRAPHICAL AND CRITICAL SOURCES:

PERIODICALS

Antipodes, June, 1999, Lars Ahlstrom, review of *Three Dollars,* p. 48.

Booklist, May 15, 1999, Carolyn Kubisz, review of *Three Dollars,* p. 1670; November 1, 2004, Donna Seaman, review of *Seven Types of Ambiguity,* p. 443.

Entertainment Weekly, December 17, 2004, Jennifer Reese, review of *Seven Types of Ambiguity,* p. 88.

Esquire, February, 2005, Tyler Cabot, review of *Seven Types of Ambiguity,* p. 38.

Kirkus Reviews, September 15, 2004, review of *Seven Types of Ambiguity,* p. 888.

Library Journal, October 15, 2004, Marc Kloszewski, review of *Seven Types of Ambiguity,* p. 55.

Newsweek, December 13, 2004, Malcolm Jones, review of *Seven Types of Ambiguity,* p. 72.

People, January 10, 2005, Kyle Smith, review of *Seven Types of Ambiguity,* p. 45.

Publishers Weekly, May 24, 1999, review of *Three Dollars,* p. 65; October 4, 2004, review of *Seven Types of Ambiguity,* p. 66; December 6, 2004, Karen Holt, "Elliot Perlman: Down Under Hero," p. 40.

Variety, April 25, 2005, Richard Kuipers, review of *Three Dollars* (film), p. 54.

ONLINE

This Swirling Sphere, http://www.thei.aust.com/ (September 16, 2005), brief profile of author.*

*   *   *

PERLMUTTER, Jerome H. 1924-2005
(Jerome Herbert Perlmutter)

OBITUARY NOTICE— See index for *CA* sketch: Born October 17, 1924, in New York, NY; died of complications from a brain tumor, October 6, 2005, in Rockville, MD. Civil servant, communications specialist, editor, and author. Perlmutter enjoyed a long career with various U.S. government agencies, working on their publications and redesigning them and many of the government's official logos. After serving in the U.S. Navy Reserve during World War II, he attended George Washington University, where he completed his B.A. in 1949. This was later followed by an M.A. in 1957 from American University. During the late 1940s and early 1950s, he held several editorial jobs, including production editor for the *NEA Journal,* editor for the *Journal of Health,* and editor-in-chief for publications of the American Association for Health, Physical Education, and Recreation. Perlmutter then began his association with governmental departments. From 1951 to 1962 he was chief editor for the U.S. Department of Agriculture, and from 1962 to 1972 he was chief of publishing and reproduction for the U.S. Department of State. While there, he published his only book, *A Practical Guide to Effective Writing* (1965). His government experience led to his appointment as federal graphics coordinator for the National Endowment for the Arts' Federal Design Improvement Program. It was in this capacity that Perlmutter worked to redesign many of the federal government's logos and publications. In addition to these positions, Perlmutter occasionally taught university-level courses, including at the U.S. Department of Agriculture Graduate School in the 1950s and at the University of Maryland in the 1960s. He also was a language consultant and writer for such organizations as the International Monetary Fund, the World Bank, and the Foreign Service Institute. After retiring from his government post in 1979, he founded Perlmutter Associates, a consulting firm where he was chief executive officer until 1990.

OBITUARIES AND OTHER SOURCES:

PERIODICALS

Washington Post, October 8, 2005, p. B7.

*   *   *

PERLMUTTER, Jerome Herbert
See PERLMUTTER, Jerome H.

*   *   *

PIFER, Alan
See PIFER, Alan J.

*   *   *

PIFER, Alan J. 1921-2005
(Alan Pifer, Alan Jay Parrish Pifer)

OBITUARY NOTICE— See index for *CA* sketch: Born May 4, 1921, in Boston, MA; died of dementia, October 31, 2005, in Shelburne, VT. As president of the Carnegie Corporation from 1967 to 1982, Pifer had a profound impact on federal policies regarding education, poverty, and the arts. After serving as a captain in the U.S. Army in Europe during World War II, he completed his B.A. at Harvard University in 1947. Pifer then attended graduate school at Emmanuel College, Oxford, for a year before taking a job as executive secretary for the U.S. Educational Commission in the United Kingdom. In 1953 he joined the Carnegie Corporation as an executive assistant, rising to the post of vice president in 1963, acting president in 1965, and president in 1967. As the leader of the Carnegie Corporation, Pifer became an influential voice among philanthropic organizations across the country. He urged such groups to take a more active position on government policies, and he himself spearheaded many efforts that influenced federal programs. Among his credits are his work directing the Carnegie Commission on Educational Television, which led to the establishment of the federally funded Public Broadcasting Service. Pifer held strong views on the importance of education, too, especially on the issues of early education, higher education, and racial equality in schools. With Pifer's backing, the Carnegie Commission on Higher Education was established; this group backed legislation and programs for funding higher education through grants, including the Pell Grant. This was in keeping with Pifer's belief that quality higher education should not be denied students who could not otherwise afford college. Pifer also championed other social issues, including women's rights and bilingual education. As chair of the University of Cape Town Fund, Inc., beginning in 1984, he worked toward providing more educational opportunities for black students in South Africa, as well. After stepping down as president of the Carnegie Corporation, he continued his association as a senior consultant, directing, in particular, a program studying the effects of the aging U.S. population. He was also on the board of trustees for the Caribbean Resources Development Foundation and on the board of directors for the Business Council for Effective Literacy, Inc., and the publisher McGraw-Hill, among many other activities. The author of such books as *The Higher Education of Blacks in the United States* (1973) and *Philanthropy in an Age of Transition: The Essays of Alan Pifer* (1984), Pifer will long be remembered for leading a revolution in philanthropic organizations across America.

OBITUARIES AND OTHER SOURCES:

PERIODICALS

Los Angeles Times, November 5, 2005, p. B15.
New York Times, November 5, 2005, p. B14.
Washington Post, November 5, 2005, p. B7.

*   *   *

PIFER, Alan Jay Parrish
See PIFER, Alan J.

*   *   *

PIXLEY, Jocelyn 1947-

PERSONAL: Born 1947. *Education:* University of Sydney, B.A., 1969, Sydney Teachers College, Dip. Ed., 1970; University of New South Wales, Ph.D. (first-class honors), 1988.

ADDRESSES: Office—School of Sociology, University of New South Wales, Sydney NSW 2052, Australia. *E-mail*—j.pixley@unsw.edu.au; Jocelyn.Pixley@hotmail.com.

CAREER: Sociologist, educator, and writer. University of New South Wales, Sydney, New South Wales, Australia, senior lecturer in sociology and school postgraduate coordinator. Member of advisory panel, Australian Survey of Social Attitudes, 2002—.

WRITINGS:

Citizenship and Employment: Investigating Post-Industrial Options, Cambridge University Press (New York, NY), 1993.
(With Michael Bittman) *The Double Life of the Family: Myth, Hope, and Experience,* Allen & Unwin (St. Leonards, New South Wales, Australia), 1997.
Emotions in Finance: Distrust and Uncertainty in Global Markets, Cambridge University Press (New York, NY), 2004.

Contributor to books, including *Society, State and Politics in Australia,* edited by Michael Muetzelfeldt, Pluto Press (Sydney, New South Wales, Australia), 1992; *The Australian Welfare State,* edited by John Wilson and others, Macmillan Education (Melbourne, Victoria, Australia), 1996; *European Citizenship and Social Exclusion,* edited by Maurice Roche and R. van Berkel, Ashgate, 1997; *Australian Way: States, Markets, and Civil Society,* edited by Bettina Cass and Paul Smyth, Cambridge University Press (Melbourne, Victoria, Australia), 1998; *Facing Australian Families,* 3rd edition, edited by W. Weeks and M. Quinn, Addison Wesley Longman (Melbourne, Victoria, Australia), 2000; *Rethinking Australian Citizenship,* edited by Wayne Hudson and John Kane, Cambridge University Press (Melbourne, Victoria, Australia), 2000; *The Politics of Australian Society: Political Issues for the New Century,* edited by P. Boreham, G. Stokes, and R. Hall, Longman/Pearson Education (Melbourne, Victoria, Australia), 2000; *Management and Organization Paradoxes,* edited by Stewart Clegg, John Benjamins (Amsterdam, Netherlands), 2002; and *Australian Social Attitudes: The First Report,* edited by D. Denemark, and others, UNSW Press (Sydney, New South Wales, Australia), 2005. Contributor to journals, including *Australian Financial Review, British Journal of Sociology, Sociological Review, Australian and New Zealand Journal of Sociology,* and *American Journal of Economics and Sociology.* Member of editorial board, *Sociological Perspectives, Journal of the Pacific Sociological Association,* 1996-2000, and *Journal of Sociology,* 2002-05.

SIDELIGHTS: Jocelyn Pixley is an Australian sociologist whose primary interest is economic sociology, including the theoretical and substantive research on money and global finance, emotions and organizations, and social policy and economic citizenship. In her book *Citizenship and Employment: Investigating Post-Industrial Options* Pixley deals with the phenomenon of mass unemployment that began in the 1990s and its effect on citizenship and democratic societies. She discusses the "post-industrialist" viewpoint that the unemployment trends are irreversible and lays out her reasoning for why she believes they are wrong. Writing in the *American Political Science Review,* Carole Pateman noted, "One of Pixley's main criticisms of the post-industrialists is that they neglect the role of the state. Their policies can be, and invariably are, turned in other directions by state intervention that is required to implement them." Pateman added that the author "makes some telling points against the post-industrialists."

In *The Double Life of the Family: Myth, Hope, and Experience* Pixley turns her attention to society's expected view of the normal family life and what it entails versus the reality. "The central objective of the book is to demonstrate that families lead a double life," wrote Sotirios Sarantakos in the *Journal of Intercultural Studies.* In the book's nine chapters, Pixley discusses topics such as the myth of the nuclear family, the high likelihood of domestic violence in the home, actual life in the home and the division of household duties, the reality of inequalities in the home, and the relationship between the family and the state. Sarantakos called the effort "a well written, well argued and . . . very informative book, which is also accessible to the uninitiated in the jargon of social sciences; most of all, it is a valuable addition to the family literature."

BIOGRAPHICAL AND CRITICAL SOURCES:

PERIODICALS

American Political Science Review, December, 1993, Carole Pateman, review of *Citizenship and*

Employment: Investigating Post-Industrial Options, p. 1046.
Journal of Intercultural Studies, October, 1998, Sotirios Sarantakos, review of *The Double Life of the Family: Myth, Hope, and Experience,* p. 230.

ONLINE

University of New South Wales School of Sociology Web site, http://sociology.arts.unsw.edu.au/ (September 16, 2005), faculty profile of author.*

*　　*　　*

PLANCHON, Roger 1931-

PERSONAL: Born September 12, 1931, in Saint-Chamond, France; son of Emile and Augusta (Nogier) Planchon; married Colette Dompietrini, 1958; children: Stéphane, Frédéric (sons). *Education:* Attended Collège des Frères des écoles chrétiennes.

ADDRESSES: Agent—c/o Author Mail, Plon, 76 rue Bonaparte, Paris 75006, France.

CAREER: Director and playwright. Worked as a bank clerk, 1947-49. Théâtre de la Comédie, Lyon, France, founder, 1951; Théâtre de la Cité (renamed Théâtre National Populaire), Villeurbain, France, codirector, 1957-72, director, 1972-95; Fondation Molière, president, 1987—European Cinematographic Center, founder, 1990. Director of plays, including: *Les chemins clos,* 1949; *Bottines et collets montés,* 1950; *La nuit des rois,* 1951; *Les joyeuses comméras de Windsor,* 1951; *Claire,* 1952; *La vie est un songe,* 1952; *Rocambole,* 1953; *La balade du grand macabre,* 1953; *Le sens de la marche,* 1953; *Le professeur Taranne,* 1953; *Burlesque-digest,* 1953; *Liliom,* 1953; (and writer) *Cartouche,* 1953; *La cruche cassée,* 1954; *Edward II,* 1954; *La bonne ame de Sé-Tchouan,* 1954; *Casque d'or,* 1954; *La belle rombière,* 1955; (and adaptation) *L'alcade de Zalaméa,* 1955; *Comment s'en débarrasser,* 1955; *L'ombre de la ravine,* 1955; *La famille Tuyau de Poêle,* 1955; *Victor; ou, les enfants au pouvoir,* 1955; *Grand-peur et misères du troisième reich,* 1956; *Les soldats,* 1956; *La leçon,* 1956; *Victimes du devoir,* 1956; *Aujourd'hui; ou, les coréens,* 1956; *Paolo-Paoli,* 1957; *Henri IV,* 1957; *Les trois mousquetaires*, 1958; *Les fourberies de Scapin*, 1958; *La seconde surprise de l'amour*, 1959; *Les ames mortes*, 1960; *George Dandin*, 1960; *Edouard II*, 1960; *Schweik dans la Deuxième Guerre mondiale*, 1960; *La seconde surprise de l'amour*, 1960; *Auguste Geai*, 1962; (and writer) *La remise*, 1962; *Le Tartuffe*, 1962; *La Villégiature*, 1963; *O'Man Chicago*, 1963; *Patte blanche*, 1963; *Troilus et Cressida*, 1964; *La fausse suivante*, 1965; *Falstaff*, 1965; *Poussière pourpre*, 1966; *Bérénice*, 1966; *Richard III*, 1966; *Dernier adieu d'Armstrong*, 1967; *Récital Dickens*, 1967; *Richard III*, 1967; (and writer) *Bleus, blancs, rouges; ou, Les libertins*, 1967; *Dans le vent*, 1967; *Le coup de Trafalgar*, 1968; *La mise en Pièces*, 1969; (and writer) *L'Infâme*, 1969; *Bérénice*, 1969; *Nicomède*, 1970; *Homme pour homme*, 1970; *The Massacre at Paris*, 1972; *La langue au chat*, 1972; (and writer) *Le cochon noir*, 1973; *Toller*, 1973; *Par-dessus bord*, 1973; *La dispute*, 1973; *La Dispute*, 1974; *Toller*, 1974; *Pardessus bord*, 1974; *A.A. Théâtre d'Arthur*, 1975; *Lear*, 1975; *Folies bourgeoises*, 1975; (and writer) *Gilles de Rais*, 1977; *Loin d'Hagondage*, 1977; *Antony and Cleopatra*, 1978; *Love's Labour's Lost*, 1978; *No Man's Land*, 1979; *Athalie*, 1979; *Dom Juan*, 1979; *Voyages chez les morts*, 1983; and *L'avare*, 1986. Also director of films, including *Louis, enfant roi* and *Lautrec*. Actor in films, including *Danton*, 1983; *The Return of Martin Guerre*, 1983; *Molière;* and *Un condamné à mort s'est échappé.*

AWARDS, HONORS: Prix Ibsen, 1974, for *Le cochon noir;* Prix Georges Lherminier, Sydicate de la Critique Dramatique, 1986, 1988; named commandeur des Arts et des Lettres; Croix de Guerre, 1939-45; named chevalier, French Légion d'Honneur.

WRITINGS:

Patte blanche (play), first produced 1963.
Le cochon noir [and] *La Remise* (plays; *La Remise* first produced 1963), Gallimard (Paris, France), 1973.
Bleus, blancs, rouges; ou, Les libertins (play; also known as *Blues, Whites, and Reds*), first produced 1967.
Dans le vent (play), 1968.
Gilles de Rais [and] *L'infâme* (plays; *L'infâme* first produced 1969), Gallimard (Paris, France), 1975.
Alice par d'obscurs chemins, Editions L'Un Dans l'Autre (Paris, France), 1986.

Lautrec (screenplay), photographs by Marianne Rosenstiehl, Plume (Paris, France), 1998.
Apprentissages: Mémoires, Plon (Paris, France), 2004.

SIDELIGHTS: Roger Planchon is a director, playwright, and actor of working-class origin who is self-taught in theater. At age seventeen, he founded his first theatrical troupe, and in 1952, with several colleagues, he built the Théâtre de la Comédie in an unused print works in Lyon, France. Planchon was cofounder and codirector of the Théâtre de la Cité in Lyon from 1957 to 1972, and director from 1972 to 1995. He was a central figure in the decentralization of French theater and such a master at theatrical promotion and production that in 1972, Théâtre de la Cité was renamed the Théâtre National Populaire (TNP).

Planchon's greatest influences were Antonin Artaud, Arthur Adamov, and, in the mid-1950s, Bertolt Brecht. Planchon became one of the first and foremost French directors to produce Brecht's plays. What he found fascinating was Brecht's political directness; Planchon believes theater to be the most political of the arts. He first produced such contemporary plays as Adamov's *Paolo Paoli* and *Professeur Taranne*, as well as Michel Vinaver's *Les coréens*, but later directed his attention to the classics. In doing so, he rejuvenated them in a Brechtian manner, recreating them in a modern context. Planchon interprets Shakespearean history and tragedy with Marxist overtones and is not afraid to take liberties with the structure of classic comedies, including those of Molière and Marivaux, to present them in a fresh light. Planchon believes the stage director is equal with the dramatist and that "scenic writing"—the deployment of movement, gesture, speech, sound, and lighting—is as important as a play's text. In some theater, indeed, he maintains that dramatic spectacle may assume primacy over text.

In 1957 Planchon and his acting troupe moved to the 1,300-seat Théâtre Municipale Villeurbain, in a Lyon suburb. Planchon's purpose has always been to bring drama to a youthful, working-class audience, and in Villeurbain, he drew audiences comprised of factory workers. His was the first national theater to be located in the provinces when the TNP, formerly located at the Palais de Chaillot in Paris, relocated to Villeurbain, where Planchon continued to pioneer the decentralization of theater.

A powerful actor and an original playwright, Planchon has written a dozen diverse plays, including his first, *La remise*, one of his "peasant" plays. The others are

L'infâme, Le cochon noir, and *Gilles de Rais.* All of these plays, including *Bleus, blancs, rouges; ou, Les libertins,* a play about the French Revolution, take place in the provinces. *La remise* is of autobiographical origin, with the character Emile Chausson based on Planchon's peasant grandfather. Chausson is so obsessed with his land that he works his wife to death and causes one of his sons to leave home and the other to commit suicide. He is killed and an inquiry held into his murder. The play uses a multiple set to convey different levels of time and reality. The title of this play means both "the return" and a storage shed or outbuilding like the one the dramatist remembered being on his grandfather's farm. Other plays of this period that have contemporary settings are *Patte blanche* and *Dans le vent.*

The colors in *Bleus, blancs, rouges; ou, Les libertins* represent the bourgeoisie, aristocracy, and common people, and the action spans the years from 1789 to 1800. Written and produced in 1967, a second, more political version was produced in 1968 at the time of the Paris riots, and the title shortened. Like *Patte blanche* and *Dans le vent,* this play does not have a linear plot. The libertines are led by Aubier d'Arbonne, a young aristocrat who has refused to consummate his marriage to a young bourgeoise. Through the machinations of his mother-in-law he is imprisoned, then freed by the revolutionaries. Eventually he and his companions emigrate but sink into poverty, finally becoming thieves, prostitutes, and traffickers in arms in order to survive. In this play, the populace is represented by popular prints in tableaux inserted between scenes. The play's perspective is of the French Revolution as seen from a distance. It is a provincial point of view. Although Planchon believed the revolution passed power from aristocracy to bourgeoisie, bypassing the common people who brought it about, this is not a thesis play.

L'infâme, which means "The Villain," is based on the actual story of a parish priest in Lorraine, the notorious Abbé Desnoyers. After impregnating a local village girl, he murdered her, cut out the fetus, then killed and disfigured it, fearing it might resemble him. This grisly murder caused a sensation throughout France in 1956. What fascinated Planchon about the case was how the murderer, while claiming to know who had committed the crime but saying he could not reveal the facts, set the police on his own trail, confessing only at the last moment. Planchon sets this play, too, in the Ardèche. *Le cochon noir* ("The Black Pig") is an historical drama that takes place during the "se-maine sanglante" (bloody week) of the 1871 Paris Commune. Planchon viewed the commune as the turning point when the proletariat came into its own and the death knell of the French countryside sounded. The plot centers on Violette, raped by the village scoundrel, Gédéon, on the day of her wedding. Believing she must not reveal what happened, she is taken for possessed and a sorcerer charged with exorcising her. After this exorcism, Violette kills herself. This play is influenced by Henrik Ibsen's *Peer Gynt.*

Produced in 1976, *Gilles de Rais* was published together with *L'infâme.* De Rais was a powerful figure, a Maréchal of France, executed in Nantes in 1440 for sexually abusing, torturing, and murdering hundreds of boys, and also for dabbling in alchemy. His trial and execution, which constitute the second half of the play, are so well presented that seeing this play is like watching a medieval morality play. This extensive scene may also be viewed as de Rais's own conception of his trial, strongly colored by imagination.

During the 1980s and thereafter, Planchon turned his sights increasingly to film. He was first attracted to this genre at the age of fifteen, upon viewing Orson Welles's *Citizen Kane.* Planchon has acted in several films. He has also directed films that include *Louis, enfant roi,* about the childhood of Louis XVI, and *Lautrec,* a film version of the life of the painter Henri de Toulouse-Lautrec. Planchon writes of his own life in his 2004 autobiography, *Apprentissages: Mémoires.*

BIOGRAPHICAL AND CRITICAL SOURCES:

BOOKS

Banham, Martin, editor, *The Cambridge Guide to World Theatre,* Cambridge University Press (New York, NY), 1988.

Bradby, David, *The Theatre of Roger Planchon,* Cambridge University Press (New York, NY), 1984.

Copfermann, Emile, *Roger Planchon,* Lausanne, 1969.

Daoust, Yvette, *Roger Planchon: Director and Playwright,* Cambridge University Press (New York, NY), 1981.

Duvignaud, Jean, *Itinéraire de Roger Planchon,* [Paris, France], 1977.

Hartnoll, Phyllis, editor, *The Oxford Companion to the Theatre,* 4th edition, Oxford University Press (New York, NY), 1983.

Hughes, Alex, and Keith Reader, editors, *Encyclopedia of Contemporary French Culture*, Routledge (New York, NY), 1998.

International Dictionary of Theatre, Volume 3: *Actors, Directors, and Designers,* St. James Press (Detroit, MI), 1996.

Planchon, Roger, *Apprentissages: Mémoires,* Plon (Paris, France), 2004.

Reid, Joyce M.H., editor, *The Concise Oxford Dictionary of French Literature,* Oxford University Press (New York, NY), 1976, pp. 616-618.

PERIODICALS

French Studies Bulletin, summer, 1987, G.J. Mallinson, "Planchon's *L'avare* and the Expectations of a Comedy," pp. 18-20.

Modern Drama, September, 1982, Rosette C. Lamon, review of *Gilles de Rais,* pp. 363-373.

Papers on French Seventeenth-Century Literature, Volume 26, issue 51, 1999, James F. Gaines, review of *Dandin,* pp. 309-317.

Sub-stance: A Review of Theory and Literary Criticism, Volume 18-19, 1977, Anne Ubersfeld, "Adamov Today: A Reconsideration of Planchon's *A.A.*," pp. 182-188.*

*　　*　　*

PRASSO, Sheridan

PERSONAL: Female. *Education:* George Washington University, B.A.; Cambridge University, M.Phil.

ADDRESSES: Home—New York, NY. *Agent*—c/o PublicAffairs, 250 W. 57th St., Ste. 1321, New York, NY 10107. *E-mail*—sheri@sheridanprasso.com.

CAREER: Journalist and editor. Worked with Associated Press in Washington, DC, Chicago, IL, and New York, NY; Agence France-Presse (AFP), Asian regional correspondent in Hong Kong, Europe/Africa desk editor, Paris, France, Cambodia bureau chief in Phnom Penh, 1991-94; *Business Week,* New York, NY, Asia editor for eight years.

MEMBER: Council on Foreign Relations, Asia Society, Japan Society, National Committee on U.S.-China Relations, Overseas Press Club.

AWARDS, HONORS: U.S.-Japan Foundation media fellow in Japan; Knight International Press fellow in China; Human Rights Press Award, for coverage of Cambodian land mine victims; shared in six awards for coverage of Asian financial crisis.

WRITINGS:

The Asian Mystique: Dragon Ladies, Geisha Girls, and Our Fantasies of the Exotic Orient (nonfiction), Public Affairs (New York, NY), 2005.

Contributor of articles to periodicals, including *New Yorker, New Republic, New York Times, Business Week,* and *Far Eastern Economic Review.*

SIDELIGHTS: Sheridan Prasso analyzes the prevalent stereotypes about Asia and Asians, and challenges Westerners to take a fresh view of the region and its people in her book *The Asian Mystique: Dragon Ladies, Geisha Girls, and Our Fantasies of the Exotic Orient.* She examines the origins of common stereotypes, which include the submissive, erotic Asian housewife, the cold and heartless "Dragon Lady" who ruthlessly manipulates people for power, and the ineffectual, effeminate Asian man. In general, the West has depicted the East as something to be dominated. In Prasso's view, many of these stereotypes originated in ancient times and continue to be seen, in various subtle and insidious ways, in modern culture. She believes they have an impact on Asian Americans in business dealings and in the workplace generally; on cross-cultural relationships, and on foreign policy and foreign relations between East and West. She cites the fact that the long-running, critically acclaimed television series *M*A*S*H*,* which was set in Korea, did not have a recurring Asian character until its final season, and the spectacle of blonde actress Uma Thurman in the movie *Kill Bill* easily defeating multiple Asian male attackers in martial-arts battles as two examples of the West's continuing problems with seeing and representing the East in a realistic manner. She stated in an interview with *Asia Source* that "we can never really understand Asian countries . . . until we rid ourselves of 'Asian Mystique,' or at least see it for what it is—the elephant in the living room that affects in some way nearly every interaction between East and West."

The author not only outlines existing stereotypes; she seeks to replace them with realistic pictures of modern life in Asia. She profiles women in Asia's business districts, middle-class neighborhoods, college campuses, and many other walks of life. Prasso stated that she felt her status as a woman and a non-Asian helped her in researching and writing her book. As she told the interviewer for *Asia Source,* "A man could not have written this book. Lots of Western men in the past have written about Asia extolling its beauties and glorifying its exoticism. As a woman, I offer a fresh, more real perspective on Asia. Because I am female, women invited me into their homes and shared their lives with me. They may not have been able to speak as openly and in the same ways with a man due to cultural mores. Plus, being a Westerner means that I can observe situations and relationships in a more objective way." Renee Graham, a reviewer for the *Boston Globe,* found *The Asian Mystique* to be "a persuasive, timely book. Unwavering and pointed, Prasso makes clear the destructive nature of stereotypes about Asia and the social, cultural, and political ramifications of allowing them to fester unchallenged."

BIOGRAPHICAL AND CRITICAL SOURCES:

PERIODICALS

Asian Review of Books, July 27, 2005, Todd Shimoda, review of *The Asian Mystique: Dragon Ladies, Geisha Girls, and Our Fantasies of the Exotic Orient.*

Audrey, July, 2005, Sheridan Prasso, "A New Perspective on the Asian Mystique."

Bookwatch, July, 2005, review of *The Asian Mystique.*

Boston Globe, June 6, 2005, Renee Graham, review of *The Asian Mystique.*

Chief Executive, May, 2005, interview with Sheridan Prasso, p. 55.

Japan Times, September 25, 2005, Stephen Mansfield, review of *The Asian Mystique.*

Kirkus Reviews, March 1, 2005, review of *The Asian Mystique,* p. 280.

Library Journal, May 1, 2005, Cynthia Harrison, review of *The Asian Mystique,* p. 106.

Seattle Post-Intelligencer, September 15, 2005, Frances Somers, "American Journalist Explores Global Stereotypes about Asian Women."

ONLINE

Asia Source, http://www.asiasource.org/ (June 13, 2005), Cindy Yoon, interview with Sheridan Prasso.

Sheridan Prasso Home Page, http://www.sheridan prasso.com (October 26, 2005).*

PRIEST, Cherie

PERSONAL: Born in Tampa, FL; partner's name, Aric. *Education:* Southern Adventist University, B.A., 1998, University of Tennessee at Chattanooga, M.A., 2002.

ADDRESSES: Home—Chattanooga, TN. *Agent*—c/o Author Mail, Tor Books, 175 5th Ave., New York, NY 10010. *E-mail*—cherie.priest@gmail.com.

CAREER: Novelist. Writer for an electronics company in Chattanooga, TN.

WRITINGS:

Four and Twenty Blackbirds (gothic novel), Marietta Publishing (Marietta, GA), 2003, revised edition, Tor (New York, NY), 2005.
Wings to the Kingdom, 2006.

Writer for role-playing projects, including *GhostOrb* and *Gnostica.*

WORK IN PROGRESS: A sequel to *Wings to the Kingdom.*

SIDELIGHTS: Cherie Priest created a modern Southern gothic in the classic tradition with her book *Four and Twenty Blackbirds.* In the story, a young woman named Eden Moore begins a search for her origins that eventually takes her on a journey across the South. She visits a swamp filled with the dead, the ruins of an old sanitarium, and other unsettling locations as she strives to discover the secret of her family's heritage. Eden has psychic visions, which seem to show her events from the past. Meanwhile, in the present she is stalked by a cousin whose mother is deeply involved in a cult of black magic practitioners. Events build to a "supernatural crescendo," according to a reviewer for *Publishers Weekly.* While offering the opinion that Priest adds "little new" to the world of gothic fiction, the reviewer stated that she crafts a story that will especially appeal to "postadolescent horror fans."

Four and Twenty Blackbirds was originally published in a briefer form, then revised and expanded for publication by Tor Books. The story is continued in *Wings to the Kingdom.*

BIOGRAPHICAL AND CRITICAL SOURCES:

PERIODICALS

Kirkus Reviews, July 15, 2005, review of *Four and Twenty Blackbirds,* p. 762.
Publishers Weekly, August 15, 2005, review of *Four and Twenty Blackbirds,* p. 38.

ONLINE

Agony Column Online, http://trashotron.com/agony/ (May 27, 2005), review of *Four and Twenty Blackbirds.*
Cherie Priest Web Log, http://cherie.twilightuniverse.com (October 25, 2005).*

* * *

PRIKKEBEEN
See GRESHOFF, Jan

* * *

PRING-MILL, Robert Deguid Forrest
See PRING-MILL, Robert D.F.

* * *

PRING-MILL, Robert D.F. 1924-2005
(Robert Deguid Forrest Pring-Mill)

OBITUARY NOTICE— See index for *CA* sketch: Born September 11, 1924, in Stapleford Tawney, Essex, England; died October 6, 2005, in Oxford, England. Educator and author. Pring-Mill was a recognized authority on the literature of Spain who was acclaimed for bringing the poetry of Pablo Neruda to academic attention. Having spent part of his childhood in Spain, he gained an affinity for that country's language and culture at an early age. However, his family retreated back to England with the onset of World War II, and Pring-Mill enlisted in the British Army when he was just seventeen. He served as an intelligence officer in India, Burma, and Malaya, then returned home to study modern languages at New College, Oxford. He earned his master's degree there in 1953, and spent his academic career at Oxford. Serving as University Lecturer in Spanish from 1952 to 1988, he was also a lecturer at New College and Exeter and a fellow and tutor at St. Catherine's College. After retiring as a lecturer, he continued his post as fellow of St. Catherine's until 2005. Pring-Mill wrote on and researched the literature and philosophy of Spain throughout its history, but was particularly noted for his expertise on the sixteenth and seventeenth century. His interests also extended to Latin America, where he had traveled extensively and become familiar with its literature. He was particularly enamored by the poetry of Neruda, who would go on to win a Nobel prize in 1971. Pring-Mill's papers about and translations of Neruda's work helped make the poet an internationally acclaimed writer and are credited as the reason why Neruda was given an honorary D.Litt. from Oxford University. In addition to Neruda, Pring-Mill also wrote about Nicaraguan poet Ernesto Cardenal, among others. For his many scholarly accomplishments, Pring-Mill was honored both in his country and abroad. He was named a fellow of the British Academy in 1988, appointed a comendador of the Orden de Isabel la Catolica in 1990, was honored by the government of Chile in 1992 when he was named an officer of the Order of Bernardo O'Higgins, and in 2004 was presented with Chile's presidential medal of honor. Other prizes include the 1956 Premi Pompeu Fabra, the 1979 Premi Citat de Palma, the 1990 Cross of St. George of the Generalitat de Catalunya, and the 1991 Premi Catalynia. Among his many publications are *Lope de Vega: Five Plays* (1961), *Neruda: A Basic Anthology* (1975), *The Scope of Spanish-American Committed Poetry* (1977), *Gracias a la vida: The Power and Poetry of Song* (1990), *Estudis sobre Ramon Llull* (1991), which won the Premi Crítica Serra d'Or, and *A Poet for All Seasons* (1993).

OBITUARIES AND OTHER SOURCES:

PERIODICALS

Independent (London, England), October 15, 2005, p. 47.
Times (London, England), November 3, 2005, p. 66.

* * *

PUSH
See DAWES, Christopher

Q-R

QUIRINA, Fiona
[A pseudonym]

PERSONAL: Female.

ADDRESSES: Home—New York, NY. *Agent*—c/o Author Mail, Penguin Group, c/o Berkley Prime Crime Publicity, 375 Hudson St., New York, NY 10014. *E-mail*—author@lydiaquess.com.

CAREER: Writer.

WRITINGS:

Sex, a Mystery, Berkley Prime Crime (New York, NY), 2005.

Also author of four mysteries and three medical thrillers under her real name (unknown).

SIDELIGHTS: Fiona Quirina is a pseudonym for a mystery and thriller writer whose real name is unknown. In her book *Sex, a Mystery,* Quirina presents a mystery involving Harvard M.B.A. graduate Lydia Quess, who loses her job with a giant food company after revealing that the company's overseas baby formula causes malnutrition. Lydia goes to work for a sex therapist as a sexual surrogate to pay the bills, including the rent for the apartment she shares as a friend with a priest named Father Paddy. Lydia's clients are successful and wealthy, and when one of them is found dead in her bed, suspicion focuses on Lydia. Her life and the lives of her clients are now opened to investigation. Knowing that she may end up being charged with a murder she did not commit, Lydia sets out on her own to investigate the crime, starting with her dead client's life.

A *Publishers Weekly* contributor noted that the author's "stylish debut combines a solid mystery, a refreshingly different heroine, a splendid supporting cast and enough sparkle to keep the pages turning." *Library Journal* reviewer Rex E. Klett noted the mystery's "fascinating, clever plot," while a contributor to *MBR Bookwatch,* called the book a "tremendous chick lit amateur sleuth romp that deftly handles a variety of social and personal issues with humor and intelligence." The reviewer went on to note that the book would be enjoyed by "fans of lighthearted with a serious undertone chic mysteries." Jenifer Hunt, writing on the *Romantic Times* Web site, commented that Quirina "has a real talent for creating characters that are both entertaining and relatable."

BIOGRAPHICAL AND CRITICAL SOURCES:

PERIODICALS

Library Journal, March 1, 2005, Rex E. Klett, review of *Sex, a Mystery,* p. 71.
MBR Bookwatch, April, 2005, review of *Sex, a Mystery.*
Publishers Weekly, February 7, 2005, review of *Sex, a Mystery,* p. 46.

ONLINE

AllReaders.com, http://www.allreaders.com/ (September 17, 2005), Harriet Klausner, review of *Sex, a Mystery.*

Fiona Quirina Home Page, http://www.lydiaquess. com (September 17, 2005).

Romantic Times Online, http://www.romantictimes. com/ (September 17, 2005), Jenifer Hunt, review of *Sex, a Mystery.*

*   *   *

RABBI DANIEL JUDSON
See JUDSON, Daniel

*   *   *

RABBIN, Robert 1950-

PERSONAL: Born May 16, 1950, in New York, NY.

ADDRESSES: Home—San Francisco, CA. *Agent*—c/o Author Mail, Global Truth Publishing, 1001 Bridge-way, Ste. 474, Sausalito, CA 95965. *E-mail*—info@ radicalsages.com.

CAREER: Writer, speaker, and spiritualist. Catalyst for Clarity, San Francisco, CA, founder, 1985; creator of *Radical Sages* Web site.

WRITINGS:

The Sacred Hub: Living in Our Real Self, New Leaders Press (San Francisco, CA), 1995, published as *The Sacred Hub: Living in Your Real Self,* Crossing Press (Freedom, CA), 1996.

(With Jo Hillyard) *The Values Workbook: Creating Personal Truth at Work,* Forethoughts, 1997.

Invisible Leadership: Igniting the Soul at Work, Acropolis Books (Lakewood, CO), 1998, revised edition published as *Igniting the Soul at Work: A Mandate for Mystics,* Hampton Roads (Charlottesville, VA), 2002.

Mentored in Silence: The Heart of Meditation, Acropolis Books (Lakewood, CO), 1999.

Echoes of Silence: Awakening the Meditative Spirit, Inner Directions (Carlsbad, CA), 2000.

(With others) *Twelve Step Wisdom at Work,* Kogan Page, 2001.

(Editor, with Deborah Masters) *The Spiritual Wisdom of Kids,* Global Truth Publishing (Mill Valley, CA), 2003.

Contributor to periodicals, including *Whole Life Times.*

SIDELIGHTS: Robert Rabbin related on his home page that at age eleven he experienced a spiritual "epiphany" that eventually led him to spend ten years with Indian Swami Muktananda, studying under the master until his death. Rabbin then passed on his knowledge by teaching, coaching, and writing. He created the *Radical Sages* Web site "as a portal through which both inner and outer directed people can find new sources of spiritual connection and meaning through action."

Among Rabbin's books is *Igniting the Soul at Work: A Mandate for Mystics,* in which he proposes exchanging the corporate greed that dominates American business for a more holistic and ethical approach. Rabbin notes that people may be afraid to use words like "spiritual" because others might judge them, but he assures readers that if they draw on their inner mystic, they can make change within themselves, as well as in their companies and coworkers.

A *Publishers Weekly* contributor noted that each chapter of *Igniting the Soul at Work* concludes with a "Personal Reflection" that offers "practical applications for questioning the way leaders view business and drawing out the inner tranquility in all of us." In a review for *Edge News* online, Maryel McKinley called the book "an amazing blessing" that suggests that "when we approach our work with a Zen-like experience, we can become masters of our destiny."

BIOGRAPHICAL AND CRITICAL SOURCES:

PERIODICALS

Publishers Weekly, November 4, 2002, review of *Igniting the Soul at Work: A Mandate for Mystics,* p. 76.

ONLINE

Edge News Online, http://www.edgenews.com/ (September 24, 2005), Maryel McKinley, review of *Igniting the Soul at Work.*

RadicalSages.com, http://www.radicalsages.com/ (September 24, 2005).*

RAFFA, Elissa A.

PERSONAL: Female. *Education:* Earned a B.S.; University of Minnesota, M.F.A.

ADDRESSES: Home—P.O. Box 59, 18010 Aegina, Greece. *E-mail*—elissa@otenet.gr.

CAREER: Educator and writer. Minnesota Online High School, Minneapolis, MN, co-director of curriculum and teaching; American College of Greece School of Continuing and Professional Studies, instructor of writing and theater arts.

AWARDS, HONORS: Fellowship in fiction, Minnesota State Arts Board, 1994; Edelstein-Keller teaching and writing fellowship, University of Minnesota, 1995; Emerging Lesbian Writers Award in Fiction, Astraea Foundation, 1995; grant from Puffin Foundation, 2005.

WRITINGS:

Freeing Vera (fiction), Permanent Press (Sag Harbor, NY), 2005.

Contributor to periodicals, including *Water-Stone Hamline Literary Review, Blink, Siren, Evergreen Chronicles,* and *Sinister Wisdom.*

WORK IN PROGRESS: Speech Acts, a novel.

SIDELIGHTS: In her debut novel, Elissa A. Raffa tells the story of Frannie D'Amato, a lesbian artist and narrator whose tale takes place during the 1970s and 1980s. An activist from a small New York town, Frannie grows up the youngest of four brothers and sisters. Frannie loves her mother, Vera, who has multiple sclerosis, but is also angry at her because she is passive and unwilling to try for a better life. Frannie's father, Anthony, is by turns, both emotionally abusive and neglecting of his family. Frannie takes the first chance she gets to leave and sets out for Chicago the day after she graduates from high school. Once there, she associates with a group of lesbian social activists and takes up the cause of fighting for disability rights. Although she has moved on and falls in love with someone, Frannie is still haunted by her family; she keeps returning home for visits with the goal of trying to change her mother's situation but cannot get her three older sisters to help. She is hurt even more when her father reveals he is a homosexual himself, and he leaves Vera for a younger man. Although Anthony seeks to form a bond with his daughter based on their mutual homosexuality, he has few redeeming qualities that would lead Frannie to accept him. A *Kirkus Reviews* contributor noted that Raffa has "a lot of rich material to work with," while a reviewer writing in *Publishers Weekly* called Raffa's effort an "earnest, angry debut novel."

Raffa told *CA:* "My maternal grandmother told wonderful stories; this and my love of reading first sparked my interest in writing. In *Living by Fiction,* Annie Dillard wrote, 'The critic is interested in the novel; the novelist is interested in his neighbors.' Marisha Chamberlain, playwright and teacher, once said that a writer is like a perverse traffic cop beckoning characters into collision with one another. These two ideas help to define my process: my characters are like people I'm acquainted but also wholly invented; I'm interested in seeing what happens when I place them in a scene with one another.

"I often write about a decade that has recently passed. *Freeing Vera* is set in the 1970s and 1980s and I wrote it in the 1990s. *Speech Acts* (working title), my new novel-in-progress, is about an American (Minnesota) small town in the 1990s. So, in addition to being a part-time expatriate seeing the United States from a distance, I'm often seeing cultural moments from a distance as well. At the same time, I'm often drawing on very immediate emotional resources—for example my current work is informed by the experience of living on a small island and of being not-quite-fluent in a language I use daily.

"I see fighting for justice as a form of loving other people and loving the world, even when the fight has no end. For me, writing is an important part of this struggle. I also love the fictional process, which weds discovery and invention—and the thought of certain very good friends reading the scenes as they develop."

BIOGRAPHICAL AND CRITICAL SOURCES:

PERIODICALS

Kirkus Reviews, June 15, 2005, *Freeing Vera,* p. 662.
Publishers Weekly, June 27, 2005, review of *Freeing Vera,* p. 41.

ONLINE

Hedgebrook Web site, http://www.hedgebrook.org/ (November 15, 2005), profile of Elissa Raffa.

*   *   *

RANSOM, Roger L. 1938-

PERSONAL: Born 1938. *Education:* Reed College, B.A., 1959; University of Washington, Ph.D., 1963.

ADDRESSES: Office—Department of History, 1212 HMNSS Bldg., University of California, Riverside, 900 University Ave., Riverside, CA 92521. *E-mail*—roger.ransom@ucr.edu.

CAREER: University of California at Riverside, professor of economics, 1968-84, professor of history, 1984—.

MEMBER: Economic History Association (president).

AWARDS, HONORS: Arthur Cole Award, Economic History Association, 1986; Guggenheim fellowship, 1987-88; Clio Award, Cliometrics Society, 1988; distinguished teaching award, University of California at Riverside, 2002-03.

WRITINGS:

NONFICTION

(With William Breit) *The Academic Scribblers: American Economists in Collision,* Holt (New York, NY), 1971, third edition, Princeton University Press (Princeton, NJ), 1998.

One Kind of Freedom: The Economic Consequences of Emancipation, Cambridge University Press (New York, NY), 1977, second edition, 2001.

Coping with Capitalism: The Economic Transformation of the United States, Prentice-Hall (Englewood Cliffs, NJ), 1981.

(Editor, with Richard Sutch and Gary M. Walton) *Explorations in the New Economic History: Essays in Honor of Douglass C. North,* Academic Press (New York, NY), 1982.

Conflict and Compromise: The Political Economy of Slavery, Emancipation, and the American Civil War, Cambridge University Press (New York, NY), 1989.

The Confederate States of America: What Might Have Been, W.W. Norton (New York, NY), 2005.

SIDELIGHTS: Roger L. Ransom is a scholar and professor whose specialty is the economic history of the United States and the history of the United States during the nineteenth century, especially during the Civil War. In *The Confederate States of America: What Might Have Been* he presents his ideas on what the modern world would be like if the South had won the war, and considers several points that could have changed the course of the conflict. If Confederate leader Stonewall Jackson had survived his wounds, for example, he might have won victory for the South. Key battles or even delays in advances of federal troops at crucial junctures could also have altered the course of the war, according to Ransom. The author goes on to imagine what a victorious South would have been like, and his vision includes a mutual defense agreement being signed with Great Britain that would probably have led to later military engagement with the North during World War I. John Carver Edwards, a reviewer for *Library Journal,* described *The Confederate States of America* as a "wild ride" that provides "provocative and compelling" material. A *Kirkus Reviews* writer recommended it as "an intriguing exercise in counterfactual history."

BIOGRAPHICAL AND CRITICAL SOURCES:

PERIODICALS

Kirkus Reviews, February 1, 2005, review of *The Confederate States of America: What Might Have Been,* p. 169.

Library Journal, March 1, 2005, John Carver Edwards, review of *The Confederate States of America,* p. 98.

ONLINE

University of California at Riverside Web site, http://history.ucr.edu/ (October 12, 2005), biographical information about Roger L. Ransom.*

REEVE, C.D.C. 1948-

PERSONAL: Born September 10, 1948. *Education:* Trinity College, Dublin, B.A., 1971, M.A., 1976; Cornell University, M.A., 1975, Ph.D. 1980.

ADDRESSES: Home—309 Lone Pine Rd., Chapel Hill, NC 27514. *Office*—Department of Philosophy, CB #3125, Caldwell Hall, University of North Carolina—Chapel Hill, Chapel Hill, NC 27599-3125. *E-mail*—cdcreeve@email.unc.edu; cdcreeve@mac.com.

CAREER: Educator and writer. Reed College, Portland, OR, professor of philosophy and humanities and chair of department, 1976-2001; University of North Carolina at Chapel Hill, adjunct professor of classics, 2002—, professor of philosophy, 2002-05, Delta Kappa Epsilon distinguished professor of philosophy, 2005—. Visiting assistant professor at Cornell University, 1981, and University of Virginia, Wise, 1981; visiting professor at University of North Carolina, 2001. Stavros Niarchos lecturer in classical philosophy at Queens College, Flushing, NY, 2000; visiting Scholar at Roanoke College, 1990; Brown University, 1991; National Endowment for the Humanities Summer Institute on Knowledge, Teaching, and Wisdom, 1993; and College of the Holly Cross, 2000.

AWARDS, HONORS: Reed College Junior Vollum fellowship, 1982-83, Senior Vollum fellowship, 1985-86, Burlington Northern Foundation Faculty Achievement Award, 1989; Outstanding Academic Book designation, *Choice,* 1994, for *Practices of Reason.*

WRITINGS:

Philosopher-Kings: The Argument of Plato's Republic, Princeton University Press (Princeton, NJ), 1988.

Socrates in the Apology: An Essay on Plato's Apology of Socrates, Hackett (Indianapolis, IN), 1989.

Practices of Reason: Aristotle's Nicomachean Ethics, Oxford University Press (New York, NY), 1992.

(Reviser) Plato, *Republic,* translated by G.M.A. Grube, Hackett (Indianapolis, IN), 1992.

(Editor, with S. Marc Cohen and Patricia Curd) *Ancient Greek Philosophy from Thales to Aristotle,* Hackett (Indianapolis, IN), 1995, published as *Readings in Ancient Greek Philosophy: From Thales to Aristotle,* 2000.

(Translator and author of introduction and notes) Aristotle, *Politics,* Hackett (Indianapolis, IN), 1998.

(Translator and author of introduction and notes) Plato, *Cratylus,* Hackett (Indianapolis, IN), 1998.

Substantial Knowledge: Aristotle's Metaphysics, Hackett (Indianapolis, IN), 2000.

Women in the Academy: Dialogues on Themes from Plato's Republic, Hackett (Indianapolis, IN), 2001.

(Editor) *The Trials of Socrates: Six Classic Texts,* Hackett (Indianapolis, IN), 2002.

(Author of introduction) Plato, *Republic* (translation; based on new standard Greek text), Hackett (Indianapolis, IN), 2004.

Love's Confusion, Harvard University Press (Cambridge, MA), 2005.

(Editor) *Plato on Love,* Hackett (Indianapolis, IN), 2006.

Contributor to books, including *Philosohers on Education,* edited by Amélie Rorty, Routledge (London, England), 1998; *Method in Ancient Philosophy,* edited by Jyl Gentzler, Clarendon Press (Oxford, England), 1998; *A Companion to the Philosophers,* edited by Robert L. Arrington, Blackwell (Oxford, England), 1999; *The Basic Works of Aristotle,* edited by Richard McKeon, Random House (New York, NY), 2001; *Political Thinkers: A History of Western Political Thought,* edited by Paul Kelly and David Boucher, Oxford University Press (Oxford, England), 2002; *The Classics of Western Philosophy,* edited by Jorge J.E. Garcia, Gregory M. Reichberg, and Bernard M. Schumacher, Blackwell, 2002; *A Companion to the Philosophy of Education,* edited by Randall R. Curren, Blackwell, 2003; and *Socrates: 2,400 Years since His Death,* edited by Sôkratês Erôtikos, European Cultural Centre of Delphi, 2004. Contributor of reviews to academic journals, including *International Philosophical Quarterly, Ethics, Philosophical Review,* and *Polis.*

WORK IN PROGRESS: An *Introductory Reader in Ancient Greek and Roman Philosophy* and several book chapters.

SIDELIGHTS: A specialist in ancient Greek philosophy, C.D.C. Reeve has written and edited numerous books on philosophy. He focuses on the work of Greek philosopher Aristotle in his book *Practices of Reason: Aristotle's Nicomachean Ethics.* In the book, Reeve discusses this masterpiece of Greek philosophical writing and sets out to clarify much of its philosophy. Reeve also presents his own view of the work, arguing against the "traditional understanding of Aristotle's view as involving a radical chorismos [or gap] between scientific knowledge and ethical knowledge," as John King-Farlow and Guangwei Ouyang noted in the *Review of Metaphysics*. As the reviewers went on to comment, "The most novel part of Reeve's book consists of his arguments for similarity between Aristotle's epistemic stands on the sciences and on ethics." In addition, King-Farlow and Ouyang wrote, "Much praise is due. We certainly congratulate Professor Reeve on a striking and distinguished contribution to Aristotelian studies." Marcia L. Homiak, writing in *Mind,* called the book "interesting and unusual," adding: "Reeve's book will be of interest to anyone who has wrestled with the question of how to integrate Aristotle's views on study with his portrait of the virtuous person as engaged in political life."

Reeve continues to explore Aristotelian philosophy in *Substantial Knowledge: Aristotle's Metaphysics.* This time the author "pursues a number of notorious problems in Aristotle, including scientific knowledge, essence, substance, God, the science of being qua being, and the historical problem of Aristotelianism," noted Helen S. Lang in the *Review of Metaphysics.* In the course of his discussion, Reeve explores such issues as Aristotle's rejection of Platonism and the idea of considering his philosophies without the existence of God as part of the analysis. In her review, Lang commented that "the great strength of this study is the clear definition of the Primacy Dilemma and the way in which the complicated (and controversial) details of the search for a solution to it never overwhelm the strong direction imparted to this study by the Dilemma." In addition to his discussion of Aristotle's philosophies, the author provides a list of Aristotle's works and bibliography, an index, and an index locorum.

In *Love's Confusion* Reeve discusses how philosophers and philosophies examine the difficult aspects of love, such as the conflicts and paradoxes love produces. In his analyses, the author draws from the works of such noted philosophers as Plato, Kant, and Sartre and examines love as presented in numerous literary works, from those of the ancient writer Homer to the modern novels of Iris Murdoch. Among the topics he discusses is the fact that married life often vacillates between boredom and romance. "Reeve . . . also

tries to shed light on the tensions between love and its troubled relatives—anxiety, jealousy, sentimentality, pornography and sadomasochism," wrote a *Publishers Weekly* contributor, who added that the "discussion" of the subject is "clear."

BIOGRAPHICAL AND CRITICAL SOURCES:

PERIODICALS

Boston Globe, February 6, 2005, George Scialabba, review of *Love's Confusion.*
Mind, January, 1994, Marcia L. Homiak, review of *Practices of Reason: Aristotle's Nicomachean Ethics,* p. 105.
Philadelphia Inquirer, July 10, 2005, Carlin Romano, review of *Love's Confusion,* p. H12.
Publishers Weekly, January 17, 2005, review of *Love's Confusion,* p. 45.
Review of Metaphysics, September, 1994, John King-Farlow and Guangwei Ouyang, review of *Practices of Reason,* p. 160; December, 2002, Helen S. Lang, review of *Substantial Knowledge: Aristotle's Metaphysics,* p. 455.

ONLINE

University of North Carolina, Chapel Hill Department of Philosophy Web site, http://philosophy.unc.edu/ (September 17, 2005), faculty profile of author.

*   *   *

REHAK, Melanie

PERSONAL: Female.

ADDRESSES: Home—Brooklyn, NY. *Agent*—The Wylie Agency, 250 W. 57th St., Ste. 2114, New York, NY 10107.

CAREER: Poet and critic.

AWARDS, HONORS: Tukman fellowship, New York Public Library Cullman Center for Scholars and Writers.

WRITINGS:

Girl Sleuth: Nancy Drew and the Women Who Created Her, Harcourt Brace (Orlando, FL), 2005.

Contributor of poetry and reviews to periodicals, including *Paris Review, New York Times Magazine, New Yorker, Partisan Review, New Republic, Vogue,* and *Nation.*

WORK IN PROGRESS: A book of poetry.

SIDELIGHTS: Melanie Rehak is a poet and critic who was inspired to create her first full-length book, *Girl Sleuth: Nancy Drew and the Women Who Created Her,* by her own devotion to the "Nancy Drew" mystery series. Rehak was intrigued by the way the series developed over time, from its debut in the 1930s to the newer installments of the 1960s and 1970s. Using fellowship funds from the New York Public Library, she researched the true story of Nancy Drew's creation and the two women, Mildred Wirt Benson and Harriet Stratemeyer Adams, who played the most important roles in writing and popularizing the series. In an interview on the Harcourt Books Web site, Rehak said: "The Nancy story couldn't be told without both Harriet and Mildred. . . . Harriet and Mildred were such fascinating people, and seeing them make their way through the times in which they lived is really inspirational"

A *Kirkus Reviews* critic noted that *Girl Sleuth* presents "the true story behind the creation of the resilient fictional girl detective" by means of a "breezy social history." A *Publishers Weekly* reviewer felt that Rehak "invigorates all the players in the Drew story, and it's truly fun to see behind the scenes."

In her online interview with Harcourt Books, Rehak maintained that Nancy Drew's enduring popularity, spanning decades and changing trends in American society, reflects the fact that the character "represents the epitome of intelligence and control over what seem to be uncontrollable situations." The author added, "I think that kind of character has endless, timeless appeal."

BIOGRAPHICAL AND CRITICAL SOURCES:

PERIODICALS

Kirkus Reviews, July 1, 2005, review of *Girl Sleuth: Nancy Drew and the Women Who Created Her,* p. 724.
Publishers Weekly, June 20, 2005, review of *Girl Sleuth,* p. 68.

ONLINE

Harcourt Books Web site, http://www.harcourtbooks. com/ (September 28, 2005), interview with Rehak.*

*   *   *

RENARD, Jean-Claude 1922-
(Jean-Claude Albert Renard)

PERSONAL: Born April 22, 1922, in Toulon, France; son of César (a military officer) and Yvonne (Rouvier) Renard; married Françoise Lainé, October 2, 1945; children: Jean-Bruno, Patrick, Emmanuel. *Education:* École Saint-Martin de France, Pontoise, licencié ès lettres.

ADDRESSES: Agent—c/o Author Mail, Éditions Mercure de France, 26, rue de Condé, 75006 Paris, France.

CAREER: Poet and lecturer. Éditions du Cerf, Paris, France, literary director, 1950-62; Éditions Casterman, Paris, literary directory, beginning 1962.

MEMBER: Académie Mallarmé, Société des Gens de Lettres, Société Européenne de Culture, Communauté Européenne des Écrivans, Union des Écrivans, PEN.

AWARDS, HONORS: Prix Catholique de Littérature, 1957; Prix Sainte-Beuve, 1966; Prix de Régnier de l'Académie Française, 1971; Prix Max-Jacob, 1974; Grand Prix de Poésie, Acadèmie Française, 1988.

WRITINGS:

Haute-Mer, Points et Contrepoints (Paris, France), 1950.

Métamorphose du monde, Points et Contrepoints (Paris, France), 1951.

Père, voici que l'homme, Éditions du Seuil (Paris, France), 1955.

Incantation du temps (poems) Éditions du Seuil (Paris, France), 1962.

Jean-Claude Renard (collection), edited by André Alter, Seghers (Paris, France), 1966.

La braise et la rivière (poems and prose), Éditions du Seuil (Paris, France), 1969.

Notes sur la foi: précédé de une situation particulière, Gallimard (Paris, France), 1973.

Mon chien m'a dit, illustrated by Yutaka Sugita, Hachette (Paris, France), 1973.

Le dieu de nuit (poems), Éditions du Seuil (Paris, France), 1973.

Connaissance des noces, Editeurs français réunis (Paris, France), 1977.

Dits d'un livre des sorts, Éditions de la Diff'rence (Paris, France), 1978.

La lumière du silence (poems), Éditions du Seuil (Paris, France), 1978.

Selected Poems, edited by Graham Dunstan Martin, Oasis Books (London, England), 1978.

Le lieu du voyageur: notes sur le mystère (essays), Éditions du Seuil (Paris, France), 1980.

Comptines et formulettes, Éditions Saint-Germain-des-Prés (Paris, France), 1981.

Une autre parole (poems), Éditions du Seuil (Paris, France), 1981.

Toutes les îles sont secrètes (poems), Éditions du Seuil (Paris, France), 1984.

Jean-Claude Renard: son oeuvre et ses amis, La bibliothèque (Lyon, France), 1985.

L'"expérience intérieure" de George Bataille, ou, La négation du mystère, Éditions du Seuil (Paris, France), 1987.

(With Marc Tardieu) *Quand le poème devient prière,* Nouvelle Cité (Paris, France), 1987.

Sous de grands vents obscurs (poems and prose), Éditions du Seuil (Paris, France), 1990.

(With Jean Mambrino and Yves-Alain Favre) *Une certaine nuit: transcendance et poésie,* Éditions Inter-Universitaires (Mont-de-Marsan, France), 1992.

Jean-Claude Renard, ou, Les secrets de la chimère (collection), criticism and interpretation by Jean Burgos and others, Nizet (Paris, France), 1992.

Ce puits que rien n'épuise (poems and prose), Éditions du Seuil (Paris, France), 1993.

Dix runes d'été (poems and prose), Mercure de France (Paris, France), 1994.

Autres notes sur la poésie, la foi et la science, Éditions du Seuil (Paris, France) 1995.

Qui ou quoi? (poems), introduction by Marie-Claire Bancquart, Cherche Midi (Paris, France), 1997.

Le temps de la transmutation: cinq poèmes, Mercure de France (Paris, France), 2001.

SIDELIGHTS: Jean-Claude Renard was considered one of the most important French poets of the latter half of the twentieth century, but his work is largely unknown to English-speaking readers because of the scarcity of translations. Renard's poetry focuses on what he considers the great mystery of life: the link between the world's spiritual and material sides, and how these balance in relation to mankind. His early work reflects his Roman Catholic background, but later poems branch out, looking at the spiritual side of life as less structured by formalized religion. Language and the ability to invoke emotions that transcend everyday life are the driving forces behind much of his work, with a focus on travel and exotic imagery that reminds the reader of the strangeness of life, nature, and the spiritual side of man's existence. Roger Cardinal, in a review of Renard's *Selected Poems* for *Modern Language Review,* remarked that "Renard's poetry impresses at once by its compulsive naming of disparate entities. With a harsh surety of manner, he points out the features of a strangely varied and yet coherent landscape, deploying a noun-dominated vocabulary to invoke things alive or inanimate, textures, movements, forces."

Renard achieves a balance in his work, referring both to spiritual images and a more secular reality that grounds his poems in the material world. A contributor to the *Times Literary Supplement* noted that "it would . . . be a mistake to read everything in his poetry as allegory. Its first and immediate meaning is also essential to it; and this is a sensuous delight in the phenomenal world, a sense of wonder at its tremulous creative potentiality." This continues to be Renard's purpose in his poetry: a search for that which is remarkable in life and for the threads that bind the miraculous to the mundane. Regarding *Toutes les îles sont secrètes,* a 1984 collection of Renard's work, David O'Connell remarked in *French Review* that "these poems display Renard's ongoing attempt to penetrate and . . . set before his reader the mystery of existence."

In an article for *French Review,* Jean R. Cranmer discussed the dividing line between Renard's religious beliefs and his poetic efforts, stating that "it is true that his poetic expression of faith does not draw upon the tenets of Catholicism to the exclusion of other religions." Cranmer further noted that "his works do not celebrate the liturgy of a particular church or poetically reaffirm an established set of beliefs" and that "the object of Renard's quest is knowledge of the unique principle, the Absolute, from which all else springs." Renard finds no reason to limit himself to religious teachings in this quest. Cranmer concluded that "Renard's poetic universe is richly colored in sensory images from the world around us. These images, however, continually transform themselves into fragments of a mystical paradise glimpsed by the poet in his desired migration to a place at the source of all creation. . . . It is here that the religious experience and the poetic experience coincide."

BIOGRAPHICAL AND CRITICAL SOURCES:

PERIODICALS

French Review, March, 1985, Michelle Rogers, "Entretien avec Jean-Claude Renard" (interview), pp. 551-557; Volume 60, 1986, David O'Connell, review of *Toutes les îles sont secrètes,* pp. 169-170; December, 1992, Jean R. Cranmer, "Jean-Claude Renard: And the World Was Made Mystère," pp. 267-274.
French Studies, October, 1993, Peter Broome, review of *Une certaine nuit: transcendance et poésie,* p. 502.
Modern Language Review, April, 1982, Roger Cardinal, review of *Selected Poems,* pp. 467-468.
Times Literary Supplement, May 15, 1969, review of *La braise et la rivière,* p. 521; July 19, 1974, review of *Le dieu de nuit,* p. 771.
World Literature Today, spring, 1985, M. Bishop, review of *Toutes les îles sont secrètes,* p. 243; winter, 1991, Maryann De Julio, review of *Sous de grands vents obscurs,* p. 82.

ONLINE

Mercure de France Web site, http://www.mercure defrance.fr/ (September 24, 2005), "Jean-Claude Renard."*

RENARD, Jean-Claude Albert
　See RENARD, Jean-Claude

*　　*　　*

REYS, Otto P.
　See GRESHOFF, Jan

*　　*　　*

RICHMAN, Alan

PERSONAL: Married Lettie Teague (an editor and columnist). *Education:* University of Pennsylvania, Philadelphia, degree (with honors), 1965.

ADDRESSES: Office—French Culinary Institute, 462 Broadway, New York, NY 10013-2618.

CAREER: Journalist and restaurant critic. *New York Times,* New York, NY, reporter; *Boston Globe,* Boston, MA, assistant managing editor; *People* magazine, writer-at-large, *Gentleman's Quarterly,* senior correspondent and restaurant critic; French Culinary Institute, New York, NY, dean of food journalism, 2004—. Sports writer for *Evening Bulletin, Montreal Star,* and *Boston Globe.* Journalist for *Portland Indiana Commercial-Review;* television cohost of *Dining Around,* Food Network. *Military service:* U.S. Army, served in Vietnam War; awarded Bronze Star.

AWARDS, HONORS: Twelve James Beard Foundation Journalism Awards for food writing, including two M.F.K. Fisher Distinguished Writing Awards; National Magazine Award.

WRITINGS:

(Author of forword) Fran McCullough and Molly Stevens, *The Best American Recipes: 2003-2004,* Houghton Mifflin (Boston, MA), 2003.
Fork It Over: The Intrepid Adventures of a Professional Eater, HarperCollins (New York, NY), 2004.

Contributor to numerous periodicals.

SIDELIGHTS: "For a decade and a half he has been one of America's most discerning, original and voracious food writers," wrote Jerry Adler of Alan Richman in *Newsweek*. Richman, who began his career as a sportswriter, sees his career in a broader light, however; as he said in an article on the French Culinary School Web site: "Whenever I'm asked what I do for a living, I don't say I'm a writer, a reporter, an editor or, heaven help me, a foodie. I say I'm a journalist. I'd love to see more people take up that cause."

Richman presents a collection of essays about food he has eaten around the world in his book *Fork It Over: The Intrepid Adventures of a Professional Eater*. On the one hand, Richman writes about his esoteric search for black truffles, but he also reviews a more down-to-earth appetite in another essay describing his hunt for North Carolina's best barbecue restaurant. Other essays discuss an expensive Chicago restaurant owned by Louis Farrakhan, a dinner with actress Sharon Stone, and his distrust of restaurants in the Hamptons. While focusing on his career, the author provides glimpses of his personal life, talking about his mother as a great cook, and how he had a good idea of what his calling might be when he had the best pastrami sandwich of his life at a Philadelphia as a kid. He also claims that, during his service in Vietnam during the war, he was the only soldier to gain weight. In addition to his essays, Richman offers tips for people eating out called the "Ten Commandments for Diners," which include such advice as never taking the waiter's word for a favorite dish and pretending to be a food critic by taking out a notebook and a pen.

"Richman's dry, witty prose will delight readers who crave good culinary writing," wrote John Charles in the *Library Journal*. A *Kirkus Reviews* contributor commented that the author's "short, simple, funny sentences both engage and surprise." The reviewer added, "His prose lets readers in on the joke without directly acknowledging it." Melissa Parcel, writing on the *BookLoons* Web site, called *Fork It Over* a "delectable treasure," noting that people "who enjoy narrative nonfiction, food lovers of all kinds, and those who are looking for an unusual and humorous writing style will thoroughly enjoy" the book. In a review in *Entertainment Weekly*, Kim Severson wrote that the author "loves lean sentences built on sharp observation and blustery opinion." Writing in *Booklist*, Mark Knoblauch noted that the author makes "deftly worded ruminations on food and restaurants." Knoblauch also

wrote that "Richman's storytelling ability serves him well." In a review in the *School Library Journal*, Barbara A. Genco commented: "This guy can flat out write—and he's funny. Just remember—don't read him with your mouth full."

BIOGRAPHICAL AND CRITICAL SOURCES:

PERIODICALS

Booklist, November 15, 2004, Mark Knoblauch, review of *Fork It Over: The Intrepid Adventures of a Professional Eater*, p. 540.
Entertainment Weekly, October 29, 2004, Kim Severson, review of *Fork It Over*, p. 72.
Kirkus Reviews, September 1, 2004, review of *Fork It Over*, p. 854.
Library Journal, October 15, 2004, John Charles, review of *Fork It Over*, p. 83.
Media Week, May 11, 1998, Lisa Granatstein, "GQ Restaurant Reviewer Richman Dresses for Awards Dinner," p. 32.
Newsweek, December 6, 2004, Jerry Adler, review of *Fork It Over*, p. 89.
Publishers Weekly, September 15, 2003, review of *The Best American Recipes: 2003-2004*, p. 59.
School Library Journal, December, 2004, Barbara A. Genco, review of *Fork It Over*, p. 54.

ONLINE

BookLoons, http://www.bookloons.com/ (September 17, 2005), Melissa Parcel, review of *Fork It Over*.
Curled Up with a Good Book, http://www.curledup.com/ (September 17, 2005), Barbara Bamberger Scott, review of *Fork It Over*.
French Culinary Institute Web site, http://www.frenchculinary.com/ (September 17, 2005), "The French Culinary Institute Appoints Alan Richman as Dean of Food Journalism and Announces New Curriculum on Food Writing."
University of Pennsylvania Web site, http://www.sas.upenn.edu/ (September 17, 2005), "From Pagano's to Pop's: Alan Richman Remembers Penn Food of the '60s."

*   *   *

RILLA, Wolf 1925-2005

OBITUARY NOTICE— See index for *CA* sketch: Born March 16, 1925, in Berlin, Germany; died October 19, 2005. Film director and author. Rilla was best known as a film director and script writer, most notably of the

1960 movie *Village of the Damned.* Born in Germany of a Jewish father, he and his family moved to England when he was a teenager to avoid the rise of the Nazis to power. Here he attended St. Catharine's, Cambridge, earning an M.A. in 1945. Rilla's father had been an actor, and this interest in movies was passed down to his son. Rilla began working for the British Broadcasting Corporation (BBC) in 1942, and was hired to work in the BBC World Service's German section during the war. Later, he moved into television, leaving the BBC in 1952 to work in movies. Initially, he was employed by the production company Group 3, but he later became an independent director who occasionally also did television shows; he also worked as a director for Cyclops Film Productions in the 1960s. In addition to adapting John Wyndham's novel *The Midwich Cuckoos* into *Village of the Damned,* which he cowrote and directed, he was the scriptwriter for such films as *Jessy* (1959), which won a Boston Film Festival award, *The World Ten Times Over* (1962), *Quarry* (1969), and *The Wheelchair* (1974). For television, Rilla worked on sitcom series in the 1970s; a novelist as well, he penned such fiction works as *Greek Chorus* (1947) and *The Dispensable Man* (1974). By the 1970s, he had retired from filmmaking and moved to France, where he ran a hotel. In addition to his film work, Rilla was also praised as the author of the useful guide *A-Z of Movie Making* (1969).

OBITUARIES AND OTHER SOURCES:

PERIODICALS

Guardian (London, England), October 25, 2005, p. 36.
Independent (London, England), October 29, 2005, p. 44.
Times (London, England), December 3, 2005, p. 76.

*   *   *

RISKIN, Boris

PERSONAL: Born in Brooklyn, NY; married; wife's name Kiki (a sculptor); children: one daughter, one son. *Education:* Attended University of Michigan.

ADDRESSES: Home—Sag Harbor, NY. *Agent*—c/o Author Mail, Five Star Books, 295 Kennedy Memorial Dr., Waterville, ME 04901. *E-mail*—Rriskin@aol.com.

CAREER: Writer. Worked at a variety of jobs, including dishwasher, busboy, factory worker, and discount clothes salesman.

WRITINGS:

Scrambled Eggs (fiction), Five Star (Waterville, ME), 2005.

Short stories have appeared in literary magazines and in *New Yorker.*

SIDELIGHTS: Boris Riskin is an established short-story writer who tells the story of retiring Shakespearean professor Jake Wanderman in the novel *Scrambled Eggs.* Although he is looking forward to retirement, the sixty-year-old Jake suddenly is confronted by his wife's declaration that she is leaving him. As narrated by Jake, who often quotes Shakespeare when under stress, he is despondent over what appears to be the end of his twenty-five-year marriage to a woman he dearly loves. In fact, Jake appears to have lost his will to do much of anything. Nevertheless, he reluctantly attends the party of a friend and meets the beautiful Cynthia Organ, whose husband, Boris, recently died. Cynthia tells Jake she has found an attaché case her husband owned containing gold bars and six Fabergé Imperial eggs worth a fortune. Before long, Jake is involved in a mystery involving the Russian mob, the FBI, and his estranged wife and her new rich, boyfriend. After getting beat up by some thugs, Jake is on the case and soon discovers his wife and her lover tied up in her lover's house, which also contains a dead FBI agent, who may actually be an imposter. "Riskin's debut is less Brighton than Coney Island, with thrills, spills and double-crosses beyond number," wrote a *Kirkus Reviews* contributor. Harriet Klausner, writing in *MBR Bookwatch,* noted that "the story line is fast-paced, but held together by the likable professor." Klausner also wrote that "sub-genre fans will enjoy this tale told by a bard filled with fun and fury."

BIOGRAPHICAL AND CRITICAL SOURCES:

PERIODICALS

Kirkus Reviews, April 1, 2005, review of *Scrambled Eggs,* p. 391.
MBR Bookwatch, May, 2005, Harriet Klausner, review of *Scrambled Eggs.*

ONLINE

Boris Riskin Home Page, http://borisriskin.com (September 17, 2005).

Harriet Klausner's Review Archive, http://harriet klausner.wwwi.com/ (September 17, 2005), Harriet Klausner, review of *Scrambled Eggs.**

*   *   *

ROBERTS, Diane 1959-

PERSONAL: Born 1959. *Education:* Graduated from Florida State University, Tallahassee; Oxford University, D.Phil.

ADDRESSES: Office—University of Alabama, Department of English, Box 870244, Tuscaloosa, AL 35487-0244. *E-mail*—droberts@english.as.ua.edu.

CAREER: Journalist, writer, and educator. University of Alabama, Tuscaloosa, member of English faculty. Commentator for National Public Radio; commentator and essayist for radio and television, including British Broadcasting Corporation (BBC) Radio, BBC World Service Radio, and BBC television.

WRITINGS:

Faulkner and Southern Womanhood, University of Georgia Press (Athens, GA), 1994.
The Myth of Aunt Jemima: Representations of Race and Region, Routledge (New York, NY), 1994.
Dream State: Eight Generations of Swamp Lawyers, Conquistadors, Confederate Daughters, Banana Republicans, and Other Florida Wildlife, Free Press (New York, NY), 2004.

Has contributed articles and essays to scholarly journals and periodicals, including *New Republic, Oxford American, Southern Living, Atlanta Journal-Constitution, Utne Reader, Southern Exposure, Content, Apalachee Quarterly, English Review, Faulkner Journal, Journal of American Studies, Southern Reader, Atlanta Weekly, St. Petersburg Times,* London *Guardian,* and *Orlando Sentinel.* Short stories appeared in *Southeastern Culture Quarterly* and *Sun Dog* magazine. Contributor to books, including *Diverse Voices,* Indiana University Press/Harvester Books (Bloomington, IN), 1991; *Southern Living. Dixie Debates,* edited by H. Taylor and R. King, New York University Press (New York, NY), 1996; and *Faulkner & Nature,* edited by Donald Kartiganer, University Press of Mississippi (Oxford, MS), 1999.

WORK IN PROGRESS: A book on secret societies in America.

SIDELIGHTS: Diane Roberts has a special interest in Southern society, culture, and literature in the United States and is the author of several books on these topics. In her book *Faulkner and Southern Womanhood,* Roberts takes a look at noted American writer William Faulkner's fascination and view of women, both in his life and his literature. The author divides her book into six chapters, each beginning with a discussion of a typical stereotype of Southern womanhood, such as the "Mammy" and the "Tragic Mullata." In the second part of each chapter, she discusses these stereotypes as presented in the works of Faulkner.

"Roberts shows how Faulkner's depictions of females reflect his society's concerns with its women," wrote Mary Wheeling White in the *Southern Literary Journal.* White went on to comment, "Even scholars not in agreement with Roberts's feminist analysis of Faulkner's fiction will learn from her examination of models of Southern womanhood. This admirable book is a useful contribution to our understanding of the novelist's troublesome cultural inheritance and his equally troublesome depictions of females in the South." Ann Goodwyn Jones, writing in the *Mississippi Quarterly,* felt that the author "has a cultural critic's fascination with history and with contexts; *Faulkner and Southern Womanhood,* in effect constructs a literary history and theory of Southern womanhood at the same time that it uses such a history to place and read Faulkner's women." Jones also called Roberts's book a "skillful and thorough examination of literary/cultural traditions and of Faulkner's work." In a review in the *Journal of English and Germanic Philology,* Deborah Clarke wrote, "This is an engaging study, with a great deal of useful contextualizing; Roberts has gathered a wide array of literary, popular, and historical documents to place Faulkner within a specific southern context."

In addition to her academic interests, Roberts is a working journalist. She used the controversy surrounding the Florida ballots in the 2000 U.S. presidential election as a springboard to examine the history of her native Florida in the book *Dream State: Eight Generations of Swamp Lawyers, Conquistadors, Confederate Daughters, Banana Republicans, and Other Florida Wildlife.* In her historical narrative, Roberts integrates much of her own family history to place the story in context as she goes from the arrival of Spanish explorer Ponce de Leon, who was looking for the mythical fountain of youth, on through to modern-day political maneuverings and social injustices. "Florida, she deftly argues, has somehow become everybody's ultimate 'second chance'—mostly in the form of perennially virgin real estate lying prostrate for exploitation," noted a *Kirkus Reviews* contributor. The reviewer went on to call the book "a raucous but also sensitive and insightful view of why the Sunshine State really is different." Boyd Childress, writing in the *Library Journal,* commented that the book is "a great way to tell the state's history." A *Publishers Weekly* contributor called Roberts's effort a "splendid unofficial history."

BIOGRAPHICAL AND CRITICAL SOURCES:

BOOKS

Roberts, Diane, *Faulkner and Southern Womanhood,* University of Georgia Press (Athens, GA), 1994.

PERIODICALS

Booklist, November 15, 2004, John Green, review of *Dream State: Eight Generations of Swamp Lawyers, Conquistadors, Confederate Daughters, Banana Republicans, and Other Florida Wildlife,* p. 550.

Journal of English and German Philology, October, 1996, Deborah Clarke, review of *Faulkner and Southern Womanhood,* p. 580.

Kirkus Reviews, September 15, 2004, review of *Dream State,* p. 906.

Library Journal, November 15, 2004, Boyd Childress, review of *Dream State,* p. 71.

Mississippi Quarterly, summer, 1994, Anne Goodwyn Jones, review of *Faulkner and Southern Womanhood,* p. 521.

Publishers Weekly, September 27, 2004, review of *Dream State,* p. 45.

Southern Literary Journal, spring, 1995, Mary Wheeling White, review of *Faulkner and Southern Womanhood,* p. 129.

Studies in American Fiction, spring, 1995, Linda Dunleavy, review of *Faulkner and Southern Womanhood,* p. 119.*

* * *

ROBINSON, Lynne

PERSONAL: Female. *Education:* Honours degree; postgraduate certificate of education.

ADDRESSES: Office—Body Control Pilates, 6 Langley Street, London, WC2H 9JA England; Fax: (0)20 7379 7551.

CAREER: Designer, illustrator, and educator. Body Control Pilates Academy, London, England, director. Contributed to development of draft national standard for Pilates in UK; teacher at Chiva Som Spa Resort, Thailand; Body Control Pilates Centre, Fortina Spa Resort, Malta, consultant. Appeared on instructional CDs, including *The Pilates Body,* 2004.

WRITINGS:

Contemporary's Working in English, Contemporary Books (Chicago, IL), 1991.

(Illustrator, with Richard Lowther) Jocasta Innes, *The Thrifty Decorator,* photography by Nadia Mackenzie, Conran Octopus (London, England), 1993.

(With Richard Lowther) *Stencilling,* photography by Pia Tryde, Trafalgar Square (North Pomfret, VT), 1995.

(With Richard Lowther) *Decorative Paint Recipes: A Step-by-Step Guide to Finishing Touches for Your Home,* Chronicle Books (San Francisco, CA), 1997.

(With Gordon Thompson) *Body Control: Using Techniques Developed by Joseph H. Pilates,* Bain-Bridge Books (Philadelphia, PA), 1998.

(With Richard Lowther) *Windows: Simple Solutions for the Home,* Chronicle Books (San Francisco, CA), 2000.

(With Gerry Convy) *Pilates Workouts,* Friedman/ Fairfax Publishers (New York, NY), 2002.

(With Helge Fisher and Paul Massey) *The Pilates Prescription for Back Pain: A Comprehensive Program for Developing and Maintaining a Healthy Back,* Ulysses Press (Berkeley, CA), 2004.

(Editor) Miranda Bass, *The Complete Classic Pilates Method: Centre Yourself with This Step-by-Step Approach to Joseph Pilates' Original Matwork Programme,* Macmillan (London, England), 2004.

(With others) *The Complete Book of Paint: Seventy Techniques, Finishes, and Designs for Your Home,* Chronicle Book (San Francisco, CA), 2005.

(With Gordon Thompson) *Pilates: A New Body in Four Weeks: A New Body Control Pilates Programme,* Pan Macmillan (London, England), 2005.

SIDELIGHTS: Lynne Robinson has expertise in interior design and the exercise regimen known as Pilates and has written books about both subjects. Her design books include *Windows: Simple Solutions for the Home,* which she wrote with Richard Lowther. Stanley Abercrombie, writing in *Interior Design,* noted that the book has "plenty of practical and attractive suggestions." Robinson is also author of *The Complete Book of Paint: Seventy Techniques, Finishes, and Designs for Your Home. Library Journal* contributor Mirela Roncevic noted that this "book makes it sound almost too easy."

Robinson first became interested in Pilates in 1992, when she was suffering from back problems. The regimen worked so well for her that she has since become an instructor in the exercise program created by Joseph Pilates. Robinson "has been at the forefront of creating the boom in Pilates in the UK and her name and image have become synonymous with Pilates," noted a biographer on the Body Control Pilates Web site. "She is firmly established as the world's top-selling Pilates author and presenter, her books and videos being sold in over thirty countries." In *The Pilates Prescription for Back Pain: A Comprehensive Program for Developing and Maintaining a Healthy Back,* which Robinson wrote with Helge Fisher and Paul Massey, the author presents a regimen that includes sample workouts augmented by diagrams and photographs. In addition, the book includes tips on preventing back problems while doing various day-to-day activities. Betsy L. Hogan, writing in *Reviewer's Bookwatch,* called the book "a no-nonsense health guide" that she "highly recommended."

BIOGRAPHICAL AND CRITICAL SOURCES:

PERIODICALS

Bookseller, February 4, 2005, review of *Pilates: A New Body in Four Weeks: A New Body Control Pilates Programme,* p. 35.

Interior Design, April, 2000, Stanley Abercrombie, review of *Windows: Simple Solutions for the Home,* p. 155.

Library Journal, March 1, 2005, Mirela Roncevic, review of *The Complete Book of Paint: Seventy Techniques, Finishes, and Designs for Your Home,* p. 109.

Reviewers Bookwatch, January, 2005, Betsy L. Hogan, review of *Pilates: A New Body in Four Weeks: A New Body-Control Pilates Programme.*

ONLINE

Body Control Pilates Web site, http://www.body control.co.uk/ (September 18, 2005).*

*   *   *

ROSENBLUM, Constance

PERSONAL: Female. *Education:* Bryn Mawr College, graduated, 1965.

ADDRESSES: Agent—c/o Author Mail, New York University Press, 838 Broadway, 3rd Fl., New York, NY 10003.

CAREER: Editor and writer. *New York Times,* New York, NY, arts and leisure section editor, then city editor, 1998—. Former culture editor for *Philadelphia Inquirer,* Philadelphia, PA.

WRITINGS:

Gold Digger: The Outrageous Life and Times of Peggy Hopkins Joyce, Metropolitan Books (New York, NY), 2000.

(Editor) *New York Stories: The Best of the City Section of the New York Times,* New York University Press (New York, NY), 2005.

SIDELIGHTS: In her book *Gold Digger: The Outrageous Life and Times of Peggy Hopkins Joyce,* Constance Rosenblum tells the story of the early-twentieth-century showgirl who worked in vaudeville, the Ziegfield follies, and eventually movies. However, the ingenue became more famous for epitomizing the "Jazz Age" and Joyce was labeled notorious for her relationships with men, including marriages to several millionaires. Joyce was born Marguerite Upton in a small town in North Carolina. Leaving home at sixteen, she quickly married, divorced, and then began a string of marriages to wealthy men, such as James Stanley Joyce. After her marriage to Joyce ended, she worked a little in films and had numerous lovers, including Charlie Chaplin and film studio head Irving Thalberg. Joyce's numerous indiscretions, however, began to hurt her career as well as her reputation, and in 1922 the Motion Picture Theater Owners of American decided to no longer show any of her films. By the end of the 1930s, she was largely forgotten. Joyce married six times in the course of her life, the last marriage being to a young bank clerk.

In a review of *Gold Digger* in the *Library Journal,* Elaine Machleder noted that "the author evokes an era of café society, Cole Porter lyrics, and passionate affairs with noblemen and titans." A *Publishers Weekly* contributor wrote that "Rosenblum not only brings her subject to vibrant life, hut also reveals how the cult of media celebrity grew in this century." Writing in *Booklist,* Donna Seaman commented that the Rosenblum includes "a shrewd analysis of Joyce's rapport with the press." Jonathan Bing, writing in *Variety* remarked that Rosenblum bases much of her book on her discovery of Joyce's personal papers and added that the author "artfully documents this original material girl's brief but incandescent waltz through the national consciousness."

Rosenblum is also the editor of *New York Stories: The Best of the City Section of the New York Times.* The book features a series of articles that have appeared in the City Section of the *New York Times* beginning in the early 1990s. Rosenblum, who edits the section, includes essays and articles from well-known writers and new writers as well. Included are both humorous

and serious pieces, their topics ranging from an essay about a blown up apartment inhabited by members of a radical group in the 1970s to the famous ability of New Yorkers to ignore even the most outlandish and strange behaviors. A *Publishers Weekly* contributor called the collection "an excellent addition to New York history and a pleasure for casual browsing." Writing in the *Library Journal,* Rita Simmons commented that "the pieces evoke a powerful sense of place,"adding that "the material is of high literary caliber."

BIOGRAPHICAL AND CRITICAL SOURCES:

PERIODICALS

Biography, fall, 2000, Leslie Chess Feller, review of *Gold Digger: The Outrageous Life and Times of Peggy Hopkins Joyce,* p. 810.
Booklist, April 1, 2000, Donna Seaman, review of *Gold Digger,* p. 1424.
Library Journal, February 15, 2000, Elaine Machleder, review of *Gold Digger,* p. 174; May 1, 2005, Rita Simmons, review of *New York Stories: The Best of the City Section of the New York Times,* p. 107.
Publishers Weekly, February 14, 2000, review of *Gold Digger,* p. 180; April 11, 2005, review of *New York Stories,* p. 45.
Variety, May 1, 2000, Jonathan Bing, review of *Gold Digger,* p. 39.*

*   *   *

ROSHI, Genpo
    See MERZEL, Dennis Genpo

*   *   *

ROSS, Alex 1970-

PERSONAL: Born January 22, 1970, in Portland, OR; son of Clark Ross (a minister); mother a commercial artist. *Education:* American Academy of Art, (Chicago, IL), graduated c. 1990.

ADDRESSES: Home—Chicago, IL. *Agent*—c/o Author Mail, DC Comics, 1700 Broadway, New York, NY 10019.

CAREER: Caroonist, graphic artist, and writer. Storyboard artist at a Chicago advertising agency, c. 1990; independent comics artist and graphic novelist, 1993—. Designer and illustrator of posters, lithographs, collectors' plates, and magazine covers; painter.

AWARDS, HONORS: Will Eisner Comics Industry Award for Best Painter/Multimedia Artist (interior art), 2000, for *Batman: War on Crime,* and Best Cover Artist, for multiple titles; National Comics Award for Top-Ten Artist Ever, 2002; other awards.

WRITINGS:

(With Kurt Busiek) *Marvels,* Marvel Comics (New York, NY), 1993.

(With Steve Darnell) *U.S.: Uncle Sam,* DC Comics (New York, NY), 1997.

(With Elliot S. Maggin, Mark Waid, and Todd Klein) *Kingdom Come* (originally published in single magazine form as *Kingdom Come,* numbers 1-4), DC Comics (New York, NY), 1997.

(With Paul Dini) *Batman: War on Crime,* DC Comics (New York, NY), 1999.

(With Mark Waid, Jerry Ordway, and others) *The Kingdom* (originally published in single magazine form in *Kingdom Come* series), DC Comics (New York, NY), 1999.

(With Paul Dini) *Superman: Peace on Earth,* DC Comics (New York, NY), 1999.

(With Mark Waid and Todd Klein) *Kingdom Come Volume 1: Strange Visitor* (originally published in single magazine form as *Kingdom Come,* number 1), millennium edition, DC Comics (New York, NY), 2000.

(With Paul Dini) *Shazam! Power of Hope,* DC Comics (New York, NY), 2000.

(With Paul Dini) *Wonder Woman: Spirit of Truth,* DC Comics (New York, NY), 2001.

(Illustrator, with Joe Bennett and Rick Veitch) Alan Moore, *Supreme: The Story of the Year,* Checker (Centerville, OH), 2002.

(With Paul Dini) *JLA: Secret Origins,* DC Comics (New York, NY), 2003.

(With Paul Dini) *JLA: Liberty and Justice,* DC Comics (New York, NY), 2003.

(With Chip Kidd) *Mythology: The DC Comics Art of Alex Ross,* introduction by M. Night Shymalan, photography by Geoff Spear, Pantheon Books (New York, NY), 2003.

Contributor to anthology *Superman and the Heroes of September 11, 2001,* edited by Paul Levitz, DC Comics (New York, NY), 2002; creator of graphic novel *Earth X,* 2001.

SIDELIGHTS: American comic-book artist Alex Ross is known as "the Norman Rockwell of comics" because of his photorealistic style. His award-winning work is often called "painted comic books" because he uses live models, light, shadow, and color to create his figures. He depicts such classic comics characters as Superman and Batman as somewhat older men, looking appropriately worn for the work they have been doing to fight crime for so many years.

Ross credits his father, a minister, for providing him with a sense of the morality involved in performing good deeds. In a biography on his home page, Ross is quoted as saying, "There was a positive effect to being around him, and his actions tied into what the superhero comics were teaching me. Superheroes aren't heroes because they're strong; they're heroes because they perform acts that look beyond themselves."

Ross was drawing by age three. He fell for comics after seeing Spider Man on a television program, and his love for superheroes—colorful characters who use their might for right—never abated. He was inspired by the work of comics artists Berni Wrightson and George Perez, as well as illustrators Andrew Loomis, Norman Rockwell, Salvador Dali, and J.C. Leyendecker. Ross credited his art-school training for his penchant for working from models. There, he developed his style of painting comics, giving them a greater sense of realism and life.

Ross collaborated with Kurt Busiek on the graphic novel *Marvels,* which looks at Marvel Comics superheroes from the point of view of an ordinary man. His next project was the comic-book series *Kingdom Come,* for DC Comics, a story about a minister who intercedes in a futuristic superhero civil war. Following that project was *U.S.: Uncle Sam,* a series about a dark side of American history.

Ross and writer Paul Dini then began work on a series of graphic novels celebrating the sixtieth anniversary of DC Comics' iconic superheroes, Superman, Batman,

Captain Marvel, Wonder Woman, and the Justice League of America (JLA). This series begins with *Superman: Peace on Earth,* in which the superhero, touched by the plight of a runaway child plagued by hunger at Christmastime, decides to embark on a twenty-four-hour mission to feed the world's hungry. However, as he faces seemingly insurmountable obstacles—dictatorships, theft, distribution difficulties, and food riots—he feels what ordinary humans feel when trying to change the world. His mission ends in failure, and he learns that even he must start small to make lasting changes. Ken Tucker, in *Entertainment Weekly,* called the book "a lovely fable of idealism." Richard von Busack, in *Metro,* described it as "the mainstream comic at its best," adding that the book "stirs feelings that lie buried underneath a crust of despair, reminding readers of the hopefulness that images of Superman once inspired." Asked by von Busack about Christian imagery in the story, Ross said it is deliberate. "There's a great aspect of Christian myth in Superman," he commented, yet "by no means should Superman have the authority to save us from ourselves. . . . We could only benefit from the example of his never-ending battle." Tom Knapp, in a review for *Rambles* online, objected to the portrayal of Superman as an older man but conceded that Ross "fills this book with lifelike images which bring an all-too-human dimension to the problems Superman faces." In a review for *Weekly Wire,* Robert Faires noted that Ross's photorealistic style is captivating, but "it is the spirit that comes through his portraits, a spirit as much a part of this character's enduring power as his ability to leap tall buildings in a single bound. This is a man of uncommon goodness." Faires called the book "as elegant and lush as a museum exhibition book."

Batman: War on Crime brings back another superhero, the Caped Crusader of Gotham City. In this book, he is reminded of the violent death of his own parents when he sees a ghetto boy named Marcus orphaned after his parents are killed in a robbery. As a result, Batman goes on a mission to break up the ghetto gangs and drug labs. Von Busack, in a review for *Metro,* said he would have preferred that Batman take on his traditional villains rather than the predominantly black men he faces in the drug raids. However, von Busack admired the fact that the original artwork for the book was auctioned to benefit the John A. Reisenbach school in Harlem. Auctioning his original art for benefits is a regular practice for Ross. Knapp found the book "moving and powerful and laden with messages" and he

said that Ross "brings characters to life with extremely vivid and realistic paintings." James R. Henry, in a review for *Comic Book,* said he was surprised by Batman's older look and thought the multiple scars revealed when he removed his shirt are problematic in maintaining Batman's secret identity as billionaire Bruce Wayne. Yet, Henry praised Ross's art, saying: "The detail is amazing: everything from light and shadow to the body language of society debutantes is dead-on accurate."

Shazam! Power of Hope is a Captain Marvel story in which the superhero visits a children's hospital and, in a series of vignettes, rights wrongs, provides hope, and takes several young patients on flying adventures. Ross's original artwork was auctioned to benefit the Make-a-Wish Foundation. Knapp found the story less interesting than the Superman and Batman episodes but still "touching" and Ross's art "startling in its ability to give life to his . . . characters." Ray Tate, in *Line of Fire Reviews,* called Ross "the N.C. Wyeth or Howard Pyle of comic books" and said his Captain Marvel drawings recall the photos taken from the 1930s films starring Tom Tyler.

Wonder Woman: Spirit of Truth reprises the female superhero, who takes on secret identities as a protestor, a Muslim woman, and a soldier as she goes about her work fighting terrorists, with her ice-blue eyes, golden lasso and bracelets, skimpy costume, and invisible plane. Randy Lander, in a review for the *Fourth Rail* online, said the creators give readers insight into her mind: "We can see that she has problems with confidence, that every battle isn't easy for her, and while she can deflect bullets . . . , she still has to contend with doubt and fear like everyone else." Knapp said Ross "has provided stunning visuals that seem unbelievably realistic. His characters seem to move, to breathe, and it's a wonder they don't leap from the page." Tate also praised Ross's art, concluding: "One simply cannot ask for a better Wonder Woman story than *Spirit of Truth.*"

Ross and Dini followed the Wonder Woman novel with *JLA: Secret Origins* which reveals the origins of DC Comics' superhero team the Justice League of America, featuring Superman, Batman, Wonder Woman, Green Lantern, the Flash, Aquaman, and others. In *Library Journal,* Steve Raiteri described Ross's artwork as "strikingly realistic and gorgeous." The second graphic novel based on the JLA, *Liberty and Justice,* finds the team battling a deadly alien bacteria unlike anything they have ever encountered. As fear and panic grip the world, even the team of superheroes comes under suspicion for causing the invasion.

BIOGRAPHICAL AND CRITICAL SOURCES:

PERIODICALS

Chicago, February, 1998, Todd Pruzan, "Notes from the Underground," p. 68.
Entertainment Weekly, November 20, 1998, Ken Tucker, review of *Superman: Peace on Earth,* p. 121; January 25, 2002, William Keck, "Glimmer Man," p. 12.
Library Journal, March 1, 2003, Steve Raiteri, review of *JLA: Secret Origins,* p. 74.
M2 Best Books, January 8, 2002, "Comic Books Pay Tribute to New York Emergency Services."
MPLS-St. Paul Magazine, September, 2001, Emily Burt and Patrick Jones, "Alternative Teen Reads," p. 168.
Publishers Weekly, October 28, 2002, review of *Supreme: The Story of the Year,* p. 53.
School Library Journal, May, 1999, Francisca Goldsmith, review of *Superman: Peace on Earth,* p. 162.
Sojourners, November-December, 1998, Nate Solloway, review of *U.S.: Uncle Sam,* p. 60.

ONLINE

Alex Ross Home Page, http://www.alexrossart.com (August 12, 2003).
Comic Book Web site, http://comicbook.100freemb.com/ (August 19, 2003), James R. Henry, review of *Batman: War on Crime.*
DC Comics Web site, http://www.dccomics.com/ (December 18, 2003).
Fourth Rail, http://www.thefourthrail.com/ (November 12, 2001), Randy Lander, review of *Wonder Woman: Spirit of Truth.*
Lambiek, http://www.lambiek.net/ (August 12, 2003), "Alex Ross."
MetroActive.com, http://www.metroactive.com/ (December 3, 1998), Richard von Busack, "Square Is Beautiful: Cartoonist Alex Ross Revives the Moral Authority of the Man of Steel" (review of *Superman: Peace on Earth*); (December 2, 1999)

Richard von Busack, "Batman in the 'Hood: Batman's War on Crime Looks a Little Too Much like the Real War on Drugs."
Rambles, http://www.rambles.net/ (March 9, 2002), Tom Knapp, review of *Wonder Woman: Spirit of Truth;* (August 19, 2003) Tom Knapp, reviews of *Superman: Peace on Earth, Batman: War on Crime,* and *Shazam! Power of Hope.*
Silver Bullet Comic Books Web site, http://www.silverbulletcomicbooks.com/ (December 2, 2000), Ray Tate, review of *Shazam! Power of Hope;* (November 17, 2001) Ray Tate, review of *Wonder Woman: Spirit of Truth.*
Weekly Wire, http://weeklywire.com/ (December 20, 1998), Robert Faires, review of *Superman: Peace on Earth.**

*   *   *

ROUART, Jean-Marie 1943-

PERSONAL: Born April 8, 1943, in Neuilly-sur-Seine, France.

ADDRESSES: Home—France. *Agent*—c/o Author Mail, Éditions Grasset & Fasquelle, 61, rue des Saints-Père, 75006 Paris, France.

CAREER: Writer and journalist. *Magazine littéraire,* writer, 1967; *Figaro,* political journalist; *Quotiedien de Paris,* director of literary pages; *Figaro littéraire,* political journalist, then director, 1986-2003.

MEMBER: Academie Française, George Duby chair, 1997.

AWARDS, HONORS: Renaudot prize, for *Avant-guerre,* 1983; Prince Pierre of Monaco prize.

WRITINGS:

NOVELS

La fuite en Pologne (novel, title means "Escape from Poland"), Grasset (Paris, France), 1974.
La blessure de Georges Aslo (novel), Grasset (Paris, France), 1975.

Les feux du pouvoir (novel), Grasset (Paris, France), 1977.

Le mythomane (novel), Grasset (Paris, France), 1980.

Avant-guerre (novel), Grasset (Paris, France), 1983.

Ils ont choisis la nuit, Grasset (Paris, France), 1985.

Le cavalier blessé (novel), Grasset (Paris, France), 1987.

La femme de proie (novel), Grasset (Paris, France), 1989.

Le voleur de jeunesse (novel), Grasset (Paris, France), 1990.

Le goût du malheur (novel), Gallimard (Paris, France), 1993.

L'invention de l'amour (novel), Grasset (Paris, France), 1997.

Une jeunesse à l'ombre de la lumière (novel), Gallimard (Paris, France), 2000.

BIOGRAPHIES

Morny: un voluptueux au pouvoir, Gallimard (Paris, France), 1995.

La noblesse des vaincus, Grasset (Paris, France), 1997.

Bernis: le cardinal des plaisirs, Gallimard (Paris, France), 1998.

Une famille dans l'impressionnisme, Gallimard (Paris, France), 2001.

Adieu à la France qui s'en va, Grasset (Paris, France), 2003.

OTHER

Omar: la construction d'un coupable (case study), Editions de Fallois (Paris, France), 1994.

(With Hélène Carrère d'Encausse and Jean d'Ormesson) *Discours de récaption de Jean-Marie Rouart et résponse de Hélène Carrère d'Encausse,* Grasset (Paris, France), 2000.

Nous ne savons pas aimer (autobiography), Gallimard (Paris, France), 2002.

Ils on choisi la nuit (case study), Grasset (Paris, France), 2003.

Libertin et chrétin: entretiens avec Marc Leboucher, Desclée de Brouwer (Paris, France), 2004.

Mes fauves, Grasset (Paris, France), 2005.

Contributor to *Paris-Match.*

SIDELIGHTS: Jean-Marie Rouart was born to a family of painters but chose to follow his own path, becoming a writer and journalist. His first novel, *La fuite en Pologne* ("Escape from Poland"), was published in 1974. He went on to write several more novels, winning the Renaudot prize in 1983 for *Avant-guerre.* In addition to his novels, he has written biographical accounts of several figures throughout French history and an autobiographical account of his own experiences with love titled *Nous ne savons pas aimer.* In an article for *World Literature Today,* reviewer Donald Dziekowicz remarked on Rouart's recounting of his love affairs, stating that the writer "candidly meditates upon his amorous affairs with nostalgic regret . . . [and] he involves himself in situations that leave him void of any caring once the sexual act is terminated."

Une jeunesse à l'ombre de la lumière also has an autobiographical feel to it, despite being labeled a novel. Anita Brookner, reviewing the book for the *Spectator,* called the volume "an autobiography interspersed with travel notes." The narrator focuses on the disappointments in his life and career. Brookner wrote that "Rouart writes, in a particularly mellifluous French, of his early years, which to him were overshadowed by failure, but failure seen through the years of later success." She concluded that the volume "proves, against the odds, that confession . . . is eminently attractive on the page."

BIOGRAPHICAL AND CRITICAL SOURCES:

BOOKS

Rouart, Jean-Marie, *Nous ne savons pas aimer,* Gallimard (Paris, France), 2002.

PERIODICALS

Booklist, September 15, 1991, Bosilika Stevanovic, review of *Le voleur de jeunesse,* p. 128; December 15, 1994, review of *Omar: la construction d'un coupable,* p. 74.

Economist, October 4, 2003, "France's Autumn Blues: Naming the Villains," p. 80.

Express International, October 7, 1993, review of *Le goût du malheur,* p. 69.

Film Quarterly, fall, 1986, review of *Ils ont choisis la nuit,* p. 64.

Spectator, December 30, 2000, Anita Brookner, review of *Une jeunesse à l'ombre de la lumière,* pp. 27-28.

Spirale, November-December, 1999, review of *Bernis: le cardinal des plaisirs,* pp. 6-7.

World Literature Today, October-December, 2003, Donald Dziekowicz, review of *Nous ne savons pas aimer,* p. 114.

ONLINE

Academie Française Web site, http://www.academie-francaise.fr/ (September 24, 2005), "Jean-Marie Rouart."

Éditions Gallimard Web site, http://www.gallimard.fr/ (September 24, 2005), "Jean-Marie Rouart."

Éditions Grasset & Fasquelle Web site, http://www.edition-grasset.fr/ (September 24, 2005), "Jean-Marie Rouart."

Jean-Marie Rouart Home Page, http://www.jean-marierouart.com (September 24, 2005).*

*   *   *

ROZWADOWSKI, Helen M.

PERSONAL: Female. *Education:* Williams College, B.A.; University of Pennsylvania, Ph.D., 1996.

ADDRESSES: Office—University of Connecticut, Avery Point Campus, 1084 Shennecossett Rd., Groton, CT 06340. *E-mail*—helen.rozwadowski@uconn.edu.

CAREER: University of Connecticut, Avery Point, Groton, CT, assistant professor of history of science and coordinator of maritime studies.

AWARDS, HONORS: Ida and Henry Schuman Prize, History of Science Society; William E. and Mary B. Ritter fellowship, Scripps Institute of Oceanography; grants from National Endowment for the Humanities, National Science Foundation, and Smithsonian Institution.

WRITINGS:

The Sea Knows No Boundaries: A Century of Marine Science under ICES, University of Washington (Seattle, WA), 2002.

(Editor, with David van Keuren) *The Machine in Neptune's Garden: Historical Perspectives on Technology and the Marine Environment,* Science History Publications (Sagamore Beach, MA), 2004.

Fathoming the Ocean: The Discovery and Exploration of the Deep Sea, Belknap Press of Harvard University (Cambridge, MA), 2005.

Contributor of scientific articles to scientific journals, including *Public Historian, Minerva, Isis,* and *History and Technology;* contributor to *Discovery On-Line.*

WORK IN PROGRESS: A book on underwater exploration during the cold war era.

SIDELIGHTS: Helen M. Rozwadowski specializes in maritime and environmental history, particularly on research involving the Atlantic Ocean during the twentieth century. It was in this era that the oceans became more than barriers to cross or sources of fish; they became frontiers for exploration and scientific endeavor. Rozwadowski's *The Sea Knows No Boundaries: A Century of Marine Science under ICES* offers a history of the International Council for the Exploration of the Sea (ICES), a body that pooled resources in order to study how the seas could be exploited without depleting fish species. More recently, ICES has studied the oceans' environmental degradation and has used gathered data to support the notion of global warming.

Fathoming the Ocean: The Discovery and Exploration of the Deep Sea examines the mid-twentieth-century scientific investigations of the Atlantic, including measurements of salinity, the effects of dredging, and the mapping of the ocean floor. The book also "addresses the social, cultural, and political aspects of this newfound interest," according to Margaret Rioux in *Library Journal.* Rioux felt that Rozwadowski's work provides an "excellent choice" for audiences interested in the history of science. A *Publishers Weekly* critic deemed *Fathoming the Ocean* an "amiable, in-depth examination of the most critical era for the development of modern oceanography" that it "should do well with maritime buffs."

BIOGRAPHICAL AND CRITICAL SOURCES:

PERIODICALS

Isis, September, 2003, Jacob Darwin Hamblin, review of *The Sea Knows No Boundaries: A Century of Marine Science under ICES,* p. 560; March, 2005,

Steven J. Dick, review of *The Machine in Neptune's Garden: Historical Perspectives on Technology and the Marine Environment*, p. 153.

Library Journal, December 1, 2004, Margaret Rioux, review of *Fathoming the Ocean: The Discovery and Exploration of the Deep Sea*, p. 157.

Publishers Weekly, January 17, 2005, review of *Fathoming the Ocean*, p. 44.

* * *

RUDACILLE, Deborah

PERSONAL: Female.

ADDRESSES: Office—Office of Corporate Communications, Johns Hopkins University, East Baltimore Campus, 901 S. Bond, Rm. 550, Baltimore, MD 21231. *E-mail*—deborah.rudacille@jhu.edu; drudaci1@jhmi.edu.

CAREER: Science writer. Johns Hopkins University, Baltimore, MD, researcher/writer, Johns Hopkins Center for Alternatives to Animal Testing, 1992-97, managing editor and newsletter writer for Institute for Cell Engineering.

WRITINGS:

(With Joanne Zurlo and Alan M. Goldberg) *Animals and Alternatives in Testing: History, Science, and Ethics,* Mary Ann Liebert (New York, NY), 1994.

The Scalpel and the Butterfly: The War between Animal Research and Animal Protection, Farrar, Straus & Giroux (New York, NY), 2000.

The Riddle of Gender: Science, Activism, and Transgender Rights, Pantheon Books (New York, NY), 2005.

SIDELIGHTS: In *The Scalpel and the Butterfly: The War between Animal Research and Animal Protection,* science writer Deborah Rudacille, who worked at the Johns Hopkins Center for Alternatives to Animal Testing, explores the battle between medical researchers who believe that testing on animals is necessary to make life-saving advances in medical science and activists who belief research on animals has been abusive and should be stopped. Rudacille takes a broad look at the issue, recounting the anti-vivisectionist movement of the nineteenth century and providing profiles of the founders of People for the Ethical Treatment of Animals (PETA). She also looks at more-radical groups opposing animal research and how they have hurt the movement. In addition, the author explores modern advances in animal research and new medical advances involving animals, such as xenotransplantation, that is, the transplantation of organs from animals to humans.

Writing in the *Library Journal,* Peggie Partello called *The Scalpel and the Butterfly* a "well-researched and-documented account." A *Publishers Weekly* contributor wrote that the book is a "cautious, useful survey" and noted that the author "seeks a middle ground" in addressing the controversy. In a review in *Booklist,* Vanessa Bush commented, "Rudacille . . . is masterful at examining the lengths to which science has been willing to go for the sake of advancements." *Isis* contributor Anita Guerrini wrote that the author "offers a thoughtful account of the ethical issues surrounding recent developments in biomedical research."

Rudacille takes a looks at the issues surrounding gender and transsexuals in *The Riddle of Gender: Science, Activism, and Transgender Rights.* The author not only includes interviews with transsexuals who are conducting research or are activists, but also discuses the history of transsexuals dating back to a famous case in the 1700s in which a man decided to live as a woman. In addition, she explores modern research into gender, such as that conducted at the Berlin Institute for Sexual Science. Writing in the *Library Journal,* Jim Van Buskirk called the book a "fascinating exploration" of the topic. A *Publishers Weekly* contributor noted that the author's "sympathetic and well-researched elucidation of . . . the tangled issue of gender variance . . . is . . . a good introduction for the educated lay reader and documented enough for the scholar," while Gilbert Taylor, writing in *Booklist,* called the book "uniquely informative."

BIOGRAPHICAL AND CRITICAL SOURCES:

PERIODICALS

Booklist, September 1, 2000, Vanessa Bush, review of *The Scalpel and the Butterfly: The War Between Animal Research and Animal Protection,* p. 33;

February 15, 2005, Gilbert Taylor, review of *The Riddle of Gender: Science, Activism, and Transgender Rights,* p. 1042.

Isis, March, 2004, Anita Guerrini, review of *The Scalpel and the Butterfly,* p. 168.

Library Journal, September 1, 2000, Peggie Partello, review of *The Scalpel and the Butterfly,* p. 245; April 1, 2005, Jim Van Buskirk, review of *The Riddle of Gender,* p. 64.

Publishers Weekly, July 31, 2000, review of *The Scalpel and the Butterfly,* p. 82; January 17, 2005, review of *The Riddle of Gender,* p. 47.

ONLINE

Brothers Judd.com, http://www.brothersjudd.com/ (September 19, 2005), review of *The Scalpel and the Butterfly.*

National Association of Science Writers Web site, http://www.nasw.org/ (November 11, 2005), review of *The Scalpel and the Butterfly.*

PrideSource.com, http://www.pridesource.com/ (November 11, 2005), review of *The Riddle of Gender.*

*   *   *

RUSCH, Sheldon M.

PERSONAL: Born in Augusta, GA; married; wife's name Katie (a poet and musician); children: Shannon, Michaela, Jackson. *Education:* University of Wisconsin, B.A.

ADDRESSES: Home—1510 W. El Rancho Dr., #97N, Mequon, WI 53092-5623. *Agent*—Sarah Lazin Books, 126 5th Ave., Ste. 300, New York, NY 10011. *E-mail*—smrusch@wi.rr.com.

CAREER: BVK Advertising, Glendale, WI, advertising copywriter. Yoga instructor, 1968—.

WRITINGS:

For Edgar (novel), Berkley Prime Crime (New York, NY), 2005.

SIDELIGHTS: A lifelong interest in the works of nineteenth-century American writer Edgar Allan Poe led Sheldon M. Rusch to write his debut novel, *For Edgar.* On his home page, Rusch noted that, as he studied Poe's life and works, he became awed "with [Poe's] absolute brilliance not only as a composer of the tales and poems, but as a scholar, philosopher, and visionary." In *For Edgar,* a homicide investigator named Elizabeth Taylor Hewitt enlists the help of a professor friend to solve a grisly series of murders, each based on a different short story by Poe. The murderer, who calls himself the Raven, leaves clues with the corpses, and she eventually threatens Hewitt and her partner. "Hewitt is a refreshing new character," noted Deborah Hern on the *Romance Reader's Connection* Web site. Hern liked the way Hewitt proves "competent and compassionate, never coming across as some kind of woman-in-charge caricature."

Several reviewers reacted favorably to *For Edgar.* For instance, a *Kirkus Reviews* contributor wrote that the title is "a startlingly effective debut, and an obvious candidate for its own Edgar," referring to the annual award for best mystery novel. In *Publishers Weekly* a critic called the book "sharply written" and commended its heroine's "hilariously outspoken" personality. Rex E. Klett concluded in *Library Journal* that *For Edgar* is an "excellent first novel [that] offers a modern-day rendering of old horrors."

BIOGRAPHICAL AND CRITICAL SOURCES:

PERIODICALS

Entertainment Weekly, August 5, 2005, Tom Sinclair, review of *For Edgar,* p. 70.

Kirkus Reviews, June 15, 2005, review of *For Edgar,* p. 667.

Library Journal, August 1, 2005, Rex E. Klett, review of *For Edgar,* p. 57.

Milwaukee Journal Sentinel, September 4, 2005, "Midwest Passages: Sheldon Rusch."

Publishers Weekly, June 27, 2005, review of *For Edgar,* p. 44.

ONLINE

Romance Reader's Connection, http://www.theromancereadersconnection.com/ (September 28, 2005), Deborah Hern, review of *For Edgar.*

Sheldon Rusch Home Page, http://www.sheldonrusch.com (October 25, 2005).*

RUSSELL, Kirk 1954-

PERSONAL: Born 1954, in CA; married Judy Rogers (a chef and restaurant owner); children: two daughters. *Education:* University of California at Berkeley, B.A., 1978. *Hobbies and other interests:* Hang gliding, mountain biking, skiing, cycling, backpacking.

ADDRESSES: Home—Berkeley, CA. *Agent*—Philip G. Spitzer Literary Agency, 50 Talmage Farm Ln., East Hampton, NY 11937. *E-mail*—kirk@kirk-russell.com.

CAREER: Novel and entrepreneur. Founder of construction company, until c. 1995.

WRITINGS:

"JOHN MARQUEZ" SERIES; NOVELS

Shell Games, Chronicle Books (San Francisco, CA), 2003.
Night Game, Chronicle Books (San Francisco, CA), 2004.
Dead Game, Chronicle Books (San Francisco, CA), 2005.

WORK IN PROGRESS: A stand-alone crime novel.

SIDELIGHTS: Kirk Russell earned a living as a builder and owner of a construction company in his native California until the mid-1990s, when he began to devote himself to fiction writing. His breakthrough as a crime novelist came when he learned of an undercover unit of state agents who work in the wilderness finding game poachers and other criminals who exploit natural resources. The protagonist in Russell's first three novels is the fictitious John Marquez, a former Drug Enforcement Agency detective who has joined the California Department of Fish and Game's elite Special Operations Unit. In an online interview with Tracy Farnsworth for *Roundtable Reviews,* Russell said that, while he does not want to preach conservation in his thrillers, "We've got some very dedicated, very genuine good people out there fighting a quiet war for wildlife."

In Russell's debut work, *Shell Games,* Marquez and his unit search for poachers who illegally harvest abalones off the shores of California. Prized for its meat, abalone has been driven to the brink of extinc-

tion by over-harvesting. As Marquez tries to find the poachers, he discovers that a former drug dealer seeking revenge is tracking him. In *Booklist* Connie Fletcher described Marquez as "far and away the most inventive new detective hero," based on his worthy but unusual occupation. A *Kirkus Reviews* critic noted that the book does not follow the usual patterns of debut thrillers. "This is not a cliché fest," the critic noted. "The story is loaded with atmosphere."

Marquez continues fighting for wildlife in *Night Game.* In this outing the detective must find and stop a ruthless gang that kills bears for bile and paws—both prized on the alternative-medicine market. A *Kirkus Reviews* contributor styled the novel a "splendid second outing in a procedural series" and concluded that the thriller demonstrates "superb suspense, culminating in an exhausting but satisfying series of chases." Fletcher, writing again for *Booklist,* emphasized that Russell reveals the California wilderness with an insight that makes his work "achingly credible." In her *All Readers* online piece, Harriet Klausner suggested that the wild California mountains "come across as sinister and dangerous as any urban noir scene."

The third Marquez procedural, *Dead Game,* finds Marquez tracking sturgeon poachers who value the endangered fish for its caviar. Russell told Jenna Glatzer on *AbsoluteWrite.com* that his books would not have been as plausible had the real California Fish and Game detectives not allowed him to accompany them on busts. "When I met the Fish and Game team something happened inside," he said. "I knew immediately this was a character I could truly care about, write, and believe in. I wanted to make a kind of modern-day hero and I saw the possibility in what this team was doing and the way they did it."

BIOGRAPHICAL AND CRITICAL SOURCES:

PERIODICALS

Booklist, July, 2003, Connie Fletcher, review of *Shell Games,* p. 1871; September 15, 2004, Connie Fletcher, review of *Night Game,* p. 214.
Kirkus Reviews, July 15, 2003, review of *Shell Games,* p. 933; August 15, 2004, review of *Night Game,* p. 773; July 1, 2005, review of *Dead Game,* p. 711.
Library Journal, October 1, 2004, Teresa L. Jacobson, review of *Night Game,* p. 65.

ONLINE

AbsoluteWrite.com, http://www.absolutewrite.com/ (October 17, 2005), Jenna Glatzer, "Interview with Kirk Russell."

All Readers, http://www.allreaders.com/ (October 17, 2005), Harriet Klausner, review of *Night Game.*

Kirk Russell Home Page, http://www.kirk-russell.com (October 17, 2005).

Roundtable Reviews Online, http://www.roundtable reviews.com/ (October 17, 2005), Tracy Farnsworth, "A Roundtable Interview with Kirk Russell."*

*   *   *

RUSTAGE, Alan
   See SPENCER, Sally

S

SAFFORD, John L. 1947-
(John Lugton Safford)

PERSONAL: Born January 6, 1947, in Pasadena, CA; son of Alton L. (an educator) and Margaret B. (a social worker) Safford; married Virginia Melrose (an educator), June, 1983; children: Joseph D., Janet A. *Education:* San Diego State University, M.A. (philosophy), 1974; California State College, San Bernardino, M.A. (history), 1980; University of California, Riverside, M.A. (political science), 1982, Ph.D., 1984. *Hobbies and other interests:* Making bows and arrows, shorin karate (third-degree black belt).

ADDRESSES: Office—Department of Social Sciences, University of South Carolina at Sumter, 200 Miller Rd., Sumter, SC 29150-2498. *E-mail*—jsafford@usc-sumter.edu.

CAREER: Writer and educator. Mount San Antonio College, Walnut, CA, instructor in philosophy, 1978-84; University of South Carolina at Sumter, faculty member, 1984—, professor of government and philosophy, 1995—. *Military service:* U.S. Army, 1967-68; served in Vietnam; received Bronze Star and Combat Infantry Badge.

MEMBER: American Political Science Association, American Philosophical Association, South Carolina Political Science Association.

WRITINGS:

Pragmatism and the Progressive Movement in the United States: The Origin of the New Social Sciences, University Press of America (Lanham, MD), 1987.

(With Hasmukh M. Raval) *Bhagavad-Gita: A Philosophical System,* W.H. Green (St. Louis, MO), 1990.

Democracy Is Dangerous: Resisting the Tyranny of the Majority, University Press of America (Lanham, MD), 2002.

(With Stanley M. Honer, Thomas C. Hunt, and Dennis L. Okholm) *Invitation to Philosophy: Issues and Options,* Wadsworth (Belmont, CA), 2006.

Contributor to journals.

WORK IN PROGRESS: The History of Epistemology; research on the relationship of religion and virtue to politics.

SIDELIGHTS: John L. Safford told *CA:* "I've always loved to read about history, philosophy, and politics. Best of all, with my job working in a university, I can call it 'research.' I enjoy teaching students who are interested in these areas. Finally, when I have something very detailed to explain, or an argument to make, I get satisfaction in writing it out as an article or a book."

*　　*　　*

SAFFORD, John Lugton
See SAFFORD, John L.

*　　*　　*

SAGINOR, Jennifer 1969(?)-

PERSONAL: Born c. 1969, in Los Angeles, CA. *Education:* Mount Vernon College, graduated.

ADDRESSES: Agent—c/o Author Mail, HarperEntertainment, 10 E. 53rd St., 7th Fl., New York, NY 10022.

CAREER: Writer. Worked in film production and development at Spelling Entertainment, Miramax Films, and Motion Picture Corporation of America.

WRITINGS:

Playground: A Childhood Lost inside the Playboy Mansion, HarperEntertainment (New York, NY), 2005.

SIDELIGHTS: In her memoir, *Playground: A Childhood Lost inside the Playboy Mansion,* Jennifer Saginor recalls her life after her mother and father divorced when she was six. Her father, a doctor to the rich and powerful in Hollywood, started taking her and her older sister to the Playboy Mansion with him. Saginor recounts how, on her first visit to the mansion as a little girl, she saw a famous actor having sex with a Playboy bunny. Over the years, Saginor would witness much that is not meant for children's eyes, including rampant drug use. Although her mother tried to prevent her ex-husband from taking their daughters to the mansion, where he seems to have a permanent open invitation, the girls enjoy the party atmosphere and often, at the behest of their father, lied to their mother about these visits. Saginor moved in with her dad full time when in high school, and eventually she was drawn into the hedonistic lifestyle, starting a relationship with an actor when she was fifteen and becoming involved in drugs.

In a review of *Playground* in *Salon.com,* Christine Smallwood noted that "one becomes not just a private witness and voyeur to Saginor's life, but a friend and confidante." Smallwood went on to comment that the author's "style creates this eavesdropping effect." Scott Eyman, writing in the *Palm Beach Post,* commented that "her characterization of her father is as a classic emotional bully, a man dependent on a proximity to fame for his identity, and who uses that proximity to score a succession of women and drugs that gradually debilitates him physically and emotionally." A *Publishers Weekly* contributor commented of the book that "readers seeking colorful general-issue dish, sleaze and bad behavior will find it in spades."

BIOGRAPHICAL AND CRITICAL SOURCES:

BOOKS

Saginor, Jennifer, *Playground: A Childhood Lost inside the Playboy Mansion,* HarperEntertainment (New York, NY), 2005.

PERIODICALS

Entertainment Weekly, May 27, 2005, Gilbert Cruz, brief review of *Playground,* p. 103; June 17, 2005, Jennifer Reese, review of *Playground,* p. 85.
Kirkus Reviews, April 1, 2005, review of *Playground,* p. 407.
Palm Beach Post, August 28, 2005, Scott Eyman, review of *Playground.*
Publishers Weekly, April 18, 2005, review of *Playground,* p. 53.
Weekly Standard, June 13, 2005, "Great Moments In Acknowledgments," p. 39.

ONLINE

Maxim Online, http://www.maximonline.com/ (September 19, 2005), Gregg Braverman, review of *Playground.*
Salon.com, http://www.salon.com (July 7, 2005), Christine Smallwood, review of *Playground.**

*   *   *

SALAMA, Hannu 1936-

PERSONAL: Born October 6, 1936, in Kouvola, Finland; son of Sulo Erland (an electrician) and Mirjam (Heino) Salama; children: Markku, Laura. *Education:* Attended Folk Academy, 1957-58.

ADDRESSES: Agent—c/o Author Mail, Otava Publishing Company, Ltd., Uudenmaankatu 10, 00120, Helsinki, Finland.

CAREER: Novelist and poet. Worked variously as an agricultural worker and electrician. *Military service:* Sergeant in Finnish armed forces, 1957.

MEMBER: Finnish Writers' Union.

AWARDS, HONORS: Literature prize, Nordic Council, 1975, for *Siinä näkijä missä tekijä;* Väinö Linna award, 1979; Eno Leino literary prize, 1985; Aleksis Kivi literature prize, 1990; Kiila award, 1987; Finnish

Writers' Union award, 1995; honorary award, Haavikko Foundation, 1997; awards from City of Tampere and from Government of Finland.

WRITINGS:

NOVELS

Se tavallinen tarina (title means "The Same Old Story"), 1961.

Juhannustanssit (title means "Midsummer Dance"), 1964.

Minä, Olli ja Orvokki (title means "Ollie, Orvokki, and Me"), 1967.

Siinä näkijä missä tekijä (title means "No Crime without a Witness"), 1972.

Kolme sukupolvea (title means "Three Generations"), Otava (Helsinki, Finland), 1978.

Vuosi elämästäni (title means "A Year of My Life"), Otava (Helsinki, Finland), 1979.

Amos ja saarelaiset (title means "Amos and the Islanders"), Otava (Helsinki, Finland), 1987.

Ottopoika (title means "Adoptive Son"), Otava, (Helsinki, Finland), 1991.

Pieni menestystarina (title means "A Small Success Story"), Otava (Helsinki, Finland), 1993.

Elämän opetuslapsia I (title means "Disciples of Life I"), Art House (Helsinki, Finland), 1997.

Elämän opetuslapsia II (title means "Disciples of Life II"), Art House (Helsinki, Finland), 1999.

"FINLANDIA CYCLE" NOVELS

Kosti Herhiläisen perunkirjoitus (title means "Inventory of Kosti Herhiläisen"), Otava (Helsinki, Finland), 1976.

Kolera on raju bändi (title means "Cholera Is a Wild Band"), Otava (Helsinki, Finland), 1977.

Pasi Harvalan tarina I (title means "Pasi Harvala's Tale I"), Otava (Helsinki, Finland), 1981.

Pasi Harvalan tarina II (title means "Pasi Harvala's Tale II"), Otava (Helsinki, Finland), 1983.

Kaivo kellarissa (title means "A Well in the Cellar"), Otava (Helsinki, Finland), 1983.

SHORT STORIES

Tienviitta ja muita novelleja: valikoima teoksista Lomapäivä, Kenttäläinen käy talossa ja kesäleski (title means "Signpost and Other Short Stories"), Otava (Helsinki, Finland), 1974.

Ihmisen ääni (title means "Voice of a Human"), Söderström (Porvoo, Finland), 1978.

Näkymä kuivaushuoneen ikkunasta (title means "A View through the Window of a Drying Room"), Otava (Helsinki, Finland), 1988.

Hyvä veli (title means "Dear John"), Otava (Helsinki, Finland), 1992.

Crime Stories, Otava (Helsinki, Finland), 1995.

POEMS

Puu balladin haudalla (title means "A Tree on the Grave of the Ballad"), Otava (Helsinki, Finland), 1963.

Villanpehmee, taskuulämmin (title means "Soft as Wool, Warm as a Pocket"), Otava (Helsinki, Finland), 1971.

Itäväylä (title means "Easter Route"), Otava (Helsinki, Finland), 1980.

Punajuova (title means "Red Thread"), Otava (Helsinki, Finland), 1985.

OTHER

Pentti Saarikoski, a Living Legend (in Finnish), Otava (Helsinki, Finland), 1975.

SIDELIGHTS: Hannu Salama is considered one of the best Finnish writers of his generation, although much of his work has been highly controversial. Although he stopped going to school early to work as a farm laborer and later in the electrical trades, he was an avid reader drawn, in particular, to existentialist writers such as Albert Camus and Jean-Paul Sartre, but also to American authors like William Faulkner, Ernest Hemingway, and John Steinbeck. Also enthusiastic about the works of Fyodor Dostoyevsky and Friedreich Nietzsche, Salama contructed his literary worldview based on his fear of hereditary schizophrenia and his highly critical view of society.

Salama antagonized Finnish society when he published *Juhannustanssit,* a highly provocative 1964 novel that exposes the shallow values of the Finnish upper class. Because of certain words he attributed to Jesus Christ in the novel, Salama was accused of blasphemy on the basis of an outdated law. Although the novelist was convicted, the sentence was suspended and later nullified by the president of Finland.

In the novel *Minä, Olli ja Orvokki*, Salama depicts a world of greed, deceit, and corruption. The story centers around Olli, a playboy whose only goal in life is to satisfy his ego. Olli is surrounded by shallow, hypocritical people who are as selfish as he is but spend their lives imagining that they are upstanding citizens. Pekka Tarkka, writing in critical study *Salama,* strongly praised the novelist as a philosophical writer in the tradition of Dostoyevsky, observing that Salama's book shows how the struggle for freedom—in particular, a freedom from capitalist exploitation—can lead to unexpected, even undesirable, consequences. As Tarkka declared, "Salama is a writer of the tragedy of freedom. His characters, whether described in the language of existentialism or of socialism, do not escape humiliation or defeat; their dreams are turned upside down. Salama's humanity lies in this empathic identification with the insulted and injured. The most important person to him is the individual making decisions in concrete situations; like Sartre, he prefers describing the consciousness of an individual to picturing the assimilation of an individual by a group."

Salama's later novel, *Siinä näkijä missä tekijä,* was well received by both the public and critics and was awarded the literature prize of the Nordic Council in 1975. In this novel Salama describes the dangerous world of the Finnish Communist movement during World War II. The book is primarily about deceit and betrayal. According to Philip Binham in *Books Abroad,* Salama excels in his descriptions of his characters. Binham especially admired the novelist's ability to present the narrative from the point of view of several characters. Naturally, as the critic pointed out, the reader encounters a story with many dimensions. "One must admire the skill," Binham asserted, "with which Salama has drawn complex threads of this theme together as well as the thoroughness, patience, and courage with which he has tackled a delicate subject that few have dared to approach."

In his five-part epic cycle, ironically named *Finlandia* after the title of musical composer Jean Sibelius's patriotic composition, Salama defies literary convention. A somewhat autobiographical work, *Finlandia* posits a narrative based on Salama's personal history against the backdrop of modern Finnish history, in particular the struggle between left-wing and right-wing political ideologies. Some of the featured characters in the cycle are alter egos of the author himself. Critics noted that, as in Salama's earlier novels, the struggles of the main characters ultimately end in defeat and despair. In *World Literature Today,* Reino Virtanen described the third novel in the cycle as a jigsaw puzzle, adding that *Pasi Harvalan tarina I* is intermittently clearly written and chaotic. According to Virtanen, "Salama evidently considers that he has a license from James Joyce and Claude Simon to move in and out between direct and indirect discourse, challenging the reader to accompany him." The protagonist of the fifth novel, *Kaivo kellarissa,* serves as Salama's alter ego: a novelist, Salminen is working on an ambitious narrative. As Virtanen observed, *Kaivo kellarissa,* "like the previous volumes of the cycle, is a personal account which includes the author's ruminations about his country's destiny and also, at a cosmic level, about the destiny of the world."

Also an acclaimed poet, Salama is known for verse that can be harshly critical of social conventions. *World Literature Today* contributor Kalevi Lappalainen described the pieces in the collection *Itäväylä* as poems with "rough edges, even cruel compositions." Citing the poet's facility with ordinary language and his occasional "wild, mad-cap effects," the critic concluded that Salama's "head-on style" in this volume merits attention. Reviewing the 1985 collection *Punajuova* in *World Literature Today,* Lappalainen again noted the poet's "uncanny slang idioms" as well as his "street-wise" sensibility but added that Salama also offers more lyrical and accessible poems in the volume. "Salama's verse," Lappalainen concluded, "creates feelings of anger and nostalgia, bringing vivid recollections of one's cherished moments to life."

BIOGRAPHICAL AND CRITICAL SOURCES:

BOOKS

Contemporary Literary Criticism, Volume 18, Thomson Gale (Detroit, MI), 1981.
Encyclopedia of World Literature in the Twentieth Century, St. James Press (Detroit, MI), 1999.
Tarkka, Pekka, *Salama,* Otava (Helsinki, Finland), 1973.
Zuck, Virpi, editor, *Dictionary of Scandinavian Literature,* Greenwood Press (New York, NY), 1990.

PERIODICALS

Books Abroad, autumn, 1973, Philip Binham, review of *Siinä näkijä missä tekijä,* p. 801.

Dimension: Contemporary German Arts and Letters, 1994, contemporary Nordic literature issue, pp. 504-505.

World Literature Today, spring, 1980, Anne Fried, review of *Vuosi elämästäni,* p. 314; autumn, 1982, Reino Virtanen, review of *Pasi Harvalan tarina I,* pp. 727-728; winter, 1982, Kalevi Lappalainen, review of *Itäväylä,* p. 153; spring, 1984, Reino Virtanen, review of *Pasi Harvalan tarina II,* p. 300; summer, 1984, Reino Virtanen, review of *Kaivo kellarissa,* p. 445; autumn, 1986, Kalevi Lappalainen, review of *Punajuova,* p. 662.*

* * *

SALEM, Elise 1955-

PERSONAL: Born May 23, 1955, in Beirut, Lebanon; daughter of Elie (a university president) and Phyllis (Sell) Salem; married Marc Manganero (divorced, 2001); children: Anthony, Thomas, Rania. *Education:* American University of Beirut, M.A., 1979; University of North Carolina at Chapel Hill, Ph.D., 1985.

ADDRESSES: Home—334 Summit Pl., Highland Park, NJ 08904. *Office*—Department of English, Fairleigh Dickinson University, Madison, NJ 07940. *E-mail*—elise@fdu.edu.

CAREER: Writer and educator. Fairleigh Dickinson University, Madison, NJ, professor of English, 1987—, assistant dean for academic planning, 2001-05.

MEMBER: Middle East Studies Association.

WRITINGS:

Constructing Lebanon: A Century of Literary Narratives, University Press of Florida (Gainesville, FL), 2003.

BIOGRAPHICAL AND CRITICAL SOURCES:

PERIODICALS

Literary Review, summer, 2003, Walter Cummins, review of *Constructing Lebanon: A Century of Literary Narratives,* p. 762.

Middle East Journal, summer, 2003, Stephen Sheehi, review of *Constructing Lebanon,* p. 511.

* * *

SANJUAN, Pedro A. 1930-
(Pedro Arroyo Sanjuan)

PERSONAL: Born August 10, 1930. *Education:* Attended Rutgers University and Columbia University; Wofford College, B.A.; Harvard University, M.A.

ADDRESSES: Agent—c/o Author Mail, Random House/Doubleday, 1745 Broadway, New York, NY 10019.

CAREER: Civil servant, artist and writer. U.S. Department of State, Washington, DC, deputy of chief of protocol, 1962, director of Office for Special Representational Services, 1962-63, director of Office of Chancery Affairs, 1963-64, State Department transition team policy coordinator; member of Inter-American Policy Coordinating Committee, 1963-66; Interlandia Corp., president, 1969-71; CLOSE-UP, executive director, 1970-71; Office of the Secretary of Defense, Washington, DC, special assistant to principal deputy assistant secretary, 1971, deputy director of policy plans for negotiations and arms control, 1971-73; assistant for strategic and economic analysis and director of Energy Task Force, 1973-75; Arms Control and Disarmament Agency (ACDA), public-affairs advisor, 1975-77; White House, Washington, DC, member of staff, 1977-78; U.S. Department of the Interior, former assistant secretary. Institute for East-West Dynamics, president; United Nations Secretariat, director of the political affairs division, c. early 1980s. Founder, resident fellow, and director of American Enterprise Institute Hemispheric Center. Host of weekly radio program, Whitney Network. *Exhibitions:* Art displayed in galleries, including Corcoran Gallery of Art, Washington, DC. *Military service:* U.S. Naval Reserve, 1956-59.

AWARDS, HONORS: American Enterprise Institute fellow.

WRITINGS:

(Guest editor) *U.S. Nuclear Export Policy: Views from Latin America,* American Enterprise Institute (Washington, DC), 1979.

Dubya & Eddie, Guignol Press, 2002.

War, Guignol Press, 2002.

Book of Clones, Guignol Press, 2002.

Fighting Geezers: A Manual for Seniors Who Don't Like Getting Pushed Around, Guignol Press, 2003.

Fables: Innocent, Shameful, Irreverent, Guignol Press, 2004.

The UN Gang: A Memoir of Incompetence, Corruption, Anti-Semitism, and Islamic Extremism at the UN Secretariat, Doubleday (New York, NY), 2005.

Contributor to periodicals, including *New York Times*, *Washington Quarterly*, and *Wall Street Journal*.

WORK IN PROGRESS: Caparrucha's War, In 2084 A.D., The Holy Rabbit, Monica Lewinsky Meets John F. Kennedy, and *Secrecy, Covertness, and Huggermuggery*.

SIDELIGHTS: A protégé of the late Senator Robert Kennedy, Pedro A. Sanjuan worked for many years in the U.S. government and the United Nations. He is also the author of several books, including self-illustrated satirical fables and lampoons, and writes about government organizations in his book *The UN Gang: A Memoir of Incompetence, Corruption, Anti-Semitism, and Islamic Extremism at the UN Secretariat*. In the book, Sanjuan—who was known as a rebel throughout his career, which included working for both Democrat and Republican administrations—relates how his real job at the United Nations differed from his official appointment. According to the author, he was directed to spy on the organization during both the Reagan and Bush administrations. He also describes a dysfunctional United Nations that he dislikes intensely. Among his many assertions are that the Russian KBG intelligence unit operated with impunity in the U.S.-based U.N. library and that the terrorist attacks that occurred on September 11, 2001, may have originated in the United Nations. "He portrays a culture that sanctions incompetence, revels in anti-Semitism, winks at drug sales in the U.N. parking garage, encourages espionage . . . while failing to execute its fundamental mission to improve the quality of life around the globe," wrote a *Kirkus Reviews* contributor. The reviewer also commented that the book would provide fodder for those seeking to reform the United Nations and called the author "as amusing as he is opinionated." Another reviewer, writing in *Publishers Weekly*, commented: "The author delivers a lively, preening, sometimes eye-opening insider's account."

BIOGRAPHICAL AND CRITICAL SOURCES:

BOOKS

Sanjuan, Pedro A., *The UN Gang: A Memoir of Incompetence, Corruption, Anti-Semitism, and Islamic Extremism at the UN Secretariat*, Doubleday (New York, NY), 2005.

PERIODICALS

Kirkus Reviews, July 1, 2005, review of *The UN Gang*, p. 725.

Publishers Weekly, July 11, 2005, review of *The UN Gang*, p. 73.

ONLINE

Pedro A. Sanjuan Home Page, http://www.pedro sanjuan.com (September 13, 2005).

Ronald Reagan Presidential Library Archives at the University of Texas, http://www.reagan.utexas.edu/ (July 2, 1981), "Nomination of Pedro A. Sanjuan to Be an Assistant Secretary of the Interior."*

*   *   *

SANJUAN, Pedro Arroyo
See SANJUAN, Pedro A.

*   *   *

SAUNDERS, Frances Stonor 1966-

PERSONAL: Born 1966. *Education:* Graduated from St Anne's College, Oxford.

ADDRESSES: Home—London, England. *Agent*—c/o Author Mail, Fourth Estate, 77-85 Fulham Palace Rd., Hammersmith, London W6 8JB, England.

CAREER: Editor, writer, and producer. Former arts editor for *New Statesman;* producer of arts documentaries for British Broadcasting Corporation, London, England.

AWARDS, HONORS: William Gladstone History Prize, Royal Historical Society, 2000, for *Who Paid the Piper?: The CIA and the Cultural Cold War.*

WRITINGS:

Who Paid the Piper?: The CIA and the Cultural Cold War, Granta Books (London, England), 1999, published as *The Cultural Cold War: The CIA and the World of Arts and Letters,* New Press (New York, NY), 2000.

Hawkwood: Diabolical Englishman, Faber & Faber (London, England), 2004, published as *The Devil's Broker: Seeking Gold, God, and Glory in Fourteenth-Century Italy,* Fourth Estate (New York, NY), 2005.

The Cultural Cold War: The CIA and the World of Arts and Letters was translated into ten languages.

SIDELIGHTS: Frances Stonor Saunders writes about the U.S. Central Intelligence Agency (CIA) and how it infiltrated various cultural organizations in her book *Who Paid the Piper?: The CIA and the Cultural Cold War,* published in the United States as *The Cultural Cold War: The CIA and the World of Arts and Letters.* In her book, Saunders describes how CIA operatives, primarily through the front organization known as the Congress for Cultural Freedom, became ensconced in mostly European cultural organizations and then set out to use art and writings in literary journals and other publications to focus on a government-sponsored agenda, such as anti-communism and anti-revolutionary movements. At the same time, these mediums were used to gloss over mistakes by the U.S. government. The operatives working within the institutions also tried to ensure that Washington's questionable international activities went unaddressed. The author reveals that the CIA spent millions of dollars in its "cultural war" efforts and shows how some respected intellectuals accepted CIA money to participate in what essentially was propaganda.

Calling *Who Paid the Piper?* "fascinating" in the *New Internationalist,* a reviewer commented that the author "deserves credit for shining a light into this dark and shoddy corner of the US-European relationship." *Monthly Review* contributor James Petras wrote that "Saunders' book provides useful information about several important questions regarding the ways in which CIA intellectual operatives defended U.S. imperialist interests on cultural fronts. It also initiates an important discussion of the long-term consequences of the ideological and artistic positions defended by CIA intellectuals." Joan Bridgman, writing in *Contemporary Review,* noted that the author "expertly weaves an impressive array of sources to show how this enterprise was funded and organised." Bridgman also pointed out that the story is not new but added, "What makes it fresh is the detail of this investigation, the concentration of the author's focus, and the drawing together of some hilarious stories about the activities carried out in this ideological battle." In his review in *History Today,* Stephen Plaice wrote, "A very bleak picture is painted here of a generation of minds that allowed itself to be coerced into equating the idea of freedom with the Pax Americana."

For her next book, Saunders delves further back in history to the tell the story of a brutal, fourteenth-century, medieval mercenary. *Hawkwood: Diabolical Englishman,* published in the United States as *The Devil's Broker: Seeking Gold, God, and Glory in Fourteenth-Century Italy,* recounts how Englishman Sir John Hawkwood came to Italy and ultimately led Florence into battle against its foes with a Machiavellian fervor as he exploited his adopted homeland for his own financial benefits. The author recounts the Englishman's early exploits and renown fighting for the English in the Hundred Years' War. When his service was over, Hawkwood decided to take a group of his fellow soldiers with him to Italy instead of returning to his relatively lowly life as a tanner. In the ensuing years, Hawkwood sold the mercenary band's services to the city of Pisa, leaders in Milan, and then in Florence, achieving such renown along the way that the pope christened him "Signore di Bagnacavallo," which means Lord Horsebath. Hawkwood was also immortalized in a fresco by Uccello that was installed in a Florence cathedral. In addition to Hawkwood's exploits, the author explores the political, economic, and social climate of the times, revealing a brutal and evengeful world.

Ian Thomson, writing a review of the book in the *Spectator,* noted that "Saunders is to be congratulated on setting the record straight, and on telling the story of Lord Horsebath so beguilingly." A *Publishers Weekly* contributor noted that the author aptly reveals the mercenary life and "the nature of their contracts, their alliances and betrayals and their democratic decision making." The reviewer added, "Equally lively is Saunders's account of the great Schism of the Church." Robert J. Andrews, writing in the *Library Journal*, commented the "Saunders does an excellent job in bringing both Hawkwood and his times to life," while a *Kirkus Reviews* contributor noted: "British author Saunders does a remarkable job of keeping straight the myriad strands of this historical cat's cradle."

BIOGRAPHICAL AND CRITICAL SOURCES:

PERIODICALS

Booklist, April 15, 2000, Mary Carroll, review of *The Cultural Cold War: The CIA and the World of Arts and Letters,* p. 1505.

Bulletin of Atomic Scientists, September, 2000, Paul D. Boyer, review of *The Cultural Cold War,* p. 59.

Canadian Dimension, March, 2000, Henry Heller, review of *Who Paid the Piper?: The CIA and the Cultural Cold War,* p. 44.

Contemporary Review, October, 1999, Joan Bridgman, review of *Who Paid the Piper?,* p. 211.

History Today, December, 1999, Stephen Plaice, review of *Who Paid the Piper?,* p. 58.

Kirkus Reviews, April 15, 2005, review of *The Devil's Broker: Seeking Gold, God, and Glory in Fourteenth-Century Italy,* p. 463.

Library Journal, June 15, 2005, Robert J. Andrews, review of *The Devil's Broker,* p. 84.

Monthly Review, November, 1999, James Petras, review of *Who Paid the Piper?,* p. 47.

New Internationalist, October, 1999, review of *Who Paid the Piper?,* p. 32.

Observer (London, England), November 21, 2004, Jane Stevenson, review of *Hawkwood: Diabolical Englishman.*

Progressive, July, 2000, Dean Bakopoulos, review of *The Cultural Cold War,* p. 44.

Publishers Weekly, February 21, 2000, review of the *The Cultural Cold War,* p. 74; April 11, 2005, review of *The Devil's Broker,* p. 42.

Spectator (London, England), December 11, 2004, Ian Thomson, review of *Hawkwood,* p. 37.

Washington Monthly, May, 2000, Robert de Neufville, review of *The Cultural Cold War,* p. 52.

World and I, September, 2000, Morton A. Kaplan, review of *The Cultural Cold War,* p. 243.

ONLINE

Asian Review of Books Online, http://www.asian reviewofbooks.com/ (September 19, 2005), James Petras, review of *Hawkwood.*

Marxism-Leninism Today, http://www.mltoday.com/ (September 19, 2005), James Petras, review of *Who Paid the Piper?**

*   *   *

SCHAAP, Jeremy 1969-

PERSONAL: Born 1969, in New York, NY; son of Dick Schaap (a journalist, radio broadcaster, and television broadcaster).

ADDRESSES: Office—ESPN Radio, ESPN Plaza, Bristol, CT 06010.

CAREER: Journalist, radio broadcaster, and television broadcaster. Entertainment & Sports Network (ESPN), New York, NY, national correspondent, 1998—, radio host of *Classic Sports Reporters* and *The Sporting Life,* television host, *Outside the Lines* and *The Sports Reporters.*

WRITINGS:

Cinderella Man: James J. Braddock, Max Baer, and the Greatest Upset in Boxing History, Houghton Mifflin (Boston, MA), 2005.

Contributor of articles to *Sports Illustrated, ESPN: The Magazine, Time, Parade,* and *New York Times.*

SIDELIGHTS: In his book *Cinderella Man: James J. Braddock, Max Baer, and the Greatest Upset in Boxing History,* Jeremy Schaap tells the story of Braddock, a mediocre boxer working during the Great Depression who beat Max Baer for the heavyweight championship in 1935. "This is one of those guys that history kind of forgot," Schaap told *Mediaweek* contributor Anne Torpey-Kemph. In his book, Schaap looks at the careers of both Baer and Braddock leading up to the big fight. He recounts how a fighter that died as the result of a deadly right-hand punch from Baer catapulted the boxer into the limelight. But Baer, according to the author, never really cared for boxing and devoted little time to physically training for the sport. Instead, the brash fighter focused on having a good time, which included dating beautiful Hollywood starlets and others. Braddock on the other hand, was the classic, quiet underdog who was dedicated to training. Braddock had given up boxing due to a broken hand that led to several follow-up defeats. He ended up working on the docks of Hoboken, New Jersey, and sometimes collecting government checks to survive. He eventually returned to the ring at the urging of his manager Joe Gould, and within twelve months, Braddock, a ten-to-one underdog to Baer, would stun the boxing world.

A *Publishers Weekly* contributor noted that Schaap "goes into captivating detail on the brawny, reserved Braddock." The reviewer added, "Not overly emotional, the story hits a nerve at just the right moments." As an *Economist* reviewer commented, "Professional boxing is sometimes a renowned noble art, and sometimes just a brutal, dirty business. In this ringside history, a classic of its kind, Jeremy Schaap throws both aspects of the fight game in sharp relief with a dramatic yet intelligent account." Jim Burns, writing in the *Library Journal,* remarked that the author "skillfully steers the men on their collision course toward a meeting that could have been conceived in Hollywood."

BIOGRAPHICAL AND CRITICAL SOURCES:

PERIODICALS

Advertising Age, May 30, 2005, James Brady, review of *Cinderella Man: James J. Braddock, Max Baer, and the Greatest Upset in Boxing History,* p. 46.

Economist (U.S.), May 7, 2005, review of *Cinderella Man,* p. 80.

Entertainment Weekly, June 10, 2005, Gilbert Cruz, "The Book on Braddock: Author Jeremy Schaap Tells a Different Story of Cinderella Man,"p. 38.

Library Journal, May 15, 2005, Jim Burns, review of *Cinderella Man,* p. 125.

Publishers Weekly, April 11, 2005, review of *Cinderella Man,* p. 42.

ONLINE

Bookreporter.com, http://www.bookreporter.com/ (September 19, 2005), W. Terry Whalin, review of *Cinderella Man.**

SCHELLE-NOETZEL, A.H.
See BRONNEN, Arnolt

*   *   *

SCHMIDT, Frederick W. 1953-
(Frederick W. Schmidt, Jr.)

PERSONAL: Born June 20, 1953, in Louisville, KY; married; children: one. *Education:* Asbury College, B.A., 1975; Asbury Theological Seminary, M.Div., 1978; Oxford University, D.Phil., 1986.

ADDRESSES: Office—Perkins School of Theology, Southern Methodist University, P.O. Box 750133, Dallas, TX 75275-0133. *E-mail*—fschmidt@smu.edu.

CAREER: Theologian, clergy, educator, and writer. Asbury Theological Seminary, Wilmore, KY, teaching fellow in biblical studies department, 1978-80; Messiah College, Grantham, PA, associate professor in religion, 1987-94; Saint George's College, dean, 1994-95; La Salle University, Philadelphia, PA, special assistant to the president, 1995-96; Washington National Cathedral, Washington, DC, canon educator and director of programs in spirituality and religious education, and acting program manager, 1997-2000; Southern Methodist University, Dallas, TX, director of spiritual life and formation and associate professor of Christian spirituality, 2000—. Ordained Methodist minister; assistant coordinator of Rural Cooperative Parish, Kingsville, OH, 1986-87; rector of Gageville United Methodist Church, Kingsville, 1986-87; staff member of St. Andrews, Harrisburg, PA, 1994-95; staff member of All Saints, Hershey, PA, 1995-96. Served on boards and committees, including at National Institutes of Health; board of examining chaplains for the Episcopal Church, USA; Clergy Leadership Project of Trinity Church, New York, NY; and board of Trustees of Christian Churches United of Tri-County Area, Harrisburg, PA.

MEMBER: American Academy of Religion (secretary-treasurer), Catholic Biblical Association, Society for the Study of Christian Spirituality, Society of Biblical Literature, Society for the Scientific Study of Religion (member of editorial board), Episcopal Church Foundation, Anglican Association of Biblical Studies, Washington Episcopal Clergy Association, Oxford Society.

AWARDS, HONORS: Excellence in Teaching Award, Messiah College, 1990; Ecumenical Service Award, Christian Churches United, 1993; Young Scholars fellow, Catholic Biblical Association, Catholic University, 1993; W.F. Albright Institute of Archaeological Research senior fellow, 1995; American Council on Education fellow, 1996, Center for Leadership Development fellow, 1996; Angus Dun fellowship, Episcopal Diocese of Washington, 1999, 2000; recipient of grants.

WRITINGS:

(As Frederick W. Schmidt, Jr.) *A Still Small Voice: Women, Ordination, and the Church,* foreword by Betty Bone Schiess, Syracuse University Press (Syracuse, NY), 1996.

(Editor) *The Changing Face of God,* Morehouse (Harrisburg, PA), 2000.

When Suffering Persists, Morehouse (Harrisburg, PA), 2001.

Conversations with Scripture: Revelation, Morehouse (Harrisburg, PA), 2005.

What God Wants for Your Life: Finding Answers to the Deepest Questions, HarperSanFrancisco (San Francisco, CA), 2005.

Contributor to *Anchor Bible Dictionary,* edited by David N. Freedman, Doubleday (New York, NY), 1992, and *North American Religions,* edited by Amanda Porterfield and Mary Farrell Bednarowski, Syracuse University Press (Syracuse, NY), 1996. Contributor to professional journals and periodicals, including *Scottish Journal of Theology, Perkins News, Living Church, Plumbline,* and *Feminist Theology.*

SIDELIGHTS: Frederick W. Schmidt is an educator and theologian whose interests include historical Jesus, spirituality, and New Testament studies. In his book *A Still Small Voice: Women, Ordination, and the Church,* Schmidt focuses on the issue of women's ordination by examining how five women and their churches have reacted to the ordination of women. To gather his data, he includes interviews with various women in which he asks about their experiences in the Roman Catholic, Episcopal, United Methodist, and Evangelical Lutheran Churches, and in the Southern Baptist Convention.

"Not surprisingly, the women complain of old-boy networks and 'black shirts' who dominate their denominations, of resistant congregations and sexist bishops, of regional variations and persistent marginalization, even where quotas exist to ensure equal gender representation on committees and boards," noted Mary Todd in a review in the *Christian Century.* Mary E. Hines, writing in *Theological Studies,* noted, "This study is valuable for its attempt to probe the reality of women's experience in ministry behind the public perception of the different denominations, and for its use of organizational theory to gain a different kind of insight into the human dynamics of church institutions." In his review in the *Sociology of Religion,* Edward C. Lehman, Jr., noted that "readers primarily interested in the oral history data—the women's stories—will find a rich source of personal testimony about women's hopes dashed by discrimination, trivialization, and marginalization. The book provides additional documentation of patterns also observed in previous research on women in ministry. The text . . . flows well."

Schmidt discusses human understanding of God's will in *What God Wants for Your Life: Finding Answers to the Deepest Questions.* The author addresses issues such as placing too much emphasis on looking for signs from God and perceiving God's will as an itemized list of do's and don'ts. Noting that the author uses a mixture "of mainline Christian theology, biblical exploration and personal stories," a *Publishers Weekly* contributor also commented: "This is an important book on Christian spiritual discernment."

BIOGRAPHICAL AND CRITICAL SOURCES:

PERIODICALS

Christian Century, November 6, 1996, Mary Todd, review of *A Still Small Voice: Women, Ordination, and the Church,* p. 1085.

Journal of Ecumenical Studies, fall, 1997, Doris Klostermaier, review of *A Still Small Voice,* p. 586.

Publishers Weekly, April 11, 2005, review of *What God Wants for Your Life: Finding Answers to the Deepest Questions,* p. 48.

Sociology of Religion, spring, 1997, Edward C. Lehman, Jr., review of *A Still Small Voice,* p. 101.

Theological Studies, March, 1997, Mary E. Hines, review of *A Still Small Voice,* p. 197.

ONLINE

Southern Methodist University Web site, http://www.smu.edu/ (September 19, 2005), information on author's career.*

SCHMIDT, Frederick W., Jr.
See SCHMIDT, Frederick W.

* * *

SCHMITT, Gerry
See CHILDS, Laura

* * *

SHAFAK, Elif 1971-

PERSONAL: Born 1971, in Strasbourg, France. *Education:* Middle East Technical University, M.Sc., Ph.D.

ADDRESSES: Agent—Marly Rusoff & Associates, Inc., P.O. Box 524, Bronxville, NY 10708.

CAREER: Writer, social scientist, and educator. Mount Holyoke College, South Hadley, MA, visiting fellow, 2002-03; University of Michigan, visiting scholar in women's studies, 2003-04.

AWARDS, HONORS: Mevlana prize, 1998, and Rumi prize, both for *Pinhan—The Sufi;* Turkish novel award, 2000, for *Mahrem.*

WRITINGS:

Sehrin aynalari, Iletisim (Istanbul, Turkey), 1999.
Bit palas (novel), Metis Yayinlari (Istanbul, Turkey), 2002, translated by Müge Göçek as *The Flea Palace,* Marion (New York, NY), 2004.
The Saint of Incipient Insanities (novel), Farrar, Straus (New York, NY), 2005.
The Gaze (novel), Marion Boyars (London, England), 2006.

Also author of novels *Pinhan—The Sufi,* c. 1998; *The Mirrors of the City;* and *Mahrem* (title means "Hide-and-Seek").

SIDELIGHTS: Elif Shafak is a novelist of Turkish descent whose works have raised the indignation of some segments of Turkish society. While modern Turkey seeks to be a secular society, Shafak's novels recall the country's older, more Islamic culture. "In Turkey, my fiction has been, from time to time, targeted by some rigidly Kemalist intellectuals who have accused me of betraying the nationalist project," the author commented in *Meridians.*

In *The Mirrors of the City,* the author draws on her time living in Spain as a young girl to tell the story of people in seventeenth-century Spain who converted to Islam. Their conversion later led to being driven from Spain to live within the Ottoman Empire. *Mahrem*—the title means "Hide-and-Seek"—is a metaphysical novel about "the sacred, and the female body that must search for its elusive autonomy while being encroached upon by the Gaze—of a masculine God, of society, of the lover," according to a contributor to *Meridians: Feminism, Race, Transnationalism.* The story covers two centuries, ending with the life of a bulimic woman who suffered sexual abuse in Istanbul as a child. Shafak's novel *The Flea Palace* was a bestseller in Turkey and focuses on the intertwining lives of people living in an apartment building. The novel's theme, according to the *Meridians* contributor, is "the seen and the unseen degradation—moral, physical, social as well as cultural—in the heart of the aging city of Istanbul."

The Saint of Incipient Insanities is the author's first novel written in English. It follows three foreign students who have come to the United States: political science student Omer, whose heritage is in the Islamic faith; Spanish dental student Piyu, who is Catholic; and Abed, a Moroccan student interested in biotechnology who is a devout Muslim. "Despite their differences in culture and language, the three men's outsider status . . . binds them together while each struggles to find where he resides in spirit," wrote a *Kirkus Reviews* contributor. Michael Spinella, writing in *Booklist,* commented that the author "presents a masterful command of language, which she uses cleverly, humorously, and engagingly." Diane Anderson-Minshall, writing in *Curve,* called the book a "heartbreaking tale . . . that centers around culture, exile, and belonging." A contributor to the *Economist* wrote that the author "has woven a tragi-comic tapestry of quirky and lovable twenty-somethings struggling to find themselves in America."

BIOGRAPHICAL AND CRITICAL SOURCES:

PERIODICALS

Booklist, September 15, 2004, Michael Spinella, review of *The Saint of Incipient Insanities,* p. 209.

Curve, December, 2004, Diane Anderson-Minshall, review of *The Saint of Incipient Insanities,* p. 52.

Economist, August 14, 2004, review of *The Saint of Incipient Insanities,* p. 75.

Kirkus Reviews, August 15, 2004, review of *The Saint of Incipient Insanities,* p. 773.

Library Journal, October 15, 2004, Edward B. St. John, review of *The Saint of Incipient Insanities,* p. 56.

Meridians: Feminism, Race, Transnationalism, spring, 2004, "Migrations: A *Meridians* Interview with Elif Shafak," p. 55.

Middle East Journal, autumn, 2004, review of *The Saint of Incipient Insanities,* p. 706; winter, 2005, Sara Hahn, review of *The Saint of Incipient Insanities,* p. 170.

Publishers Weekly, September 13, 2004, review of *The Saint of Incipient Insanities,* p. 56.

ONLINE

Marion Boyars Publishers Web site, http://www. marionboyars.co.uk/ (September 14, 2005).*

*   *   *

SHANGHVI, Siddharth Dhanvant 1977-

PERSONAL: Born 1977, in Mumbai, India. *Education:* University of Westminster, M.A.; San Jose State University, M.S.

ADDRESSES: Agent—c/o Author Mail, Weidenfeld & Nicolson, Orion Publishing Group, Orion House, Upper St. Martin's Ln., London WC2H 9EA, England.

CAREER: Writer. Has worked as a chef, a kennel boy, and a storyteller.

AWARDS, HONORS: Betty Trask Award, Society of Authors, 2004, for *The Last Song of Dusk.*

WRITINGS:

The Last Song of Dusk (novel), Arcade Publishing (New York, NY), 2004.

Contributor of articles to newspapers and magazines, including *Sunday Times of India, Elle,* and *San Francisco Chronicle.*

SIDELIGHTS: Siddharth Dhanvant Shanghvi received substantial acclaim for his first novel, *The Last Song of Dusk,* which received the Betty Trask Award, a prestigious British prize given to outstanding first novels penned by writers under agethirty-five. The story begins in the 1920s in India with the marriage of an attractive couple, bride Anuradha Patwardhan and groom Vardhamaan Gandharva, who believe they will have a wonderful life together, as in a fairy tale. Reality interferes with their dreams, however, as they endure the death of their first child and the hostility of Vardhamaan's stepmother. Shanghvi follows them through their difficulties and tells the stories of other family members, including Anuradha's beautiful and beguiling artist cousin, Nandini, and the couple's second son, Shloka. Shanghvi's fictional characters encounter some from real life, such as Mohandas Gandhi and Virginia Woolf, and the author adds touches of magic realism.

Several critics praised the novel as creative and compelling. "Shanghvi enchants readers with delectable images and sensual scenes," observed Faye A. Chadwell in *Library Journal,* while *Newsweek International* reviewer Vibhuti Patel found it a "lush" work that "truly satisfies." Deborah Donovan, writing in *Booklist,* described *The Last Song of Dusk* as "marvelously inventive," combining social satire, complex family history, romance, and a bit of fantasy. A *Kirkus Reviews* commentator called it "insistently readable," with "gorgeous atmospheric and verbal trappings." *Verve* magazine contributor Sangita P. Advani summed up the novel and its author by saying that readers will find "a simply unputdownable story, a writing talent that is dew in its ability to moisten the heart as it glistens over the tale."

BIOGRAPHICAL AND CRITICAL SOURCES:

PERIODICALS

Booklist, September 1, 2004, Deborah Donovan, review of *The Last Song of Dusk,* p. 64.

Library Journal, December 1, 2004, Faye A. Chadwell, review of *The Last Song of Dusk,* p. 103.

Newsweek International, December 13, 2004, Vibhuti Patel, review of *The Last Song of Dusk,* p. 57.

Publishers Weekly, August 9, 2004, Charles Hix, profile of Siddharth Dhanvant Shanghvi, p. 131; September 13, 2004, review of *The Last Song of Dusk,* p. 56.

Verve, September, 2004, Sangita P. Advani, interview with Siddharth Dhanvant Shanghvi.

ONLINE

Siddharth Dhanvant Shanghvi Home Page, http://www.siddharths.com (September 29, 2005).*

*   *   *

SHAW, Steven A. 1969-
(Steven Anthony Shaw)

PERSONAL: Born June 10, 1969. *Education:* Law degree.

ADDRESSES: Agent—c/o Author Mail, HarperCollins Publishers, 10 E. 53rd St., 7th Fl., New York, NY 10022. *E-mail*—steven@fat-guy.com.

CAREER: Food columnist and restaurant reviewer. Publisher of *fat-guy.com;* cofounder of Web site *egullet;* founder, online eGullet Culinary Institute (eGCI). Previously worked as a lawyer.

AWARDS, HONORS: James Beard Foundation Journalism Award for Internet Writing, 2002, for story "A Week in the Gramercy Tavern Kitchen."

WRITINGS:

The Menu New York: The Best Restaurants and Their Menus, Ten Speed Press (Berkeley, CA), 2003.

Turning the Tables: Restaurants from the Inside Out, HarperCollins (New York, NY), 2005.

Contributor of articles to periodicals, including *Elle* and *Saveur.*

SIDELIGHTS: Steven A. Shaw began his career as a lawyer but turned to his true passion when he became a food writer. In his book *Turning the Tables: Restaurants from the Inside Out,* the author presents insider secrets on how to get the best food and service in restaurants. For example, the author offers tips such as making sure to sit at the Sushi bar of a restaurant to get to know the chef and, as a result, perhaps get served the best food. The author also gives a close-up look at a restaurant's operations, such as the food preparation and its ultimate delivery to the table. "Hanging out with the reservationist . . . , assisting in the kitchen of Manhattan's renowned Gramercy Tavern and counting the number of eggs used on a Sunday at the Tavern on the Green, Shaw . . . soaks up the atmosphere," wrote a *Kirkus Reviews* contributor. In a review for *Newsweek,* Anna Kuchment wrote that the author "tells you how to get exceptional service every time." A *Publishers Weekly* contributor commented that "this opinionated diner's tour is sure to appeal to chowhounds in general." Deborah M. Ebster, writing in the *Library Journal,* commented: "In his penetrating first book, . . . Shaw decodes the secrets of the food world," and called the effort a "delicious read for restaurant goers." *Bookloons* online contributor Mary Ann Smyth found the book to be a "handy guide," adding that "you will consider the investment you make in these pages well spent."

BIOGRAPHICAL AND CRITICAL SOURCES:

PERIODICALS

Fortune, August 8, 2005, Kate Bonamici, review of *Turning the Tables: Restaurants from the Inside Out,* p. 111.

Fort Wayne Journal Gazette, August 28, 2005, Jonathan Yardley, review of *Turning the Tables.*

Kirkus Reviews, May 15, 2005, review of *Turning the Tables,* p. 579.

Library Journal, August 1, 2005, Deborah M. Ebster, review of *Turning the Tables,* p. 115.

Newsweek, August 29, 2005, review of *Turning the Tables,* p. 80.

Publishers Weekly, May 16, 2005, review of *Turning the Tables,* p. 47.

ONLINE

BookLoons, http://www.bookloons.com/ (September 14, 2005), Mary Ann Smyth, review of *Turning the Tables.*

Morning News Online, http://www.themorningnews. org/ (September 2, 2003), Rosecrans Baldwin, interview with author.*

*   *   *

SHAW, Steven Anthony
See SHAW, Steven A.

*   *   *

SHEALY, Daniel
(Daniel L. Shealy)

PERSONAL: Male. *Education:* Newberry College, B.A.; University of South Carolina at Columbia, M.A., Ph.D.

ADDRESSES: Office—University of North Carolina at Charlotte, Department of English, 9201 University City Blvd., Charlotte, NC 28223-0001.

CAREER: University of North Carolina at Charlotte, professor of English and associate dean of graduate school.

WRITINGS:

(Editor with Joel Myerson and Madeleine B. Stern) Louisa May Alcott, *The Selected Letters of Louisa May Alcott,* introduction by Madeleine B. Stern, Little, Brown (Boston, MA), 1987.
(Editor with Joel Myerson and Madeleine B. Stern) Louisa May Alcott, *A Double Life: Newly Discovered Thrillers of Louisa May Alcott,* introduction by Madeleine B. Stern, Little, Brown (Boston, MA), 1988.
(Editor with Joel Myerson and Madeleine B. Stern) Louisa May Alcott, *The Journals of Louisa May Alcott,* introduction by Madeleine B. Stern, Little, Brown (Boston, MA), 1989.
(Editor with Joel Myerson and Madeleine B. Stern) Louisa May Alcott, *Louisa May Alcott: Selected Fiction,* introduction by Madeleine B. Stern, Little, Brown (Boston, MA), 1990.

(Editor with Joel Myerson and Madeleine B. Stern) Louisa May Alcott, *Freaks of Genius: Unknown Thrillers of Louisa May Alcott,* Greenwood Press (New York, NY), 1991.
(Editor) Louisa May Alcott, *Louisa May Alcott's Fairy Tales and Fantasy Stories,* University of Tennessee Press (Knoxville, TN), 1992.
(Editor with Madeleine B. Stern) Louisa May Alcott, *From Jo March's Attic: Stories of Intrigue and Suspense,* Northeastern University Press (Boston, MA), 1993, published as *The Lost Stories of Louisa May Alcott,* Carol Publishing Group (Secaucus, NJ), 1995.
(Editor) Louisa May Alcott, *Flower Fables* (fairy tales), illustrated by Leah Palmer Preiss, Okey-Doke Productions (New York, NY), 1998.
(Editor with Joel Myerson) Louisa May Alcott, *The Inheritance* (novel), Penguin Books (New York, NY), 1998.
(Editor and contributor) *Alcott in Her Own Time: A Biographical Chronicle of Her Life, Drawn from Recollections, Interviews, and Memoirs by Family, Friends, and Associates,* University of Iowa Press (Iowa City, IA), 2005.

Contributor of articles to journals, including *Resources for American Literary Study.*

SIDELIGHTS: Daniel Shealy has a particular interest in nineteenth-century American literature, especially the works of Louisa May Alcott (1832-1888). Alcott is best known for writing *Little Women,* the enduringly popular novel about the four March sisters—Meg, Jo, Beth, and Amy—coming of age in a poor but loving New England family during and after the U.S. Civil War. However, Alcott also wrote fairy tales and thrillers, and in contrast to the morally uplifting tone of her most famous work, some of the latter are rather lurid, although the forces of good win out eventually. Shealy and his collaborators have collected Alcott's lesser-known writings as well as her journals, letters, and other biographical information. In doing so, they seek to provide insight into the woman and her craft.

One of Shealy's achievements, with coeditor Joel Myerson, was discovering and publishing *The Inheritance,* a novel Alcott wrote in her teens that was long believed to be lost. The two researchers came upon the manuscript while compiling the author's correspondence. Discussing this novel, critic Ellen Marsh noted in *Humanities* that "Myerson and Shealy say that Alcott's early fiction was inspired by the melodramas of the nineteenth century theater, and by the gothic and sentimental fiction popular at the time. This juvenile work presages themes that the author would develop in her mature writings." In this tale of an orphaned young woman who is taken into the home of an English nobleman, "the virtues of honesty, trust, fidelity, and self-sacrifice appear . . . as they do throughout Alcott's fiction," Marsh observed.

In *From Jo March's Attic: Stories of Intrigue and Suspense*, Shealy and coeditor Madeleine B. Stern bring to audiences some of the melodramatic stories Alcott published in popular magazines before she experienced her great success with *Little Women*. (In *Little Women*, Alcott's alter ego, Jo March, supports herself for a time by writing similar stories.) While these tales have righteousness emerge victorious in the end, along the way they deal with "sizzling passions," related a *Publishers Weekly* reviewer, who praised the collection's "informative introduction and bibliography."

For *Alcott in Her Own Time: A Biographical Chronicle of Her Life, Drawn from Recollections, Interviews, and Memoirs by Family, Friends, and Associates*, Shealy compiles thirty-six accounts by people who had known Alcott. He supplements these accounts with "a detailed, informative introduction to Alcott's life" and "a perceptive analysis of her influence and legacy," reported Kathryn R. Bartelt in *Library Journal*. Bartelt stated that Shealy's work, which includes commentary on each contributor, will significantly enhance readers' understanding of Alcott. A *Publishers Weekly* critic pointed out that the pieces included in the book indicate that Alcott, who used her family and friends as models for the characters in *Little Women*, portrayed them quite accurately, and added that the narratives display Alcott's sense of humor in the face of her childhood poverty and ill health in middle age. The critic concluded by writing, "This valuable book will be a boon to devotees and scholars."

BIOGRAPHICAL AND CRITICAL SOURCES:

PERIODICALS

Humanities, July-August, 1997, Ellen Marsh, "Louisa May Alcott's Long-Lost Novel," about *The Inheritance*.

Library Journal, May 15, 2005, Kathryn R. Bartelt, review of *Alcott in Her Own Time: A Biographical Chronicle of Her Life, Drawn from Recollections, Interviews, and Memoirs by Family, Friends, and Associates*, p. 117.
Publishers Weekly, November 2, 1990, Sybil Steinberg, review of *Louisa May Alcott: Selected Fiction*, p. 63; September 20, 1993, review of *From Jo March's Attic: Stories of Intrigue and Suspense*, p. 62; April 25, 2005, review of *Alcott in Her Own Time*, p. 47.

ONLINE

University of North Carolina at Charlotte, Department of English Web site, http://www.english.uncc.edu/ (September 28, 2005), brief biography of Daniel Shealy.

*   *   *

SHEALY, Daniel L.
   See SHEALY, Daniel

*   *   *

SHENGOLD, Nina

PERSONAL: Children: Maya. *Education:* Graduated from Wesleyan University.

ADDRESSES: Home—NY. *Agent*—Phyllis Wender, Rosenstone Wender, 38 E. 29th St., 10th Fl., New York, NY 10016.

CAREER: Playwright, writer, editor, and artistic director. Worked for Young-Adult Conservation Corps, Olympic Reforestation Inc., and on a salmon troller in southeast Alaska. Actors & Writers (theatre company), artistic director; *Chronogram*, book editor.

AWARDS, HONORS: ABC Playwright Award, and *LA Weekly* Award, both c. 1984, both for *Homesteaders*; Writers Guild Award, for teleplay *Labor of Love*.

WRITINGS:

COEDITOR WITH ERIC LANE

The Actor's Book of Scenes from New Plays, Penguin Books (New York, NY), 1988.

Moving Parts: Monologues from Contemporary Plays, Penguin Books (New York, NY), 1992.

The Actor's Book of Gay and Lesbian Plays, Penguin Books (New York, NY), 1995.

Plays for Actresses, Vintage (New York, NY), 1997.

Take Ten: New Ten-minute Plays, Vintage (New York, NY), 1997.

Leading Women: Plays for Actresses II, Vintage (New York, NY), 2002.

Take Ten II: More Ten-Minute Plays, Vintage (New York, NY), 2003.

Talk to Me: Monologue Plays, Vintage (New York, NY), 2004.

Under 30: Plays for a New Generation, Vintage (New York, NY), 2004.

OTHER

Homesteaders (play), S. French (New York, NY) 1984.

(Editor) *The Actor's Book of Contemporary Stage Monologues,* Penguin Books (New York, NY), 1987.

(With Michael Ryan) *Michael Ryan: Between Living and Dreaming, 1982-1994,* Waanders Publishers (Zwolle), 1994.

Clearcut (novel), Anchor Books (New York, NY), 2004.

Romeo/Juliet (play; adapted from William Shakespeare's *Romeo and Juliet*), Broadway Play Publishing (New York, NY), 2004.

Finger Foods (collection of plays), Playscripts (New York, NY), 2006.

Also co-author, with Nicole Quinn and Rondout Valley High School Drama Club, of play *War at Home: Students Respond to September 11th;* author of one-act plays, including *No Shoulder, Lush Life, Lives of the Great Waitresses, Finger Food,* and *Emotional Baggage.* Author of television scripts, including *Labor of Love, Blind Spot,* and *Unwed Father.* Adaptor of Jane Smiley's novella *Good Will* for *American Playhouse,* Public Broadcasting Service. Contributor of stories and essays to periodicals, including *Lifetime, New Woman, Femina, Living Fit, Prima Materia, Upstate House,* and *Woodstock Times.*

SIDELIGHTS: Nina Shengold is a novelist and playwright who has written for the stage and for television. Commenting on the life of a playwright, and in particular on the collaborative nature of playwriting, Shengold noted on the *Writers Guild of America East* Web site, "Some years ago, I started signing my first drafts. Painters handwrite their names on their canvasses; why shouldn't I? It's an affectation, I guess, but it keeps me in touch with a radical notion: pride of authorship."

Shengold is also coeditor, with Eric Lane, of a number of books featuring plays for specific groups of actors. In *Plays for Actresses,* Shengold and Lane present seven plays and ten one-acts that are especially suited to female performers. *Leading Women: Plays for Actresses II* includes twenty-two plays that premiered from 1990 through 2001. Elizabeth Stifter, writing in the *Library Journal,* noted that "these pieces are an excellent representation of the poignant writing available for actresses." *Under 30: Plays for a New Generation* focuses on plays written specifically for actors under the age of thirty. Overall, the volume includes sixteen plays and excerpts from four others. Larry Schwartz, writing in the *Library Journal,* called the collection "fresh and gripping." *Talk to Me: Monologue Plays* features works by such writers as Neil Labute, Jose Rivera, David Ives, David Cale, Danny Hoch, and Anna Deavere Smith. *Booklist* contributor Jack Helbig noted that the collection will be "of interest to both actors, especially those looking for new audition pieces, and readers eager to keep up with current trends in American theater."

In her first novel, *Clearcut,* Shengold sets her story in the Pacific Northwest, where the author once lived and worked. The plot revolves around a ménage a trois that develops when the rugged Earley Ritter picks up a hitchhiker name Reed Alton and eventually becomes involved with Reed's girlfriend, Zan. "Shengold has a keen familiarity with this moist, woodsy region of the country, and the sexual tension among the three rough-and-ready lovers resonates thrillingly with the landscape," wrote a *Kirkus Reviews* contributor. The reviewer went on to call the novel "a nouveau hippie tale with boldness and spunk." Kevin Greczek, writing in the *Library Journal,* commented that the author "does a good job presenting Earley's struggles" and "evoking pathos for a misanthrope from the wilds."

BIOGRAPHICAL AND CRITICAL SOURCES:

PERIODICALS

Booklist, October 15, 2004, Jack Helbig, review of *Talk to Me: Monologue Plays,* p. 380.

Kirkus Reviews, May 1, 2005, review of *Clearcut,* p. 504.

Library Journal, September 1, 1997, Ming-ming Shen Kuo, review of *Plays for Actresses,* p. 183; July, 2002, Elizabeth Stifter, review of *Leading Women: Plays for Actresses II,* p. 80; August, 2004, Larry Schwartz, review of *Under 30: Plays for a New Generation,* p. 82; December 1, 2004, Larry Schwartz, review of *Talk to Me,* p. 116; July 1, 2005, Kevin Greczek, review of *Clearcut,* p. 71.

School Library Journal, April, 2005, Francisca Goldsmith, review of *Under 30,* p. 164.

ONLINE

Dollee.com, http://www.doollee.com/ (September 14, 2005), information on Shengold's plays.

Nina Shengold Home Page, http://www.ninashengold. com (September 14, 2005).

Writers Guild of America East Web site, http://www. wgaeast.org/ (November 10, 2005), transcript of speech by Shengold.

*   *   *

SHIMELD, Thomas J. 1977-
(Thomas Jay Shimeld)

PERSONAL: Born May 25, 1977, in Nashua, NH; son of Thomas Edward III (an air-traffic controller and government worker) and Janice Marie (a flight attendant and postal worker; maiden name, Finney) Shimeld; married Jennifer Ann Leavitt (an art consultant), May 15, 2002. *Ethnicity:* "Caucasian." *Education:* Tufts University, B.A., 2000; Salem State College, graduate study, 2000—. *Politics:* Democrat. *Religion:* Roman Catholic. *Hobbies and other interests:* Performing magic, juggling, barbershop singing.

ADDRESSES: Home—3 Chestnut St., No. 3, Beverly, MA 01915. *E-mail*—shimeld_leavitt@msn.com.

CAREER: Writer and actor. Magician and actor throughout New England, 1988—. Substitute teacher at public schools in Beverly, MA, 2001-04; CVS Pharmacy, pharmacy technician, 2003—. Cofounder, publisher, editor, and columnist for *Fiz Bin: An Independent Magazine for and by the Young Magician,* 1996-98.

MEMBER: International Brotherhood of Magicians, International Jugglers Association, Society of American Magicians, Golden Key.

AWARDS, HONORS: Named volunteer of the year, Merrimack, NH, Young Men's Christian Association, 1995-96.

WRITINGS:

Walter B. Gibson and the Shadow, McFarland and Co. (Jefferson, NC), 2003.

Work represented in anthologies, including *Treasured Poems of America,* 1995.

WORK IN PROGRESS: Writing poetry for Sparrowgrass Poetry Forum; *Fli-Rite,* an "aviation/family history"; *Magical Moments* and *See in 3D,* both children's picture books.

SIDELIGHTS: Thomas J. Shimeld told *CA:* "Everything I have written seems to be need-based. This can be interpreted on a few different levels.

"My writing has often been sparked by a simple hole in the field of interest that has been revealed to me in my current circumstances. My children's books are a good example of this. *Magical Moments* gives the reader an idea of how one actually becomes a magician. The need for this book was discovered while I was teaching a kindergarten unit on magic and magnets. There were plenty of reading materials with magical themes and talking animals, but none on the actual magic a magician performs. So I wrote one. My *See in 3D* manuscript came about in much the same way when I discovered the dimensional shapes while teaching mathematics.

"A need of a different kind sparked my research and writing of *Walter B. Gibson and the Shadow.* My magic mentor, Wendel W. Gibson, revealed his uncle Walter's life to me. The more he spoke, the more need I saw for a biography of this prolific writer and magician. Walter Gibson selflessly wrote under so many pseudonyms, including Maxwell Grant, under which he created and wrote 283 novels of 'The Shadow,' yet his name remained relatively unknown. I thought this should change.

"After the biography was published, I found I knew more about the Gibson family than my own. My manuscript *Fli-Rite* is an attempt to satisfy my own need to know my family history while presenting a personal history of aviation.

"Of all my needs, there is a deep desire to write. The words simply well up in my mind and spill onto the page. A miniature notebook carried with me helps catch the drips when and wherever they occur. The need to write seeps into my day-to-day life, flowing around my work and family, filling up the moments."

*   *   *

SHIMELD, Thomas Jay
See SHIMELD, Thomas J.

*   *   *

SHONE, Tom 1967-

PERSONAL: Born 1967, in Horsham, England.

ADDRESSES: Home—Brooklyn, NY. *Agent*—c/o Free Press Publicity, 1230 Avenue of the Americas, New York, NY 10020.

CAREER: Writer. *Sunday Times*, London, England, film critic, 1994-99.

WRITINGS:

Blockbuster: How Hollywood Learned to Stop Worrying and Love the Summer (nonfiction), Free Press (New York, NY) 2004.

Contributor of articles to newspapers and magazines, including *New York Times*, London *Daily Telegraph*, *New Yorker*, and *Vogue*.

SIDELIGHTS: Tom Shone's *Blockbuster: How Hollywood Learned to Stop Worrying and Love the Summer* examines the influence of the big-budget action films that have dominated the summer schedule since the mid-1970s. Shone makes a case that such movies as *Jaws, Star Wars,* and *Raiders of the Lost Ark* reinvigorate the U.S. film industry, not only because they draw large audiences but because they are often better than many of the offerings critics laud, particularly in the 1960s and early 1970s. He also emphasizes that the profits from these popular movies help guarantee a place for more eccentric films, as they have played a role in the rise of multiscreen theaters, which show both so-called blockbusters and smaller-scale art films. Shone particularly admires directors Steven Spielberg, George Lucas, and James Cameron, and he interviews them and many other filmmakers for his book, while also offering extensive analyses of blockbuster films and how they are made.

Some reviewers praised Shone's writing, despite having reservations about his thesis. "Whether you're convinced by this or not, it's extremely refreshing to find a critic willing to stake out such unfashionable ground and then spend 392 pages defending it," remarked Toby Young in *Spectator.* Young added, "Shone helps his cause immeasurably by being a gifted writer." Reviewer Sukhdev Sandhu, writing in *New Statesman,* considered blockbuster films to be "genetically modified, supersize cinema: . . . succulent and filling, but still able to leave you just as hungry as when you first started." The critic reported, however, that Shone's book "is a spirited and intelligent account of their emergence." Benjamin Svetkey, writing in *Entertainment Weekly,* pointed out that Shone makes "a clever, entertaining argument," while David Siegfried in *Booklist* called the author's "biting analyses" "on target." In addition, a *Publishers Weekly* reviewer noted that Shone "writes with verve," while reviewer Toby Young concluded that "for anyone interested in film, this book is a must read."

BIOGRAPHICAL AND CRITICAL SOURCES:

PERIODICALS

Booklist, November 15, 2004, David Siegfried, review of *Blockbuster: How Hollywood Learned to Stop Worrying and Love the Summer,* p. 538.

Entertainment Weekly, December 3, 2004, Benjamin Svetkey, review of *Blockbuster,* p. 97.

Kirkus Reviews, September 15, 2004, review of *Blockbuster,* p. 906.

New Statesman, October 11, 2004, Sukhdev Sandhu, "Supersize Cinema," review of *Blockbuster,* p. 50.

Publishers Weekly, September 27, 2004, review of *Blockbuster,* p. 44.

Spectator, October 9, 2004, Toby Young, "Both the First and the Last Word," review of *Blockbuster,* p. 49.

ONLINE

Simon & Schuster Web site, http://www.simonsays. com/ (September 28, 2005), brief biography of Tom Shone.*

*   *   *

SIENKIEWICZ, Bill 1958-
(Boleslaw William Felix Robert Sienkiewicz)

PERSONAL: Name pronounced sin-KEV-itch; born May 3, 1958, in Blakely, PA. *Education:* Attended Newark School of Fine and Industrial Arts.

ADDRESSES: Agent—c/o Author Mail, Diamond Comic Distributors, Inc., 1966 Greenspring Dr., Ste. 300, Timonium, MD 21093.

CAREER: Comic-book illustrator and writer, 1978—, illustrator for DC Comics, Marvel Comics, Image Comics, Epic Comics, Oni Press, Kitchen Sink, Publishing, and others; independent commercial artist for book and magazine publishers, including Doubleday, St. Martin's Press, Avon, Viking Penguin, *Rolling Stone, Spin, Outdoor Life, ESPN, Reader's Digest, Guitar, National Lampoon,* and others. Animator and production, Web site, and character designer for clients, including Hanna-Barbera Animation, DIC Animation, MTV, Sunbow Animation, CBS Television, and Cyclops Entertainment. Set designer, storyboard artist, and consultant for films including: *The Matrix, Unforgiven, The Mummy, Highway to Hell, The Yards, The Green Mile,* and *American Pimp,* and for television networks. *Exhibitions:* Works exhibited at Carson Street Gallery, Pittsburgh, PA, 1988-89; Words and Pictures Museum, Northampton, MA, 1994; Museum of Fine Art, Rio de Janeiro, Brazil, 1995; and Gijon, Asturias, Spain, 1997. Participant in group exhibits, including Jimi Hendrix traveling exhibit, 1997-98; and many others.

AWARDS, HONORS: Eagle Award for Best New Artist, 1981, for Best Artist, 1982, 1983; Yellow Kid award (Italy), 1986, and Jack Kirby Award for Best Artist, 1987, both for *Elektra: Assassin*; Gran Guigiri award (Lucca, Italy), 1986; March of Dimes Award for charity work, 1988; Alpe de Huiz award (Grenoble, France), 1991; Emmy Award nominations for production and character design on *Where in the World Is Carmen Sandiego?* 1995, 1996; other awards.

WRITINGS:

COMIC-BOOK SERIES

(With Frank Miller) *Daredevil in Love and War* (originally published in single issues), Marvel Comics (New York, NY), 1986.

(With Frank Miller) *Elektra: Assassin* (originally published in single issues), Epic Comics (New York, NY), 1987.

(With Alan Moore) *Brought to Light,* (includes *Shadowplay: The Secret Team*; bound with *Flashpoint: The La Penca Bombing,* by Joyce Brabner and Thomas Yeates), Eclipse (Forestville, CA), 1989.

(With Chris Claremont) *The New Mutants: The Demon Bear Saga* (originally published in single issues), Marvel Comics (New York, NY), 1990.

(Adaptor with Dan Chichester and Willie Schubert; and illustrator) Herman Melville, *Moby Dick,* First Publishing (Chicago, IL), 1990.

Stray Toasters (originally in single volues beginning 1988), Epic Comics (New York, NY), 1991.

Wolverine: Inner Fury (originally published in single issues), art by D.G. Chichester, Marvel Comics (New York, NY), 1992.

(With Dennis O'Neil, Rodolfo Damaggio, and Pat Garrahy) *The Official Comic Adaptation of the Warner Bros. Picture Batman & Robin,* DC Comics (New York, NY), 1997.

Contributor to Marvel Comics' *New Mutants* series, 1984-86; creator of comic strip "Slow down Sir," in *Epic Illustrated,* 1986; contributor to Alan Moore's *Big*

Numbers, 1990; contributor of story *A River in Egypt* to *Oni Double Feature,* Oni Press, 1998. Author/illustrator of *Moon Knight* comic-book series, 1980-84.

ILLUSTRATOR:

Frank Herbert, *Dune* (comic-book adaptation of film by David Lynch; originally published as "Marvel Comics Super Special," number 36), Marvel Comics (New York, NY), 1984.

Martin I. Green, *Voodoo Child: The Illustrated Legend of Jimi Hendrix,* Penguin Group (New York, NY), 1995.

Martin I. Green, *Santa: My Life & Times: An Illustrated Autobiography,* Avon Books (New York, NY), 1998.

Contributor to books, including Joe Kelly, *Green Lantern Legacy: The Last Will and Testament of Hal Jordan,* DC Comics (New York, NY), 2002.

ILLUSTRATOR; "RACE AGAINST TIME" NOVEL SERIES

J.J. Fortune, *Escape from Raven Castle,* Dell (New York, NY), 1984.

J.J. Fortune, *Pursuit of the Deadly Diamonds,* Dell (New York, NY), 1984.

J.J. Fortune, *Search for Mad Jack's Crown,* Dell (New York, NY), 1984.

J.J. Fortune, *Evil in Paradise,* Dell (New York, NY), 1984.

WORK IN PROGRESS: The anthology *Vuja de* (working title); anniversary re-release of *Stray Toasters;* a new comic series, with Frank Miller, titled *Drop Dead* (working title); a Web project for creators of the film *The Matrix.*

SIDELIGHTS: American comic-book writer and illustrator Bill Sienkiewicz is known for his innovative use of a variety of techniques, such as creating collages from objects and pictures and mixing this medium with acrylic and oil painting. One of only a few comic-book artists who paint their drawings, Sienkiewicz has won major awards in the United States, Italy, and France, and his work has been exhibited all over the world. He is best known in comics for his

work on the series *Elektra: Assassin* and for his four-part solo series *Stray Toasters,* both of which have been published collectively in single volumes. Sienkiewicz has also illustrated books and magazines, provided artwork for U.S. Olympic teams, and provided artwork for television and films.

Sienkiewicz's early work, with its free brushstrokes and fine pen lines, was influenced by Neal Adams. One of the earliest comic-book series Sienkiewicz drew was *Moon Knight,* which was published from 1980 to 1984. After his early career in comics in the 1980s, Sienkiewicz left the field for a time to study art in depth in Paris. This study led to his developing techniques for painting comics. In a feature for *Words and Pictures Museum* online, Sienkiewicz is quoted as saying: "I think that artists, in general, have a responsibility in our society to expose people to new ways of seeing things. Comic artists have that responsibility too."

Elektra: Assassin, which Sienkiewicz created with writer Frank Miller, features a female villain who is the daughter of an ambassador slain by terrorists. Driven to a life of crime by this incident, Elektra uses her martial arts training to work as a hired assassin. In this role, she clashes with the Marvel Comics character Daredevil, who, as it turns out, is a man she once loved.

Sienkiewicz worked with legendary graphic novelist Alan Moore on *Shadowplay: The Secret Team,* a graphic documentary about a secret team said to direct a covert war in Nicaragua during President Ronald Reagan's administration. The docudrama is bound with Joyce Brabner and Tom Yeates's *Flashpoint: The La Penca Bombing* to form a single volume called *Brought to Light.* It was written in conjunction with a lawsuit filed by the Christic Institute against the U.S. government in the late 1980s. A *Publishers Weekly* contributor called Sienkiewicz's drawings "viciously parodic" and the documentary "a scathing black comedy" of Central Intelligence Agency (CIA) history as a shadow government. Keith R.A. DeCandido, in *Library Journal,* said both books will "shatter any illusions" about U.S. involvement in covert activities.

In the 1980s, Sienkiewicz also illustrated a series of novels for adolescent readers. In the "Race against Time" books, written by J.J. Fortune, a teen boy named Stephen Lane spends weekends with his adventurous

Uncle Richard and Richard's girlfriend. The three must complete their escapades before the boy's parents return on Sunday afternoons.

Sienkiewicz wrote and illustrated, with others, a graphic adaptation of Herman Melville's *Moby Dick*. He also won acclaim for his illustrations for Martin I. Green's graphic novel about rock guitarist Jimi Hendrix. This latter book represented a return to comics by Sienkiewicz in 1995 after a long absence in which he devoted time to commercial art and worked in television and film. Called *Voodoo Child: The Illustrated Legend of Jimi Hendrix*, the book also contains a compact disk of previously unrecorded songs written and performed by Hendrix before his death by drug overdose in 1971, at age twenty-seven. Jas Obrecht, in *Guitar Player*, observed that Sienkiewicz "makes eye-arresting use of illustration, lyrics, and Jimi's handwritten letters" in his artwork. A *Publishers Weekly* contributor called it "lavishly and beautifully illustrated." Gordon Flagg, in *Booklist*, welcomed Sienkiewicz's return to the graphic-novel medium, saying that his "imaginative, evocative full-color illustration and narrative mastery" brought substantial weight to the project.

One of Sienkiewicz's 2002 projects was his work, with Brent Anderson, illustrating Joe Kelly's graphic novel *Green Lantern Legacy: The Last Will and Testament of Hal Jordan*. This story chronicles the life of the great Green Lantern, otherwise known as Hal Jordan, a tragic hero. The story i told—beginning at Jordan's funeral—through the eyes of Jordan's betrayed confidant, Tom Kalmaku. Jordan, it seems, has left behind a son, who is gifted with great powers, and Tom's challenge is to protect him from an alien assassin before the boy can use his gift. A reviewer for *Hillcity Comics* called the 112-page graphic novel "a sweeping tale of family, friends, vengeance . . . and redemption."

BIOGRAPHICAL AND CRITICAL SOURCES:

BOOKS

Clute, John, and Peter Nicholls, *Encyclopedia of Science Fiction*, second edition, Palgrave Macmillan, 1993.

PERIODICALS

Booklist, Gordon Flagg, review of *Voodoo Child: The Illustrated Legend of Jimi Hendrix*, p. 377.

Guitar Player, February, 1996, Jas Obrecht, review of *Voodoo Child*, p. 130.
Library Journal, March 15, 1990, Keith R.A. DeCandido, reviews of *Brought to Light*, *Elektra: Assassin*, and *Stray Toasters*, p. 55.
Publishers Weekly, February 17, 1989, Penny Kaganoff, review of *Shadowplay: The Secret Team*, p. 73; November 20, 1995, review of *Voodoo Child*, p. 64.
School Library Journal, May, 1984, Therese Bigelow, reviews of *Escape from Raven Castle*, *Pursuit of the Deadly Diamonds*, *Search for Mad Jack's Crown*, and *Revenge in the Silent Tomb*, p. 88; September, 1984, review of *Evil in Paradise*, p. 88.

ONLINE

Bill Sienkiewicz Home Page, http://www.bill sienkiewicz.com (December 18, 2003).
Hillcity Comics Web site, http://www.hillcity-comics. com/ (August 19, 2003), review of *Green Lantern Legacy: The Last Will and Testament of Hal Jordan*.
Lambiek, http://www.lambiek.net/ (August 12, 2003), "Bill Sienkiewicz."
Words and Pictures Museum Web site, http://www. wordsandpictures.org/ (December 18, 2003), "Words and Pictures Exhibit: *Elektra: Assassin*."*

* * *

SIENKIEWICZ, Boleslaw William Felix Robert See SIENKIEWICZ, Bill

* * *

SIM, Dave 1956-

PERSONAL: Born 1956, in Hamilton, Ontario, Canada; married Deni Loubert (divorced).

ADDRESSES: Office—c/o Aardvark-Vanaheim, Inc., P.O. Box 1674, Station C, Kitchener, Ontario N2G 4R2, Canada.

CAREER: Comic-book writer, illustrator, and publisher, 1977—.

AWARDS, HONORS: Kirby Award for Best Black-and-White series, 1985, 1987, Harvey Award, for Best Cartoonist, 1992, Eisner Award for Best Graphic Album, 1994, Ignatz Award for Outstanding Artist, 1998, and Shuster Award for Outstanding Comic-book Achievement, 2005, all for *Cerebus*.

WRITINGS:

(With Barry Windsor-Smith, Chester Brown, and Gerhard) *Cerebus World Tour Book*, Aardvark-Vanaheim (Kitchener, Ontario, Canada), 1995.
(With Gerhard) *Cerebus Guide to Self-Publishing*, Aardvark-Vanaheim (Kitchener, Ontario, Canada), 1997.

Contributor to *Alan Moore: Portrait of an Extraordinary Gentleman*, Abiogenesis Press, 2002.

"CEREBUS THE AARDVARK" SERIES; COLLECTIONS: ILLUSTRATED WITH GERHARD

Cerebus, Volume 1, Aardvark-Vanaheim (Kitchener, Ontario, Canada), 1986.
High Society, Volume 2, Aardvark-Vanaheim (Kitchener, Ontario, Canada), 1986.
Church & State I, Volume 3, Aardvark-Vanaheim (Kitchener, Ontario, Canada), 1986.
Church & State II, Volume 4, Aardvark-Vanaheim (Kitchener, Ontario, Canada), 1987.
Jaka's Story, Volume 5, Aardvark-Vanaheim (Kitchener, Ontario, Canada), 1989.
Melmoth, Volume 6, Aardvark-Vanaheim (Kitchener, Ontario, Canada), 1990.
Mothers & Daughters, Book 1: Flight, Volume 7, Aardvark-Vanaheim (Kitchener, Ontario, Canada), 1993.
Mothers & Daughters, Book 2: Women, Volume 8, Aardvark-Vanaheim (Kitchener, Ontario, Canada), 1993.
Cerebus Number Zero, Aardvark-Vanaheim (Kitchener, Ontario, Canada), 1993.
Mothers & Daughters, Book 3: Reads, Volume 9, Aardvark-Vanaheim (Kitchener, Ontario, Canada), 1994.
Mothers & Daughters, Book 4: Minds, Volume 10, Aardvark-Vanaheim (Kitchener, Ontario, Canada), 1996.

Guys, Volume 11, Aardvark-Vanaheim (Kitchener, Ontario, Canada), 1996.
Rick's Story, Volume 12, Aardvark-Vanaheim (Kitchener, Ontario, Canada), 1999.
Going Home, Volume 13, Aardvark-Vanaheim (Kitchener, Ontario, Canada), 2000.
Form & Void, Volume 14, Aardvark-Vanaheim (Kitchener, Ontario, Canada), 2001.
Latter Days, Volume 15, Aardvark-Vanaheim (Kitchener, Ontario, Canada), 2002.
The Last Days, Volume 16, Aardvark-Vanaheim (Kitchener, Ontario, Canada), 2004.

SIDELIGHTS: Canadian comics writer Dave Sim began an innovative venture into self-publishing in 1977, with his then wife, Deni Loubert, creating the award-winning *Cerebus the Aardvark* series. Comprising sixteen volumes when it ended in 2004, the series was a collaboration between Sim and a background illustrator and business partner, known only as Gerhard, which began working together in 1984. In 1986 the two began compiling monthly installments of *Cerebus the Aardvark* into "phone books"—300-to 600-page graphic novels, published by Sim's publishing house, Aardvark-Vanaheim, Inc. To aid other creative artists, Sim is an active supporter of the Comic Books Legal Defense Fund, which helps to fairly compensate and restore rights to artists who created commercially exploited comics characters for which they have received little or no recognition or royalties and defends artists whose work is censored.

Sim's artistic influences have included the cartoonists Jules Feiffer, Bernard Krigstein, Barry Windsor-Smith, and Will Eisner, as well as authors Gore Vidal, Norman Mailer, James Brooks, and others. Sim's wide range of literary interests are revealed in the intricate, intelligent storytelling he accomplishes in *Cerebus the Aardvark*.

The often controversial series follows the daily life of Sims' main character and is a somewhat bitter, though humorous, masculine commentary on politics, relationships with women, religion, creativity, aging, and literary history. Sim has devised characters based on such writers as Oscar Wilde, Ernest Hemingway, and F. Scott Fitzgerald, in addition to characters based on actors Groucho and Chico Marx, singer Mick Jagger, comedian Rodney Dangerfield, and many others. Tim Blackmore, in *Canadian Children's Literature*, wrote that "Sim creates out of an intertextual stream. He blends people he knows, other creators' characters, people from public life, synthesizing them all into his own work." Douglas Wolk, in *Publishers Weekly,* called the series "a brilliant, mindbendingly intricate, alternately hysterically funny and infuriating saga." In a review for *Village Voice,* Richard Gehr observed, "Assisted and inspired by Gerhard, . . . Sim has oscillated between tension and rest, density and minimalism, tradition and innovation. While the early issues reflect Sim's sword-and-sorcery infatuation, *Church and State* simmers as close to real time as a comic has dared." Blackmore called the series "a battleground between high and low culture."

Commenting on Sim's black-and-white artwork, Lloyd Rose wrote in the *Atlantic Monthly* that Sim "poses his characters to be looked at: your eye wants to linger over them rather than move on." Rose also noted Sim's "cinematographer's eye," saying that he "swoops in for close-ups, gazes down from a ceiling corner, focuses on a detail of movement . . . like an animation director who happens to be drawing comic books." Yet, said Rose, Sim is "more like a writer illustrating his own stories than a comics artist who thinks mostly in visual terms. . . . There's a streak of Lewis Carroll in Sim—the politicians and flunkies have all the fantastic reality of the court of the Queen of Hearts." Keith R.A. DeCandido, in *Library Journal,* called the *Cerebus the Aardvark* series "one of the most literate and beautifully drawn comics ever created."

Set in European city-states during the Middle Ages, *Cerebus the Aardvark* was originally created as a parody of Robert E. Howard's comic-book series *Conan the Barbarian,* but it quickly took on new directions as a lampoon of other heroes and supermen and earned the status of a cult following. Cerebus, also known as the "earth-pig," is a greedy, power hungry, and lustful little creature living in a world of humans. In his struggle for power and wealth, he eventually becomes prime minister (in *High Society*) and then pope (in *Church & State*) of his human world. Bound by no rules in his office as pope, he can marry and divorce at will and once demonstrates his infallibility by throwing a baby to his death in front of a crowd. Sim delves into the history of Western religion in his series. He also earned a reputation as a misogynist because Cerebus, and later Sim in his own voice, expounds on the negative qualities of girls and women, marriage and family, from a male sociopolitical

viewpoint, reaching a crescendo with the *Mothers & Daughters* books. Michael Rawdon, in a review for *Spies,* found *Mothers & Daughters* to be "boring" but "inflammatory," although admitting that the art is "lovely."

The first collected volume, *Cerebus* includes the first twenty-five monthly issues of the comic. It introduces the furry aardvark, whose lust for gambling and alcohol leads him to interact with a number of other superhero and fantasy characters as well as politicians and comedians. Some of the series' basic characters are introduced in *Cerebus,* so readers who want to follow the entire epic should start with this collection. DeCandido, in another *Library Journal* review, found it "marred by crude stories and cruder art," although he said that in Sim's subsequent volumes the art is "magnificent." A reviewer for *Grovel* online wrote, "It's well worth getting past these earlier stories as the improvement in quality made further into the book is enormous. By the time you get to the end of this volume, you should be well and truly attached to Cerebus." Art Kleiner, writing in the *Whole Earth Review,* said Sim's characters "are portrayed with depth and complexity" and that Sim has a "graceful ear for the rhythms of their speech." Jack Lechner, writing in the *Village Voice Literary Supplement,* thought Sim's "prevailing style is a sort of elegant deadpan, describing chaotic action within great formal spaces." He wrote, "*Cerebus* gives you the opera and the Marx Brothers to disrupt it."

High Society, according to DeCandido, deals with "the nuances and peculiarities of political power." In this collection, Cerebus becomes prime minister, gives up his sword and medallions for a tuxedo, and moves into the Regency Hotel. As Blackmore commented, "Cerebus's move uptown was the first of many shocks to the fan community which had cheered on the grouchy little killer aardvark." Cerebus is later evicted from his position of power and goes wandering.

After his appointment as pope in *Church & State,* Cerebus's life continues with a love relationship in *Jaka's Story.* Domesticity, personal power, repressive government, and religious totalitarianism are dealt with here. Jaka is a pub dancer. Oscar Wilde appears in the story and is sentenced to hard labor for possessing no artistic license. Cerebus and Jaka are parted, but they come back together again at the end of *Rick's Story.*

Following *Jaka's Story* is *Melmoth,* a tribute to Oscar Wilde and a contemplation of existence, loss of power over the self, and death. Blackmore viewed it as in part a discussion of AIDS.

Sim brings Cerebus back to the forefront and launches into his *Mothers & Daughters* story arc with the first volume, *Flight.* The story continues with *Women, Reads,* and *Minds.* In *Reads,* Sim conducts a lengthy discussion of the "feeling" aspect of the feminine and its dominion over the "thinking" aspect of the masculine. It is this volume that became so controversial for its degradation of women and marriage.

In *Going Home,* Cerebus returns to his birthplace of Sand Hills Creek, a name created from "Sand Hills," the former name of Kitchener, Ontario, where Sim lives and works, and "Stoney Creek," the town where Sim lived as a young child. *Form & Void* follows *Going Home. The Last Days,* the final issue—number 300—in what was, to date, the longest-running self-published series in North American comics, concludes with Cerebus's death.

As Blackmore wrote, "Sim's isolation is a key factor in the development of *Cerebus.* Remote from even the meagre support offered by the comics community, . . . Sim is one working in opposition to many. . . . Sim's cloister has performed the double function of setting him apart and keeping him safe. The positioning of the individual against those around him is *Cerebus's* leitmotif. . . . What follows is an attempt to . . . understand the way the text and its author respond to each other; how Sim can produce his world which produces *Cerebus,* and yet *Cerebus* produces Sim's world."

Sim also wrote a guide for prospective comics self-publishers titled *Cerebus Guide to Self-Publishing.* Speaking about self-publishing in an interview for *Two-Handed Man,* Sim said, "I single out the creativity vs. business thing only because, to me, it's the cart you have to get before the horse. Until you find a way to bind and limit business you are just asking for trouble, asking for your innovation to be limited by business, hamstrung by business, blunted by business, deflected by business. If in later years, . . . someone sees something in my work that seems . . . innovative . . . well, I'm pretty sure they will also see that what I achieved was only possible through self-publishing and, hopefully, I will have saved a handful of future creators from hitting a brick wall at their innovative peak."

In his *Two-Handed Man* interview, Sim responded to a question about what his experience has taught him about the comics medium. The medium has "Versatility for the asking," he explained. "Twenty-three years in and I haven't scratched the surface."

BIOGRAPHICAL AND CRITICAL SOURCES:

BOOKS

Clute, John, and Peter Nicholls, *Encyclopedia of Science Fiction,* second edition, Palgrave Macmillan, 1993.

PERIODICALS

Atlantic Monthly, August, 1986, Lloyd Rose, "Comic Books for Grown-Ups" (review of *Cerebus*), p. 77.
Canadian Children's Literature, issue 71, 1993, Tim Blackmore, "*Cerebus:* From Aardvark to Vanaheim, Reaching for Creative Heaven in Dave Sim's Hellish World," pp. 57-78.
Library Journal, March 15, 1990, Keith R.A. DeCandido, review of *Cerebus, High Society,* and *Church & State,* p. 53; June 1, 1991, Keith R.A. DeCandido, review of *Jaka's Story,* p. 134; June 15, 1992, Keith R.A. DeCandido, review of *Melmoth,* p. 76; July, 1993, Keith R.A. DeCandido, review of *Flight,* p. 79.
Publishers Weekly, December 18, 2000, Douglas Wolk, "D.I.Y. Works for Sim's 'Cerebus,'" p. 37.
Village Voice, April 19, 1988, Richard Gehr, "Money Changes Everything: Earth-Pig Brings Home the Bacon," p. 58.
Village Voice Literary Supplement, June, 1985, Jack Lechner, review of *Cerebus,* p. 3.
Whole Earth Review, fall, 1986, Art Kleiner, review of *Cerebus the Aardvark,* p. 98.

ONLINE

Comics Journal, http://www.tcj.com/ (August 12, 2003), Tom Spurgeon, "Dave Sim Interview, excerpted from Issues 184 and 192."
Dave Sim Misogyny Page, http://www.theabsolute.net/ (October 2, 2003), "The Merged Void: Writings from *Reads.*"

Grovel, http://www.grovel.org.uk/ (August 19, 2003), review of *Cerebus.*

Lambiek, http://www.lambiek.net/ (August 12, 2003), "Dave Sim."

Mars Import Web site, http://www.marsimport.com/ (December 4, 2003), "Dave Sim."

Spies.com, http://www.spies.com/ (August 10, 1997), Michael Rawdon, review of *Cerebus 196.*

Two-Handed Man Online, http://www.twohandedman. com/ (June, 2000), "27 Years with an Aardvark: *Two-Handed Man* Interviews Dave Sim."*

*   *   *

SIMPSON, William W.

PERSONAL: Male.

ADDRESSES: Office—Conscious Living Foundation, 1110 Oberlin Dr., Glendale, CA 91205.

CAREER: Writer, educator, and administrator. Conscious Living Foundation, Glendale, CA, founder and director, 2002—.

WRITINGS:

From the Path: Verses on the Mystic Journey (poetry), PageFree Publishing, Inc. (Otsego, MI), 2004.

WORK IN PROGRESS: A book titled *Stepping out of the Whirlwind—A Beginner's Manual for a Conscious Life.*

SIDELIGHTS: William W. Simpson writes about a variety of spiritual disciplines. He has studied both Chan and Zen Buddhism as well as Zen meditation. Since 1975, he has been a practitioner of Kriya Yoga meditation, and he is founder and director of the California-based Conscious Living Foundation, an organization that offers programs and techniques for personal growth, relaxation, meditation, and spiritual living. He has taught several classes at the foundation, and has also recorded a number of the foundation's audio products, including readings of poetry, prayers, and affirmations.

From the Path: Verses on the Mystic Journey is "a wonderful and moving collection of poetry and verse with a mystical bent," commented Marie Jones on *Bookideas.com.* The sixty-six poems span a variety of religious ideas, focusing more on ideas of spirituality rather than on any one particular branch of religious faith. Topics cover both practical and metaphysical concepts familiar to those who follow a spiritual life. "And So I Sit" looks at the difficulties of consistently maintaining a spiritual practice; "To Rest in You" celebrates the inner peace and joy that comes from knowing and communing with the divine; "Another Kind of Love" considers that it is the unconditional giving and receiving of love that propels one's spiritual growth. For those readers who are just starting out on their spiritual quest, Simpson also offers a chapter titled "First Steps," in which he shares practical techniques for spiritual growth and transformation, including praying, using affirmations, meditating, and more.

Simpson "has a gift with words and delights the senses with descriptions of emotions and feelings not easily captured in phrases," Jones stated. The book "is full of philosophy, lessons of life as well as moments of spiritual awakening and consciousness," commented Robert Denson III on the *Sunpiper Press* Web site. Simpson "is well aware that spirituality is a journey, that one never arrives," remarked Jeremy M. Hoover in *Reviewer's Bookwatch.* "The poems in this book are food for the soul," Hoover stated, "providing both inlet and outlet for contemporary journeying with the divine."

BIOGRAPHICAL AND CRITICAL SOURCES:

PERIODICALS

Reviewer's Bookwatch, May, 2005, Jeremy M. Hoover, review of *From the Path: Verses on the Mystic Journey.*

ONLINE

Bookideas.com, http://www.bookideas.com/ (September 25, 2005), Marie Jones, review of *From the Path: Verses on the Mystic Journey.*

Conscious Living Foundation Web site, http://www.consciouslivingfoundation.org/ (September 25, 2005), biography of William W. Simpson.

Sunpiper Press Web site, http://www.sunpiperpress. com/ (September 25, 2005), Robert Denson III, review of *From the Path.*

*   *   *

SINGH, Nalini 1977-

PERSONAL: Born September 7, 1977, in Suva, Fiji. *Ethnicity:* "Indo-Fijian." *Education:* University of Auckland, B.A., LL.B. (with honors), 2001.

ADDRESSES: Agent—c/o Author Mail, Silhouette Books, P.O. Box 5190, Buffalo, NY 14240-5190. *E-mail*—nalini@nalinisingh.com.

CAREER: Romance writer.

MEMBER: Romance Writers of New Zealand.

WRITINGS:

ROMANCE NOVELS

Desert Warrior, Silhouette Books (Buffalo, NY), 2003.
Awaken to Pleasure, Silhouette Books (Buffalo, NY), 2004.
Awaken the Senses, Silhouette Books (Buffalo, NY), 2005.
Craving Beauty, Silhouette Books (Buffalo, NY), 2005.
Secrets in the Marriage Bed, Silhouette Books (Buffalo, NY), 2006.

WORK IN PROGRESS: Slave to Sensation, for Berkley.

*   *   *

SMITH, Haywood 1949-

PERSONAL: Born 1949, in Atlanta, GA; married (divorced); children: one son.

ADDRESSES: Home—Boston, MA. *Agent*—c/o Author Mail, St. Martin's Press, 175 5th Ave., New York, NY 10010. *E-mail*—haywood100@aol.com.

CAREER: Novelist. Former real-estate agent.

AWARDS, HONORS: Maggie Award.

WRITINGS:

Shadows in Velvet (historical romance novel), St. Martin's Paperbacks (New York, NY), 1996.
Secrets in Satin (historical romance novel), St. Martin's Paperbacks (New York, NY), 1997.
Damask Rose (historical romance novel), Five Star (Unity, ME), 1999.
Dangerous Gifts (historical romance novel), St. Martin's Press (New York, NY), 1999.
Highland Princess (historical romance novel), St. Martin's Paperbacks (New York, NY), 2000.
Border Lord (historical romance novel), St. Martin's Paperbacks (New York, NY), 2001.
Queen Bee of Mimosa Branch (novel), St. Martin's Press (New York, NY), 2002.
The Red Hat Club (novel), St. Martin's Press (New York, NY), 2003.
The Red Hat Club Rides Again (novel), St. Martin's Press (New York, NY), 2005.

WORK IN PROGRESS: Ladies of the Lake; the final book of the "Red Hat Club" trilogy; two more humorous women's fiction novels.

SIDELIGHTS: Haywood Smith did not initially set out to become a novelist. However, motivated by a midlife crisis that left her tired and unhappy with her career as a real estate broker, she changed her profession. "I started writing after a midlife assessment in 1989, at my fortieth birthday," she said in an interview on the *Barnes and Noble* Web site. Her self-assessment prompted her to quit her job in real estate and pursue her dream of writing fiction, despite warnings of the difficulty of breaking into publishing and stories of the volatility of the fiction market. The Georgia chapter of Romance Writers of America (RWA) helped steer her toward the resources that would help her hone her writing craft. Despite the help and encouragement, "it took me five years to learn how to 'get it right.'" Smith remarked in the *Barnes and Noble* Web site interview. A three-minute pitch session at an RWA conference landed her an agent, and within weeks, publishers were showing interest in Smith's work. Her first book, an historical romance titled *Shadows in Velvet,* appeared in 1996.

Shadows in Velvet is set in seventeenth-century France, where civil unrest threatens to overflow at any moment. Convent-raised Anne-Marie de Bourbon-Corbay finds it difficult to cope with the materialistic and corrupt world she occupies after an arranged marriage to her cousin, Philippe. The two become embroiled in deadly civil unrest that sets the range of French classes, from commoners to nobles, against the rule of Cardinal Mazarin and Anne of Austria. "Rich in history, romance and fine narrative drive, this is an impressive debut that explores new territory" in the romance genre, noted a *Publishers Weekly* reviewer.

Secrets in Satin takes place during the English Civil War. When Edward Garrett Viscount Creighton sees Elizabeth, Countess of Ravenwold, dance on the grave of her recently deceased husband, he believes her to be cold and unpleasant. However, he is shocked when King Charles I compels him to marry her. Unaware of her former husband's abuse, Garrett does not warm to his new bride, and neither does she find anything to like in her new, unwanted husband. However, as the two cohabitate, Garrett begins to realize that he has misjudged his first wife, and he begins the slow process of nurturing a relationship. Before the two can reach any new understanding, war erupts and requires Garrett's presence, threatening the newly meaningful marriage between Elizabeth and Garrett. Smith provides "intelligent, sensitive—but not saccharine—historical romance for readers who expect more from the genre," commented a *Publishers Weekly* reviewer.

The Red Hat Club chronicles the lives and views of a group of five middle-aged women who have been friends since their high-school days. Vivacious, determined, intelligent, and still sexy and full of life, the women meet for lunch wearing their gaudiest clothes and red hats, in honor of Jenny Joseph's poem "Warning," which characterizes red hats and purple clothing as symbols of defiance of aging and social stagnation. Their loosely framed secret society gathers for food, drinks, and gossip; adheres (more or less) to a twelve-point code of conduct, including minding one's own business and telling no lies; and serves as social and moral support during tough times and crises. During one meeting, the ladies discover that one of their own is in the midst of a home-life crisis of giant proportions. Red Hat member Diane has discovered her husband cheating on her and needs to arrange his comeuppance. The five begin plotting how to visit unequivocal revenge on Diane's husband. Along with corporate exec Teeny, divorcee SuSu, happily married Linda, and married narrator Georgia, Diane begins looking for documents to prove her banker husband's infidelity, as well as revealing his hidden cache of funds and his hidden property assets. A *Kirkus Reviews* contributor called the book "rowdy southern feminist fantasy for women of a certain age."

The irrepressible members of the Red Hat Club return in *The Red Hat Club Rides Again.* When the ladies discover that their old friend, Pru, is suffering from the effects of drug addiction, they plot a way to come to her rescue. Four of the five jet off to Las Vegas, Nevada, where they pull Pru from the depths of a seedy casino and help her with her recovery. Family crises erupt around them and personal challenges loom, but they remain loyal to their sister-in-crisis and help Pru when she needs it most. A month-long ocean cruise devoted to plastic surgery and physical transformation caps the Red Hatters' good deeds. "Smith's lilting twang and kitchen-sink wisdom permeate every paragraph," observed a *Kirkus Reviews* contributor. "For all their mischief, these women on the verge of second adolescence retain core values of Southern womanhood: goodness, graciousness and grandchildren," observed a *Publishers Weekly* reviewer. The *Kirkus Reviews* critic noted that "even if Smith's is a well-explored genre, her adventurous tale of six middle-aged Atlanta women remains a welcome ride."

Smith told *CA:* "I have been a lifelong reader of all genres and classics, and am influenced by everything I've ever read. I also love movies and think very cinematically when I write. I have osteoarthritis and work in a recliner with a large monitor and cordless mouse andkeyboard.

"I plan each book based on a 'high concept' idea, then I structure the characterizations, conflicts, subplots, andevents into a brief synopsis.After that's approved by my editor, I brainstorm a detailed outline with my critique partner, Betty Cothran. Once that's in place, I sit down and write. Ideally, it's like being a director with an improvisational cast of characters. I know the objectives for each scene, and I sit back and record what plays out in my imagination. I do two rewrites, then send the material, chapter by chapter, for critique, then do a third rewrite and send in the final manuscript.

"I try to write every day, except when I'm on the road. I do two out-of-town appearances a month, except for a month-long book tour with the release of each new book.

"The most surprising thing I've learned is that I could write funny and romantic books while going through a devastating divorce, the loss of my father, and several serious surgeries, but I give most of the credit to my Christian faith—plus a boatload of anti-depressants.

"The objective of all my books is to bring laughter and encouragement to my readers."

"I love all my books. If I didn't, I couldn't very well expect my readers to! But if I had to pick. . . Of my historicals, I loved my first, *Shadows in Velvet* the best, because I had the luxury of unlimited research and time, and it's the most historical of my romance novels. Of my women's fiction, *Queen Bee of Mimosa Branch* is close to my heart, because the divorced heroine was further along in the healing process than I was, and she acted as my guide for becoming whole after the death of a thirty-three-year marriage."

BIOGRAPHICAL AND CRITICAL SOURCES:

PERIODICALS

Booklist, February 15, 1999, Catherine Sias, review of *Dangerous Gifts,* p. 1047; September 15, 2002, Carol Haggas, review of *Queen Bee of Mimosa Branch,* p. 209; September 1, 2003, Carol Haggas, review of *The Red Hat Club,* p. 62; February 1, 2005, Carol Haggas, review of *The Red Hat Club Rides Again,* p. 943.
Kirkus Reviews, September 15, 2002, review of *Queen Bee of Mimosa Branch,* p. 1344; July 15, 2003, review of *The Red Hat Club,* p. 934; January 15, 2005, review of *The Red Hat Club Rides Again,* p. 81.
Library Journal, May 15, 1997, Kristin Ramsdell, review of *Secrets in Satin,* p. 68; September 1, 2002, Rebecca Sturm Kelm, review of *Queen Bee*

of Mimosa Branch, p. 216; September 1, 2003, Shelley Mosley, review of *The Red Hat Club,* p. 211; March 1, 2005, Shelley Mosley, review of *The Red Hat Club Rides Again,* p. 80.
MBR Bookwatch, March, 2005, Harriet Klausner, review of *The Red Hat Club Rides Again.*
Publishers Weekly, May 27, 1996, review of *Shadows in Velvet,* p. 75; March 10, 1997, review of *Secrets in Satin,* p. 64; March 9, 1998, review of *Damask Rose,* p. 65; February 8, 1999, review of *Dangerous Gifts,* p. 210; September 2, 2002, review of *Queen Bee of Mimosa Branch,* p. 52; September 15, 2003, review of *The Red Hat Club,* p. 45; February 28, 2005, review of *The Red Hat Club Rides Again,* p. 43.

ONLINE

Barnes and Noble Web site, http://www.barnes andnoble.com/ (September 25, 2005), interview with Haywood Smith.
Haywood Smith Home Page, http://www.haywood smith.net (September 25, 2005).
Reading Group Guides, http://www.readinggroup guides.com/ (September 25, 2005), brief biography of Haywood Smith.
Romance Reader, http://www.romancereader.com/ (April 30, 1998), review of *Damask Rose*; (February 8, 1999) review of *Dangerous Gifts*; (April 26, 2001) review of *Border Lord.*
Romantic Times, http://www.romantictimes.com/ (September 25, 2005), biography of Haywood Smith.

*   *   *

SMITH, Maya
See MOYNIHAN, Maura

*   *   *

SORRENTINO, Christopher 1963-

PERSONAL: Born 1963, in New York, NY; son of Gilbert Sorrentino (novelist).

ADDRESSES: Home—San Francisco, CA. *Agent*—c/o Author Mail, Farrar, Straus & Giroux, 19 Union Square W., New York, NY 10003.

CAREER: Writer.

WRITINGS:

Sound on Sound (novel), Dalkey Archive Press (Normal, IL), 1995.
Trance (novel), Farrar, Straus (New York, NY), 2005.

SIDELIGHTS: In his first novel, *Sound on Sound,* Christopher Sorrentino tells the story of a rock band named Hi Fi that rises to fame after an infamous night playing at a New York bar called Cheaters. A decade later, writer Paul Marzio begins to investigate that night at Cheaters and recount the hazy events that fueled the band's success. A *Publishers Weekly* contributor called the novel "ambitious," pointing out that it is written to reflect "a mulitlayered recording session." The reviewer went on to note that "the story is flawlessly executed."

Sorrentino fictionalizes the real-life story of heiress Patty Hearst's kidnapping in 1973 by the Symbionese Liberation Army (SLA) in his novel *Trance.* Sorrentino stays close to the actual historical account and provides perspectives on the events through the eyes of several characters, including the kidnap victim, who has gone from hostage to willing comrade in the SLA, and a sportswriter who is an SLA sympathizer and trying to get a book deal to write about the group. The novel is a "consistently entertaining account of a media sensation," wrote a *Kirkus Reviews* contributor. Andrew O'Hehir, writing for the *Salon.com,* called the novel "ambitious and powerfully written," and went on to note that the author's "eye and ear for the period are terrifying." In a review in the *Seattle Weekly,* Patrick Enright called the novel "a brilliant, hallucinatory fever dream of Americana," while a *Publishers Weekly* contributor found the book to be "a tour de force, announcing a mature and ambitious talent."

BIOGRAPHICAL AND CRITICAL SOURCES:

PERIODICALS

Kirkus Reviews, May 1, 2005, review of *Trance,* p. 504.
Publishers Weekly, March 6, 1995, review of *Sound on Sound,* p. 55; June 6, 2005, review of *Trance,* p. 37.
Seattle Weekly, July 2-August 7, 2005, Patrick Enright, review of *Trance.*

ONLINE

Salon.com, http://www.salon.com/ (August 24, 2005), Andrew O'Hehir, review of *Trance.*
Write Stuff, http://www.altx.com/int2/ (October 27, 2005), Alexander Laurence, "Interview with Christopher Sorrentino."*

*   *   *

SPENCER, Sally 1949-
  (Alan Rustage, James Garcia Woods)

PERSONAL: Born 1949, in Cheshire, England.

ADDRESSES: Home—Spain. *Agent*—c/o Author Mail, Severn House Publishers, 9-15 High St., Sutton, Surrey SM1 1DF, England. *E-mail*—sally@sallyspencer.com.

CAREER: Writer. Formerly a school teacher in England and Iran.

WRITINGS:

NOVELS

The Morgan Horse, J.A. Allen (London, England), 1994.
A Picnic in Eden, Orion (London, England), 1995.
The Silent Land, Severn House (Sutton, England), 1996.
The Paradise Job, Severn House (Sutton, England), 1999.

"MARSTON" TRILOGY

Salt of the Earth, Orion (London, England), 1993.
Up Our Street, Orion (London, England), 1994.
Those Golden Days, Orion (London, England), 1996.

"LONDON" SERIES

Old Father Thames, Orion (London, England), 1995.
South of the River, Orion (London, England), 1997.

"INSPECTOR WOODEND" SERIES

The Salton Killings, Severn House (Sutton, England), 1998.

Murder at Swann's Lake, Severn House (Sutton, England), 1999.

The Dark Lady, Severn House (Sutton, England), 2000.

Death of a Cave Dweller, Severn House (Sutton, England), 2000.

The Golden Mile to Murder, Severn House (Sutton, England), 2001.

Dead on Cue, Severn House (Sutton, England), 2001.

Death of an Innocent, Severn House (Sutton, England), 2002.

The Red Herring, Severn House (Sutton, England), 2002.

The Enemy Within, Severn House (Sutton, England), 2003.

A Death Left Hanging, Severn House (Sutton, England), 2003.

The Witch Maker, Severn House (Sutton, England), 2004.

The Butcher Beyond, Severn House (Sutton, England), 2004.

Dying in the Dark, Severn House (Sutton, England), 2005.

Also author of series title *Stone Killer,* 2005.

"INSPECTOR BLACKSTONE" SERIES; AS ALAN RUSTAGE

A Rendezvous with Death, Severn House (Sutton, England), 2003.

Blackstone and the Tiger, Severn House (Sutton, England), 2003.

Blackstone and the Golden Egg, Severn House (Sutton, England), 2004.

Blackstone and the Firebug, Severn House (Sutton, England), 2004.

"INSPECTTOR RUIZ" SERIES; AS JAMES GARCIA WOODS

The General's Dog, Robert Hale (London, England), 1999.

A Murder of No Consequence, Robert Hale (London, England), 1999.

The Fifth Column, 2002.

ADAPTATIONS: The Silent Land has been adapted for audiocassette by Magna.

SIDELIGHTS: Sally Spencer is a prolific mystery and crime novelist who also writes under the pseudonyms Alan Rustage and James Garcia Woods. Writing as herself, Spencer is the author of a number of novels featuring Inspector Woodend that are set in the 1960s. The first in the series, *The Salton Killings,* revolves around a serial killer who is committing murders in the small village of Salton. Inspector Woodend from Scotland Yard is called in to help. Working with his partner, Detective Sergeant Rutter, Woodend has a horrifying confrontation with the killer as he solves the case. John Rowen, writing in *Booklist,* commented that the author's "epilogue is a real stunner, promising more from a very talented writer." In *Murder at Swann's Lake,* an ex-criminal who is now a club owner is murdered, and Woodend begins to suspect that the murder may not have anything to do with the victim's criminal past but rather his current family life. In *Death of a Cave Dweller,* Woodend and Rutter are looking for the killer of a guitarist in a new hit rock band in Liverpool. *Booklist* contributor John Rowen noted that the author's "characters are diverse, intriguing, and believable; her plots never fail to surprise; and the procedural details are grittily realistic."

The Dark Lady features Woodend on the case of a German who is murdered near an English manor for reasons that may have something to do with World War II, which ended sixteen years earlier. In a review for *Library Journal,* Rex E. Klett called the book "a very successful British procedural." Rowen, writing in *Booklist,* commented: "Excellent work from a too-little-known author."

The Golden Mile to Murder finds Woodend assigned to a case in the hinterlands of England after getting on the wrong side of his superiors because of his efforts on a sensitive case. This time he is trying to solve the murder of a local detective. A *Publishers Weekly* contributor noted that the book "does carry a jolly good sting in its tail that should give the reader a shiver or two." In *Dead on Cue,* Woodend tries to solve the murder of a television actor. A *Kirkus Reviews* contributor noted that "Woodend's steady but unsentimental determination make Spencer's low-key latest a model puzzler."

In *The Red Herring,* Woodend is investigating the murder of a history teacher and the subsequent kidnapping of a student. He battles with his own regret at not being able to rescue another kidnap victim years before. "Spencer's finest hour: a tightly plotted puzzler with surprises at every turn," wrote a *Kirkus Reviews* contributor. *Death of an Innocent* finds Woodend in trouble with his superiors and suspended for suspected bribery as he works on the case of a man and woman murdered by a cold-hearted killer. A *Kirkus Reviews* contributor noted: "Title notwithstanding, there's more than enough guilt to go around in Spencer's chilling ninth." Woodend works on a thirty-year-old case to clear the name of a woman who was hanged for murder in *A Death Left Hanging.* Emily Melton, writing in *Booklist,* commented that the novel contains "a richly layered plot, complex and engaging characters, and a shocking conclusion."

The Enemy Within features Woodend on the trail of a murderer who hides his victims in the bonfires used to celebrate Great Britain's Guy Fawkes Night. "Spencer's careful balance of menace from without and within makes her latest a standout," noted a *Kirkus Reviews* contributor. *The Witch Maker* is a story about the murder of a person who makes witch effigies for burning as part of an historical reenactment. Emily Melton, writing in *Booklist,* called the effort "a first-rate addition to an entertaining series." In *The Butcher Beyond,* Woodend goes on vacation with his wife to Spain, only to witness a man thrown off a balcony, leading him to investigate a case that may involve a global conspiracy. A *Kirkus Reviews* contributor wrote: "Whether he's sipping una cerveza or downing a pint of best bitter, dogged Woodend's a treat for fans of truth-and-justice detection." *Dying in the Dark* details Woodend's investigation of a raped and murdered secretary, but the investigation is hindered when his colleague Rutter is suspected of killing his own wife. *Booklist* contributor Melton commented that the author "writes deftly and skillfully, offering up intriguingly multidimensional characters and a cleverly constructed plot."

In her novel *The Paradise Job,* Spencer leaves Woodend behind to tell the story of Frank Mason. Harried by his wife and mistress, Mason wants to escape his life by running off to Scotland. He plans a bank heist to get the money to fund his new life. John Rowen, writing in *Booklist,* found that the "characters are well developed," and that "the story moves at a good pace." Writing as Alan Rustage, Spencer has also penned several mysteries featuring Scotland Yard detective Sam Blackstone. These stories are set in Victorian England. In *A Rendezvous with Death,* Blackstone is on the murder case of the Honorable Charles Montcliffe, who had his throat cut during the Queen Victoria's Jubilee celebration. Rex Klett, writing in the *Library Journal,* noted that the novel "features a nicely captured Victorian ethos, solid prose, and winning subplot diversions." In *Blackstone and the Golden Egg* Blackstone is on the trail of whoever killed the person guarding a Fabergé egg owned by the Prince of Wales. A *Kirkus Reviews* contributor noted that the author "has several pleasing surprises in store" for readers. *Blackstone and the Firebug* relates Blackstone's efforts to track down a blackmailing firebug, all the while trying to keep from getting fired by his boss Sir Roderick Todd. A *Kirkus Reviews* contributor wrote that "politics as usual . . . keeps Rustage's, or Spencer's, latest transgendered entry simmering nicely."

BIOGRAPHICAL AND CRITICAL SOURCES:

PERIODICALS

Booklist, August, 1998, John Rowen, review of *The Salton Killings,* p. 1977; March 1, 2000, John Rowen, review of *The Paradise Job,* p. 1199; June 1, 2000, John Rowen, review of *Death of a Cave Dweller,* p. 1865; January 1, 2001, John Rowen, review of *The Dark Lady,* p. 926; July, 2001, John Rowen, review of *The Golden Mile to Murder,* p. 1989; January 1, 2002, John Rowen, review of *Dead on Cue,* p. 820; May 1, 2003, Emily Melton, review of *A Death Left Hanging,* p. 1554; May 1, 2004, Emily Melton, review of *The Witch Maker,* p. 1519; October 1, 2004, Emily Melton, review of *The Butcher Beyond,* p. 315; March 15, 2005, Emily Melton, review of *Dying in the Dark,* p. 1271.

Coventry Evening Telegraph, February 19, 2000, Sandra Jury, review of *Old Father Thames,* p. 16.

Kirkus Review, July 1, 1998, review of *The Salton Killings,* p. 936; June 15, 1999, review of *Murder at Swann's Lake,* p. 924; June 1, 2000, review of *Death of a Cave Dweller,* p. 756; November 15, 2000, review of *The Dark Lady,* p. 1580; December 1, 2001, review of *Dead on Cue,* p. 2001; May 15, 2002, review of *The Red Herring,* p. 710; December 1, 2002, review of *Death of an Innocent,* p. 1739; May 15, 2003, review of *A Death Left Hanging,* p. 720; September 1, 2003, review of *A Rendezvous with Death,* p. 1105; November 15, 2003, review of *The Enemy Within,* p. 1343; May 1, 2004, review of *The Witch Maker,* p. 426; December 1, 2004, review of *The Butcher Beyond,* p. 1123; February 15, 2005, review of *Blackstone and the Golden Egg,* p. 203; May 1, 2005, review of *Dying in the Dark,* p. 515; July 15, 2005, review of *Blackstone and the Firebug,* p. 769.

Library Journal, January 1, 2001, Rex Klett, review of *The Dark Lady,* p. 162; August, 2001, Rex Klett, review of *The Golden Mile to Murder,* p. 169; January, 2003, Rex E. Klett, review of *Death of an Innocent,* p. 164; October 1, 2003, Rex Klett, review of *A Rendezvous with Death,* p. 120; December, 2003, Rex Klett, review of *The Enemy Within,* p. 172; June 1, 2004, Rex Klett, review of *The Witch Maker,* p. 108; January 1, 2005, Rex Klett, review of *The Butcher Beyond,* p. 85.

Publishers Weekly, June 22, 1998, Sybil Steinberg, review of *The Salton Killings,* p. 88; June 28, 1999, review of *The Salton Killings,* p. 59; December 18, 2000, Jeff Zaleski, review of *The Dark Lady,* p. 59; July 16, 2001, review of *The Golden Mile to Murder,* p. 161; January 14, 2002, review of *Dead on Cue,* p. 43; June 17, 2002, review of *The Red Herring,* p. 46; June 30, 2003, p. 61.

ONLINE

Alan Rustage Home Page, http://www.alanrustage.com (October 17, 2005).

Allison & Busby Web site, http://www.allisonbusby.ltd. uk/ (September 23, 2004).

James Garcia Woods Home Page, http://www.james garciawoods.com (October 17, 2005).

Mystery Reader, http://www.themysteryreader.com/ (January 27, 2002), Jane Davis, review of *Dead on Cue.*

Sally Spencer Home Page, http://www.sallyspencer. com (September 16, 2004).*

*   *   *

STERN, Stewart 1922-

PERSONAL: Born March 22, 1922, in New York, NY; married; wife's name Marilee. *Education:* Attended University of Iowa.

ADDRESSES: Agent—c/o Author Mail, Grove/ Atlantic, Inc., 841 Broadway, 4th Fl., New York, NY 10003.

CAREER: Writer for film and television. Faculty member at University of Washington and Sundance Institute Screenwriters Lab. *Military service:* U.S. Army, served during World War II.

AWARDS, HONORS: Academy Award nomination for Best Screenplay, 1968, for *Rachel, Rachel;* Emmy Award for best dramatic writing, Academy of Television Arts and Sciences, 1976, for *Sybil.*

WRITINGS:

SCREENPLAYS

(With Alfred Hayes) *Teresa,* Metro-Goldwyn-Mayer, 1951.

Benjy, Paramount, 1951.

Rebel without a Cause (based on the novel by Robert M. Linder), Warner Bros., 1955.

The Rack (adapted from a teleplay by Rod Serling), Metro-Goldwyn-Mayer, 1956.

The James Dean Story, Warner Bros., 1957.

Thunder in the Sun, Paramount, 1959.

The Outsider, Universal, 1961.

The Ugly American (based on the novel by Eugene Burdick and William J. Lederer), Universal, 1963.

Rachel, Rachel (adapted from the novel *A Jest of God* by Margaret Laurence), Warner Bros./Seven Arts, 1968.

(With Dennis Hopper) *The Last Movie,* Alta-Light Productions/Universal, 1971.

Summer Wishes, Winter Dreams, Raster Pictures/ Columbia, 1973.

OTHER

Thunder Silence (television script), *Televison Playhouse,* National Broadcasting Company, 1954.

Sybil (television script; based on the book by Flora Rheta Schreiber), National Broadcasting Company, 1976.

A Christmas to Remember (television script; adapted from the novel *The Melodeon* by Glendon Swarthout), Columbia Broadcasting System, 1978.

No Tricks in My Pocket: Paul Newman Directs, Grove Press (New York, NY), 1989.

SIDELIGHTS: Stewart Stern has written screenplays for some of the most memorable films of mid-twentieth century America. His first script, *Teresa,* which was nominated for an Academy award, tells the story of a troubled U.S. soldier who brings his Italian war bride back to New York City after World War II. The film, which was described as "uncompromisingly realistic" by a contributor to the *Dictionary of Literary Biography,* follows the soldier's treatment by a psychiatrist who helps him cope with his life. Stern had been asked by producer Arthur Loew, Sr., to provide comments on the existing script, and Loew was so impressed by Stern's contributions that he asked the aspiring writer to revise the entire screenplay. Stern drew on his own combat experiences—he served as an infantryman in the Battle of the Bulge—and also visited veterans' hospitals to research the effects of combat fatigue. The resulting screenplay was hailed for its psychological depth, an element that became a hallmark of Stern's subsequent work.

Stern's next major screenwriting project was *Rebel without a Cause,* a film that reflects the misunderstood American teens of the 1950s. The story, based on a book by Robert M. Lindner, concerns three alienated adolescents, played by James Dean, Natalie Wood, and Sal Mineo. Defying their parents, the youths act out in dangerous ways that get them into trouble with the authorities. In the end, a juvenile psychiatrist helps the parents reach a new understanding of the stresses facing modern teenagers. When Dean, a good friend of Stern's, died in a car crash in 1955, Stern wrote the documentary tribute *The James Dean Story.* It was the first film directed by Robert Altman.

The Rack, which Stern adapted from a teleplay by Rod Serling, returns to the subject of the psychological trauma of war. The film tells the story of a Korean War veteran on trial for collaborating with the enemy. The captain, who had been subjected to psychological torture by his North Korean captors, must also confront his troubled childhood and his sense of guilt. Stern also wrote the screenplays for *Thunder in the Sun,* about Basque immigrants in the American West, and *The Outsider,* about American Indian Ira Hayes, one of the marines who raised the flag at Iwo Jima.

Stern went on to write the screenplay for *The Ugly American,* based on the novel by Eugene Burdick and William J. Lederer. Starring Marlon Brando as a U.S. ambassador to a troubled Asian country, the film exposes political and personal corruption. Stern's next project allowed him to focus on more domestic concerns. *Rachel, Rachel,* adapted from the novel *A Jest of God* by Margaret Laurence, tells the story of an inhibited thirty-five-year-old schoolteacher who finally discovers her sexuality. Directed by Paul Newman and starring Joanne Woodward, the film became a huge commercial and critical hit. It received Oscar nominations for best actress, best director, and best screenplay.

For his next project, Stern accepted an invitation from actor Dennis Hopper to write a film about how a remote village in South America is affected after a Hollywood company shoots a movie there on location. Despite the story's potential, *The Last Movie* was Stern's greatest career disappointment. Hopper made drastic changes in the script, and, according to the *Dictionary of Literary Biography* contributor, "failed in his attempt to recapture the alienation of [his earlier success] *Easy Rider.*" Stern's last film project was the original screenplay for *Summer Wishes, Winter Dreams,* about a neurotic middle-aged woman who must confront the failure of her marriage. Although it was not a box office success, the film won critical praise.

Among Stern's more notable later scripts was the adaptation of Flora Rheta Schreiber's book *Sybil* for television. Starring Sally Field as a woman living with multipersonality disorder and Joanne Woodward as the psychiatrist who treats her, the television film won Stern an Emmy award for best dramatic writing. *Sybil* also won for best dramatic special; Field won for best actress.

BIOGRAPHICAL AND CRITICAL SOURCES:

BOOKS

Brown, Kent R., *The Screenwriter as Collaborator: The Career of Stewart Stern,* Arno (New York, NY), 1980.

Dictionary of Literary Biography, Volume 26: *American Screenwriters,* Thomson Gale (Detroit, MI), 1984, pp. 229-303.

PERIODICALS

American Film, October, 1983, "Dialogue on Film: Stewart Stern," pp. 20-22.
Michigan Quarterly Review, fall, 1999, William Baer, "On *Rebel without a Cause:* A Conversation with Stewart Stern," p. 580.*

* * *

STUEBNER, Stephen

PERSONAL: Male.

ADDRESSES: Home—Boise, ID. *Agent*—c/o Author Mail, Caxton Press, 312 Main St., Caldwell, ID 83605.

CAREER: Writer.

WRITINGS:

Idaho Impressions, photography by Mark W. Lisk, foreword by Cecil D. Andrus, Graphic Arts Center (Portland, OR), 1997.
Mountain Biking in Idaho, Falcon (Helena, MT), 1999.
Cool North Wind: Morley Nelson's Life with Birds of Prey, Caxton Press (Caldwell, ID), 2002.
Salmon River Country, photographs by Mark Lisk, Caxton Press (Caldwell, ID), 2004.

SIDELIGHTS: Stephen Stuebner is a freelance writer who often writes about the outdoors. He has also collaborated with photographer Mark W. Lisk for the "coffee table" books *Idaho Impressions* and *Salmon River Country.* The latter book focuses on the largely unspoiled wilderness area in Idaho that covers nearly as much area as the state of Ohio. Commenting on *Salmon River Country* in an interview with Jeanne Huff for the *Idaho Statesman,* Stuebner noted: "I thought it would be good to put a face to the Salmon River country by profiling some of the Salmon River legends." Among these legends are such notables as musician and composer Carole King. The book also includes stories about colorful Idaho locals, such as Sheila Mills, who is known as the "Dutch Oven Queen" for her idea of making casseroles for eating on river-rafting trips. Stuebner also provides general nature essays about the area, and the book includes more than one hundred photographs by Lisk. Jo-Anne Mary Benson, writing in the *Library Journal,* called the book a "delightful work," while a *Wisconsin Bookwatch* contributor wrote that the book is "a true and highly recommended treat for the armchair traveler." The reviewer added that the book could also be used to help plan an adventure vacation. Commenting on the book in the *Idaho Statesman,* Huff wrote: "The book is peppered throughout with stories amid the breathtaking photographs. It feels as if the reader is actually floating, backpacking or skiing, taking a breather here and there to chat with the locals."

BIOGRAPHICAL AND CRITICAL SOURCES:

PERIODICALS

Idaho Statesman, March 8, 2005, Jeanne Huff, "Photographer Mark Lisk and Author Steve Stuebner Turn Their Attention to One of the Most Beautiful Parts of Idaho."
Library Journal, March 1, 2005, Jo-Anne Mary Benson, review of *Salmon River Country,* p. 102.
Wisconsin Bookwatch, January, 2005, review of *Salmon River Country.**

* * *

SUBERMAN, Stella 1922-

PERSONAL: Born February 7, 1922, in Union City, TN; daughter of Morris Aaron (a merchant) and Rebecca (a homemaker; maiden name, Burstein) Kaufman; married Jack Suberman (a professor of English literature), January 31, 1942; children: Rick Ian. *Ethnicity:* "Jewish." *Education:* Attended University of Miami, Coral Gables, and Florida State College for Women. *Politics:* Democrat.

ADDRESSES: Home—700 NE 5th Ave., Boca Raton, FL 33432. *E-mail*—suberman@att.net.

CAREER: Writer. North Carolina Museum of Art, Raleigh, public information officer, 1960-66; University of Miami, Coral Gables, FL, worked at Lowe Art Gallery, 1968-70.

WRITINGS:

The Jew Store (memoir), Algonquin Books of Chapel Hill (Chapel Hill, NC), 1998.
When It Was Our War: A Soldier's Wife on the Home Front (memoir), Algonquin Books of Chapel Hill (Chapel Hill, NC), 2003.

WORK IN PROGRESS: A memoir of World War II veterans and the GI Bill.

SIDELIGHTS: Stella Suberman told *CA:* "I wrote my first memoir, *The Jew Store,* because I wanted to tell a story that had never been told in a personal way. The story would recall the Jewish immigration experience in the American South, especially as it related to 'Jew stores,' which is what the locals called those modest dry goods stores operated by Jewish immigrants. These stores began to be seen in the late nineteenth century, but it was the 1920s and 1930s that were their golden years, the time when almost every southern town had one. Using my own family for the narrative thrust, I wanted to tell how these unworldly Jewish immigrants fresh from the *shtetls* of eastern Europe struggled to come to terms with equally unworldly rural southerners, many of whom had never before seen a Jew.

"I thought my next memoir, *When It Was Our War: A Soldier's Wife on the Home Front,* was a story that needed to be told as well. It was the story of World War II told from my point of view—that of a young woman who followed her Air Corps husband from air base to air base, and then, when he was sent overseas for combat, led the home-front life. I thought it was especially important to recall that we once *had* a wartime home front, since we currently have almost none. I wanted furthermore to tell the story through the eyes of a member of an ethnic minority to enable me to depart from the usual glowing accounts of wartime America and to give a more realistic picture. As a Jewish wife, I perceived the scene somewhat differently from the mainstream soldier's wife, and what I saw was truly the best and the worst of America.

"I am influenced by any writer whom I can respect for his or her writing skills and for his or her implacable search for the truth, with all sentiment cast aside.

"My writing process is to stay in bed after I awake in the morning until I have my plans for where my writing is going that day. When those plans are more or less acceptable, I get up, have breakfast, leave the dishes in the sink (and the bed unmade), and rush to my computer keyboard, upon which I plunk away until early afternoon. With this process I never have writer's block because, by the time I get out of bed, my next pages are out there waiting for me, and I can't wait to see them on the screen."

BIOGRAPHICAL AND CRITICAL SOURCES:

PERIODICALS

Booklist, September 1, 2003, Roland Green, review of *When It Was Our War: A Soldier's Wife on the Home Front,* p. 51.
Kirkus Reviews, June 15, 2003, review of *When It Was Our War,* p. 853.
Library Journal, September 1, 2003, Elizabeth Morris, review of *When It Was Our War,* p. 178.
School Library Journal, May, 2004, Francisca Goldsmith, review of *When It Was Our War,* p. 178.

T

TAK, Sagetarius en Joost
See GRESHOFF, Jan

* * *

TALBERT, David E. 1964(?)-

PERSONAL: Born c. 1964 (some sources say 1966), in Washington, DC; married; wife's name Lyn (an actress). *Education:* Morgan State University, B.A.

ADDRESSES: Home—Sherman Oaks, CA. *Agent*—c/o Author Mail, Simon & Schuster, 1230 Avenue of the Americas, New York, NY 10020. *E-mail*—info@ davidetalbert.com.

CAREER: Novelist, playwright, and director. Urban Broadway theatre series, artistic director and executive producer, 2001—. Director of films, including *A Woman like That,* and of music videos. Recordings include *His Woman, His Wife,* Gospo Centric Records, 2000. Radio broadcaster in San Francisco Bay Area.

AWARDS, HONORS: National Association for the Advancement of Colored People Best Playwright Theater Award, five-time recipient; Urban World Films Award for best dramatic feature, for *A Woman like That.*

WRITINGS:

Tellin' It like It 'Tiz (play), produced in Berkeley, CA, 1991.

The Fabric of a Man (play), produced in Los Angeles, CA, 2001.

(And director) *Love Makes Things Happen* (musical play), produced in Los Angeles, CA, 2002.

Baggage Claim (novel), Simon & Schuster (New York, NY), 2003.

Love on Lay-a-Way (musical play), produced in Los Angeles, CA, 2004.

Love on the Dotted Line (novel), Simon & Schuster (New York, NY), 2005.

Author of plays, including *He Say She Say, but What Does God Say?* (musical) 1996; *Mr. Right Now* (musical), 1999; *His Woman, His Wife* (musical), 2000; *A Fool and His Money; What Goes around Comes Around; Talk Show Live;* and *Lawd Ha' Mercy.*

ADAPTATIONS: He Say She Say, but What Does God Say? was the basis for the television situation comedy *Good News,* UPN, beginning 1997.

WORK IN PROGRESS: The Things That Happen When Grandma Prays, a play; writing and directing *First Sunday,* a comedy film.

SIDELIGHTS: Novelist and playwright David E. Talbert is also a producer and director of "several successful musicals that were sometimes tagged as gospel theater, but which he preferred to call 'soul' plays," commented a biographer in *Contemporary Black Biography.* The great-grandson of a Pentecostal preacher, Talbert offers both inspiration and entertainment with his religious-themed plays.

After attending a performance of the musical *Beauty Shop,* Talbert determined that he could write a play that was not only funny but which was also thought-provoking, spiritually aware, and refined. He began writing his first play the very night he returned from the theatre and in 1991 *Tellin' It like It 'Tiz* premiered in Berkeley, California. "The story and its focus on relationships between a group of African-American men and women [is] set in a women's clothing store and a barbershop," noted the *Contemporary Black Biography* contributor. The play was successful and features spiritual ideas, but is considered for mature audiences only.

Other plays, some with a more conventional spiritual message, have followed. *He Say She Say, but What Does God Say?* premiered in 1996. In the play, the pastor of the debt-encumbered True Vine Full Gospel Church watches helplessly as a local drug kingpin acquires enough real estate to force the church out of existence. However, when the drug dealer is shot during a bad deal, he repents and graciously gives the pastor enough money to save his church and his ministry. This play served as the basis for *Good News,* a situation comedy that aired on the UPN network in 1997. A *Fool and His Money* focuses on the effects of too little self-control in handling a financial windfall. *Mr. Right Now* demonstrates how a sincere woman can make bad choices in searching for her perfect mate, and how perfect choices can sometimes be overlooked because they are so close at hand. *The Fabric of a Man* relates how romantic success can still elude someone who is increasingly successful in business.

Talbert's debut novel, *Baggage Claim,* concerns the unique dilemma of Montana Moore, a flight attendant who has to find a husband in thirty days in order to save face with her family. Growing up in an old-fashioned family setting where most women are married by the age of twenty-five, the thirty-five-year-old Montana is considered an aberration and a woman who is dangerously close to beyond hope. Though she has enjoyed her life of far-ranging travel, and has met more than one interesting, eligible man in her life, a spate of marriages of people close to her has made her reconsider the single life. Two of her friends have recently gotten married; her mother has just entered into her fourth marriage; and her younger sister has recently announced her engagement. Echoes of wedding bells have made her determined to find a suitable fiancée to show off at her sister's upcoming wedding party.

With the help of her fellow flight attendants, Montana manipulates her schedule to put her on planes carrying former boyfriends. All the while, faithful friend William watches with bemusement as Montana moves with skill and grace among her potential suitors. Despite Montana's efforts, however, none of the men are suitable. "Talbert's flair for storytelling and comedic timing make his debut novel a page-turner," commented Melissa Ewey Johnson in *Black Issues Book Review.*

Morgan and Marcus, the lead characters of Talbert's second novel, *Love on the Dotted Line,* are unmarried, but are a serious couple nonetheless. Contract lawyer Morgan and investment banker Marcus are young, good looking, and prosperous, and share what Morgan thinks is a solid relationship. However, one day Morgan spies the tennis bracelet she thought was to be her birthday present decorating the arm of another woman. Her only conclusion: Marcus is cheating on her. Though she refuses to stay down for long, the breakup still comes as a shock. When she meets former pro athlete Charles and their interaction seems destined to move toward the more serious, she wants him to sign a pre-relationship contract that guarantees he will remain faithful to her. A *Publishers Weekly* reviewer commented favorably on the novel's "thin but amusing plot."

Talbert sees his novel writing, in relation to his dramatic work, as "less of a transition, and more of an expansion," as he stated in an interview on the *Morgan State University Spokesman Online.* "I was never one to be boxed in. The theater will always be my first passion, but gifts and talents are transferable."

BIOGRAPHICAL AND CRITICAL SOURCES:

BOOKS

Contemporary Black Biography, Volume 34, Thomson Gale (Detroit, MI), 2002.

PERIODICALS

Back Stage West, May 17, 2001, Lori Talley, "Keeping It Real," profile of David E. Talbert, p. 3; May 2, 2002, Lori Talley, "Making Things Happen: David E. Talbert's Latest Musical Has Attracted the Talents of Kenneth 'Babyface' Edmonds," p. 2.

Black Issues Book Review, January-February, 2004, Melissa Ewey Johnson, review of *Baggage Claim,* p. 51.

Ebony, February, 2004, review of *Baggage Claim,* p. 26.

Essence, June, 2000, Ytasha L. Womack, profile of David E. Talbert, p. 66.

Jet, April 1, 2002, review of *Love Makes Things Happen,* p. 56.

Kirkus Reviews, August 15, 2003, review of *Baggage Claim,* p. 1043.

Publishers Weekly, April 11, 2005, review of *Love on the Dotted Line,* p. 34.

Video Business, April 18, 2005, Krystal Hunt, "With a Little Faith," p. 13.

ONLINE

AllReaders.com, http://www.allreaders.com/ (September 25, 2005), Harriet Klausner, review of *Baggage Claim.*

David E. Talbert Home Page, http://www.davide talbert.com (September 25, 2005).

Morgan State University Spokesman Online, http://www.msuspokeseman.com/ (October 18, 2003), Loren Jackson, interview with David E. Talbert.*

*   *   *

TANNING, Dorothea 1910-

PERSONAL: Born August 25, 1910, in Galesburg, IL; married Homer Shannon (divorced); married Max Ernst (a painter), 1946 (died, 1976). *Education:* Attended Knox College; studied at Art Institute of Chicago.

ADDRESSES: *Home*—New York, NY. *Agent*—c/o Author Mail, Graywolf Press, 2402 University Ave., Ste. 203, Saint Paul, MN 55114.

CAREER: Novelist, poet, and artist. *Exhibitions:* Works exhibited at Julien Levy Gallery, New York, NY, 1944; Galerie les Pas Perdus, Paris, France, 1950; Alexandre Iolas Gallery, New York, NY, 1953; Galerie Furstenberg, Paris, 1954; Musée des Beaux-Arts, 1956; Galerie Edouard Loeb, Paris, 1959; Galerie der Spiegel, Cologne, Germany, 1963; Galerie d'Art Moderne, Basel, Switzerland, 1966; Casino Communal, Knokke-le-Zoute, Belgium, 1967; Le Point Cardinal, Paris, 1970; Centre National d'Art Contemporain, Paris, 1974; Gimpel & Weitzenhoffer Gallery, New York, NY, 1979; Stephen Mazoh Gallery, New York, NY, 1983; Kent Fine Art, New York, NY, 1987, 1988; Stephen Schlesinger Gallery, New York, NY 1989; Runkel-Hue-Williams, London, England, 1989; New York Public Library, New York, NY, 1992; Konsthall, Malmo, Sweden, 1993; and Metropolitan Museum of Art, New York, NY, 2002. Works included in permanent collections of Museum of Modern Art; Tate Gallery, London; Georges Pompisou Center, Paris; Menil Collection, Houston, TX; and Philadelphia Museum of Art.

WRITINGS:

Birthday (memoir), Lapis Press (Santa Monica, CA), 1986, expanded edition published as *Between Lives: An Artist and Her World,* W.W. Norton (New York, NY), 2001.

(Author of chronology and commentary) Roberta Waddell and Louisa Wood Ruby, editors, *Dorothea Tanning: Hail, Delirium!: A Catalogue Raisonné of the Artist's Illustrated Books and Prints, 1942-1991,* Miriam and Ira D. Wallach Division of Art, Prints and Photographs, New York Public Library (New York, NY), 1992.

(Illustrator) James Merrill and others, *Another Language of Flowers: Paintings* (poetry), Braziller (New York, NY), 1998.

Chasm: A Weekend (novel), Overlook Press (Woodstock, NY), 2004.

A Table of Content (poems), Graywolf Press (St. Paul, MN), 2004.

Contributor to books, including *Best American Poetry 2000,* edited by David Lehman and Rita Dove, Scribner (New York, NY), 2000. Contributor of poetry to periodicals, including *New Republic, Partisan Review, Yale Review, Parnassus, New Yorker, Poetry,* and *Paris Review.*

SIDELIGHTS: Novelist, memoirist, and poet Dorothea Tanning is also a noted painter and sculptor often associated with the surrealism movement of the early-twentieth century. "The juxtaposition of familiar and fantastic objects set in barren landscapes or Victorian interiors, rendered with a uniform treatment notable for sharp outlines and careful finish, links these paintings to the 'magic realism' of the Surrealists," commented a biographer in *Contemporary Women Artists.* In addition, she has also been a printmaker and a costume designer for a number of ballet companies in New York City. Tanning is best known for paintings such as "Birthday," in which the artist is depicted in self-portrait, breasts exposed, a somewhat pensive and doubtful expression on her face, dressed in a skirt of vines and leaves, and standing in front of an endlessly repeated series of open doors. In the foreground, a demonic-looking winged creature, seemingly a combination of bird and cat, stands threateningly, as if ready to attack. It was this painting that first brought her to the attention of surrealism pioneer Max Ernst, whom she married in 1946. They remained married until Ernst's death in 1976.

Between Lives: An Artist and Her World is an expansion of Tanning's earlier memoir, *Birthday.* In this book, "Tanning uses language like paint, limning scenes dreamy in hue yet acute in detail and metaphoric in their images," telling colorful stories from her earliest days to her current life as a vibrant, creative nonagenarian, according to *Booklist* reviewer Donna Seaman. The author recalls numerous aspects of her life and work, including her association with some of the greatest creative artists of the twentieth century, such as Virgil Thompson, Dylan Thomas, Truman Capote, Man Ray, Igor Stravinsky, and George Balanchine. She fondly remembers her second husband, Ernst, and their many years together. "She is self-effacing," noted a *Publishers Weekly* contributor, "finding Ernst's life and story more interesting than her own, but describes their shared life poetically." The memoir is "never merely gossipy or needlessly name-dropping," observed Martin R. Kalfatovic in *Library Journal.* Tanning simply refers matter-of-factly to those luminaries she truly did know, and who in turn held her in high esteem.

Tanning's oeuvre includes sculptures as well as paintings, and in her more advanced years she also emerged as a novelist and poet of note. *New Yorker* contributor Jane Kramer noted that Tanning will sometimes ironically refer to herself as the "oldest living emerging poet." Her book of poetry, *A Table of Content,* contains works "like collages, softly surreal, delicately personal, but somehow perfectly right," observed *Library Journal* reviewer Louis McKee. Demonstrating what a *Publishers Weekly* contributor called "a curious mix of numerous styles," Tanning explores images and ideas of family, love, life, place, regret, and lost opportunity. In some of her poems, she demonstrates a "straightfor-

ward, unmannered approach to the deconstruction of icons, references and symbols," commented the *Publishers Weekly* critic, while in others she speaks in a quieter voice, punctuating explorations of loss and regret. The collection will "admirably serve to introduce her to a whole new generation of readers," attested a reviewer in *Wisconsin Bookwatch.*

Tanning has also taken up the mantle of novelist, albeit one with a surrealistic tinge to her writing. In *Chasm: A Weekend* seven-year-old Destina Meridian has witchcraft in her background, being the descendant of a woman tried for practicing the dark arts in 1692 Massachusetts. She lives in the Arizona desert with her father, Raoul, and Nelly, a woman who is presented as the girl's governess but is actually Raoul's sexual plaything. When Raoul invites the beautiful Nadine and her ne'er-do-well fiancée Albert to spend a weekend at his desert estate, the two houseguests find their familiar lives transformed. Nadine becomes entranced by the desert landscape and captivated by the charismatic but ultimately despicable Raoul. He even convinces her to cut off her long blonde hair to satisfy one of his fetishes. Separated from Nadine, Albert wanders through the enormous house, where he encounters the mysterious Destina. The child shows him a box full of peculiar items, such as lizard claws, reptile skins, and tiny eyes preserved in bottles. She describes the friend in the desert who brings these items to her, and to Albert the description sounds like that of a lion. A raucous dinner party leads the guests to their separate fates, with Albert and Nadine searching the desert for Destina's lion friend and Raoul, once again, with Nelly. Tanning's "roots as a surrealist painter are evident throughout her creepy, erotically charged first novel," observed reviewer Emily Mead in *Entertainment Weekly.* Tanning "describes the desert with poetic precision," noted a *Kirkus Reviews* critic. "While her plot wavers at times, she concludes with a series of truly gruesome set pieces and a final moment of grace." The reviewer declared the book to be a "spare gothic jewel."

BIOGRAPHICAL AND CRITICAL SOURCES:

BOOKS

Bailly, George Christophe, *Dorothea Tanning,* translated by Richard Howard and Robert C. Morgan, Braziller (New York, NY), 1995.

Contemporary Women Artists, St. James Press (Detroit, MI), 1999.

PERIODICALS

Art Business News, March, 2005, "Reviewing the History of Surrealism in the USA," p. 78.

Art Criticism, 1987, Donald B. Kuspit, "Dorothea Tanning's Occult Drawings."

Art in America, November-December, 1974, Linda Nochlin, "Dorothea Tanning at the CNAC."

ARTnews, March, 1988, John Gruen, "Among the Sacred Monsters."

Arts, September, 1983, Ann Gibson, "Dorothea Tanning: The Impassioned Double Entendre."

Bomb, fall, 1990, interview with Dorothea Tanning.

Booklist, July, 2001, Donna Seaman, review of *Between Lives: An Artist and Her World,* p. 1968.

Entertainment Weekly, October 22, 2004, Emily Mead, review of *Chasm: A Weekend,* p. 101.

Feminist Art Journal, spring, 1974, Cindy Nemser, "In Her Own Image."

Kirkus Reviews, August 15, 2004, review of *Chasm,* p. 775.

Library Journal, October 15, 2001, Martin R. Kalfatovic, review of *Between Lives,* p. 73; May 15, 2004, Louis McKee, review of *A Table of Content,* p. 91.

New Yorker, May 3, 2004, Jane Kramer, "Self Inventions," profile of Dorothea Tanning, p. 40.

Publishers Weekly, June 4, 2001, review of *Between Lives,* p. 66; June 21, 2004, review of *A Table of Content,* p. 59.

Wisconsin Bookwatch, August, 2004, review of *A Table of Content.*

Woman's Art Journal, spring-summer, 1981, Paula Lumbard, "Dorothea Tanning: On the Threshold to a Darker Place."

Women's Art, September-October, 1995, Alison Rowley, "Lapses of Taste."

ONLINE

Salon.com, http://www.salon.com/ (February 11, 2002), John Glassie, "Oldest Living Surrealist Tells All," interview with Dorothea Tanning.*

*   *   *

TAYLOR, Kate 1962-

PERSONAL: Born July 22, 1962, in Boulougne-sur-Seine, Provence, France; daughter of J.H. (a diplomat) and Mary (a writer, editor, and homemaker) Taylor; married Joel Sears (an advertising copywriter), March 10, 2001. *Ethnicity:* "Anglo-Saxon Scots" *Education:* University of Toronto, B.A., 1983; University of Western Ontario, London, M.A., 1985.

ADDRESSES: *Office*—Globe and Mail, 444 Front St. W., Toronto, Ontario M5V 2S9, Canada. *E-mail*—ktaylor@globeandmail.ca.

CAREER: *Hamilton Spectator,* Hamilton, Ontario, Canada, copy editor, 1986-89; *Globe & Mail,* Toronto, Ontario, copy editor, 1989-91, arts reporter, 1991-95, theater critic, 1995-2003, arts columnist, 2003—.

AWARDS, HONORS: Nathan Cohen Award for Excellence in Theatre Criticism, Canadian Theatre Critics Association, 1996, for long review, 1999, for short review; Commonwealth Writers Prize, 2004, for *Madame Proust and the Kosher Kitchen.*

WRITINGS:

Painters (juvenile), Fitzhenry & Whiteside (Toronto, Ontario, Canada), 1989.

Madame Proust and the Kosher Kitchen (novel), Doubleday Canada (Toronto, Ontario, Canada), 2003.

SIDELIGHTS: Canadian journalist Kate Taylor, a veteran critic and arts reporter for Toronto's *Globe & Mail,* became a novelist with the publication of *Madame Proust and the Kosher Kitchen,* inspired, she told *CA,* by her "own affection for Proust." The fictional diary of the mother of French novelist Marcel Proust is woven into two stories set in the present time. In one, a Jewish refugee named Sarah Segal is smuggled into Toronto in 1942 by her parents, who ultimately die in a Nazi concentration camp. Sarah marries and raises a family in Canada, although she is haunted by her past. The other story features Marie, a translator who is captivated by Proust's writings. Marie is a friend of Sarah's grown son, Maxime, and she is also the person who discovers Jeanne Proust's diaries in a Paris archive.

Calling *Madame Proust and the Kosher Kitchen* a "magnificent first novel," London *Times* reviewer Michael Arditti praised Taylor for sensitively addressing themes of sexual and religious identity, while also showing "how events in a writer's life and themes in his work have resonance for subsequent generations." London *Sunday Telegraph* contributor Jessica Mann also praised the work, citing the author's "meticulous research" and noting that Taylor's "well-written, melancholy story contains a lot to admire." Calling the novel a "moving meditation on Parisian and Toronto history," *Maclean's* critic Brian Bethune noted that an historical theme is appropriate "in a novel colored by the presence of Marcel Proust, the original obsessed-with-the-past writer."

BIOGRAPHICAL AND CRITICAL SOURCES:

PERIODICALS

Globe & Mail (Toronto, Ontario, Canada), January 25, 2003, T.F. Rigelhof, review of *Madame Proust and the Kosher Kitchen.*

Maclean's, March 24, 2003, Brian Bethune, review of *Madame Proust and the Kosher Kitchen*, p. 52.

Sunday Telegraph (London, England), February 9, 2003, Jessica Mann, review of *Madame Proust and the Kosher Kitchen.*

Times (London, England), February 19, 2003, Michael Arditti, review of *Madame Proust and the Kosher Kitchen*, p. 13.

Times Literary Supplement, January 31, 2003, Toby Lichtig, review of *Madame Proust and the Kosher Kitchen*, p. 22.

ONLINE

University of Western Ontario Web site, http://communications.uwo.ca/ (August 15, 2005), profile of Taylor.*

*   *   *

TEMPLE, Lou Jane

PERSONAL: Married; children: Reagan, Jed.

ADDRESSES: Home—Kansas City, MO. *Agent*—Penguin Group, c/o Berkley Prime Crime Publicity, 375 Hudson St., New York, NY 10014.

CAREER: Chef, restauranter, and writer. Former owner of Café Lulu, Kansas City, MO; guest chef at Culinary Institute of America and James Beard Foundation; currently develops menus for new restaurants.

WRITINGS:

(With A. Cort Sinnes) *The Big Platter Cookbook: Cooking and Entertaining for a Crowd,* Stewart, Tabori & Chang (New York, NY), 2004.

The Spice Box (novel), Berkley Prime Crime (New York, NY), 2005.

Death du Jour (mystery novel), Berkley Prime Crime (New York, NY), 2006.

"HEAVEN LEE" MYSTERY SERIES

Death by Rhubarb, St. Martin's Paperbacks (New York, NY), 1996.

Revenge of the Barbecue Queens, St. Martin's Paperbacks (New York, NY), 1997.

A Stiff Risotto, St. Martin's Paperbacks (New York, NY), 1997.

Bread on Arrival, St. Martin's Press (New York, NY), 1998.

The Cornbread Killer, St. Martin's Minotaur (New York, NY), 1999.

Red Beans and Vice, St. Martin's Minotaur (New York, NY), 2001.

Death Is Semisweet, St. Martin's Minotaur (New York, NY), 2002.

Contributor to periodicals, including *Kansas City* magazine.

SIDELIGHTS: Mystery novelist Lou Jane Temple is a chef and restaurateur who consults with restaurants in developing new and innovative menus. She uses her considerable kitchen skills to literary effect in the "Heaven Lee" series of food-themed culinary mysteries. The books are centered around the cooking adventures and sleuthing skills of ex-attorney Heaven Lee, a chef and restaurant owner in Kansas City, Missouri, whose real name is Katherine O'Malley. Heaven Lee is introduced in *Death by Rhubarb*, Temple's first book. At Café Heaven, Lee's Kansas City restaurant, both the inside business and the catering arm are busy and successful. After a difficult stretch of personal and business problems, Heaven thinks she is finally past her problems and is looking forward to nurturing her flourishing business. When her first ex-husband's date is poisoned in the cafe, however, her newfound happiness comes crashing down. To save her restaurant and herself, Heaven becomes an amateur sleuth determined to uncover the perpetrator behind the murder. A colorful cast of neighborhood regulars band together to help out. Temple also inaugurates her recurring technique of including detailed recipes for dishes associated with the novel at hand. In her story, "Temple develops a sense of community, often absent in urban settings, which is crucial to catching the killer," observed a *Publishers Weekly* reviewer.

In *Bread on Arrival* Heaven indulges her current passion for bread-making. As she studies the subtleties of the baking arts, she attends the ARTOS breadmakers' conference held in town. The ARTOS members endorse all-natural breads and disdain mass-produced commercial breads. Foul play is suspected when General Irwin Mills, the chief of an experimental grain laboratory, falls to his death in front of hundreds of ARTOS attendees. When Heaven discovers a fellow attendee face down and dead in an enormous pan of dough, she must investigate and locate the killer before more bakers and dough-pullers wind up dead. Meanwhile, Heaven has to deal with her boyfriend, Hank, a Vietnamese physician twenty years her junior, and her daughter's much-older lover, a rock musician twenty years her senior. "Heaven is a likable protagonist, and Temple knows how to construct an entertaining plot," commented reviewer Stuart Miller in *Booklist*.

The Cornbread Killer finds Heaven in a frenzy of work as she and the town prepare for a jazz festival and black heritage celebration. When disreputable and thoroughly disliked events planner Evelyn Edwards is found electrocuted, Heaven calls in colleagues Mona Kirk and Detective Bonnie Weber to help determine if the frying was accidental or a deliberate murder. Matters deteriorate quickly when a documentary film crew arrives, Charlie Parker's irreplaceable plastic saxophone disappears from the local jazz museum, two musical imposters are discovered, and a number of old jazz musicians with still-raw grudges come to town. Perhaps worse, a mysterious stranger is buying up all the ethnic foods in town, running Heaven dangerously short on the supplies she will need for the festival. "An abundance of interesting action, characters, and recipes will place this high on the acquisitions list," com-

mented Rex E. Klett in *Library Journal*. "Temple's writing is light, fluffy, and as delicious as a chocolate soufflé," remarked *Booklist* contributor Jenny McLarin.

The Christmas season does not mean a moratorium on murder in *Death Is Semisweet*. A local family of chocolatiers, the Fosters, is in turmoil over an internal dirty deal: the eldest brothers deceived the younger siblings into selling them their shares of the company, after which the older brothers took the company public and made a fortune. When the company sends up an ostentatious pink blimp to celebrate its fiftieth anniversary, someone literally shoots it out of the sky. Heaven Lee witnesses the crash that kills the pilot of the airship, and decides her investigative skills are needed to uncover the problems in the chocolate company. While snooping around the factory, she overhears the Foster brothers complaining of a bad deal with an African cocoa supplier. Worse, she finds her old friend, Stephanie Simpson, a distant Foster relative, standing with murder weapon in hand as the supplier floats dead in a vat of chocolate. Heaven is faced with the challenge of saving her old pal and sewing up the Foster family rift, all the while dealing with the never-ending complications of her own life. "Fans of the series are sure to be entertained," noted GraceAnne A. DeCandido in *Booklist*.

The Spice Box marks Temple's departure from the "Heaven Lee" series and the first book of a new food-themed historical mystery series. In U.S. civil war-era New York, Bridget Heaney has been hired as assistant cook in the mansion of wealthy merchant Isaac Gold. Her first day on the job gets off to an inauspicious start as she discovers Gold's youngest son, Seth, dead and stuffed inside a dough box. An incompetent police force inspires Gold to undertake his own investigation, with Bridget's help. While the mismatched duo searches for clue to Seth's murder, Bridget seeks information on her missing sister's whereabouts. They search for Seth's lover, Katherine, as well, but her dead body is soon discovered, too. As they continue to investigate, the boundary between employer and servant continues to blur. The spice box of the novel's title provides a tantalizing clue. A *Publishers Weekly* contributor called the book "memorable." Temple's work "expertly weaves together a fully realized look at the ghettoizing of Irish immigrants, Sephardic Judaism and New York during the Civil War," noted Oline H. Cogdill in the *South Florida Sun-Sentinel*. Temple has "written a delectable culinary historical mystery," concluded Harriet Klausner in *MBR Bookwatch*.

BIOGRAPHICAL AND CRITICAL SOURCES:

PERIODICALS

Booklist, September 15, 1998, Stuart Miller, review of *Bread on Arrival,* p. 202; December 1, 1999, Jenny McLarin, review of *The Cornbread Killer,* p. 688; July, 2001, GraceAnne A. DeCandido, review of *Red Beans and Vice,* p. 1989; September 1, 2002, GraceAnne A. DeCandido, review of *Death is Semisweet,* p. 64.

Kirkus Reviews, July 15, 2002, review of *Death Is Semisweet,* p. 999; April 1, 2005, review of *The Spice Box,* p. 391.

Library Journal, November 1, 1998, Rex E. Klett, review of *Bread on Arrival,* p. 128; January, 2000, Rex E. Klett, review of *The Cornbread Killer,* p. 166; September 1, 2002, Rex E. Klett, review of *Death Is Semisweet,* p. 219.

MBR Bookwatch, April, 2005, Harriet Klausner, review of *The Spice Box.*

Pittsburgh Post-Gazette, March 27, 2005, Suzanne Martinson, "That's Entertainment: *Big Platter Cookbook* Helps Hosts Limit the Stress When Feeding a Group."

Publishers Weekly, June 10, 1996, review of *Death by Rhubarb,* p. 96; March 10, 1997, review of *Revenge of the Barbecue Queens,* p. 64; September 7, 1998, review of *Bread on Arrival,* p. 88; November 22, 1999, review of *The Cornbread Killer,* p. 45; July 2, 2001, review of *Red Beans and Vice,* p. 56; April 4, 2005, review of *The Spice Box,* p. 47.

South Florida Sun-Sentinel, June 8, 2005, Oline H. Cogdill, review of *The Spice Box.*

ONLINE

Murder Express, http://www.murderexpress.net/ (October 23, 2005), biography of Lou Jane Temple.

Mystery Reader, http://www.themysteryreader.com/ (October 23, 2005), Jennifer Monahan Winberry, review of *The Spice Box.*

Romantic Times Online, http://www.romantictimes. com/ (October 23, 2005), Toby Bromberg, review of *Death Is Semisweet* and *The Cornbread Killer.**

TEW, Philip 1954-

PERSONAL: Born February 17, 1954, in Enfield, Middlesex, England; married Caroline Patti McAlister, June 26, 1976 (divorced May 8, 1981); children: George Alister. *Ethnicity:* "Londoner." *Education:* University of Leicester, B.A. (with honors), 1976, M.Phil., 1986; Leicester Polytechnic, postgraduate certificate of education, 1977; University of Westminster, Ph.D., 1997. *Politics:* "Lapsed anarchist." *Religion:* "Gnostic/spiritualist." *Hobbies and other interests:* Cycling, swimming, television, pubs and restaurants.

ADDRESSES: Office—School of English, University of Central England, Perry Barr., Birmingham B42 2SU, England. *E-mail*—philip.tew@uce.ac.uk; tewp@ ukf.net.

CAREER: Writer and educator. Schoolteacher in Leicestershire and London, England, 1977-82; English teacher at secondary school in London, 1982-90; University of Wolverhampton, Wolverhampton, England, senior lecturer in English and American studies and section head for American literature, 1990-94; Tufts University, Medford, MA, tutor at University College London, 1995-97; University of Westminster, Westminster, England, visiting lecturer in English and American literature and creative writing, 1994-2000; University of Debrecen, Debrecen, Hungary, senior lecturer, 2000-01, honorary reader, beginning 2001; Szeged University, Szeged, Hungary, visiting British Council tutor in English literature, 2000-01; University of Central England, Birmingham, reader in English and aesthetics. Freelance television researcher and producer, 1997-2001. United Kingdom Network for Modern Fiction Studies, director.

MEMBER: Royal Society of Arts (fellow), North East Modern Languages Association.

WRITINGS:

B.S. Johnson: A Critical Reading, St. Martin's Press (New York, NY), 2001.

(Editor, with Rod Mengham and Richard Lane, and contributor) *Contemporary British Fiction Post-1979: A Critical Introduction,* Polity Press (Cambridge, England), 2003.

The Contemporary British Novel, Continuum (London, England), 2004.

Contributor to books, including *Focus: Papers in English Literary and Cultural Studies,* edited by Maria Kurdi, Gabriella Hartvig, and Andrew C. Rouse, University of Pecs Press, 2000; *Beckett and Philosophy,* edited by Richard J. Lane, Palgrave (London, England), 2002; *Pastiches, Parodies, and Other Imitations,* edited by Marius Buning, Matthijs Engelberts, and Sjef Houppermans, Rodopi (New York, NY), 2002; *The City of Dreadful Night,* by James Thomson, Agraphia (London, England), 2003; and *After Postmodernism,* de Gruyter (New York, NY), 2003. Coeditor of book series "The New British Novel," for Palgrave Macmillan. Contributor to periodicals, including *Review of Contemporary Fiction, Critical Survey, Hungarian Journal for English and American Studies,* and *New Formations: Journal of Culture/Theory/ Politics.*

WORK IN PROGRESS: Jim Crace, a monograph, for Manchester University Press; editing *British Fiction Today,* with Rod Mengham, Continuum (London, England), completion expected in 2006.

SIDELIGHTS: Philip Tew told *CA:* "The primary motivation for writing must be to inform readers and try to inspire them to think critically in an engaged fashion, seeing literary texts in relation to life-world experiences. Among my other motivations is a desire to reflect a meta-realist and theoretical understanding of literary exegesis, avoiding and opposing the relativism of postmodernism. Overall the intention is to engage an ideological understanding of literary texts and contexts that is nevertheless illuminating. I am committed to bringing to the fore neglected and unfashionable authors, critics, and ways of reading. I remain opposed to conservative critics who wish to respect the literary text so that it may simply speak for itself, which of course is paradoxical since any text opens a paradoxical space that invites its interrogation, without simply being one relativistic version of plural means that cannot be either judged or situated. All texts, literary or factual, are at least residually contextual and may be judged by value systems.

"Who or what particularly influences my work? For helping me to understand the philosophic and exegetical contexts of literature, such critics and theorists as Matthew Arnold, F.R. Leavis, Ernst Cassirer, Maurice Merleau-Ponty, Jurgen Habermas, Pierre Bourdieu, Edward Pols, and Roy Bhaskar. Also, some fairly obvious Anglo-American literary figures such as William Shakespeare, Laurence Sterne, Samuel Taylor Coleridge, John Keats, Charles Dickens, Walt Whitman, Emily Dickinson, Willa Cather, Thomas Hardy, Katharine Mansfield, Virginia Woolf, Evelyn Waugh, B.S. Johnson, Muriel Spark, and the contemporary British writers Jonathan Coe, Jim Crace, Jenny Diski, and Will Self, since they all inspire me to think creative fiction enhances our experience and mutual self-knowledge (intersubjectivity).

"My writing process is at times laborious, but at others transcendent. I find criticism can be creative or at the very least challenging. I remain in some senses a frustrated novelist who finds ideological possibilities in literary criticism. I work fairly assiduously through texts, but I have been known to read them backwards. One piece of advice I offer to students that comes from my own dialectical thinking is that, if an exegetical idea will not go anywhere, or is not persuasive, just try its opposite and see what that suggests to you. I am conscious that one should not simply be descriptive of literary texts, since people are capable of reading primary literary texts themselves, and most of them are not that complicated!

"What inspired me to write on the subjects I have chosen? First, it is the dialectical possibilities that the primary texts offer, and the understandings of life. Alternatively, it is because people ask me to, and something attracts me. In terms of critical writing, I think in some ways I find an impulse from a necessity to balance recent intellectual thought, in that some of us had to resist the extremities and stupidities of the poststructuralist and postmodernist period of thought that for some strange reason dominated the humanities until the end of the last century from about 1980. I still maintain that literature informs and is informed by life, not simply languages."

BIOGRAPHICAL AND CRITICAL SOURCES:

PERIODICALS

Review of Contemporary Fiction, summer, 2002, Richard J. Murphy, review of *B.S. Johnson: A Critical Reading,* p. 249.

THOMAS, Diane C.
(Diane Coulter Thomas)

PERSONAL: Born in Oakland, CA; married Bill Osher (a writer, editor, and college administrator). *Education:* Georgia State University, B.A.; Columbia University, M.F.A.

ADDRESSES: Home—GA. *Agent*—c/o Author Mail, Toby Press, P.O. Box 8531, New Milford, CT 06776-8531. *E-mail*—diane@dianecoulterthomas.com.

CAREER: Novelist, journalist, and editor. Worked as a freelance writer and editor producing advertising copy, public relations materials, training manuals, and other materials. *Atlanta Journal,* entertainment editor; *Atlanta* magazine, editorial associate; *Human Ecologist,* editor.

WRITINGS:

Atlanta, a City for the World, corporate profiles by Pamela A. Keene, foreword by Mayor Andrew Young, Windsor Publications (Northridge, CA), 1988.
(With Thomas M. Camden and Bill Osher) *How to Get a Job in Atlanta: The Insider's Guide,* Surrey Books (Chicago, IL), 1990, 2nd edition, 1992.
The Year the Music Changed, Toby Press (New Milford, CT), 2005.

Contributor to periodicals such as *Redbook* and *Rolling Stone.*

SIDELIGHTS: Novelist Diane C. Thomas is also a journalist whose work has focused largely on Atlanta, Georgia. Born in California, Thomas arrived in Atlanta when she was four years old. She was the entertainment editor, reviewing movies and plays, for the *Atlanta Constitution,* which later merged with another local paper to form the *Atlanta Journal-Constitution.* She has also worked as an editorial associate for *Atlanta* magazine and written two book-length works related to Atlanta. *Atlanta, a City for the World* describes Atlanta's business and cultural climate, and *How to Get a Job in Atlanta: The Insider's Guide* provides in-depth advice on searching for and finding

work within the unique environment of Atlanta. Her other work includes an advertising copywriting, technical writing, public-relations writing, and editing.

Thomas's debut work of fiction, *The Year the Music Changed,* is a "sweet and gripping first novel," remarked a contributor in *Kirkus Reviews.* Achsa McEachern, a fourteen-year-old girl living in rural America, writes a fan letter to Elvis Presley after she hears the singer perform "That's All Right, Mama." To her surprise, Presley writes back, and the novel chronicles the fourteen months of ongoing correspondence between the two. At first, Presley mistakes Achsa for a man because of her name and proficiency with language. Even after he finds out differently, he still encourages her to keep writing to him. "The result is a touching, funny, . . . tender exchange between two people trying to find their way through thorny emotional terrain," noted Eleanor J. Bader in *Library Journal.*

Achsa details her difficulties at school, the cleft palate that impairs her, the tumultuous family situation she lives in, the social ostracism she experiences because of her deformity, her plainness, and her keen intellect. Presley writes to her of life on the road and his single-minded determination to succeed in the music business. The two find a grateful confidante in each other as each teeters on the brink of a new and unfamiliar world. Like Presley, who knows deep within himself that he will succeed, Achsa "knows that she's destined for better things than high-school popularity," the *Kirkus Reviews* critic noted. A *Publishers Weekly* reviewer called the book a "warm, lively and immensely readable novel that will especially touch fans of 'the King.'"

Though the popular perception of the 1950s is that it was a time of conformity, family tranquility, and even repression, Thomas observes that a great deal of dissent and nonconformity lurked under the surface of docile Americana. "That's what I wanted to write about, that fascinating underside of the 1950s, how things are never what they seem—or what most people wish us to believe." she remarked in an interview on her home page. "There really did seem to be one year where the music completely changed character." "We went into it with Perry Como and Patti Page and came out of it with Little Richard and Chuck Berry."

BIOGRAPHICAL AND CRITICAL SOURCES:

PERIODICALS

Kirkus Reviews, July 1, 2005, review of *The Year the Music Changed,* p. 709.

Library Journal, May 1, 2005, Eleanor J. Bader, review of *The Year the Music Changed,* p. 78.

Publishers Weekly, June 27, 2005, review of *The Year the Music Changed,* p. 37.

ONLINE

Diane Coulter Thomas Home Page, http://www.dianecoulterthomas.com (October 8, 2005).*

*   *   *

THOMAS, Diane Coulter
    See THOMAS, Diane C.

*   *   *

THOMAS, Raju G.C. 1940-

PERSONAL: Born February 21, 1940, in Bhopal, Madhya Pradesh, India; immigrated to United States, naturalized citizen, 1986; married, wife's name, Suzanne. *Education:* University of Bombay, B.A., 1960, M.A. (industrial and monetary economics), 1962; London School of Economics, B.Sc.Econ., 1965; University of Southern California, M.A. (international relations), 1972; University of California, Los Angeles, Ph.D., 1976.

ADDRESSES: Home—Glendale, WI. *Office*—Dept. of Political Science, Marquette University, P.O. Box 1881, Milwaukee, WI 53201. *E-mail*—raju.thomas@marquette.edu.

CAREER: Commercial executive with Forbes, Forbes, Campbell & Company, Bombay, India, and Avery India Limited, Calcutta, India, 1965-68; Hofstra University, New York, NY, lecturer in political science, 1974-75; Marquette University, Milwaukee, WI, assistant professor, 1976, associate professor, 1981-86, assistant department chairman, 1985-88, professor of political science, 1986—, codirector of UW-Milwaukee/Marquette Center for International Studies, 1994-97, Allis Chalmers Distinguished Professor of International Affairs, 2000—. National Advisory Council on South Asian Affairs, Washington, DC, vice chairman, 1996—; lecturer worldwide. University of California, Los Angeles, and University of Southern California, visiting associate professor, summer, 1983; Marquette University, acting department chairman, summers, 1987, 1989; Massachusetts Institute of Technology, visiting scholar, 1988-89.

MEMBER: International Institute for Strategic Studies, International Studies Association, American Political Science Association, Association for the Study of Nationalities, Association for Asian Studies, Arms Control Association, Indian Council of World Affairs, London School of Economics Club.

AWARDS, HONORS: Ford Foundation fellow, 1980-81; Institute for the Study of World Politics grant, 1982-83; Research Institute on International Change research grant, 1985-86; Marquette University summer faculty fellowships, 1987, 1991; Harvard University fellow, 1988-89; International Institute for Strategic Studies grant, 1991-92; U.S. Institute of Peace grant, 1991-92; Los Alamos National Laboratory grant, 1991; National Endowment for the Humanities grant, 1995.

WRITINGS:

The Defence of India: A Budgetary Perspective of Strategy and Politics, Macmillan (Delhi, India), 1978.

(Editor) *The Great-Power Triangle and Asian Security,* Lexington Books (Lexington, MA), 1983.

Indian Security Policy, Princeton University Press (Princeton, NJ), 1986.

(Editor, with Bennett Ramberg) *Energy and Security in the Industrializing World,* University Press of Kentucky (Lexington, KY), 1990.

(Editor) *Perspectives on Kashmir: The Roots of Conflict in South Asia,* Westview Press (Boulder, CO), 1992.

(Editor, with H. Richard Friman) *The South Slav Conflict: History, Religion, Ethnicity, and Nationalism* ("Garland Reference Library of Social Science" series), Garland (New York, NY), 1996.

Democracy, Security, and Development in India, St. Martin's Press (New York, NY), 1996.

(Editor) *The Nuclear Non-proliferation Regime: Prospects for the Twenty-first Century,* St. Martin's Press (New York, NY), 1998.

(Editor, with Amit Gupta) *India's Nuclear Security,* Lynne Rienner (Boulder, CO), 2000.

(Editor, with D.R. SarDesai) *Nuclear India in the Twenty-first Century,* Palgrave (New York, NY), 2002.

(Editor and contributor) *Yugoslavia Unraveled: Sovereignty, Self-Determination, Intervention,* Lexington Books (Lanham, MD), 2003.

Contributor to books by others, including *Exiting the Balkan Thicket,* edited by Gary Dempsey, CATO Institute Press (Washington, DC), 2001, and *The New Balkans: Disintegration and Reconstruction,* edited by George Kourvetaris and Victor Roudometof, Columbia University Press (New York, NY), 2002; contributor to journals, including *World Affairs, Mediterranean Quarterly, Washington Quarterly, Harvard International Review, Survival, Nuclear Times, Asian Survey, Journal of Strategic Studies, Bulletin of Atomic Scientists,* and *Pacific Affairs.*

WORK IN PROGRESS: With Stanley Wolpert, *Encyclopedia of India,* four volumes.

SIDELIGHTS: As a professor of international affairs, Raju G.C. Thomas is a scholar of international politics, security, and the global economy, particularly as it relates to his native India. In addition to his teaching responsibilities and role as a lecturer at schools in the United States and abroad, Thomas has written extensively on his area of expertise and has published books as well as edited collections of works by other writers on contemporary world affairs.

In *Energy and Security in the Industrializing World* Thomas and coeditor Bennett Ramberg present "a valuable collection of analysis . . . and data" on the energy policy and national security of such nations as India, Pakistan, Argentina, Brazil, South Africa, and South Korea, according to *New Scientist* contributor Michael Grubb. The book details such issues as links to nuclear weapons programs, oil scarcity and consequent price fluctuations, and the political rhetoric revolving around each nation's position on nuclear

weaponry. While Grubb found the collection to be somewhat dated, he also praised the "consistency in the way these issues are approached."

Based on a series of lectures Thomas gave in the early 1990s, *Democracy, Security, and Development in India* focuses on the efforts of India to deal with national security, civil liberties, and a developing economy in the years since it gained its independence from Great Britain. Noting that the "Indian experiment" goes against the commonly held belief that there exists "a strong association between development and democracy," *Political Science Quarterly* contributor Stephen Philip Cohen commended Thomas's book because it "asks the right questions and tentatively offers some answers to one of the great emerging questions . . . the survival of a democratic India."

Thomas and D.R. SarDesai coedited *Nuclear India in the Twenty-first Century,* the contributors to which met in Los Angeles after the 1998 test in India. The Indian, American, British, and French authors probe the desirability of nuclear testing and whether India should have taken this step. Individual chapters discuss weaponry and comparisons of nuclear programs, and the book includes a condensed version of George Perkovich's 1999 book *India's Nuclear Bomb,* which provides an introduction to the issue and examines events leading up to India's 1974 nuclear test. Arabinda Acharya wrote in *Contemporary Southeast Asia* that *Nuclear India in the Twenty-first Century* "is an attempt to reassess India's nuclear weapons programme from a strategic, political, technological, and economic perspective."

Thomas is the editor of and contributor to *Yugoslavia Unraveled: Sovereignty, Self-Determination, Intervention,* a collection by scholars—nearly all American—who closely study the dissolution of Yugoslavia. As Andrew C. Janos noted in *Perspectives on Political Science,* "Most of the chapters are well researched and richly annotated. Although this by itself does not validate their arguments, it does testify to the seriousness of the enterprise and hence cannot be overlooked easily in debates about Balkan politics and the larger issue of humanitarian interventionism."

BIOGRAPHICAL AND CRITICAL SOURCES:

PERIODICALS

American Political Science Review, March, 1988, Aaron Karp, review of *Indian Security Policy,*

p. 349; March, 1999, George H. Quester, review of *The Nuclear Non-proliferation Regime: Prospects for the Twenty-first Century,* p. 245.

Contemporary Southeast Asia, December, 2002, Arabinda Acharya, review of *Nuclear India in the Twenty-first Century,* p. 621.

New Scientist, March 23, 1991, Michael Grubb, review of *Energy and Security in the Industrializing World,* p. 53.

Pacific Affairs, summer, 2003, Robert S. Anderson, review of *Nuclear India in the Twenty-first Century,* p. 317.

Perspectives on Political Science, spring, 2004, Andrew C. Janos, review of *Yugoslavia Unraveled: Sovereignty, Self-Determination, Intervention,* p. 116.

Political Science Quarterly, spring, 1998, Stephen Philip Cohen, review of *Democracy, Security, and Development in India,* p. 156.

Studies in Comparative International Development, summer, 1998, Sumit Ganguly, review of *Democracy, Security, and Development in India,* p. 125.*

*   *   *

TÖTÖSY de ZEPETNEK, Steven 1950-

PERSONAL: Born November 22, 1950, in Budapest, Hungary; son of Magdalena Haidekker (an accountant); married Joanne E. Toms (a director), December 10, 1976; children: Chantal Patricia, Julia Olga. *Education:* University of Western Ontario, B.A., 1980; Carleton University, M.A., 1983; University of Ottawa, B.Ed., 1984; University of Alberta, Ph.D., 1989.

ADDRESSES: Home—8 Sunset Rd., Winchester, MA 01890. *Office*—Dept. of Media Studies, University of Halle-Wittenberg, Rudolf-Breitscheid-Strasse 10, D-06110 Halle, Germany. *E-mail*—steven.totosy@medienkomm.uni-halle.de.

CAREER: Editor and writer. University of Alberta, Edmonton, Alberta, Canada, 1984-2000, began as lecturer, became professor, assistant director, then associate director of Research Institute of Comparative Literature, 1989-97; Northeastern University, Boston, MA, lecturer, 2000-01, 2002-05; University of Halle-Wittenberg, Halle, Germany, professor of media and culture studies, 2002—. Founder and editor of *CLCWeb: Comparative Literature and Culture* (online journal), 1999—. Teacher of online courses in literature, communication studies, and media studies for several American universities.

MEMBER: International Comparative Literature Association, Modern Language Association of America, Canadian Comparative Literature Association.

WRITINGS:

(With others) *Préfaces et manifestes littéraires* (conference proceedings; title means "Prefaces and Literary Manifestoes"), Research Institute of Comparative Institute (Edmonton, Alberta, Canada), 1990.

(With others) *Literatures of Lesser Diffusion: Proceedings of a Conference,* Research Institute of Comparative Institute (Edmonton, Alberta, Canada), 1990.

(With others) *Women's Writing and the Literary Institution* (conference papers), Research Institute of Comparative Institute (Edmonton, Alberta, Canada), 1992.

The Social Dimensions of Fiction: On the Rhetoric and Function of Prefacing Novels in the Nineteenth-Century Canadas, Vieweg (Braunschweig, Germany), 1993.

A Zepetneki Tötösy család adattára: Records of the Tötösy de Zepetnek Family, Jozsef Attila University (Szeged, Hungary) 1993.

(Editor, with Jennifer W. Jay) *East-Asian Cultural and Historical Perspectives: Histories and Society/Culture and Literatures* (conference papers), University of Alberta (Edmonton, Alberta, Canada), 1997.

(Editor, with Irene Sywenky) *The Systemic and Empirical Approach to Literature and Culture as Theory and Application* (conference papers), University of Alberta (Edmonton, Alberta, Canada), 1997.

Wen xue yan jiu de he fa hua: yi zhong xin shi yong zhu yi: zheng ti hua he jing yan zhu yi wen xue yu wen hua yan jiu fang fa (translations of lectures given at Peking University, 1995-96), Beijing da xue chu ban she (Beijing, China), 1997.

(Editor, with Yiu-nam Leung) *Canadian Culture and Literature: And a Taiwan Perspective* (conference papers), University of Alberta (Edmonton, Alberta, Canada), 1998.

Comparative Literature: Theory, Method, Application, Rodopi (Atlanta, GA), 1998.

(Editor) *Comparative Central-European Culture* (conference papers), Purdue University Press (West Lafayette, IN), 2002.

(Editor) *Comparative Literature and Comparative Cultural Studies,* Purdue University Press (West Lafayette, IN), 2003.

(Editor, with Louise O. Vasvári) *Imre Kertész and Holocaust Literature,* Purdue University Press (West Lafayette, IN), 2005.

(Editor) *Comparative Cultural Studies and Michael Ondaatje's Writing,* Purdue University Press (West Lafayette, IN), 2005.

Canadian Review of Comparative Literature, editor, 1989-97; contributor to periodicals, including *Modern Fiction Studies, MELUS, Mosaic,* and *Essays on Canadian Writing.*

SIDELIGHTS: As a scholar and educator, Steven Tötösy de Zepetnek focuses on comparative culture and literature, as well as on media theory and communications. Many of his books, including *Comparative Literature: Theory, Method, Application,* and the edited volumes *Comparative Literature and Comparative Cultural Studies* and *Comparative Central European Culture,* combine these interests.

In *Comparative Literature* Tötösy de Zepetnek presents a theoretical framework and methodology for approaching the analysis of literary works as they relate to culture. Useful in specific theoretical contexts—such as feminist studies, translation studies, and ethnic and minority studies—Tötösy de Zepetnek includes numerous applications of this methodology—which he calls the Systematic and Empirical Approach to Literature and Culture—in practice. Reviewing *Comparative Literature* for *symploke,* Nicolae Harsanyi called Tötösy de Zepetnek's approach "innovative" and especially useful in the study of "cultural studies dealing with East Central Europe." The critic added that the author's "ubiquitous voice, alert pace of argumentation, subtle humor and irony enhance his persuasiveness."

BIOGRAPHICAL AND CRITICAL SOURCES:

PERIODICALS

Ariel, October, 1999, Estelle Dansereau, review of *Comparative Literature: Theory, Method, Application,* p. 168.

symploke, winter-spring, 1999, Nicolae Harsanyi, review of *Comparative Literature,* p. 215.

University of Toronto Quarterly, winter, 2000, Richard Cavell, review of *Comparative Literature,* p. 313.

ONLINE

Comparative Literature and Culture Web site, http://clcwebjournal.lib.purdue.edu/ (August 24, 2005), information on life and works of Tötösy de Zepetnek.

*　　*　　*

TOWNSEND, Camilla 1965-

PERSONAL: Born 1965. *Education:* Bryn Mawr College, B.A. (summa cum laude), 1985; Rutgers University, Ph.D., 1995.

ADDRESSES: Office—Colgate University, Department of Native American Studies, 12 Hascall Hall, 13 Oak Dr., Hamilton, NY 13346. *E-mail*—ctownsend@mail.colgate.edu.

CAREER: Instituto Nacionale Eliseo Picado, Matagalpa, Nicaragua, faculty member, 1987-88; Colgate University, Hamilton, NY, assistant professor of history and acting director of Native American studies, 1995—.

AWARDS, HONORS: Fulbright Commission grant for study in Ecuador, 1992-93; American Association for University Women dissertation fellow, 1993-94; Research fellow, Philadelphia Center for Early American Studies, 1994-95; National Endowment for the Humanities fellowship, 2003.

WRITINGS:

Tales of Two Cities: Race and Economic Culture in Early Republican North and South America: Guayaquil, Ecuador, and Baltimore, Maryland, University of Texas Press (Austin, TX), 2000.

Pocahontas and the Powhatan Dilemma, Hill & Wang (New York, NY), 2004.

Contributor to periodicals, including *Colonial Latin-American Review, Latin American Perspectives, Procesos,* and *Journal of Women's History.* Member of editorial board, *History Compass* Web site.

SIDELIGHTS: Writer, historian, and university professor Camilla Townsend is a comparativist who studies colonial Latin America within the context of the New World and its developments. In her book *Tales of Two Cities: Race and Economic Culture in Early Republican North and South America: Guayaquil, Ecuador, and Baltimore, Maryland* she considers "the disparity of economic development existing between the United States and Latin America," according to Carlos Perez in *History: Review of New Books.* Using a "comparative approach that helps illuminate the recondite paths of divergent economic development," Townsend explores in detail everyday life and economic activity in two similar cities, Baltimore, Maryland, and Guayaquil, Ecuador, from 1820 to 1835. She divides the economic and social strata of the two cities into the elite; the middling ranks consisting of professionals, artisans, and entrepreneurs; and the poor.

Much of the book looks at how the three levels interacted, and especially how the poor fared in terms of their relationships with the elite and the middling ranks. Townend's analysis focuses largely on two individuals, Ana Yagual of Guayaquil and Frederick Bailey, a former slave, of Baltimore. "Townsend describes the two cities through the two men's nineteenth-century eyes, giving us a sense of how the lower classes conceptualized urban space and their relationship to the elite and middling ranks," Perez noted. He called the book a "unique and valuable contribution to the field" and a "provocative and thought-provoking work" of economic history and analysis.

Townsend's interests also extend to colonial America. In *Pocahontas and the Powhatan Dilemma* she reconsiders the long-held conceptions of how the Jamestown settlers interacted with the natives, how John Smith portrayed his role in the colonization, and how the often-repeated legend of Pocahontas may not be historically accurate. Townsend "writes with a sharp sword and a crackling whip" and "refuses to believe anything just because so many people have repeated it," remarked John Leonard in *Harper's.* "What emerges is an unpretty picture of a Jamestown colony"

that wanted to use the natives as serfs, a boasting John Smith who consistently exaggerated his effect on native women, and an Algonquin tribe that deeply distrusted the white settlers, and rightly so. Smith's account of his interactions with Pocahontas may well be outright fabrication, designed to "satisfy their own need to believe that the Indians loved and admired them (or their cultural forebears), without resentments, without guile," Townsend wrote. Townsend "has written this book in part to dispel the mythology about Pocahontas and her people, and to try to give us a realistic understanding of the dynamics between the conquerors and the conquered," observed a reviewer on the *Curled Up with a Good Book* Web site. A *Kirkus Reviews* contributor noted that the book serves as an example of "colonial history that admirably complicates the history of Indian/white relations in Virginia."

BIOGRAPHICAL AND CRITICAL SOURCES:

BOOKS

Townsend, Camilla, *Pocahontas and the Powhatan Dilemma,* Hill & Wang (New York, NY), 2004.

PERIODICALS

Harper's, October, 2004, John Leonard, review of *Pocahontas and the Powhatan Dilemma,* p. 92.

History: Review of New Books, fall, 2000, Carlos Perez, review of *Tales of Two Cities: Race and Economic Culture in Early Republican North and South America: Guayaquil, Ecuador, and Baltimore, Maryland,* p. 20.

Kirkus Reviews, August 15, 2004, review of *Pocahontas and the Powhatan Dilemma,* p. 797.

ONLINE

Colgate University Department of Native American Studies Web site, http://departments.colgate.edu/ (October 23, 2005), biography of Camilla Townsend.

Curled Up with a Good Book, http://www.curledcup. com/ (October 23, 2005), review of *Pocahontas and the Powhatan Dilemma.*

History Compass Web site, http://www.history-compass.com/ (October 23, 2005), biography of Camilla Townsend.*

* * *

TROWBRIDGE, James
See FENDER, J.E.

* * *

TUCKER, Tom 1944-

PERSONAL: Born February 11, 1944, in St. Louis, MO; son of Buell (a claims adjuster) and Susie (a teacher) Tucker; married Diane Sherer (a choreographer), August 10, 1968; children: Matthew, Joseph, Bonnie. *Ethnicity:* "White." *Education:* Attended Harvard University; earned B.A. (magna cum laude); Washington University (St. Louis, MO), M.A.

ADDRESSES: Home—143 S. Ridgecrest St., Rutherfordton, NC 28139. *E-mail*—tomtucker_1@lycos.com.

CAREER: Writer. Worked as camera operator and special-effects technician, 1978-85; Casey & O'Connell, creative director and copywriter, 1985-89; Isothermal Community College, instructor in English and technical writing, 1989—, writer-in-residence, 2002—.

AWARDS, HONORS: Woodrow Wilson fellow; Blumenthal Reader Award, 1991; first prize, Gardner Webb Playwriting Contest, 1993; summer faculty fellow, National Aeronautics and Space Administration, 1998, 1999; Bakken fellow, 2000.

WRITINGS:

Brainstorm! The Stories of Twenty American Kid Inventors (juvenile), Farrar, Straus & Giroux (New York, NY), 1995, 2nd edition, 1998.
Touchdown: The Development of Propulsion Controlled Aircraft at NASA Dryden, National Aeronautics and Space Administration (Washington, DC), 1999.

The Eclipse Project, National Aeronautics and Space Administration (Washington, DC), 2000.
Bolt of Fate: Benjamin Franklin and His Electric Kite Hoax, Public Affairs Books (New York, NY), 2003.

Contributor of nine scripts for Golden Video series "Our Dwelling Place," and additional scripts for other videotapes, and plays. Contributor of technical articles, poetry, short fiction, and reviews to periodicals, including *Sports Illustrated, Ploughshares, Screen, Filmmakers Newsletter,* and *Technical Photography.*

SIDELIGHTS: Tom Tucker told *CA:* "*Bolt of Fate: Benjamin Franklin and His Electric Kite Hoax* began when I first noticed how much unraveled when you started looking at authentic eighteenth-century sources behind the story of Benjamin Franklin's electrical kite and his lightning rod. I was working on a space-launch history for the National Aeronautics and Space Administration out at their Mojave Desert site when the idea first glimmered. At the time, any chance of pursuing it seemed remote.

"When I finally started the project, I was in a rural part of North Carolina, far from archives. My research sometimes diminished to interlibrary loan requests and personal pleas by phone to archivists to photocopy crumbling eighteenth-century booklets. It moved at a snail's pace, financed on a shoestring. Often I depended on the remarkable generosity of scholars and other specialists contacted by phone who—even if they disagreed with my revisionist approach—were fascinated enough by my questions to offer their assistance. The resulting book was not intended as debunking; it uncovers the adventure and triumph of a self-taught tradesman wrestling for recognition from the silk-coat connoisseurs who ruled over international science in Franklin's era. And the immensely powerful tale of the kite, as the imaginative Franklin developed it, would later become crucial to the success of the American Revolution and the establishment of the Republic.

"All of my books concern the history of science and invention. All of them give a human context to the process of intellectual discovery. I have written some about baseball—and may do so again—but I am especially interested in the process of invention and discovery in a group context and the dramatic and sometimes melodramatic way that ideas transcend and develop beyond their individual creators."

BIOGRAPHICAL AND CRITICAL SOURCES:

PERIODICALS

American Scientist, January-February, 2004, Shawn Carlson, review of *Bolt of Fate: Benjamin Franklin and His Electric Kite Hoax,* p. 77.

Booklist, August, 1995, Mary Harris Veeder, review of *Brainstorm! The Stories of Twenty American Kid Inventors,* p. 1945.

Contemporary Review, October, 2004, review of *Bolt of Fate,* p. 255.

Forbes, July 7, 2003, Susan Adams, review of *Bolt of Fate,* p. 139.

Isis, March, 2004, Martin L. Levitt, review of *Bolt of Fate,* p. 132.

New Scientist, June 28, 2003, Christine Finn, review of *Bolt of Fate,* p. 52.

New Yorker, June 30, 2003, Adam Gopnik, review of *Bolt of Fate,* p. 96.

Weatherwise, January-February, 2004, Randy Cerveny, review of *Bolt of Fate,* p. 48.

*   *   *

TWINING, James 1972-

PERSONAL: Born December, 1972, in London, England; married; children: Amelia. *Education:* Christ Church, Oxford, graduated, 1995. *Hobbies and other interests:* Collecting brass and iron plates or plaques from old safes and store rooms.

ADDRESSES: Agent—James Twining—Private Mail, c/o Curtis Brown, 28-29 Haymarket, London SW1Y 4SP, England. *E-mail*—mail@jamestwining.com.

CAREER: Novelist and entrepreneur. UBS (investment bank), financial advisor for four years; business owner until 2002.

AWARDS, HONORS: Named among Best of Young British Entrepreneurs, *New Statesman.*

WRITINGS:

The Double Eagle (novel), HarperCollins (New York, NY), 2005.

The Black Sun (novel), HarperCollins (New York, NY), 2006.

WORK IN PROGRESS: Three more books in the "Tom Kirk" series.

SIDELIGHTS: James Twining is a former financial consultant and entrepreneur who sold his business in 2002 to turn his attention full time to writing novels. His debut, *The Double Eagle,* is "an old-fashioned well-written thriller about a treasure hunt but with a twist," commented a reviewer for *Shots* online. In the novel, five exceptionally rare gold coins have turned up missing from the vaults at Fort Knox. The coins are twenty-dollar "Double Eagle" gold pieces, which were minted as legal U.S. tender until 1933. That year, President Franklin D. Roosevelt removed the country's currency from the gold standard, recalled all the coins, and had them melted down. However, some of the coins escaped melting; at least one fell into private hands and five were stored at Fort Knox. With the coins now worth more than eight million dollars each, their theft is vexing to the Federal Bureau of Investigation (FBI) and the other government agencies that were supposed to keep them secure.

When one of the coins shows up lodged in the throat of an ex-priest in Paris, the theft of the other specimens is discovered. The FBI assigns Special Agent Jennifer Browne to the case. Browne's position with the agency is in turmoil because of the accidental shooting death of a fellow agent. Solving the case of the missing coins could be the victory she needs to salvage her career. The agency suspects the coin heist involves renowned burglar Tom Kirk, a brilliant thief who is eyeing retirement, but there is nothing to link him directly to the case. Browne travels to London to meet with Kirk and solicit his assistance in finding the coins, but things begin badly when a sample coin that Browne was carrying is stolen. Uneasy in their new alliance to recover the Double Eagles, Browne and Kirk find themselves betrayed and at the same time pursued through international locales by some dangerous characters with murderous intentions.

"Despite a highly theatrical and overly protracted finale, this is an auspicious beginning for a fledgling series," noted a *Publishers Weekly* reviewer. "*The Double Eagle* just may be the fun book of the year," commented Joe Hartlaub on *Bookreporter.com.* "Twining has a nice, light touch that makes the book a pleasant diversion," concluded Ron Bernas in the *Detroit Free Press.*

Positive reviews of *The Double Eagle* sparked several sequels, beginning with *The Black Sun* and continuing on for at least three more installments.

BIOGRAPHICAL AND CRITICAL SOURCES:

PERIODICALS

Detroit Free Press, September 11, 2005, Ron Bernas, "Trite Tale Has Light Touch," review of *The Double Eagle.*

Kirkus Reviews, July 1, 2005, review of *The Double Eagle,* p. 709.

Publishers Weekly, July 25, 2005, review of *The Double Eagle,* p. 42.

Rocky Mountain Press, September 9, 2005, Peter Mergendahl, review of *The Double Eagle.*

ONLINE

Bookreporter.com, http://www.bookreporter.com/ (October 23, 2005), Joe Hartlaub, review of *The Double Eagle.*

James Twining Home Page, http://www.jamestwining.com (October 23, 2005).

Shots Online, http://www.shotsmag.co.uk/ (October 23, 2005), review of *The Double Eagle.**

U-V

ULLMAN, Larry 1972-
(Larry E. Ullman)

PERSONAL: Born February 23, 1972, in Cedar Rapids, IA; married April 20, 1996; wife's name Jessica (a speech language pathologist). *Ethnicity:* "White." *Education:* Northeast Missouri State University, B.A., 1994. *Politics:* "Independent." *Hobbies and other interests:* Reading, home improvement, sports, movies, music.

ADDRESSES: Agent—c/o Author Mail, Peachpit Press, Inc., 1249 8th St., Berkeley, CA 94710. *E-mail*—larryullman@mac.com.

CAREER: Writer. Borders Bookstore, Chicago, IL, trainer, 1994-97; Georgetown University, Washington, DC, librarian assistant, 1997-99; DMC Insights, Inc., Waldorf, MD, director, 1999—.

WRITINGS:

PHP for the World Wide Web: Visual QuickStart Guide, Peachpit Press (Berkeley, CA), 2001.
PHP Advanced for the World Wide Web: Visual Quick-Pro Guide, Peachpit Press (Berkeley, CA), 2002.
MySQL: Visual QuickStart Guide, Peachpit Press (Berkeley, CA), 2003.
PHP and MySQL for Dynamic Web Sites: Visual QuickPro Guide, Peachpit Press (Berkeley, CA), 2003.
(With Marc Liyanage) *Mac OS X Panther Timesaving Techniques for Dummies,* Wiley (New York, NY), 2004.
(With Marc Liyanage) *C Programming: Visual Quick-Start Guide,* Peachpit Press (Berkeley, CA), 2005.
(With Andreas Signor) *C++ Programming: Visual QuickStart Guide,* Peachpit Press (Berkeley, CA), 2005.

SIDELIGHTS: Larry Ullman told *CA:* "Despite the fact that I've only ever taken one computer course, I have an affinity for computing which, when coupled with my degree in English, has allowed me to write computer books. The modest success I've had with these books is due to my ability to convey concepts in a less-'techie' way, explaining somewhat complex ideas in a lay person's manner. It just goes to show that you never know where you'll end up, and that good writing skills are an asset in nearly any field.

"I've also been very fortunate to develop a relationship with a great publisher—Peachpit Press. By working with an organization of such integrity, I have had opportunities I might not otherwise have had. Furthermore, being able to work with the smart, talented people there has made my job much, much easier.

"A final note: through maintaining an active dialogue with readers, I have learned much as an author. While such interactions can be both time-consuming and tedious, they've given me the feedback I need to be a better writer."

BIOGRAPHICAL AND CRITICAL SOURCES:

PERIODICALS

Reviewer's Bookwatch, December, 2004, John Burroughs, review of *C Programming: Visual Quick-Start Guide.*

ULLMAN, Larry E.
See ULLMAN, Larry

*   *   *

URE, Louise 1952(?)-

PERSONAL: Born c. 1952; married. *Education:* Graduate of University of Arizona, Dijon University, and American Graduate School of International Management. *Hobbies and other interests:* Rescuing golden retrievers, racing vintage racecars.

ADDRESSES: Home—San Francisco, CA. *Agent*—c/o Author Mail, Mysterious Press, 1271 Avenue of the Americas, New York, NY 10020. *E-mail*—Louise@louiseure.com.

CAREER: Writer. Account manager with an advertising agency for twenty-five years.

WRITINGS:

Forcing Amaryllis (mystery novel), Mysterious Press (New York, NY), 2005.

SIDELIGHTS: Louise Ure's debut mystery novel, *Forcing Amaryllis,* is "a surprisingly tender tale of sisterly vengeance," noted a *Publishers Weekly* reviewer. As a trial consultant, thirty-three-year-old Calla Gentry's job involves scouring pools of potential jurors for individuals who will be most sympathetic and advantageous to her firm's clients. Though her job is often physically and emotionally draining, Calla endures it for the sake of her sister, Amaryllis, who remains in a coma ever since attempting suicide seven years earlier after a vicious rape that was never reported or solved. Calla ekes out a living while making sure Amaryllis is as comfortable as possible.

Though Calla specializes in jury selection for civil cases, a personnel crunch mandates that she take on a criminal trial. The client, Raymond Cates, is the son of a wealthy Texas rancher and is on trial for the rape and murder of a women he met in a bar. As she delves into the case, Calla begins to suspect that Cates is not only guilty of the murder he is currently defending

himself against, but that he may also be the shadowy attacker who nearly killed Amaryllis. Despite her personal conflict—how can she construct an effective and sympathetic jury when she believes Cates is guilty?—she continues on with the case and begins digging deeper into the arrogant defendant's background. Assisting her are Anthony Strike, a handsome private investigator and potential romantic interest, and a coterie of old friends with connections in the right places. Even though other suspects arise, including one who matches a victim's identification but who has an alibi, a distinctive physical feature of Cates's becomes a recurring theme in the cases Calla researches. This lends greater credibility to her suspicions of his guilt. With a desperate need for closure of her sister's case, and with the cold flame of revenge still burning, Calla continues her investigation until she, too, is put in mortal danger.

Ure compares the job of the trial consultant with that of the advertiser and marketer. "In marketing and advertising we have to define the target audience—figure out which people are most likely to buy the product," she stated in an interview on her home page. "That's the same thing a jury consultant does. He finds the juror who is most likely to agree with his client's story and point of view."

"Ure is that rare and unusual author who knows exactly what is required in the construction of a mystery story, and her first novel is a prize," commented Alan Paul Curtis on the *Who Dunnit* Web site. The book "provides a thoughtful look at rape victims, showing how even women's well-honed instincts about men can fail," observed reviewer Oline H. Cogdill in the *South Florida Sun-Sentinel.* As *Library Journal* reviewer Rex E. Klett commented, "The story plays out with increasing intensity but has a surprising twist." Another reviewer on the *Who Dunnit* Web site stated that Ure "not only knows how to structure a mystery, but writes it well and maintains our interest throughout." *Forcing Amaryllis* "will provide you with enough suspense to keep you going and make you want more," concluded Andrea Sisco on the *Arm Chair Interviews* Web site.

BIOGRAPHICAL AND CRITICAL SOURCES:

PERIODICALS

Kirkus Reviews, May 1, 2005, review of *Forcing Amaryllis,* p. 516.

Library Journal, May 1, 2005, Rex E. Klett, review of *Forcing Amaryllis,* p. 66.

MBR Bookwatch, May, 2005, Harriet Klausner, review of *Forcing Amaryllis.*

Publishers Weekly, May 2, 2005, review of *Forcing Amaryllis,* p. 180.

South Florida Sun-Sentinel, August 24, 2005, Oline H. Cogdill, review of *Forcing Amaryllis.*

ONLINE

Arm Chair Interviews, http://www.armchairinterviews. com/ (October 23, 2005), Andrea Sisco, review of *Forcing Amaryllis.*

BookLoons, http://www.bookloons.com/ (October 23, 2005), Hilary Williamson, review of *Forcing Amaryllis.*

Curled Up with a Good Book, http://www.curledup. com/ (October 23, 2005), review of *Forcing Amaryllis.*

Louise Ure Home Page, http://www.louiseure.com (October 23, 2005).

Who Dunnit, http://www.who-dunnit.com/ (October 23, 2005), profile of Louise Ure; Alan Paul Curtis, review of *Forcing Amaryllis.*

Woman's Day Online, http://www.womansday.com/ (October 23, 2005), "Believe It, Achieve It," profile of Louise Ure.*

*   *   *

VALANTASIS, Richard

PERSONAL: Male. *Education:* Hope College, B.A.; Harvard University, Th.M., Th.D.

ADDRESSES: Office—ILIFF School of Theology, 2201 South University Blvd., Denver, CO 80210-4798. *E-mail*—rvalantasis@iliff.edu.

CAREER: Episcopal priest, historian, and educator. Ordained Episcopal priest, 1974; ILIFF School of Theology, professor of New Testament and Christian origins, 1999—, Clifford E. Baldridge professor of biblical studies, 2005—. Former dean, Hartford Seminary.

MEMBER: American Academy of Religion, Society of Biblical Literature, Studiorum Novi Testamentum Societas.

WRITINGS:

Spiritual Guides of the Third Century: A Semiotic Study of the Guide-Disciple Relationship in Christianity, Neoplatonism, Hermetism, and Gnosticism, Fortress Press (Minneapolis, MN), 1991.

(Editor, with Vincent L. Wimbush) *Asceticism,* Oxford University Press (New York, NY), 1995.

The Gospel of Thomas, Routledge (New York, NY), 1997.

(Editor) *Religions of Late Antiquity in Practice,* Princeton University Press (Princeton, NJ), 2000.

Centuries of Holiness: Ancient Spirituality Refracted for a Postmodern Age, Continuum (New York, NY), 2005.

The New Q: A Fresh Translation with Commentary, T&T Clark (New York, NY), 2005.

The Beliefnet Guide to Gnosticism and Other Vanished Christianities, preface by Marcus Borg, Three Leaves Press (New York, NY), 2006.

SIDELIGHTS: Educator and Episcopal priest Richard Valantasis is a religious scholar and historian who studies the history and literature of formative Christianity. He concentrates his research on issues related to the many varieties of religious experience and expression, social organization in religious contexts, and literary works of early Christians in a Greco-Roman environment.

Valantasis is also known for his theories on asceticism and his wide writings on the subject. He served as coeditor, with Vincent L. Wimbush, of the book *Asceticism,* a collection of thirty-two scholarly essays on the many facets of a religious practice that even the experts have difficulty defining. A working definition of asceticism in a religious context would be the deliberate and systematic self-discipline and self-denial of physical gratifications in order to attain a greater understanding of the spiritual, and the attainment of a higher spiritual state. Based on papers presented at a 1993 conference at Union Theological Seminary in New York, New York, "the book reflects the collaboration of historians, phenomenologists, psychologists, sociologists, and anthropologists of religion, as well as researchers in cultural studies, postmodernist criticism, archaeology, and psychophysiology," noted reviewer Christopher Queen in *Philosophy East and West.* Asceticism manifests itself in a wide variety of ways, through devoted daily prayer, fasting, celibacy, voluntary poverty, pilgrimage, endurance of physical pain and deprivation, and more. The book contains chapters on the origins and meaning of asceticism, hermeneutics, aesthetics, and politics. Editors Wimbush and Valantasis provide introductions to each chapter, helping to place the work in context. They also provide an introductory essay outlining the history of the study of asceticism.

The book emerges as "an ambitious attempt to approach the protean phenomenon of asceticism from a perspective at once inter-religious, cross-cultural and multi-disciplinary," commented John A. Newton in *Journal of Ecclesiastical History*. The authors discuss asceticism in a variety of religious expressions, including Hindu, Buddhist, Jewish, Hellenistic, and Islamic traditions, with a focus on many manifestations of Christian asceticism. Among the book's topics are the role of female ascetics, the life of Christ as an ascetic, the interconnection between politics and asceticism, the hope of transformation, and the experiences of modern ascetics. "Perhaps inevitably as a pioneer intellectual endeavour, it raises more questions than it answers," Newton observed, "but it is a valuable resource and suggests an ample agenda for future research." "No other volume in the field of ascetical studies offers so much," Queen concluded. "The book reveals scholarship that is engaged, conversational, located, and rich," commented Margaret R. Miles in the *Journal of Religion*. Scholars and readers, she continued, "will gain a breadth of vision and an increment of precision from the questions brought to, and gathered from, these in-depth studies."

The Gospel of Thomas provides a detailed study of the Nag Hammadi version of the gospel and its connection to a number of known fragments extant in Greek texts. Valantasis suggests that the Gospel of Thomas was not an obscure and little-known Gnostic text, but instead existed in at least two different, divergent forms as early as A.D. 200, and in three forms when considering the Nag Hammadi text. Valantasis explores the contradictory nature of some of the statements present in the Gospel of Thomas. He also provides an analytical scheme for assessing the diverse collection of sayings in the gospel that are attributed to Jesus. Valantasis "has opened up new perspectives regarding the date and purpose of the Gospel, and his short well-constructed work is to be warmly welcomed," commented reviewer W.H.C. Frend in the *Journal of Ecclesiastical History*.

Centuries of Holiness: Ancient Spirituality Refracted for a Postmodern Age contains one hundred short essays on a variety of topics in Christian spiritual and religious practice. The "beautifully written entries" range across many ideas and disciplines, noted Graham Christian in *Library Journal*, but the work also applies an Orthodox sensibility to the analysis of other religious traditions.

BIOGRAPHICAL AND CRITICAL SOURCES:

PERIODICALS

Journal of Ecclesiastical History, April, 1997, John A. Newton, review of *Asceticism*, p. 316; July, 1998, W.H.C. Frend, review of *The Gospel of Thomas*, p. 502.
Journal of Religion, January, 1997, Margaret R. Miles, review of *Asceticism*, p. 131.
Journal of the American Oriental Society, October-December, 1997, Sara J. Denning-Bolle, review of *Asceticism*, p. 694.
Journal of Theological Studies, April, 1997, Ann Loades, review of *Asceticism*, p. 376.
Library Journal, March 1, 2005, Graham Christian, review of *Centuries of Holiness: Ancient Spirituality Refracted for a Postmodern Age*, p. 94.
Philosophy East and West, January, 1999, Christopher Queen, review of *Asceticism*, p. 75.

ONLINE

ILIFF School of Theology Web site, http://www.iliff.edu/ (September 25, 2005), biography of Richard Valantasis.

*   *   *

VAN DER ALM, Aart
See DONKER, Anthonie

*   *   *

VAN RIPER, A. Bowdoin 1963-

PERSONAL: Born March 17, 1963, in Boston, MA; son of Anthony King (a teacher and freelance writer) and Janice Patricia (a social worker and homemaker; maiden name, Riley) Van Riper; married Julie R. Newell (a professor of history); children: Katharine P.;

(stepson) Josef C. Mundt. *Education:* Brown University, A.B., 1985; University of Wisconsin—Madison, M.A., 1987, Ph.D., 1990. *Politics:* "FDR/LBJ Democrat." *Religion:* Unitarian-Universalist. *Hobbies and other interests:* Sailing, hiking, reading, movies, local history.

ADDRESSES: Office—Department of Social and International Studies, Southern Polytechnic State University, 1100 S. Marietta Parkway, Marietta, GA 30060.

CAREER: Writer and educator. Southern Polytechnic State University, Marietta, GA, adjunct professor of science, technology, and society. Volunteer for Friends of Red Top Mountain State Park and other organizations and institutions.

MEMBER: American Historical Association, History of Science Society, Film and History League, Martha's Vineyard Historical Society, Vineyard Haven Yacht Club.

WRITINGS:

Men among the Mammoths: Victorian Science and the Discovery of Human Prehistory, University of Chicago Press (Chicago, IL), 1993.
Science and Popular Culture: A Reference Guide, Greenwood Press (Westport, CT), 2002.
Imagining Flight: Aviation and Popular Culture, Texas A&M University Press (College Station, TX), 2004.
Rockets and Missiles: The Life Story of a Technology, Greenwood Press (Westport, CT), 2004.

Contributor of more than fifty articles and reviews to periodicals and reference books.

WORK IN PROGRESS: Invasion USA: The History of an American Nightmare, completion expected c. 2006; research on depictions of science and technology in American popular culture, with a special emphasis on portrayals of scientists and engineers; research on subjects related to technological disasters, technology and war, and controlling nature.

SIDELIGHTS: A. Bowdoin Van Riper told *CA:* "I grew up spending summers in a house that had been built in the 1880s and remodeled by my grandparents when they bought it in 1940. Exploring its nooks and crannies on rainy days, I loved to discover traces of mysterious things from the past: fragments of anthracite in the basement storage closets (left over from the days of coal furnaces), buckets of sand in the attic (left over from preparation for World War II air raids that never happened), a square-cut nail wedged between two boards in the garage (left over from the days when the 'family car' had been a horse and buggy), and so on. Being an historian is, for me, an extension of those rainy-day treasure hunts: you find odd bits and pieces of the past and use them to try and understand how people lived and acted and thought 'back in the day.' It's like being a detective . . . except that nobody shoots at you in dark alleys.

"I try to write the kind of books that I like to read: books that show you something you've looked at all your life . . . then show you how it got to be that way, and how it's connected to other things you might never have thought it was connected to. Authors like John McPhee, Henry Petroski, Stephen Jay Gould, and John Stilgoe are my literary heroes. They can make anything (no matter how complex) seem understandable and anything (no matter how familiar) seem new."

BIOGRAPHICAL AND CRITICAL SOURCES:

PERIODICALS

Air Power History, fall, 2004, William A. Nardo, review of *Imagining Flight: Aviation and Popular Culture,* p. 54.
Antiquity, March, 1994, Cyprian Broodbank, review of *Men among the Mammoths: Victorian Science and the Discovery of Human Prehistory,* p. 149.

*   *   *

VISMAN, Janni

PERSONAL: Female. *Education:* Attended Slade School of Fine Art.

ADDRESSES: Home—London, England. *Agent*—c/o Author Mail, Bloomsbury Publishing, 38 Soho Square, London W1D EHB, England.

CAREER: Novelist.

WRITINGS:

Sex Education (novel), Bloomsbury (London, England), 2002.

Yellow (novel), Bloomsbury (London, England), 2004, Viking (New York, NY), 2005.

WORK IN PROGRESS: A new novel, set in the near future, that features a love triangle complicated by aspects of mystery and the supernatural.

SIDELIGHTS: Novelist Janni Visman is the author of *Yellow,* a psychological thriller in which "claustrophobia, sexual obsession and paranoia are the linchpins" of the story, commented a *Publishers Weekly* reviewer. Stella, the protagonist of *Yellow,* is an aromatherapist and massage therapist who suffers from a litany of fears and phobias, including severe agoraphobia. She refuses to leave her apartment, and her entire world is contained within the walls of her London flat. Stella's clients come to her, and she has food and necessities delivered. Even Ivan, her boyfriend, is willing to coexist with Stella on her terms and within the boundaries of the world she has created for herself. "I wanted her various obsessions to be her 'magic' to keep the world (and herself) at bay," Visman remarked on the *Backstory* Web site.

Stella and Ivan decide to take their relationship to the next level, and he moves in with her. Part of the rules of cohabitation are that there will be no stories told about their past and no questions about anything that occurred before they met. However, Stella finds these rules too difficult to follow when Ivan begins wearing an identification bracelet inscribed with the initials "S.-L."; a gift from a former lover with the same initials as Stella. She begins to ask about the other S.L., and her obsession with her grows into a strangely thrilling sexual game with Ivan. She enlists the aid of her sister, Skye, to follow Ivan around the city and report on what he does. Unexplained discoveries, such as a photograph of an unknown woman and a large sum of hidden cash, complicate matters. As the stress of the mystery exacerbates Stella's phobias and odd behaviors, she strives to transform herself into what she imagines the other S.L. to be. The reader is led to wonder if Ivan is really cheating on Stella, or if she is simply descending further into uncontrolled madness. A *Kirkus Reviews* critic called the book "captivating . . . but with a mordant hipness that marks the welcome U.S. debut of British novelist Visman."

Some critics responded well to Visman's storyline and writing style but found Stella to be a difficult character to embrace. A reviewer commented in *Publishers Weekly* that Visman delivers a well-written, taut narrative, "but Stella is too grating to hold readers' sympathy, even when she deserves it." Even Visman herself reacted to the unpleasantness that surrounded Stella; admitting that writing a novel with a character as dysfunctional as Stella was draining. "When I finally delivered the manuscript I was relieved no major rewrites were required," Visman remarked on the *Backstory* Web site. "I was so desperate to get out of Stella's head and her flat."

BIOGRAPHICAL AND CRITICAL SOURCES:

PERIODICALS

Herizons, fall, 2004, Jillian Ridington, review of *Yellow,* p. 34.

Kirkus Reviews, April 15, 2005, review of *Yellow,* p. 450.

Library Journal, May 15, 2005, Elaine Bender, review of *Yellow,* p. 109.

Publishers Weekly, May 2, 2005, review of *Yellow,* p. 176.

ONLINE

Backstory, http://mjroseblog.typepad.com/backstory/ (October 9, 2005), interview with Janni Visman.

BookBrowse, http://www.bookbrowse.com/ (October 9, 2005), interview with Janni Visman.*

* * *

VOET, H.L.
    See GRESHOFF, Jan

* * *

VOORNE, J.J. van
    See GRESHOFF, Jan

W

WAITE, Gary K. 1955-

PERSONAL: Born March 20, 1955, in Vancouver, British Columbia, Canada; son of Robert Waite (in the Royal Canadian Air Force) and Audrey (Flynn) Waite; married Catherine Cressman, August 27, 1977 (divorced, 1984); married Katherine Hayward (a university tutor), August 7, 1992; children: Jessica Parker (stepdaughter), Eleanor. *Ethnicity:* Irish-Scottish *Education:* Ontario Bible College (now Tyndale College), B.Th., 1978; University of Waterloo, B.A., 1980, M.A. 1981, Ph.D., 1987. *Politics:* "New Democratic Party." *Hobbies and other interests:* Walking, reading mystery novels, photography.

ADDRESSES: Home—New Brunswick, Canada. *Office*—Dept. of History, University of New Brunswick, 9 MacAuley Ln., 120, Fredericton, New Brunswick E3B 5A3, Canada. *E-mail*—waite@unb.ca.

CAREER: University of Waterloo, Waterloo, Ontario, Canada, 1986-87, began as instructor, became assistant professor; University of New Brunswick, Fredericton, New Brunswick, Canada, assistant professor, 1987-91, associate professor, 1991-96, professor of history, 1996—. Visiting fellow, Clare Hall, Cambridge, 2001.

MEMBER: Canadian Society for Renaissance Studies, Canadian Historical Association, Sixteenth-Century Studies Conference Association.

AWARDS, HONORS: University of New Brunswick merit awards, 1991, 2002, and research scholarship, 2005; life fellow of Clare Hall, Cambridge.

WRITINGS:

David Joris and Dutch Anabaptism, 1524-1543, Wilfred Laurier University Press (Waterloo, Ontario, Canada), 1990.

(Editor and translator) *The Anabaptist Writings of David Joris, 1535-1543,* Herald Press (Scottdale, PA), 1994.

Reformers on Stage: Popular Drama and Religious Propaganda in the Low Countries of Charles V, 1515-1556, University of Toronto Press (Toronto, Ontario, Canada), 2000.

Heresy, Magic, and Witchcraft in Early Modern Europe, Palgrave Macmillan (New York, NY), 2003.

Contributor to books, including *Profiles of Anabaptist Women: Sixteenth-Century Reforming Pioneers,* edited by C. Arnold Snyder and Linda H. Hecht, Wilfrid Laurier University Press, 1996; *Oxford Encyclopedia of the Reformation,* Oxford University Press, 1996; *Rederijkers: conformisten en rebellen. Literatuur, cultuur en stedelijke netwerken (1400-1650),* Amsterdam University Press, 2003; *Confessional Sanctity (c.1550-c.1800),* Philipp von Zabern, 2003; *ABC-CLIO Encyclopedia of Witchcraft: The Western Tradition,* ABC-CLIO, 2003; and *Urban Theatre in the Low Countries, 1400-1625,* Brepols Publishers, 2006. Contributor to periodicals, including *Fides et Historia, Social History, Dutch Review of Church History, Canadian Journal of History, Church History, Ecuminist, Mennonite Quarterly Review,* and *Renaissance et Réforme.*

WORK IN PROGRESS: Eradicating the Devil's Minions: The Persecution of Anabaptists and Witches in Reformation Europe.

SIDELIGHTS: Gary K. Waite is a professor and historian who specializes in religious history and the effect of religion on European societies during the Protestant Reformation and the early modern period. He focuses on the literature and culture of the 1500s in several of his books, particularly *Reformers on Stage: Popular Drama and Religious Propaganda in the Low Countries of Charles V, 1515-1556.* In this work, Waite studies the texts of eighty dramas written to be produced by small, local acting societies in Antwerp and Amsterdam during the period under scrutiny. Supporting his analysis with records gleaned from other primary-source materials, the author argues that the plays depict a society wherein the tastes of the merchant and artisan classes, rather than those of the nobility, determined the culture. Noting that the plays Waite explores "became subtle propaganda for reform" in the hands of both Protestant and Roman Catholic groups, *Church History* contributor James H. Forse explained that such propaganda remained subtle to allow acting societies to perform freely—and thereby disseminate their religious beliefs. Citing Waite's "careful scholarship" and "attention to the social and political framework" of the plays, Forse praised *Reformers on Stage* as "a valuable addition to studies linking drama and the Reformation in Early Modern Europe." Waite's more recent book, *Heresy, Magic, and Witchcraft in Early Modern Europe,* further enhances understanding of the period by exploring the religious conflicts that led to witch hunting, persecution, and a rising belief in the supernatural.

Waite told *CA:* "After the death of my father in 1957, my brother and I were raised by our mother in Toronto. Thanks to a widow's pension and a place in a low-income housing development, we were able to have a good life and to look forward to post-secondary education. My involvement in an evangelical church as a youth led to enrollment in a bible college after high school. Graduating with a bachelor's degree from Ontario Bible College (now Tyndale College, Toronto) in 1978, my first wife and I moved to Waterloo, Ontario, where I began my studies in history at the University of Waterloo. Throughout my academic training, I gradually withdrew from my evangelical beliefs, although the history of religion and religious beliefs has remained one of my major research interests. Under the supervision of Dr. Werner O. Packull, I defended my Ph.D. dissertation in December, 1986, on the subject of the sixteenth-century Dutch radical religious reformer David Joris.

"My research and writing interests have broadened considerably since my Ph.D. work, although I retain a deep fascination with the impact of the religious impulse in history. After revising my dissertation and translating some of the key early writings of Joris, I returned to the subject of sixteenth-century religious drama and its impact as propaganda during the early Reformation in the Netherlands. In the meantime, I began teaching courses on the history of the witch hunts in early modern Europe, and this sparked my most recent research into the history of religious fervour, doubt, and intolerance and their role in sparking fears of diabolical conspiracies and a desire to persecute both heretics and witches. This research has resulted in *Heresy, Magic, and Witchcraft in Early Modern Europe,* as well as a second volume on the persecution of the Anabaptists and witches in early modern Europe.

"Although I am proud of my work on Joris and Dutch drama, I think that I would have to point to my *Heresy, Magic, and Witchcraft in Early Modern Europe,* as my favourite book to date. Intended for a wider audience than my more specialized studies, it takes a fairly simple argument about why early-modern Europeans became obsessed with conspiracy theories and runs with it, offering new insights into the potential dangers of religious fervour.

"My life experience and academic research have made me an advocate of religious tolerance and understanding and an opponent of intolerance in any guise. My politics are definitely left of center, and as a member of the New Democratic Party, I promote the development of a society that cares for all its members in such a way that all citizens, regardless of social or familial background, are able to reach their potential."

BIOGRAPHICAL AND CRITICAL SOURCES:

PERIODICALS

American Historical Review, June, 1992, Keith L. Sprunger, review of *David Joris and Dutch Anabaptism, 1524-1543,* p. 869; April, 2002, Andrew Pettegree, review of *Reformers on Stage: Popular Drama and Religious Propaganda in the Low Countries of Charles V, 1515-1556,* p. 635.

Canadian Journal of History, December, 1991, James M. Stayer, review of *David Joris and Dutch Anabaptism, 1524-1543,* p. 500.

Catholic Historical Review, July, 1995, James M. Stayer, reviews of *David Joris and Dutch Anabaptism, 1524-1543* and *The Anabaptist Writings of David Joris, 1535-1543,* p. 445.

Church History, December, 1992, Lee Daniel Snyder, review of *David Joris and Dutch Anabaptism, 1524-1543,* p. 448; June, 1996, Walter Klaassen, review of *The Anabaptist Writings of David Joris, 1535-1543,* p. 272; September, 2002, James H. Forse, review of *Reformers on Stage,* p. 657.

English Historical Review, June, 2004, Julian Goodare, review of *Heresy, Magic, and Witchcraft in Early Modern Europe,* p. 791.

Journal of Ecclesiastical History, July, 1992, Alistair Hamilton, review of *David Joris and Dutch Anabaptism, 1524-1543,* p. 484.

Sixteenth-Century Journal, fall, 1991, H. Wayne Pipkin, review of *David Joris and Dutch Anabaptism, 1524-1543,* p. 597; fall, 1995, John D. Roth, review of *The Anabaptist Writings of David Joris, 1535-1543,* p. 706.

*   *   *

WALKER, Sue 1960-

PERSONAL: Born 1960, in Edinburgh, Scotland.

ADDRESSES: Agent—c/o Author Mail, William Morrow & Company, 10 E. 53rd St., 7th Fl., New York, NY 10022.

CAREER: Novelist and investigative journalist. Worked for British Broadcasting Corporation, London, England, formerly on staff of news and current-affairs department.

WRITINGS:

The Reunion (thriller novel), William Morrow (New York, NY), 2004.
Fidra's Archive, Gardners Books, 2005.

SIDELIGHTS: Novelist and television journalist Sue Walker is the author of *The Reunion,* a thriller that explores how terrible events from the past have cast a shadow over the outwardly successful adulthood of the story's characters. The book, which *Library Journal* reviewer Jane la Plante called a "cleverly plotted novel," relates the deeply troubled past and tainted present of a group of former teen psychiatric patients living in Edinburgh, Scotland. During the 1970s, the eight teenagers were treated in an experimental psychiatric facility called The Unit. In 1977, however, a horrific event during an ostensibly therapeutic camping trip near Loch Fyne scarred their minds and lives, and created a bond between them that neither time nor distance can break. "Walker shows her characters as deeply troubled kids and as variously disturbed adults plagued by guilty memories of a camping trip gone wrong," observed a *Publishers Weekly* reviewer.

The story begins in the present when former Unit patient Innes Haldane receives a telephone message from friend and former Unit patient Isabella "Abby" Velasco. Innes does not immediately return the call, but shortly thereafter she learns that Abby is dead from an apparent suicide. Unconvinced that Abby would have killed herself, she leaves her job in London to investigate. Innes discovers that before Abby's death, she had started dating another Unit graduate, Danny Rintoul. Danny, however, is now also a suspected suicide. Innes then finds out about another Unit member who nearly perished in a fire that left her husband and children dead. Other plotlines involve two more former Unit members: Alex Baxendale, a cold and calculating stockbroker who is fighting to keep from revealing his knowledge of the past, and Dr. Simon Caldwell, who is searching for his kidnapped daughter. Meanwhile, Innes must discover whether the events of decades ago are in any way responsible for the increasing number of deaths happening now.

In a text that combines flashbacks between past and present, along with case notes, letters, therapists' observations, and newspaper reports, the story of the terrible day in 1977, and its long-term effects on the young men and women who were there, is pieced together. La Plante called *The Reunion* a "compelling story" and "a suspenseful, satisfying read," while *Booklist* reviewer Jennifer Mattson concluded that "this first novelist peels back the layers with confidence and polish."

BIOGRAPHICAL AND CRITICAL SOURCES:

PERIODICALS

Booklist, August, 2004, Jennifer Mattson, review of *The Reunion,* p. 1908.

Kirkus Reviews, August 15, 2004, review of *The Reunion,* p. 776.

Library Journal, October 1, 2004, Jane la Plante, review of *The Reunion,* p. 74.

Publishers Weekly, September 20, 2004, review of *The Reunion,* p. 45.

ONLINE

AllReaders.com, http://www.allreaders.com/ (October 23, 2005), Harriet Klausner, review of *The Reunion.**

* * *

WALSH, Helen 1977-

PERSONAL: Born 1977, in Warrington, England. *Education:* Liverpool University, graduated.

ADDRESSES: Agent—c/o Author Mail, Canongate Books, 14 High St., Edinburgh EH1 1TE, Scotland.

CAREER: Novelist and social worker. Worked at a film and literary agency and at various call centers.

WRITINGS:

Brass (novel), Canongate (Edinburgh, Scotland), 2004.

SIDELIGHTS: Novelist Helen Walsh's debut novel, *Brass,* is the dark, coming-of-age story of Millie, a young woman from Liverpool who must face unwanted change and difficult decisions in her life. The story is fueled by drugs and sex, shot through with an undercurrent of youthful nihilism, and punctuated with the desire for the forbidden and the taboo. "There's no denying that *Brass* is as loud an entrance into the publishing world as a first-time novelist can make," commented Vanessa Craft in an *IdeasFactory Base* Web site interview with Walsh.

Walsh herself lived part of her life as a rebel who sought out places and experiences that were at times unsavory. Born to a Malaysian mother and an English father, she was a well-behaved child and superior student until she discovered the club scene and drugs when she was thirteen, noted Claire Sawers in *Scotland on Sunday.* "Her next decade was spent getting high, teasing older guys, stealing, terrifying her parents and, above all else, running in desperation from the goodie-goodie image that everyone held of her," Sawers reported. Walsh had her first Ecstasy tablet before her first period or her first kiss. She moved to Barcelona at age sixteen, where she worked as a "fixer," a sort of intermediary who helped introduce men to transvestite prostitutes (notably, the title of her book, *Brass,* is a slang term for prostitute). She worked a number of dead-end jobs, interrupted by destructive drinking binges and deteriorating psychological stability. She sought help after waking up one morning and realizing that she had stabbed herself. She was diagnosed with depression and started taking antidepressants, which helped her find some order in her life. "Creativity provided relief" for Walsh's depression and tension, reported Colin Walters in the *Sunday Herald.* "At the kitchen table, she began to write. 'Brass purged me. Although I was lonely and debilitated by depression, *Brass* came out really easy.' Nine months later, after 'a painless, gorgeous process,' *Brass* was ready," Walters stated.

The wild and gorgeous Millie, the protagonist in *Brass,* is disturbed by changes in her life. Her mother has abruptly left the family, and her best friend Jamie is in the process of renouncing his partying ways to marry and settle down. Her grief at her perceived loss of Jamie and the trauma of her mother's departure spark a rapid spiral into a depraved world of drugs, prostitutes, sexual predation (Millie becomes a rapist who convinces herself that her victims encourage her), and self-destruction. A *Kirkus Reviews* contributor called the book a "fast-paced, gritty look at the back streets of Liverpool that could benefit from more depth and less dirt. Still, newcomer Walsh's energy and language give an entertaining ride."

Even though Walsh spent part of her life on the seamier side, *Brass* "isn't autobiographical—which sometimes isn't what journalists want to hear," she remarked in an interview with Vanessa Craft for *IdeasFactory.com.*

A reviewer in the London *Guardian* called the book a "very noisy piece of writing indeed, not so much executed as spewed by a woman who is, without a shadow of a doubt, a force of nature." London *Tele-*

graph reviewer David Isaacson stated that Walsh "has exploited some very raw material to good literary, if not always literate, effect," concluding that "*Brass* is compelling and disturbing." "Certain episodes are undeniably shocking, but beautifully poetic prose quickly proves this girl's plight is far more than a hard-hitting hard-luck story," noted Sawers. The book's "depiction of predatory female sexual behavior is, at times, shockingly edgy, and the prose is never less than exquisite," commented *Booklist* reviewer Joanne Wilkinson. A *Publishers Weekly* reviewer remarked that "Millie's . . . commentary on the . . . sexual and intellectual power of postadolescent women heralds the arrival of a promising new voice from the darker fringes of anti-girlhood."

BIOGRAPHICAL AND CRITICAL SOURCES:

PERIODICALS

Booklist, October 15, 2004, Joanne Wilkinson, review of *Brass,* p. 391.

Entertainment Weekly, November 5, 2004, Jennifer Reese, review of *Brass,* p. 88.

Esquire, December, 2004, Beth Greenfield, "A Writer We Love," interview with Helen Walsh, p. 58.

Guardian (London, England), April 3, 2004, Sarah Adams, "Where There's Muck . . . ," review of *Brass.*

Kirkus Reviews, September 1, 2004, review of *Brass,* p. 836.

Library Journal, November 1, 2004, Prudence Peiffer, review of *Brass,* p. 78.

Publishers Weekly, September 13, 2004, review of *Brass,* p. 56.

Scotland on Sunday, March 21, 2004, Claire Sawers, "One Girl's Journey toward Self-Destruction," review of *Brass.*

Sunday Herald (Glasgow, Scotland), March 7, 2004, Colin Waters, "The Grave Side of Helen Walsh."

Telegraph (London, England), February 5, 2004, David Isaacson, "Out of Her Mind, She Rages," review of *Brass*; February 5, 2004, Ivo Stourton, "Every Kind of Intoxication," review of *Brass.*

ONLINE

British Broadcasting Corporation Web site, http://www.bbc.co.uk/ (October 9, 2004), Michael Williams, profile of Helen Walsh.

IdeasFactory.com, http://www.ideasfactory.com/ (October 9, 2005), Vanessa Craft, "Brass in Pocket," profile of Helen Walsh.

*   *   *

WALTERS, Guy 1971-

PERSONAL: Born August 8, 1971, in London, England; married Annabel Venning (an author); children: two.

ADDRESSES: Home—Warminster, Wiltshire, England. *Agent*—Tif Loehnis, 29 Adam and Eve Mews, London W8 6UG, England. *E-mail*—guy@guywalters.com.

CAREER: Times, London, England, journalist, 1992-2000; freelance writer, 2000—.

WRITINGS:

The Leader (novel), Headline (London, England), 2003.

The Occupation (novel), Headline (London, England), 2004.

(Editor, with James Owen) *The Voice of War* (anthology), 2004.

The Traitor (novel), Simon & Schuster (New York, NY), 2005.

WORK IN PROGRESS: A fourth novel, *The Colditz Legacy; Berlin Games,* a history of the 1936 Berlin Olympics; editing a second anthology, with James Owen.

SIDELIGHTS: Guy Walters is a former London *Times* journalist who uses his experience as a newsman to explore alternate histories of the twentieth century. His first novel, *The Leader,* asks the question, "What would have happened to England if Edward VIII had refused to abdicate in 1937, had insisted on marrying the American divorcée Wallis Simpson, and had allied the country with the fascist leaders Benito Mussolini and Adolf Hitler?" In Walters' re-imagining of the political situation leading up to World War II, Britain has become a fascist state. Oswald Moseley, leader of the fascist Blackshirts, has seized power with the help of the king. For his part, Edward VIII, who historically flirted with fascism and made friends with prominent fascists, now leads a nation that has incarcerated its Jewish population in concentration camps and sent its opposition political leaders into prison on the Isle of Man in the middle of the Irish Sea. "The ability of fascism to insinuate itself into British society and pit work mates, families and friends against each other in an atmosphere of suspicion and distrust," remarked Paul French in the *Asian Review of Books,* "is well detailed."

One of these political leaders is James Armstrong, former conservative chief whip and a World War I veteran with a strong war record. Moseley rails against Armstrong's supporters, accusing them of Jewish ancestry or Communist sympathies (although most are neither Jewish nor Communists). His accusations lead to Armstrong's arrest and imprisonment. After escaping confinement, however, Armstrong begins to organize the scattered resistance movements across the country, ranging from the working classes of London's East End to the wealthy of the westernmost suburbs. "When we meet Armstrong's eventual East End collaborators they are not Communists either," stated critic L.J. Hurst in *Vector.* "However, Walters throws an international spanner into the works—what do the real Communists—that is, the Stalinists and Stalin himself—want for Britain?" The complications have Armstrong pitted against the fascists on the one hand and the Communists on the other, while trying to restore British traditions of democracy.

In *The Traitor* Walter again approaches an historical subject with a unique twist. His focus this time is on the leader of a Fascist-led British force that is mobilized to fight on the Eastern Front against the Russians. The traitor in question is Captain John Lockhart, who was captured by British during a partisan raid in the Balkans. Lockhart turns to the Nazis when they convince him that, should he serve in their force, they will release his wife from a concentration camp in Belgium. In his own mind, however, Lockhart remains a British patriot, determined to use his position to undermine the Nazi war machine from within. "Walters," wrote a *Publishers Weekly* critic, "delivers a fast-paced, exciting story filled with action, intricate plot twists, deception and betrayal."

BIOGRAPHICAL AND CRITICAL SOURCES:

PERIODICALS

Kirkus Reviews, May 1, 2005, review of *The Traitor,* p. 507.

Publishers Weekly, June 20, 2005, review of *The Traitor,* p. 57.
Vector, May-June, 2004, L.J. Hurst, review of *The Leader.*

ONLINE

Asian Review of Books Online, http://www.asian reviewofbooks.com/ (October 23, 2005), Paul French, review of *The Leader.*
Guy Walters Home Page, http://www.guywalters.com (October 23, 2005).*

*   *   *

WHARTON, Peter 1951(?)-

PERSONAL: Born c. 1951, in England; married; children: three. *Education:* University of North Wales, graduated, 1973; trained at Merrist Wood Agricultural College.

ADDRESSES: Home—South Surrey, British Columbia, Canada. *Office*—Rm. 106, Campbell Building, University of British Columbia Botanical Garden and Centre for Plant Research, 6804 Southwest Marine Dr., Vancouver, British Columbia V6T 1Z4, Canada. *E-mail*—Peter.Wharton@ubc.ca.

CAREER: David C. Lam Asian Garden, University of British Columbia, Vancouver, British Columbia, Canada, curator, 1975—.

WRITINGS:

(With Brent Hine and Douglas Justice) *The Jade Garden: New and Notable Plants from Asia,* Timber Press (Portland, OR), 2005.

SIDELIGHTS: Peter Wharton was born and raised in England, where he studied forestry and trained as an arborist. In 1975, he immigrated to Canada, where he has served as the curator at the University of British Columbia's David C. Lam Asian Garden. Wharton's

work includes extensive research in the plants of China, and he has traveled there on a number of field expeditions, as well as to South Korea and northern Vietnam.

In *The Jade Garden: New and Notable Plants from Asia,* which he wrote with Brent Hine and Douglas Justice, Wharton examines the history of Asian plants that have been introduced to North American and European climates over the years, and he discusses new plants that are also suitable for transplant from Asia to the West. He includes thoughtful tips regarding the landscape in China and how best to replicate the natural environments to increase the chance of successful cultivation of the native Asian plant life. Brian Lym, in a review for *Library Journal,* called the book "an authoritative, ground-breaking work that will delight horticultural connoisseurs and those interested in Asian flora and natural history." A contributor for *Asian Review of Books* remarked that "this is a nifty and highly recommended book for plant and garden enthusiasts wishing to expand their knowledge of Asian greenery."

BIOGRAPHICAL AND CRITICAL SOURCES:

PERIODICALS

Library Journal, June 15, 2005, Brian Lym, review of *The Jade Garden: New and Notable Plants from Asia,* p. 89.

ONLINE

Asian Review of Books Online, http://www.asian reviewofbooks.com/ (October 25, 2005), "Peter Wharton."
University of British Columbia Botanical Garden and Centre for Plant Research Web site, http://www. ubcbotanicalgarden.org/ (October 25, 2005), "Peter Wharton."*

*   *   *

WILSON, August 1945-2005 (Frederick August Kittel)

OBITUARY NOTICE— See index for *CA* sketch: Born April 27, 1945, in Pittsburgh, PA; died of liver cancer, October 2, 2005, in Seattle, WA. Author. Wilson was a Pulitzer Prize-winning playwright who was most famous for his ten-play cycle of works covering the twentieth-century African-American experience. He himself came from mixed parents—his father was a white German immigrant and his mother was black—and he experienced racial discrimination as a boy growing up in Pittsburgh. The situation worsened after his mother divorced and remarried, this time to a black sewer worker. The family moved to a predominantly white neighborhood, where the young Wilson met prejudice from both his peers and his teachers. When one teacher accused him of plagiarizing a paper he turned in, Wilson quit school at the age of fifteen. He continued his education, however, by spending many hours in the public library, where he discovered the books of such authors as Langston Hughes, Ralph Ellison, James Baldwin, and Malcolm X. Such writing inspired him to write as well. After a year serving in the U.S. Army, he began to write in earnest, changing his name from Freddie Kittel to August Wilson, using his middle name and his mother's maiden name. He became active in a collective of Pittsburgh poets and, in 1968, cofounded the theater company Black Horizons on the Hill, where he served as script writer and director for the next ten years. Wilson's first play, *Recycle,* was produced in Pittsburgh in 1973. However, the playwright struggled for many years before finding his footing. His theater work earned him little money, and he had to supplement his income with a variety of odd jobs. He also began publishing poems and contributing to anthologies. In 1978, he moved to Minneapolis and worked for the African-American Penumbra Theatre company. He soon began submitting plays to the National Playwrights Conference for consideration, including *Jitney,* which later premiered in Pittsburgh in 1982, but again found rejection. With *Ma Rainey's Black Bottom* (1984), however, Wilson finally gained notice. It premiered at the Yale Repertory Theatre, where many of the playwright's other works would also debut. Settling down in Seattle, over the next twenty years Wilson produced the plays that would all be considered part of a cycle of works capturing the African American experience. Although, with a few exceptions, the characters in each of the plays are not seen in the other dramas, the plays are tied together by the common setting of the Hill District and by themes concerning identity and black history. After he had written the first two plays, Wilson noticed that he was setting each work in a different decade; he decided he would do well to continue this pattern, thus writing a play for each decade of the twentieth century. The dramas each earned prestigious prizes, including the Pulitzer Prize and Drama Desk Outstanding New Play award for *Fences* (1985), an Antonia Perry

("Tony") Award nomination and New York Drama Critics Circle Best Play awards for *Joe Turner's Come and Gone* (1986), a Tony nomination, Drama Desk Outstanding Play Award, and a second Pulitzer prize for *The Piano Lesson* (1987), and Tony nominations for *Two Trains Running* (1990), *Seven Guitars* (1995), *King Hedley II* (2000), *Gem of the Ocean* (2003), and *Radio Golf* (2005). Many other New York Drama Critics awards were also received among Wilson's other prizes. Wilson more recently also received the *Chicago Tribune* Literary Prize in 2004. Having become a prominent figure in black theater by the 1980s, Wilson used his fame to express his beliefs in the importance of an independent black theater community that was not reliant on Broadway. One of the results of his lectures and debates on this issue was the emergence of the African Grove Institute for the Arts, a nonprofit group that supports the black performing arts. Though his life was cut short by liver cancer, Wilson managed to complete his cycle of twentieth-century African American life in plays that will likely continue to be performed for generations to come.

OBITUARIES AND OTHER SOURCES:

PERIODICALS

Chicago Tribune, October 3, 2005, section 1, pp. 1, 7.
Los Angeles Times, October 3, 2005, pp. A1, A14-15.
New York Times, October 3, 2005, pp. A1, A23.
Times (London, England), October 4, 2005, p. 61.

*   *   *

WINTLE, Edwin John 1963(?)-

PERSONAL: Born c. 1963.

ADDRESSES: Home—New York, NY. *Agent*—Mitchell Waters, Curtis Brown, Ltd., 10 Astor Pl., New York, NY 10003. *E-mail*—Edwin@edwinjohnwintle.com.

CAREER: Actor and lawyer; Curtis Brown Ltd., New York, NY, film agent, 1998—.

WRITINGS:

Breakfast with Tiffany: An Uncle's Memoir, Miramax Books (New York, NY), 2005.

WORK IN PROGRESS: A novel.

SIDELIGHTS: Edwin John Wintle started his career as an actor and lawyer before he finally settled into a job as a film agent for New York City-based Curtis Brown, Ltd. He decided to become an author when he had the idea to write a memoir chronicling his experiences with his then-thirteen-year-old niece, who had moved into his New York City apartment. The move came after Wintle visited his newly divorced sister and her two daughters in Connecticut, only to find that his sister was at a loss as to how to handle Tiffany, a "wild child" who had been skipping school and was failing her classes. Wintle agreed to take Tiffany in, and his niece showed up with a hangover a week later. *Breakfast with Tiffany: An Uncle's Memoir* tells of Wintle's experiences in raising the troubled teenager, from dealing with her drug use to setting parameters about sexual conduct, school, the people she spent her time with, and her home life. What makes Wintle's situation more difficult is that he himself is a single, gay man. This put him in the position of having to maintain a double standard about what was acceptable relationship behavior for his niece versus for himself as an adult. The book also addresses Wintle's relationships with other family members, as well as Tiffany's own hopes and dreams, which are illustrated through snippets of her letters and poems.

Wintle allowed himself to be open and honest in the writing of his book. In an interview for *Bookslut.com,* he explained: "One of the stories in the book is the ripping open of my heart, which is a journey toward vulnerability. The whole thing was about having this teenager come to me and turn me inside-out. In the book I mention that I feel like I'm a bundle of jagged nerves, I'm an open wound. So, if anything, it was trying to do the opposite, it was trying to keep a lid on some of the vulnerability. I felt vulnerable the entire time writing the memoir, because I was going inward, I was plumbing the depths of my past, journey, and struggles." An *Observer* contributor noted that "Wintle is strongest when nailing the blindingly cavalier self-confidence of teen tyranny. He's trying to protect Tiffany but, running on hormone overload and ricocheting between unexpected sweetness and uncontrollable fury, she considers him to be a control freak." A contributor for *Publishers Weekly* wrote of the end result that "the lighthearted tone makes a serious subject amusing, and Wintle is charmingly self-deprecating." Michelle Green similarly remarked in

People that the author's "dead-on wit sparks the narrative, and his neurotic but creative approach to child-rearing is bracing." A contributor for *Entertainment Weekly* recommended the book as "one of the most unconventional—and heartwarming—parenting guides ever."

BIOGRAPHICAL AND CRITICAL SOURCES:

BOOKS

Wintle, Edwin John, *Breakfast with Tiffany: An Uncle's Memoir*, Miramax Books (New York, NY), 2005.

PERIODICALS

Daily Variety, November 7, 2003, David Rooney, "Breakfast at Miramax," p. 1.
Entertainment Weekly, June 17, 2005, Tina Jordan, review of *Breakfast with Tiffany*, p. 87; June 24, 2005, review of *Breakfast with Tiffany*, p. 127.
Kirkus Reviews, May 1, 2005, review of *Breakfast with Tiffany*, p. 531.
People, June 27, 2005, Michelle Green, review of *Breakfast with Tiffany*, p. 47.
Publishers Weekly, April 25, 2005, review of *Breakfast with Tiffany*, p. 48.

ONLINE

Beatrice.com, http://www.beatrice.com/ (October 25, 2005), "Edwin John Wintle."
Bookslut.com, http://www.bookslut.com/ (October 25, 2005), "Edwin John Wintle."
Edwin John Wintle Home page, http://www.edwinjohnwintle.com (October 25, 2005).
National Public Radio Web site, http://www.npr.org/ (October 25, 2005), "Edwin John Wintle."
Observer Online, http://www.observer.co.uk/ (October 25, 2005), "Edwin John Wintle."
San Diego Union-Tribune Online, http://www.signonsandiego.com/ (October 25, 2005), "Edwin John Wintle."

*   *   *

WOLF, Bernard 1930-

PERSONAL: Born 1930, in New York, NY.

ADDRESSES: Office—Bernard Wolf Photography, 240 E. 27th St., New York, NY 10016. *E-mail*—bernardwolf@bernardwolfphotography.com.

AWARDS, HONORS: Notable Children's Trade Book citation, National Council for Social Studies/Children's Book Council, 1978, for *Adam Smith Goes to School;*. American Library Association honr, 1991, for books on the handicapped.

WRITINGS:

JUVENILE; AND PHOTOGRAPHER

The Little Weaver of Agato: A Visit with an Indian Boy Living in the Andes Mountains of Ecuador, Cowles Book Company (New York, NY), 1969.
Jamaica Boy, Cowles Book Company (New York, NY), 1971.
Daniel and the Whale Hunters: The Adventures of a Portuguese Boy in a Whaling Town in the Azores, Random House (New York, NY), 1972.
Tinker and the Medicine Men: The Story of a Navajo Boy of Monument Valley, Random House (New York, NY), 1973.
Don't Feel Sorry for Paul, Lippincott (Philadelphia, PA), 1974.
Connie's New Eyes, Lippincott (Philadelphia, PA), 1976.
Anna's Silent World, Lippincott (Philadelphia, PA), 1977.
In This Proud Land: The Story of a Mexican-American Family, Lippincott (Philadelphia, PA), 1978.
Adam Smith Goes to School, Lippincott (Philadelphia, PA), 1978.
Michael and the Dentist, Four Winds Press (New York, NY), 1980.
Firehouse, Morrow (New York, NY), 1983.
Cowboy, Morrow (New York, NY), 1985.
Amazing Grace: Smith Island and the Chesapeake Watermen, Macmillan (New York, NY), 1986.
In the Year of the Tiger, Macmillan (New York, NY), 1988.
Beneath the Stone: A Mexican Zapotec Tale, Orchard Books (New York, NY), 1994.
Homeless, Orchard Books (New York, NY), 1995.
HIV Positive, Dutton Children's Books (New York, NY), 1997.
If I Forget Thee, O Jerusalem, Dutton Children's Books (New York, NY), 1998.
Cuba: After the Revolution, Dutton Children's Books (New York, NY), 1999.
Coming to America: A Muslim Family's Story, Lee & Low Books (New York, NY), 2003.

Contributor to periodicals, including *Travel and Camera, House Beautiful, Fortune,* and *Camera 35.*

SIDELIGHTS: Photographer Bernard Wolf has written and illustrated books for children, many of which introduce young readers to new cultures or ways of life. In such books as *The Little Weaver of Agato: A Visit with an Indian Boy Living in the Andes Mountains of Ecuador, Jamaica Boy,* and *Tinker and the Medicine Men: The Story of a Navajo Boy of Monument Valley,* Wolf presents a view into the daily lives of children in traditional societies. Other books, such as *Don't Feel Sorry for Paul, Connie's New Eyes,* and *Anna's Silent World,* describe the lives of children who live with physical disabilities.

In recent years, Wolf has confronted more controversial topics, such as homelessness and the AIDS epidemic. His *Homeless* received enthusiastic reviews in *Booklist* and in *Horn Book,* where contributor Ellen Fader praised the book's sympathetic but unpatronizing tone. A reviewer for *Publishers Weekly,* however, felt that the book fails to explain some basic issues relating to homelessness, such as temporary housing and public-assistance benefits. *HIV Positive,* which follows a twenty-nine-year-old mother with full-blown AIDS as she goes about her life and cares for her children, earned much critical admiration. Stephanie Zvirin in *Booklist* noted that Wolf avoids sentimentalizing his subject and steers clear of any political slant, creating a book Zvirin hailed as a "real achievement that brings the tragedy home full force." A contributor to *Publishers Weekly* found Wolf's editorializing to be a small flaw in the book, but added that its "cumulative effect . . . is potent and bittersweet."

Cuba: After the Revolution also received significant attention. A *Publishers Weekly* reviewer described the book as a "complex portrait" of contemporary Cuban society and noted that Wolf's photographs are particularly effective in capturing the diversity of Havana's people and landscape. The writer added, however, that although Wolf shows the paradoxes of Cuban life, he does not adequately explain them. Randy Meyer in *Booklist* made a similar point, observing that while Wolf describes Cuba as a 'troubled island,' he avoids any discussion of politics. In Meyer's view, this evasion makes the book's optimistic message unclear.

Two of Wolf's titles address issues relating to religion. *If I Forget Thee, O Jerusalem* "brings alive" the history of that holy city, according to *Booklist* critic Ilene

Cooper. Cooper noted that Wolf chooses "details that will capture children's imaginations" and presents a "balanced" discussion of issues that have divided Jews, Christians, and Muslims—who all hold the city sacred. *Coming to America: A Muslim Family's Story* focuses on the daily life of an Egyptian Muslim family now residing in New York City. Though the book takes a social rather than religious perspective, it does explain basic elements of Islamic practice, including mosque attendance on Fridays. In *School Library Journal,* Coop Renner praised Wolf's depictions of the family as individuals; this approach, Renner noted, emphasizes that "differences of religion do not signify differences in humane behavior, love of family, or appreciation for hard work." A writer for *Kirkus Reviews* observed that Wolf considers such problems as language, economic strain, and homesickness, but "with no mention prejudice or current politics." Nevertheless, the critic found the book insightful and informative.

BIOGRAPHICAL AND CRITICAL SOURCES:

PERIODICALS

Booklist, March 15, 1994, Mary Harris Veeder, review of *Beneath the Stone: A Mexican Zapotec Tale,* p. 1346; February 15, 1995, Stephanie Zvirin, review of *Homeless,* p. 1088; March 15, 1997, Stephanie Zvirin, review of *HIV Positive,* p. 1240; October 1, 1998, Ilene Cooper, review of *If I Forget Thee, O Jerusalem,* p. 341; September 1, 1999, Randy Meyer, review of *Cuba: After the Revolution,* p. 131; April 1, 2003, John Peters, review of *Coming to America: A Muslim Family's Story,* p. 1395.

Horn Book, December, 1983, Kate M. Flanagan, review of *Firehouse,* p. 728; May-June, 1995, Ellen Fader, review of *Homeless,* p. 346; May-June, 2003, Roger Sutton, review of *Coming to America,* p. 372.

Kirkus Reviews, April 15, 2003, review of *Coming to America,* p. 613.

Language Arts, March, 1987, Janet Hickman, review of *Amazing Grace: Smith Island and the Chesapeake Watermen,* p. 314.

New York Times, November 13, 1983, Sherwin D. Smith, review of *Firehouse,* p. 48.

Publishers Weekly, September 30, 1983, Jean F. Mercier, review of *Firehouse,* p. 115; December 12,

1986, review of *Amazing Grace,* p. 58; March 20, 1995, review of *Homeless,* p. 61; April 21, 1997, review of *HIV Positive,* p. 72; March 31, 2003, review of *Coming to America,* p. 64.

School Library Journal, November, 1983, Phyllis Sue Alpert, review of *Firehouse,* p. 84; April, 1985, Pat Harrington, review of *Cowboy,* p. 94; February, 1987, Don Reaber, review of *Amazing Grace,* p. 86; August, 1988, Mary Mueller, review of *In the Year of the Tiger,* p. 112; August, 1994, Lauren Mayer, review of *Beneath the Stone,* p. 153; August 9, 1999, review of *Cuba,* p. 354; May, 2003, Coop Renner, review of *Coming to America,* p. 143.

School Science and Mathematics, January, 1988, Charles E. Lamb, review of *Cowboy,* p. 76.

ONLINE

Bernard Wolf Home Page, http://www.bernardwolf photography.com (September 23, 2005).

*   *   *

WOODS, James Garcia
    See SPENCER, Sally

Y-Z

YAKOVLEV, Alexander 1923-2005
(Alexandr Nikolayevich Yakovlev)

OBITUARY NOTICE— See index for *CA* sketch: Born December 2, 1923, in Korolyevo, Russia; died October 18, 2005, in Moscow, Russia. Diplomat, government official, and author. A formerly ardent Communist Party member, Yakovlev became a democratizing voice in the USSR and an important ally to Soviet leader Mikhail Gorbachev during the age of glasnost. Growing up under Josef Stalin's oppressive rule, he nevertheless became a staunch idealist, especially after his role as a soldier fighting against the Germans at the Battle of Leningrad, where he was severely wounded. After World War II, he joined the Communist Party and earned a history degree from the Academy of Social Sciences. Yakovlev worked as a member of his local Yaroslavl district committee of the Party until 1953, when he was promoted to head of the department of science and culture. He became involved primarily in propaganda and the media and was so trusted by Party officials that in 1958 he was allowed to study for a year at Columbia University. Yakovlev was all the more contemptuous of America after having lived there a year, and was highly critical of U.S. foreign and economic policies. Returning to the USSR, he wrote histories that painted America in an ugly light. During the 1960s, Yakovlev served in several governmental posts, including in the department of propaganda and agitation (agitprop), as head of radio and television from 1964 to 1965, and as first deputy head and then acting head of agitprop from 1965 to 1973. By the early 1970s, however, his attitudes were beginning to change, and in 1972 he went so far as to criticize nationalistic and anti-Semitic policies in his country. As a kind of punishment, he was removed from his propaganda post and made ambassador to Canada, where he remained for the next decade. From 1983 to 1985 he also worked as the director of the Institute for World Economy and International Relations. It was while in Canada that Yakovlev first met the young rising star, Gorbachev. The two became friends, and when Gorbachev was elected general secretary of the Communist Party, Yakovlev was invited to return to the Soviet Union. He was put back in charge of propaganda for a year, and from 1986 to 1991 was a member of the powerful central committee. The 1980s brought many changes to the Soviet Union; with pressur from U.S. President Ronald Reagan, Gorbachev, along with Yakovlev, started to institute new policies that provided greater freedoms to Soviet citizens. These policies became collectively known as glasnost and "perestroika." After a few years of progress, however, Gorbachev started to fear that the shift toward democracy was coming too swiftly and was threatening national stability; Yakovlev, however, took the opposite position and founded the Democratic Reform Movement, leaving the Communist Party altogether in 1991. Gorbachev's hesitance proved to be the wrong move politically; he started to surround himself with hardliners who, in 1991, betrayed him with a coup attempt. Though the coup failed, Gorbachev was removed from office. The Soviet Union by then had already lost influence in Eastern Europe; now the country itself fell apart as former republics sought independence. Yakovlev allied himself with the new president, Boris Yeltsin, and headed the state's television network, Russian Public TV, Ltd., until 1995, when he could no longer tolerate the government's influence in limiting media freedoms. He spent his last years focusing on his writing and working for the Presidential Committee on Rehabilitation of Victims of Political Repression. Among Yakovlev's books available in English are *Realism as the Land of Perestroika* (1990), *What We Were Going to Do in the Soviet Union* (1991), and *Striving for Law in a Lawless Land: Memoirs of a Russian Reformer* (1996).

OBITUARIES AND OTHER SOURCES:

BOOKS

Yakovlev, Alexander, *Striving for Law in a Lawless Land: Memoirs of a Russian Reformer*, M.E. Sharpe, 1996.

PERIODICALS

Los Angeles Times, October 19, 2005, p. B10.
New York Times, October 19, 2005, p. A20.
Washington Post, October 20, 2005, p. B8.

*   *   *

YAKOVLEV, Alexandr Nikolayevich
See YAKOVLEV, Alexander

*   *   *

YOUNG, Audrey

PERSONAL: Female. *Education:* University of Washington, M.D., 1998.

ADDRESSES: Home—Seattle, WA. *Office*—Harborview Medical Center, 325 9th Ave., Campus Box 359780, Seattle, WA 98104. *E-mail*—auyoung@ u.washington.edu.

CAREER: University of Washington, Seattle, and Boise Veterans Administration Medical Center, Boise, ID, intern, 1999-2002; Harbor Medical Center, Seattle, attending physician and acting instructor of medicine.

WRITINGS:

What Patients Taught Me: A Medical Student's Journey, Sasquatch Books (Seattle, WA), 2004.

SIDELIGHTS: Audrey Young's book *What Patients Taught Me: A Medical Student's Journey* recounts the first four years of her medical education. It tracks her progress through medical school and explains how she struggled to learn not just the science behind her career, but also the reasons for the behavior of her patients, even when it seemed to go against medical sense. Michelle Green, in a review for *People*, remarked that Young is "a fine storyteller" who "tempers pathos with the life-and-death scenes that ER junkies crave." Green went on to write that Young's effort is a "keenly observed account of her first four years of training."

BIOGRAPHICAL AND CRITICAL SOURCES:

BOOKS

Young, Audrey, *What Patients Taught Me: A Medical Student's Journey*, Sasquatch Books (Seattle, WA), 2004.

PERIODICALS

Booklist, September 1, 2004, Donna Chavez, review of *What Patients Taught Me*, p. 34.
Kirkus Reviews, August 15, 2004, review of *What Patients Taught Me*, p. 799.
People, November 15, 2004, Michelle Green, review of *What Patients Taught Me*, p. 48.

ONLINE

Seattle Weekly Online, http://www.seattleweekly.com/ (October 25, 2005), "Audrey Young."
University of Washington Web site, http://depts. washington.edu/ (October 25, 2005), "Audrey Young."*

*   *   *

ZHOU, Jinghao 1955-

PERSONAL: Born March 6, 1955, in China; naturalized U.S. citizen; married Sai Gong; children: Lingjia, Yifang. *Ethnicity:* "Asian." *Education:* Baylor University, Ph.D., 2000.

ADDRESSES: Home—4045 Scandling Center, Geneva, NY 14456. *Office*—222 Stern Hall, Hobart and William Smith Colleges, Geneva, NY 14456. *E-mail*—zhou@hws.edu.

CAREER: Writer and educator. Wuhan University, Wuhan, China, chief editor, 1983-85, lecturer, 1985-91; Union Theological Seminary, Richmond, VA, study master, 1992-95; minister at Baptist church in Washington, DC, 1995-96; Belsky & Pudum Law Firm, Baltimore, MD, legal assistant, 1996-97; Hobart and William Smith Colleges, Geneva, NY, assistant professor, 2001—.

MEMBER: Association for Asian Studies, Association of Chinese Political Studies.

WRITINGS:

Remaking China's Public Philosophy for the Twenty-first Century, Praeger Publishers (Westport, CT), 2003.

WORK IN PROGRESS: Remaking China's Public Philosophy and Chinese Women's Liberation.

SIDELIGHTS: Jinghao Zhou told *CA:* "After I was assigned to a factory as a worker when I was sixteen years old in 1971, I swore to myself that I wanted to become an intellectual. Then I began self-studying and writing, because I did not have any choice during the turbulent years. At the beginning, I wrote everything, including poems, novels, dramas, and essays. Gradually, I realized that writing is one important tool that could change not only personal status but also social and political systems. I have kept this naive idea for more than thirty years and will continue to pursue it in my remaining years either in the United States or in China."

*   *   *

ZOMEREN BADIUS, J. van
   See GRESHOFF, Jan